Rodale's
GARDEN
PROBLEM SOLVER
Vegetables, Fruits, and Herbs
by Jeff Ball

Illustrations by Pamela and Walter Carroll and Robin Brickman

Photographs by Liz Ball

Rodale Press, Emmaus, Pennsylvania

Printed in the United States of America on acid-free ∞, recycled paper ♻

Cover design: Stan Green/Green Graphics
Cover Photographer: Mitch Mandel/RSI
Book design: Denise Mirabello

If you have any questions or comments concerning this book, please
write:
    Rodale Press
    Book Readers' Service
    33 East Minor Street
    Emmaus, PA 18098

Library of Congress Cataloging-in-Publication Data

Ball, Jeff.
    Rodale's garden problem solver : vegetables, fruits, and herbs /
by Jeff Ball ; illustrations by Pamela and Walter Carroll and Robin
Brickman ; photographs by Liz Ball.
        p.   cm.
    Bibliography: p.
    Includes index.
    ISBN 0-87857-762-9   hardcover
    ISBN 0-87596-699-3   paperback
    1. Garden pests—Control—Handbooks, manuals, etc.   2. Gardens—
Management—Handbooks, manuals, etc.   3. Vegetables—Diseases
and pests—Handbooks, manuals, etc.   I. Title.
SB603.5.B35   1988
635′.049—dc19   88-1714
                                                      CIP

Distributed in the book trade by St. Martin's Press

12 14 16 18 20 19 17 15 13 11   hardcover
 2   4   6   8 10   9   7   5   3   paperback

Contents

Acknowledgments

An enormous amount of information had to be reviewed, summarized, and reorganized to prepare this book. It was definitely a team effort. Every member of my team made significant contribution to the production effort.

Most good gardening books have lots of pearls of problem-solving wisdom sprinkled throughout their pages. However, finding those pearls can be a difficult and time-consuming task. Fortunately, my dear mother-in-law, Ad Geigle, has the patience to go through every line of every page of a gardening book to find those handy problem-solving tips offered by experienced gardeners. Not only was her search thorough, but she made all her deadlines, a record I don't always achieve.

Sorting out all the insects from all the diseases for all the plants was Mike Wisniewski's job, and he did it well. He even went out and bought his own personal computer for this task, a dedication to detail and accuracy not found in many research assistants.

Lois Murray is my keyboard operator. She put all the notes from Ad and Mike into my database so I could begin to sort and adjust and manipulate that huge pile of data.

It didn't really feel like a book until Liz Ball finished her loving but hard-nosed editing. That editing was critical, but it is her photography that puts the finishing touches on my work. All the helpful and descriptive photos in this book were shot by Liz, my wife and writing partner.

There are dozens of people at Rodale Press who work on any book that is published by that company, and they all work with high personal standards. I thank them all, but I want to take special note of the contribution of Denise Mirabello, who is responsible for designing this book. It is very difficult to design a reference book for easy retrieval of information and I feel that she did a brilliant job—a special thanks to her.

Introduction

After paging through this book and seeing the many problems that could occur in your garden, you may wonder why you should even try to grow anything. Collected in one place, the number of insect pests, weird diseases, and other problems that exist can intimidate even the most enthusiastic gardener. Maybe it would be easier just to ignore all of these possible problems and forge on blindly, hoping for the best. On the conviction that knowledge is the best defense against a disappointing gardening season, I have tried to provide you with a comprehensive reference book to consult when a problem occurs.

In most cases, you are not going to be overwhelmed with problems. In any established garden with 15 to 20 different food crops, you might have to cope with four or five pest insects, three or four disease problems, and maybe a pest animal or two. After a few years of experience with these problems you'll find that you can limit their damage without having to use any materials that would be toxic to you or your backyard ecosystem. As you will see in chapters 7 and 8, many routine garden activities, such as watering, fertilizing, weeding, and planting, can be performed in a manner that will serve to prevent problems while also serving the basic needs of your plants. If you water early in the day, apply the proper amounts of fertilizer, and use lots of mulch, you will be taking good care of your plants and simultaneously preventing disease and insect problems.

Use this book as a practical, working tool: that means write in it. When you see in a magazine a new technique for controlling corn earworms, make a note in the corn earworm section of this book. When you read about a new variety of cucumber that is resistant to powdery mildew and will grow well in your area, make a note in the cucumber entry.

This is a book that should sit on top of the refrigerator rather than on the bookshelf in the den. You may have muddy shoes when you need to find out which insecticide you should use for asparagus beetles, and your refrigerator is probably closer to the back door than the den is.

One of the most important points I hope you take from this book is that it is easier to prevent most problems than it is to let everything go and then try to solve the problem once it appears. General, simple garden routines such as fall garden cleanup, mulching, and foliar spraying prevent most of the insect and disease problems that can occur in any garden. Good problem prevention takes very little extra time over and above the normal food gardening activities. So although this book is dedicated to helping you solve problems, its real story is about how to prevent those problems in the first place.

You should need to use this book less and less as the years go by. You will have learned how to prevent serious problems in your food garden, and will be able to grow bountiful crops of vegetables, fruit, and herbs undaunted by pesky insects or devastating diseases.

BASIC MEDICINE KIT

This book describes dozens and dozens of different techniques, tools, and supplies that you might use to remedy the various problems listed for each vegetable, fruit, berry, and herb. However, if you want to be generally prepared for the most common situations, you should have certain basic supplies on hand. Every spring, check your stock of gardening tools and materials and make sure you have the following items:

1. A bottle of seaweed extract (use a fresh supply each year).

2. A bottle of liquid fertilizer, such as fish emulsion (will keep for 2 to 3 years).

3. A bottle of insecticidal soap concentrate (will keep indefinitely).

4. A bottle of *Bacillus thuringiensis*, or BT, in either liquid or wettable powder form (use a fresh supply each year).

5. A bottle of pyrethrum insecticide (will keep for 3 to 4 years).

6. A bottle of flowable sulfur fungicide (will keep for 1 year).

7. A bottle of copper-based fungicide (will keep indefinitely).

8. A bottle of dormant oil, if you have fruit trees (will keep indefinitely).

9. A generous pile of finished compost.

10. At least one package of agricultural fleece.

11. A good sprayer with at least a 1-gallon capacity.

12. At least one bird feeder to keep the songbirds in the area.

13. Sufficient organic mulch material to cover the garden.

Of course there are other items you could acquire, but these are the basic problem-solving and problem-preventing supplies. Keep fertilizers, pesticides, and fungicides in well-sealed containers, stored away from direct sunlight, in a location where they will not be exposed to dramatic changes in temperature. Extreme cold or heat can shorten a product's shelf life.

How to Use This Book

Rodale's Garden Problem Solver has two functions. It is designed to give you quick, immediate solutions to problems that occur in your garden, and it is a resource for learning long-range solutions and preventive practices that will help you establish a problem-free garden for the future.

This book has been designed and organized so that it will be easy for you to find answers quickly. Although you could sit down and figure out how to use the book just by looking through it, I'd like to save you that trouble by explaining briefly the steps you should follow for the most efficient and effective use of this guide.

1. Once you spot the symptoms of some disease or insect problem on a plant—such as yellow, wilted leaves—turn to the entry for that plant in chapter 1, Vegetables; chapter 2, Fruits and Berries; or chapter 3, Herbs.

2. Look for the symptom in the entry. In every plant entry, the symptom of a problem appears on a line by itself, and it is underlined.

3. Beneath the symptom, you will find its cause, whether it is an insect pest, a disease, or a nutrient deficiency.

4. Beneath the cause, you will find further discussion of the problem, with a solution for immediate control.

5. For further information about the insect pest or the disease, and for other options for controlling and preventing the problem, turn to chapter 4, Insects, or chapter 5, Diseases, which contain entries for the most common insect pests and the most common diseases, listed in alphabetical order. Note: these chapters do not contain entries for insect pests or diseases that are specific to only one or two plants. In those cases, the information about the pest or disease can be found in the entry for the plant it affects.

6. For information on controlling damage from deer and other wildlife, turn to chapter 6, Animal Pests.

In addition to offering solutions to garden problems, each plant entry contains valuable information on growing, which will help you to provide the right environment for your crops so that you will have fewer problems. Harvesting and storage tips are also given, so that you can get the most flavor from your produce.

The last two chapters of this book discuss basic garden management techniques, which will teach you how to run a pest-free, disease-free garden, and help you to produce the best vegetables, fruit, berries, and herbs possible. And don't forget the Hardiness Zone map, the source list of gardening supplies, and the list of books under Recommended Reading in the back of the book. From cover to cover, this reference is a quick, easy-to-use source of useful information.

PART 1

Plant Problems

CHAPTER 1

Vegetables

Most vegetables are vulnerable to attack by certain insects and certain diseases. It is important to remember that not all pest insects attack every vegetable. Each vegetable plant is potentially bothered by a very limited number of pest insects and a similarly limited number of destructive diseases. In many cases, these pests and diseases don't even represent a death threat. For instance, although the ubiquitous aphid does tend to hang around most of the plants in the garden, it will not wipe out the entire garden, nor will the other insect pests do so. You need to realize that there is not an army of pest insects out there ready to move in and eliminate your entire food garden in one night (although deer have been known to commit such atrocities). Therefore, insects and diseases can be relegated to the status of minor nuisances if you know how to handle them. That is what this book is about: keeping insects, diseases, and other problems in the vegetable garden controlled to the level where they are only minor problems.

As you use this book, think about what *problem* means to you. Insects, animals, diseases, and the environment create situations that are relative to our own definitions of what is a real problem. If there are a few holes in the leaves of the bean plants, but the beans are fine, do you have a problem? If the seedlings are chomped off at the base and have completely disappeared, is that a problem? Most of us would probably say no to the first situation and definitely yes to the second. Only experience will enable you to determine your particular standards for what constitutes a real problem in your food garden. The more you can tolerate minor damage, the easier and less demanding your problem-solving tasks will be.

There will always be bugs in your garden—good ones and bad ones. There will always be spores, bacteria, and viruses in your garden—good ones and bad ones. Your challenge as a vegetable gardener is to create an ecosystem in your backyard that allows for a healthy balance between the good guys and the bad guys so that the damage that does occur is below your personal standards of what you feel constitutes a problem that needs attention. As you refer to this chapter, you will learn about gardening techniques and practices that will help you attain that balance between the forces of evil (cucumber beetles and downy mildew) and the forces of good (lady bugs and beneficial soil fungi) that rage in that quiet but productive piece of your property you call the vegetable garden.

3

VEGETABLE Asparagus
Asparagus officinalis

DESCRIPTION AND ENVIRONMENT

Height   5 to 6 feet
Spread   3 feet
Shade Tolerance   Needs only 5 hours of sun a day (partial shade).
Frost Tolerance   Hardy
Preferred pH   6.0 to 7.5

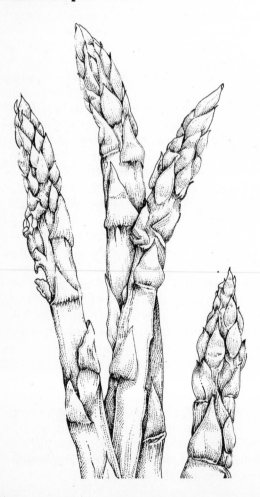

PLANTING

Spring Planting Time   From 4 to 6 weeks before last spring frost until hot weather sets in.
Fall Planting Time   Not appropriate for asparagus.
Planting Depth   6 to 8 inches
Spacing of Plants in Rows   18 inches; rows should be 3 to 4 feet apart.
Spacing of Plants in Beds   Asparagus is best planted in rows for maximum access to sunlight.
Best Soil Temperature for Germination 60°F to 85°F
Days to Germination   7 to 21
Weeks to Transplanting   12 to 14
Time to Maturity   3 years
Greenhouse Varieties   Asparagus cannot be grown in the greenhouse.
Container Varieties   Asparagus cannot be grown in containers.

PLANT MANAGEMENT

Water Requirements for Good Production

Make sure the plants get 1 inch of water every week from rain or by watering. (See chapter 8 for more information on watering.)

Water Requirements for Maximum Production

This plant can use a lot of water. For maximum production, make sure it gets between 1 and 1½ inches of water a week.

Feeding Requirements for Good Production

Apply compost or a slow-acting general-purpose fertilizer in spring before the spears begin to pop up. In addition, apply a foliar spray of liquid seaweed extract two or three times during the growing season. (See chapter 8 for more information on feeding.)

Feeding Requirements for Maximum Production

This plant is considered a heavy feeder, and for maximum production can use, in addition to the spring feeding mentioned above, a light supplement (either a side-dressing or foliar spray) every 2 weeks during its growing season. In addition, apply a foliar spray of liquid seaweed extract two or three times during the growing season.

Reduced Yield

Weeds
Weed competition in new asparagus beds during the first 6 weeks of growth causes the plants to produce fewer leaves during the first year and reduces the number of new spears for two more seasons. Keep new asparagus beds free of weeds.

MOST COMMON INSECT PESTS

Yellow Foliage

Aphid
If the foliage turns yellow and its growth becomes stunted, look for ants on the plant. They are a sign that your asparagus has aphids. Ants are attracted to the sticky honeydew secreted by aphids. Look for clusters of aphids on the undersides of young leaves. They are soft-bodied, pear-shaped insects about the size of a pinhead, and may be green, brown, or pink. For light infestations, spray vigorously with water early in the morning, three times, once every other day. For heavy infestations, use a commercial insecticidal soap every 2 to 3 days until aphids are under control.

Defoliated Plants

Asparagus Beetle
Defoliated plants and misshapen young spears indicate that the asparagus beetle is attacking your plants. The asparagus beetle has an oblong shape and is ¼ inch long. Its hard wing covers meet in a straight line in the middle of its back. It is blue-black with four white spots or stripes and reddish margins. Early handpicking makes a sizable dent in the asparagus beetle infestation right away. The pests emerge in the spring (for example in late April or early May in the north). Pyrethrum paralyzes asparagus beetles on contact. Usually two applications during the evening, 3 to 4 days apart, will control the problem.

Leaves Stippled Yellow

Mite
Leaves of asparagus that have mites become stippled, yellow, and dry, and sometimes pale yellow spots or blotches appear. Mites are not insects but arachnids, and are about the size of a grain of black pepper. They may be red, black, or brown. They feed by sucking out the plant's juices. In sucking chlorophyll out of the leaves, they cause small white dots to appear. In addition, they inject toxins into the leaves, which discolors and distorts them. To control infestations, spray plants with a forceful spray of water three times, once every three days, to knock mites from the leaves. If mites are still present, spray with insecticidal soap three times, once every 5 to 7 days.

MOST COMMON DISEASES

Reddish Brown Masses on Ferns

Asparagus Rust
Seen after the cutting season, the spores of the rust disease create reddish brown masses on the ferns of

the plant. When these areas are touched, they give off a dusty cloud. In late summer, black masses of spores may be produced. The disease retards fern growth, causes early maturity, and reduces food storage in the crown of the plant. Cut the diseased tops to the ground and burn them. Try applying a sulfur spray twice, 5 to 7 days apart, to reduce spread of the disease.

Resistant Varieties. California 500, Martha Washington, Mary Washington, Seneca Washington, Viking, and Waltham Washington.

HARVEST AND STORAGE

When to Harvest

Start harvesting asparagus the third year after planting. Collect the thick, green spears 6 to 8 inches tall; do not harvest thin spears (smaller than a pencil). Heads should be tight and spears brittle. Snap the spears at ground level at the most tender part or use a very sharp knife to cut spears just below the soil surface, being careful not to cut into adjacent spears. During the third year of growth, harvest spears for only 2 weeks. The fourth year harvest for 4 weeks, and during the fifth and subsequent years, you can harvest for 6 to 8 weeks.

Yield for 25-Foot Row   7 to 12 pounds
Volume vs. Weight   1 bushel equals 40 pounds.
Weight of 1-Quart Canning Jar   2 to 3 pounds
Number of Quarts Stored from 1 Bushel   13 to 20
Best Fresh Storage Methods   Wrap stems in moist toweling. Refrigerate in plastic bags or in covered containers, or store standing upright in a glass of water covered with a plastic bag. Asparagus will keep fresh for 2 to 3 days.
Best Long-Term Storage Method   Asparagus freezes well and can be kept frozen for up to 12 months.
Second-Best Long-Term Storage Method   Canned asparagus will keep for more than 12 months.
Seed Storage   3 years

VEGETABLE *Bean, Lima* *Phaseolus limensis*

DESCRIPTION AND ENVIRONMENT

Height   Bush, 10 to 15 inches; pole, 8 to 15 feet.
Spread   Bush, 4 to 8 inches; pole, 6 to 8 inches.
Root Depth   36 to 48 inches, bush and pole.
Shade Tolerance   Needs full sun.
Frost Tolerance   None
Preferred pH   6.0 to 7.0

PLANTING

Spring Planting Time   At least 2 weeks after last expected frost; any root disturbance will hinder growth, so handle seedlings as little as possible. When thinning, cut rather than pull unwanted seedlings.

Fall Planting Time   At least 12 weeks before first expected frost.

Succession Planting Plant bush varieties every week or two. Pole beans need only one planting.

Planting Depth 1½ to 2 inches

Spacing of Plants in Rows Bush, 6 inches; pole, 12 to 18 inches, depending on variety.

Spacing of Plants in Beds Bush, 4 inches.

Best Soil Temperature for Germination 65°F to 85°F

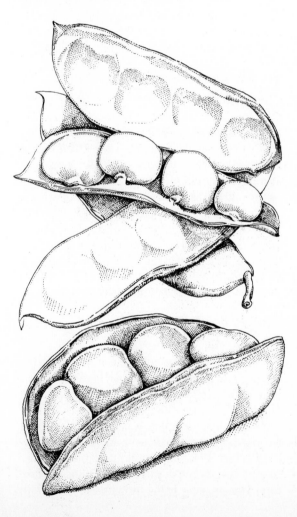

Best Soil Temperature for Growing 70°F to 80°F

Best Air Temperature for Growing 60°F to 80°F during the day.

Days to Germination 7 to 12

Weeks to Transplanting 3 to 5

Days to Maturity Bush, 75 to 80; pole, 85 to 90.

Greenhouse Varieties Lima beans don't grow well in the greenhouse.

Container Varieties Bush Baby, Fordhook Bush Lima, Fordhook 242, and Henderson.

Container Size 12 inches wide, 8 to 10 inches deep, with 1½ to 2 quarts of soil. Pole limas will need a trellis of some kind.

Poor Growth

Low Air Temperature

Lima beans are cold sensitive. If growth is poor, you may have planted them in soil that was too cold. To grow well, limas need 2½ months of warm weather with daytime averages of 70°F to 80°F. The best soil temperature for germination is 65°F to 85°F. You should delay your lima bean sowing until at least 2 weeks after the last frost.

PLANT MANAGEMENT

Water Requirements for Good Production

Make sure the plants get 1 inch of water every week from rain or by watering. Critical watering periods are during pollination and pod development; lack of water may cause pod drop. (See chapter 8 for more information on watering.)

Water Requirements for Maximum Production

Lima beans can use lots of water. For maximum production, give your plants 1 to 1½ inches of water each week.

Feeding Requirements

Apply compost or a slow-acting general-purpose fertilizer in spring. Spray plants with liquid seaweed extract two or three times during the growing season. This plant is a light feeder, so it needs little or no supplemental fertilizer over and above the one application of slow-acting fertilizer in the spring. (See chapter 8 for more information on feeding.)

MOST COMMON INSECT PESTS

Foliage Curls, Puckers, Turns Yellow

Aphid

If the foliage on your plants curls, puckers, and turns yellow, and the foliage and blooms become stunted, look for ants. They are a sign that your plants have aphids. Ants are attracted to a sticky honeydew secreted by aphids. These insects have soft, pear-shaped bodies about the size of a pinhead. They may be green, brown, or pink. You will find them in clusters on the undersides of young leaves. For light infestations, spray the plants vigorously with water in the early morning, three times, once every other day. For heavy infestations, apply a commercial insecticidal soap every 2 to 3 days until aphids are under control.

Small Ragged Holes in Leaves

Cabbage Looper

Small ragged holes in leaves indicate that your plants may be infested with cabbage loopers. The cabbage looper is a 1½-inch-long caterpillar that is light green with long yellowish stripes on its back. It loops as it walks. Spray plants with *Bacillus thuringiensis* (BT) every 2 weeks until the problem is solved.

Damage to Buds and Young Plants

Corn Earworm

Corn earworms can cause damage to flower buds and young plants and may stunt the growth of your beans. The corn earworm may be white, green, or red. It has spines and is 1½ inches long. The best control is to spray young leaves with a light horticultural oil mixed with *Bacillus thuringiensis* (BT) twice, 3 to 5 days apart.

Plants Die from Disease

Cucumber Beetle

The cucumber beetle causes minor physical damage to plants, but it can spread diseases that quickly kill them. It is ¼ inch long, oblong, and yellow with black stripes or spots. The best way to control cucumber beetles and the diseases they carry is to prevent them from feeding on young plants. Spread a covering, such as agricultural fleece, over your plants from germination until the plants start to bloom.

Seedling Stems Severed

Cutworm

Cutworms completely sever the stems of seedlings and transplants at or below the soil surface. They are 1- to 2-inch, dull-colored, plump, soft-bodied larvae that curl up when disturbed. Cutworms feed at night and hide in the soil during the day. To control cutworms, use barriers or traps to prevent access to seedlings. To protect individual plants, surround them with a collar, or make a trap by sprinkling cornmeal or bran meal around each plant. (See chapter 4 for more information on collars and meal traps.)

Resistant Varieties. Baby Fordhook and Baby White.

Tiny Holes in Leaves

Flea Beetle

If you find several little holes or perforations in the leaves of your plants, the plants may have flea beetles. Flea beetles are $\frac{1}{10}$ inch long, shiny, and black, and may have yellow or white markings. They are very active and jump like fleas when disturbed. Their feeding can destroy small plants rapidly. Apply pyrethrum every 2 to 3 days until infestation is under control. Usually two or three applications will take care of the problem. In the spring, cover plants with a barrier, such as agricultural fleece, to keep flea beetles off your bean plants. The cover should be removed by the time the plants begin to bloom.

Skeletonized Leaves

Japanese Beetle
If the leaves of your beans have been skeletonized, suspect the Japanese beetle. This shiny metallic-green beetle is about ½ inch long and has copper-brown wings. Set up pheromone beetle traps, making sure traps are no closer than 50 feet from vulnerable crops. Handpick stragglers or use pyrethrum if traps cannot handle the infestation. If Japanese beetles are a regular problem in your garden, set up the traps a week before emergence.

Mexican Bean Beetle
If the stems, pods, and leaves of your beans have all been chewed, and the leaves look skeletonized, check your plants for the Mexican bean beetle. The adult is ¼ inch long and round, and has yellow to gold to copper coloring with 16 black dots in three rows down its back. It looks somewhat like a lady bug. It lays yellow eggs in clusters on the undersides of leaves. The hump-backed, fuzzy larvae are orange or yellow and measure about ⅓ inch in length. Both the adults and larvae chew holes in the leaves. To control Mexican bean beetles, handpick early arrivals, with special attention to the easy-to-spot bright yellow eggs. If the infestation gets out of control, make two applications of pyrethrum, 3 days apart.

Weakened Plants

Leafhopper
Both adult leafhoppers and nymphs pierce leaves, buds, and stems and suck the sap and chlorophyll from cells, causing plants to weaken. Adults are green, wedge-shaped insects, ¼ to ⅓ inch long, that hold their wings in a rooflike position above their bodies. They are very active and move sideways. Nymphs resemble adults. To control serious infestations, apply insecticidal soap laced with isopropyl alcohol every 3 to 4 days. In early spring, apply a preventive spray of insecticidal soap and seaweed extract and cover seedlings with an agricultural fleece barrier for the first month of growth to deny leafhoppers access to your plants.
Resistant Varieties. Fordhook.

White or Brown Tunnels in Leaves

Leafminer
White or brown tunnels or blotches on the leaves of bean plants are symptoms of leafminers. Adult leafminers are black flies, about ¹⁄₁₀ inch long, usually with yellow stripes. They lay eggs on the undersides of leaves. Yellowish larvae hatch and tunnel inside the leaves, feeding between the upper and lower surfaces of leaves, which causes the tunnels or blotches. There can be stem damage below the soil. Remove and destroy the infested leaves. To prevent leafminers, use agricultural fleece over seeded areas or transplants.

Leaves Stippled Yellow

Mite
Leaves of lima beans that have mites become stippled, yellow, and dry, and sometimes pale yellow spots or blotches appear. Mites are not insects but arachnids, and are about the size of a grain of black pepper. They may be red, black, or brown. They feed by sucking out the plant's juices. In sucking chlorophyll out of the leaves, they cause small white dots to appear. In addition, they inject toxins into the leaves, which discolors and distorts them. To control infestations, spray plants with a forceful spray of water three times, once every three days, to knock mites from the leaves. If mites are still present, spray with insecticidal soap three times, once every 5 to 7 days.

Stunted Plants, Yellow Leaves

Nematode
Plants infected with nematodes are stunted and the leaves become yellow prematurely, and if they do survive to maturity, they produce low yields. Roots of affected plants have root knots. Nematodes are

microscopic whitish, translucent worms barely visible to the naked eye. They live in the soil and attack plant roots. Work 3 to 4 inches of compost (especially leaf mold) into the soil, fertilize with fish emulsion, and plant early in the season.

Large Ragged Holes in Leaves

Slug

Large ragged holes in the leaves or stems are a sign of slugs. They work their way from the bottom of a plant up. Look for trails of slime on the leaves and on the soil near the plants as further evidence of the presence of slugs. Slugs are 1 to 2 inches long and look like snails without shells. They may be brown, gray, white, pale yellow, purple, or nearly black with brown specks. You can control them by handpicking if you get them early in the season. The best way to control their damage is to set up a barrier to deny them access to the garden. Use hardware cloth, ashes, sand, or some other barrier. You can also make traps to catch slugs. (See the entry Slug in chapter 4 for information on making slug traps.)

Black Spots on Leaves

Tarnished Plant Bug

Black spots and pitting can be seen on the leaves, stem tips, buds, and fruit of infested plants. This pest can also deform roots, blacken terminal shoots, and ruin flowers. The adult tarnished plant bug is a ¼-inch-long, oval, flat, brownish insect, mottled with yellow and black. It sucks on blossom stems and other plant parts. Tarnished plant bugs are highly mobile. The nymphs are pale yellow, and the eggs are long and curved and inserted in stems, tips, and leaves. Sprays must be used early in the morning when bugs are least active. Try three applications of pyrethrum, one every 3 days, to handle nymphs and adults. The best way to control this pest is by fall and spring cleanup to prevent it from occurring in the first place.

Discolored Blossoms

Thrip

Thrips puncture petals and leaves to suck the sap, causing considerable discoloration and disfiguration. Leaves may become bleached and will wilt. Thrips are only ¹⁄₂₅ inch long. What is visible are their dark fecal pellets. To control them, spray with insecticidal soap every 3 days for 2 weeks. For serious infestations, use pyrethrum.

Holes in Seeds

Weevil

Weevil damage is usually not noticed until storage, when you will notice small holes in bean seeds. The adult weevil is brown or dark green, with mottling, and ¹⁄₁₀ to ½ inch long, depending on the species. It lays its eggs in holes chewed in the bean pods. The white larvae feed inside the seeds and emerge during storage. Inspect plants regularly, and as soon as weevils appear, spray with pyrethrum twice, 3 to 4 days apart, making sure to cover all leaf surfaces.

Weakened Plants, Yellow Leaves

Whitefly

Plants that have whiteflies weaken, their leaves turn yellow, and they die. Honeydew secreted by whiteflies encourages fungus. Molds often develop following an attack. Adult whiteflies are about the size of a pinhead and are mothlike, with dusty white wings. When an infested plant is shaken, it appears as if dandruff were flying off the leaves. Nymphs are yellowish, legless, flat, and oval, resembling scale at certain stages. To control infestations, spray plants with insecticidal soap spray every 2 to 3 days for 2 weeks. Use it also early in the season to prevent whiteflies. Spray every 2 weeks for the first months of the plant's life. Pyrethrum may be used as a last resort. Make two applications, 3 to 4 days apart.

Plants Wilt and Die

Wireworm

If your bean plants wilt and die, suspect the wireworm. Wireworms are the larvae of click beetles. They are

⅓ to 1½ inches long, dark brown to yellowish, jointed, hard shelled, and cylindrical. They chew on the roots of beans. Trap them with pieces of potato speared on the ends of sticks. (See the entry Wireworm in chapter 4 for information on how to use potato traps.) Plant a cover crop for long-term control.

MOST COMMON DISEASES

Black, Sunken Spots on Pods

Anthracnose
Beans infected with anthracnose develop round, black, sunken spots on pods and stems. Also, the veins on the undersides of leaves turn black. Apply an approved fungicide such as copper dust or liquid copper spray every 7 to 10 days. Do not work near plants when they are wet.
Resistant Varieties. Charlevoix Dark Red Kidney and Seafarer (navy bean).

Large Brown Blotches on Leaves

Bacterial Blight
The symptoms of bacterial blight include large brown blotches on the leaves, possibly bordered with yellow or red; water-soaked spots on pods; and sometimes seed discoloration. One species of bacterial blight, called halo blight, causes a yellow halo to form around the leaf spots. Bacterial blight cannot be cured. Remove and destroy infected and surrounding plants. Delay and plant for a fall crop to avoid blight.

Wilted Leaves

Bacterial Wilt
Bacterial wilt usually kills seedlings. If your plants are more than 3 inches tall, bacterial wilt will cause the leaves to become limp, wilt, and die. Wilting occurs especially during the warm part of the day. This disease cannot be cured. Remove and destroy plants immediately. Wash your hands and any tools in a bleach solution (one part household bleach to four parts water) before touching other plants. Pre-

vent bacterial wilt by following clean garden practices and planting seeds that are certified wilt-free.

Brown Spore Masses on Undersides of Leaves

Bean Rust
Initially, after plants become infected with bean rust, small, whitish, slightly raised spots appear, which turn to many small, reddish orange to brown spore masses after a few days. These can be seen primarily on the undersides of leaves and sometimes the stem. The leaves rapidly yellow, dry up, and drop. Avoid handling wet plants. Apply a sulfur spray or undiluted sulfur dust every 7 to 10 days until the disease is under control.

Mottled, Elongated Leaves

Common Mosaic
Signs of common mosaic include mottled, elongated leaflets, puckered along the midrib; distorted pods, leaves, and petioles; and dwarfed leaves or plants, with the eventual death of the plants. Common mosaic cannot be cured. Remove and destroy the infected and surrounding plants. Prevent common mosaic by controlling aphids, which transmit this disease, and by following clean gardening practices.

Curled, Puckered Leaves

Curly Top
Leaves that are puckered and curl downward, are cupped, or look like small green balls, indicate curly top. This disease dwarfs and kills young plants. Curly top cannot be cured. Remove and destroy infected and surrounding plants.

Seedlings Die

Damping-Off
Seedlings that have damping-off simply topple over. You will see a watery soft rot on the stem at the soil line. There is no cure for this disease. Remove and destroy all infected plants. When starting seeds

indoors, use commercial potting soil or pasteurize your own potting soil in an oven. Disinfect tools in heated water or a bleach solution (one part household bleach to four parts water). Provide soil with adequate drainage and use a fan for better air circulation. For direct seeding, make sure soil is well drained and warm. You might try spreading pasteurized soil or a sterile vermiculite in furrows where you plant your seeds.

White, Cottony Patches on Pods

Downy Mildew

Downy mildew produces white, cottony patches on bean pods; some may have a purple border. The upper surfaces of older leaves will have yellowish or light green areas. In seedlings, purplish lesions develop on the leaves and stems, which become covered with the white downy fungus. Plants die very rapidly after contracting this disease. If you catch the infection early, apply a copper-based fungicide to diseased and surrounding plants every 7 to 10 days until harvest. Remove and destroy any plants with a serious infection.
Resistant Varieties. Eastland and Thaxter.

Seeds Do Not Germinate

Seed Rot

Seed rot will prevent your bean seeds from germinating. It occurs when soil is too moist and not at the proper temperature for germination. If necessary, make a shallow ditch, fill it with commercial sterilized potting mix, and sow seeds in that mixture.

HARVEST AND STORAGE

When to Harvest

If you will be using lima beans fresh from the garden, pick them when the pods are well filled and plump but still bright colored. The end of the pod should feel spongy when squeezed between your fingers. Fresh beans can be picked for 3 to 4 weeks. If you will be drying your beans, let the pods pass the mature stage, and pick them when they are dry and papery.

Yield for 25-Foot Row   Bush, 6 to 8 pounds; pole, 10 to 20 pounds.
Volume vs. Weight   1 bushel equals 32 pounds.
Weight of 1-Quart Canning Jar   3 to 5 pounds
Number of Quarts Stored from 1 Bushel   6 to 10
Best Fresh Storage Method   Refrigerate unshelled lima beans in plastic bags; they will keep for 2 weeks.
Best Long-Term Storage Method   Shelled lima beans can be frozen for up to 12 months.
Other Long-Term Storage Methods   Dried beans will keep for more than 12 months; limas can also be canned or used in pickles.
Seed Storage   3 years

VEGETABLE Bean, Snap   *Phaseolus vulgaris*

DESCRIPTION AND ENVIRONMENT

Height   Bush, 10 to 15 inches; pole, 8 to 15 feet.

Spread   Bush, 4 to 8 inches; pole, 6 to 8 inches.

Root Depth   36 to 48 inches, bush and pole.
Shade Tolerance   Needs full sun.
Frost Tolerance   None
Preferred pH   5.8 to 6.5

PLANTING

Spring Planting Time 1 to 2 weeks after last expected frost. Any root disturbance will hinder growth, so handle seedlings as little as possible. When thinning, cut rather than pull unwanted seedlings.

Fall Planting Time 12 weeks before first expected frost.

Succession Planting Plant bush beans once a week. Pole beans need only one planting each season.

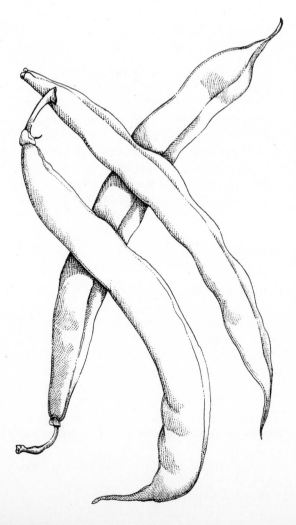

Planting Depth 1 to 1½ inches for spring planting; 2 inches for fall planting.

Spacing of Plants in Rows 4 to 6 inches for bush or pole.

Spacing of Plants in Beds Bush, 3 inches.

Best Soil Temperature for Germination 60°F to 85°F

Best Soil Temperature for Growing 70°F to 80°F

Best Air Temperature for Growing 60°F to 80°F during day.

Days to Germination 4 to 10

Weeks to Transplanting Direct-seed only.

Days to Maturity 52 to 70 for bush and pole, though pole tend to mature later than most varieties of bush bean.

Greenhouse Varieties Snap beans don't grow well in the greenhouse.

Container Varieties Bush Romano, Contender, Provider, and Tendercrop Stringless are good container bush varieties. Pole beans will need a trellis to climb.

Container Size 8 inches wide, 8 to 10 inches deep.

Stunted Plants

Planted Too Early

If germination is poor, and those plants that do germinate don't do very well, you may have planted the beans in soil that was too cold. The soil should be at least 50°F, but 60°F is even better. If you planted them in 40°F soil, they may never grow well even if they do germinate; the cold soil causes permanent shock. The first 2 or 3 hours that the seeds are in the soil are critical. If the soil temperature borders on being warm enough, don't plant in the morning, but wait until after noon. Soil can warm up as much as 20°F during a sunny day. (See chapter 7 for information on using tunnels and cloches to extend the growing season.)

PLANT MANAGEMENT

Water Requirements

Make sure the plants get 1 inch of water every week from rain or by watering. Critical times to be sure watering is consistent are during pollination and pod development. (See chapter 8 for more information on watering.)

Feeding Requirements

Apply compost or a slow-acting general-purpose fertilizer in spring. Spray plants with liquid seaweed extract two or three times during the growing season. This plant is a light feeder, so it needs little or no supplemental fertilizer over and above the one application of slow-acting fertilizer in the spring. (See chapter 8 for more information on feeding.)

MOST COMMON INSECT PESTS

Foliage Curls, Puckers, Turns Yellow

Aphid

If the foliage on your plants curls, puckers, and turns yellow, and the foliage and blooms become stunted, look for ants. They are a sign that your plants have aphids. Ants are attracted to a sticky honeydew secreted by aphids. These insects have soft, pear-shaped bodies about the size of a pinhead. They may be green, brown, or pink. You will find them in clusters on the undersides of young leaves. For light infestations, spray the plants vigorously with water in the early morning, three times, once every other day. For heavy infestations, apply a commercial insecticidal soap every 2 to 3 days until aphids are under control.

Small Ragged Holes in Leaves

Cabbage Looper

Small ragged holes in leaves indicate that your plants may be infested with cabbage loopers. The cabbage looper is a 1½-inch-long caterpillar that is light green with long yellowish stripes on its back. It loops as it walks. Spray plants with *Bacillus thuringiensis* (BT) every 2 weeks until the problem is solved.

Damage to Buds and Young Plants

Corn Earworm

Corn earworms can cause damage to flower buds and young plants and may stunt the growth of your beans. The corn earworm may be white, green, or even red. It has spines and is 1½ inches long. The best control is to spray young leaves with a light horticultural oil mixed with *Bacillus thuringiensis* (BT) twice, 3 to 5 days apart.

Plants Die from Disease

Cucumber Beetle

The cucumber beetle causes minor physical damage to plants, but it can spread diseases that quickly kill them. It is ¼ inch long, oblong, and yellow with black stripes or spots. The best way to control cucumber beetles and the diseases they carry is to prevent them from feeding on young plants. Spread a covering, such as agricultural fleece, over your plants from germination until the plants start to bloom. Once the bug is allowed to bite the plant, the disease is transmitted and the plant will die.

Seedling Stems Severed

Cutworm

Cutworms completely sever the stems of seedlings and transplants at or below the soil surface. They are 1- to 2-inch, dull-colored, plump, soft-bodied larvae that curl up when disturbed. Cutworms feed at night and hide in the soil during the day. To control cutworms, use barriers or traps to prevent access to seedlings. To protect individual plants, surround them with a collar, or make a trap by sprinkling cornmeal or bran meal around each plant. (See chapter 4 for more information on collars and meal traps.)

Resistant Varieties. Gold Crop, Idaho Refugee, Regal, and Wade.

Tiny Holes in Leaves

Flea Beetle

If you find many little holes or perforations in the leaves of your plants, the plants may have flea beetles. Flea beetles are $1/10$ inch long, shiny, and black, and may have yellow or white markings. They are very active and jump like fleas when disturbed. Their feeding can destroy small plants rapidly. Apply pyrethrum every 2 to 3 days to control infestations. Usually two or three applications will take care of the problem. In the spring, cover plants with a barrier, such as agricultural fleece, to keep flea beetles off your bean plants, at least until bloom time.

Skeletonized Leaves

Japanese Beetle

If the leaves of your beans have been skeletonized, suspect the Japanese beetle. This shiny metallic-green beetle is about $1/2$ inch long and has copper-brown wings. Set up pheromone beetle traps, making sure traps are no closer than 50 feet from vulnerable crops. Handpick stragglers or use pyrethrum if traps cannot handle the infestation. If Japanese beetles are a regular problem in your garden, set up the traps a week before emergence.

Mexican Bean Beetle

If the stems, pods, and leaves of your beans have all been chewed, and the leaves look skeletonized, check your plants for the Mexican bean beetle. The adult is $1/4$ inch long, round, and has yellow to gold to copper coloring with 16 black dots in three rows down its back. It looks somewhat like a lady bug. It lays yellow eggs in clusters on the undersides of leaves. The hump-backed, fuzzy larvae are orange or yellow and measure about $1/3$ inch in length. Both the adults and larvae chew holes in the leaves. To control Mexican bean beetles, handpick early arrivals, with special attention to the easy-to-spot bright yellow eggs. If the infestation gets out of control, make two applications of pyrethrum, 3 days apart.

Resistant Varieties. Black Valentine, Idaho Refugee, Logan, Supergreen, and Wade.

Weakened Plants

Leafhopper

Both adult leafhoppers and nymphs pierce leaves, buds, and stems and suck the sap and chlorophyll from cells, causing plants to weaken. The leaves may develop white or yellow mottling. Adults are green, wedge-shaped insects, $1/4$ to $1/3$ inch long, that hold their wings in a rooflike position above their bodies. They are very active and move sideways. Nymphs resemble adults. To control serious infestations, apply insecticidal soap laced with isopropyl alcohol every 3 to 4 days. In early spring, apply a preventive spray of insecticidal soap and seaweed extract and cover seedlings with an agricultural fleece barrier for the first month of growth to deny leafhoppers access to your plants.

White or Brown Tunnels in Leaves

Leafminer

White or brown tunnels or blotches on the leaves of bean plants are symptoms of leafminers. Adult leafminers are black flies, about $1/10$ inch long, usually with yellow stripes. They lay eggs on the undersides of leaves. Yellowish larvae hatch and tunnel inside the leaves, feeding between the upper and lower surfaces of leaves, which causes the tunnels or blotches. There can be stem damage below the soil. Remove and destroy the infested leaves. To prevent leafminers, use agricultural fleece over seeded areas or transplants.

Leaves Stippled Yellow

Mite

Leaves of snap beans that have mites become stippled, yellow, and dry, and sometimes pale yellow spots or blotches appear. Mites are not insects but arachnids, and are about the size of a grain of black pepper. They may be red, black, or brown. They feed by sucking out the plant's juices. In sucking chlorophyll out of the leaves, they cause small white dots to appear. In addition, they inject toxins into the leaves, which discolors and distorts them. To control infestations, spray plants with a forceful spray of water three times, once every three days, to knock mites from the leaves. If mites are still present, spray with insecticidal soap three times, once every 5 to 7 days.

Stunted Plants, Yellow Leaves

Nematode

Plants infected with nematodes are stunted and the leaves become yellow prematurely, and if they do survive to maturity, they produce low yields. Roots of affected plants have root knots. Nematodes are microscopic whitish, translucent worms barely visible to the naked eye. They live in the soil and attack plant roots. Plant resistant varieties early in the season and work 3 to 4 inches of compost (especially leaf mold) into the soil. Fertilize with fish emulsion.

Large Ragged Holes in Leaves

Slug

Large ragged holes in the leaves or stems are a sign of slugs. They work their way from the bottom of a plant up. Look for trails of slime on the leaves and on the soil near the plants as further evidence of the presence of slugs. Slugs are 1 to 2 inches long and look like snails without shells. They may be brown, gray, white, pale yellow, purple, or nearly black with brown specks. You can control them by handpicking if you get them early in the season. The best way to control their damage is to set up a barrier to deny them access to the garden. Use hardware cloth, ashes, sand, or some other barrier. You can also make traps to catch slugs. (See the entry Slug in chapter 4 for information on making slug traps.)

Black Spots on Leaves

Tarnished Plant Bug

Black spots and pitting can be seen on the leaves, stem tips, buds, and fruit of infested plants. This pest can also deform roots, blacken terminal shoots, and ruin flowers. The adult tarnished plant bug is a ¼-inch-long, oval, flat, brownish insect, mottled with yellow and black. It sucks on blossom stems and other plant parts. Tarnished plant bugs are highly mobile. The nymphs are pale yellow, and the eggs are long and curved and inserted in stems, tips, and leaves. Sprays must be used early in the morning when bugs are least active. Try three applications of pyrethrum, one every 3 days, to handle nymphs and adults. The best way to control this pest is by fall and spring cleanup to prevent it from occurring in the first place.

Discolored Blossoms

Thrip

Thrips puncture petals and leaves to suck the sap, causing considerable discoloration and disfiguration. Leaves may become bleached and will wilt. Thrips are only ¹⁄₂₅ inch long. What is visible are their dark fecal pellets. To control them, spray with insecticidal soap every 3 days for 2 weeks. For serious infestations, use pyrethrum.

Holes in Seeds

Weevil

Weevil damage is usually not noticed until storage, when you will notice small holes in bean seeds. The adult weevil is brown or dark green, with mottling. It lays its eggs in holes chewed in the bean pods. The white larvae feed inside the seeds and emerge during storage. Inspect plants regularly, and as soon as weevils appear, spray with pyrethrum twice, 3 to 4 days apart, making sure to cover all leaf surfaces.

Weakened Plants, Yellow Leaves

Whitefly

Plants that have whiteflies weaken, their leaves turn yellow, and they die. Honeydew secreted by whiteflies encourages fungus. Molds often develop following an attack. Adult whiteflies are about the size of a pinhead and are mothlike, with dusty white wings. When an infested plant is shaken, it appears as if dandruff were flying off the leaves. Nymphs are yellowish, legless, flat, and oval, resembling scale at certain stages. To control infestations, spray plants with insecticidal soap spray every 2 to 3 days for 2 weeks or until the whiteflies are under control. Use it also early in the season, as soon as plants are in the garden, to prevent whiteflies. Spray every 2 weeks for the first months of the plant's life. Pyrethrum may be used as a last resort. Make two applications, 3 to 4 days apart.

Plants Wilt and Die

Wireworm

If your bean plants wilt and die, suspect the wireworm. Wireworms are the larvae of click beetles. They are $\frac{1}{3}$ to $1\frac{1}{2}$ inches long, dark brown to yellowish, jointed, hard-shelled, and cylindrical. They chew on the roots of beans. Trap them with pieces of potato speared on the ends of sticks. (See the entry Wireworm in chapter 4 for more information on how to use potato traps.) Plant a cover crop for long-term control.

MOST COMMON DISEASES

Black, Sunken Spots on Pods

Anthracnose

Beans infected with anthracnose develop round, black, sunken spots on pods and stems. These spots are about ½ inch in diameter and usually are covered by a salmon-colored ooze during moist conditions. Also, the veins on the undersides of leaves turn black. Apply an approved sulfur- or copper-based fungicide every 7 to 10 days. Do not work near plants when they are wet.
Resistant Varieties. Charlevoix Dark Red Kidney, Flo, and Seafarer (navy bean).

Large Brown Blotches on Leaves

Bacterial Blight

The symptoms of bacterial blight include large brown blotches on the leaves, possibly bordered with yellow or red; water-soaked spots on pods; and sometimes seed discoloration. One species of bacterial blight, called halo blight, causes a yellow halo to form around the leaf spots. Bacterial blight cannot be cured. Remove and destroy infected and surrounding plants. Delay planting to avoid blight; plant for a fall crop.
Resistant Varieties. Seafarer (navy bean) and Tendergreen (some types).

Wilted Leaves

Bacterial Wilt

Bacterial wilt usually kills seedlings. If your plants are more than 3 inches tall, bacterial wilt will cause the leaves to become limp, wilt, and die. Wilting occurs especially during the warm part of the day. This disease cannot be cured. Remove and destroy plants immediately. Wash your hands and any tools in a bleach solution (one part household bleach to four parts water) before touching other plants. Prevent bacterial wilt by following clean garden practices and planting seeds that are certified wilt-free.
Resistant Varieties. Tendergreen.

Brown Spore Masses on Undersides of Leaves

Bean Rust

Initially, after plants become infected with bean rust, small, whitish, slightly raised spots appear, which turn to many small, reddish orange to brown spore masses after a few days. These can be seen primarily on the undersides of leaves and sometimes on the stem. The leaves rapidly yellow, dry up, and drop. Avoid handling wet plants. Apply a sulfur spray or undiluted sulfur dust every 7 to 10 days until the disease is under control.
Resistant Varieties. Cherokee Wax (yellow), Dade, Harvester, Kentucky Wonder, some types of Tendergreen, U.S. No. 3, and White Kentucky Wonder 191.

Mottled, Elongated Leaves

Common Mosaic

Signs of common mosaic include mottled, elongated leaflets, puckered along the midrib; distorted pods, leaves, and petioles; and dwarfed leaves or plants, with the eventual death of the plants. Common mosaic cannot be cured. Remove and destroy the infected and surrounding plants. Plant resistant varieties.

Resistant Varieties. Blue Lake (pole), Contender, Golden Wax Improved, Great Northern, Greensleeves, Idaho Refugee, Robust, Roma II, Tendercrop, Topcrop, U.S. No. 5, and Wisconsin Refugee.

Curled, Puckered Leaves

Curly Top

Leaves that are puckered and curl downward, are cupped, or look like small green balls, indicate curly top. This disease dwarfs and kills young plants. Mature plants do not usually show symptoms, and will usually live. Curly top cannot be cured. Remove and destroy infected and surrounding plants.

Resistant Varieties. Cape, Great Northern, Red Mexican, and University of Idaho.

Seedlings Die

Damping-Off

Seedlings that have damping-off simply topple over. You will see a watery soft rot on the stem at the soil line. There is no cure for this disease. Remove and destroy all infected plants. When starting seeds indoors, use commercial potting soil or pasteurize your own potting soil in an oven. Disinfect tools in heated water or a bleach solution (one part household bleach to four parts water). Provide soil with adequate drainage and use a fan for better air circulation. For direct seeding, make sure soil is well drained and warm. You might try spreading pasteurized soil or a sterile vermiculite in furrows where you plant your seeds.

Seeds Do Not Germinate

Seed Rot

Seed rot will prevent your bean seeds from germinating. It occurs when soil is too moist and the soil temperature is too cold for germination. If necessary, make a shallow ditch, fill it with commercial sterilized potting mix, and sow seeds in that mixture.

HARVEST AND STORAGE

When to Harvest

Bush varieties will be ready to harvest 2 to 3 weeks after they first bloom. Pods should be long, slender, and velvety. They should snap readily, but the tips should still be pliable. Green beans should have a bright green color, and wax beans, a pale yellow color. Harvest before the seeds fill out the pods. Pole beans and bush wax beans mature more slowly than green bush beans. Don't pick beans when the plants are wet from rain or you could spread any disease that might be carried on the plant. Bush beans can be harvested for 2 to 4 weeks. Pole beans are harvested right through the season until the first frost. It is critical that you keep pole beans picked. Do not allow them to get fat and dry on the vine, or you will not continue to get beans throughout the season. If you will be drying your beans, let the pods pass the mature stage, and pick them when they are dry and papery.

Yield for 25-Foot Row   Bush, 20 to 30 pounds; pole, 50 to 70 pounds.

Volume vs. Weight   1 bushel equals 30 pounds.

Weight of 1-Quart Canning Jar   1½ to 2 pounds

Number of Quarts Stored from 1 Bushel   15 to 20

Best Fresh Storage Method   In plastic bags, beans will keep for 2 to 5 days in the refrigerator.

Best Long-Term Storage Method   Beans can be frozen for up to 12 months.

Other Long-Term Storage Methods Canned beans will keep for more than 12 months; dried will keep for several years; beans can also be pickled.

Seed Storage   3 years

VEGETABLE Beet *Beta vulgaris*

DESCRIPTION AND ENVIRONMENT

Height   6 to 12 inches
Spread   4 to 8 inches
Root Depth   Most roots to 2 feet; some reaching down to 5 feet.

Shade Tolerance   Needs full sun.
Frost Tolerance   Hardy; can withstand some short-term subfreezing temperatures.
Preferred pH   6.0 to 7.5

PLANTING

Spring Planting Time   2 to 4 weeks before last expected frost.

Fall Planting Time   8 to 10 weeks before first expected frost.

Succession Planting   Plant beets every 2 to 3 weeks until midsummer.

Planting Depth   1½ to 2 inches

Spacing of Plants in Rows   6 inches

Spacing of Plants in Beds   2 to 4 inches

Best Soil Temperature for Germination   50°F to 75°F

Best Soil Temperature for Growing 60°F to 75°F

Best Air Temperature for Growing 50°F to 75°F

Days to Germination   7 to 10

Weeks to Transplanting   Direct seeding is best.

Days to Maturity   50 to 80

Greenhouse Varieties   Beets do not grow well in the greenhouse.

Container Varieties   Baby Canning and Spinel Baby Beets are well suited for growing in containers. Pick them when they are about the size of a golf ball.

Container Size   6 to 12 inches deep.

PLANT MANAGEMENT

Water Requirements

Make sure plants get 1 inch of water every week from rain or by watering. Be consistent in watering. (See chapter 8 for more information on watering.)

Feeding Requirements for Good Production

Apply compost or a slow-acting general-purpose fertilizer in the spring, and give supplemental light feedings (either a side-dressing or foliar spray) monthly through the growing season. (See chapter 8 for more information on feeding.)

Feeding Requirements for Maximum Production

Beets are heavy feeders. In addition to the spring feeding mentioned above, give your plants a light supplement (either a side-dressing or foliar spray) every 2 weeks during the growing season. When tops are 4 to 5 inches high, go light on nitrogen, which encourages leaf growth. Spray plants with liquid seaweed extract two or three times during the growing season.

Long, Tapered Roots

Potassium Deficiency

Potassium-deficient beet roots grow long and tapered instead of bulbous. To remedy this problem quickly, spray the plants with seaweed extract. Side-dress plants with wood ashes. (See chapter 8 for more information on potassium deficiency.)

MOST COMMON INSECT PESTS

Defoliated Plants, Tunnels in Roots

Carrot Weevil

Carrot weevils chew holes in the leaves, eventually defoliating beet plants except for the ribs of leaves and stems. The larvae tunnel into beet roots. The adult weevil is brown, ⅕ inch long, with a hard shell.

The larvae are whitish grubs with brown heads and no legs. They burrow into the tops and roots of beets. To control infestations, spray beet plants with pyrethrum as soon as adult beetles appear in spring. To deny weevils access to your beets in the first place, cover the beet plants with agricultural fleece early in the season. Apply juvenile state nematodes to prevent infestation of the roots by the grubs. (See chapter 4 for more information on parasitic nematodes.)

Tiny Holes in Leaves

Flea Beetle

If you find several little holes or perforations in the leaves of your plants, the plants may have flea beetles. Flea beetles are ¹/₁₀ inch long, shiny, and black, and may have yellow or white markings. They are very active and jump like fleas when disturbed. Their feeding can destroy small plants rapidly. Apply pyrethrum, making two applications 3 to 4 days apart, to control infestations. In the spring, cover plants with a barrier, such as agricultural fleece, to keep flea beetles off your beet plants.

Weakened Plants

Leafhopper

Both adult leafhoppers and nymphs pierce leaves, buds, and stems and suck the sap and chlorophyll from cells, causing plants to weaken. The beet leafhopper is pale green or yellow, about ⅛ inch long, and has slender, long hind legs that enable it to jump quickly into the air. When flying, it looks like a tiny white fly. To control serious infestations, apply insecticidal soap laced with isopropyl alcohol every 2 to 3 days for 2 weeks. In early spring, apply a preventive spray of insecticidal soap and seaweed extract and cover seedlings with an agricultural fleece barrier for the first month of growth to deny leafhoppers access to your plants.

White or Brown Tunnels in Leaves

Leafminer

White or brown tunnels or blotches on leaves are signs that your beets have leafminers. The leaves may turn yellow and blotched and look blistered or curled. Leafminers are small black flies, usually with yellow stripes. The tiny yellowish larvae feed between the upper and lower surfaces of leaves, causing the tunnels or blotches to appear. You may also find stem damage below the soil. Remove the infested leaves before the larvae mature. The best way to control leafminers, though, is to screen out the adult flies by covering seeded areas with agricultural fleece.

Leaves Stippled Yellow

Mite
Leaves of beets that have mites become stippled, yellow, and dry, and sometimes pale yellow spots or blotches appear. Mites are not insects but arachnids, and are about the size of a grain of black pepper. They may be red, black, or brown. They feed by sucking out the plant's juices. In sucking chlorophyll out of the leaves, they cause small white dots to appear. In addition, they inject toxins into the leaves, which discolors and distorts them. To control infestations, spray plants with a forceful spray of water three times, once every other day, to knock mites from the leaves. If mites are still present, spray with insecticidal soap three times, once every 5 to 7 days.

Weakened Plants, Yellow Leaves

Whitefly
Plants that have whiteflies weaken, their leaves turn yellow, and they die. Honeydew secreted by whiteflies encourages fungus. Molds often develop following an attack. Adults are about the size of a pinhead and are mothlike, with dusty white wings. When an infested plant is shaken, it appears as if dandruff were flying off the leaves. Nymphs are yellowish, legless, flat, and oval, resembling scale at certain stages. To control infestations, spray plants with insecticidal soap spray every 2 to 3 days for 2 weeks. Use it also early in the season to prevent whiteflies. Spray every 2 weeks for the first months of the plant's life. Pyrethrum may be used as a last resort. Make two applications, 3 to 4 days apart.

Plants Wilt and Die

Wireworm
If your beets wilt and die, suspect the wireworm. Wireworms are the larvae of click beetles. They are $\frac{1}{3}$ to $1\frac{1}{2}$ inches long, dark brown to yellowish, jointed, hard shelled, and cylindrical. They chew on the roots of many plants. Trap them with pieces of potato speared on the ends of sticks. (See the entry Wireworm in chapter 4 for more information on how to use potato traps.) Plant a cover crop for long-term control.

MOST COMMON DISEASES

Corky Spots on Beets

Scab
Beet plants with scab develop corky spots on the root surfaces. Maintain uniform soil moisture, and lower the soil pH to 5.3 or less by adding manure or other organic material.

HARVEST AND STORAGE

When to Harvest

It's best to harvest beets when they are fairly small, 1 to 2 inches in diameter; larger roots are sweeter, but also tougher and woodier. Beets should be smooth, firm, and round with a slender taproot. Their color should be rich and deep red (golden in some varieties). You can pick beets for 4 to 6 weeks before they become too woody.

Yield for 24-Square-Foot Bed 30 to 40 pounds

Yield for 25-Foot Row 25 to 30 pounds

Volume vs. Weight 1 bushel (without tops) equals 52 pounds.

Weight of 1-Quart Canning Jar 2 to 3 pounds

Number of Quarts Stored from 1 Bushel 17 to 26

Best Fresh Storage Method   Cut off the tops to 2 inches above the root, and refrigerate beets in plastic bags. They will keep for 1 to 2 weeks.

Best Long-Term Storage Method   Beets can be stored in damp sand in a cool (32°F to 40°F), humid (95 percent) place such as a root cellar for 2 to 5 months. They may also be kept in the garden for 3 to 4 months under at least 1 foot of organic mulch.

Other Long-Term Storage Methods   Frozen beets are only fair in quality but will keep for about 8 months. Canned beets will keep for more than 12 months. Beets can be pickled as well.

Seed Storage   4 to 6 years

NOTES AND RESEARCH

The highest yield of baby beets is obtained when they are sown at a rate of 10 to 15 seeds per square foot. For larger, more mature beets, the best spacing is 5 to 10 seeds per square foot.

VEGETABLE **Broccoli**   *Brassica ruvo,* Botrytis Group

DESCRIPTION AND ENVIRONMENT

Height   18 inches
Spread   15 to 24 inches
Root Depth   18 to 36 inches
Shade Tolerance   Needs only 5 hours of sun a day (partial shade).
Frost Tolerance   Hardy, will withstand some subfreezing temperatures.
Preferred pH   6.0 to 7.5

PLANTING

Spring Planting Time   From 4 to 6 weeks before last expected frost to 2 to 3 weeks after last frost.

Fall Planting Time   From 14 to 17 weeks before first expected frost. Shade young plants if summers are very hot (average temperatures over 85°F).

Succession Planting   If the summers do not get too hot (average temperatures over 85°F), plant more broccoli 1 month after the first planting. Otherwise, wait for fall planting.

Planting Depth   ¼ to ½ inch
Spacing of Plants in Rows   14 to 24 inches; rows 24 inches apart.
Spacing of Plants in Beds   15 to 18 inches
Best Soil Temperature for Germination   50°F to 65°F
Best Soil Temperature for Growing   65°F to 75°F
Best Air Temperature for Growing   Day, 60°F to 75°F; night, 50°F to 65°F.
Days to Germination   3 to 10
Weeks to Transplanting   6 to 8
Days to Maturity   110 after direct seeding; 60 to 80 after transplanting.

Greenhouse Varieties   Broccoli does not grow well in the greenhouse.

Container Varieties   Any variety is suitable for growing in containers, but the Crusader Hybrid tends to be smaller and more compact than most. Provide good drainage and keep the broccoli plants cool and moist.

Container Size   20 inches deep.

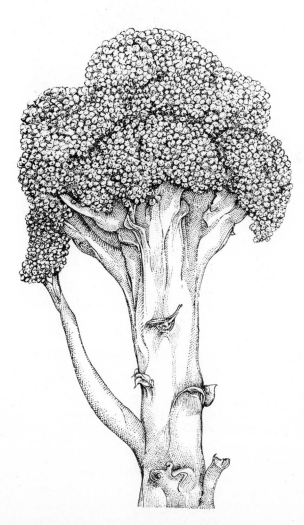

Small Heads

Compacted Clay Soil
Broccoli planted in heavy clay soil will produce small heads. You can improve clayey soil by adding compost, sand, or peat moss.

Late or Early Transplanting
If your broccoli plants produce heads less than 2 inches across (known as buttoning), you may have transplanted seedlings too early or too late. Seedlings must be transplanted by the time they are 4 to 6 weeks old or they will become potbound, which causes them to produce small heads. On the other hand, if they are transplanted too early, the cold temperatures will cause buttoning. To be certain this doesn't occur, you can plant a buttoning-resistant variety or use row covers to raise the temperature enough to prevent buttoning.
Resistant Varieties. Premium Crop.

Planted Too Closely
If your broccoli heads are small, you may be planting them too closely together. Larger plants require a lot of space, as much as 24 inches apart, in rows 24 inches apart. If your garden is small, you can place your plants as little as 12 inches apart, giving you modest heads but more broccoli per square foot of garden. These closely spaced plants may need additional nitrogen. Mulching benefits broccoli, especially if temperatures climb above 75°F. An organic mulch keeps roots cool and provides water at a more even rate. To produce the best-yielding plants, keep weeds out of the garden, at least for the first month.

No Heads

High Air Temperature
Hot weather may prevent your broccoli from producing any heads. Broccoli prefers cool temperatures, especially at night. Organic mulch helps cool the soil, and shading material gives modest help in protecting plants from the heat of the direct sun.

Uneven Ripening

Sudden Rise in Air Temperature

A sudden rise in air temperature that occurs when heads are forming can greatly harm your crop. Temperatures of 90°F can produce stalks of uneven lengths, and one part of a head might have tight flower buds while another part may have buds that are almost ready to open. In addition, maturity dates will be erratic.

Delayed Maturity

Seedling Container Too Small

Broccoli transplants placed in containers that are too small (less than 12 inches deep) may mature slowly. Use larger containers, which will produce sturdier plants.

PLANT MANAGEMENT

Water Requirements for Good Production

Make sure plants get 1 inch of water every week from rain or by watering. (See chapter 8 for more information on watering.)

Water Requirements for Maximum Production

This plant can use lots of water. For maximum production, give it up to 1½ inches of water each week. Critical watering periods are during head development and early in the season to prevent buttoning.

Feeding Requirements for Good Production

Apply compost or a slow-acting general-purpose fertilizer in spring. Give plants supplemental light feedings (either a side-dressing or foliar spray) monthly throughout the growing season. (See chapter 8 for more information on feeding.)

Feeding Requirements for Maximum Production

Broccoli is a heavy feeder. For maximum production, in addition to the spring feeding mentioned above, give plants a light supplement every 2 weeks during the growing season. A critical period during which a supplemental feeding greatly improves broccoli plants is 3 weeks after transplanting; go light on nitrogen, though. Spray plants with liquid seaweed extract two or three times during the growing season.

No Heads

Calcium Deficiency

If your broccoli plants do not produce heads, the cause may be a calcium deficiency. To prevent this problem from occurring next season, spread crushed limestone over the soil and till it in. (See chapter 8 for more information on calcium deficiency.)

Improper Watering

Improper watering, meaning inconsistent watering, can prevent head formation. Early in the season, broccoli needs at least an inch of water a week. Broccoli planted for fall harvest needs slightly less water, but the supply must be steady.

Fibrous Spears

Lack of Water

If you don't meet the watering needs of your broccoli, it will be fibrous. Water your plants lavishly for succulent spears. Commercial growers give their plants 1 to 1½ inches of water a week to get prime specimens for market.

Light Green or Yellow Leaves

Nitrogen Deficiency

If the leaves of your broccoli seedlings are light green or yellow in color, they are probably suffering from a nitrogen deficiency. Nitrogen and phosphorus deficiencies are the most common nutrient problems in broccoli. To remedy the problem quickly, spray plants with fish emulsion or another liquid fertilizer. (See chapter 8 for more information on nitrogen deficiency.)

Hollow Stems, Uneven Heads

Excess Nitrogen
Rapid leaf and shoot growth and a delay in the development of heads are the first signs that your broccoli plants have received too much nitrogen. This may result in hollow stems and uneven heads with a depression in the center. In rainy weather this depression can collect water and become a site for diseases. If your soil is high in nitrogen, choose varieties that are less susceptible to the problems caused by excess nitrogen.
Resistant Varieties. Emperor and Green Dwarf #36.

Purplish Color on Undersides of Leaves

Phosphorus Deficiency
Purplish coloring on the undersides of broccoli seedlings is a sign of phosphorus deficiency. Phosphorus and nitrogen deficiencies are the most common nutrient problems in broccoli. To remedy the problem quickly, spray plants with fish emulsion or other liquid fertilizer. (See chapter 8 for more information on phosphorus deficiency.)

MOST COMMON INSECT PESTS

Foliage Curls, Puckers, Turns Yellow

Aphid
If the foliage on your broccoli plants curls, puckers, and turns yellow, and plant growth becomes stunted, look for ants. They are a sign that your plants might have aphids. Ants are attracted to a sticky honeydew secreted by aphids. Broccoli plants are particularly bothered by cabbage aphids, which have soft, pear-shaped bodies about the size of a pinhead, are green to powdery blue in color, and are covered with a fine whitish wax. You will find them in clusters on the undersides of young leaves and in the heads. For light infestations, spray plants vigorously with water in the early morning, three times, once every other day. Heavy infestations can be dealt with by applying commercial insecticidal soap every 2 to 3 days until aphids are under control.

Small Ragged Holes in Leaves

Cabbage Looper
Small ragged holes in leaves indicate that your plants may be infested with cabbage loopers. Later in the season, the worms bore into developing broccoli heads. The cabbage looper is a 1½-inch-long caterpillar that is light green with long yellowish stripes on its back. It loops as it walks. Spray *Bacillus thuringiensis* (BT) on infested plants every 2 weeks until heads form.

Brown Tunnels in Stems

Cabbage Maggot
Brown tunnels in the stem just below soil level indicate cabbage maggots. Seedlings become yellow, growth is stunted, and plants lack vigor. The infested plants wilt during the heat of the day, and eventually die. The cabbage maggot is a small, white, legless worm about ¼ inch long. The adult resembles a housefly. Maggots tunnel into plant roots and stems. Bacterial diseases such as black leg may result, causing the plants to wilt. To control infestations, apply wood ashes or a lime drench (1 cup of lime in 1 quart of water; let sit overnight) around the root ball of each plant. The best control is to prevent flies from laying eggs in the first place. Spread a barrier, such as agricultural fleece, over transplants, or place a collar around the stem of each plant. (See chapter 4 for information on how to construct these collars.)

Seedling Stems Severed

Cutworm
Cutworms completely sever the stems of seedlings and transplants at or below the soil surface. They are 1- to 2-inch, dull-colored, plump, soft-bodied larvae that curl up when disturbed. Cutworms feed at night and hide in the soil during the day. To control cutworms, use barriers or traps to prevent

access to seedlings. To protect individual plants, surround them with a collar, or make a trap by sprinkling cornmeal or bran meal around each plant. (See chapter 4 for more information on collars and meal traps.)

Tiny Holes in Leaves

Flea Beetle
If you find many little holes or perforations in the leaves of your plants, the plants may have flea beetles. Flea beetles are $1/10$ inch long, shiny and black, and may have yellow or white markings. They are very active and jump like fleas when disturbed. Their feeding can destroy small plants rapidly. Apply pyrethrum, making two applications, 3 to 4 days apart, to control infestations. In the spring, cover seedlings with a barrier, such as agricultural fleece, to deny flea beetles access to your plants.
Resistant Varieties. Atlantic, Coastal, De Cicco, Gem, and Italian Green Sprouting.

Wilted Leaves with Black Spots

Harlequin Bug
If the leaves of your plants develop yellowish or black spots and then wilt and die, suspect the harlequin bug. This insect is ¼ inch long and shaped like a shield, with a triangle on its back. It has patterned markings in black and red. Harlequin bugs emit a foul odor. To control infestations, spray plants with an insecticidal soap laced with isopropyl alcohol every 2 to 3 days for 2 weeks. Apply insecticidal soap twice, 5 to 7 days apart, in early spring to prevent harlequin bugs.
Resistant Varieties. Atlantic, Coastal, Gem, and Grande.

Large Ragged Holes in Leaves

Imported Cabbage Worm
Imported cabbage worms chew large ragged holes in broccoli leaves, and they may bore into the heads, leaving trails of dark green frass, or excrement. The worm is light green with one yellow stripe, and measures 1¼ inches long. The adult is a common white butterfly with three to four black spots on its wings that is active during the day. To control infestations, apply *Bacillus thuringiensis* (BT) every 10 to 14 days until the pests are under control. Prevent cabbage worms by spraying plants with BT early in the season, every 2 weeks from transplanting until heads form, and covering transplants with an agricultural fleece barrier.

Slug
Large ragged holes in the leaves or stems can also be a sign of slugs. They work their way from the bottom of a plant up. Look for trails of slime on the leaves and on the soil near the plants as further evidence of the presence of slugs. Slugs are 1 to 2 inches long and look like snails without shells. They may be brown, gray, white, pale yellow, purple, or nearly black with brown specks. You can control them by handpicking if you get them early in the season. The best way to control their damage is to set up a barrier to deny them access to the garden. Use hardware cloth, ashes, sand, or some other barrier. You can also make traps to catch slugs. (See the entry Slug in chapter 4 for information on making slug traps.)

Leaves Stippled Yellow

Mite
Leaves of broccoli that have mites become stippled, yellow, and dry, and sometimes pale yellow spots or blotches appear. Mites are not insects but arachnids, and are about the size of a grain of black pepper. They may be red, black, or brown. They feed by sucking out the plant's juices. In sucking chlorophyll out of the leaves, they cause small white dots to appear. In addition, they inject toxins into the leaves, which discolors and distorts them. To control infestations, spray plants with a forceful spray of water three times, once every other day, to knock mites from the leaves. If mites are still present, spray with insecticidal soap three times, once every 5 to 7 days.

Chewed Foliage

Weevil

If the leaves of your broccoli plants are chewed to the stem, suspect the vegetable weevil. This pest is gray to brownish in color with a V-shaped mark near the tip of its wing covers. It is about ½ inch long and has a long snout. Weevils feed at night and hide during the day. As they appear, spray with pyrethrum twice, 3 to 4 days apart.

Weakened Plants, Yellow Leaves

Whitefly

Plants that have whiteflies weaken, their leaves turn yellow, and they die. Honeydew secreted by whiteflies encourages fungus. Molds often develop following an attack. Adults are about the size of a pinhead and are mothlike, with dusty white wings. When an infested plant is shaken, it appears as if dandruff were flying off the leaves. Nymphs are yellowish, legless, flat, and oval, resembling scale at certain stages. To control infestations, spray plants with insecticidal soap spray every 2 to 3 days for 2 weeks. Use it also early in the season to prevent whiteflies. Spray every 2 weeks for the first months of the plant's life. Pyrethrum may be used as a last resort. Make two applications, 3 to 4 days apart.

MOST COMMON DISEASES

Dark Patches on Leaves

Black Leg

The leaves and stems of broccoli plants infected with black leg have well-defined dark patches over which many tiny black dots are scattered. The edges of leaves will wilt and turn bluish or red. Sunken areas develop on the stem near the ground, which girdle the stem. The entire plant may wilt or topple over. Fixed copper fungicides are sometimes effective in controlling this disease. Apply as directed on the package. If this treatment does not halt the disease, remove and destroy the infected plants.

Yellow, Wedge-shaped Areas on Leaves

Black Rot

The leaves of broccoli plants infected with bacterial black rot develop yellow, wedge-shaped areas with darkened veins; then they wilt. The vascular bundles in leaves and stems are black and bad smelling. Young plants may not produce heads, and the heads on older plants that become infected will rot. Black rot cannot be cured. Remove and destroy the infected and surrounding plants. Micronized sulfur helps to control the spread of black rot to other plants. Apply the sulfur to unaffected plants every 7 days until harvest.

Resistant Varieties. Emperor Hybrid.

Poor Crop Development

Club Root

In general, plants that have club root exhibit the effects of a malfunctioning root system: wilting, poor development, and small heads. Under the soil you will find misshapen roots with club-shaped swellings. Try to prevent this disease by following clean gardening practices, dipping young transplants in a fungicidal solution, and rotating plants (the fungus persists in the soil for 7 years). Club root is more of a problem with plants growing in acid soil. Test your soil, and if the pH is too low, add lime.

Seedlings Die

Damping-Off

Seedlings that have damping-off simply topple over. You will see a watery soft rot on the stem at the soil line. There is no cure for this disease. Remove and destroy all infected plants. When starting seeds indoors, use commercial potting soil, or pasteurize your own potting soil in an oven. Disinfect tools in a bleach solution (one part household bleach to four parts water). Soak seeds in brine (1 cup of salt in 1 quart of water), or lime and wood solution (1 cup of lime and wood ashes in 1 quart of water). Provide soil with adequate drainage and use a fan for better air circulation. For direct seeding, make sure soil is well drained and warm. You might try spreading pasteurized soil or a sterile vermiculite in furrows where you plant your seeds.

White Downy Substance on Leaves

Downy Mildew

Yellowish or light green leaf spots appear on the upper surface of older leaves in plants with downy mildew. These spots turn brown, with bluish black, lacelike markings, and become covered with white downy mold in moist conditions. The heads are shaggy. Seedlings infected with downy mildew develop purplish lesions on leaves and stems, which become covered with a white downy fungus. Plants die very rapidly after contracting the disease. If you catch the infection early, apply a copper-based fungicide to diseased and surrounding plants every 7 to 10 days until harvest. Remove and destroy any plants with a serious infection.

Resistant Varieties. Citation, Emperor, Futura, Green Dwarf, and Orion.

Water-soaked Spots on Leaves

Leaf Spot

Broccoli plants that have leaf spot develop water-soaked spots that later grow in size and take on a brownish or purplish gray color. Leaf spot cannot be cured. Remove and destroy infected and surrounding plants.

Part of Plant Rots

Rhizoctonia

Rhizoctonia in crucifers is characterized by darkened and girdled areas on the stem near the soil line. Affected plants are weak, produce small heads, and sometimes wilt and die. Bottom rot develops on plants after they have been transplanted to the garden. Dark, slightly sunken spots develop on basal leaves near the soil. In moist conditions the rot spreads to adjacent leaves and causes the head to rot. Rhizoctonia also commonly causes damping-off, a watery soft rot on the stem at the soil line. Rhizoctonia cannot be controlled. Remove and destroy infected plants. To prevent rhizoctonia from becoming a problem, avoid planting broccoli in short rotations where bottom rot and damping-off have been a problem. Pasteurizing the soil used to raise seedlings and solarizing the garden soil also help to control rhizoctonia. (See chapter 5 for more information on soil pasteurization and solarization.)

Seeds Do Not Germinate

Seed Rot

Seed rot will prevent your broccoli seeds from germinating. It occurs when soil is too moist and too cold for germination. If necessary, make a shallow ditch, fill it with commercial sterilized potting mix, and sow seeds in that mixture.

Yellow Lower Leaves

Yellows

The symptoms of yellows are similar to those of black rot. The lower leaves of plants turn yellow, then brown, and finally drop. Broccoli heads may appear stunted and taste bitter. Yellows cannot be cured. Remove and destroy infected and surrounding plants.

HARVEST AND STORAGE

When to Harvest

Cut the central head while buds are still compact and not showing any yellow color. More side shoots will form after the main head is cut, giving you up to 8 weeks of harvest period. Cut the bottom of the main stem at an angle to prevent rotting at the cut end.

Yield for 24-Square-Foot Bed   15 to 25 pounds

Yield for 25-Foot Row   15 to 25 pounds
Volume vs. Weight   1 bushel equals 24 to 36 pounds.
Weight of 1-Quart Canning Jar   2 to 3 pounds
Number of Quarts Stored from 1 Bushel   12
Best Fresh Storage Method   Always soak broccoli briefly in cold salted water to drive out any worms that may be hiding in the head. Place the trimmed broccoli in a cup or glass of water and refrigerate. Otherwise, rinse and store in a clear plastic bag. It will keep for 10 to 14 days.
Best Long-Term Storage Method   Broccoli can be frozen for 12 months.
Second-Best Long-Term Storage Method   Broccoli can be pickled.
Seed Storage   5 years

Yellow Flowers in Head

Harvested Too Late
To maintain peak production, continually harvest side sprouts before the yellow flowers open. Compact heads and side sprouts whose buds are still tight and firm have the best flavor and also last longest in the freezer. Premium Crop and Citation are two varieties that hold the tight-bud stage well in the garden, making them top choices for gardeners who can't harvest every day.

Low Yield

Improper Harvesting
To increase your broccoli yield, remove the growing point (the central stalk) before a head forms. Studies with Green Duke broccoli showed that later harvesting (70 days after planting) produced the highest number of side shoots, but early pinching (42 days after planting, when the plant has three leaves) produced fewer but larger side shoots and the highest overall yield.

VEGETABLE *Brussels Sprouts*   *Brassica oleracea,* Gemmifera Group

DESCRIPTION AND ENVIRONMENT

Height   36 to 48 inches
Spread   24 inches
Root Depth   18 to 36 inches
Shade Tolerance   Some; needs a minimum of 6 hours of sun a day.
Frost Tolerance   Hardy, can take some subfreezing temperatures.
Preferred pH   6.0 to 7.5

PLANTING

Spring Planting Time   4 to 6 weeks before last expected frost to 2 to 3 weeks after frost.

Fall Planting Time   17 weeks before first frost; short-season gardeners should always use transplants.

Planting Depth   ¼ to ½ inch

Spacing of Plants in Rows   14 to 24 inches

Spacing of Plants in Beds   15 to 18 inches

Best Soil Temperature for Germination   65°F to 75°F

Best Air Temperature for Growing Day, 60°F to 70°F; night, 50°F to 60°F.

Days to Germination   3 to 10

Weeks to Transplanting   5 to 8

Days to Maturity   80 to 90 after transplanting.

Greenhouse Varieties   Brussel sprouts cannot be grown in the greenhouse.

Container Varieties   All varieties of brussels sprouts can be grown in containers.

Container Size   12 inches wide and 12 inches deep.

PLANT MANAGEMENT

Water Requirements

Make sure plants get 1 inch of water every week from rain or by watering. (See chapter 8 for more information on watering.)

Feeding Requirements for Good Production

Apply compost or a slow-acting general-purpose fertilizer in spring and give plants supplemental light feedings (either side-dressings or foliar spray) monthly throughout the growing season. (See chapter 8 for more information on feeding.)

Feeding Requirements for Maximum Production

Brussels sprouts are heavy feeders. In addition to the spring feeding mentioned above, give them a light supplement every 2 weeks during the growing season. Critical times during which supplemental feedings greatly improve brussels sprouts are 3 weeks after transplanting and again when sprouts begin to appear. Spray plants with liquid seaweed extract two or three times during the growing season.

Bronze Leaves

Potassium Deficiency

Signs of potassium deficiency in brussels sprouts include bronzing of leaf borders that spreads inward. Leaf margins will become parched, and brown spots will appear on the leaves. To remedy the problem quickly, apply a foliar spray of fish emulsion or other liquid fertilizer. Side-dress plants with wood ashes. (See chapter 8 for more information on potassium deficiency.)

MOST COMMON INSECT PESTS

Foliage Curls, Puckers, Turns Yellow

Aphid

If the foliage on your brussels sprouts curls, puckers, and turns yellow, and plant growth becomes stunted, look for ants. They are a sign that your plants might have aphids. Ants are attracted to a sticky honeydew secreted by aphids. Brussels sprouts are bothered particularly by cabbage aphids, which have soft, pear-shaped bodies about the size of a pinhead, are green to powdery blue in color, and are covered with a fine whitish wax. You will find them in clusters on the undersides of young leaves and in the heads. For light infestations, spray plants vigorously with water in the early morning three times, once every other day. Heavy infestations can be dealt with by applying commercial insecticidal soap every 2 to 3 days.

Small Ragged Holes in Leaves

Cabbage Looper

Small ragged holes in leaves indicate that your plants may be infested with cabbage loopers. Later in the season, the worms bore into the developing sprouts of brussels sprouts. The cabbage looper is a 1½-inch-long caterpillar that is light green with long yellowish stripes on its back. It loops as it walks. Spray *Bacillus thuringiensis* (BT) on infested plants every 2 weeks until heads form.

Brown Tunnels in Stems

Cabbage Maggot

Brown tunnels in the stem just below soil level indicate cabbage maggots. Seedlings become yellow, growth is stunted, and plants lack vigor. The infested plants wilt during the heat of the day, and eventually die. The cabbage maggot is a small, white, legless worm about ¼ inch long. The adult resembles a housefly. Maggots tunnel into plant roots and stems. Bacterial diseases such as black leg, which causes dark patches on leaves, and soft rot, which causes plant decomposition, may result, causing the plants to wilt. To control infestations, apply wood ashes or a lime drench (1 cup of lime in 1 quart of water; let sit overnight) around the root ball of each plant. The best control is to prevent flies from laying eggs in the first place. Spread a barrier, such as agricultural fleece, over transplants, or place a collar around the stem of each plant. (See chapter 4 for information on how to construct these collars.)

Seedling Stems Severed

Cutworm

Cutworms completely sever the stems of seedlings and transplants at or below the soil surface. They are 1- to 2-inch, dull-colored, plump, soft-bodied larvae that curl up when disturbed. Cutworms feed at night and hide in the soil during the day. To control cutworms, use barriers or traps to prevent access to seedlings. To protect individual plants, surround them with a collar, or make a trap by sprinkling cornmeal or bran meal around each plant. (See chapter 4 for more information on collars and meal traps.)

Tiny Holes in Leaves

Flea Beetle

If you find many little holes or perforations in the leaves of your plants, the plants may have flea beetles. Flea beetles are ¹⁄₁₀ inch long, shiny, and black, and may have yellow or white markings. They are very active and jump like fleas when disturbed. Their feeding can destroy small plants rapidly. Apply pyrethrum, making two applications, 3 to 4 days apart, to control infestations. In the spring, cover transplants with a barrier, such as agricultural fleece, to deny flea beetles access to your plants.

Wilted Leaves with Black Spots

Harlequin Bug

If the leaves of your plants develop white blotches or black spots and then wilt and die, suspect the harlequin bug. This insect is ¼ inch long and shaped like a shield, with a triangle on its back. It has patterned markings in black and red. Harlequin bugs emit a foul odor. To control infestations, spray plants with an insecticidal soap laced with isopropyl alcohol every 2 to 3 days for 2 weeks. Apply insecticidal soap twice, 5 to 7 days apart, in early spring to prevent harlequin bugs.

Large Ragged Holes in Leaves

Imported Cabbage Worm
Imported cabbage worms chew large ragged holes in the leaves of brussels sprouts, and they may bore into the sprouts, leaving trails of dark green frass, or excrement. The worm is light green with one yellow stripe and measures 1¼ inches long. The adult is a common white butterfly with three to four black spots on its wings that is active during the day. To control infestations, apply *Bacillus thuringiensis* (BT) every 10 to 14 days until the pests are under control. Prevent cabbage worms by spraying seedlings with BT from transplanting until sprouts form and covering plants with an agricultural fleece barrier.

Slug
Large ragged holes in the leaves or stems can also be a sign of slugs. They work their way from the bottom of a plant up. Look for trails of slime on the leaves and on the soil near the plants as further evidence of the presence of slugs. Slugs are 1 to 2 inches long and look like snails without shells. They may be brown, gray, white, pale yellow, purple, or nearly black with brown specks. You can control them by handpicking if you get them early in the season. The best way to control their damage is to set up a barrier to deny them access to the garden. Use hardware cloth, ashes, sand, or some other barrier. You can also make traps to catch slugs. (See the entry Slug in chapter 4 for information on making slug traps.)

Leaves Stippled Yellow

Mite
Leaves of brussels sprouts that have mites become stippled, yellow, and dry, and sometimes pale yellow spots or blotches appear. Mites are not insects but arachnids, and are about the size of a grain of black pepper. They may be red, black, or brown. They feed by sucking out the plant's juices. In sucking chlorophyll out of the leaves, they cause small white dots to appear. In addition, they inject toxins into the leaves, which discolors and distorts them. To control infestations, spray plants with a forceful spray of water three times, once every other day, to knock mites from the leaves. If mites are still present, spray with insecticidal soap three times, once every 5 to 7 days.

Chewed Foliage

Weevil
If the leaves of your brussels sprouts are chewed to the stem, suspect the vegetable weevil. This pest is gray to brownish in color with a V-shaped mark near the tip of its wing covers. It is about ½ inch long and has a long snout. Weevils feed at night and hide during the day. As they appear, spray with pyrethrum twice, 3 to 4 days apart.

Weakened Plants, Yellow Leaves

Whitefly
Plants that have whiteflies weaken, their leaves turn yellow, and they die. Honeydew secreted by whiteflies encourages fungus. Molds often develop following an attack. Adults are about the size of a pinhead and are mothlike, with dusty white wings. When an infested plant is shaken, it appears as if dandruff were flying off the leaves. Nymphs are yellowish, legless, flat, and oval, resembling scale at certain stages. To control infestations, spray plants with insecticidal soap spray every 2 to 3 days for 2 weeks. Use it also early in the season to prevent whiteflies. Spray every 2 weeks for the first months of the plant's life. Pyrethrum may be used as a last resort. Make two applications, 3 to 4 days apart.

MOST COMMON DISEASES

Dark Patches on Leaves

Black Leg

The leaves and stems of brussels sprouts infected with black leg have well-defined dark patches over which many tiny black dots are scattered. The edges of leaves will wilt and turn bluish or red. Sunken areas develop on the stem near the ground, which girdle the stem. The entire plant may wilt or topple over. Fixed copper fungicides are sometimes effective in controlling this disease. Apply as directed on the package. If this treatment does not halt the disease, remove and destroy the infected plants.

Yellow, Wedge-shaped Areas on Leaves

Black Rot

The leaves of brussels sprouts infected with bacterial black rot develop yellow, wedge-shaped areas with darkened veins; then they wilt. The vascular bundles in leaves and stems are black and bad smelling. Young plants may not produce sprouts, and the sprouts on older plants that become infected will rot. Black rot cannot be cured. Remove and destroy the infected and surrounding plants. Micronized sulfur helps to control the spread of black rot to other plants. Apply the sulfur to unaffected plants every 7 days until harvest.

Poor Crop Development

Club Root

In general, plants that have club root exhibit the effects of a malfunctioning root system: wilting and poor development. The sprouts of brussels sprouts will be small. Under the soil you will find misshapen roots with club-shaped swellings. Try to prevent this disease by following clean gardening practices, dipping young transplants in a fungicidal solution, and rotating plants (the fungus persists in the soil for 7 years). Club root is more of a problem with plants growing in acid soil. Test your soil, and if the pH is too low, add lime. Apply approved soil fungicides to control the disease in infected plants.

Seedlings Die

Damping-Off

Seedlings that have damping-off simply topple over. You will see a watery soft rot on the stem at the soil line. There is no cure for this disease. Remove and destroy infected plants. When starting seeds indoors, use commercial potting soil, or pasteurize your own potting soil in an oven. Disinfect tools in a bleach solution (one part household bleach to four parts water). Soak seeds in brine (1 cup of salt in 1 quart of water), or lime and wood solution (1 cup of lime and wood ashes in 1 quart of water). Provide soil with adequate drainage and use a fan for better air circulation. For direct seeding, make sure soil is well drained and warm. You might try spreading pasteurized soil or a sterile vermiculite in furrows where you plant your seeds.

Water-soaked Spots on Leaves

Leaf Spot

Brussels sprouts that have leaf spot develop water-soaked spots that later grow in size and take on a brownish or purplish gray color. Leaf spot cannot be cured. Remove and destroy infected and surrounding plants.

Part of Plant Rots

Rhizoctonia

Rhizoctonia in crucifers is characterized by darkened and girdled areas on the stem near the soil line. Affected plants are weak, produce small heads, and sometimes wilt and die. Bottom rot develops on plants after they have been transplanted to the garden. Dark, slightly sunken spots develop on basal leaves near the soil. In moist conditions the rot spreads to adjacent leaves and causes the head to rot. Rhizoctonia also commonly causes damping-off, a watery soft rot on the stem at soil level. Rhizoctonia cannot be controlled. Remove and destroy infected plants. To prevent rhizoctonia from becoming a problem, avoid planting brussels sprouts in short rotations where bottom rot and damping-off have been a problem. Pasteurizing the soil used to raise seedlings and solarizing the garden soil also help to control rhizoctonia. (See chapter 5 for more information on soil pasteurization and solarization.)

Seeds Do Not Germinate

Seed Rot
Seed rot will prevent your brussels sprout seeds from germinating. It occurs when soil is too moist and too cold for germination. If necessary, make a shallow ditch, fill it with commercial sterilized potting mix, and sow seeds in that mixture.

Yellow Lower Leaves

Yellows
The symptoms of yellows are similar to those of black rot. The lower leaves of plants turn yellow, then brown, and finally drop. The sprouts of brussels sprouts may appear stunted and taste bitter. Yellows cannot be cured. Remove and destroy infected and surrounding plants.

HARVEST AND STORAGE

When to Harvest
Harvest sprouts when they are bright green, firm, compact, and an inch or so in diameter; sprouts larger than that have passed their prime. Pick the lowest sprouts first. Frost vastly improves the flavor. After picking the lower stem, mound dirt around the base of the plant to keep the top-heavy plant from toppling over. The harvesting period for brussels sprouts lasts for 8 to 10 weeks.

Yield for 24-Square-Foot Bed   18 to 25 pounds

Yield for 25-Foot Row   12 to 20 pounds

Volume vs. Weight   A 4-quart box equals 6 pounds.

Weight of 1-Quart Canning Jar   2 pounds

Number of Quarts Stored from 1 Bushel   3

Best Fresh Storage Method   Refrigerate brussels sprouts in plastic bags; they will keep for 3 to 5 weeks.

Best Long-Term Storage Method   Brussels sprouts can be frozen for 12 months.

Second-Best Long-Term Storage Method   Pickling

Seed Storage   5 years

VEGETABLE *Cabbage*   *Brassica oleracea,* Capitata Group

DESCRIPTION AND ENVIRONMENT

Height   12 to 15 inches

Spread   2 to 3½ feet

Root Depth   Roots can grow as deep as 18 to 36 inches, but the majority of the roots will be confined to the upper 12 inches.

Shade Tolerance   Needs only 5 hours of sun a day (partial shade).

Frost Tolerance   Hardy; withstands some subfreezing temperatures.

Preferred pH   6.0 to 7.5

PLANTING

Spring Planting Time   4 to 6 weeks before last expected frost to 2 to 3 weeks after frost.

Fall Planting Time   13 to 14 weeks before first expected frost.

Succession Planting   Plant transplants 2 months after the first planting and then again in late summer to get three harvests of cabbage.

Planting Depth   ¼ inch

Spacing of Plants in Rows   14 to 24 inches

Spacing of Plants in Beds   15 to 18 inches

Best Soil Temperature for Germination   50°F to 75°F

Best Soil Temperature for Growing 65°F to 75°F

Best Air Temperature for Growing   Day, 60°F to 75°F; night, 50°F to 65°F.

Days to Germination   4 to 10

Weeks to Transplanting   6 to 8

Days to Maturity   About 140 after direct seeding; 60 to 90 after transplanting.

Greenhouse Varieties   Cabbage does not grow well in the greenhouse.

Container Varieties   Baby Head or Dwarf Morden are good container varieties. When growing cabbage in containers, avoid hot, dry areas, and keep plants cool and moist.

Container Size   8 to 10 inches wide, 12 inches deep.

PLANT MANAGEMENT

Water Requirements for Good Production

Make sure plants get 1 inch of water every week from rain or by watering. (See chapter 8 for more information on watering.)

Water Requirements for Maximum Production

For best production, cabbage can use lots of water. Give them 1 to 1½ inches of water each week. A critical watering period occurs during head development, but too much water later in head development will cause heads to split.

Feeding Requirements for Good Production

Apply compost or a slow-acting general-purpose fertilizer in spring, and give cabbage supplemental light feedings (either side-dressings or foliar spray) monthly throughout the growing season. (See chapter 8 for more information on feeding.)

Feeding Requirements for Maximum Production

Cabbage are heavy feeders. For maximum production, in addition to the spring feeding mentioned above, give plants a light supplement (either a side-dressing or foliar spray) every 2 weeks during the growing season. Spray plants with liquid seaweed extract two or three times during the growing season.

Bronze Leaves

Potassium Deficiency

Signs of potassium deficiency in cabbage include bronzing of leaf borders that spreads inward. Leaf margins will become parched, and brown spots will appear on the leaves. To remedy the problem quickly, apply a foliar spray of fish emulsion or other liquid fertilizer. Side-dress plants with wood ashes. (See chapter 8 for more information on potassium deficiency.)

MOST COMMON INSECT PESTS

Foliage Curls, Puckers, Turns Yellow

Aphid

If the foliage on your cabbage plants curls, puckers, and turns yellow, and plant growth becomes stunted, look for ants. They are a sign that your plants might have aphids. Ants are attracted to a sticky honeydew secreted by aphids. Cabbage plants are particularly bothered by cabbage aphids, which have soft, pear-shaped bodies about the size of a pinhead, are green to powdery blue in color, and are covered with a fine whitish wax. You will find them in clusters on undersides of young leaves and in the heads. For light infestations, spray plants vigorously with water in the early morning, three times, once every other day. Heavy infestations can be dealt with by applying commercial insecticidal soap every 2 to 3 days until the problem is under control.

Small Ragged Holes in Leaves

Cabbage Looper

Small ragged holes in leaves indicate that your plants may be infested with cabbage loopers. Later in the season, the worms bore into developing cabbage heads. The cabbage looper is a 1½-inch-long caterpillar that is light green with long yellowish stripes on its back. It loops as it walks. Spray *Bacillus thuringiensis* (BT) on infested plants every 2 weeks until heads form.

Resistant Varieties. Abbot and Cobb No. 5, Green Winter, Mammoth Red Rock, Red Acre, Red Danish, Rioverdi, Savoy, and Savoy Chieftain.

Wilted Plants

Cabbage Maggot

Plants infested with cabbage maggots will wilt during the heat of the day. Brown tunnels in the stem just below soil level are further evidence that this pest has attacked your cabbage. Seedlings become yellow, growth is stunted, and plants lack vigor. Eventually they will die. The cabbage maggot is a small, white, legless worm about ¼ inch long. The adult resembles a housefly. Maggots tunnel into plant roots and stems. Bacterial diseases such as black leg, which causes dark patches on leaves, and soft rot, which causes plant decomposition, may result, causing the plants to wilt. To control infestations, apply wood ashes or a lime drench (1 cup of lime in 1 quart of water; let sit overnight) around the root ball of each plant. The best control is to prevent flies from laying eggs in the first place. Spread a barrier, such as agricultural fleece, over the transplants in spring, or place a collar around the stem of each plant. (See chapter 4 for instructions on how to construct these collars.)

Resistant Varieties. Early Jersey.

Seedling Stems Severed

Cutworm

Cutworms completely sever the stems of seedlings and transplants at or below the soil surface. They are 1- to 2-inch, dull-colored, plump, soft-bodied larvae that curl up when disturbed. Cutworms feed at night and hide in the soil during the day. To control cutworms, use barriers or traps to prevent access to seedlings. To protect individual plants, surround them with a collar, or make a trap by sprinkling cornmeal or bran meal around each plant. (See chapter 4 for more information on collars and meal traps.)

Tiny Holes in Leaves

Flea Beetle

If you find many little holes or perforations in the leaves of your plants, the plants may have flea beetles. Flea beetles are $\frac{1}{10}$ inch long, shiny, and black, and may have yellow or white markings. They are very active and jump like fleas when disturbed. Their feeding can destroy small plants rapidly. Make two applications of pyrethrum, 3 to 4 days apart, to control infestations. In the spring, cover seedlings with a barrier, such as agricultural fleece, to deny flea beetles access to your plants.
Resistant Varieties. Copenhagen Market 86, Early Jersey Wakefield, Ferry's Round Dutch, Mammoth Red Rock, Savoy Perfection Drumhead, and Stein's Early Flat Dutch.

Wilted Leaves with Black Spots

Harlequin Bug

If the leaves of your plants develop white blotches or black spots and then wilt and die, suspect the harlequin bug. This insect is ¼ inch long and shaped like a shield, with a triangle on its back. It has patterned markings in black and red. Harlequin bugs emit a foul odor. To control infestations, spray plants with an insecticidal soap laced with isopropyl alcohol every 2 to 3 days for 2 weeks. Apply insecticidal soap twice, 5 to 7 days apart, in early spring to prevent harlequin bugs.
Resistant Varieties. Copenhagen Market 86, Early Jersey Wakefield, Headstart, Savoy Perfection Drumhead, and Stein's Early Flat Dutch. (Michihli Chinese cabbage is quite susceptible to the harlequin bug.)

Large Ragged Holes in Leaves

Imported Cabbage Worm

Imported cabbage worms chew large ragged holes in cabbage leaves, and they may bore into the heads, leaving trails of dark green frass, or excrement. The worm is light green with one yellow stripe, and measures 1¼ inches long. The adult is a common white butterfly with three to four black spots on its wings that is active during the day. To control infestations, apply *Bacillus thuringiensis* (BT) every 10 to 14 days until the cabbage worms are under control. Prevent cabbage worms by spraying seedlings with BT early in the season, every 2 weeks from transplanting until heads form, and covering plants with an agricultural fleece barrier.
Resistant Varieties. Mammoth Red Rock, Savoy, and Savoy Chieftain.

Slug

Large ragged holes in the leaves or stems can also be signs of slugs. They work their way from the bottom of a plant up. Look for trails of slime on the leaves and on the soil near the plants as further evidence of the presence of slugs. Slugs are 1 to 2 inches long and look like snails without shells. They may be brown, gray, white, pale yellow, purple, or nearly black with brown specks. You can control them by handpicking if you get them early in the season. The best way to control their damage is to set up a barrier of hardware cloth, ashes, sand, or some other material to deny them access to the garden. You can also make traps to catch slugs. (See the entry Slug in chapter 4 for information on making slug traps.)

White or Brown Tunnels in Leaves

Leafminer

White or brown tunnels or blotches on leaves are signs that your cabbage plants have leafminers. The leaves may turn yellow and blotchy and look blistered or curled. Leafminers are small black flies usually with yellow stripes. The tiny yellowish larvae feed between the upper and lower surfaces of leaves, causing the tunnels or blotches to appear. You may also find stem damage below the soil.

Remove the infested leaves before the larvae mature. The best way to control leafminers, though, is to screen out the adult flies by covering seedlings with agricultural fleece.

Leaves Stippled Yellow

Mite

Leaves of cabbage infested with mites become stippled, yellow, and dry, and sometimes pale yellow spots or blotches appear. Mites are not insects but arachnids, and are about the size of a grain of black pepper. They may be red, black, or brown. They feed by sucking out the plant's juices. In sucking chlorophyll out of the leaves, they cause small white dots to appear. In addition, they inject toxins into the leaves, which discolors and distorts them. To control infestations, spray plants with a forceful spray of water three times, once every other day, to knock mites from the leaves. If mites are still present, spray with insecticidal soap at least three times once every 5 to 7 days.

Chewed Foliage

Weevil

If the leaves of your cabbage plants are chewed to the stem, suspect the vegetable weevil. This pest is gray to brownish in color with a V-shaped mark near the tip of its wing covers. It is about ½ inch long and has a long snout. It feeds at night and hides during the day. As weevils appear, spray with pyrethrum twice, 3 to 4 days apart.

MOST COMMON DISEASES

Dark Patches on Leaves

Black Leg

The leaves and stems of cabbage plants infected with black leg have well-defined dark patches over which many tiny black dots are scattered. The edges of leaves will wilt and turn bluish or red. Sunken areas develop on the stem near the ground, which girdle the stem. The entire plant may wilt or topple over. Fixed copper fungicides are sometimes effective in controlling this disease. Apply them as directed on the package label. If this treatment does not halt the disease, remove and destroy the infected plants.

Yellow, Wedge-shaped Areas on Leaves

Black Rot

The leaves of cabbage plants infected with bacterial black rot develop yellow, wedge-shaped areas with darkened veins; then they wilt. The vascular bundles in leaves and stems are black and bad smelling. Young plants may not produce heads, and the heads on older plants that become infected will rot. Black rot cannot be cured. Remove and destroy the infected and surrounding plants. Micronized sulfur helps to control the spread of black rot to other plants. Apply the sulfur to unaffected plants every 7 days until harvest.

Resistant Varieties. Bravo, Custodian, Hancock, Jadekeeper, Lariat, Regalia, Safekeeper Hybrid, and Survivor Hybrid.

Poor Crop Development

Club Root

In general, plants that have club root exhibit the effects of a malfunctioning root system: wilting, poor development, and small heads. Under the soil you will find misshapen roots with club-shaped swellings. Try to prevent this disease by following clean gardening practices and rotating plants (the fungus persists in the soil for 7 years). Club root is more of a problem with plants growing in acid soil. Test your soil; if the pH is too low, add lime. Apply approved soil fungicides to control the disease in infected plants.

Seedlings Die

Damping-Off

Seedlings that have damping-off simply topple over. You will see a watery soft rot on the stem at the soil line. There is no cure for this disease. Remove and destroy infected plants. When starting seeds indoors, use commercial potting soil, or pasteurize your own potting soil in an oven. Disinfect tools in heated water or a bleach solution (one part household bleach to four parts water). Soak seeds in brine (1 cup of salt in 1 quart of water) or lime and wood solution (1 cup of lime and wood ashes in 1 quart of water). Provide soil with adequate drainage and use a fan for better air circulation. For direct seeding, make sure soil is well drained and warm. You might try spreading pasteurized soil or a sterile vermiculite in furrows where you plant your seeds.

Yellow Leaves

Fusarium Wilt

Fusarium wilt (also called yellows or fusarium yellows) causes seedlings to wilt. When older plants contract this disease, they lose vitality; leaves turn yellow, then brown, and then drop off. Lower leaves are affected first. Some plants will produce some fruit, but in most cases you should remove and destroy infected plants. Fusarium wilt is carried in the soil, so using resistant varieties is the best approach to overall control of this disease in your garden. Solarizing the soil also helps. (See chapter 5 for information on solarization.)

Resistant Varieties. Charleton Wakefield, Globe, Harvester Queen, Hercules, Hybrid Blueboy, Jersey Queen, Marion Market, Resistant Detroit, Stonehead, Wisconsin All Season, and Wisconsin Golden Acre.

Water-soaked Spots on Leaves

Leaf Spot

Cabbage plants that have leaf spot develop water-soaked spots that later grow in size and take on a brownish or purplish gray color. Leaf spot cannot be cured. Remove and destroy infected and surrounding plants.

Part of Plant Rots

Rhizoctonia

Rhizoctonia in crucifers is characterized by darkened and girdled areas on the stem near the soil line. Affected plants are weak, produce small heads, and sometimes wilt and die. Bottom rot develops on plants after they have been transplanted to the garden. Dark, slightly sunken spots develop on basal leaves near the soil. In moist conditions the rot spreads to adjacent leaves and causes the head to rot. Rhizoctonia also commonly causes damping-off, a watery soft rot on the stem at soil level. Rhizoctonia cannot be controlled. Remove and destroy infected plants. To prevent rhizoctonia from becoming a problem, avoid planting cabbage in short rotations where bottom rot and damping-off have been a problem. Pasteurizing the soil used to raise seedlings and solarizing the garden soil also help to control rhizoctonia. (See chapter 5 for more information on soil pasteurization and solarization.)

Seeds Do Not Germinate

Seed Rot

Seed rot will prevent your cabbage seeds from germinating. It occurs when soil is too moist and too cold for germination. If necessary, make a shallow ditch, fill it with commercial sterilized potting mix, and sow seeds in that mixture.

HARVEST AND STORAGE

When to Harvest

Harvest white cabbage when the heads are hard, tight-leaved, compact, heavy for their size, and greenish white in color. Harvest red cabbage when the heads are hard, tight-leaved, compact, and reddish purple in color. Harvest Savoy cabbage when the leaves are crumpled and dark green in color. Split heads have passed their prime. The harvest period for cabbage can last from 4 to 6 weeks, depending on the variety.

Yield for 24-Square-Foot Bed   24 to 50 pounds

Yield for 25-Foot Row   30 to 50 pounds

Weight of 1-Quart Canning Jar   2 to 3 pounds

Best Fresh Storage Method   Refrigerate cabbage heads in plastic bags; they will keep for 1 to 2 weeks.

Best Long-Term Storage Method   You can store cabbage in a root cellar, with the heads down and the roots up, or store them in a buried cache, covered with straw or leaves. They will keep for 4 months.

Second-Best Long-Term Storage Method   Pickling (as sauerkraut).

Seed Storage   5 years

VEGETABLE Carrot   *Daucus carota*

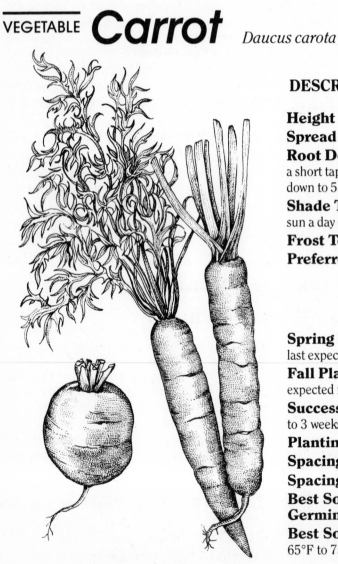

DESCRIPTION AND ENVIRONMENT

Height   12 to 18 inches

Spread   1 to 2 feet

Root Depth   Most roots limited to 2 feet; has a short taproot with some fibrous roots reaching down to 5 feet.

Shade Tolerance   Needs only 5 hours of sun a day (partial shade).

Frost Tolerance   Hardy

Preferred pH   5.5 to 6.5

PLANTING

Spring Planting Time   2 to 4 weeks before last expected frost.

Fall Planting Time   13 weeks before first expected frost.

Succession Planting   Start carrots every 2 to 3 weeks throughout the season.

Planting Depth   ¼ inch

Spacing of Plants in Rows   2 inches

Spacing of Plants in Beds   2 to 3 inches

Best Soil Temperature for Germination   55°F to 75°F

Best Soil Temperature for Growing   65°F to 75°F

Best Air Temperature for Growing
45°F to 75°F

Days to Germination   10 to 17

Days to Maturity   70 to 80

Greenhouse Varieties   Carrots cannot be grown in the greenhouse.

Container Varieties   The short-rooted or round varieties are best for containers; avoid the long, slender carrots. Baby Finger Nantes, Gold Nugget, Oxheart, Short 'N' Sweet, and Tiny Sweet grow well in containers.

Container Size   At least 10 to 12 inches deep; better carrots will be produced in deeper containers.

Stumpy, Short, or Misshapen Carrots

Compacted Soil

In addition to selecting a variety of the proper length and preparing a loose soil, there's a trick that can help produce attractive carrots: Sow the seeds shallowly, between ¼ and ½ inch deep. Cover them with another ¼ to ½ inch of organic matter, and keep the seeds evenly moist until they germinate. When the seedlings reach about 1 inch tall (the roots at this stage are slender threads) withhold water until the plants start to wilt; then resume normal watering until harvest. This practice encourages downward root growth.

Seeds Do Not Germinate

Crusted Soil

Sometimes a crust forms over the top layer of soil, making it impossible for the fine carrot seeds to sprout through. An easy way to break the crust is to mix radish seeds with the carrot seeds during sowing. Radishes germinate fast, and they'll push through the soil in a few days, forging the way for the slower-germinating carrots. In 3 weeks, the radishes should be ready to harvest. Pull any before that time if they are crowding the young carrots.

Misshapen Carrots

Heavy Soil

If your carrots are misshapen, your soil may be too heavy. Add sand to the area where carrots will be grown. Even in relatively heavy soil, you can improve the shape and length of your carrots by raking up a raised, flat-topped row.

Fall Crop Does Poorly

Too Much Heat and Light

Because they are cool-loving crops, carrots planted in the summer for a fall harvest will do poorly if exposed to too much heat and light. Protect them with shade netting for the first month or so.

PLANT MANAGEMENT

Water Requirements

Make sure carrots get 1 inch of water every week from rain or by watering. Uniform watering is important for good root enlargement. Reduce watering when carrots are three-quarters their final size to lessen the chance of splitting. (See chapter 8 for more information on watering.)

Feeding Requirements

Apply compost or a slow-acting general-purpose fertilizer in spring. This plant is a light feeder, so it needs little or no supplemental fertilizer. If you wish, you can give your carrots supplemental light feedings (either side-dressings or foliar spray) monthly throughout the growing season. If you do feed your carrots during the season, cut back on nitrogen later in the season to reduce splitting; do not give plants any nitrogen once they are three-quarters grown. Spray plants with liquid seaweed extract two or three times during the growing season. (See chapter 8 for more information on feeding.)

Hairy, Tough Carrots

Lack of Water

When the soil isn't kept moist enough, the main roots develop many small feeder roots to soak up whatever moisture they can get. At the same time, the roots form extra tissue to carry water and so they become tough. For crisp, hairless carrots, water thoroughly as soon as the top 4 inches of soil have dried out.

Curled Leaves

Potassium Deficiency

If carrot leaves curl and their margins turn brown, and the inner portions become grayish green and finally bronzed, your carrots probably are suffering from a potassium deficiency. To remedy the problem quickly, spray plants with fish emulsion or another liquid fertilizer. Side-dress plants with wood ashes. (See chapter 8 for more information on potassium deficiency.)

MOST COMMON INSECT PESTS

Rotted or Dwarfed Plants

Carrot Rust Fly

The maggots of the carrot rust fly chew roots, causing plants to be dwarfed. Soft-rot bacteria may become a problem, and when that happens, the entire plant quickly decomposes. The carrot rust fly is a black fly, 1/5 inch long, with long yellow hairs, a yellow head, and yellow legs. The maggots are 1/3 inch long and yellow to white in color. The flies lay eggs in the crowns of the plants. Once plants have been attacked, there is little the gardener can do. Destroy infested plants, rotate crops, and protect new plantings with netting or a similar barrier. Try adjusting planting dates to avoid the pest at its peak.

Defoliated Plants

Carrot Weevil

Carrot weevils defoliate plants, beginning at the crown. After a plant has been attacked, only the ribs of leaves and stems remain. Larvae tunnel into the tops and roots of carrots. The adult carrot weevil is 1/5 inch long, brown, and has a hard shell. The larvae are pale in color, with brown heads and no legs. Control infestations by spraying carrot plants with pyrethrum as soon as adult beetles appear in spring. Try to deny weevils access early in the season by covering seedlings with agricultural fleece. Parasitic nematodes may help to prevent infestation of the roots. (See chapter 4 for more information on parasitic nematodes.)

Parsleyworm

The leaves of plants infested with parsleyworms are chewed so that often only the bare stems remain. The parsleyworm is a 2-inch caterpillar that is green with a yellow-dotted black band across each segment. It gives off an odor and projects orange horns when upset. These bright, large caterpillars are easy to handpick in the early morning. You can also apply *Bacillus thuringiensis* (BT) as a powder or a spray every 10 to 14 days until the pest is under control.

Weakened Plants

Leafhopper

Both adult leafhoppers and nymphs pierce leaves, buds, and stems and suck the sap and chlorophyll from cells, causing plants to weaken. Adults are green, wedge-shaped insects, 1/4 to 1/3 inch long, that hold their wings in a rooflike position above their bodies. They are very active and move sideways. Nymphs resemble adults. To control serious infestations, apply insecticidal soap laced with isopropyl alcohol every 2 to 3 days for 2 weeks. In early spring, apply a preventive spray of insecticidal soap and seaweed extract and cover seedlings with an agricultural fleece barrier for the first month of growth to deny leafhoppers access to your plants.

Stunted Plants, Yellow Leaves

Nematode

If your carrot plants are stunted, and the leaves are yellow, suspect nematodes. Nematodes are microscopic whitish, translucent worms barely visible to the naked eye. They live in the soil and attack the roots of the plant, causing galls (swellings) to develop on the roots. To prevent nematodes, use resistant varieties, work 3 or 4 inches of compost (especially leaf mold) into the garden, fertilize with fish emulsion, and plant early in the season.

Chewed Foliage

Weevil

If the leaves of your carrots are chewed to the stem, suspect the vegetable weevil. This pest is gray to brownish in color with a V-shaped mark near the tip of its wing covers. It is about ½ inch long and has a long snout. It feeds at night and hides during the day. As weevils appear, spray with pyrethrum twice, 3 to 4 days apart.

Plants Wilt and Die

Wireworm

If your carrots wilt and die, suspect the wireworm. Wireworms are the larvae of click beetles. They are ⅓ to 1½ inches long, dark brown to yellowish, jointed, hard shelled, and cylindrical. They chew on the roots of many plants. Trap them with pieces of potato speared on the ends of sticks. (See the entry Wireworm in chapter 4 for more information on how to use potato traps.) Plant a cover crop for long-term control.

MOST COMMON DISEASES

Seedlings Die

Damping-Off

Seedlings that have damping-off simply topple over. You will see a watery soft rot on the stem at the soil line. There is no cure for this disease. Remove and destroy infected plants. Soak seeds in brine (1 cup of salt in 1 quart of water) or lime and wood solution (1 cup of lime and wood ashes in 1 quart of water). Before seeding, make sure soil is well drained and warm. You might try spreading pasteurized soil or a sterile vermiculite in furrows where you plant your seeds.

Yellow to White Spots on Seedling Leaves

Leaf Blight

Yellow to white spots on the margins of seedling leaves that become brown and take on a water-soaked appearance are a sign that your plant has leaf blight. Spots may girdle taproots also. The affected roots may appear water-soaked, and may have lesions, dark spots, craters, or pustules. Leaf blight cannot be cured. To prevent this disease in the future, soak seeds in hot water (126°F) for 10 minutes before planting. Thin seedlings to the proper space and keep the garden soil well cultivated. Build healthy soil to fight off disease symptoms.
Resistant Varieties. Spartan Premium.

HARVEST AND STORAGE

When to Harvest

Fall carrots taste better than spring carrots. Even though sugar content is greater in mature roots, pick carrots while they are small, no more than 1 to 1½ inches in diameter. Carrots should be firm but tender and well colored. The harvest period for most carrots lasts about 6 to 8 weeks. For best flavor, don't harvest fall carrots until the ground has had a good frost.

Yield for 24-Square-Foot Bed   25 to 40 pounds
Yield for 25-Foot Row   20 to 25 pounds
Volume vs. Weight   1 bushel, without tops, equals 50 pounds.
Weight of 1-Quart Canning Jar   2 to 3 pounds
Number of Quarts Stored from 1 Bushel   16 to 20

Best Fresh Storage Method   Cut off the tops and discard them; then wash and refrigerate carrots in plastic bags. They will keep for at least 2 to 4 weeks.

Best Long-Term Storage Method   Do not wash carrots. Cut the tops to ½ to 2 inches. Store them in dry sawdust, dry straw, moist sand, or moist peat moss, in a place with a temperature of 32°F to 40°F and a relative humidity of 90 to 95 percent. Keep the sand or peat moss moist. Carrots should keep for 6 months.

Other Storage Methods   Carrots can be stored in the garden under mulch all winter.

Frozen carrots will keep for 8 months. Carrots can also be pickled.

Seed Storage   3 years

NOTES AND RESEARCH

U.S. Department of Agriculture (USDA) experiments have found that carrots in cold storage stay sweeter longer if they are exposed to fresh air once a day. Ethylene, a by-product of plant respiration, builds up around stored carrots and in some way reduces their sweetness. If you're a carrot connoisseur, uncover your carrots and expose them to fresh air for a couple of minutes each day.

VEGETABLE **Cauliflower**   *Brassica oleracea,* Botrytis Group

DESCRIPTION AND ENVIRONMENT

Height   18 to 24 inches
Spread   2 to 2½ feet
Root Depth   Shallow; 18 to 36 inches.
Shade Tolerance   Some tolerance; needs at least 6 hours of sun a day.
Frost Tolerance   Half-hardy; will stand some light freezing.
Preferred pH   6.0 to 7.5

PLANTING

Spring Planting Time   2 to 3 weeks before last spring frost; if using transplants, use only seedlings with a tiny bud in the center. If the seedling doesn't have a bud, no head will form.
Fall Planting Time   14 weeks before first fall frost.

Planting Depth   ¼ to ½ inch
Spacing of Plants in Rows   14 to 24 inches
Spacing of Plants in Beds   15 to 18 inches
Best Soil Temperature for Germination   50°F to 75°F
Best Soil Temperature for Growing 65°F to 75°F
Best Air Temperature for Growing Day, 60°F to 70°F; night, 50°F to 70°F.
Days to Germination   4 to 10
Weeks to Transplanting   5 to 7
Days to Maturity   50 to 95 days after transplanting.
Greenhouse Varieties   Cauliflower cannot be grown in the greenhouse.
Container Varieties   Cauliflower cannot be grown in containers.

Small Heads

Planted Too Closely

The optimum spacing for cauliflower is 24 plants per 100 square feet. If you plant them too closely, the heads will be small.

Head Turns Yellow

Over-Exposed to Sun

When the head does appear above ground level, small incurving leaves will close around it to protect it from the sun. As the head enlarges, you should shield it from the sun by bringing the largest leaves up over it and tying them in an upright position with soft string. Watch carefully after the leaves have been tied to make sure the heads do not

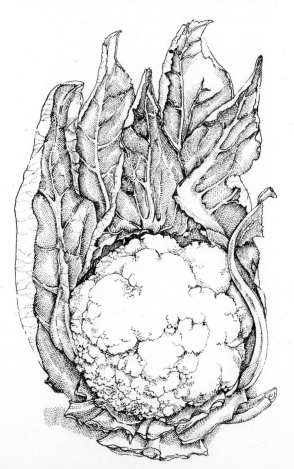

overdevelop. In hot weather, the head should be ready in 3 to 5 days after tying the leaves. In cool weather, it may take as long as 2 weeks for the head to reach acceptable size.

Buttoning

Various Possible Causes

Buttoning (extremely small heads) can result from several conditions: soil temperatures below 50°F; a soil too low in nitrogen; an excess of salt in the soil; weed competition; or a prolonged hot, dry spell. Transplant seedlings no more than 30 days after germination. Black plastic mulch raises the soil temperature to about 70°F. Check daily and don't allow the temperature inside row covers to exceed 75°F. If button heads form, leave the plants alone; they may produce normal-sized heads later.

PLANT MANAGEMENT

Water Requirements

Make sure plants get 1 inch of water every week from rain or by watering. Critical watering periods are early in the season, to prevent buttoning, and during head development. (See chapter 8 for more information on watering.)

Feeding Requirements for Good Production

Apply compost or a slow-acting general-purpose fertilizer in spring, then give supplemental light feedings (side-dressings or foliar spray) monthly throughout the growing season. (See chapter 8 for more information on feeding.)

Feeding Requirements for Maximum Production

Cauliflower is a heavy feeder and can use, in addition to the spring feeding mentioned above, a light supplement every 2 weeks during the growing season. Also, spray plants with liquid seaweed extract two or three times during the growing season.

Browning of Head

Boron Deficiency

Cauliflower planted in boron-deficient soil will grow very slowly. The tips of leaves will die back, and leaves will become distorted. You will see browning of the cauliflower head. To remedy this problem quickly, apply a foliar spray of liquid seaweed extract every 2 weeks until symptoms disappear. For long-term results, add granite dust or rock phosphate to the soil, or plant cover crops of vetch or clover in the fall. Do not add lime to a boron-deficient soil, as the soil is likely to be near alkaline already. (See chapter 8 for more information on boron deficiency.)

MOST COMMON INSECT PESTS

Foliage Curls, Puckers, Turns Yellow

Aphid

If the foliage on your cauliflower curls, puckers, and turns yellow, and plant growth becomes stunted, look for ants. They are a sign that your plants might have aphids. Ants are attracted to a sticky honeydew secreted by aphids. Cauliflower plants are particularly bothered by cabbage aphids, which have soft, pear-shaped bodies about the size of a pinhead, are green to powdery blue in color, and are covered with a fine whitish wax. You will find them in clusters on the undersides of young leaves and in the heads. For light infestations, spray plants vigorously with water in the early morning, three times, once every other day. Heavy infestations can be dealt with by applying commercial insecticidal soap every 2 to 3 days until the problem is under control.

Small Ragged Holes in Leaves

Cabbage Looper

Small ragged holes in leaves indicate that your plants may be infested with cabbage loopers. Later in the season, the worms bore into developing cauliflower heads. The cabbage looper is a 1½-inch-long caterpillar that is light green with long yellowish stripes on its back. It loops as it walks. Spray *Bacillus thuringiensis* (BT) on infested plants every 2 weeks until heads form.

Plants Wilt during Heat of Day

Cabbage Maggot

Plants infested with cabbage maggots will wilt during the heat of the day. Brown tunnels in the stem just below soil level are further evidence that this pest has attacked your cauliflower. Seedlings become yellow, growth is stunted, and plants lack vigor. Eventually they will die. The cabbage maggot is a small, white, legless worm about ¼ inch long. The adult resembles a housefly. Maggots tunnel into plant roots and stems. Bacterial diseases such as black leg, which causes dark patches on leaves, and soft rot, which causes plant decomposition, may result, causing the plants to wilt. To control infestations, apply wood ashes or a lime drench (1 cup of lime in 1 quart of water; let sit overnight) around the root ball of each plant. The best control is to prevent flies from laying eggs in the first place. Spread a barrier, such as agricultural fleece, over the seedlings, or place a collar around the stem of each plant. (See chapter 4 for instructions on how to construct these collars.)

Seedling Stems Severed

Cutworm

Cutworms completely sever the stems of seedlings and transplants at or below the soil surface. They are 1- to 2-inch, dull-colored, plump, soft-bodied larvae that curl up when disturbed. Cutworms feed at night and hide in the soil during the day. To control cutworms, use barriers or traps to prevent access to seedlings. To protect individual plants, surround them with a collar, or make a trap by sprinkling cornmeal or bran meal around each plant. (See chapter 4 for more information on collars and meal traps.)

Tiny Holes in Leaves

Flea Beetle

If you find many little holes or perforations in the leaves of your plants, the plants may have flea beetles. Flea beetles are 1/10 inch long, shiny, and black, and may have yellow or white markings. They are very active and jump like fleas when disturbed. Their feeding can destroy small plants rapidly. Make two applications of pyrethrum, 3 to 4 days apart, to control infestations. In the spring, cover seedlings with a barrier, such as agricultural fleece, to deny flea beetles access to your plants.

Resistant Varieties. Early Snowball A and Snowball X.

Wilted Leaves with Black Spots

Harlequin Bug

If the leaves of your plants develop white blotches or black spots, and then wilt and die, suspect the harlequin bug. This insect is ¼ inch long and shaped like a shield, with a triangle on its back. It has patterned markings in black and red. Harlequin bugs emit a foul odor. To control infestations, spray plants with an insecticidal soap laced with isopropyl alcohol every 2 to 3 days for 2 weeks. Apply insecticidal soap twice, 5 to 7 days apart, in early spring to prevent harlequin bugs.

Large Ragged Holes in Leaves

Imported Cabbage Worm

Imported cabbage worms chew large ragged holes in cauliflower leaves, and they may bore into the heads, leaving trails of dark green frass, or excrement. The worm is light green with one yellow stripe, and measures 1¼ inches long. The adult is a common white butterfly with three to four black spots on its wings that is active during the day. To control infestations, apply *Bacillus thuringiensis* (BT) every 10 to 14 days until cabbage worms are under control. Prevent cabbage worms by spraying seedlings with BT early in the season, every 2 weeks from transplanting until heads form, and covering plants with an agricultural fleece barrier.

Slug

Large ragged holes in the leaves or stems are a sign of slugs. They work their way from the bottom of a plant up. Look for trails of slime on the leaves and on the soil near the plants as further evidence of the presence of slugs. Slugs are 1 to 2 inches long and look like snails without shells. They may be brown, gray, white, pale yellow, purple, or nearly black with brown specks. You can control them by handpicking if you get them early in the season. The best way to control their damage is to set up a barrier of hardware cloth, ashes, sand, or some other material to deny them access to the garden. You can also make traps to catch slugs. (See the entry Slug in chapter 4 for information on making slug traps.)

Leaves Stippled Yellow

Mite

Leaves of cauliflower plants infested with mites become stippled, yellow, and dry, and sometimes pale yellow spots or blotches appear. Mites are not insects but arachnids, and are about the size of a grain of black pepper. They may be red, black, or brown. They feed by sucking out the plant's juices. In sucking chlorophyll out of the leaves, they cause small white dots to appear. In addition, they inject toxins into the leaves, which discolors and distorts them. To control infestations, spray plants with a forceful spray of water three times, once every other day, to knock mites from the leaves. If mites are still present, spray with insecticidal soap at least three times once every 7 to 10 days.

Chewed Foliage

Weevil

If the leaves of your cauliflower plants are chewed to the stem, suspect the vegetable weevil. This pest is gray to brownish in color with a V-shaped mark near the tip of its wing covers. It is about ½ inch long and has a long snout. It feeds at night and hides during the day. As weevils appear, spray with pyrethrum twice, 3 to 4 days apart.

MOST COMMON DISEASES

Dark Patches on Leaves

Black Leg

Plants infected with black leg develop sunken areas on the stem near the ground, which girdle the stem.

Gray spots speckled with black dots appear on the leaves and stems. The edges of leaves wilt and turn bluish or red, and the entire plant may wilt or topple over. Fixed copper fungicides are sometimes effective. Follow application directions on package. If this treatment does not halt the disease, remove and destroy the infected plants.

Yellow, Wedge-shaped Areas on Leaves

Black Rot

Black rot affects young as well as mature plants. Infected seedlings turn yellow and die. On older plants, yellow, wedge-shaped areas develop at the leaf margins and expand toward the center of the leaf. These areas later turn brown and die, and the leaves fall off. The vascular bundles in leaves and stems are black and bad smelling. Young plants may not produce heads, and the heads on older plants that become infected will rot. Black rot cannot be cured. Remove and destroy the infected and surrounding plants. Micronized sulfur helps to control the spread of black rot to other plants. Apply the sulfur to unaffected plants every 7 days until harvest.

Poor Crop Development

Club Root

In general, aboveground parts of plants exhibit the effects of a malfunctioning root system: wilting, poor development, and small heads. Under the soil you will find misshapen roots with club-shaped swellings. Try to prevent this disease by following clean gardening practices and rotating plants (the fungus persists in the soil for 7 years). Club root is more of a problem with plants growing in acid soil. Test your soil, and if the pH is too low, add lime. Club root can be controlled with approved soil fungicides.

Seedlings Die

Damping-Off

Seedlings that have damping-off simply topple over. You will see a watery soft rot on the stem at the soil line. There is no cure for this disease. Remove and destroy infected plants. When starting seeds indoors, use commercial potting soil, or pasteurize your own potting soil in an oven. Disinfect tools in a bleach solution (one part household bleach to four parts water). Soak seeds in brine (1 cup of salt in 1 quart of water), or lime and wood solution (1 cup of lime and wood ashes in 1 quart of water). Provide soil with adequate drainage and use a fan for better air circulation. For direct seeding, make sure soil is well drained and warm. You might try spreading pasteurized soil or a sterile vermiculite in furrows where you plant your seeds.

Plants Die

Downy Mildew

Cauliflower seedlings develop purplish lesions on the leaves and stems, which become covered with white downy fungus. Plants die very rapidly after contracting this disease. If you catch the infection early, apply a copper-based fungicide to diseased and surrounding plants every 7 to 10 days until harvest. Remove and destroy any plants with a serious infection.

Small Gray-Brown Spots on Heads

Leaf Spot

Small gray-brown spots on cauliflower heads indicate leaf spot. There is no cure. Remove and destroy infected and surrounding plants.

Part of Plant Rots

Rhizoctonia

Rhizoctonia in crucifers is characterized by darkened and girdled areas on the stem near the soil line. Affected plants are weak, produce small heads, and sometimes wilt and die. Bottom rot develops on plants after they have been transplanted to the garden. Dark, slightly sunken spots develop on basal leaves near the soil. In moist conditions the rot spreads to adjacent leaves and causes the head to rot. Rhizoctonia also commonly causes damping-off, a watery soft rot on the stem at the soil line. Rhizoctonia cannot be controlled. Remove and destroy infected plants. To prevent rhizoctonia from becoming a problem, avoid planting cauliflower in short rotations where bottom rot and damping-off have been a problem. Pasteurizing the soil used to raise seedlings and solarizing the garden soil also help to control rhizoctonia. (See chapter 5 for more information on soil pasteurization and solarization.)

Seeds Do Not Germinate

Seed Rot

Seed rot will prevent your cauliflower seeds from germinating. It occurs when soil is too moist and cold for germination. If necessary, make a shallow ditch, fill it with commercial sterilized potting mix, and sow seeds in that mixture.

Yellow Lower Leaves

Yellows

The symptoms of yellows are similar to those produced by black rot. The lower leaves of infected plants turn yellow, then brown, and finally drop. The heads may appear stunted and will taste bitter. Yellows cannot be cured. Remove and destroy infected and surrounding plants.
Resistant Varieties. Early Snowball.

HARVEST AND STORAGE

When to Harvest

To blanch cauliflower, which is the process that keeps the heads white, tie outer leaves over the head when the curd is 2 to 3 inches in diameter. Check plants every few days, and pick the head when it is firm and white. Harvest cauliflower as soon as it is ready; the head deteriorates quickly. The harvest period lasts only about 1 to 2 weeks, depending on the variety and the weather.

Yield for 24-Square-Foot Bed   11 to 25 pounds

Yield for 25-Foot Row   12 to 16 pounds

Volume vs. Weight   1 bushel equals 12 pounds; 2 medium-sized heads equal 4 pounds.

Weight of 1-Quart Canning Jar   2 to 3 pounds

Number of Quarts Stored from 1 Bushel   4 to 6

Best Fresh Storage Method   Refrigerate cauliflower in plastic bags; it will keep for 5 to 10 days.

Best Long-Term Storage Method Frozen cauliflower will keep for 12 months.

Other Long-Term Storage Methods Cauliflower can be pickled, or you can store it with roots intact in a cold, moist pit or cellar.

Seed Storage   5 years

VEGETABLE **Celery** *Apium graveolens* var. *dulce*

DESCRIPTION AND ENVIRONMENT

Height   16 inches
Spread   8 to 12 inches
Root Depth   Roots are generally shallow and fibrous, limited to the upper 6 inches of the soil, with some going down as deep as 18 inches.

Shade Tolerance   Needs only 5 hours of sun a day (partial shade).

Frost Tolerance   Hardy

Preferred pH   6.0 to 7.5

PLANTING

Spring Planting Time   2 to 3 weeks before last expected frost.

Fall Planting Time   19 weeks before first expected frost.

Succession Planting   Plant every month for a succession of celery all season long. It is best to use transplants. Celery likes some shading in the heat of the summer.

Planting Depth   ⅛ inch

Spacing of Plants in Rows   10 to 12 inches

Spacing of Plants in Beds   6 to 9 inches

Best Soil Temperature for Germination   50°F to 70°F; for best germination, soak seeds in water overnight.

Best Soil Temperature for Growing 60°F to 70°F

Best Air Temperature for Growing   Day, 65°F to 75°F; night, 60°F to 65°F.

Days to Germination   9 to 21

Weeks to Transplanting   10

Days to Maturity   125 after direct seeding.

Greenhouse Varieties   Celery does not grow well in the greenhouse.

Container Varieties   Celery does not grow well in containers.

PLANT MANAGEMENT

Water Requirements for Good Production

Make sure the plants get 1 inch of water every week from rain or by watering. (See chapter 8 for more information on watering.)

Water Requirements for Maximum Production

This plant can use lots of water. Give it between 1 and 1½ inches of water each week.

Feeding Requirements for Good Production

Apply compost or a slow-acting general-purpose fertilizer in spring, then give your celery plants supplemental light feedings (either side-dressings or foliar spray) monthly throughout the growing season. (See chapter 8 for more information on feeding.)

Feeding Requirements for Maximum Production

Celery is a heavy feeder. In addition to the spring feeding mentioned above, it can use a light supplement every 2 weeks during the growing season. Critical times during which supplemental feedings can benefit plants are 3 weeks after setting plants out and again 6 weeks later. Spray plants with liquid seaweed extract two or three times during the growing season.

Cracked Stems

Boron Deficiency

Celery planted in boron-deficient soil will grow very slowly. The tips of leaves die back, and the leaves become distorted. Stems crack. To remedy the deficiency quickly, spray plants with liquid seaweed extract every 2 weeks until symptoms disappear. For a long-term solution, add granite dust or rock phosphate to the soil, or plant cover crops of vetch or clover in the fall. You can also mix rock phosphate into the compost pile. Do not add lime to a boron-deficient soil, as the soil is likely to be nearly alkaline already. (See chapter 8 for more information on boron deficiency.)

Slender Stalks

Phosphorus Deficiency

Slender stalks and poor root development are signs of a phosphorus deficiency in celery. This deficiency occurs temporarily in cold, wet soils. To remedy the problem quickly, spray plants with diluted fish emulsion or another liquid fertilizer, and apply some fast-acting wood ashes. (See chapter 8 for more information on phosphorus deficiency.)

MOST COMMON INSECT PESTS

Foliage Curls, Puckers, Turns Yellow

Aphid

If the foliage on your plants curls, puckers, and turns yellow, and the foliage and blooms become stunted, look for ants. They are a sign that your plants have aphids. Ants are attracted to a sticky honeydew secreted by aphids. These insects have soft, pear-shaped bodies about the size of a pinhead. They may be green, brown, or pink. You will find them in clusters on the undersides of young leaves. For light infestations, spray the plants vigorously with water in the early morning, three times, once every other day. For heavy infestations, apply a commercial insecticidal soap every 2 to 3 days until aphids are under control.

Rotted or Dwarfed Plants

Carrot Rust Fly

The maggots of the carrot rust fly chew roots, causing plants to be dwarfed. Soft-rot bacteria may become a problem, and when that happens, the entire plant quickly decomposes. The carrot rust fly is a black fly, ⅕ inch long, with long yellow hairs, a yellow head, and yellow legs. The maggots are ⅓ inch long and yellow to white in color. The flies lay eggs in the crowns of the plants. Once plants have been attacked, there is little the gardener can do. Destroy infested plants, rotate crops, and protect new plantings with netting or a similar barrier. Try adjusting planting dates to avoid the pest at its peak.

Defoliated Plants

Carrot Weevil

The larvae of carrot weevils chew celery hearts and tunnel into the tops. Plants become defoliated, starting with the crowns. Ribs of leaves and stems remain. The adult carrot weevil is ⅕ inch long and brown and has a hard shell. The larvae are pale in color, with brown heads and no legs. Control infestations by spraying celery plants with pyrethrum as soon as adult beetles appear in spring. Try to deny weevils access early in the season by covering seedlings with agricultural fleece.

Parsleyworm

The leaves of plants infested with parsleyworms are chewed so that often only the bare stems remain. The parsleyworm is a 2-inch caterpillar that is green with a yellow-dotted black band across each segment. It gives off an odor and projects orange horns when upset. These bright, large caterpillars are easy to handpick in the early morning. You can also apply *Bacillus thuringiensis* (BT) as a powder or a spray every 10 to 14 days until the pest is under control.

Leaves Folded and Closed by Webs

Celery Leaftier

Leaves that are folded over and closed by webs are signs that your plants are infested with celery leaftiers. This pest chews holes in the leaves and stems of celery plants. The leaftier is a pale green caterpillar with a white stripe down its back. As it grows to its full length of ¾ inch, its color changes to yellow. The adult moth is small and brown with dark wavy lines on its wings. It is active at night and lays eggs on the undersides of leaves. The eggs resemble fish scales. Handpicking usually controls this pest, since it appears in low numbers. Also remove any rolled or folded leaves, which may be sheltering caterpillars. *Bacillus thuringiensis* (BT) helps to control this pest. Apply as a powder or spray every 10 to 14 days until leaftiers are under control. For heavy infestations, dust with pyrethrum twice, 3 to 4 days apart.

Weakened Plants

Leafhopper

Both adult leafhoppers and nymphs pierce leaves, buds, and stems and suck the sap and chlorophyll from cells, causing plants to weaken. The leaves may develop white or yellow mottling. Adults are green, wedge-shaped insects, ¼ to ⅓ inch long, that hold their wings in a rooflike position above their bodies. They are very active and move sideways. Nymphs resemble adults. To control serious infestations, apply insecticidal soap laced with isopropyl alcohol every 3 to 4 days. In early spring, apply a preventive spray of insecticidal soap and seaweed extract, and cover seedlings with an agricultural fleece barrier for the first month of growth to deny leafhoppers access to your plants.

Leaves Stippled Yellow

Mite

Leaves of celery infested with mites become stippled, yellow, and dry, and sometimes pale yellow spots or blotches appear. Mites are not insects but arachnids, and are about the size of a grain of black pepper. They may be red, black, or brown. They feed by sucking out the plant's juices. In sucking chlorophyll out of the leaves, they cause small white dots to appear. In addition, they inject toxins into the leaves, which discolors and distorts them. To control infestations, spray plants with a forceful spray of water three times, once every other day, to knock mites from the leaves. If mites are still present, spray with insecticidal soap at least three times once every 7 to 10 days.

Large Ragged Holes in Leaves

Slug

Large ragged holes in the leaves or stems are a sign of slugs. They work their way from the bottom of a plant up. Look for trails of slime on the leaves and on the soil near the plants as further evidence of the presence of slugs. Slugs are 1 to 2 inches long and look like snails without shells. They may be brown, gray, white, pale yellow, purple, or nearly black with brown specks. You can control them by handpicking if you get them early in the season. The best way to control their damage is to set up a barrier of hardware cloth, ashes, sand, or some other material to deny them access to the garden. You can also make traps to catch slugs. (See the entry Slug in chapter 4 for information on making slug traps.)

Black Spots on Leaves

Tarnished Plant Bug

Black spots and pitting can be seen on the leaves and stem tips of infested plants. This pest can also deform roots and blacken terminal shoots. The adult tarnished plant bug is a ¼-inch-long, oval, flat, brownish insect, mottled with yellow and black. It sucks on plant parts. Tarnished plant bugs are highly mobile. The nymphs are pale yellow, and the eggs are long and curved and inserted in stems, tips, and leaves. Sprays must be used early in the morning when bugs are least active. Try three applications of pyrethrum, one every 3 days, to handle nymphs and adults. The best way to control this pest is by fall and spring cleanup to prevent it from occurring in the first place.

MOST COMMON DISEASES

Water-soaked Areas on Leaves

Black Heart

Celery plants infected with black heart exhibit water-soaked areas on the tips of the youngest leaves. These areas turn brown and may spread until all the leaves are affected. Add calcium to the soil. The best sources are natural ground limestone, dolomite limestone, wood ashes, bone meal, or oyster shells. Check pH levels so that you don't add so much material that it creates a pH imbalance. Spray celery with kelp or seaweed extract.

Seedlings Die

Damping-Off

Seedlings that have damping-off simply topple over. You will see a watery soft rot on the stem at the soil line. There is no cure for this disease. Remove and destroy infected plants. When starting seeds indoors, use commercial potting soil, or pasteurize your own potting soil in an oven. Disinfect tools in a bleach solution (one part household bleach to four parts water). Soak seeds in brine (1 cup of salt in 1 quart of water) or lime and wood solution (1 cup of lime and wood ashes in 1 quart of water). Provide soil with adequate drainage and use a fan for better air circulation. For direct seeding, make sure soil is well drained and warm. You might try spreading pasteurized soil or a sterile vermiculite in furrows where you plant your seeds.

Small Yellow Spots on Leaves

Early Blight

Celery plants infected by early blight have circular, small, yellow spots on the leaves of seedlings, which rapidly enlarge up to ½ inch. Color of the spots changes from yellow to brown with a grayish cast in the center. The spots can grow together and kill the leaves. In addition, sunken lesions may develop on the stalks, and growth of the plant is stunted. As soon as you spot symptoms, begin applying a copper-based fungicide every 7 to 10 days until symptoms are gone.
Resistant Varieties. Emerson Pascal and Green Giant Hybrid.

Stunted Plants, Yellow Leaves

Fusarium Wilt

Celery plants infected by fusarium wilt show stunted, one-sided growth and yellowing, and the vascular strands become reddish brown from the roots to the leaves. You should remove and destroy infected plants. Fusarium wilt is generally carried in the soil, so using resistant varieties is the best approach to preventing fusarium wilt in celery.
Resistant Varieties. Green petiole varieties or Ornell 19, and Emerson Pascal, Florida Golden, Forbes Golden Plume, Golden Pascal, Michigan Golden, and Tall Golden Plume.

Black Spots on Leaves

Late Blight

Late blight appears on seedlings as small, round, yellow spots on the leaves. The spots turn almost black in 2 weeks. Once you spot the symptoms, apply a copper-based fungicide every 7 to 10 days until harvest.
Resistant Varieties. Emerson Pascal and Green Giant Hybrid.

Water-soaked Stalks, Pink Growth

Pink Rot

Celery plants infected with pink rot develop water-soaked spots on the stalks, and you will see a cottony pink growth at the base of the stalks. Stems will rot and taste bitter. Damping-off, a watery soft rot on the stem at the soil line, may occur in an infected seedbed. Remove and destroy infected plants. Avoid successive plantings of celery, lettuce, and cabbage.

ting off the roots right below the crown. The harvest period for celery lasts 6 to 8 weeks, depending on the variety and the weather. You can get a second crop of celery if you harvest it by cutting it off at the ground instead of pulling it up by the roots. The stumps soon grow new shoots, which you can continue to harvest until the first snowfall.

HARVEST AND STORAGE

When to Harvest

Celery stalks should be rigid, crisp, tightly packed, and glossy, with good heart formation. A few stalks can be picked from the outside of the plant as needed, once they reach the desired size, or an entire plant can be harvested by lifting it and cut-

Yield for 24-Square-Foot Bed   20 to 40 pounds
Yield for 25-Foot Row   12 to 20 pounds
Best Fresh Storage Method   Refrigerate celery in plastic bags; it will keep for at least 2 to 4 weeks.
Seed Storage   5 years

VEGETABLE *Chard*   *Beta vulgaris,* Cicla Group

DESCRIPTION AND ENVIRONMENT

Height   24 to 30 inches
Spread   3½ feet
Root Depth   36 to 48 inches
Shade Tolerance   Needs only 5 hours of sun a day (partial shade).
Frost Tolerance   Hardy; withstands light freezing.
Preferred pH   6.0 to 7.5

Planting Depth   ½ to ¾ inch
Spacing of Plants in Rows   10 to 15 inches
Spacing of Plants in Beds   6 to 9 inches
Best Soil Temperature for Germination   40°F to 70°F
Best Soil Temperature for Growing   60°F to 70°F
Best Air Temperature for Growing   45°F to 70°F
Days to Germination   7 to 14
Weeks to Transplanting   3 to 4
Days to Maturity   55 to 60
Greenhouse Varieties   Chard cannot be grown in the greenhouse.
Container Varieties   Any variety.
Container Size   8 to 12 inches deep.

PLANTING

Spring Planting Time   2 to 4 weeks before last expected frost.
Fall Planting Time   6 weeks or more before first expected frost. Chard grows well after first frost.

PLANT MANAGEMENT

Water Requirements

Make sure the plants get 1 inch of water every week from rain or by watering. (See chapter 8 for more information on watering.)

Feeding Requirements

Apply compost or a slow-acting general-purpose fertilizer in spring. Chard is a light feeder, but benefits from a foliar spray of liquid seaweed extract two or three times during the growing season. As an option, you can give supplemental light feedings (side-dressings or foliar spray) monthly throughout the growing season. (See chapter 8 for more information on feeding.)

MOST COMMON INSECT PESTS

Foliage Curls, Puckers, Turns Yellow

Aphid

If the foliage on your plants curls, puckers, and turns yellow, and the foliage and blooms become stunted, look for ants. They are a sign that your plants have aphids. Ants are attracted to a sticky honeydew secreted by aphids. These insects have soft, pear-shaped bodies about the size of a pinhead. They may be green, brown, or pink. You will find them in clusters on the undersides of young leaves. For light infestations, spray the plants vigorously with water in the early morning, three times, once every other day. For heavy infestations, apply a commercial insecticidal soap every 2 to 3 days until aphids are under control.

Defoliated Plants

Carrot Weevil

Carrot weevils defoliate plants, beginning at the crown. After a plant has been attacked, only the ribs of leaves and stems remain. Larvae tunnel into the tops and roots of chard. The adult carrot weevil is $\frac{1}{5}$ inch long, brown, and has a hard shell. The larvae are pale in color, with brown heads and no legs. Control infestations by spraying chard plants with pyrethrum as soon as adult beetles appear in spring. Try to deny weevils access early in the season by covering seedlings with agricultural fleece. Parasitic nematodes may help to prevent infestation of the roots. (See chapter 4 for more information on parasitic nematodes.)

Shotgun-like Holes in Leaves

European Corn Borer

European corn borers chew the leaves of plants, giving them the appearance of having shotholes.

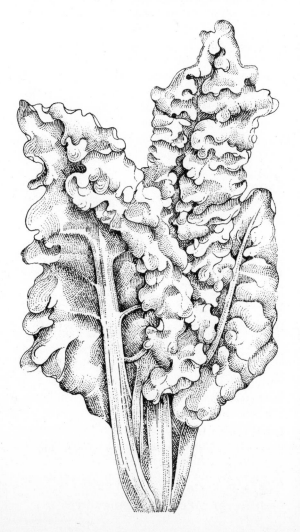

The borer is a grayish to pink caterpillar with a darker head and spots on each segment. White eggs are laid in groups on the undersides of foliage. The adult is a yellowish nocturnal moth with ½-inch wings that have dark bands. Apply *Bacillus thuringiensis* (BT) as soon as you spot the eggs on the undersides of leaves, and continue making applications every 7 to 10 days.

Tiny Holes in Leaves

Flea Beetle

If you find many little holes or perforations in the leaves of your plants, the plants may have flea beetles. Flea beetles are 1/10 inch long, shiny, and black, and may have yellow or white markings. They are very active and jump like fleas when disturbed. Their feeding can destroy small plants rapidly. Make two applications of pyrethrum, 3 to 4 days apart, to control infestations. In the spring, cover seedlings with a barrier, such as agricultural fleece, to deny flea beetles access to your plants.

Weakened Plants

Leafhopper

Both adult leafhoppers and nymphs pierce leaves, buds, and stems and suck the sap and chlorophyll from cells, causing plants to weaken. The beet leafhopper, which also attacks chard, is pale green or yellow, about ⅛ inch long, and has slender, long hind legs that enable it to jump quickly into the air. When flying, it looks like a tiny white fly. To control serious infestations, apply insecticidal soap laced with isopropyl alcohol every 3 to 4 days. In early spring, apply a preventive spray of insecticidal soap and seaweed extract and cover seedlings with an agricultural fleece barrier for the first month of growth to deny leafhoppers access to your plants.

White or Brown Tunnels in Leaves

Leafminer

White or brown tunnels or blotches on leaves are signs that your chard has leafminers. The leaves may turn yellow and blotchy and look blistered or curled. Leafminers are small black flies, usually with yellow stripes. The tiny yellowish larvae feed between the upper and lower surfaces of leaves, causing the tunnels or blotches to appear. You may also find stem damage below the soil. Remove the infested leaves before the larvae mature. The best way to control leafminers, though, is to screen out the adult flies, using a barrier such as agricultural fleece.

Large Ragged Holes in Leaves

Slug

Large ragged holes in the leaves or stems are a sign of slugs. They work their way from the bottom of a plant up. Look for trails of slime on the leaves and on the soil near the plants as further evidence of the presence of slugs. Slugs are 1 to 2 inches long and look like snails without shells. They may be brown, gray, white, pale yellow, purple, or nearly black with brown specks. You can control them by handpicking if you get them early in the season. The best way to control their damage is to set up a barrier of hardware cloth, ashes, sand, or some other material to deny them access to the garden. You can also make traps to catch slugs. (See the entry Slug in chapter 4 for information on making slug traps.)

Black Spots on Leaves

Tarnished Plant Bug

Black spots and pitting can be seen on the leaves, stem tips, buds, and fruit of infested plants. This pest can also deform roots and blacken terminal shoots. The adult tarnished plant bug is a ¼-inch-long, oval, flat, brownish insect, mottled with yellow and black. It sucks on plant parts. Tarnished plant bugs are highly mobile. The nymphs are pale yellow, and the eggs are long and curved and inserted in stems, tips, and leaves. Sprays must be used early in the morning when bugs are least active. Try three applications of pyrethrum, one every 3 days, to handle nymphs and adults. The best way to control this pest is by fall and spring cleanup to prevent it from occurring in the first place.

Chewed Foliage

Weevil

If the leaves of your chard are chewed to the stem, suspect the vegetable weevil. This pest is gray to brownish in color with a V-shaped mark near the tip of its wing covers. It is about ½ inch long and has a long snout. It feeds at night and hides during the day. As weevils appear, spray with pyrethrum twice, 3 to 4 days apart.

Weakened Plants, Yellow Leaves

Whitefly

Plants that have whiteflies weaken, their leaves turn yellow, and they die. Honeydew secreted by whiteflies encourages fungus. Molds often develop following an attack. Adults are about the size of a pinhead, and mothlike, with dusty white wings. When an infested plant is shaken, it appears as if dandruff were flying off the leaves. Nymphs are yellowish, legless, flat, and oval, resembling scale at certain stages. To control infestations, spray plants with insecticidal soap spray every 2 to 3 days for 2 weeks. Use it also early in the season to prevent whiteflies. Spray every 2 weeks for the first months of the plant's life. Pyrethrum may be used as a last resort. Make two applications, 3 to 4 days apart.

MOST COMMON DISEASES

White Downy Substance on Leaves

Downy Mildew

Chard infected with downy mildew will have yellowish or light green areas on the upper surfaces of older leaves. Seedlings develop purplish lesions on the leaves and stems, which become covered with white downy fungus. Plants die very rapidly after contracting downy mildew. If you catch the infection early, apply a copper-based fungicide to diseased and surrounding plants every 7 to 10 days until harvest. Remove and destroy any plants with a serious infection.

HARVEST AND STORAGE

When to Harvest

When chard reaches 8 to 10 inches, pick the outer leaves as needed, or cut the entire plant 1½ inches above the ground.

Yield for 25-Foot Row   15 to 25 pounds
Volume vs. Weight   1 bushel equals 12 pounds.
Best Fresh Storage Method   Refrigerate chard in plastic bags; it will keep for 7 to 10 days.

VEGETABLE *Chinese Cabbage*

Brassica pekinensis

DESCRIPTION AND ENVIRONMENT

Height   Up to 20 inches.
Spread   5 inches or more.
Root Depth   Shallow, 18 to 36 inches.
Shade Tolerance   Needs at least 6 hours of

sun a day (partial shade).
Frost Tolerance   Hardy; can survive subfreezing weather for short periods of time.
Preferred pH   6.0 to 7.0

PLANTING

Spring Planting Time   4 to 6 weeks before last expected frost. While some of the newer varieties can be planted in early spring, most will bolt with the first hot days and so are best planted in summer for fall cropping.

Fall Planting Time   11 weeks before first expected frost. Chinese cabbage grows well after first frost.

Planting Depth   ¼ inch

Spacing of Plants in Rows   12 to 15 inches

Spacing of Plants in Beds   10 to 12 inches

Best Soil Temperature for Germination   50°F to 75°F

Best Soil Temperature for Growing 60°F to 70°F

Best Air Temperature for Growing 55°F to 70°F

Days to Germination   4 to 10

Weeks to Transplanting   4; some varieties of Chinese cabbage dislike transplanting when young.

Days to Maturity   65 to 70 after direct seeding; 40 to 50 after transplanting.

Greenhouse Varieties   Any variety of Chinese cabbage can be grown in a cool greenhouse.

Container Varieties   Almost any variety can be grown in containers, but try the Bok Choy, Michihli, and Wong Bok varieties for easy success.

Container Size   20 inches deep.

Plants Bolt

Hot Temperatures

Chinese cabbage planted in spring can bolt and go to seed before they are harvested if temperatures get too high. To prevent this from happening, cover plants with shading material, such as agricultural fleece, whenever the air temperature exceeds 70°F. Place the shading material over some kind of support so there is good air circulation under the material. Remove the cover when the temperature goes down again. Shade plants from about 10 or 11 A.M. until 5 or 6 P.M.

Plants Don't Produce Heads

Hot Temperatures

Hot weather can prevent certain heading varieties of Chinese cabbage from producing heads. Loosely tying up all but the outer leaves reduces the light to the inner leaves and gives a 100 percent heading rate. The leaves are tied up the same way cauliflower is tied. Do this about 30 days after 21-day-old seedlings are set out in the garden.

PLANT MANAGEMENT

Water Requirements

Make sure Chinese cabbage get 1 inch of water every week from rain or by watering. (See chapter 8 for more information on watering.)

Feeding Requirements

Apply compost or a slow-acting general-purpose fertilizer in spring. Chinese cabbage is a light feeder, but can benefit from a foliar spray of liquid seaweed extract two or three times during the growing season. You can also give your plants supplemental light feedings (side-dressings or foliar spray) monthly throughout the growing season, but this is optional. (See chapter 8 for more information on feeding.)

MOST COMMON INSECT PESTS

Foliage Curls, Puckers, Turns Yellow

Aphid
If the foliage on your plants curls, puckers, and turns yellow, and the foliage and blooms become stunted, look for ants. They are a sign that your plants have aphids. Ants are attracted to a sticky honeydew secreted by aphids. These insects have soft, pear-shaped bodies about the size of a pinhead. They may be green, brown, or pink. Cabbage aphids also attack Chinese cabbage. They are green to powdery blue in color and are covered with a fine whitish wax. You will find them in clusters on the undersides of young leaves. For light infestations, spray the plants vigorously with water in the early morning, three times, once every other day. For heavy infestations, apply a commercial insecticidal soap every 2 to 3 days until aphids are under control.

Small Ragged Holes in Leaves

Cabbage Looper
Small ragged holes in leaves indicate that your plants may be infested with cabbage loopers. Later in the season, the worms bore into developing heads. The cabbage looper is a 1½-inch-long caterpillar that is light green with long yellowish stripes on its back. It loops as it walks. Spray *Bacillus thuringiensis* (BT) on infested plants every 2 weeks until loopers are under control.

Brown Tunnels in Stem

Cabbage Maggot
Brown tunnels in the stem just below soil level indicate cabbage maggots. Seedlings become yellow, growth is stunted, and plants lack vigor. The infested plants wilt during the heat of the day, and eventually die. The cabbage maggot is a small, white, legless worm about ¼ inch long. The adult resembles a housefly. Maggots tunnel into plant roots and stems. Bacterial diseases such as black leg, which causes dark patches on leaves, and soft rot, which causes plant decomposition, may result, causing the plants to wilt. To control infestations, apply wood ashes or a lime drench (1 cup of lime in 1 quart of water; let sit overnight) around the root ball of each plant. The best control is to prevent flies from laying eggs in the first place. Spread a barrier, such as agricultural fleece, over the seedlings in spring, or place a collar around the stem of each plant. (See chapter 4 for instructions on how to construct these collars.)

Seedling Stems Severed

Cutworm
Cutworms completely sever the stems of seedlings and transplants at or below the soil surface. They are 1- to 2-inch, dull-colored, plump, soft-bodied larvae that curl up when disturbed. Cutworms feed at night and hide in the soil during the day. To control cutworms, use barriers or traps to deny them access to seedlings. To protect individual plants, surround them with a collar, or make a trap by

sprinkling cornmeal or bran meal around each plant. (See chapter 4 for more information on collars and meal traps.)

Tiny Holes in Leaves

Flea Beetle
If you find many little holes or perforations in the leaves of your plants, the plants may have flea beetles. Flea beetles are $1/10$ inch long, shiny and black, and may have yellow or white markings. They are very active and jump like fleas when disturbed. Their feeding can destroy small plants rapidly. Make two applications of pyrethrum, 3 to 4 days apart, to control infestations. In the spring, cover seedlings with a barrier, such as agricultural fleece, to deny flea beetles access to your plants.

Wilted Leaves with Black Spots

Harlequin Bug
If the leaves of your plants develop white blotches or black spots and then wilt and die, suspect the harlequin bug. This insect is ¼ inch long and shaped like a shield, with a triangle on its back. It has patterned markings in black and red. Harlequin bugs emit a foul odor. To control infestations, spray plants with an insecticidal soap laced with isopropyl alcohol every 2 to 3 days for 2 weeks. Apply insecticidal soap twice, 5 to 7 days apart, in early spring to prevent harlequin bugs.

Large Ragged Holes in Leaves

Imported Cabbage Worm
Imported cabbage worms chew large ragged holes in Chinese cabbage leaves, and they may bore into the heads, leaving trails of dark green frass, or excrement. The worm is light green with one yellow stripe, and measures 1¼ inches long. The adult is a common white butterfly with three to four black spots on its wings that is active during the day. To control infestations, apply *Bacillus thuringiensis* (BT) every 10 to 14 days until the pests are gone. Prevent cabbage worms by spraying seedlings with BT early in the season, every 2 weeks from trans-planting until heads form, and covering them with an agricultural fleece barrier.

Slug
Large ragged holes in the leaves or stems are signs of slugs. They work their way from the bottom of a plant up. Look for trails of slime on the leaves and on the soil near the plants as further evidence of the presence of slugs. Slugs are 1 to 2 inches long and look like snails without shells. They may be brown, gray, white, pale yellow, purple, or nearly black with brown specks. You can control them by handpicking if you get them early in the season. The best way to control their damage is to set up a barrier of hardware cloth, ashes, sand, or some other material to deny them access to the garden. You can also make traps to catch slugs. (See the entry Slug in chapter 4 for information on making slug traps.)

Chewed Foliage

Weevil
If the leaves of your Chinese cabbage are chewed to the stem, suspect the vegetable weevil. This pest is gray to brownish in color with a V-shaped mark near the tip of its wing covers. It is about ½ inch long and has a long snout. It feeds at night and hides during the day. As weevils appear, spray with pyrethrum twice, 3 to 4 days apart.

MOST COMMON DISEASES

Dark Patches on Leaves

Black Leg
Plants infected with black leg develop sunken areas on the stem near the ground, which girdle the stem. Gray spots speckled with black dots appear on the leaves and stems. The edges of leaves wilt and turn bluish or red, and the entire plant may wilt or topple over. Fixed copper fungicides are sometimes effective in controlling this disease. Use as directed on the label. If this treatment does not halt the disease, remove and destroy the infected plants.

Yellow, Wedge-shaped Areas on Leaves

Black Rot

The leaves of Chinese cabbage plants infected with black rot develop yellow, wedge-shaped areas with darkened veins; then they wilt. The vascular bundles in leaves and stems are black and bad smelling. Young plants may not produce heads, and the heads on older plants that become infected will rot. Black rot cannot be cured. Remove and destroy the infected and surrounding plants. Micronized sulfur helps to control the spread of black rot to other plants. Apply the sulfur to unaffected plants every 7 days until harvest.

Poor Crop Development

Club Root

In general, plants that have club root exhibit the effects of a malfunctioning root system: wilting and poor development. Under the soil you will find misshapen roots with club-shaped swellings. Try to prevent this disease by following clean gardening practices, dipping young transplants in fungicidal solution, and rotating plants (the fungus persists in the soil for 7 years). Club root is more of a problem with plants growing in acid soil. Test your soil; if the pH is too low, add lime. Apply approved soil fungicides to control the disease in infected plants.

Seedlings Die

Damping-Off

Seedlings that have damping-off simply topple over. You will see a watery soft rot on the stem at the soil line. There is no cure for this disease. Remove and destroy infected plants. When starting seeds indoors, use commercial potting soil, or pasteurize your own potting soil in an oven. Disinfect tools in heated water or a bleach solution (one part household bleach to four parts water). Provide soil with adequate drainage and use a fan for better air circulation. For direct seeding, make sure soil is well drained and warm. You might try spreading pasteurized soil or a sterile vermiculite in furrows where you plant your seeds.

Water-soaked Spots on Leaves

Leaf Spot

Chinese cabbage plants that have leaf spot develop water-soaked spots that later grow in size and take on a brownish or purplish gray color. Leaf spot cannot be cured. Remove and destroy infected and surrounding plants.

Part of Plant Rots

Rhizoctonia

Rhizoctonia is characterized by darkened and girdled areas on the stem near the soil line. Affected plants are weak, produce small heads, and sometimes wilt and die. Bottom rot develops on plants after they have been transplanted to the garden. Dark, slightly sunken spots develop on basal leaves near the soil. In moist conditions the rot spreads to adjacent leaves and causes the head to rot. Rhizoctonia also commonly causes damping-off, a watery soft rot on the stem at the soil line. Rhizoctonia cannot be controlled. Remove and destroy infected plants. To prevent rhizoctonia from becoming a problem, avoid planting Chinese cabbage in short rotations where bottom rot and damping-off have been a problem. Pasteurizing the soil used to raise seedlings and solarizing the garden soil also help to control rhizoctonia. (For more information on soil pasteurization and solarization, see chapter 5.)

Seeds Do Not Germinate

Seed Rot

Seed rot will prevent your Chinese cabbage seeds from germinating. It occurs when soil is too moist and cold for germination. If necessary, make a shallow ditch, fill it with commercial sterilized potting mix, and sow seeds in that mixture.

Yellow Lower Leaves

Yellows

The symptoms of yellows are similar to those of black rot. The lower leaves of plants turn yellow, then brown, and finally drop. Cabbage heads may appear stunted and taste bitter. Yellows cannot be cured. Remove and destroy infected and surrounding plants.

HARVEST AND STORAGE

When to Harvest

Cut heading types of Chinese cabbage as soon as they reach usable size. For nonheading types, harvest a few outer leaves at a time, or cut the entire plant for a single harvest. Cook the very tender and sweet stalks like asparagus, and the leaves like spinach. Heading types are used just like any cabbage. The harvest period for Chinese cabbage lasts from 3 to 6 weeks, depending on variety.

Yield for 24-Square-Foot Bed   20 to 30 pounds
Yield for 25-Foot Row   15 to 25 pounds
Best Fresh Storage Method   Refrigerate

Chinese cabbage in plastic bags; it will keep for 2 to 3 weeks.

Best Long-Term Storage Method
Chinese cabbage can be stored with heads down and roots up under straw and soil in a root cellar or cool cellar, where it will keep for up to 3 months. Chinese cabbage can be transplanted into a cold frame for winter harvests.

Seed Storage   5 years

NOTES AND RESEARCH

One of the most confusing groups of vegetables are those known as Chinese cabbage. There are heading types *(Brassica pekinensis)* and non-heading types *(B. chinensis)*. Heading types include short, round varieties generally known as *wong bok* or *napa*, and tall, slender ones called *michihli* or *tientsin*. The non-heading types have celerylike stalks and are called *pac choy* or *bok choy*. The names are often mixed up, so it pays to compare catalog descriptions.

VEGETABLE *Collard*   *Brassica oleracea,* Acephala Group

DESCRIPTION AND ENVIRONMENT

Height   24 to 30 inches
Spread   24 inches
Shade Tolerance   Needs full sun.
Frost Tolerance   Very hardy.
Preferred pH   5.5 to 6.8

PLANTING

Spring Planting Time   4 weeks before to 2 weeks after last expected frost.

Fall Planting Time   8 to 10 weeks before first expected frost. Collards grow well after first frost.
Planting Depth   ¼ to ½ inch
Spacing of Plants in Rows   12 to 15 inches
Spacing of Plants in Beds   10 to 12 inches
Weeks to Transplanting   6 to 8
Greenhouse Varieties   Collards are not grown in the greenhouse.

Container Varieties Any variety can be grown in containers.
Container Size 12 inches deep.

PLANT MANAGEMENT

Water Requirements

Make sure collards get 1 inch of water every week from rain or by watering. (See chapter 8 for more information on watering.)

Feeding Requirements

Apply compost or a slow-acting general-purpose fertilizer in spring. Collards are light feeders, but benefit from foliar spray of liquid seaweed extract two or three times during the growing season. You can give collards supplemental light feedings (side-dressings or foliar spray) monthly throughout the growing season, but this is not necessary. (See chapter 8 for more information on feeding.)

MOST COMMON INSECT PESTS

Foliage Curls, Puckers, Turns Yellow

Aphid

If the foliage on your plants curls, puckers, and turns yellow, and the foliage and blooms become stunted, look for ants. They are a sign that your plants have aphids. Ants are attracted to a sticky honeydew secreted by aphids. These insects have soft, pear-shaped bodies about the size of a pinhead. They may be green, brown, or pink. Cabbage aphids also attack collards. They are green to powdery blue in color and are covered with a fine whitish wax. You will find aphids in clusters on the undersides of young leaves. For light infestations, spray the plants vigorously with water in the early morning, three times, once every other day. For heavy infestations, apply a commercial insecticidal soap every 2 to 3 days until aphids are under control.

Small Ragged Holes in Leaves

Cabbage Looper

Small ragged holes in leaves indicate that your plants may be infested with cabbage loopers. The cabbage looper is a 1½-inch-long, light green caterpillar with long yellowish stripes on its back. It loops as it walks. Spray *Bacillus thuringiensis* (BT) on infested plants every 2 weeks until the problem is solved.

Brown Tunnels in Stems

Cabbage Maggot

Brown tunnels in the stem just below soil level indicate cabbage maggots. Seedlings become yellow, growth is stunted, and plants lack vigor. The infested plants wilt during the heat of the day, and eventually die. The cabbage maggot is a small, white, legless worm about ¼ inch long. The adult resembles a housefly. Maggots tunnel into plant roots and stems. Bacterial diseases such as black leg, which causes dark patches on leaves, and soft rot, which causes plant decomposition, may result, causing the plants to wilt. To control infestations, apply wood ashes or a lime drench (1 cup of lime in 1 quart of water; let sit overnight) around the root ball of each plant. The best control is to prevent flies from laying eggs in the first place. Spread a barrier, such as agricultural fleece, over the transplants, or place a collar around the stem of each plant. (See chapter 4 for instructions on how to construct these collars.)

Seedling Stems Severed

Cutworm

Cutworms completely sever the stems of seedlings and transplants at or below the soil surface. They are 1- to 2-inch, dull-colored, plump, soft-bodied larvae that curl up when disturbed. Cutworms feed at night and hide in the soil during the day. To control cutworms, use barriers or traps to prevent access to seedlings. To protect individual plants, surround them with a collar, or make a trap by sprinkling cornmeal or bran meal around each plant. (See chapter 4 for more information on collars and meal traps.)

Tiny Holes in Leaves

Flea Beetle

If you find many little holes or perforations in the leaves of your plants, the plants may have flea beetles. Flea beetles are $\frac{1}{10}$ inch long, shiny, and black, and may have yellow or white markings. They are very active and jump like fleas when disturbed. Their feeding can destroy small plants rapidly. Make two applications of pyrethrum, 3 to 4 days apart, to control infestations. In the spring, cover plants with a barrier, such as agricultural fleece, to deny flea beetles access to your plants.

Resistant Varieties. Georgia, Georgia LS, and Vates.

Wilted Leaves with Black Spots

Harlequin Bug

If the leaves of your plants develop white blotches or black spots and then wilt and die, suspect the harlequin bug. This insect is ¼ inch long and shaped like a shield, with a triangle on its back. It has patterned markings in black and red. Harlequin bugs emit a foul odor. To control infestations, spray plants with an insecticidal soap laced with isopropyl alcohol every 2 to 3 days for 2 weeks. Apply insecticidal soap twice, 5 to 7 days apart, in early spring to prevent harlequin bugs.

Resistant Varieties. Green Glaze, Morris Improved Heading, and Vates.

Large Ragged Holes in Leaves

Imported Cabbage Worm

Imported cabbage worms chew large ragged holes in collards, leaving trails of dark green frass, or excrement. The worm is light green with one yellow stripe, and measures 1¼ inches long. The adult is a common white butterfly with three to four black spots on its wings that is active during the day. To control infestations, apply *Bacillus thuringiensis* (BT) every 10 to 14 days until the pest is removed. Prevent cabbage worms by spraying plants with BT early in the season, every 2 weeks from transplanting until crowns form, and covering them with an agricultural fleece barrier.

Leaves Stippled Yellow

Mite

Leaves of collards infested with mites become stippled, yellow, and dry, and sometimes pale yellow spots or blotches appear. Mites are not insects but arachnids, and are about the size of a grain of black pepper. They may be red, black, or brown. They feed by sucking out the plant's juices. In sucking chlorophyll out of the leaves, they cause small white dots to appear. In addition, they inject toxins into the leaves, which discolors and distorts them. To control infestations, spray plants with a forceful spray of water three times, once every other day, to knock mites from the leaves. If mites are still present, spray with insecticidal soap three times, once every 5 to 7 days.

Chewed Foliage

Weevil

If the leaves of your collards are chewed to the stem, suspect the vegetable weevil. This pest is gray to brownish in color with a V-shaped mark near the tip of its wing covers. It is about ½ inch long and has a long snout. It feeds at night and hides during the day. As weevils appear, spray with pyrethrum twice, 3 to 4 days apart.

MOST COMMON DISEASES

Dark Patches on Leaves

Black Leg

Plants infected with black leg develop sunken areas on the stem near the ground, which girdle the stem. Gray spots speckled with black dots appear on the leaves and stems. The edges of leaves wilt and turn bluish or red, and the entire plant may wilt or topple over. Fixed copper fungicides are sometimes effective in controlling this disease. Use the application directions on the label. If this treatment does not halt the disease, remove and destroy the infected plants.

Yellow, Wedge-shaped Areas on Leaves

Black Rot

Black rot affects young as well as mature plants. Infected seedlings turn yellow and die. On older plants, yellow, wedge-shaped areas develop at the leaf margins and expand toward the center of the leaf. These areas later turn brown and die, and the leaves fall off. The vascular bundles in leaves and stems are black and bad smelling. Black rot cannot be cured. Remove and destroy the infected and surrounding plants. Micronized sulfur helps to control the spread of black rot to other plants. Apply the sulfur to unaffected plants every 7 days until harvest.

Poor Crop Development

Club Root

In general, plants that have club root exhibit the effects of a malfunctioning root system: wilting and poor development. Under the soil you will find misshapen roots with club-shaped swellings. Try to prevent this disease by following clean gardening practices and rotating plants (the fungus persists in the soil for 7 years). Club root is more of a problem with plants growing in acid soil. Test your soil, and if the pH is too low, add lime. Apply approved soil fungicides to control the disease in infected plants.

Seedlings Die

Damping-Off

Seedlings that have damping-off simply topple over. You will see a watery soft rot on the stem at the soil line. There is no cure for this disease. Remove and destroy infected plants. When starting seeds indoors, use commercial potting soil, or pasteurize your own potting soil in an oven. Disinfect tools in heated water or a bleach solution (one part household bleach to four parts water). Provide soil with adequate drainage and use a fan for better air circulation. For direct seeding, make sure soil is well drained and warm. You might try spreading pasteurized soil or a sterile vermiculite in furrows where you plant your seeds.

Water-soaked Spots on Leaves

Leaf Spot

Collards that have leaf spot develop water-soaked spots that later grow in size and take on a brownish or purplish gray color. Leaf spot cannot be cured. Remove and destroy infected and surrounding plants.

Part of Plant Rots

Rhizoctonia

Rhizoctonia is characterized by darkened and girdled areas on the stem near the soil line. Affected plants are weak, produce small heads, and sometimes wilt and die. Bottom rot develops on plants after they have been transplanted to the garden. Dark, slightly sunken spots develop on basal leaves near the soil. In moist conditions the rot spreads to adjacent leaves and causes the head to rot. Rhizoctonia also commonly causes damping-off, a watery soft rot on the stem at the soil line. Rhizoctonia cannot be controlled. Remove and destroy infected plants. To prevent rhizoctonia from becoming a problem, avoid planting collards in short rotations where bottom rot and damping-off have been a problem. Pasteurizing the soil used to raise seedlings and solarizing the garden soil also help to control rhizoctonia. (See chapter 5 for more information on soil pasteurization and solarization.)

Seeds Do Not Germinate

Seed Rot

Seed rot will prevent your collard seeds from germinating. It occurs when soil is too moist and cold for germination. If necessary, make a shallow ditch, fill it with commercial sterilized potting mix, and sow seeds in that mixture.

Yellow Lower Leaves

Yellows

The symptoms of yellows are similar to those of black rot. The lower leaves of plants turn yellow, then brown, and finally drop. Collards may appear stunted and taste bitter. Yellows cannot be cured. Remove and destroy infected and surrounding plants.

HARVEST AND STORAGE

When to Harvest

All the green parts of the collard plant are edible. You can pick the inner rosette only, or wait until the plants are 1 foot tall and pick the largest leaves. With collards planted for fall, wait to pick until after the first fall frost, which improves flavor.

NOTES AND RESEARCH

Studies have shown that collards intercropped with beans had more wasp parasites, four times fewer aphids, and less aphid damage than when planted alone. One study indicated that a catnip border reduced cabbage flea beetles on collards.

VEGETABLE # Corn   *Zea mays*

DESCRIPTION AND ENVIRONMENT

Height   6 to 8 feet
Spread   1½ to 4 feet
Root Depth   Most are shallow, 18 to 36 inches, but some deep, fibrous roots reach down as far as 7 feet.

Shade Tolerance   Needs full sun.

Frost Tolerance   Tender; injured by light frost.

Preferred pH   5.5 to 7.5

PLANTING

Spring Planting Time   From last expected frost to 2 to 3 weeks after frost.

Succession Planting   Make a second planting 3 weeks after the first, and a third planting 4 weeks later.

Planting Depth   2 inches

Spacing of Plants in Rows   12 to 18 inches

Spacing of Plants in Beds   18 inches

Best Soil Temperature for Germination   55°F to 85°F

Best Soil Temperature for Growing 75°F to 85°F

Best Air Temperature for Growing 50°F to 95°F

Days to Germination   6 to 10

Weeks to Transplanting   4

Days to Maturity   70 to 90

Greenhouse Varieties   Corn cannot be grown in the greenhouse.

Container Varieties   Space-saving varieties can be grown in containers.

Container Size   21 inches wide, 8 inches deep; you must grow at least three plants per container to assure pollination.

Delayed Ripening, Flat Flavor

Cool Air Temperatures
If you are having a cold summer, you can have trouble with warm weather crops such as corn. Such plants will delay their ripening and will produce flat-flavored crops.

PLANT MANAGEMENT

Water Requirements
Make sure corn gets 1 inch of water every week from rain or by watering. Watering is critical during silking, tasseling, and ear development. (See chapter 8 for more information on watering.)

Feeding Requirements for Good Production

Apply compost or a slow-acting general-purpose fertilizer in spring; then give the plants supplemental light feedings (either side-dressings or foliar spray) monthly throughout the growing season. (See chapter 8 for more information on feeding.)

Feeding Requirements for Maximum Production

Corn is a heavy feeder. In addition to the spring feeding mentioned above, it can use a light supplement every 2 weeks during the growing season. Apply a foliar spray of liquid seaweed extract two or three times during the growing season.

Pale Leaves, Turning Yellow

Nitrogen Deficiency

If leaves are pale and turn yellow, especially the lower leaves, and if growth is stunted, your corn plants may be deficient in nitrogen. To remedy the problem quickly, spray plants with diluted fish emulsion or another liquid fertilizer. (See chapter 8 for more information on nitrogen deficiency.)

Yellow Leaves, Missing Kernels

Phosphorus Deficiency

A yellowing of leaves similar to that which occurs from nitrogen deficiency may also be a sign of a phosphorus deficiency. In addition, the ears of corn will show missing kernels. Phosphorus deficiencies generally occur in acid soils. To remedy the problem quickly, spray plants with diluted fish emulsion or another liquid fertilizer, and add some wood ashes around the plants; they will quickly release phosphorus into the soil. (See chapter 8 for more information on phosphorus deficiency.)

MOST COMMON INSECT PESTS

Foliage Curls, Puckers, Turns Yellow

Aphid

If the foliage on your plants curls, puckers, and turns yellow, and plant growth becomes stunted, look for ants. They are a sign that your corn might have aphids. Ants are attracted to a sticky honeydew secreted by aphids. These insects have soft, pear-shaped bodies about the size of a pinhead. They may be green, brown, or pink. You will find them in clusters on the undersides of young leaves. For light infestations, spray plants vigorously with water in the early morning, three times, once every other day. Heavy infestations can be dealt with by applying commercial insecticidal soap every 2 to 3 days until aphids are under control.

Stunted Growth, Damaged Ears

Corn Earworm

Damage to buds and young plants is an early sign of corn earworms. Damp castings (excrement) can be seen near silk on the ears. Plant growth may be stunted, and later, corn ears are destroyed from the tip down. The corn earworm is 1½ inches long and may be white, green, or red. It has four prolegs, and spines along its body. The best strategy for controlling earworms is to apply a light horticultural oil spray mixed with *Bacillus thuringiensis* (BT) every 2 weeks from when the corn is knee-high until ears begin to form. Then apply a drop of mineral oil to the silks of each ear, after the silks have dried.

Resistant Varieties. Aristogold, Calumet, Country Gentleman, Dixie 18, Iona, Seneca Chief, Seneca Scout, Silver Cross Bantam, Staygold, and Victory Golden.

Plants Wilt and Collapse

Cucumber Beetle

The larvae of cucumber beetles, also known as corn rootworms, attack the roots of corn plants, causing the plants to wilt and collapse. Cucumber beetles are ¼ inch long, oblong, and yellow, with black stripes or spots. The adults lay eggs at the base of the plants. To control cucumber beetles, prevent the beetles from feeding on young plants. The critical period is from germination until the plants start to bloom. Use an agricultural fleece barrier to deny the beetles access to the plants. Remove the barrier when plants are about a foot tall.

Seedling Stems Severed

Cutworm

Cutworms completely sever the stems of seedlings and transplants at or below the soil surface. They are 1- to 2-inch, dull-colored, plump, soft-bodied larvae that curl up when disturbed. Cutworms feed at night and hide in the soil during the day. To control cutworms, use barriers or traps to prevent access to seedlings. To protect individual plants, surround them with a collar, or make a trap by sprinkling cornmeal or bran meal around each plant. (See chapter 4 for more information on collars and meal traps.)

Tassels Eaten

European Corn Borer

European corn borers chew the leaves and tassels of corn plants. Later in the season, they bore into stalks and ears. You may find a sawdustlike trail around the stalk and notice a gradual wilting of the plants. European borers are grayish to pink with dark heads and spots on each segment. The adult is a yellowish brown moth. Females lay their white eggs in groups on the undersides of leaves. These borers are difficult to control and easier to prevent. *Bacillus thuringiensis* (BT) is effective if used before the insect bores into the stalks. For long-term control, clean up the garden in the fall, rotate crops, and maintain a healthy population of predators. (See chapter 4 for information on predators.)
Resistant Varieties. Apache, Bellringer, Burgundy Delight, Butter and Sugar, Calumet, Country Gentleman, Quicksilver, Stowell's Evergreen, Sweet Sue, and Tablevee.

Tiny Holes in Leaves

Flea Beetle

If you find several little holes or perforations in the leaves of your plants, the plants may have flea beetles.

Flea beetles are $\frac{1}{10}$ inch long, shiny, and black, and may have yellow or white markings. They are very active and jump like fleas when disturbed. Their feeding can destroy small plants rapidly. Apply pyrethrum three times, 2 to 3 days apart. In the spring, cover seedlings with a barrier, such as agricultural fleece, to deny flea beetles access to your plants.

Whitened, Withered Leaves

Thrip

Whitened leaves are a sign that your corn plants may be infested with thrips. These insects are only $\frac{1}{25}$ inch long, and are recognized by their dark fecal pellets and by the damage they create. Thrips scrape the surfaces of leaves and suck the juices, leaving the tissue whitened and weak. A spray of insecticidal soap every 3 days for 2 weeks should control infestations. For serious problems, make two applications of pyrethrum, 3 to 4 days apart.

Sudden Wilting of Plant

White Grub

A sudden wilting of your corn plants, when all other conditions seem fine, may indicate the presence of white grubs. These pests are the fat, whitish larvae of the june beetle. They are $\frac{3}{4}$ to $1\frac{1}{2}$ inches long and they feed on the roots of plants. To control infestations, make one application of beneficial nematodes, which go below the surface of the soil to attack the grubs. (See chapter 4 for more information on parasitic nematodes.) Milky spore disease spread on the soil around the plants will control white grubs, but it takes 3 to 5 years to have a complete effect.

Wilting and Poor Development of Plant

Wireworm

Young corn plants infested with wireworms will wilt, discolor, and die. Wireworms are $\frac{1}{3}$ to $1\frac{1}{2}$ inches long, dark brown to yellowish, jointed, hard shelled, and cylindrical. They bore into the underground stems and roots, damaging them and causing poor development of the plant. The best control is to trap wireworms with pieces of potato speared on the ends of sticks. (See the entry Wireworm in chapter 4 for more information on how to use potato traps.)

MOST COMMON DISEASES

Wilted Leaves

Bacterial Wilt

If the leaves of your corn plants wilt on dry days and develop long, pale streaks, your plants probably are infected with bacterial wilt. This disease blocks the vascular systems of plants. It is transmitted by flea beetles, so try to prevent their access to the plant by covering plants with a barrier, such as agricultural fleece. Bacterial wilt cannot be cured. Remove and destroy infected plants immediately. Wash hands and any tools in a bleach solution (one part household bleach to four parts water) before touching other plants. Prevent bacterial wilt by following clean garden practices and planting seeds that are certified wilt-free.

Resistant Varieties. Bantam, Carmelcross, Country Gentleman, F-M Cross, Golden Beauty, Golden Cross Bantam, Ioana, Iochief, Marcross, N.K. 199, Seneca Chief, Silver Queen, and most white, late-maturing varieties.

Grayish White Galls on Plant

Smut

White or grayish white galls (swellings) of varying size on any aerial part of a corn plant are symptoms of smut. Seedling infection results in distorted and dwarfed plants. Cut out the galls and apply a sulfur-or copper-based fungicide every 7 to 10 days after discovering the disease. Badly affected plants should be removed and destroyed.

Resistant Varieties. Bantam, Country Gentleman, Gold Cup, Golden Cross, and Silver Queen.

HARVEST AND STORAGE

When to Harvest

Ears are ripe when the silks look dry and brown. Husks should be moist and green, and kernels, bright and plump. Press the kernels with a thumbnail; they should spurt a milky juice. Corn past its prime has starchy, doughy kernels. Flavor is best when picked in the late afternoon. The harvest period for corn is 1 to 2 weeks, depending on variety. Keep ears cool and cook within an hour of picking.

Yield for 24-Square-Foot Bed   12 to 20 pounds, including the cob.

Yield for 25-Foot Row   12 to 20 pounds, including the cob.

Volume vs. Weight   1 bushel equals 35 pounds in the husks.

Weight of 1-Quart Canning Jar   4 to 5 pounds

Best Fresh Storage Method   Corn can be kept fresh in the refrigerator if husked and stored in tightly sealed plastic bags; it will retain its flavor for up to a week.

Best Long-Term Storage Methods   Corn can be frozen, canned, or pickled, and will keep for 12 months in any of these forms.

Second-Best Long-Term Storage Method   Dried corn will keep for 12 months or more.

Seed Storage   1 to 2 years

NOTES AND RESEARCH

Quack grass, *Agropyrens repens,* reduces corn yields. Corn growing in areas infested with quack grass develops symptoms of nutrient deficiency even if the nutrients are present, because the quack grass renders soil nutrients unavailable.

Crabgrass and other species of *Digitaria* are often infected with viruses that can spread to corn, barley, and other crops.

VEGETABLE # *Cucumber*   *Cucumis sativus*

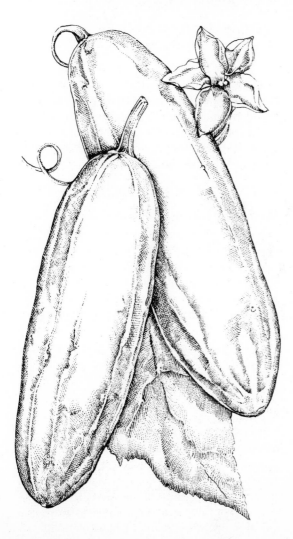

DESCRIPTION AND ENVIRONMENT

Height   6 to 8 inches

Spread   On ground, 12 to 20 square feet; on trellis, 12 to 15 inches.

Root Depth   Most roots are in the top 12 inches of the soil, with a taproot that can grow from 2 to 3 feet deep.

Shade Tolerance   Needs only 5 hours of sun a day (partial shade).

Frost Tolerance   Very tender, needs temperatures above 70°F to grow well.

Preferred pH   6.0 to 7.5

PLANTING

Spring Planting Time   1 week before last expected frost. Cucumber roots are very sensitive to any disturbance, so transplant seedlings before they become rootbound, and avoid deep cultivation.

Fall Planting Time   11½ weeks before first expected frost.

Succession Planting   Plant cucumbers every 2 weeks until midsummer.

Planting Depth   ¾ to 1 inch

Spacing of Plants in Rows   24 to 48 inches

Best Soil Temperature for Germination   65°F to 85°F

Best Soil Temperature for Growing
70°F to 80°F

Best Air Temperature for Growing
Day, 60°F to 80°F; night, 60°F to 70°F.

Days to Germination   3 to 10

Weeks to Transplanting   2 to 4

Days to Maturity   50 to 70

Greenhouse Varieties   Special varieties of cucumbers have been developed for growing in the greenhouse. They include Burpless Early Pik, Crispy Salty, Pot Luck, Patio Pik, and Tiny Dill Cuke.

Container Varieties   Space-saving varieties such as Bush Crop, Patio Pic, Pot Luck, and Spacemaster grow well in containers. Keep soil moist, especially while fruit is setting.

Container Size   8 inches wide, 12 inches deep.

Poor Germination

Seed Orientation
Cucumber seeds are sensitive to their orientation when planted. Those planted with the radicle (root) end uppermost show better emergence and produce larger seedlings than those planted with the radicle end down. Horizontally planted seeds perform nearly as well as the latter.

PLANT MANAGEMENT

Water Requirements for Good Production

Make sure cucumbers get 1 inch of water every week from rain or by watering. (See chapter 8 for more information on watering.)

Water Requirements for Maximum Production

This plant thrives with lots of water, so for maximum production give it 1 to 1½ inches of water each week. Critical watering periods are during flowering and fruit development.

Feeding Requirements for Good Production

Apply compost or a slow-acting general-purpose fertilizer in spring; then give cucumbers supplemental light feedings (side-dressings or foliar spray) monthly throughout the growing season. (See chapter 8 for more information on feeding.)

Feeding Requirements for Maximum Production

This plant is a heavy feeder and, in addition to the spring feeding mentioned above, can use a light supplement every 2 weeks during the growing season. Important times for supplemental feedings are when the vines first begin to run and when blossoms set. Spray plants with liquid seaweed kelp extract two or three times during the growing season.

Pale Leaves, Turning Yellow

Nitrogen Deficiency
If the leaves on your cucumber plants are pale and turning yellow, especially the lower leaves, your cucumbers are probably suffering from nitrogen deficiency. Plant growth will be stunted, with smaller than normal leaves being produced. The roots will turn brown, and fruit will be pointed at the blossom end. To quickly solve the problem, spray plants with dilute fish emulsion or another liquid fertilizer. (See chapter 8 for more information on nitrogen deficiency.)

Bronze Leaves

Potassium Deficiency
Bronzing and dying of leaf margins is a sign of potassium deficiency in cucumbers. The fruit will develop enlarged tips (opposite of a nitrogen-deficient plant). To quickly solve the problem, spray plants with fish emulsion or another liquid fertilizer, and spread wood ashes around plants. (See chapter 8 for more information on potassium deficiency.)

MOST COMMON INSECT PESTS

Foliage Curls, Puckers, Turns Yellow

Aphid

If the foliage on your plants curls, puckers, and turns yellow, and the foliage and blooms become stunted, look for ants. They are a sign that your plants have aphids. Ants are attracted to a sticky honeydew secreted by aphids. These insects have soft, pear-shaped bodies about the size of a pinhead. They may be green, brown, or pink. You will find them in clusters on the undersides of young leaves. For light infestations, spray the plants vigorously with water in the early morning, three times, once every other day. For heavy infestations, apply a commercial insecticidal soap every 2 to 3 days until aphids are under control.

Plants Die from Disease

Cucumber Beetle

The cucumber beetle causes minor physical damage to plants, but it can spread diseases that quickly kill the plant. It is ¼ inch long, oblong, and yellow, with black stripes or spots. The best way to control cucumber beetles and the diseases they carry is to prevent them from feeding on young plants. Spread a covering, such as agricultural fleece, over your plants from germination until the plants start to bloom.
Resistant Varieties. Ashley, Chipper, Fletcher, Niagara, and Stono.

Large Ragged Holes in Leaves

Slug

Large ragged holes in the leaves or stems are signs of slugs. They work their way from the bottom of a plant up. Look for trails of slime on the leaves and on the soil near the plants as further evidence of the presence of slugs. Slugs are 1 to 2 inches long and look like snails without shells. They may be brown, gray, white, pale yellow, purple, or nearly black with brown specks. You can control slugs by handpicking if you get them early in the season.

The best way to control their damage is to set up a barrier of hardware cloth, ashes, sand, or some other material to deny them access to the garden. You can also make traps to catch slugs. (See the entry Slug in chapter 4 for information on making slug traps.)

Wilted, Dried-up Leaves

Squash Bug

The leaves on cucumbers infested with squash bugs wilt, dry up, and turn black, with damage increasing until the vine dies. Adult squash bugs are flat-backed, shield-shaped, brown to black bugs with a light-colored outline on their abdomens. They are ½ to ¾ inch long and lay brown or red shiny eggs on the undersides of leaves. Adults and nymphs suck juices from leaves, causing them to wilt and dry up. To control infestations, handpick pests from the undersides of leaves. If this doesn't work, apply insecticidal soap every 2 to 3 days for 2 weeks. Deny the bugs access to cucumbers by covering plants with a barrier such as agricultural fleece. Remove the barrier when plants begin to bloom.

Sudden Wilting of Plants

Squash Vine Borer

Sudden wilting of all or part of a cucumber vine can be caused by squash vine borers. You can tell borers are at work by the moist, sawdustlike debris, called frass, piled up outside their small holes. Squash vine borers are fat white caterpillars with brown heads, about 1 inch long. They tunnel into the stems to feed. The adult is an orange-and-black, clear-winged moth with black stripes on its abdomen. It lays brown, flat eggs on the stem. Inject *Bacillus thuringiensis* (BT) into the stem of infested plants with a hypodermic needle. Slit the stems, remove the borers, and cover the wounds with soil. Try to deny the moth access to the plant with an agricultural fleece or netting barrier, which must be removed at flowering to allow pollination.

MOST COMMON DISEASES

Water-soaked Spots on Leaves

Angular Leaf Spot

Cucumbers infected with angular leaf spot develop water-soaked spots that turn tan and gray, and then drop out, leaving ragged holes. Rounded spots form on fruit and may exude a thick ooze. The infection will spread into the seed cavity, making the fruit inedible. Remove and destroy infected and surrounding plants.

Resistant Varieties. Bounty, Carolina, Liberty Hybrid, Score, Stokes Early Hybrid, Sweet Slice Hybrid, and many more.

Leaves Become Brown

Anthracnose

The anthracnose fungus attacks all parts of the plant above the ground. Small water-soaked spots develop on the leaves. They enlarge and turn brown, and eventually the leaves shrivel and die. Sunken lesions form on the stems, and circular, black, sunken spots appear on the fruit. During moist conditions, these spots become covered with the salmon-colored fungus. Do not work near plants when they are wet. As soon as you spot the problem, apply a fixed copper- or sulfur-based fungicide every 7 to 10 days. If this does not control the disease, remove and discard infected plants.

Resistant Varieties. Bounty, Calypso, Carolina, County Fair, Dasher II, Flurry, Gemini Hybrid, Lucky Strike, Marketsett, Monarch, Pik-Rite, Pioneer Hybrid, Poinsett, Score, Spear-it, Sprint 440, Stokes Early Hybrid, Victory Hybrid, and many more.

Plants Wilt Quickly

Bacterial Wilt

Cucumber plants infected with bacterial wilt may wilt so quickly that they will be dried up but still green. Bacterial wilt blocks the vascular system of the plant. It is transmitted by spotted and striped cucumber beetles. Try to deny the beetles access to your cucumbers. Cover transplants or a seeded area with netting or agricultural fleece and leave it on until harvest. If possible in your growing season, plant late, after cucumber beetles lay their eggs. Bacterial wilt cannot be cured. Remove and destroy plants immediately. Wash your hands and any tools in a bleach solution (one part household bleach to four parts water) before touching other plants. Prevent bacterial wilt by following clean garden practices and planting seeds that are certified wilt-free.

Resistant Varieties. Saladin.

Downy Purple Spots on Leaves

Downy Mildew

Cucumber plants infected with downy mildew have irregularly shaped yellow to brown spots on the tops of leaves, usually at the centers of the plants. Under moist conditions, downy purple spots appear on the undersides of leaves. The leaves die as these spots increase in size. Downy mildew spreads rapidly from the crown toward new growth. Plants die very rapidly after contracting this disease. If you catch the infection early, apply a copper-based fungicide to diseased and surrounding plants every 7 to 10 days until harvest. Remove and destroy any plants with a serious infection.

Resistant Varieties. Ashley, Burpee Hybrid, Cherokee 7, Comanche, Dublin, Fletcher, Gemini Hybrid, High Mark II, Burpee's M & M Hybrid, Marketmore 76, Palmetto, Palomar, Pioneer, Poinsett, Poinsett 76, Salty, Santee, Saticoy, Slicemaster, Smoothie, Stono, Streamliner Hybrid, and Suyo Long.

Yellow-Green Mottling of Leaves

Mosaic

Symptoms of mosaic in cucumbers include a yellow-green mottling of the leaves near the growing terminals, a similar mottling of the fruit, and stunting of the plant. Mosaic cannot be cured. Remove and destroy infected and surrounding plants. Control aphids and cucumber beetles, because they spread mosaic. The following weeds also carry mosaic:

bittersweet, chickweed, ground cherry, horse nettle, jimson weed, mints, nightshade, pokeweed, ragweed, and wild cucurbits.

Resistant Varieties. Burpee Hybrid, Burpee Pickler, Bush Champion, Challenger, China, Comanche, Dublin, Early Set, Gemini Hybrid, High Mark II, Marketmore 70, Pacer, Pot Luck, Saladin, Salty, Slicemaster, SMR, Spacemaster, Spartan Dawn, Tablegreen 65, and Victory.

White Spots on Undersides of Leaves

Powdery Mildew

Cucumbers infected with powdery mildew develop round, white spots on the undersides of leaves. Eventually the entire leaf becomes covered with these powdery areas. As soon as you discover the disease, remove and destroy the infected parts. Disinfect your hands and your pruning tool in a bleach solution (one part household bleach to four parts water) after each cut. In addition to pruning, apply a copper-based fungicide every 7 to 10 days until 3 to 4 weeks before harvest. Researchers in Japan found that a baking-soda spray applied once a week controlled powdery mildew in cucurbits. To make the solution, mix 1 teaspoon of baking soda in 1 quart of water. Limit overhead sprinkling to early in the day, and do not work around plants when they are wet. Thin plants to let in sun and air.

Resistant Varieties. Bounty, Burpee's M & M Hybrid, Burpless Hybrid, Calypso, County Fair, Gemini Hybrid, Liberty Hybrid, Marketmore 76, Park's Comanche Hybrid, Patio Pik, Pik-Rite, Premier, Royal, Sprint 440, Supersett, Sweet Success, Ultraslice Early, and Victory.

Sunken Green Spots on Cucumbers

Scab

Cucumbers infected with scab develop water-soaked spots on leaves, which may cause them to wilt. Stems may develop small cankers. Scab cannot be controlled. Remove and destroy infected plants.

Resistant Varieties. Bounty, Calypso, Carolina, County Fair, Early Triumph, Gemini Hybrid, Highmoor, Lucky Strike, Maine No. 2, Burpee's M & M Hybrid, Marketmore 80, Northern Pickling, Pacer, Salty, Salvo Hybrid, Slicemaster, Spacemaster, Victory Hybrid, Wisconsin SR 6, and Wisconsin SR 10.

HARVEST AND STORAGE

When to Harvest

Cucumbers are at their best when they are dark green, firm, and of moderate size; overripe fruit is yellow and tough. Picking increases a vine's production. The harvest period for cucumbers lasts for 4 to 6 weeks.

Yield for 24-Square-Foot Bed 40 to 70 pounds

Yield for 25-Foot Row 40 to 70 pounds; however, if you use a trellis, a 25-foot-long trellis will yield over 100 pounds of cucumbers, depending on the variety.

Best Fresh Storage Method Cucumbers keep best in a cool, moist environment with temperatures ranging from 40°F to 50°F and a humidity of 95 percent. Refrigerate them in plastic bags. They will keep for 5 to 10 days.

Best Long-Term Storage Method Pickled

Seed Storage 5 years

NOTES AND RESEARCH

Cucumbers are somewhat reluctant climbers. To hold cucumbers to a trellis, tie heavy twine through the springs of two clothespins and clamp the pins to the trellis on each side of the vine. This method lets you adjust the tension on the twine and move it up or down the trellis without tying and untying a lot of knots hidden by foliage.

VEGETABLE Eggplant

Solanum melongena

DESCRIPTION AND ENVIRONMENT

Height   24 inches
Spread   3 to 4 feet
Root Depth   4 to 7 feet
Shade Tolerance   Needs full sun.
Frost Tolerance   Very tender.
Preferred pH   5.5 to 6.5

PLANTING

Spring Planting Time   1 to 3 weeks after last expected frost; make sure that seedlings are never chilled.

Fall Planting Time   14 weeks before first expected frost.

Planting Depth   ¼ to ½ inch

Spacing of Plants in Rows   18 to 24 inches

Spacing of Plants in Beds   12 to 18 inches

Best Soil Temperature for Germination   65°F to 85°F

Best Soil Temperature for Growing   75°F to 85°F

Best Air Temperature for Growing   Day, 70°F to 85°F; night, 65°F to 75°F.

Days to Germination   6 to 14

Weeks to Transplanting   6 to 10

Days to Maturity   120 from seed; 80 to 90 from transplanting.

Greenhouse Varieties   Eggplants do not grow well in the greenhouse.

Container Varieties   Space-saving varieties such as Dusky and Morden Midget grow well in containers. When grown in containers, eggplants need full sun, lots of water, and weekly fertilizing.

Container Size   12 inches deep.

PLANT MANAGEMENT

Water Requirements for Good Production

Make sure eggplants get 1 inch of water every week from rain or by watering. (See chapter 8 for more information on watering.)

Water Requirements for Maximum Production

This plant likes lots of water, so for maximum productivity give it 1 to 1½ inches of water each week and water consistently. The most critical watering period is from flowering through harvest.

Feeding Requirements for Good Production

Apply compost or a slow-acting general-purpose fertilizer in spring, and give eggplants supplemental light feedings (side-dressings or foliar spray) monthly throughout the growing season. (See chapter 8 for more information on feeding.)

Feeding Requirements for Maximum Production

Eggplants are heavy feeders. In addition to the spring feeding mentioned above, they can use a light supplement every 2 weeks during the growing season. They will especially benefit from a supplement 3 weeks after setting them out. Apply a foliar spray of liquid seaweed extract two or three times during the growing season.

MOST COMMON INSECT PESTS

Foliage Curls, Puckers, Turns Yellow

Aphid

If the foliage on your plants curls, puckers, and turns yellow, and the foliage and blooms become stunted, look for ants. They are a sign that your plants have aphids. Ants are attracted to a sticky honeydew secreted by aphids. These insects have soft, pear-shaped bodies about the size of a pinhead. They may be green, brown, or pink. You will find them in clusters on the undersides of young leaves. For light infestations, spray the plants vigorously with water in the early morning, three times, once every other day. For heavy infestations, apply a commercial insecticidal soap every 2 to 3 days until aphids are under control.

Defoliated Plants

Colorado Potato Beetle

Defoliated plants and skeletonized leaves are signs of Colorado potato beetles. These insects are ⅓ inch long and have a convex shape. They are yellow with black stripes and an orange head covering. The best control is to handpick the first arrivals in spring and use pyrethrum spray if the infestation becomes heavy. Usually, two applications of pyrethrum, applied 3 to 4 days apart, will control the beetles.

Plant Dies of Disease

Cucumber Beetle

The cucumber beetle causes minor damage to plants, but it can spread diseases that quickly kill the plants. It is ¼ inch long, oblong, and yellow with black stripes or spots. The best way to control cucumber beetles and the diseases they carry is to prevent them from feeding on young plants. Spread a covering, such as agricultural fleece, over your plants from germination until the plants start to bloom. If your plants do become infested with cucumber beetles, dust frequently with pyrethrum to control adults and larvae.

Seedling Stems Severed

Cutworm

Cutworms completely sever the stems of seedlings and transplants at or below the soil surface. They are 1- to 2-inch, dull-colored, plump, soft-bodied larvae that curl up when disturbed. Cutworms feed at night and hide in the soil during the day. To control cutworms, use barriers or traps to deny them access to seedlings. To protect individual plants, surround them with a collar, or make a trap by sprinkling cornmeal or bran meal around each plant. (See chapter 4 for more information on collars and meal traps.)

Tiny Holes in Leaves

Flea Beetle

If you find several little holes or perforations in the leaves of your plants, the plants may have flea beetles.

Flea beetles are ¹/₁₀ inch long, shiny, and black, and may have yellow or white markings. They are very active and jump like fleas when disturbed. Their feeding can destroy small plants rapidly. Apply pyrethrum, making two applications, 3 to 4 days apart, to control infestations. In the spring, cover plants with a barrier, such as agricultural fleece, to keep flea beetles off your eggplants. Remove the barrier at bloom time.

Wilted Leaves with Black Spots

Harlequin Bug

If the leaves of your plants develop white blotches or black spots, and then wilt and die, suspect the harlequin bug. This insect is ¼ inch long and shaped like a shield, with a triangle on its back. It has patterned markings in black and red. Harlequin bugs emit a foul odor. To control infestations, spray plants with an insecticidal soap laced with isopropyl alcohol every 2 to 3 days for 2 weeks. Apply insecticidal soap twice, 5 to 7 days apart, in early spring to prevent harlequin bugs.

Weakened Plants

Leafhopper

Both adult leafhoppers and nymphs pierce leaves, buds, and stems and suck the sap and chlorophyll from cells, causing plants to weaken. Adults are green, wedge-shaped insects, ¼ to ⅓ inch long, that hold their wings in a rooflike position above their bodies. They are very active and move sideways. Nymphs resemble adults. To control serious infestations, apply insecticidal soap laced with isopropyl alcohol every 2 to 3 days for 2 weeks. In early spring, apply a preventive spray of insecticidal soap and seaweed extract, and cover seedlings with an agricultural fleece barrier for the first month of growth to deny leafhoppers access to your plants.

Leaves Stippled Yellow

Mite

Leaves of eggplants infested with spider mites become stippled, yellow, and dry, and sometimes pale yellow spots or blotches appear. Mites are not insects but arachnids, and are about the size of a grain of black pepper. They may be red, black, or brown. They feed by sucking out the plant's juices. In sucking chlorophyll out of the leaves, they cause small white dots to appear. In addition, they inject toxins into the leaves, which discolors and distorts them. To control infestations, spray plants with a forceful spray of water three times, once every other day, to knock mites from the leaves. If mites are still present, spray with insecticidal soap three times, once every 7 to 10 days.

Holes in Leaves

Tomato Hornworm

Holes in leaves and sometimes on fruit is a sign that your eggplants may be infested with tomato hornworms. To spot them early, look for dark-colored droppings on the foliage, and spray the plants with water, causing the worms to thrash about and give away their location. The tomato hornworm is a large green caterpillar with white stripes and a horn projecting from its rear. It measures 3 to 5 inches long. Hornworms are easy to see, so handpicking early in the season usually controls them. Spraying plants with *Bacillus thuringiensis* (BT) every 10 to 14 days also reduces hornworms. If the infestation gets out of hand, use pyrethrum, making two applications, 3 to 4 days apart.

Weakened Plants, Yellow Leaves

Whitefly

Plants that have whiteflies weaken, their leaves turn yellow, and they die. Honeydew secreted by whiteflies encourages fungus. Molds often develop following an attack. Adults are about the size of a pinhead, and mothlike, with dusty white wings. When an infested plant is shaken, it appears as if dandruff were flying off the leaves. Nymphs are yellowish, legless, flat, and oval, resembling scale at certain stages. To control infestations, spray plants with insecticidal soap spray every 2 to 3 days for 2 weeks. Use it also early in the season on seedlings to prevent whiteflies. Spray every 2 weeks for the first months of the plant's life. Pyrethrum may be used as a last resort. Make two applications, 3 to 4 days apart.

MOST COMMON DISEASES

Brown Spots on Leaves

Fruit Rot
Eggplants infected with fruit rot develop brown or gray spots on their leaves, and large, ringed, tan or brown spots covered with small pustules form on the fruit. Fruit rot cannot be cured. Remove and destroy infected and surrounding plants. Use resistant varieties. A 4-year crop rotation plan may also prevent this disease from invading your garden. **Resistant Varieties.** Florida Beauty and Florida Market.

Wilted Leaves

Verticillium Wilt
The leaves of plants infected with this disease wilt in the heat of the day and recover toward night. They eventually die and fall off. A cross-section of the stem will show discoloration. Remove and destroy infected plants. A sulfur fungicide used every 7 to 10 days once the symptoms have been noticed has some effect in controlling this disease, but prevention practices will be more effective in the long run. Avoid growing eggplants in soil where tomatoes or potatoes have recently been grown.

HARVEST AND STORAGE

When to Harvest

Bigger eggplants are not better eggplants. Pick the fruit whenever it reaches a usable size, 3 to 5 inches long and 4 to 6 inches in diameter. The skin should be shiny and deep purple in color; dull skin and brown seeds are signs of overripe fruit. The harvest period for eggplants lasts all season until the first frost.

Yield for 24-Square-Foot Bed 40 to 80 pounds
Yield for 25-Foot Row 30 to 70 pounds
Seed Storage 5 years

VEGETABLE **Kale** *Brassica oleracea,* Acephala Group

DESCRIPTION AND ENVIRONMENT

Height 8 to 12 inches
Spread 8 to 12 inches
Shade Tolerance Needs only 5 hours of sun a day (partial shade).

Frost Tolerance Very hardy; can survive heavy frosts.

Preferred pH 6.0 to 7.0

PLANTING

Spring Planting Time 5 weeks before to 2 weeks after last expected frost.

Fall Planting Time 6 to 8 weeks before first expected frost; the flavor of the fall crop is best after first frost.

Planting Depth ¼ to ½ inch

Spacing of Plants in Rows 12 to 18 inches

Spacing of Plants in Beds 10 to 15 inches

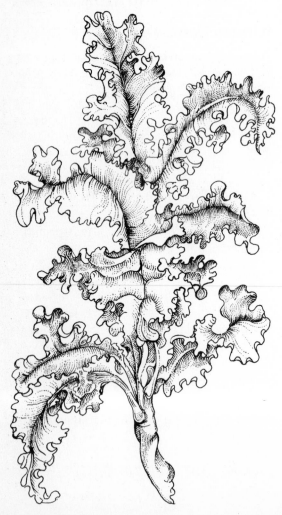

Weeks to Transplanting 6 to 8

Best Soil Temperature for Germination 40°F to 70°F

Best Soil Temperature for Growing 60°F to 70°F

Best Air Temperature for Growing 40°F to 70°F

Days to Maturity 55 to 75 days after direct seeding; 30 to 40 days after transplanting.

Greenhouse Varieties Kale does not grow well in the greenhouse.

Container Varieties Any variety can be grown in containers.

Container Size 8 inches wide, 8 inches deep.

PLANT MANAGEMENT

Water Requirements for Good Production

Make sure the plants get 1 inch of water every week from rain or by watering. (See chapter 8 for more information on watering.)

Water Requirements for Maximum Production

Kale likes lots of water, so for maximum productivity give it 1 to 1½ inches of water each week.

Feeding Requirements for Good Production

Apply compost or a slow-acting general-purpose fertilizer in spring, and give plants supplemental light feedings (side-dressings or foliar spray) monthly throughout the growing season. (See chapter 8 for more information on feeding.)

Feeding Requirements for Maximum Production

Kale is a heavy feeder, and, in addition to the spring feeding mentioned above, it can use a light supplement every 2 weeks during the growing season. Kale will especially benefit from a side-dressing when the plants are 6 to 8 inches high. In addition, apply a foliar spray of liquid seaweed extract two or three times during the growing season.

MOST COMMON INSECT PESTS

Foliage Curls, Puckers, Turns Yellow

Aphid

If the foliage on your plants curls, puckers, and turns yellow, and the foliage and blooms become stunted, look for ants. They are a sign that your plants have aphids. Ants are attracted to a sticky honeydew secreted by aphids. These insects have soft, pear-shaped bodies about the size of a pinhead. They may be green, brown, or pink. Cabbage aphids also attack kale. They are green to powdery blue in color and are covered with a fine whitish wax. You will find them in clusters on the undersides of young leaves. For light infestations, spray the plants vigorously with water in the early morning, three times, once every other day. For heavy infestations, apply a commercial insecticidal soap every 2 to 3 days until aphids are under control.

Small Ragged Holes in Leaves

Cabbage Looper

Small ragged holes in leaves indicate that your plants may be infested with cabbage loopers. The cabbage looper is a 1½-inch-long caterpillar that is light green with long yellowish stripes on its back. It loops as it walks. Spray *Bacillus thuringiensis* (BT) on infested plants every 2 weeks until the problem is solved.

Tiny Holes in Leaves

Flea Beetle

If you find many little holes or perforations in the leaves of your plants, the plants may have flea beetles. Flea beetles are 1/10 inch long, shiny, and black, and may have yellow or white markings. They are very active and jump like fleas when disturbed. Their feeding can destroy small plants rapidly. Apply pyrethrum, making two applications, 3 to 4 days apart, to control infestations. In the spring, cover plants with a barrier, such as agricultural fleece, to deny flea beetles access to your plants.
Resistant Varieties. Dwarf Green Curled Scotch, Dwarf Siberian, Early Siberian, and Vates are resistant to the striped flea beetle specifically.

Wilted Leaves with Black Spots

Harlequin Bug

If the leaves of your plants develop white blotches or black spots, and then wilt and die, suspect the harlequin bug. This insect is ¼ inch long and shaped like a shield, with a triangle on its back. It has patterned markings in black and red. Harlequin bugs emit a foul odor. To control infestations, spray plants with an insecticidal soap laced with isopropyl alcohol every 2 to 3 days for 2 weeks. Apply insecticidal soap twice, 5 to 7 days apart, in early spring to prevent harlequin bugs.
Resistant Varieties. Vates.

Large Ragged Holes in Leaves

Imported Cabbage Worm

Imported cabbage worms chew large ragged holes in the leaves of kale, trailing dark green frass, or excrement, behind them. The worm is light green with one yellow stripe, and measures 1¼ inches long. The adult is a common white butterfly with three to four black spots on its wings that is active during the day. To control infestations, apply *Bacillus thuringiensis* (BT) every 10 to 14 days until the pest is removed. Prevent cabbage worms by spraying transplants with BT every 2 weeks until heads form and covering them with an agricultural fleece barrier.

Skeletonized Leaves

Mexican Bean Beetle

Skeletonized leaves on your kale plants indicate Mexican bean beetles. The adult is ¼ inch long, round, and has yellow to gold to copper coloring

with 16 black dots in three rows down its back. It looks somewhat like a lady bug. It lays yellow eggs in clusters on the undersides of leaves. The hump-backed, fuzzy larvae are orange or yellow and measure about ⅓ inch in length. Both the adults and larvae chew holes in the leaves. To control Mexican bean beetles, handpick early arrivals with special attention to the easy-to-spot bright yellow eggs. If the infestation gets out of control, make two applications of pyrethrum, 3 days apart.
Resistant Varieties. Dwarf Siberian.

Chewed Foliage

Weevil
If the leaves of your kale are chewed to the stem, suspect the vegetable weevil. This pest is gray to brownish in color with a V-shaped mark near the tip of its wing covers. It is about ½ inch long and has a long snout. It feeds at night and hides during the day. As weevils appear, spray with pyrethrum twice, 3 to 4 days apart.

MOST COMMON DISEASES

Spots at Base of Stems

Black Leg
Plants infected with black leg develop sunken areas on the stem near the ground, which girdle the stem. Gray spots speckled with black dots appear on the leaves and stems. The edges of leaves wilt and turn bluish or red, and the entire plant may wilt or topple over. Fixed copper fungicides are sometimes effective in controlling this disease. Apply as directed on the package. If this treatment does not halt the disease, remove and destroy the infected plants.

HARVEST AND STORAGE

When to Harvest

Kale should have crisp, tender leaves of a bright green to blue-green color typical of the variety. Frost improves flavor, so wait to harvest until after the first frost.

Yield for 24-Square-Foot Bed   15 to 30 pounds
Yield for 25-Foot Row   5 to 12 pounds
Volume vs. Weight   1 bushel equals 18 pounds.
Weight of 1-Quart Canning Jar   2 to 3 pounds
Number of Quarts Stored from 1 Bushel   6 to 9
Best Fresh Storage Method   Refrigerate kale in perforated plastic bags; it will keep for 10 to 14 days.
Best Long-Term Storage Method Mulched kale will survive in the garden for 2 months from first frost.
Other Long-Term Storage Methods Kale can be frozen or canned, and will keep for 12 months.
Seed Storage   5 years

VEGETABLE *Kohlrabi*   *Brassica oleracea,* Gongylodes Group

DESCRIPTION AND ENVIRONMENT

Height   12 to 18 inches

Spread   2 to 3 feet

Root Depth   7 to 8½ feet
Shade Tolerance   Needs only 5 hours of sun a day (partial shade).

Frost Tolerance   Hardy
Preferred pH   6.0 to 7.0

PLANTING

Spring Planting Time   5 weeks before to 2 weeks after last expected frost.
Fall Planting Time   10 weeks before first expected frost.
Planting Depth   ½ inch

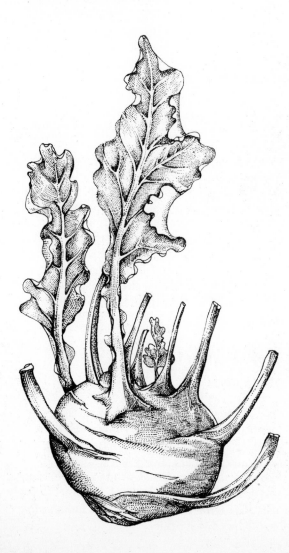

Spacing of Plants in Rows   Kohlrabi that is planted too close together will not get the light it needs for good bulb formation. Thin plants to stand at least 6 inches apart; 12 inches to produce the largest bulbs possible.
Spacing of Plants in Beds   6 to 9 inches
Best Soil Temperature for Germination   50°F to 75°F
Best Soil Temperature for Growing   65°F to 75°F
Best Air Temperature for Growing   40°F to 75°F
Days to Germination   5 to 10
Weeks to Transplanting   6 to 8
Days to Maturity   45 to 60 after direct seeding; 25 to 35 after transplanting.
Greenhouse Varieties   Kohlrabi cannot be grown in the greenhouse.
Container Varieties   Kohlrabi cannot be grown in containers.

PLANT MANAGEMENT

Water Requirements for Good Production

Make sure the plants get 1 inch of water every week from rain or by watering. (See chapter 8 for more information on watering.)

Water Requirements for Maximum Production

Kohlrabi likes a lot of water, so for maximum size, give it 1 to 1½ inches of water each week.

Feeding Requirements for Good Production

Apply compost or a slow-acting general-purpose fertilizer in spring, and give plants supplemental light feedings (side-dressings or foliar spray) monthly throughout the growing season. (See chapter 8 for more information on feeding.)

Feeding Requirements for Maximum Production

Kohlrabi is a heavy feeder. In addition to the spring feeding mentioned above, it benefits from a light supplement every 2 weeks during the growing season. Spray plants with liquid seaweed extract two or three times during the growing season.

MOST COMMON INSECT PESTS

Foliage Curls, Puckers, Turns Yellow

Aphid

If the foliage on your plants curls, puckers, and turns yellow, and the foliage and blooms become stunted, look for ants. They are a sign that your plants have aphids. Ants are attracted to a sticky honeydew secreted by aphids. These insects are about the size of a pinhead and have soft, pear-shaped bodies. They may be green, brown, or pink. Cabbage aphids also attack kohlrabi. They are green to powdery blue in color and are covered with a fine whitish wax. You will find aphids in clusters on the undersides of young leaves. For light infestations, spray the plants vigorously with water in the early morning three times, once every other day. For heavy infestations, apply a commercial insecticidal soap every 2 to 3 days until aphids are under control.

Small Ragged Holes in Leaves

Cabbage Looper

Small ragged holes in leaves indicate that your plants may be infested with cabbage loopers. The cabbage looper is a 1½-inch-long light green caterpillar with long yellowish stripes on its back. It loops as it walks. Spray *Bacillus thuringiensis* (BT) on plants every 2 weeks until the problem is solved.

Brown Tunnels in Stems

Cabbage Maggot

Brown tunnels in the stem just below soil level indicate cabbage maggots. Seedlings become yellow, growth is stunted, and plants lack vigor. The infested plants wilt during the heat of the day, and eventually die. The cabbage maggot is a small, white, legless worm about ¼ inch long. The adult resembles a housefly. Maggots tunnel into plant roots and stems. Bacterial diseases such as black leg, which causes dark patches on leaves, and soft rot, which causes plant decomposition, may result, causing the plants to wilt. To control infestations, apply wood ashes or a lime drench (1 cup of lime in 1 quart of water; let sit overnight) around the root ball of each plant. The best control is to prevent flies from laying eggs in the first place. Spread a barrier, such as agricultural fleece, over the seedlings, or place a collar around the stem of each plant. (See chapter 4 for information on how to construct these collars.)

Seedling Stems Severed

Cutworm

Cutworms completely sever the stems of seedlings and transplants at or below the soil surface. They are 1- to 2-inch, dull-colored, plump, soft-bodied larvae that curl up when disturbed. Cutworms feed at night and hide in the soil during the day. To control cutworms, use barriers or traps to deny them access to seedlings. To protect individual plants, surround them with a collar, or make a trap by sprinkling cornmeal or bran meal around each plant. (See chapter 4 for more information on collars and meal traps.)

Tiny Holes in Leaves

Flea Beetle

If you find many little holes or perforations in the leaves of your plants, the plants may have flea beetles. Flea beetles are ¹/₁₀ inch long, shiny, and black, and may have yellow or white markings. They are very active and jump like fleas when disturbed. Their feeding can destroy small plants rapidly. Apply pyrethrum, making two applications, 3 to 4 days apart, to control infestations. In the spring, cover plants with a barrier, such as agricultural fleece, to deny flea beetles access to your plants.

Wilted Leaves with Black Spots

Harlequin Bug

If the leaves of your plants develop white blotches or black spots, and then wilt and die, suspect the harlequin bug. This insect is ¼ inch long and shaped like a shield, with a triangle on its back. It has patterned markings in black and red. Harlequin bugs emit a foul odor. To control infestations, spray plants with an insecticidal soap laced with isopropyl alcohol every 2 to 3 days for 2 weeks. Apply insecticidal soap twice, 5 to 7 days apart, in early spring to prevent harlequin bugs.

Large Ragged Holes in Leaves

Imported Cabbage Worm

Imported cabbage worms chew large ragged holes in kohlrabi leaves, trailing dark green frass, or excrement, behind them. The worm is light green with one yellow stripe, and measures 1¼ inches long. The adult is a common white butterfly with three to four black spots on its wings that is active during the day. To control infestations, apply *Bacillus thuringiensis* (BT) every 10 to 14 days until the pest is removed. Prevent cabbage worms by spraying plants with BT early in the season, every 2 weeks from transplanting until heads form, and covering them with an agricultural fleece barrier.

Leaves Stippled Yellow

Mite

Leaves of kohlrabi plants infested with mites become stippled, yellow, and dry, and sometimes pale yellow spots or blotches appear. Mites are not insects but arachnids, and are about the size of a grain of black pepper. They may be red, black, or brown. They feed by sucking out the plant's juices. In sucking chlorophyll out of the leaves, they cause small white dots to appear. In addition, they inject toxins into the leaves, which discolors and distorts them. To control infestations, spray plants with a forceful spray of water three times, once every other day, to knock mites from the leaves. If they are still present, spray with insecticidal soap three times, once every 5 to 7 days.

Chewed Foliage

Weevil

If the leaves of your kohlrabi are chewed to the stem, suspect the vegetable weevil. This pest is gray to brownish in color with a V-shaped mark near the tip of its wing covers. It is about ½ inch long and has a long snout. It feeds at night and hides during the day. As weevils appear, spray with pyrethrum twice, 3 to 4 days apart.

MOST COMMON DISEASES

Dark Patches on Leaves

Black Leg

Plants infected with black leg develop sunken areas on the stem near the ground, which girdle the stem. Gray spots speckled with black dots appear on the leaves and stems. The edges of leaves wilt and turn bluish or red, and the entire plant may wilt or topple over. Fixed copper fungicides are sometimes effective in controlling this disease. Follow the application directions on the label. If this treatment does not halt the disease, remove and destroy the infected plants.

Yellow, Wedge-shaped Areas on Leaves

Black Rot

Black rot affects young as well as mature plants. Infected seedlings turn yellow and die. On older plants, yellow, wedge-shaped areas develop at the leaf margins and expand toward the center of the leaf. These areas later turn brown and die, and the leaves fall off. The vascular bundles in leaves and stems are black and bad smelling. Young plants may not produce bulbs, and the bulbs on older plants that become infected will rot. Black rot cannot be cured. Remove and destroy the infected and surrounding plants. Micronized sulfur helps to control the spread of black rot to other plants. Apply the sulfur to unaffected plants every 7 days until harvest.

Resistant Varieties. Grand Duke Hybrid.

Poor Crop Development

Club Root

In general, plants that have club root exhibit the effects of a malfunctioning root system: wilting, poor development, and smaller bulbs. Under the soil you will find misshapen roots with club-shaped swellings. Apply approved soil fungicides to control the disease in infected plants. Try to prevent this disease by following clean gardening practices and rotating plants (the fungus persists in the soil for 7 years). Club root is more of a problem with plants growing in acid soil. Test your soil, and if the pH is too low, add lime.

Seedlings Die

Damping-Off

Seedlings that have damping-off simply topple over. You will see a watery soft rot on the stem at the soil line. There is no cure for this disease. Remove and destroy infected plants. When starting seeds indoors, use commercial potting soil, or pasteurize your own potting soil in an oven. Disinfect tools in a bleach solution (one part household bleach to four parts water). Provide soil with adequate drainage and use a fan for better air circulation. For direct seeding, make sure the soil is well drained and warm. You might try spreading pasteurized soil or a sterile vermiculite in furrows where you plant your seeds.

Water-soaked Spots on Leaves

Leaf Spot

Kohlrabi plants infected with leaf spot develop water-soaked spots that later grow in size and take on a brownish or purplish gray color. Leaf spot cannot be cured. Remove and destroy infected and surrounding plants.

Part of Plant Rots

Rhizoctonia

Rhizoctonia is characterized by darkened and girdled areas on the stem near the soil line. Affected plants are weak, produce small heads, and sometimes wilt and die. Bottom rot develops on plants after they have been transplanted to the garden. Dark, slightly sunken spots develop on basal leaves near the soil. In moist conditions the rot spreads to adjacent leaves and causes the head to rot. Rhizoctonia also commonly causes damping-off, a watery soft rot on the stem at the soil line. Rhizoctonia cannot be controlled. Remove and destroy infected plants. To prevent rhizoctonia from becoming a problem, avoid planting kohlrabi in short rotations where bottom rot and damping-off have been a problem. Pasteurizing the soil used to raise seedlings and solarizing the garden soil also help to control rhizoctonia. (See chapter 5 for more information on soil pasteurization and solarization.)

Seeds Do Not Germinate

Seed Rot

Seed rot will prevent your kohlrabi seeds from germinating. It occurs when soil is too moist and cold for germination. If necessary, make a shallow ditch, fill it with commercial sterilized potting mix, and sow seeds in that mixture.

Yellow Lower Leaves

Yellows

The symptoms of yellows are similar to those of black rot. The lower leaves of plants turn yellow, then brown, and finally drop. Kohlrabi may appear stunted and the bulb will taste bitter. Yellows cannot be cured. Remove and destroy infected and surrounding plants.

HARVEST AND STORAGE

When to Harvest

The bulb should never be allowed to grow larger than a golf ball or tennis ball, depending on the variety. If the bulb is too large, it will be woody. It should be tender and easily marked when pressed with a fingernail. The harvest period for kohlrabi usually lasts 2 to 3 weeks.

Yield for 24-Square-Foot Bed 20 to 40 pounds

Yield for 25-Foot Row 15 to 20 pounds

Best Fresh Storage Method Refrigerate kohlrabi in plastic bags; it will keep for 1 to 2 weeks.

Best Long-Term Storage Method Kohlrabi will keep in the root cellar or a cool cellar for 3 months.

Second-Best Long-Term Storage Method Dice kohlrabi into ½-inch pieces, blanch for 2 minutes, and pack for freezer storage; it will keep for about 4 months.

Seed Storage 5 years

VEGETABLE Lettuce *Lactuca sativa*

DESCRIPTION AND ENVIRONMENT

Height 4 to 8 inches
Spread 6 to 12 inches
Root Depth 18 to 36 inches, but the taproot can grow to 5 feet long.
Shade Tolerance Needs only 5 hours of sun a day (partial shade).
Frost Tolerance Hardy
Preferred pH 6.0 to 7.5

PLANTING

Spring Planting Time 2 to 4 weeks before to 3 weeks after last expected frost.

Fall Planting Time 6 to 8 weeks before first expected frost.

Succession Planting Plant lettuce every 2 weeks, shifting to warm weather varieties for the summer months. Lettuce can be grown through warm weather if shaded by agricultural fleece, cheesecloth, or some other shading material. Oak Leaf lettuce is heat resistant.

Planting Depth ¼ to ½ inch
Spacing of Plants in Rows Leaf, 2 to 3 inches; head, 10 to 12 inches.
Spacing of Plants in Beds Leaf, 6 to 9 inches; head, 10 to 12 inches.
Best Soil Temperature for Germination 45°F to 75°F
Best Soil Temperature for Growing 65°F to 75°F
Best Air Temperature for Growing Day, 55°F to 75°F; night, 50°F to 55°F.
Days to Germination 2 to 10
Weeks to Transplanting 4 to 6
Days to Maturity Leaf, 40 to 50; head, 70 to 75.
Greenhouse Varieties Looseleaf varieties such as Arctic King, North Pole, and Parris Cos perform the best.

Container Varieties   Any variety grows well in containers; partial shade and constant moisture are keys to success.

Container Size   8 inches wide, 6 to 8 inches deep.

Plants Bolt

Air Temperature Too High

Lettuce is composed primarily of water. When the weather is hot and dry, lettuce loses moisture rapidly,

which causes stress. The plant responds by starting to bolt to seed. Bolting causes a chemical change in the plant, resulting in a bitter flavor. By planting lettuce in wide beds with a heavy organic mulch layer, you can delay this process. The microclimate around the plants will be a bit cooler, and water loss will occur more slowly. Planting lettuce in a shady spot can also help, but drying winds may still cause problems. Covering the plants with shade netting or agricultural fleece will filter the sunlight and thus reduce temperature and retard moisture loss. It will also provide some wind protection.

Seedlings Too Large

Seedlings Started Too Early

If the seedlings are ready to transplant before weather and soil conditions are appropriate, you can hold seedlings for up to 2 weeks by storing them in the refrigerator at about 34°F. The plants stop growing, but are not harmed.

PLANT MANAGEMENT

Water Requirements

This plant doesn't need as much water as most. For best production, give it ½ to 1 inch of water a week, which is less than is normally required by garden vegetables. Watering is critical during head development of loosehead and iceberg types. Leaf lettuce should be consistently watered throughout the growing season. (See chapter 8 for more information on watering.)

Feeding Requirements for Good Production

Apply compost or a slow-acting general-purpose fertilizer in the spring, then give supplemental light feedings (side-dressings or foliar spray) monthly throughout the growing season. (See chapter 8 for more information on feeding.)

Feeding Requirements for Maximum Production

Lettuce is a heavy feeder. In addition to the spring feeding mentioned above, it likes a light supplement every 2 weeks during the growing season. Important times to side-dress lettuce plants are 3 weeks after transplanting and, for loosehead and iceberg types, as the heads form. Apply a foliar spray of liquid seaweed extract two or three times during the growing season.

MOST COMMON INSECT PESTS

Foliage Curls, Puckers, Turns Yellow

Aphid

If the foliage on your plants curls, puckers, and turns yellow, and the foliage and blooms become stunted, look for ants. They are a sign that your plants have aphids. Ants are attracted to a sticky honeydew secreted by aphids. These insects are about the size of a pinhead and have soft, pear-shaped bodies. They may be green, brown, or pink. You will find them in clusters on the undersides of young leaves. For light infestations, spray the plants vigorously with water in the early morning three times, once every other day. For heavy infestations, apply a commercial insecticidal soap every 2 to 3 days until aphids are under control.
Resistant Varieties. Avoncrisp and Avondefiance.

Small Ragged Holes in Leaves

Cabbage Looper

Small ragged holes in leaves indicate that your plants may be infested with cabbage loopers. Later in the season caterpillars bore into the developing heads of head lettuce. The cabbage looper is a 1½-inch-long caterpillar that is light green with long yellowish stripes on its back. It loops as it walks. Spray *Bacillus thuringiensis* (BT) on infested plants every 2 weeks until the problem is solved.

Seedling Stems Severed

Cutworm

Cutworms completely sever the stems of seedlings and transplants at or below the soil surface. They are 1- to 2-inch, dull-colored, plump, soft-bodied larvae that curl up when disturbed. Cutworms feed at night and hide in the soil during the day. To control cutworms, use barriers or traps to deny them access to seedlings. To protect individual plants, surround them with a collar, or make a trap by sprinkling cornmeal or bran meal around each plant. (See chapter 4 for more information on collars and meal traps.)

Weakened Plants

Leafhopper

Both adult leafhoppers and nymphs pierce leaves, buds, and stems and suck the sap and chlorophyll from cells, causing plants to weaken. Adults are green, wedge-shaped insects, ¼ to ⅓ inch long, that hold their wings in a rooflike position above their bodies. They are very active and move sideways. Nymphs resemble adults. To control serious infestations, apply insecticidal soap laced with isopropyl alcohol every 2 to 3 days for 2 weeks. In early spring, apply a preventive spray of insecticidal soap and seaweed extract, and cover seedlings with an agricultural fleece barrier for the first month of growth to deny leafhoppers access to your plants.

White or Brown Tunnels in Leaves

Leafminer

White or brown tunnels or blotches on leaves are signs that your lettuce has leafminers. The leaves may turn yellow and blotchy and look blistered or curled. Leafminers are small black flies, usually with yellow stripes. The tiny yellowish larvae feed between the upper and lower surfaces of leaves, causing the tunnels or blotches to appear. You may also find stem damage below the soil. Remove the infested leaves before the larvae mature. The best way to control leafminers, though, is to screen out the adult flies with some type of light material, such as agricultural fleece. Place the fleece over the seedlings.

Large Ragged Holes in Leaves

Slug
Large ragged holes in the leaves of your lettuce plants are signs of slugs. They work their way from the bottom of a plant up. Look for trails of slime on the leaves and on the soil near the plants as further evidence of the presence of slugs. Slugs are 1 to 2 inches long and look like snails without shells. They may be brown, gray, white, pale yellow, purple, or nearly black with brown specks. You can control them by handpicking if you get them early in the season. The best way to control their damage is to set up a barrier of hardware cloth, ashes, sand, or some other material to deny them access to the garden. You can also make traps to catch slugs. (See the entry Slug in chapter 4 for information on making slug traps.)

Wilting, Poor Development

Wireworm
Lettuce plants that look wilted and show poor development may be infested with wireworms. The larvae of click beetles, these pests are $\frac{1}{3}$ to $1\frac{1}{2}$ inches long, dark brown to yellowish, jointed, hard shelled, and cylindrical. They chew on the roots of lettuce plants. The best control is to trap wireworms with pieces of potato speared on the ends of sticks. (See the entry Wireworm in chapter 4 for information on how to use potato traps.)

MOST COMMON DISEASES

Rust-Colored Spots on Leaves

Bottom Rot
Lettuce infected with bottom rot develops rust-colored spots on the lower leaves, which spread until the whole plant is rotted. Harvest infected plants; use the good parts and destroy the rest. Clean up the garden at the end of the season and rotate crops. **Resistant Varieties.** Canasta, King Crown, and Nancy.

Seedlings Die

Damping-Off
Seedlings that have damping-off simply topple over. You will see a watery soft rot on the stem at the soil line. There is no cure for this disease. Remove and destroy infected plants. When starting seeds indoors, use commercial potting soil, or pasteurize your own potting soil in an oven. Disinfect tools in a bleach solution (one part household bleach to four parts water). Provide soil with adequate drainage and use a fan for better air circulation. For direct seeding, make sure soil is well drained and warm. You might try spreading pasteurized soil or a sterile vermiculite in furrows where you plant your seeds.

Pale Yellow Areas on Upper Leaves

Downy Mildew
Downy mildew affects both seedlings and mature lettuce plants. The symptoms appear first on the oldest leaves. Look for light green or pale yellow areas on the upper surfaces of leaves, and for spots with downy white growth on the undersides. If you catch the infection early, apply a copper-based fungicide to diseased and surrounding plants every 7 to 10 days until harvest. Remove and destroy any plants with a serious infection.
Resistant Varieties. Crisp Mint (romaine); Grand Rapids (looseleaf); Hot Weather (butterhead); Salinas (butterhead); Tania (butterhead); Valmaine Cos (romaine); and Valverde (head).

Yellow and Green Mottling of Leaves

Mosaic
Lettuce plants infected with mosaic have mottled yellow and green leaves. Overall, the plants develop a yellowish cast, and growth is stunted. In head lettuce, no head forms. Mosaic cannot be cured. Remove

and destroy infected and surrounding plants. Aphids spread mosaic, so control them in your garden. **Resistant Varieties.** Nancy and Parris Island Cos.

Seeds Do Not Germinate

Seed Rot

Seed rot will prevent lettuce seeds from germinating. It occurs when soil is too moist and cold for germination. If necessary, make a shallow ditch, fill it with commercial sterilized potting mix, and sow seeds in that mixture.

Wilted Plants, Stunted Growth

Yellows

Wilting plants and stunted growth are symptoms of fusarium yellows. Plants will develop white hearts and become lopsided, and their vascular system will turn brown. Pull and destroy infected plants. Yellows is often transmitted by leafhoppers, so keep them away from lettuce with some kind of barrier, such as agricultural fleece. Control weeds and try not to plant lettuce near carrots or asters, which are also susceptible to yellows.

HARVEST AND STORAGE

When to Harvest

Head lettuce is ready as soon as the heads have

formed and are firm when squeezed. Pick heads before the seed stalk breaks through the top. You can start harvesting a few outer leaves of leaf lettuce as soon as they reach usable size, about 2 inches long. Continue to harvest outer leaves until the seed stalk appears—about 4 to 6 weeks. The harvest period for head lettuce is the same.

Yield for 24-Square-Foot Bed   25 to 30 pounds for both leaf and head lettuce.

Yield for 25-Foot Row   Leaf, 25 to 30 pounds; head, 12 pounds.

Best Fresh Storage Method   Refrigerate lettuce in a plastic bag or a container with a lid; it will keep for over a week.

Seed Storage   5 years

NOTES AND RESEARCH

Lettuce is sensitive to toxic chemicals found in various plant residues, including broccoli, broad beans, vetch, wheat, rye, and barley. Where decomposing material touches developing lettuce roots, lesions occur.

VEGETABLE **Okra** *Abelmoschus esculentus*

DESCRIPTION AND ENVIRONMENT

Height   6 feet

Spread   4 to 6 feet

Root Depth   4 to 4½ feet

Shade Tolerance   Needs full sun.

Frost Tolerance   Very tender; cannot tolerate any frost at all.

Preferred pH   7.0 to 7.5

PLANTING

Spring Planting Time   From frost-free date to 4 weeks after.

Planting Depth   1 inch

Spacing of Plants in Rows   12 to 24 inches

Spacing of Plants in Beds   12 to 18 inches

Best Soil Temperature for Germination   70°F to 95°F

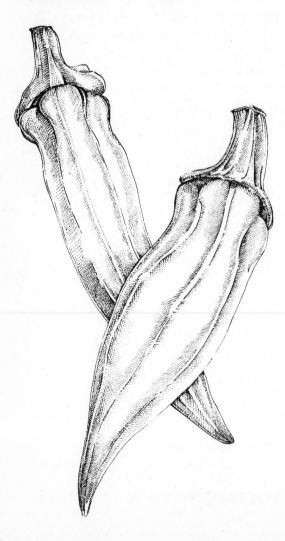

Days to Germination   7 to 14

Weeks to Transplanting   6 to 8

Days to Maturity   55 to 65 after direct seeding.

Pods Fall Off Early

Air Temperature Too Low

Okra grows in cool weather, but it doesn't produce enough pollen to set seed at soil temperatures below 70°F and air temperatures below 75°F, so the pods drop off. Since early planting does not increase production, time your next crop so the first bloom coincides with summer temperatures.

PLANT MANAGEMENT

Water Requirements

Make sure okra gets 1 inch of water every week from rain or by watering. (See chapter 8 for more information on watering.)

Feeding Requirements

Apply compost or a slow-acting general-purpose fertilizer in spring; then give okra supplemental light feedings (side-dressings or foliar spray) monthly throughout the growing season. Apply a foliar spray of liquid seaweed extract two or three times during the growing season. (See chapter 8 for more information on feeding.)

MOST COMMON INSECT PESTS

Holes in Leaves

Corn Earworm

Corn earworms chew buds and leaves of young plants, stunting their growth. The corn earworm is a white, green, or red worm with four prolegs. It is ½ inch long, and has spines on its body. To control these pests, spray plants with light horticultural oil mixed with *Bacillus thuringiensis* (BT) twice, 3 to 5 days apart.

Skeletonized Leaves

Japanese Beetle

Japanese beetles chew leaves between the veins, leaving them skeletonized. They also eat flowers. They are ½-inch-long, shiny, metallic green beetles with copper-brown wings. Set up beetle traps a week prior to their emergence in your area, making sure the traps are no closer than 50 feet to vulnerable crops. Handpick stragglers. Use pyrethrum if traps cannot handle the infestation. Two applications, 3 to 4 days apart, should control the problem.

Stunted Plants, Yellow Leaves

Nematode

Plants infected with nematodes are stunted, their leaves yellow prematurely, and root knots develop. If plants survive to maturity, they produce low yields. Nematodes are microscopic whitish, translucent worms, barely visible to the naked eye. They live in the soil and attack plant roots. Use resistant varieties, and add 3 to 4 inches of compost (especially leaf mold) to the garden. This encourages the growth of fungi that attack nematodes. Fertilize with fish emulsion, which repels nematodes, and if your late spring temperatures are high enough to support blossoming, plant your okra a bit earlier in the season.

HARVEST AND STORAGE

When to Harvest

Pick okra pods when they are white or bright green in color, depending on the variety, and less than 4½ inches long. They should be tender enough to bend under light pressure.

Best Fresh Storage Method   Store in a cool, damp place, or refrigerate okra in perforated plastic bags; it will keep for 3 to 4 days.

Best Long-Term Storage Method   Okra can be frozen or pickled.

Seed Storage   5 years

VEGETABLE **Onion** *Allium cepa*

DESCRIPTION AND ENVIRONMENT

Height   24 to 36 inches
Spread   6 to 18 inches
Root Depth   1½ to 3 feet
Shade Tolerance   Needs only 5 hours of sun a day (partial shade).
Frost Tolerance   Hardy; can survive some light frosts.
Preferred pH   6.0 to 7.5

PLANTING

Spring Planting Time   Sets, 3 weeks before to 2 weeks after last expected frost; seeds, after last frost.

Fall Planting Time   Plant a second crop 8 weeks after the spring planting for fall scallions.

Planting Depth   Sets, about 1 inch; seeds, ¼ to ½ inch.

Spacing of Plants in Rows   2 to 3 inches

Spacing of Plants in Beds   Bulb, 3 to 5 inches; bunching, 2 to 3 inches.

Best Soil Temperature for Germination   50°F to 80°F

Best Soil Temperature for Growing   65°F to 75°F

Best Air Temperature for Growing   Day, 60°F to 85°F; night, 55°F to 60°F.

Days to Germination   4 to 12

Weeks to Transplanting   4 to 8; keep seedling tops trimmed to ½ to 1 inch until a week before planting outdoors.

Days to Maturity   80 to 120 after direct seeding; 30 to 40 from sets.

Greenhouse Varieties   Try any variety.

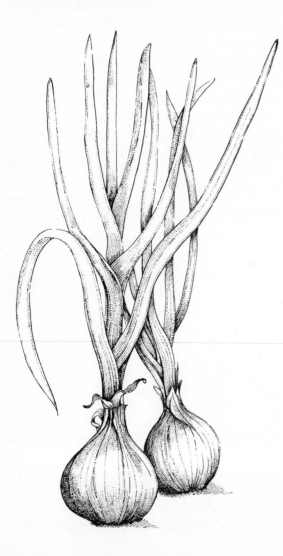

Container Varieties   Any variety can be grown in containers, but bunching onions are more productive in small spaces. Try Beltsville Bunching, Japanese Bunching, and White Pearl.

Container Size   10 to 12 inches deep.

PLANT MANAGEMENT

Water Requirements

Make sure onions get 1 inch of water every week from rain or by watering. It is especially important when bulbs enlarge. Stop watering when tops fall, or ripening may be delayed. (See chapter 8 for more information on watering.)

Feeding Requirements

Apply compost or a slow-acting general-purpose fertilizer in spring, and give onions supplemental light feedings (side-dressings or foliar spray) monthly throughout the growing season. Important times to give onions side-dressings are 3 weeks after setting out, when tops are 6 to 8 inches tall, and when bulbs start to swell. Spray onions with liquid seaweed extract two or three times during the growing season. (See chapter 8 for more information on feeding.)

MOST COMMON INSECT PESTS

Damage to Lower Part of Stem

Onion Maggot

Onion maggots burrow into and destroy the lower part of the onion stem near the bulb. These white maggots are about ⅓ inch long and legless. To prevent onion maggots from becoming a serious problem, don't plant onions close together or in rows, which allows the maggots to move easily from plant to plant.

Large Ragged Holes in Leaves

Slug

Large ragged holes in the leaves of your onion plants are signs of slugs. They work their way from the bottom of a plant up. Look for trails of slime on the leaves and on the soil near the plants as further evidence of the presence of slugs. Slugs are 1 to 2 inches long and look like snails without shells. They may be brown, gray, white, pale yellow, purple, or nearly black with brown specks. You can control them by handpicking if you get them early in the season. The best way to control their damage is to set up a barrier of hardware cloth, ashes, sand, or some other material to deny them access to the garden. You can also make traps to catch slugs. (See the entry Slug in chapter 4 for information on making slug traps.)

Whitened, Withered Foliage

Thrip

If the foliage of your onions becomes bleached or silvery and withers, suspect thrips. These insects are only $\frac{1}{25}$ inch long and so are recognized by the dark fecal pellets they produce and the damage they create. To control them, spray with insecticidal soap every 3 days for 2 weeks. If the infestation is heavy, apply pyrethrum twice, 3 to 4 days apart.

Sudden Wilting of Plant

White Grub

A sudden wilting of your onion plants may indicate white grubs. Look for these fat, whitish larvae. They are $\frac{3}{4}$ to $1\frac{1}{2}$ inches long and feed on the underground parts of plants. To control them, make one application of beneficial nematodes. (See chapter 4 for more information on parasitic nematodes.) Milky spore disease can be applied to the soil around onions, but it takes 3 to 5 years for this treatment to be effective.

Wilting, Poor Development of Plants

Wireworm

If your onion plants show signs of wilting and poor development, they may be infested with wireworms. The larvae of click beetles, these pests are $\frac{1}{3}$ to $1\frac{1}{2}$ inches long, dark brown to yellowish, jointed, hard shelled, and cylindrical. They chew on the underground parts of onion plants. The best control is to trap wireworms with pieces of potato speared on the ends of sticks. (See the entry Wireworm in chapter 4 for information on how to use potato traps.)

MOST COMMON DISEASES

Soft, Brown Tissue at Neck

Botrytis Rot

The neck tissue on the bulb becomes soft and brownish and may shrivel. Often a gray to brown mold develops on the surface of bulbs. Leaves may appear water-soaked. Remove any infected plants from the garden to control spread of the disease. When storing onions, make sure the necks are completely dry.

Seedlings Die

Damping-Off

Seedlings that have damping-off simply topple over. You will see a watery soft rot on the stem at the soil line. There is no cure for this disease. Remove and destroy infected plants. When starting seeds indoors, use commercial potting soil, or pasteurize your own potting soil in an oven. Disinfect tools in a bleach solution (one part bleach to four parts water). Provide soil with adequate drainage and use a fan for better air circulation. For direct seeding, make sure soil is well drained and warm. You might try spreading pasteurized soil or a sterile vermiculite in furrows where you plant your seeds.

Yellow or Gray Spots on Leaves

Downy Mildew

Symptoms of downy mildew in onions usually appear

after leaves are 6 inches long. The oldest leaves are affected first. Yellow or gray elongated spots appear on these leaves; the spots later become covered with a white to purplish mold during cool weather. The leaves drop over and dry up.

Tops Wilted

Pink Root

Onions infected with pink root are stunted, and their tops wilt. The roots are pinkish or red, and eventually rot. Once the soil is infected, do not grow any bulb crops. Remove and destroy infected plants. Select tolerant and resistant varieties, and make sure your soil is well drained.

Resistant Varieties. Brown Beauty, Granada, Granex 33, Nebuka (Welsh onion), Texas Grano 502pr, Vega, and Yula.

Elongated Dark Area at Base of Seedlings

Smut

Smut produces elongated, dark, slightly thickened areas at the base of the seedling leaf as it emerges from the soil. As new leaves are infected they become swollen and bend downward. Raised, black lesions appear near the bases of the scales on plants that are starting to bulb. Protect young seedlings with a fungicide drench or dust applied directly in the furrow with the seeds or sets. Remove and destroy infected plants.

Resistant Varieties. Texas Early Grano 502.

HARVEST AND STORAGE

When to Harvest

For use as scallions, harvest onions when bulbs are ¼ to ⅝ inch in diameter. For boiling or pickling, harvest when bulbs measure 1 to 1½ inches in diameter. For storage, harvest when the tops fall over and turn brown, and cure before harvesting and storing. (Information on curing is given below.) Onions should be clean, hard, well-shaped globes with dry, papery skins. The color varies with the type. Onions can be harvested all season long.

Onions and garlic keep best if properly cured before harvest. As the tops begin to yellow, push them over with the back of a rake. This action forces the bulbs into their final maturing stage. About 3 weeks after bending the tops, dig up the onions. Lay them on newspapers in a dry, shady place for 10 days. The tops and roots can then be trimmed, and the onions stored for winter-long use.

Yield for 24-Square-Foot Bed   25 to 50 pounds

Yield for 25-Foot Row   15 to 20 pounds

Volume vs. Weight   1 bushel equals 50 pounds.

Best Fresh Storage Method   Store onions in net bags in a cool, dry, dark place with a temperature of about 35°F; they will keep for at least 1 month.

Best Long-Term Storage Method   Canned, dried, or pickled, onions will keep for 12 months.

Seed Storage   1 to 2 years

Onions Rot in Storage

Damp, Warm Storage Area

Onions in storage require cool temperatures and dry air. Store them in a cellar where the temperatures get at least as cold as 45°F during the winter; 32°F is ideal. Onions can be piled two layers deep in slatted boxes or hung in mesh bags, but bulbs get best ventilation when the stems have been braided. After onions have been harvested, and left to dry out so tops are still pliable but not brittle, braid onions together.

VEGETABLE # *Parsnip*   *Pastinaca sativa*

DESCRIPTION AND ENVIRONMENT

Height   12 to 18 inches

Spread   10 to 15 inches

Root Depth   Parsnips produce a short taproot with some fibrous roots reaching down to 5 feet, but most roots are limited to 2 feet.

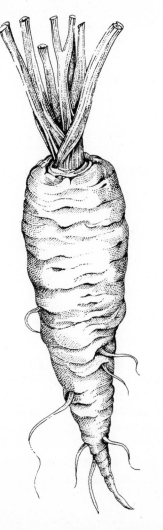

Shade Tolerance   Needs only 5 hours of sun a day (partial shade).

Frost Tolerance   Hardy

Preferred pH   6.0 to 8.0

PLANTING

Spring Planting Time   2 to 4 weeks before last expected frost to 4 weeks after.

Planting Depth   ½ inch

Spacing of Plants in Rows   3 to 4 inches

Spacing of Plants in Beds   4 to 6 inches

Best Soil Temperature for Germination   50°F to 70°F

Best Soil Temperature for Growing 55°F to 70°F

Days to Germination   15 to 25

Weeks to Transplanting   4 to 6

Days to Maturity   120 to 170

PLANT MANAGEMENT

Water Requirements

Make sure parsnips get 1 inch of water every week from rain or by watering. (See chapter 8 for more information on watering.)

Feeding Requirements

Apply compost or a slow-acting, general-purpose fertilizer in spring. This plant is a light feeder and needs little or no supplemental feedings, but parsnips will benefit from a foliar spray of liquid seaweed extract two or three times during the growing season. (See chapter 8 for more information on feeding.)

MOST COMMON INSECT PESTS

Foliage Curls, Puckers, Turns Yellow

Aphid

If the foliage on your plants curls, puckers, and turns yellow, and the foliage and blooms become stunted, look for ants. They are a sign that your plants have aphids. Ants are attracted to a sticky honeydew secreted by aphids. These insects are about the size of a pinhead and have soft, pear-shaped bodies. They may be green, brown, or pink. You will find them in clusters on the undersides of young leaves. For light infestations, spray the plants vigorously with water in the early morning three times, once every other day. For heavy infestations, apply a commercial insecticidal soap every 2 to 3 days until aphids are under control.

Rotted or Dwarfed Plants

Carrot Rust Fly

The maggots of the carrot rust fly chew roots, causing plants to be dwarfed. Soft-rot bacteria may become a problem, and when that happens, the entire plant quickly decomposes. The carrot rust fly is a black fly, ⅕ inch long, with long yellow hairs, a yellow head, and yellow legs. The maggots are ⅓ inch long and yellow to white in color. The flies lay eggs in the crown of the plants. Once plants have been attacked, there is little the gardener can do; destroy infested plants. Prevent access to the plants by spreading agricultural fleece or a fine nylon mesh over the garden where parsnips have just been planted.

Defoliated Plants

Carrot Weevil

Carrot weevils defoliate plants, beginning at the crown. After a plant has been attacked, only the ribs of leaves and stems remain. Larvae tunnel into the tops and roots of parsnips. The adult carrot weevil is ⅕ inch long, brown, and has a hard shell. The larvae are pale in color, with brown heads and no legs. Control infestations by spraying parsnip plants with pyrethrum as soon as adult beetles appear in spring. Try to deny weevils access early in the season by covering seedlings with agricultural fleece. Parasitic nematodes may help to prevent infestation of the roots. (See chapter 4 for more information on parasitic nematodes.)

Parsleyworm

The leaves of parsnip plants infested with parsleyworms are chewed so that often only the bare stems remain. The parsleyworm is a 2-inch caterpillar that is green with a yellow-dotted black band across each segment. It gives off an odor and projects orange horns when upset. These bright, large caterpillars are easy to handpick in the early morning. You can also apply *Bacillus thuringiensis* (BT) as a powder or a spray every 10 to 14 days until the pest is under control.

HARVEST AND STORAGE

When to Harvest

For best flavor, harvest parsnips after a few hard frosts. Pull when roots are white, smooth, firm, clean, and tapered, and when they are about an inch in diameter. Overwintered roots must be dug before new growth starts in spring.

Yield for 24-Square-Foot Bed   100 roots

Yield for 25-Foot Row   70 roots

Volume vs. Weight   1 bushel equals 50 pounds.

Best Fresh Storage Method   Refrigerate parsnips in plastic bags; they will keep for 3 to 4 weeks.

Best Long-Term Storage Method   Store parsnips in a root cellar, or mulch them and leave them in the ground; they will keep for 4 to 5 months.

Seed Storage   2 years

VEGETABLE Pea *Pisum sativum*

DESCRIPTION AND ENVIRONMENT

Height   Garden, 2 to 4 feet; snap, 4 to 6 feet.
Spread   6 to 10 inches, both garden and snap.
Shade Tolerance   Needs full sun.
Frost Tolerance   Very hardy
Preferred pH   6.0 to 7.0

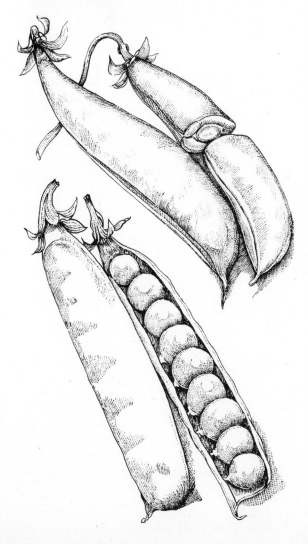

PLANTING

Spring Planting Time   4 to 6 weeks before last expected frost to 2 to 3 weeks after frost.
Fall Planting Time   12 weeks before first expected frost.
Succession Planting   Plant every 3 weeks until late spring, and again in late summer.
Planting Depth   1 to 2 inches; 2 inches for fall crop.
Spacing of Plants in Rows   1 to 4 inches
Spacing of Plants in Beds   6 inches
Best Soil Temperature for Germination   40°F to 75°F
Best Soil Temperature for Growing 60°F to 75°F
Best Air Temperature for Growing 55°F to 75°F
Days to Germination   6 to 15
Weeks to Transplanting   Direct-seed only.
Days to Maturity   55 to 90
Greenhouse Varieties   Peas do not grow well in the greenhouse.
Container Varieties   Space-saving varieties such as Laxton's Progress, Little Marvel, SugarBon, SugarMel, and SugarRae grow well in containers. Dwarf peas still require a low trellis or some other means of support to keep air circulating through the vines. Keep soil moist once flowers appear, and keep plants picked to encourage production.
Container Size   12 inches deep.

Plants Die for No Apparent Reason

High Temperatures
If your peas showed no signs of disease, but die before pods form, hot weather may have killed the plants before they could produce a full crop. Planting earlier will solve the problem.

Poor Production in Fall Crop

Too Much Heat and Light

Peas and other cool-loving crops will not grow well in high temperatures. Peas planted for a fall harvest benefit from the protection of shade netting and a thick organic mulch for the first month or so.

PLANT MANAGEMENT

Water Requirements

Peas don't need as much water as most garden vegetables. For best production give them ½ to 1 inch of water a week. Critical watering periods for peas are during flowering, seed enlargement, and pod development. (See chapter 8 for more information on watering.)

Feeding Requirements

Apply compost or a slow-acting general-purpose fertilizer in spring. Peas are light feeders and need little or no supplemental fertilizer, but they will benefit from a foliar spray of liquid seaweed extract two or three times during the growing season. (See chapter 8 for more information on feeding.)

MOST COMMON INSECT PESTS

Foliage Curls, Puckers, Turns Yellow

Aphid

If the foliage on your plants curls, puckers, and turns yellow, and the foliage and blooms become stunted, look for ants. They are a sign that your plants have aphids. Ants are attracted to a sticky honeydew secreted by aphids. These insects are about the size of a pinhead and have soft, pear-shaped bodies. They may be green, brown, or pink. You will find them in clusters on the undersides of young leaves. For light infestations, spray the plants vigorously with water in the early morning, three times, once every other day. For heavy infestations, apply a commercial insecticidal soap every 2 to 3 days until aphids are under control.

Resistant Varieties. Champion of England, Laurier, Melting Sugar, and Prince of Wales.

Wilted Plants

Cabbage Maggot

Plants infested with cabbage maggots will wilt during the heat of the day. Brown tunnels in the stem just below soil level are further evidence that this pest has attacked your peas. Seedlings become yellow, growth is stunted, and plants lack vigor. Eventually they will die. The cabbage maggot is a small, white, legless worm about ¼ inch long. The adult resembles a housefly. Maggots tunnel into plant roots and stems. Bacterial diseases such as black leg, which causes dark patches on the leaves, and soft rot, which causes plant decomposition, may result, causing the plants to wilt. To control infestations, mix heaping teaspoonfuls of wood ashes 1 inch into the soil around each plant, or pour a cupful of lime drench (1 cup of lime in 1 quart of water; let sit overnight) around the root ball of each plant. The best control is to prevent flies from laying eggs in the first place. Spread a barrier, such as agricultural fleece, over the plants, or place a collar around the stem of each plant. (See chapter 4 for instructions on constructing these collars.)

Plants Die from Disease

Cucumber Beetle

The cucumber beetle causes minor physical damage to plants, but it can spread diseases that quickly kill them. It is ¼ inch long, oblong, and yellow with black stripes or spots. The best way to control cucumber beetles and the diseases they carry is to prevent them from feeding on young plants. Spread a covering, such as agricultural fleece, over your plants from germination until the plants start to bloom.

Holes in Blossoms

Weevil

If the blossoms on your pea plants have holes chewed in them, suspect the pea weevil. This pest is a brownish, fat beetle, spotted with white and black. It is about ⅕ inch long. It feeds at night and hides during the day. As weevils appear, spray with pyrethrum twice, 3 to 4 days apart.

Plants Wilt and Die

Wireworm

If your pea plants wilt and die, suspect the wireworm. Wireworms are the larvae of click beetles. They are ⅓ to 1½ inches long, dark brown to yellowish, jointed, hard shelled, and cylindrical. They chew on the roots of peas. Trap them with pieces of potato speared on the ends of sticks. (See the entry Wireworm in chapter 4 for more information on how to use potato traps.) Plant a cover crop for long-term control.

MOST COMMON DISEASES

Purple Specks on Pods

Ascochyta Blight

Small purple lesions, no larger than specks, form on the leaves and pods of peas infected with ascochyta blight. The stems develop elongated, purplish black lesions that may grow and girdle stems, weakening them so that they are easily broken. Affected leaves eventually shrivel and dry. Stems and roots may be afflicted at ground level with a bluish black foot rot. Apply either a sulfur- or copper-based fungicide every 7 to 10 days until symptoms disappear or until 3 to 4 weeks before harvest.

Purplish Stems

Bacterial Blight

Symptoms of bacterial blight in peas include purplish or nearly black areas on the stem near the soil line; discolored areas at the nodes; small, water-soaked spots on leaves; and yellow to brown water-soaked spots on pods. Bacterial blight cannot be cured. Remove and destroy infected and surrounding plants. To prevent bacterial blight, use certified seeds, and do not work around plants while they are wet.

Yellow Leaves

Fusarium Wilt

This disease is no longer a formidable problem for peas because of the availability of resistant varieties; however, if you aren't growing a resistant variety, symptoms include yellow leaves and wilted plants. A cross-section of stems would show lemon-yellow discoloration. Some plants will produce some fruit, but in most cases you should remove and destroy infected plants. Fusarium wilt is generally carried in the soil, so using resistant varieties is the best approach. Solarizing the soil also helps. (See chapter 5 for information on solarization.)

Resistant Varieties. Alaska, Alderman, Bolero, Dwarf Gray Sugar, Freezonian, Frosty, Greater Progress, Green Arrow, Little Marvel, Mars, Novella, Perfection, Pride, Sparkle, Thomas Laxton, Venus, Wando, and Wisconsin Early Sweet.

White, Powdery Mold on Leaves

Powdery Mildew

If the leaves, stems, and pods of your peas are covered by a white, powdery mold, your plants have powdery mildew. When pods are affected, the seeds may turn gray or brown. As soon as you discover the disease, remove and destroy the infected parts. Disinfect your pruning tool in a bleach solution (one part household bleach to four parts water) after each cut. In addition to pruning, apply a sulfur- or copper-based fungicide every 7 to 10 days until 4 weeks before harvest. Limit overhead sprinkling to early in the day, and do not work around plants when they are wet. Thin plants to let in sun and air. **Resistant Varieties.** Grenadier, Knight, Maestro, Olympia, Oregon Sugar Pod, Snappy, Snowflake, SugarBon, and Sugar Daddy.

Brown Lower Stems

Root Rot

Various root rots attack peas, causing the lower stems and roots to turn brown or black. Plants become yellowed and gangly, and the roots and lower stems rot. Peas may die before pods form. Remove and destroy infected plants.

HARVEST AND STORAGE

When to Harvest

Garden peas should be harvested when pods are fairly well filled but still bright green. The raw peas should taste sweet. Harvest lower pods first. Consistent picking increases production. The harvest period for garden peas lasts 1 to 2 weeks.

The older the snap pea, the sweeter—up to a point. Harvest snap peas before they touch each other in the pod for the sweetest flavor and crunchiest texture. Pods should appear crisp, slender, and bright green, with immature peas. The harvest period for peas lasts 1 to 2 weeks.

Yield for 24-Square-Foot Bed　5 to 15 pounds

Yield for 25-Foot Row　4 to 10 pounds

Volume vs. Weight　1 bushel equals 30 pounds.

Weight of 1-Quart Canning Jar　2 to 3 pounds

Number of Quarts Stored from 1 Bushel　10 to 15

Best Fresh Storage Method　Peas are best when used quickly after harvesting, but they can be refrigerated in plastic bags, and will keep for 2 to 4 days.

Long-Term Storage Methods　Peas can be frozen, canned, or dried; they will keep for 12 months in any of these forms.

Seed Storage　3 years

NOTES AND RESEARCH

Peas suffer stunting, wilting, or even death when they come in contact with black walnut roots. Allelopathic reactions occur within a circle one and a half times the distance from the trunk to the outermost branches.

To hold Sugar Snaps and other reluctant climbers close to wire trellises, tie heavy twine through the springs of two clothespins and clamp the pins to the trellis on each side of the vine. This method lets you adjust the tension on the twine and move it up or down the trellis without tying and untying a lot of knots hidden by foliage.

VEGETABLE **Pepper**　*Capsicum annuum*

DESCRIPTION AND ENVIRONMENT

Height　15 to 36 inches

Spread　24 inches

Root Depth　The fibrous spreading roots of peppers are generally confined to the top 8 inches, but sometimes extend 4 feet deep.

Shade Tolerance　Needs at least 6 hours of sun a day.

Frost Tolerance　Very tender; cannot tolerate any frost.

Preferred pH　6.0 to 7.0

PLANTING

Spring Planting Time　1 to 3 weeks after last expected frost.

Planting Depth　¼ to ½ inch

Spacing of Plants in Rows　12 to 24 inches

Spacing of Plants in Beds　12 to 15 inches

Best Soil Temperature for Germination　65°F to 85°F

Best Soil Temperature for Growing

Seedlings can be set out when the average night temperature is 55°F and the soil temperature has reached 60°F or above; however, the best soil temperature range is from 70°F to 80°F.

Best Air Temperature for Growing   Day, 65°F to 85°F; night, 60°F to 75°F.

Days to Germination   8 to 20

Weeks to Transplanting   6 to 8

Days to Maturity   60 to 90 for direct seeded; 50 to 75 after transplanting.

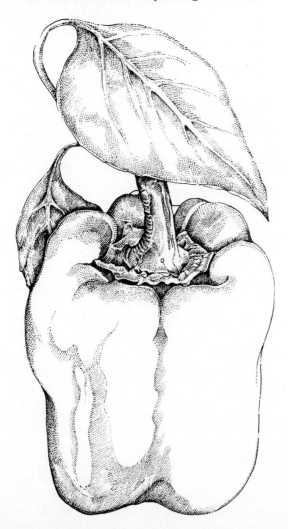

Greenhouse Varieties   Peppers do not grow well in the greenhouse.

Container Varieties   Space-saving varieties such as Canape, Gypsy Hybrid, Italian Sweet, Pepper Pot, or any hot pepper variety grow well in containers. Full sun, warm temperatures, and lots of water during fruit set are important.

Container Size   12 inches deep.

PLANT MANAGEMENT

Water Requirements

Make sure peppers get 1 inch of water every week from rain or by watering. Consistency in watering is important from flowering through harvest and fruit development. (See chapter 8 for more information on watering.)

Feeding Requirements

Apply compost or a slow-acting, general-purpose fertilizer in spring, and give plants supplemental light feedings (side-dressings or foliar spray) monthly throughout the growing season. Peppers will especially benefit from supplemental feedings 3 weeks after transplanting and after the first fruit sets. Spray plants with liquid seaweed extract two or three times during the growing season. (See chapter 8 for more information on feeding.)

Grayish Green Color on Leaves

Phosphorus Deficiency

Peppers that have very narrow, grayish green leaves are probably deficient in phosphorus. Plants may fail to flower or produce fruit, and if they do, the fruit will be smaller and more slender than usual. Phosphorus deficiencies generally occur in acid soils. Temporary deficiencies occur in cold, wet soils. To remedy the problem quickly, apply a foliar spray of dilute fish emulsion or another liquid fertilizer, and spread wood ashes around the plants. (See chapter 8 for more information on phosphorus deficiency.)

MOST COMMON INSECT PESTS

Foliage Curls, Puckers, Turns Yellow

Aphid

If the foliage on your plants curls, puckers, and turns yellow, and the foliage and blooms become stunted, look for ants. They are a sign that your plants have aphids. Ants are attracted to a sticky honeydew secreted by aphids. These insects are about the size of a pinhead and have soft, pear-shaped bodies. They may be green, brown, or pink. You will find them in clusters on the undersides of young leaves. For light infestations, spray the plants vigorously with water in the early morning three times, once every other day. For heavy infestations, apply a commercial insecticidal soap every 2 to 3 days until aphids are under control.

Seedling Stems Severed

Cutworm

Cutworms completely sever the stems of seedlings and transplants at or below the soil surface. They are 1- to 2-inch, dull-colored, plump, soft-bodied larvae that curl up when disturbed. Cutworms feed at night and hide in the soil during the day. To control cutworms, use barriers or traps to deny them access to seedlings. To protect individual plants, surround them with a collar, or make a trap by sprinkling cornmeal or bran meal around each plant. (See chapter 4 for more information on collars and meal traps.)

Shotgun-like Holes in Leaves

European Corn Borer

European corn borers chew the leaves of plants, giving them the appearance of having shotholes. The borer is a grayish to pink caterpillar with a darker head and spots on each segment. White eggs are laid in groups on the undersides of foliage. The adult is a yellowish nocturnal moth with ½-inch wings that have dark bands. Apply *Bacillus thuringiensis* (BT) as soon as you spot the eggs on the undersides of leaves, and continue making applications every 7 to 10 days.

Tiny Holes in Leaves

Flea Beetle

If you find many little holes or perforations in the leaves of your plants, the plants may have flea beetles. Flea beetles are $\frac{1}{10}$ inch long, shiny, and black, and may have yellow or white markings. They are very active and jump like fleas when disturbed. Their feeding can destroy small plants rapidly. Apply pyrethrum, making two applications, 3 to 4 days apart, to control infestations. In the spring, cover plants with a barrier, such as agricultural fleece, to deny flea beetles access to your plants.

White or Brown Tunnels in Leaves

Leafminer

White or brown tunnels or blotches on leaves are signs that your peppers have leafminers. The leaves may turn yellow and blotchy and look blistered or curled. Leafminers are small black flies, usually with yellow stripes. The tiny yellowish larvae feed between the upper and lower surfaces of leaves, causing the tunnels or blotches to appear. You may also find stem damage below the soil. Remove the infested leaves before the larvae mature. The best way to control leafminers, though, is to screen out the adult flies with a barrier such as agricultural fleece. Place the fleece over the seedlings; it can remain on peppers throughout the growing season.

Leaves Stippled Yellow

Mite

Leaves of peppers infested with mites become stippled, yellow, and dry, and sometimes pale yellow spots or blotches appear. Mites are not insects but arachnids, and are about the size of a grain of black pepper. They may be red, black, or brown. They feed by sucking out the plant's juices. In sucking chlorophyll out of the leaves, they cause small white dots to appear. In addition, they inject toxins into the leaves, which discolors and distorts them. To control infestations, spray plants with a forceful spray of water three times, once every other day, to knock mites from the leaves. If mites are still present, spray with insecticidal soap three times, once every 5 to 7 days.

Holes in Leaves

Tomato Hornworm

Holes in leaves and sometimes on fruit are signs that your peppers may be infested with tomato hornworms. To spot them early, look for dark-colored droppings on the foliage, and spray the plants with water, causing the worms to thrash about and give away their location. The tomato hornworm is a large green caterpillar with white stripes and a horn projecting from its rear. It measures 3 to 5 inches long. These pests are easy to see, so handpicking early in the season usually controls them. Spraying plants with *Bacillus thuringiensis* (BT) also reduces hornworms, and if the infestation gets out of hand, use pyrethrum, making two applications, 3 to 4 days apart.

Misshapen and Discolored Pods

Weevil

If your peppers have large misshapen and discolored pods, suspect the pepper weevil. This pest is shiny brown or black in color. It is about ⅛ inch long and has a long snout. It feeds at night and hides during the day. As weevils appear, spray with pyrethrum twice, 3 to 4 days apart.

MOST COMMON DISEASES

Black Spots on Peppers

Anthracnose

Sometimes dark watery spots develop on leaves, but usually anthracnose affects the fruit. Dark, sunken spots form on the fruit, which becomes covered with pink spore masses. As soon as you spot the problem, apply a fixed copper or sulfur-based fun-

gicide every 7 to 10 days until 3 to 4 weeks before harvest. If this does not control the disease, remove and discard infected plants.

Yellow-Green Spots on Leaves

Bacterial Spot

Small yellow-green spots appear on the young leaves of peppers infected with bacterial spot. Older leaves exhibit larger spots with dead, straw-colored centers and dark margins. Bacterial spot cannot be cured. The first line of defense, if the disease is identified early in its development, is to apply a copper-based fungicide every 7 to 10 days until 3 to 4 weeks before harvest. Prune the infected parts immediately, disinfecting tools and hands in a bleach solution (one part bleach to four parts water) between each cut. If good results don't show up after a second spraying, the plant must be destroyed. Prevent bacterial spot by following good fall cleanup practices and by planting resistant varieties.
Resistant Varieties. Early Calwonder, Long Red Cheyenne, Red Chili, and Sunnybrook.

Shriveled Blossom Ends

Blossom End Rot

If the blossom ends of the fruit become soft and spotted and eventually shrivel, your peppers have blossom end rot. Water plants evenly (consistently) and only as needed. Check the pH of the soil; it should be between 6.0 and 7.0. If it's below 6.0, add limestone, which contains calcium.

Mottled Green and Yellow Leaves

Mosaic

Mottled green and yellow leaves are a sign that your peppers have mosaic. The growth of infected plants is stunted. Mosaic cannot be cured. Remove and destroy the infected and surrounding plants. To prevent mosaic, follow good fall cleanup practices and plant resistant varieties.
Resistant Varieties. Bellringer, Keystone Resistant Giant, and Yolo Wonder.

Mottled Leaves and Fruit

Tobacco Mosaic

Symptoms of tobacco mosaic can vary. Young plants have malformed leaflets. Older plants exhibit mottling (dark green), and the leaflets tend to be stringy and fernlike, or pointed. Overall, the plants exhibit a slightly grayish appearance, and the fruit may be mottled, or may ripen unevenly. Tobacco mosaic cannot be cured. Remove and destroy the infected and surrounding plants. To prevent tobacco mosaic, plant resistant varieties, follow good fall cleanup practices, and keep tobacco users away from your garden.

Resistant Varieties. Annabell, Bell Captain, Big Bertha, California Wonder, Emerald Giant, Gypsy Hybrid, Lady Bell, Ma Belle, Melody, Ringer, and Yolo Wonder.

HARVEST AND STORAGE

When to Harvest

The skin of peppers should be firm and shiny. The bigger the pepper, the thicker the skin. Fruit is green at an early stage and becomes red or yellow when mature. Hot peppers do not get hotter the longer they're left on the plant. Harvesting lasts for the entire season until first frost.

Yield for 24-Square-Foot Bed   15 to 20 pounds for sweet peppers; 20 to 25 for hot peppers.

Yield for 25-Foot Row   12 to 15 pounds for sweet peppers; 16 to 20 pounds for hot peppers.

Volume vs. Weight   1 bushel equals 25 pounds.

Number of Quarts Stored from 1 Bushel   18

Best Fresh Storage Method   Refrigerate peppers in plastic bags; they will keep for 1 to 2 weeks.

Best Long-Term Storage Method   Can, dry, or pickle peppers; they will keep for 12 months in any of these forms.

Seed Storage   2 years

NOTES AND RESEARCH

Peppers suffer stunting, wilting, or even death when they come in contact with black walnut roots. Allelopathic reactions occur within a circle one and a half times the distance from the trunk to the outermost branches.

A researcher has found that if pepper plants are thinned to leave only a few peppers at the initial fruit-setting stage, yields are increased. Thinning to six peppers per plant resulted in highest early yields, while thinning to four peppers per plant resulted in highest late yields. Average fruit size was also increased by thinning.

VEGETABLE **Potato**   *Solanum tuberosum*

DESCRIPTION AND ENVIRONMENT

Height   24 to 30 inches
Spread   24 inches
Shade Tolerance   Needs full sun.

Frost Tolerance   Very tender; cannot tolerate any frost.

Preferred pH   5.0 to 6.5

Plants Do Not Thrive

High pH

Potatoes prefer acid soil. Do not use ashes or lime in soil in which potatoes are to be raised because these will increase the soil's alkalinity.

PLANTING

Spring Planting Time   4 to 6 weeks before last expected frost.

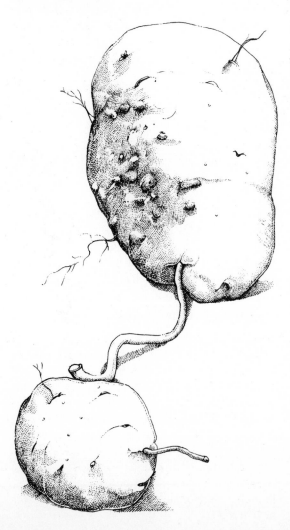

Planting Depth   4 inches

Spacing of Plants in Rows   12 to 15 inches; you can also plant potatoes in trenches 6 inches wide, 4 to 8 inches deep, and 30 to 36 inches apart.

Spacing of Plants in Beds   10 to 12 inches

Best Soil Temperature for Germination   60°F to 65°F

Best Air Temperature for Growing 60°F to 80°F

Days to Germination   10 to 15

Days to Maturity   80 to 140

Greenhouse Varieties   Potatoes cannot be grown in the greenhouse.

Container Varieties   Potatoes cannot be grown in containers.

PLANT MANAGEMENT

Water Requirements for Good Production

Make sure potatoes get 1 inch of water every week from rain or by watering. (See chapter 8 for more information on watering.)

Water Requirements for Maximum Production

Potatoes like lots of water, so for maximum productivity give them 1 to 1½ inches of water each week. Critical watering periods are during tuber set and tuber enlargement.

Feeding Requirements

Apply compost or a slow-acting general-purpose fertilizer in spring. Potatoes are light feeders and need little or no supplemental fertilizer. If you do wish to give them a supplement, the best time is when plants bloom. Apply a foliar spray of liquid seaweed extract two or three times during the growing season. (See chapter 8 for more information on feeding.)

Small Potatoes

Calcium Deficiency

Undersized potatoes may indicate a calcium deficiency in your soil. Adding calcium to soils can increase average potato size and quality, as well as decrease susceptibility of tubers to bacterial soft rot, which causes plant decomposition, and internal brown spots. Soluble calcium works best. (See chapter 8 for more information on calcium deficiency.)

Hollow Heart

Environmental Causes

A hollow heart (a lens- or star-shaped cavity at the center of the tuber) results when conditions such as high rainfall (especially after drought), excessive fertilization, or wide spacing overstimulate growth. Varieties that produce large tubers, such as Katahdin and Kennebec, are most susceptible. Early varieties like Norland, and midseason varieties like Superior and Chieftain, produce smaller tubers and are much less prone to the disorder. Avoid overfeeding, but maintain high potassium levels and keep the soil evenly moist.

MOST COMMON INSECT PESTS

Foliage Curls, Puckers, Turns Yellow

Aphid

If the foliage on your plants curls, puckers, and turns yellow, and the foliage and blooms become stunted, look for ants. They are a sign that your plants have aphids. Ants are attracted to a sticky honeydew secreted by aphids. These insects are about the size of a pinhead and have soft, pear-shaped bodies. They may be green, brown, or pink. You will find them in clusters on the undersides of young leaves. For light infestations, spray the plants vigorously with water in the early morning three times, once every other day. For heavy infestations,

apply a commercial insecticidal soap every 2 to 3 days until aphids are under control.
Resistant Varieties. British Queen, De Soto, Early Pinkeye, Houma, and Irish Daisy.

Defoliated Plants

Colorado Potato Beetle

Defoliated plants and skeletonized leaves are signs of Colorado potato beetles. These insects are $\frac{1}{3}$ inch long and have a convex shape. They are yellow with black stripes and an orange head covering. The best control is to handpick the first arrivals in spring and use pyrethrum spray if the infestation becomes heavy. Usually, two applications of pyrethrum, applied 3 to 4 days apart, will control the beetles.
Resistant Varieties. Katahdin and Sequoia.

Plants Die from Disease

Cucumber Beetle

The cucumber beetle causes minor physical damage to plants, but it can spread diseases that quickly kill them. It is $\frac{1}{4}$ inch long, oblong, and yellow with black stripes or spots. The best way to control cucumber beetles and the diseases they carry is to prevent them from feeding on young plants. Spread a covering, such as agricultural fleece, over your plants from germination until the plants start to bloom.

Seedling Stems Severed

Cutworm

Cutworms completely sever the stems of seedlings and transplants at or below the soil surface. They are 1- to 2-inch, dull-colored, plump, soft-bodied larvae that curl up when disturbed. Cutworms feed at night and hide in the soil during the day. To control cutworms, use barriers or traps to deny them access to seedlings. To protect individual plants, surround them with a collar, or make a trap by sprinkling cornmeal or bran meal around each plant. (See chapter 4 for more information on collars and meal traps.)

Shotgun-like Holes in Leaves and Stalks

European Corn Borer

European corn borers chew the leaves of plants, giving them the appearance of having shotholes. In addition, in potatoes, they bore into the stalks. The borer is a grayish to pink caterpillar with a darker head and spots on each segment. White eggs are laid in groups on the undersides of foliage. The adult is a yellowish nocturnal moth with ½-inch wings that have dark bands. Apply *Bacillus thuringiensis* (BT) as soon as you spot the eggs on the undersides of leaves, and continue making applications every 7 to 10 days.

Tiny Holes in Leaves

Flea Beetle

If you find several little holes or perforations in the leaves of your plants, the plants may have flea beetles. Flea beetles are $1/10$ inch long, shiny, and black, and may have yellow or white markings. They are very active and jump like fleas when disturbed. Their feeding can destroy small plants rapidly. Apply pyrethrum, making two applications, 3 to 4 days apart, to control infestations. In the spring, cover plants with a barrier, such as agricultural fleece, to keep flea beetles off of your potato plants.
Resistant Varieties. Sequoia.

Skeletonized Leaves

Japanese Beetle

Japanese beetles chew leaves between the veins leaving them skeletonized. They also eat flowers. They are ½-inch-long, shiny, metallic green beetles with copper-brown wings. Set up beetle traps a week prior to their emergence in your area, making sure the traps are no closer than 50 feet to vulnerable crops. (See the entry Japanese Beetle in chapter 4 for more information on these traps.) Handpick stragglers. Use pyrethrum if traps cannot handle the infestation; two applications, 3 to 4 days apart, should control the problem. The larvae of Japanese beetles are grayish white grubs with dark brown heads and two rows of spines that form a V on the

underside of the last abdominal segment. They feed on the tubers. One application of juvenile stage nematodes should control the larvae. (See chapter 4 for information on parasitic nematodes.)

Weakened Plants

Leafhopper

Both adult leafhoppers and nymphs pierce leaves, buds, and stems and suck the sap and chlorophyll from cells, causing plants to weaken. Adults are green, wedge-shaped insects, $1/4$ to $1/3$ inch long, that hold their wings in a rooflike position above their bodies. They are very active and move sideways. Nymphs resemble adults. To control serious infestations, apply insecticidal soap laced with isopropyl alcohol every 2 to 3 days for 2 weeks. In early spring, apply a preventive spray of insecticidal soap and seaweed extract and cover seedlings with an agricultural fleece barrier for the first month of growth to deny leafhoppers access to your plants.
Resistant Varieties. Delus, Plymouth, Pungo, Sebago, and Sequoia (Sequoia is susceptible to aphids, though).

Stunted Plants, Yellow Leaves

Nematode

Plants infected with nematodes are stunted, the leaves yellow prematurely, and root knots develop on roots. If plants survive to maturity, they produce low yields. Nematodes are microscopic whitish, translucent worms, barely visible to the naked eye. They live in the soil and attack plant roots. Use resistant varieties, and add 3 to 4 inches of compost (especially leaf mold) to the garden. Fertilize with fish emulsion, and plant early in the season.

Holes in Leaves

Tomato Hornworm

Holes in leaves are a sign that your potatoes may be infested with tomato hornworms. To spot them early, look for dark-colored droppings on the foliage, and spray the plants with water, causing the worms to thrash about and give away their location. The tomato hornworm is a large green caterpillar with white stripes and a horn projecting from its rear. It measures 3 to 5 inches long. Hornworms are easy to see, so handpicking early in the season usually controls them. Dusting plants with *Bacillus thuringiensis* (BT) also reduces hornworms; dust plants every 10 to 14 days until pests are gone. If the infestation gets out of hand, use pyrethrum. Apply twice, 3 to 4 days apart.

Sudden Wilting of Plant

White Grub
A sudden wilting of your potato plants may indicate white grubs. Look for these fat, whitish larvae. They are ¾ to 1½ inches long and feed on the underground parts of plants. To control them, make one application of beneficial nematodes. (See chapter 4 for information on parasitic nematodes.) Milky spore disease can be applied to the soil around potatoes, but it takes 3 to 5 years for this treatment to be effective.

Wilting, Poor Development of Plants

Wireworm
If your potato plants show signs of wilting and poor development, they may be infested with wireworms. The larvae of click beetles, these pests are ⅓ to 1½ inches long, dark brown to yellowish, jointed, hard shelled, and cylindrical. They chew on the underground parts of potato plants. The best control is to trap wireworms with pieces of potato speared on the ends of sticks. (See the entry Wireworm in chapter 4 for information on how to use potato traps.)

MOST COMMON DISEASES

Streaks inside Tubers

Black Heart
The insides of potato tubers with black heart have dark gray, purple, or black areas. In potatoes, the disease is caused by insufficient oxygen in the center of the tubers, a result of waterlogged soil or temperatures that are too high. Black heart cannot be eliminated from potatoes. To prevent the disease, provide good soil drainage and do not leave tubers in or on hot soil (over 90°F).

Yellow, Curled Leaves

Black Leg
On older plants infected with black leg, yellowing occurs between leaf veins, and the leaf margins brown and curl upward. When young plants are affected, stunting and erratic growth may occur. Infected plants may wilt during hot weather. The stems may turn an inky black and become soft and mushy just above and below the soil line. Fixed copper fungicides are sometimes effective. Follow the application directions on the label. If this treatment does not halt the disease, remove and destroy the infected plants.

Russet Skin

Common Scab
The surfaces of potato tubers infected with scab have brown, roughened, irregularly shaped areas that may be raised and warty, level with the surface, or sunken. These lesions may affect just a small part of the tuber surface, or they may completely cover it. To control this disease, maintain optimum soil moisture, and lower the soil pH to 5.3 or less. Scab on potatoes can increase in soils with a high pH. Don't add ashes to the soil, because they make it more alkaline. Soybeans grown on infected soil and turned under increase soil acidity and set beneficial bacteria and fungi in competition with the scab.

Resistant Varieties. Cayuga, Cherokee, Early Gem, Menominee, Norchip, Norgold Russet, Norland, Ontario Rhine Red, Seneca, and Superior.

Dark Spots on Older Leaves

Early Blight
The first signs of early blight in potatoes are circular or irregular dark spots that develop on older leaves. As these spots enlarge, they develop concentric rings, giving a target effect. Collar rot, with dark, girdling lesions, develops at the soil line, and tubers develop shallow decayed areas in the form of

small circular lesions surrounded by puckered skin. As soon as you spot symptoms, begin applying a copper-based fungicide every 7 to 10 days according to the directions on the package.

Resistant Varieties. Chieftain and Norgold Russet.

Brownish Black Areas on Leaves

Late Blight

Purplish or brownish black areas on the blade of the leaflet or leaf stalk or on the stem indicate late blight. Pale halos surround these blackened areas. The lower leaves are affected first. Once you spot the symptoms, apply a copper-based fungicide every 7 to 10 days until harvest. After harvesting, do not let culled potatoes remain in or near the field; volunteer plants can spread the disease. Destroy any potatoes that have been infected.

Resistant Varieties. Essex, Kennebec, Ona, Pungo, Saco, and Sebago.

Mottled Light and Dark Green Leaves

Mosaic

A mottled light and dark green pattern on curled or crinkled leaves indicates that your potato plants have mosaic. Brown specks may appear on tubers, and the plants will yellow, droop, and die. Mosaic cannot be cured. Remove and destroy infected and surrounding plants. Control aphids in the garden because they spread mosaic.

Resistant Varieties. Cherokee, Chippewa, Earlaine, Huoma, Katahdin, Kennebec, Ona, Penobscot, Pungo, Saco, and Sebago.

Brown Cankers on Young Sprouts

Rhizoctonia

Potatoes infected with rhizoctonia develop brown cankers that prevent some potato sprouts from emerging, causing uneven germination of plants in the garden. Cankers and girdling appear on roots, stolons, and stems, and brown, sunken, dead areas develop on mature stalks. The stem cankers prevent the normal functioning of the plant and cause stunting, purple discoloration of the foliage, and the formation of aerial tubers. You will find black or brown sclerotia on the skin of infected tubers. There

is no cure for rhizoctonia. Pull and destroy all infected plants. Shallow planting gives some control by encouraging rapid emergence. Avoid planting potatoes in heavy, poorly drained soils, and delay planting until warm weather.

Yellow Foliage

Ring Rot

Wilting of leaflets, stems, and stalks occurs in potatoes that have ring rot. The foliage turns yellow, and the leaf margins turn brown and die. Yellowish discolored areas develop next to the vascular ring in potato tubers. As the disease progresses, a yellow, cheesy mass can be squeezed out of the ring in a cut tuber. Aboveground symptoms show up late in the season and sometimes not at all. Ring rot cannot be cured. Destroy infected plants and tubers. Disinfect tools, follow good fall cleanup practices, and rotate your potato growing site.

Resistant Varieties. Katahdin and Sebago.

Fusarium Wilt

Fusarium wilt in potatoes causes yellow foliage, brown discoloration of the vascular system, and wilting of the leaves and stems. Tubers show internal browning of the vascular ring. Remove and destroy infected plants. To prevent this disease, provide good soil drainage, and control cucumber beetles, which transmit fusarium wilt, with an agricultural fleece barrier spread over the plants from germination until bloom time.

Brown Lesions on Tubers

Scab

The surfaces of scab-infected tubers have brown, rough, irregularly shaped areas that may be raised and warty, level with the surface, or sunken. The lesions may completely cover the tuber. Remove and destroy infected plants.

Old Leaves Yellow and Die

Verticillium Wilt

Late in the season, the older, lower leaves of potatoes infected with verticillium wilt become yellow and die. The leaflets curl and roll, and show tipburn.

The inside of the stem turns yellow or brown. A sulfur fungicide used every 7 to 10 days once the symptoms have been noticed has some effect in controlling this disease, but prevention practices will be more effective in the long run. Do not plant potatoes where other infected plants have grown. Maintain a soil high in organic matter, and clean up the garden well in the fall.

Resistant Varieties. Green Mountain, Katahdin, Ona, Pontiac, Rhinered, and Shoshoni.

HARVEST AND STORAGE

When to Harvest

A week or two after blooming, dig for new potatoes. For storage potatoes, wait to harvest until the tops have died down. Don't delay harvest too long though; once tubers freeze, they become watery and unusable. Potatoes should be nicely shaped and firm, with no green discoloration under skin. Discard any green tubers.

Yield for 25-Foot Row   30 to 50 pounds
Volume vs. Weight   1 bushel equals 50 pounds, or 150 potatoes.
Best Fresh Storage Method   Store potatoes in a cool, dry, dark, well-ventilated place. They will keep for 2 months. A temperature of around 40°F is best. Use potatoes before they sprout.
Best Long-Term Storage Method
Potatoes will keep for 6 months in a root cellar. To prevent black heart, make sure there is adequate ventilation and that temperatures are well above freezing.

VEGETABLE **Pumpkin**   *Cucurbita pepo* var. *pepo*

DESCRIPTION AND ENVIRONMENT

Height   18 to 24 inches
Spread   One plant can spread over 50 to 100 square feet, depending on the variety.
Root Depth   Most of the roots are in the top 12 inches of soil, but the taproot can grow 2 to 3 feet deep.
Shade Tolerance   Needs full sun.
Frost Tolerance   Very tender; cannot tolerate any frost.
Preferred pH   6.0 to 7.0

PLANTING

Spring Planting Time   As soon as all danger of frost has passed.

Planting Depth   1 to 2 inches
Spacing of Plants in Rows   Plant in hills with 3 to 4 plants, keeping hills 6 to 8 feet apart.
Spacing of Plants in Beds   Plant in hills with 3 to 4 plants, keeping hills 6 to 8 feet apart.
Best Soil Temperature for Germination   65°F to 85°F
Best Soil Temperature for Growing   75°F to 85°F
Best Air Temperature for Growing   50°F to 90°F
Days to Germination   7 to 10
Weeks to Transplanting   4
Days to Maturity   110 to 120
Greenhouse Varieties   Pumpkins cannot be grown in the greenhouse.

Container Varieties Pumpkins cannot be grown in containers.

PLANT MANAGEMENT

Water Requirements for Good Production

Make sure pumpkins get 1 inch of water every week from rain or by watering. (See chapter 8 for more information on watering.)

Water Requirements for Maximum Production

Pumpkins like a lot of water, so for maximum productivity give them 1 to 1½ inches of water each week.

Feeding Requirements for Good Production

Apply compost or a slow-acting general-purpose fertilizer in spring, and give the plants supplemental light feedings (side-dressings or foliar spray) monthly throughout the growing season. (See chapter 8 for more information on feeding.)

Feeding Requirements for Maximum Production

Pumpkins are heavy feeders. In addition to the spring feeding mentioned above, they can use a light supplement every 2 weeks during the growing season. Apply a foliar spray of liquid seaweed extract two or three times during the growing season.

MOST COMMON INSECT PESTS

Foliage Curls, Puckers, Turns Yellow

Aphid

If the foliage on your plants curls, puckers, and turns yellow, and the foliage and blooms become stunted, look for ants. They are a sign that your plants have aphids. Ants are attracted to a sticky honeydew secreted by aphids. These insects are about the size of a pinhead and have soft, pear-shaped bodies. They may be green, brown, or pink. You will find them in clusters on the undersides of young leaves. For light infestations, spray the plants vigorously with water in the early morning three times, once every other day. For heavy infestations, apply a commercial insecticidal soap every 2 to 3 days until aphids are under control.

Plants Die from Disease

Cucumber Beetle

The cucumber beetle causes minor physical damage to plants, but it can spread diseases that quickly

kill plants. It is ¼ inch long, oblong, and yellow with black stripes or spots. The best way to control cucumber beetles and the diseases they carry is to prevent them from feeding on young plants. Spread a covering, such as agricultural fleece, over your plants from germination until the plants start to bloom.
Resistant Varieties. Dickinson Field, King of the Mammoth, and Mammoth Chili.

Wilted, Dried-up Leaves

Squash Bug
The leaves on pumpkins that are infested with squash bugs wilt, dry up, and turn black, and damage increases until the vine dies. Adult squash bugs are flat-backed, shield-shaped, brown to black bugs with a light-colored outline on their abdomens. They are ½ to ¾ inch long and lay brown or red shiny eggs on the undersides of leaves. Adults and nymphs suck juices from leaves, causing them to wilt and dry up. To control infestations, handpick pests from the undersides of leaves. If this doesn't control squash bugs, apply insecticidal soap every 2 to 3 days for 2 weeks. Prevent access to pumpkins by applying a preventive spray and covering plants with a barrier such as agricultural fleece. Remove the barrier when plants begin to bloom.

Sudden Wilting of Plants

Squash Vine Borer
Sudden wilting of all or part of a pumpkin vine can be caused by squash vine borers. You can tell borers are at work by the moist, sawdustlike debris, called frass, piled up outside their small holes. Squash vine borers are fat, white caterpillars with brown heads, about 1 inch long. They tunnel into the stems to feed. The adult is an orange-and-black, clear-winged moth with black stripes on its abdomen. It lays brown, flat eggs on the stem. Inject *Bacillus thuringiensis* (BT) into the stem of infested plants with a hypodermic needle. Slit the stems, remove the borers, and cover the wounds with soil. Try to deny the moth access to the plant with an agricultural fleece or netting barrier, which must be removed at flowering to allow pollination.
Resistant Varieties. Dickson, Green Striped Cushaw,

Kentucky Field, Large Sweet Cheese, and Sweet Potato.

MOST COMMON DISEASES

Water-soaked Spots on Leaves

Angular Leaf Spot
Pumpkins infected with angular leaf spot develop water-soaked spots on their leaves, which turn tan and gray, and then drop out, leaving ragged holes. Spots develop also on fruit. The spots are rounded, and may exude a thick, oozing substance. The infection will go into the seed cavity, making the fruit inedible. Angular leaf spot overwinters in seed and plant debris and spreads during wet weather. There is no cure for this disease, so remove and destroy all infected plants.

Black Leaves

Anthracnose
The anthracnose fungus attacks all parts of the plant above the ground. The first symptoms are usually black specks on the oldest leaves; eventually, the entire leaf becomes black and shriveled. Dark red, slightly sunken, water-soaked spots develop on leaves and stems, and pinkish red spots appear on leaves and runners in moist weather. The infected fruit may have round, sunken lesions, in which pink spore masses may also be seen. Do not work near plants when they are wet. As soon as you spot the problem, apply a fixed copper or sulfur-based fungicide every 7 to 10 days until 3 to 4 weeks before harvest. If this does not control the disease, remove and discard infected plants.

Quick Wilting of Plants

Bacterial Wilt
Pumpkins infected with bacterial wilt may wilt so quickly that they will be dried up but still green. White sticky material oozes from the stem when it is cut. Bacterial wilt blocks the vascular system of the plant. The disease cannot be cured. Remove and destroy plants immediately. Wash your hands and any tools in a bleach solution (one part house-

hold bleach to four parts water) before touching other plants. Bacterial wilt is transmitted by spotted and striped cucumber beetles. Try to prevent the beetles from getting to your pumpkins by covering them with agricultural fleece until the plants start to bloom.

Stunted, Curled Leaves

Curly Top
The young leaves of diseased plants are stunted and curled, but may be normal in color. The older leaves are often yellowed. Stems are shorter then normal, and plants are stunted and bushy and fail to produce. Curly top cannot be cured. Remove and destroy infected and surrounding plants. Next time, use resistant varieties.

Downy Purple Spots on Leaves

Downy Mildew
Pumpkins infected with downy mildew have irregularly shaped yellow spots on the upper surfaces of their leaves, and under moist conditions, downy purple spots appear on the undersides. The leaves die as the spots increase in size. Seedlings develop purplish lesions on leaves and stems, and a white downy substance covers these areas. Plants die very rapidly after contracting downy mildew. If you catch the infection early, apply a copper-based fungicide to diseased and surrounding plants every 7 to 10 days until harvest. Remove and destroy any plants with a serious infection.

Whitish Spots on Undersides of Leaves

Powdery Mildew
Circular, whitish spots on the undersides of leaves are signs of powdery mildew. As the disease progresses, the spots increase in number and size, grow together, progress to the upper surfaces, and finally cover entire leaves with white, powdery growth. As soon as you discover the disease, remove and destroy the infected parts. Disinfect your pruning tool in a bleach solution (one part household bleach to four parts water) after each cut. In addition to pruning, apply a sulfur-based fungicide every 7 to 10 days if you are growing a sulfur-tolerant pumpkin variety (check with your County Extension agent: If your pumpkins are not sulfur tolerant, use a copper-based fungicide). Limit overhead sprinkling to early in the day, and do not work around plants when they are wet. Thin plants to let in sun and air.

Dark, Oozing Spots on Pumpkins

Scab
Symptoms of scab include the appearance of water-soaked spots on leaves, which may cause them to wilt. Stems may develop small cankers. Young fruit develops gray, slightly sunken spots. As the plant matures, these spots darken, become more sunken, and develop a greenish velvety mold. Remove and destroy infected plants. Prevent scab with good fall cleanup and crop rotation.

HARVEST AND STORAGE

When to Harvest

Wait to harvest until the pumpkins are a uniform orange color. Ripe fruit gives a sharp thud when rapped with the knuckles. Pumpkins for storage should have tough shells that resist denting. Unless frost threatens, don't harvest pumpkins until the vine dies.

Yield for 25-Foot Row 30 to 40 pounds

Volume vs. Weight 1 bushel equals 40 pounds.

Weight of 1-Quart Canning Jar 2½ to 3 pounds

Number of Quarts Stored from 1 Bushel 13 to 26

Best Fresh Storage Method Before storage, cure pumpkins in a warm, well-ventilated room for 1 to 2 weeks, then store them in a cool, dry place; they will keep for several months.

Best Long-Term Storage Methods Pumpkins can be frozen, canned, or dried; they will keep for 8 to 12 months in any of these forms.

Second-Best Long-Term Storage Method In a dry root cellar, pumpkins will keep for 5 months.

Radish

Raphanus sativus

DESCRIPTION AND ENVIRONMENT

Height   6 to 8 inches
Spread   6 inches
Shade Tolerance   Needs at least 6 hours of sun a day (partial shade).

Frost Tolerance   Hardy
Preferred pH   5.0 to 6.0

PLANTING

Spring Planting Time   4 to 6 weeks before last expected frost.

Fall Planting Time   7 weeks before first expected frost.

Succession Planting   Plant radishes every 10 days until warm weather arrives (average air temperature over 70°F), and then start again in the late summer for some fall successions, planting every 10 days.

Planting Depth   ½ inch

Spacing of Plants in Rows   2 to 3 inches

Spacing of Plants in Beds   2 to 3 inches

Best Soil Temperature for Germination   40°F to 85°F

Best Soil Temperature for Growing
65°F to 75°F

Best Air Temperature for Growing
45°F to 75°F

Days to Germination   3 to 10

Days to Maturity   20 to 40

Greenhouse Varieties   French Breakfast and Sparkler.

Container Varieties   Try Cherry Belle, Early Scarlet Globe, French Breakfast, or Sparkler. The round red- and white-tipped varieties do well in containers. Stay away from large winter radishes like Daikon. Don't let container radishes dry out. Underwatering leads to cracked, pithy roots.

Container Size 4 to 6 inches deep.

Radishes Go to Seed

High Temperatures

Radishes do not grow well in hot weather (air temperature over 75°F). This problem can be eased by covering the plants with fine netting or agricultural fleece to shade them from the direct sun. Using organic mulch also helps to cool the soil.

PLANT MANAGEMENT

Water Requirements

Make sure the plants get 1 inch of water every week from rain or by watering. (See chapter 8 for more information on watering.)

Feeding Requirements

Apply compost or a slow-acting general-purpose fertilizer in spring. This plant is a light feeder, so it needs little or no supplemental fertilizer. Apply a foliar spray of liquid seaweed extract two or three times during the growing season. (See chapter 8 for more information on feeding.)

Pale Leaves, Turning Yellow

Nitrogen Deficiency

If the leaves of your radishes are pale and turning yellow, suspect a nitrogen deficiency. Plants will be stunted, with small and narrow leaves and weak, slender stems. The roots will be small and pale in color. To remedy the problem quickly, apply a foliar spray of diluted fish emulsion or another liquid fertilizer. (See chapter 8 for more information on nitrogen deficiency.)

Reddish Purple Color on Leaves

Phosphorus Deficiency

A reddish purple color on leaves, especially the undersides, veins, and stems, indicates a phosphorus deficiency. Stems will be thin and radishes will fail to produce decent bulbs. Phosphorus deficiencies generally occur in acid soils and also temporarily in cold, wet soils. To remedy the problem quickly, spray radishes with diluted fish emulsion or another liquid fertilizer. In addition, spread wood ashes around the plants. (See chapter 8 for more information on phosphorus deficiency.)

Dark Green Centers of Leaves

Potassium Deficiency

If radish leaves appear dark green in the center while the edges curl and turn pale yellow to brown, your plants are suffering from a potassium deficiency. An extreme potassium deficiency is indicated by deep yellow leaves and stems. The leaves may grow thick and leathery. Roots are more bulbous than normal. Radish roots are undersized, and edges of the older leaves are dead. To remedy the problem quickly, spray the plants with diluted fish emulsion or some other liquid fertilizer, and apply side-dressings of wood ashes or greensand. (See chapter 8 for more information on potassium deficiency.)

MOST COMMON INSECT PESTS

Foliage Curls, Puckers, Turns Yellow

Aphid

If the foliage on your plants curls, puckers, and turns yellow, and the foliage and blooms become stunted, look for ants. They are a sign that your plants have aphids. Ants are attracted to a sticky honeydew secreted by aphids. These insects are about the size of a pinhead and have soft, pear-shaped bodies. They may be green, brown, or pink. You will find them in clusters on the undersides of young leaves. For light infestations, spray the plants vigorously with water in the early morning three times, once every other day. For heavy infestations, apply a commercial insecticidal soap every 2 to 3 days until aphids are under control.

Small Ragged Holes in Leaves

Cabbage Looper

Small ragged holes in leaves indicate that your plants may be infested with cabbage loopers. The cabbage looper is a 1½-inch-long caterpillar that is light green with long yellowish stripes on its back. It loops as it walks. Spray *Bacillus thuringiensis* (BT) on infested plants every 2 weeks until the problem is solved.

Plant Wilts during Heat of Day

Cabbage Maggot

Plants infested with cabbage maggots will wilt during the heat of the day. Brown tunnels in the stem just below soil level are further evidence that this pest has attacked your radishes. Seedlings become yellow, growth is stunted, and plants lack vigor. Eventually they will die. The cabbage maggot is a small, white, legless worm about ¼ inch long. The adult resembles a housefly. Maggots tunnel into plant roots and stems. Bacterial diseases such as black leg, which causes dark patches on leaves, and soft rot, which causes plant decomposition, may result, causing the plants to wilt. To control infestations, mix heaping teaspoonfuls of wood ashes 1 inch into the soil around the plant, or pour a cupful of lime drench (1 cup of lime in 1 quart of water; let sit overnight) around the root ball of each plant. The best control is to prevent flies from laying eggs in the first place. Spread a barrier, such as agricultural fleece, over the seedlings.

Seedling Stems Severed

Cutworm

Cutworms completely sever the stems of seedlings and transplants at or below the soil surface. They are 1- to 2-inch, dull-colored, plump, soft-bodied larvae that curl up when disturbed. Cutworms feed at night and hide in the soil during the day. To control cutworms, use barriers or traps to deny them access to seedlings. To protect individual plants, surround them with a collar, or make a trap by sprinkling cornmeal or bran meal around each plant. (See chapter 4 for more information on collars and meal traps.)

Tiny Holes in Leaves

Flea Beetle

If you find many little holes or perforations in the leaves of your plants, the plants may have flea beetles. Flea beetles are 1/10 inch long, shiny, and black, and may have yellow or white markings. They are very active and jump like fleas when disturbed. Their feeding can destroy small plants rapidly. Apply pyrethrum, making two applications, 3 to 4 days apart, to control infestations. In the spring, cover plants with a barrier, such as agricultural fleece, to deny flea beetles access to your plants.
Resistant Varieties. Champion and Sparkler.

Wilted Leaves with Black Spots

Harlequin Bug

If the leaves of your plants develop white blotches or black spots, and then wilt and die, suspect the harlequin bug. This insect is ¼ inch long and shaped like a shield, with a triangle on its back. It has patterned markings in black and red. Harlequin bugs emit a foul odor. To control infestations, spray plants with an insecticidal soap laced with isopropyl alcohol every 2 to 3 days for 2 weeks. Apply insecticidal soap twice, 5 to 7 days apart, in early spring to prevent harlequin bugs.

Resistant Varieties. Champion, Cherry Belle, Globemaster, Red Devil, and White Icicle.

Large Ragged Holes in Leaves

Imported Cabbage Worm

Imported cabbage worms chew large ragged holes in radish leaves, trailing dark green frass, or excrement, behind them. The worm is light green with one yellow stripe, and measures 1¼ inches long. The adult is a common white butterfly with three to four black spots on its wings that is active during the day. To control infestations, apply *Bacillus thuringiensis* (BT) every 10 to 14 days until the pest is removed. Prevent cabbage worms by spraying the plant with BT twice, 5 to 7 days apart, by the time radishes are over an inch tall, and covering plants with an agricultural fleece barrier.

White or Brown Tunnels in Leaves

Leafminer

White or brown tunnels or blotches on leaves are signs that your radishes have leafminers. The leaves may turn yellow and blotched and look blistered or curled. Leafminers are small black flies, usually with yellow stripes. The tiny yellowish larvae feed between the upper and lower surfaces of leaves, causing the tunnels or blotches to appear. You may also find stem damage below the soil. Remove the infested leaves before the larvae mature. The best way to control leafminers, though, is to screen out the adult flies by covering seeded areas with agricultural fleece.

Leaves Stippled Yellow

Mite

Leaves of radishes infested with mites become stippled, yellow, and dry, and sometimes pale yellow spots or blotches appear. Mites are not insects but arachnids, and are about the size of a grain of black pepper. They may be red, black, or brown. They feed by sucking out the plant's juices. In sucking chlorophyll out of the leaves, they cause small white dots to appear. In addition, they inject toxins into the leaves, which discolors and distorts them. To control infestations, spray plants with a forceful spray of water three times, once every other day, to knock mites from the leaves. If mites are still present, spray with insecticidal soap three times, once every 5 to 7 days.

Damage to Lower Part of Stem

Onion Maggot

Onion maggots burrow into and destroy the lower part of the radish stem near the bulb. These white maggots are about ⅓ inch long and legless. To prevent onion maggots from becoming a serious problem, don't plant radishes close together or in rows, which allows the maggots to move easily from plant to plant.

MOST COMMON DISEASES

Small Yellow Areas on Leaves

Downy Mildew

Leaf symptoms of downy mildew appear as small yellowish areas that later turn brown with bluish black, lacelike markings. In moist weather, a whitish downy mold develops on the undersides of leaves. Inner root tissue is discolored. The roots can become discolored internally, sometimes with a netlike brown or black area. In the advanced stages of this disease, the skin of the radish develops small cracks, becomes rough, and may split. If you catch the infection early, apply a copper-based fungicide to diseased and surrounding plants every 7 to 10 days until harvest. Remove and destroy any plants with a serious infection.

HARVEST AND STORAGE

When to Harvest

Harvest radishes once they reach a usable size; large, overgrown roots split or turn spongy. Black radishes should be firm, smooth, round, and black. Red radishes should also be firm, smooth, and round and should have a good red color. Harvest them when they reach ¾ to 1⅛ inches in diameter. White radishes should be firm, slender, and white, measuring 3 to 4 inches in length. The harvest period for radishes lasts 1 to 2 weeks, depending upon the variety.

Yield for 25-Foot Row   8 to 12 pounds
Best Fresh Storage Method   Refrigerate radishes in plastic bags; they will keep for 2 weeks.
Best Long-Term Storage Method Pickled radishes will keep for years.
Seed Storage   3 years

VEGETABLE **Rutabaga**   *Brassica napus*

DESCRIPTION AND ENVIRONMENT

Height   15 inches
Spread   15 inches
Shade Tolerance   Needs at least 6 hours of sun a day (partial shade).
Frost Tolerance   Hardy
Preferred pH   6.0 to 8.0

PLANTING

Spring Planting Time   6 weeks before last expected frost.

Fall Planting Time   16 weeks before first expected frost.
Planting Depth   ¼ inch
Spacing of Plants in Rows   8 to 12 inches
Spacing of Plants in Beds   6 to 9 inches
Best Soil Temperature for Germination   65°F to 75°F
Days to Germination   7 to 15
Days to Maturity   90 to 100
Greenhouse Varieties   Rutabagas cannot be grown in the greenhouse.

Container Varieties Rutabagas cannot be grown in containers.

PLANT MANAGEMENT

Water Requirements

Make sure the plants get 1 inch of water every week

from rain or by watering. (See chapter 8 for more information on watering.)

Feeding Requirements

Apply compost or a slow-acting general-purpose fertilizer in spring. Rutabagas are light feeders, so they need little or no supplemental fertilizer. Apply a foliar spray of liquid seaweed extract two or three times during the growing season. (See chapter 8 for more information on feeding.)

MOST COMMON INSECT PESTS

Foliage Curls, Puckers, Turns Yellow

Aphid

If the foliage on your rutabagas curls, puckers, and turns yellow, and plant growth becomes stunted, look for ants. They are a sign that your plants might have aphids. Ants are attracted to a sticky honeydew secreted by aphids. Rutabagas are particularly bothered by cabbage aphids, which have soft, pear-shaped bodies about the size of a pinhead, are green to powdery blue in color, and are covered with a fine whitish wax. You will find them in clusters on undersides of young leaves. For light infestations, spray plants vigorously with water in the early morning three times, once every other day. Heavy infestations can be dealt with by applying commercial insecticidal soap every 2 to 3 days until aphids are under control.

Small Ragged Holes in Leaves

Cabbage Looper

Small ragged holes in leaves indicate that your plants may be infested with cabbage loopers. The cabbage looper is a 1½-inch-long caterpillar that is light green with long yellowish stripes on its back. It loops as it walks. Spray *Bacillus thuringiensis* (BT) on infested plants every 2 weeks until heads form.

Plant Wilts during Heat of Day

Cabbage Maggot

Plants infested with cabbage maggots will wilt during the heat of the day. Brown tunnels in the stem just below soil level are further evidence that this pest has attacked your rutabagas. Seedlings become yellow, growth is stunted, and plants lack vigor. Eventually, they will die. The cabbage maggot is a small, white, legless worm about ¼ inch long. The adult resembles a housefly. Maggots tunnel into plant roots and stems. Bacterial diseases such as black leg, which causes dark patches on leaves, and soft rot, which causes plant decomposition, may result, causing the plants to wilt. To control infestations, mix heaping teaspoonfuls of wood ashes 1 inch into the soil around the plant, or pour a cupful of lime drench (1 cup of lime in 1 quart of water; let sit overnight) around the root ball of each plant. The best control is to prevent flies from laying eggs in the first place. Spread a barrier, such as agricultural fleece, over the plants, or place a collar around the stem of each plant. (For instructions on how to construct these collars, see chapter 4.)

Seedling Stems Severed

Cutworm

Cutworms completely sever the stems of seedlings and transplants at or below the soil surface. They are 1- to 2-inch, dull-colored, plump, soft-bodied larvae that curl up when disturbed. Cutworms feed at night and hide in the soil during the day. To control cutworms, use barriers or traps to deny them access to seedlings. To protect individual plants, surround them with a collar, or make a trap by sprinkling cornmeal or bran meal around each plant.

(See chapter 4 for more information on collars and meal traps.)

Tiny Holes in Leaves

Flea Beetle

If you find many little holes or perforations in the leaves of your plants, the plants may have flea beetles. Flea beetles are ¹⁄₁₀ inch long, shiny, and black, and may have yellow or white markings. They are very active and jump like fleas when disturbed. Their feeding can destroy small plants rapidly. Apply pyrethrum, making two applications, 3 to 4 days apart, to control infestations. In the spring, cover plants with a barrier, such as agricultural fleece, to deny flea beetles access to your plants.

Wilted Leaves with Black Spots

Harlequin Bug

If the leaves of your plants develop white blotches or black spots, and then wilt and die, suspect the harlequin bug. This insect is ¼ inch long and shaped like a shield, with a triangle on its back. It has patterned markings in black and red. Harlequin bugs emit a foul odor. To control infestations, spray plants with an insecticidal soap laced with isopropyl alcohol every 2 to 3 days for 2 weeks. Apply insecticidal soap twice, 5 to 7 days apart, in early spring to prevent harlequin bugs.

Large Ragged Holes in Leaves

Imported Cabbage Worm

Imported cabbage worms chew large ragged holes in rutabaga leaves. Look for trails of dark green frass, or excrement, which are further evidence of their presence. The worm is light green with one yellow stripe, and measures 1¼ inches long. The adult is a common white butterfly with three to four black spots on its wings that is active during the day. To control infestations, apply *Bacillus thuringiensis* (BT) every 10 to 14 days until the pest is removed. Prevent cabbage worms by spraying transplants with BT early in the season and covering plants with an agricultural fleece barrier.

HARVEST AND STORAGE

When to Harvest

Dig rutabagas whenever they reach a usable size, about the size of a tennis ball. Never let roots get bigger than 5 to 7 inches in diameter or they will get woody. The best flavor develops after rutabagas are touched by frost.

Yield for 25-Foot Row   25 pounds

Best Fresh Storage Method   Store rutabagas in a cool, dry place; they will keep for 3 to 5 weeks.

Best Long-Term Storage Method   Store rutabagas in a humid root cellar, or mulch your plants and leave them in the garden; they will keep for 4 to 6 months.

Second-Best Long-Term Storage Method   Canned rutabagas will keep for more than 12 months.

VEGETABLE *Spinach*   *Spinacia oleracea*

DESCRIPTION AND ENVIRONMENT

Height   4 to 6 inches
Spread   6 to 8 inches
Root Depth   Most of the plant's roots are usually limited to the upper 1 foot of soil, but the taproot measures up to 5 feet long.
Shade Tolerance   Needs only 5 hours of sun a day (partial shade).
Frost Tolerance   Very hardy; can tolerate heavy frosts.
Preferred pH   6.5 to 7.5

PLANTING

Spring Planting Time   3 to 6 weeks before last expected frost.
Fall Planting Time   6 to 8 weeks before first expected frost.
Succession Planting   Plant spinach every 2 weeks until temperatures rise above 65°F and the days lengthen. Start the succession again in late August or early September for a fall crop.
Planting Depth   ¼ inch
Spacing of Plants in Rows   4 to 8 inches

Spacing of Plants in Beds   4 to 6 inches
Best Soil Temperature for Germination   40°F to 75°F
Best Soil Temperature for Growing 60°F to 70°F
Best Air Temperature for Growing 40°F to 75°F
Days to Germination   6 to 14
Weeks to Transplanting   4 to 6
Days to Maturity   40 to 60

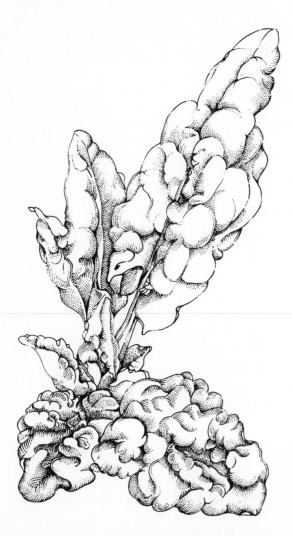

Greenhouse Varieties   Spinach does not grow well in the greenhouse.

Container Varieties   Any variety can be grown in containers. Spinach must have cool, moist conditions. A good hot-weather substitute is New Zealand spinach.

Container Size   4 to 6 inches deep.

Poor Germination in Summer

High Temperatures

Spinach seeds germinate best at low temperatures. For a fall crop, you can pre-germinate spinach seeds in the refrigerator. Keep seeds in damp paper towels for a week, then plant them.

PLANT MANAGEMENT

Water Requirements

This plant doesn't need much water; for best production give it ½ to 1 inch of water a week, which is less than most garden vegetables require. (See chapter 8 for more information on watering.)

Feeding Requirements for Good Production

Apply compost or a slow-acting general-purpose fertilizer in the spring, and give spinach supplemental light feedings (side-dressings or foliar spray) monthly throughout the growing season. (See chapter 8 for more information on feeding.)

Feeding Requirements for Maximum Production

Spinach is a heavy feeder. In addition to the spring feeding mentioned above, it likes a light supplement every 2 weeks during the growing season. An important time to give spinach a supplemental feeding is when the plants are about half grown. Apply a foliar spray of liquid seaweed extract two or three times during the growing season.

MOST COMMON INSECT PESTS

Foliage Curls, Puckers, Turns Yellow

Aphid

If the foliage on your plants curls, puckers, and turns yellow, and the foliage and blooms become stunted, look for ants. They are a sign that your plants have aphids. Ants are attracted to a sticky honeydew secreted by aphids. These insects are about the size of a pinhead and have soft, pear-shaped bodies. They may be green, brown, or pink. You will find them in clusters on the undersides of young leaves. For light infestations, spray the plants vigorously with water in the early morning three times, once every other day. For heavy infestations, apply a commercial insecticidal soap every 2 to 3 days until aphids are under control.

Tiny Holes in Leaves

Flea Beetle

If you find many little holes or perforations in the leaves of your plants, the plants may have flea beetles. Flea beetles are $1/10$ inch long, shiny, and black, and may have yellow or white markings. They are very active and jump like fleas when disturbed. Their feeding can destroy small plants rapidly. Apply pyrethrum, making two applications, 3 to 4 days apart, to control infestations. In the spring, cover plants with a barrier, such as agricultural fleece, to deny flea beetles access to your plants.

Weakened Plants

Leafhopper

Both adult leafhoppers and nymphs pierce leaves, buds, and stems and suck the sap and chlorophyll from cells, causing plants to weaken. Adults are green, wedge-shaped insects, $1/4$ to $1/3$ inch long, that hold their wings in a rooflike position above their bodies. They are very active and move sideways.

Nymphs resemble adults. To control serious infestations, apply insecticidal soap laced with isopropyl alcohol every 2 to 3 days for 2 weeks. In early spring, apply a preventive spray of insecticidal soap and seaweed extract, and cover seedlings with an agricultural fleece barrier for the first month of growth to deny leafhoppers access to your plants.

White or Brown Tunnels in Leaves

Leafminer

White or brown tunnels or blotches on leaves are signs that your spinach has leafminers. The leaves may turn yellow and blotchy and look blistered or curled. Leafminers are small black flies, usually with yellow stripes. The tiny yellowish larvae feed between the upper and lower surfaces of leaves, causing the tunnels or blotches to appear. You may also find stem damage below the soil. Remove the infested leaves before the larvae mature. The best way to control leafminers, though, is to screen out the adult flies with some type of light material, such as agricultural fleece. Place the fleece over seedlings.

MOST COMMON DISEASES

Yellow, Curled Leaves

Blight

Yellowed and curled leaves, stunted plants, and reduced yields are all symptoms of blight in spinach. There is no cure for blight. Remove and destroy all infected plants. Blight is transmitted by aphids, so control these insects by spraying plants with water, or applying insecticidal soap every 2 or 3 days until they are under control. Select resistant varieties.

Seedlings Die

Damping-Off

Seedlings that have damping-off simply topple over. You will see a watery soft rot on the stem at the soil line. There is no cure for this disease. Remove and destroy infected plants. Make sure the soil is well drained and warm. You might try spreading pasteurized soil or a sterile vermiculite in furrows where you plant your seeds.

Yellow Leaf Spots

Downy Mildew

Spinach plants infected with downy mildew develop yellow leaf spots with fuzzy purple growth on the undersides of leaves. In addition, purplish lesions form on the leaves and stems, which become covered with a downy white fungus. Plants die very rapidly after contracting this disease. If you catch the infection early, apply a copper-based fungicide to diseased and surrounding plants every 7 to 10 days until harvest. Remove and destroy any plants with a serious infection.

Resistant Varieties. Califlay, Dixie Market, Dixie Savoy, High Pack, Hybrid No. 7, Hybrid No. 424, Hybrid No. 425, Indian Summer Hybrid, Kent, Marathon, Melody Hybrid, and Texas Early Hybrid 7.

Yellow Plant

Fusarium Wilt

Spinach plants infected with fusarium wilt turn yellow, and the lower leaves lose their firmness and wilt. A brown discoloration appears in water channels of leaves. Remove and destroy infected plants. Fusarium wilt is generally carried in the soil, so using resistant varieties is the best approach to preventing this problem. Solarizing the soil also helps. (See chapter 5 for more information on solarization.)

HARVEST AND STORAGE

When to Harvest

Pick outer leaves a few at a time once they're large enough to use. The mineral content of spinach leaves, including nitrogen, phosphorus, potassium, and magnesium, fluctuates during the day. It tends to drop after sunrise and hit a minimum in late afternoon; then it increases to a maximum at dawn. If you're trying to get the most minerals from your spinach, pick it early in the morning. The harvest period for spinach lasts about 2 weeks, depending on the variety.

Yield for 25-Foot Row   10 to 15 pounds
Volume vs. Weight   1 bushel equals 18 pounds.
Weight of 1-Quart Canning Jar   2 to 3 pounds
Number of Quarts Stored from 1 Bushel   6 to 9
Best Fresh Storage Method   Refrigerate spinach in plastic bags; it will keep for up to 2 weeks.
Best Long-Term Storage Method   Freeze or can spinach; it will keep for 12 months.

VEGETABLE **Squash, Summer** *Cucurbita pepo*

DESCRIPTION AND ENVIRONMENT

Height   30 to 40 inches
Spread   12 to 16 square feet
Root Depth   The taproot is usually confined to the upper 2 feet, but can grow 6 feet deep.

Shade Tolerance   Needs full sun.
Frost Tolerance   Tender; cannot tolerate any frost.
Preferred pH   6.0 to 8.0

PLANTING

Spring Planting Time   From frost-free date to 4 weeks after.

Fall Planting Time   10 weeks before first expected frost.

Planting Depth   ½ inch

Spacing of Plants in Rows   18 to 24 inches

Spacing of Plants in Beds   12 to 18 inches

Best Soil Temperature for Germination   65°F to 85°F

Best Soil Temperature for Growing   70°F to 85°F

Best Air Temperature for Growing   Day, 70°F to 85°F; night, 60°F to 75°F.

Days to Germination   3 to 12

Weeks to Transplanting   4

Days to Maturity   45 to 60

Greenhouse Varieties   Squash does not grow well in the greenhouse.

Container Varieties   Try Early Yellow Summer Crookneck, Goldbar Straightneck, Park's Creamy, and Scallopine.

Container Size   24 inches deep.

Meager Harvest

Few Male Blossoms

Early zucchini are produced from unpollinated female flowers. The blossoms of most zucchini hybrids are all female when the plants first flower. Pick some of the first tender young zucchini as soon as they begin to form. This encourages male flowers to develop, which should begin to appear within several weeks and which will pollinate the female blossoms. Let later-developing zucchini grow, and your crop's total production will increase.

PLANT MANAGEMENT

Water Requirements for Good Production

Make sure the plants get 1 inch of water every week from rain or by watering. (See chapter 8 for more information on watering.)

Water Requirements for Maximum Production

Summer squash likes lots of water. For maximum productivity, give it 1 to 1½ inches of water each week. Critical watering periods are during bud development and flowering.

Feeding Requirements for Good Production

Apply compost or a slow-acting general-purpose fertilizer in spring, and give the plants supplemental light feedings (side-dressings or foliar spray) monthly throughout the growing season. (See chapter 8 for more information on feeding.)

Feeding Requirements for Maximum Production

Summer squash is a heavy feeder. In addition to the spring feeding mentioned above, it likes a light supplement every 2 weeks during the growing season. Important periods for giving plants supplemental feedings are when the plants are about 6 inches tall, and when they bloom. Apply a foliar spray of liquid seaweed extract two or three times during the growing season.

Small Squash Drop Off

Overwatering

If small squash soften and drop off before they reach harvest size, you are probably overwatering the plants. When squash plants get too much water, they produce huge, lush leaves but meager fruit. A small zucchini on an overwatered vine will often turn yellow, rot, and fall off as it reaches thumb size. Let the plants dry out until leaves begin to droop a little. Within a week or 10 days, the problem should be resolved.

Young Squash Spoil

Wet Squash

If fruit rots before becoming ripe, it has probably been exposed to too much wetness for too long. Avoid this by growing vining types on a trellis. For bush types, set fruit on pieces of wood and use drip irrigation if possible.

MOST COMMON INSECT PESTS

Foliage Curls, Puckers, Turns Yellow

Aphid

If the foliage on your plants curls, puckers, and turns yellow, and the foliage and blooms become stunted, look for ants. They are a sign that your plants have aphids. Ants are attracted to a sticky honeydew secreted by aphids. These insects are about the size of a pinhead and have soft, pear-shaped bodies. They may be green, brown, or pink. You will find them in clusters on the undersides of young leaves. For light infestations, spray the plants vigorously with water in the early morning three times, once every other day. For heavy infestations, apply a commercial insecticidal soap every 2 to 3 days until aphids are under control.

Holes in Leaves

Corn Earworm

Corn earworms chew holes in the leaves of summer squash plants, and they damage buds and young plants. Plant growth may be stunted. The corn earworm is 1½ inches long and may be white, green, or red. It has four prolegs and has spines along its body. Apply a light horticultural oil spray mixed with *Bacillus thuringiensis* (BT) every 2 weeks until the pest is removed.

Plant Dies of Disease

Cucumber Beetle

The cucumber beetle causes minor physical damage to plants, but it can spread diseases that quickly kill the plants. It is ¼ inch long, oblong, and yellow with black stripes or spots. The best way to control cucumber beetles and the diseases they carry is to prevent them from feeding on young plants. Spread a covering, such as agricultural fleece, over your plants from germination until the plants start to bloom. If your plants do become infested with cucumber beetles dust frequently with pyrethrum to control adults and larvae.

Resistant Varieties. Varieties resistant to the spotted cucumber beetle include Bennings Green Tint Scallop, Black Zucchini, Early Golden Bush Scallop, Long Cozella, Seneca Prolific, Summer Crookneck, and Summer Straightneck.

Those resistant to the striped cucumber beetle include Bennings Green Tint Scallop, Cozella Hybrid, Early Golden Bush Scallop, Early Prolific Straightneck, Early Yellow Summer Crookneck, Long Cocozelle, Marine Black Zucchini, Short Cocozelle, Summer Crookneck, U Conn, White Bush Scallop, and Zucchini.

Weakened Plants

Leafhopper
Both adult leafhoppers and nymphs pierce leaves, buds, and stems and suck the sap and chlorophyll from cells, causing plants to weaken. Adults are green, wedge-shaped insects, ¼ to ⅓ inch long, that hold their wings in a rooflike position above their bodies. They are very active and move sideways. Nymphs resemble adults. To control serious infestations, apply insecticidal soap laced with isopropyl alcohol every 2 to 3 days for 2 weeks. In early spring, apply a preventive spray of insecticidal soap and seaweed extract, and cover seedlings with an agricultural fleece barrier for the first month of growth to deny leafhoppers access to your plants.

Skeletonized Leaves

Mexican Bean Beetle
If the leaves of squash plants look skeletonized, check your plants for the Mexican bean beetle. The adult is ¼ inch long, round, and has yellow to gold to copper coloring with 16 black dots in three rows down its back. It looks somewhat like a lady bug. It lays yellow eggs in clusters on the undersides of leaves. The hump-backed, fuzzy larvae are orange or yellow and measure about ⅓ inch in length. Both

the adults and larvae chew holes in the leaves. To control Mexican bean beetles, handpick early arrivals, with special attention to the easy-to-spot bright yellow eggs. If the infestation gets out of control, make two applications of pyrethrum, 3 days apart.

Wilted, Dried-up Leaves

Squash Bug
The leaves on plants infested with squash bugs wilt, dry up, and turn black, and the damage increases until the vine dies. Adult squash bugs are flat-backed, shield-shaped, brown to black bugs with a light-colored outline on their abdomens. They are ½ to ¾ inch long and lay brown or red shiny eggs on the undersides of leaves. Adults and nymphs suck juices from leaves, causing them to wilt and dry up. To control infestations, handpick pests from the undersides of leaves. If this doesn't control squash bugs, apply insecticidal soap every 2 to 3 days for 2 weeks. In spring, apply a preventive spray made with insecticidal soap and seaweed extract (see the entry Squash Bug in chapter 4) and cover plants with a barrier, such as agricultural fleece, to deny squash bugs access to your plants. Remove the barrier when plants begin to bloom.

Resistant Varieties. Early Golden Bush Scallop, Early Prolific Straightneck, Early Summer Crookneck, and Sweet Cheese.

Sudden Wilting of Plant

Squash Vine Borer
Sudden wilting of all or part of a squash vine can be caused by squash vine borers. You can tell borers are at work by the moist, sawdustlike debris, called frass, piled up outside their small holes. Squash vine borers are fat, white caterpillars with brown heads, about 1 inch long. They tunnel into the stems to feed. The adult is an orange-and-black, clear-winged moth with black stripes on its abdomen. It lays brown, flat eggs on the stem. Inject *Bacillus thuringiensis* (BT) into the stem of infested plants with a hypodermic needle. Slit the stems, remove the borers, and cover the wounds with soil. Try to

deny the moth access to the plant with an agricultural fleece or netting barrier, which must be removed at flowering to allow pollination.

Discolored Blossoms

Thrip
Thrips puncture petals and leaves to suck the sap, causing considerable discoloration and disfiguration. Leaves may become bleached and will wilt. Thrips are only 1/25 inch long. What is visible are their dark fecal pellets. To control them, spray with insecticidal soap every 3 days for 2 weeks. For serious infestations, use pyrethrum.

Weakened Plants, Yellow Leaves

Whitefly
Plants that have whiteflies weaken, their leaves turn yellow, and they die. Honeydew secreted by whiteflies encourages fungus. Molds often develop following an attack. Adults are about the size of a pinhead, and mothlike, with dusty white wings. When an infested plant is shaken, it appears as if dandruff were flying off the leaves. Nymphs are yellowish, legless, flat, and oval, resembling scale at certain stages. To control infestations, spray plants with insecticidal soap spray every 2 to 3 days for 2 weeks. Use it also early in the season during the first months of the plant's life to prevent whiteflies. Spray every 2 weeks. Pyrethrum may be used as a last resort. Make two applications, 3 to 4 days apart.

MOST COMMON DISEASES

Brown Leaves

Anthracnose
The anthracnose fungus attacks all parts of the plant above the ground. Small water-soaked spots develop on the leaves. They enlarge and turn brown, and eventually the leaves shrivel and die. Sunken lesions form on the stems, and circular, black, sunken spots appear on the fruit. During moist conditions, these spots become covered with salmon-colored fungus. Do not work near plants when they are wet. As soon as you spot the problem, apply a fixed copper or sulfur-based fungicide every 7 to 10 days until 3 to 4 weeks before harvest. If this does not control the disease, remove and discard infected plants.

Gradual Wilting of Single Leaf

Bacterial Wilt
When summer squash becomes infected with bacterial wilt, usually a single leaf gradually wilts and dies followed by the vine and then the whole plant. Plants are often stunted. Bacterial wilt cannot be cured. Remove and destroy infected plants immediately. Wash hands and any tools in a bleach solution (one part household bleach to four parts water) before touching any other plants. Bacterial wilt is transmitted by spotted and striped cucumber beetles. Try using a barrier, such as agricultural fleece, to deny the beetles access to plants. Prevent bacterial wilt by following clean garden practices and planting seeds that are certifiably wilt-free.

Downy Purple Spots on Leaves

Downy Mildew
Squash plants infected with downy mildew have irregularly shaped yellow spots on the upper surfaces of their leaves and downy purple spots on the undersides. Seedlings develop purplish lesions on leaves and stems, and a white downy substance covers these areas. The disease spreads from the crown to the new growth. Plants die very rapidly after contracting downy mildew. If you catch the infection early, apply a copper-based fungicide to diseased and surrounding plants every 7 to 10 days until harvest. Remove and destroy any plants with a serious infection.

Yellow Spots on Leaves

Mosaic

Mosaic is most common in straightneck and crookneck summer squash. Yellow spots appear on leaves and sometimes on fruit. Plants are stunted. Mosaic cannot be cured. Remove and destroy infected and surrounding plants. Resistant varieties are available. Aphids and cucumber beetles spread mosaic. Control aphids with sprays of water or applications of insecticidal soap every 7 to 10 days until harvest, and prevent cucumber beetles with barriers, such as agricultural fleece.

White Spots on Undersides of Leaves

Powdery Mildew

Squash plants infected with powdery mildew develop round, white spots on the undersides of leaves. Eventually the entire leaf becomes covered with powdery mildew. Fruit ripens prematurely and has poor flavor and texture. Use resistant varieties. As soon as you discover the disease, remove and destroy the infected parts. Disinfect your pruning tool in a bleach solution (one part household bleach to four parts water) after each cut. In addition to pruning, apply a sulfur-based fungicide twice, 5 to 7 days apart, if you are growing a sulfur-tolerant variety (check with your County Extension agent), or use a copper-based fungicide every 7 to 10 days until 3 to 4 weeks before harvest. Researchers in Japan found that a baking-soda spray applied once a week controlled powdery mildew in cucurbits. To make the solution, mix 1 teaspoon of baking soda in 1 quart of water. Limit overhead sprinkling to early in the day, and do not work around plants when they are wet. Thin plants to let in sun and air.

Dark, Oozing Spots on Squash

Scab

Scab produces water-soaked spots on leaves, which may cause them to wilt. Stems may develop small cankers. Young squash develop gray, slightly sunken spots. As the plant matures, these spots darken, become more sunken, and develop a greenish velvety mold. There is no cure for scab. Remove and destroy infected plants. Try to prevent scab by following good fall cleanup practices and by using a 3-year crop rotation plan.

HARVEST AND STORAGE

When to Harvest

Summer squash tastes best when young and tender, about 8 inches long. Fruit should be firm and glossy, and the rind dark green or bright yellow and tender. You should be able to dent the rind easily with your thumbnail. Patty Pan squash should be light yellow in color and 4 inches or less in diameter.

Poor Flavor

Low Air Temperature

If you are having a cold summer, you may have trouble with warm weather crops such as squash. These plants will delay their ripening and will produce flat-flavored fruit.

Yield for 25-Foot Row   20 to 40 pounds
Volume vs. Weight   1 bushel equals 40 pounds.
Weight of 1-Quart Canning Jar   2 to 4 pounds
Number of Quarts Stored from 1 Bushel   10 to 20
Best Fresh Storage Method   Refrigerate summer squash in plastic bags; it will keep for 5 to 10 days.
Seed Storage   4 to 5 years

Squash, Winter

Cucurbita maxima (Buttercup, Hubbard);
C. mixta (Cushaw); *C. moschata* (Butternut); *C. pepo* (Acorn)

DESCRIPTION AND ENVIRONMENT

Height   12 to 15 inches
Spread   12 to 20 square feet, depending on variety.

Root Depth   Most of the roots of winter squash are in the top 12 inches of the soil, but the taproot can grow from 2 to 3 feet deep.
Shade Tolerance   Needs full sun.
Frost Tolerance   Very tender; cannot tolerate frost.
Preferred pH   6.0 to 8.0

PLANTING

Spring Planting Time   2 weeks after last expected frost.
Fall Planting Time   13 weeks before first expected frost.
Planting Depth   ½ inch
Spacing of Plants in Rows   24 to 48 inches
Spacing of Plants in Beds   24 to 36 inches
Best Soil Temperature for Germination   65°F to 85°F
Best Soil Temperature for Growing 75°F to 85°F
Best Air Temperature for Growing Day, 70°F to 85°F; night, 60°F to 75°F.
Days to Germination   4 to 10
Weeks to Transplanting   3 to 4
Days to Maturity   85 to 100; 60 to 80 after transplanting.
Greenhouse Varieties   Squash does not grow well in the greenhouse.
Container Varieties   Space-saving bush varieties such as Butterbush grow well in containers.
Container Size   24 inches deep.

PLANT MANAGEMENT

Water Requirements for Good Production

Make sure the plants get 1 inch of water every week from rain or by watering. (See chapter 8 for more information on watering.)

Water Requirements for Maximum Production

Winter squash likes lots of water. For maximum production, give your plants 1 to 1½ inches of water each week. Critical watering periods are during bud development and flowering.

Feeding Requirements for Good Production

Apply compost or a slow-acting general-purpose fertilizer in the spring, and then give your plants supplemental light feedings (side-dressings or foliar spray) monthly throughout the growing season. (See chapter 8 for more information on feeding.)

Feeding Requirements for Maximum Production

Winter squash is a heavy feeder. In addition to the spring feeding mentioned above, it likes a light supplement every 2 weeks during the growing season. Important periods for giving plants supplemental feedings are when plants start to produce vines and at blossom set. Apply a foliar spray of liquid seaweed extract two or three times during the growing season.

MOST COMMON INSECT PESTS

Foliage Curls, Puckers, Turns Yellow

Aphid

If the foliage on your plants curls, puckers, and turns yellow, and the foliage and blooms become stunted, look for ants. They are a sign that your plants have aphids. Ants are attracted to a sticky honeydew secreted by aphids. These insects are about the size of a pinhead and have soft, pear-shaped bodies. They may be green, brown, or pink. You will find them in clusters on the undersides of young leaves. For light infestations, spray the plants vigorously with water in the early morning three times, once every other day. For heavy infestations, apply a commercial insecticidal soap every 2 to 3 days until aphids are under control.

Holes in Leaves

Corn Earworm

Corn earworms chew holes in the leaves of winter squash plants, and they damage buds and young plants. Plant growth may be stunted. The corn earworm is 1½ inches long and may be white, green, or red. It has four prolegs and has spines along its body. Apply a light horticultural oil spray mixed with *Bacillus thuringiensis* (BT) every 2 weeks until the pest is removed.

Plant Dies of Disease

Cucumber Beetle

The cucumber beetle causes minor physical damage to plants, but it can spread diseases that quickly kill the plants. It is ¼ inch long, oblong, and yellow with black stripes or spots. The best way to control cucumber beetles and the diseases they carry is to prevent them from feeding on young plants. Spread a covering, such as agricultural fleece, over your plants from germination until the plants start to bloom. If your plants do become infested with cucumber beetles, dust frequently with pyrethrum to control adults and larvae.

Resistant Varieties. Varieties resistant to the spotted cucumber beetle include Blue Hubbard, Green Hubbard, and Royal Acorn.

Those resistant to the striped cucumber beetle include Butternut and Royal Acorn.

Weakened Plants

Leafhopper

Both adult leafhoppers and nymphs pierce leaves, buds, and stems and suck the sap and chlorophyll from cells, causing plants to weaken. Adults are green, wedge-shaped insects, ¼ to ⅓ inch long, that hold their wings in a rooflike position above their bodies. They are very active and move sideways. Nymphs resemble adults. To control serious infestations, apply insecticidal soap laced with isopropyl alcohol. In early spring, apply a preventive spray of insecticidal soap and seaweed extract, and cover seedlings with an agricultural fleece barrier for the first month of growth to deny leafhoppers access to your plants.

Skeletonized Leaves

Mexican Bean Beetle

If the leaves of squash plants look skeletonized, check your plants for the Mexican bean beetle. The adult is ¼ inch long, round, and has yellow to gold to copper coloring with 16 black dots in three rows down its back. It looks somewhat like a lady bug. It lays yellow eggs in clusters on the undersides of leaves. The hump-backed, fuzzy larvae are orange or yellow and measure about ⅓ inch in length. Both the adults and larvae chew holes in the leaves. To control Mexican bean beetles, handpick early arrivals, with special attention to the easy-to-spot bright yellow eggs. If the infestation gets out of control, make two applications of pyrethrum, 3 days apart.

Wilted, Dried-up Leaves

Squash Bug

The leaves on plants infested with squash bugs wilt, dry up, and turn black, and damage increases until the vine dies. Adults are flat-backed, shield-shaped, brown to black bugs with a light-colored outline on their abdomens. They are ½ to ¾ inch long and lay brown or red shiny eggs on the undersides of leaves. Adults and nymphs suck juices from leaves, causing them to wilt and dry up. To control infestations,

handpick pests from the undersides of leaves. If this doesn't work, apply insecticidal soap every 2 to 3 days for 2 weeks. In spring, apply a preventive spray of insecticidal soap and seaweed extract (see the entry Squash Bug in chapter 4) and cover plants with a barrier, such as agricultural fleece, to deny squash bugs access to your plants. Remove the barrier when plants begin to bloom.

Sudden Wilting of Plant

Squash Vine Borer

Sudden wilting of all or part of a squash vine can be caused by squash vine borers. You can tell borers are at work by the moist, sawdustlike debris, called frass, piled up outside their small holes. Squash vine borers are fat, white caterpillars with brown heads, about 1 inch long. They tunnel into the stems to feed. The adult is an orange-and-black, clear-winged moth with black stripes on its abdomen. It lays brown, flat eggs on the stem. Inject *Bacillus thuringiensis* (BT) into the stem of infested plants with a hypodermic needle. Slit the stems, remove the borers, and cover the wounds with soil. Try to deny the moth access to the plant with an agricultural fleece or netting barrier, which must be removed at flowering to allow pollination.
Resistant Varieties. Butternut and Hubbard.

Discolored Blossoms

Thrip

Thrips puncture petals and leaves to suck the sap, causing considerable discoloration and disfiguration. Leaves may become bleached and will wilt. Thrips are only 1/25 inch long. What is visible are their dark fecal pellets. To control them, spray with insecticidal soap every 3 days for 2 weeks. For serious infestations, use pyrethrum.

Weakened Plants, Yellow Leaves

Whitefly

Plants that have whiteflies weaken, their leaves turn yellow, and they die. Honeydew secreted by whiteflies encourages fungus. Molds often develop following an attack. Adults are about the size of a pinhead, and mothlike, with dusty white wings. When an infested plant is shaken, it appears as if dandruff were flying off the leaves. Nymphs are yellowish, legless, flat, and oval, resembling scale at certain stages. To control infestations, spray plants with insecticidal soap spray every 2 to 3 days for 2 weeks. Use it also early in the season on seedlings to prevent whiteflies. Spray every 2 weeks for the first month of the plants' lives. Pyrethrum may be used as a last resort. Make two applications, 3 to 4 days apart.

MOST COMMON DISEASES

Water-soaked Spots on Leaves

Angular Leaf Spot
Plants infected with angular leaf spot develop water-soaked spots on their leaves, which turn tan and gray, and then drop out, leaving ragged holes. Spots form on the fruit. The spots are rounded and may exude a thick ooze. The infection will spread to the seed cavity, making the squash inedible. Angular leaf spot cannot be cured. Immediately remove and destroy infected plants.

Brown Leaves

Anthracnose
The anthracnose fungus attacks all parts of the plant above the ground. Small water-soaked spots develop on the leaves. They enlarge and turn brown, and eventually the leaves shrivel and die. Sunken lesions form on the stems, and circular, black, sunken spots appear on the fruit. During moist conditions, these spots become covered with salmon-colored fungus. Do not work near plants when they are wet. As soon as you spot the problem, apply a fixed copper or sulfur-based fungicide every 7 to 10 days. If this does not control the disease, remove and discard infected plants.

Gradual Wilting of Single Leaf

Bacterial Wilt
When winter squash becomes infected with bacterial wilt, usually a single leaf gradually wilts and dies, followed by the vine and then the whole plant. Plants are often stunted. Bacterial wilt cannot be cured. Remove and destroy infected plants immediately. Wash hands and any tools in a bleach solution (one part household bleach to four parts water) before touching any other plants. Bacterial wilt is transmitted by spotted and striped cucumber beetles. Try using a barrier, such as agricultural fleece, to deny the beetles access to plants. Prevent bacterial wilt by following clean garden practices and planting seeds that are certifiably wilt-free.
Resistant Varieties. Buttercup, Butternut, and Table Queen.

Downy Purple Spots on Leaves

Downy Mildew
Squash plants infected with downy mildew have irregularly shaped yellow spots on the upper surfaces of their leaves and downy purple spots on the undersides. Seedlings develop purplish lesions on leaves and stems, and a white downy substance covers these areas. The disease spreads from the crown to the new growth. Plants die very rapidly after contracting downy mildew. If you catch the infection early, apply a copper-based fungicide to diseased and surrounding plants every 7 to 10 days until harvest. Remove and destroy any plants with a serious infection.

Yellow Spots on Leaves

Mosaic
Winter squash infected with mosaic develop yellow spots on leaves and sometimes on the fruit. Plants are stunted. Mosaic cannot be cured. Remove and destroy infected and surrounding plants. Resistant varieties are available. Aphids and cucumber beetles spread mosaic. Control aphids with sprays of water or applications of insecticidal soap every 7 to 10 days until harvest, and prevent cucumber beetles with barriers, such as agricultural fleece.

White Spots on Undersides of Leaves

Powdery Mildew

Squash plants infected with powdery mildew develop round, white spots on the undersides of leaves. Eventually the entire leaf becomes covered with powdery mildew. Fruit ripens prematurely and has poor flavor and texture. Use resistant varieties. As soon as you discover the disease, remove and destroy the infected parts. Disinfect your pruning tool in a bleach solution (one part household bleach to four parts water) after each cut. In addition to pruning, apply a sulfur-based fungicide if you are growing a sulfur-tolerant variety (check with your County Extension agent), or use a copper-based fungicide every 7 to 10 days. Researchers in Japan found that a baking-soda spray applied once a week controlled powdery mildew in cucurbits. To make the solution, mix 1 teaspoon of baking soda in 1 quart of water. Limit overhead sprinkling to early in the day, and do not work around plants when they are wet. Thin plants to let in sun and air.

Dark, Oozing Spots on Squash

Scab

Scab produces water-soaked spots on leaves, which may cause them to wilt. Stems may develop small cankers. Young squash develop gray, slightly sunken spots. As the plant matures, these spots darken, become more sunken, and develop a greenish vel-vety mold. There is no cure for scab. Remove and destroy infected plants.

HARVEST AND STORAGE

When to Harvest

Winter squash is ready to harvest when the stem begins to shrivel and takes on a grayish color. Press the rind with your fingernail; it should resist denting. Pick winter squash before the first hard frost and cure before storing by letting it lie in the sun for at least 3 days, turning it each day. The Acorn, Buttercup, and Hubbard squash have a dark green rind. The Butternut has a beige rind, and the Chayote, a pale green rind.

Yield for 25-Foot Row   30 to 40 pounds
Volume vs. Weight   1 bushel equals 11 pounds.
Weight of 1-Quart Canning Jar   1½ to 2½ pounds
Number of Quarts Stored from 1 Bushel   3 to 7
Best Long-Term Storage Method   Store winter squash in a cool, dry place; it will keep for up to 5 months.
Seed Storage   4 to 5 years

VEGETABLE **Sweet Potato**   *Ipomoea batatas*

DESCRIPTION AND ENVIRONMENT

Height   10 to 12 inches
Spread   4 to 8 square feet
Shade Tolerance   Needs full sun.

Frost Tolerance   Very tender; cannot tolerate any frost.
Preferred pH   5.0 to 6.0

PLANTING

Spring Planting Time 1 to 3 weeks after last expected frost. If you are growing sprouts for transplanting, detach sprouts from the seed potato when they are 4 to 8 inches tall and have four to five leaves and roots. Plant them in an individual pot until you are ready to put them into the garden.

Planting Depth 4 to 5 inches
Spacing of Plants in Rows 12 to 16 inches

Spacing of Plants in Beds 10 to 12 inches
Best Soil Temperature for Germination 60°F to 85°F
Best Soil Temperature for Growing 75°F to 85°F
Best Air Temperature for Growing 65°F to 95°F
Days to Germination 8 to 12 days
Weeks to Transplanting 6 to 8
Days to Maturity 150 to 175 after direct seeding; 100 to 125 after transplanting.
Greenhouse Varieties Sweet potatoes cannot be grown in the greenhouse.
Container Varieties Sweet potatoes cannot be grown in containers.

PLANT MANAGEMENT

Water Requirements

Make sure sweet potatoes get 1 inch of water every week from rain or by watering. (See chapter 8 for more information on watering.)

Feeding Requirements

Apply compost or a slow-acting general-purpose fertilizer in spring. Sweet potatoes are light feeders and need little or no supplemental fertilizer. Apply a foliar spray of liquid seaweed extract two or three times during the growing season. (See chapter 8 for more information on feeding.)

MOST COMMON INSECT PESTS

Stunted Plant, Yellow Leaves

Nematode
Plants infected with nematodes become stunted and the leaves yellow prematurely. The roots of affected plants have root knots. If they do survive to

maturity, the plants will produce low yields. Nematodes are microscopic whitish, translucent worms, barely visible to the naked eye. They live in the soil and attack plant roots. Use resistant varieties. Work 3 to 4 inches of compost (especially leaf mold) into the soil, fertilize with fish emulsion, and plant early in the season.

Holes in Leaves, Pitted Potatoes

Weevil

If the leaves of your sweet potatoes have holes chewed in them and sweet potatoes are pitted, suspect the sweet potato weevil. This pest has a dark blue head and wing covers, and a reddish orange body and legs. It is about ¼ inch long. It feeds at night and hides during the day. As weevils appear, spray with pyrethrum twice, 3 to 4 days apart.

Wilting, Poor Development of Plants

Wireworm

If your sweet potato plants show signs of wilting and poor development, they may be infested with wireworms. The larvae of click beetles, these pests are ⅓ to 1½ inches long, dark brown to yellowish, jointed, hard shelled, and cylindrical. They chew on the underground parts of the plants. The best control is to trap wireworms with pieces of potato speared on the ends of sticks. (See the entry Wireworm in chapter 4 for information on how to use potato traps.)

develops black cankers on the subsurface portions of the stem. Sulfur-based fungicides will control black rot; apply them every 7 to 10 days until 3 to 4 weeks before harvest.
Resistant Varieties. Allgold.

Pitted Potatoes

Soil Rot

Sweet potatoes infected with soil rot, or scurf, develop pits on tubers. Dark lesions may form on the underground portions of stems. By the time the disease is detected, it is too late to control it. Remove and destroy all infected plants. Maintain soil acidity below 5.5 and use resistant varieties.
Resistant Varieties. Allgold.

Young Plants Die

Stem Rot

Young plants infected with stem rot may die after transplanting. The surviving plants first show a few bright leaves around the crown, then dwarfed leaves and a dwarfed crown, and later, badly rotted stems. Remove and destroy infected plants. To prevent stem rot, plant resistant varieties and follow good fall cleanup practices.
Resistant Varieties. Southern Queen, Triumph, and Yellow Stransburg.

MOST COMMON DISEASES

Yellowish Foliage

Black Rot (fungal)

Symptoms of black rot in sweet potatoes appear on the foliage and on the fleshy roots. The foliage becomes yellowish and sickly. On roots, depressed circular spots of various sizes develop. These spots appear grayish black when dry and greenish black when moist. The entire plant turns yellow and often

HARVEST AND STORAGE

When to Harvest

Harvest sweet potatoes after frost kills the vines. Tubers should be medium-sized (6 to 8 inches), smooth, firm, and should have a good shape. Those potatoes that you store should not be washed, and should be handled carefully to prevent damage. Cure sweet potatoes by placing them in an unused cold frame or a heated room at 85°F to 90°F for 7 to 10 days.

Volume vs. Weight 1 bushel equals 50 pounds.

Weight of 1-Quart Canning Jar 2 to 3 pounds

Number of Quarts Stored from 1 Bushel 16 to 25

Best Fresh Storage Method Store sweet potatoes in a cool, dry place, making sure they don't touch each other; they will keep for 4 months.

Best Long-Term Storage Method Sweet potatoes can be frozen for up to 6 months, or processed and canned for over a year.

VEGETABLE *Tomato* *Lycopersicon lycopersicum*

DESCRIPTION AND ENVIRONMENT

Height Determinate, 3 to 4 feet; indeterminate, 7 to 15 feet.

Spread 24 to 36 inches

Root Depth Most of the roots are found in the top 8 inches, but some fibrous spreading roots extend 4 to 6 feet deep.

Shade Tolerance Needs 8 or more hours of full sun a day.

Frost Tolerance Tender, cannot tolerate any frost.

Preferred pH 6.0 to 7.0

PLANTING

Spring Planting Time 2 to 4 weeks after frost-free date.

Planting Depth ¼ to ½ inch

Spacing of Plants in Rows 18 to 24 inches

Spacing of Plants in Beds 12 to 18 inches (intensive planting on trellis).

Best Soil Temperature for Germination 65°F to 85°F

Best Soil Temperature for Growing 70°F to 80°F

Best Air Temperature for Growing Day, 65°F to 85°F; night, 60°F to 70°F.

Days to Germination   6 to 14
Weeks to Transplanting   6 to 10
Multiple Transplants   Tomatoes benefit by being transplanted two or three times before finally being placed in the garden.
Days to Maturity   70 to 90, after direct seeding; 70, after transplanting.
Greenhouse Varieties   Try Patio, Small Fry, and Tiny Tim.
Container Varieties   Try Patio VF, Pixie, Small Fry VFN, Sweet 100, Toy Boy, Tumblin' Tom, Yellow Pear, and others designed for containers.
Container Size   Dwarf varieties, 6 inches deep; standard varieties, at least 24 inches deep.

Delayed Ripening, Flat Flavor

Cool Air Temperatures

If you are having a cold summer (average temperature 65°F or below), you may have trouble with warm weather crops such as tomatoes. Ripening will be delayed and flavor of fruit will be flat. Cover plants with agricultural fleece at dusk to hold in extra heat overnight. Remove fleece in the morning.

Blistered Skin

Sunscald

Blistering of the skin on tomatoes is a sign of sunscald. Tomatoes must have some protection from extended exposure to the direct rays of the sun. Training a trellised tomato plant to two stems is one solution. Two stems are left unpruned instead of one. This provides enough foliage to eliminate most sunscald problems, and gives you a greater yield from each plant.

PLANT MANAGEMENT

Watering Requirements for Good Production

Make sure the plants get 1 inch of water per week by watering or from the rain. (See chapter 8 for more information on watering.)

Watering Requirements for Maximum Production

This plant likes lots of water, so for maximum production give it between 1 and 1½ inches of water each week. During the period from flowering through harvest, it is critical that your tomatoes get an even supply of water. Older, late-maturing varieties require less water.

Feeding Requirements for Good Production

Apply compost or a slow-acting general-purpose fertilizer in spring, and give plants supplemental light feedings (either side-dressings or foliar spray) monthly throughout the growing season. (See chapter 8 for more information on feeding.)

Feeding Requirements for Maximum Production

This plant is a heavy feeder, and, in addition to the spring feeding mentioned above, it likes a light supplement every 2 weeks during its growing season. Periods during which supplemental feeding are especially important occur 2 to 3 weeks after transplanting, before the first harvesting, and 2 weeks after the first harvesting. Go light on nitrogen. Spray plants with liquid seaweed extract two or three times during the growing season.

Catfacing

Environmental Stress

Catfacing, a spiderweb of tan scars on the fruit skin, results when environmental stresses during bloom cause young fruit to develop more than the usual number of cells. Exposure of plants to temperatures below 55°F or above 85°F are the most frequent causes, but drought, high winds, and the herbicide 2-4-D can also produce catfacing. Heavy use of fertilizers high in ammonia, such as uncomposted poultry manure, may contribute to the problem. The best way to prevent catfacing is to plant resistant varieties.

Resistant Varieties. Big Set, Burpee's VF, Flora-Dade, Floradel, and Floramerica.

Pale Leaves, Turning Yellow

Nitrogen Deficiency
If the leaves of your tomato plants are pale and turning yellow, especially the lower leaves, suspect a nitrogen deficiency. Plants will grow slowly and produce small leaves. The stems are stunted and brown, and flower buds turn yellow and drop off. Yield will be reduced. To remedy the problem quickly, spray plants with diluted fish emulsion or another liquid fertilizer. (See chapter 8 for more information on nitrogen deficiency.)

Reddish Purple Color on Leaves

Phosphorus Deficiency
A reddish purple color on the leaves, especially on the undersides, veins, and stems, indicates a phosphorus deficiency. In addition, the leaves are small and the stems thin and fibrous. Tomato plants will be late in flowering and producing fruit. Phosphorus deficiencies generally occur in acid soils and temporarily in cold, wet soils. To remedy the problem quickly, spray plants with diluted fish emulsion or a liquid fertilizer, and add wood ashes to the soil. (See chapter 8 for more information on phosphorus deficiency.)

Slow Growth, Low Yield

Potassium Deficiency
Slow growth and low yield are signs of a potassium deficiency. Young leaves become crinkled, and older leaves turn pale grayish green and develop a yellowish green color along the margins. Bronze spots appear between longer veins on the leaves. These spots may become bright orange and turn brittle. The leaves turn brown and die. Stems grow hard and woody, and fail to increase in diameter. Roots are brown and underdeveloped, and the fruit may ripen unevenly and lack solidity. To solve this problem quickly, apply a foliar spray of fish emulsion or some other liquid fertilizer, and side-dress the plants with

wood ashes. (See chapter 8 for more information on potassium deficiency.)

MOST COMMON INSECT PESTS

Foliage Curls, Puckers, Turns Yellow

Aphid
If the foliage on your plants curls, puckers, and turns yellow, and the foliage and blooms become stunted, look for ants. They are a sign that your plants have aphids. Ants are attracted to a sticky honeydew secreted by aphids. These insects are about the size of a pinhead and have soft, pear-shaped bodies. They may be green, brown, or pink. You will find them in clusters on the undersides of young leaves. For light infestations, spray the plants vigorously with water in the early morning three times, once every other day. For heavy infestations, apply a commercial insecticidal soap every 2 to 3 days until aphids are under control.

Defoliated Plants

Colorado Potato Beetle
Defoliated plants and skeletonized leaves are signs of Colorado potato beetles. These insects are 1/3 inch long and have a convex shape. They are yellow with black stripes and an orange head covering. The best control is to handpick the first arrivals in spring and use pyrethrum spray if the infestation becomes heavy. Make two applications, 3 to 4 days apart.

Damage to Buds and Young Plants

Corn Earworm
Damaged buds and young plants are signs of corn earworms. Plant growth may be stunted. The corn earworm is 1½ inches long and may be white, green, or red. It has four prolegs, and has spines along its body. To control corn earworms, apply *Bacillus thuringiensis* (BT) every 10 to 14 days until the pest is removed.

Seedling Stems Severed

Cutworm

Cutworms completely sever the stems of seedlings and transplants at or below the soil surface. They are 1- to 2-inch, dull-colored, plump, soft-bodied larvae that curl up when disturbed. Cutworms feed at night and hide in the soil during the day. To control cutworms, use barriers or traps to deny them access to seedlings. To protect individual plants, surround them with a collar, or make a trap by sprinkling cornmeal or bran meal around each plant. (See chapter 4 for more information on collars and meal traps.)

Tiny Holes in Leaves

Flea Beetle

If you find several little holes or perforations in the leaves of your plants, the plants may have flea beetles. Flea beetles are $\frac{1}{10}$ inch long, shiny, and black, and may have yellow or white markings. They are very active and jump like fleas when disturbed. Their feeding can destroy small plants rapidly. Apply pyrethrum to control infestations. Make two applications, 3 to 4 days apart. In the spring, cover plants with a barrier, such as agricultural fleece, to prevent access to your plants.
Resistant Varieties. Oxheart and Pearson A.

Leaves Stippled Yellow

Mite

Leaves of tomato plants infested with mites become stippled, yellow, and dry, and sometimes pale yellow spots or blotches appear. Mites are not insects but arachnids, and are about the size of a grain of black pepper. They may be red, black, or brown. They feed by sucking out the plant's juices. In sucking chlorophyll out of the leaves, they cause small white dots to appear. In addition, they inject toxins into the leaves, which discolors and distorts them. To control infestations, spray plants with a forceful spray of water three times, once every other day, to knock mites from the leaves. If mites are still present, spray with insecticidal soap at least three times every 5 to 7 days.
Resistant Varieties. Campbell 135 and Kewalo.

Stunted Plants, Yellow Leaves

Nematode

Plants infected with nematodes are stunted, the leaves become yellow prematurely, and if they do survive to maturity, they produce low yields. The roots of affected plants have root knots. Nematodes are microscopic whitish, translucent worms, barely visible to the naked eye. They live in the soil and attack the roots of plants. Nematodes cannot be controlled once they have infested a plant. To prevent them, use resistant varieties, add 3 to 4 inches of compost (especially leaf mold) to the soil, fertilize with fish emulsion, and plant early in the season.
Resistant Varieties. Beefmaster, Better Boy, Better Bush, Better Girl, Big Pick, Celebrity, and Dombello.

Large Ragged Holes in Leaves

Slug

Large ragged holes in the leaves of your tomato plants are signs of slugs. They work their way from the bottom of a plant up. Look for trails of slime on the leaves and on the soil near the plants as further evidence of the presence of slugs. Slugs are 1 to 2 inches long and look like snails without shells. They may be brown, gray, white, pale yellow, purple, or nearly black with brown specks. You can control them by handpicking if you get them early in the season. The best way to control their damage is to set up a barrier of hardware cloth, ashes, sand, or some other material to deny them access to the garden. You can also make traps to catch slugs. (See the entry Slug in chapter 4 for information on making slug traps.)

Holes in Leaves

Tomato Hornworm

Holes in leaves and sometimes on fruit are a sign that your tomatoes may be infested with tomato hornworms. To spot them early, look for dark-colored droppings on the foliage, and spray the plants with water, causing the worms to thrash about and give away their location. The tomato hornworm is a large green caterpillar with white stripes and a horn projecting from its rear. It measures 3 to 5 inches long. Hornworms are easy to see, so handpicking early in the season usually controls them. Dusting plants with *Bacillus thuringiensis* (BT) also reduces hornworms; dust plants every 10 to 14 days until pests are gone. If the infestation gets out of hand, use pyrethrum. Apply twice, 3 to 4 days apart.

Weakened Plants, Yellow Leaves

Whitefly

Plants that have whiteflies weaken, their leaves turn yellow, and they die. Honeydew secreted by whiteflies encourages fungus. Molds often develop following an attack. Adults are about the size of a pinhead, and mothlike, with dusty white wings. When an infested plant is shaken, it appears as if dandruff were flying off the leaves. Nymphs are yellowish, legless, flat, and oval, resembling scale at certain stages. To control infestations, spray plants with insecticidal soap spray every 2 to 3 days for 2 weeks. Use it also early in the season to prevent whiteflies. Spray seedlings every 2 weeks for the first months of the plants' lives. Pyrethrum may be used as a last resort. Make two applications, 3 to 4 days apart.

MOST COMMON DISEASES

Water-soaked Spots on Tomatoes

Anthracnose

Depressed, circular, water-soaked spots appear on the ripe or ripening fruit of tomatoes that are infected with anthracnose. These spots look like they were made with a match head or a pencil eraser. The lesions on infected ripe fruit darken from the center outward as the fungus develops. The spots enlarge to about ¼ inch, and the fungus spreads internally to produce soft rot, which causes plant decomposition.

Do not work near plants when they are wet. As soon as you spot the problem, apply a fixed copper or sulfur-based fungicide every 7 to 10 days until 3 to 4 weeks before harvest. If this does not control the disease, remove and discard infected plants.

Plants Do Not Set Fruit

Blossom Drop

Tomato plants that do not set fruit may have blossom drop, an environmental disease. Spray plants with one application of seaweed extract.

Botrytis Fruit Rot

Botrytis starts as blossom blight, causing discolored petals and wilted fruit stems. Small water-soaked spots, most often seen at the base, develop on fruit. They enlarge and eventually become covered with a grayish mold. Sulfur or fixed-copper fungicides provide a good degree of control, provided the application is properly timed so that it catches the fungus early in its spring development. Apply fungicides when symptoms first appear.

Wilting of Leaf Margins

Bacterial Canker

On plants of all sizes, the first symptom of bacterial canker is wilting of the margins of the leaflets and lower leaves. Wilting begins on one side of the leaf; the margins become dry, and eventually entire leaves curl upward, turn brown, wither, and die. Diseased plants may wilt and die early, but many survive, though stunted and wilted. As the disease progresses, cankers form on the stem. Small, raised, snowy dots appear on the surface of the fruit, and the centers of those dots break open and become brown and rough, with the white color persisting as a halo. Fruit that is small, stunted, and deformed has been affected internally. Bacterial canker cannot be cured, so if pruning doesn't stop the disease, the plant must be destroyed. When pruning, clean tools in a bleach solution (one part household bleach to four parts water) after each cut. To prevent bacterial canker, follow good fall cleanup practices and implement a 3- to 4-year crop rotation plan.

Water-soaked Areas on Leaves

Bacterial Spot

The leaves of tomato plants infected with bacterial spot show minute water-soaked areas, which later become angular, turn black, and develop a greasy appearance. On green fruit, minute, black, raised spots develop. These spots enlarge, become irregular in shape, are light brown to black in color, and have a rough, pitted appearance. Bacterial spot cannot be cured. The first line of defense, if the disease is identified early in its development, is to apply a copper-based fungicide every 7 to 10 days until 3 to 4 weeks before harvest. Prune the infected parts immediately, disinfecting tools and hands in a bleach solution (one part household bleach to four parts water) after each cut. If good results don't show up after a second spraying of fungicide, the plant or tree must be destroyed. Try to prevent bacterial spot by following good fall cleanup practices.

Rapid Wilting

Bacterial Wilt

Tomatoes infected with this disease wilt rapidly and die without showing any signs of yellowing or spotting of the leaves. Bacterial wilt is difficult to distinguish from a wilt caused by environmental problems. The difference is that environmental problems occur more slowly. If conditions in your garden are good and you notice *rapid* wilting of your tomato plants, suspect bacterial wilt. Bacterial wilt cannot be cured. Remove infected plants immediately and destroy them. Wash hands and any tools in a bleach solution (one part household bleach to four parts water) before touching other plants. Prevent bacterial wilt by planting resistant varieties and by following good fall cleanup practices.

Blossom End of Tomatoes Darken

Blossom End Rot

The fruit of tomato plants infected with blossom end rot shows darkened areas at the blossom end. These areas eventually become sunken, black, and leathery. Blossom end rot is caused by inconsistent or uneven watering or by a calcium deficiency. Water plants evenly (consistently) and only as needed. Check the pH of the soil; it should be between 6.0 and 7.0. If it's below 6.0, add limestone, which contains calcium.

Resistant Varieties. Flora-Dade, Harvestvee, Hotset, Manalucie, Moira, Olympic, Porter, Summer Prolific, Summerset, and others.

Curled, Twisted Leaves

Curly Top

The foliage of seedlings infected with curly top yellows, curls, and twists, and the seedlings usually die. Leaflets of older plants that become infected twist and roll upward, exposing their undersides. The foliage becomes stiff and leathery, and the entire plant assumes a dull yellow appearance. Branches and stems are abnormally erect. Leaf stalks bend downward and the veins in the leaflets turn purple. Plant growth is stunted, and either no fruit sets, or the fruit that is produced ripens prematurely. Curly top cannot be cured. Remove and destroy infected and surrounding plants. Prevent curly top by growing resistant varieties. Also, control whiteflies and leafhoppers, which can transmit the disease.

Resistant Varieties. Owyhee and Payette.

Seedlings Die

Damping-Off

Seedlings that have damping-off simply topple over. You will see a watery soft rot on the stem at the soil line. There is no cure for this disease. Remove and destroy infected plants. When starting seeds indoors, use commercial potting soil, or pasteurize your own potting soil in an oven. Disinfect tools in a bleach solution (one part household bleach to four parts water). Provide soil with adequate drainage and use a fan for better air circulation. For direct seeding, make sure the soil is well drained and warm. You might try spreading pasteurized soil or a sterile vermiculite in furrows where you plant your seeds.

Dark Spots on Older Leaves

Early Blight
Tomatoes infected by early blight develop collar rot—dark, girdling lesions on the stem at the soil line. The foliage infection appears first as circular or irregular dark spots on older leaves. As these spots enlarge, a series of concentric rings develops, forming a target pattern. Often these spots grow together. Cankers develop on fruit stems, branches, and large stems. Green or ripe fruit cracks at the stem. As soon as you spot early blight, begin applying a copper-based fungicide every 7 to 10 days as directed on the label.
Resistant Varieties. Early Cascade, Floradel, Floramerica, Manalucie, New Hampshire, New Yorker, Nova, Southland, Sprint, Surecrop, Vista, West Virginia, and others.

Yellow Leaves

Fusarium Wilt
Yellowing of the leaves occurs in tomatoes infected with fusarium wilt. This yellowing spreads upward from the base of the plant as the disease progresses. It may occur on only one side of a leaf midrib or on one side of a plant. The leaves wilt noticeably before they die, and the whole plant eventually dies. Some plants will produce some fruit, but in most cases you should remove and destroy infected plants. Fungicides are not effective against fusarium fungi. Prevent fusarium by planting resistant varieties and following sanitary gardening practices.
Resistant Varieties. Ace 55, Beefeater Hybrid, Beefmaster, Better Boy, Better Girl, Burpee's Big Girl, Campbell's 17, Floradel, Homestead, H 1350, KC 146, Kokomo, Manalucie, Manapal, Marion, and Supersonic.

Water-soaked Patches on Older Leaves

Late Blight
Greenish black, water-soaked patches develop on the older leaves of tomatoes infected with late blight. These spots enlarge, and in moist weather may show white, downy growth of the fungus on their surface. On the fruit, you will see large dark-colored spots that are firm and have a rough surface. Use a copper-based fungicide every 7 to 10 days as directed on the label.
Resistant Varieties. Early: Floradel, Manahill, Manalucie, and Southland. Late: New Hampshire, New Yorker, Nova, Surecrop, and West Virginia.

Yellow, Bushy Plants

Mosaic
Stunted, yellow, bushy plants and a shoestring appearance of the leaves are signs of mosaic in tomatoes. Mosaic cannot be cured. Remove and destroy the infected and surrounding plants. Aphids spread mosaic. Control aphids with a spray of water or applications of insecticidal soap every 7 to 10 days until harvest.
Resistant Varieties. Beefmaster, Moto-red, Ohio M-12, Ohio M-39, Park's Whopper, Quick Pick, Tropic, Vendor, and others.

Thickened, Upward-rolled Older Leaves

Psyllid Yellows
The older leaves of infected tomatoes thicken and roll upward. Young leaves curl, the plant is spindly, and the fruit is soft. This is a disease carried to the plant by psyllids, so to prevent it from occurring, control psyllids with a garlic spray, applied weekly throughout the season if necessary. Keep the area free of ground cherry and other weeds.

Water-soaked Spots

Septoria Leaf Spot
The leaf spots of septoria begin as small yellow specks, which later enlarge, becoming brown with a yellow border. They can be either circular or irregular in shape, and often have a black dot in the center. You will see them scattered all over the older leaves of infected tomato plants. Apply copper dust or a liquid copper spray fungicide every 7 to 10 days after discovering the disease until 3 to 4 weeks before harvesting.

White or Yellowish Patch on Tomatoes

Sunscald

Sunscald is an environmental disease that most commonly appears on green fruit. A white or yellowish patch develops on the side of fruit facing the sun. In severe cases, the affected area shrinks and forms a large grayish spot with a papery surface. To prevent sunscald, prune above the first group of leaves on the sucker rather than at the base when you prune suckers. This will provide more foliage to shade tomatoes.

Malformed Leaves on Young Plants

Tobacco Mosaic

The symptoms of tobacco mosaic vary. Young plants have malformed leaflets. Older plants exhibit mottling (dark green), and the leaflets tend to be stringy and fernlike or pointed. Overall, the plants exhibit a slightly grayish appearance, and the fruit may be mottled, or may ripen unevenly. Tobacco mosaic cannot be cured. Remove and destroy the infected and surrounding plants. To prevent tobacco mosaic, plant resistant varieties, follow good fall cleanup practices, and keep tobacco users away from your garden.

Resistant Varieties. Big Pick, Buffalo, Celebrity, Dombello, Park's Extra Early Hybrid, Sierra, and Vendor.

HARVEST AND STORAGE

When to Harvest

Ripe fruit will have rich color and feel firm. The size of ripened tomatoes is governed by variety. Tomatoes will ripen after picking, but vine-ripened fruit tastes the best.

Yield for 25-Foot Row   30 to 50 pounds
Volume vs. Weight   1 bushel equals 53 pounds.
Weight of 1-Quart Canning Jar   2 to 3 pounds
Number of Quarts Stored from 1 Bushel   17 to 26
Best Fresh Storage Method   Keep unripe tomatoes at room temperature but out of the sun. When they ripen, refrigerate tomatoes. They will keep for a week.
Best Long-Term Storage Methods   Tomatoes can be frozen, dried, canned, or pickled, and will keep for 8 to 12 months.
Seed Storage   2 years

NOTES AND RESEARCH

Research is showing that using air currents to vibrate seedlings reduces their spindliness. In one study, seedlings, after developing their first true leaves, were set by a fan for two 1-hour periods (one in the morning and one in the evening) every day. After 6 weeks, their height was measured and was found to be 40 percent less than that of controls, which received no vibration treatment.

VEGETABLE  *Brassica rapa*, Rapifera Group

DESCRIPTION AND ENVIRONMENT

Height   10 to 15 inches
Spread   6 to 8 inches
Shade Tolerance   Needs only 5 hours of sun a day (partial shade).
Frost Tolerance   Very hardy
Preferred pH   6.0 to 8.0

PLANTING

Spring Planting Time   4 to 6 weeks before last expected frost.

Fall Planting Time   6 to 8 weeks before first expected frost.

Succession Planting   Plant every 3 weeks until midsummer.

Planting Depth   ½ inch

Spacing of Plants in Rows   2 to 3 inches

Spacing of Plants in Beds   2 to 3 inches

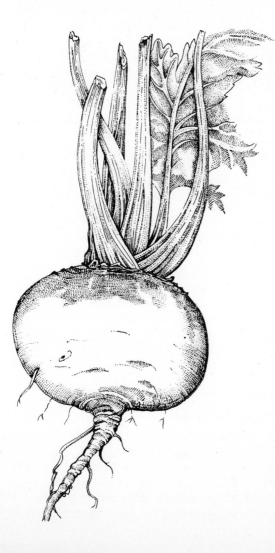

Best Soil Temperature for Germination   60°F to 75°F

Days to Germination   3 to 10

Days to Maturity   30 to 75

Greenhouse Varieties   Turnips do not grow well in the greenhouse.

Container Varieties   Any variety can be grown in containers.

Container Size   10 to 12 inches deep.

PLANT MANAGEMENT

Water Requirements

Make sure the plants get 1 inch of water every week from rain or by watering. Periods during which watering is critical occur at the beginning of root development and during root enlargement. (See chapter 8 for more information on watering.)

Feeding Requirements

Apply compost or a slow-acting general-purpose fertilizer in spring. Turnips are light feeders. They need little or no supplemental fertilizer over and above the one application of slow-acting fertilizer in the spring. Spray plants with liquid seaweed extract two or three times during the growing season. (See chapter 8 for more information on feeding.)

Black Heart

Boron Deficiency

Turnips grown in a boron-deficient soil will have a very slow growth rate. Dieback and leaf distortion will occur and black heart (a blackening of the inside of the turnip) will develop. To remedy this problem quickly, apply a foliar spray of liquid seaweed extract every 2 weeks until the symptoms disappear. For long-term results, add granite dust to the soil, or plant cover crops of vetch or clover in the fall. Add rock phosphate to the compost pile and to the garden in the fall. Do not add lime to boron-deficient soil, as the soil is probably already close to alkaline. (See chapter 8 for more information on boron deficiency.)

MOST COMMON INSECT PESTS

Foliage Curls, Puckers, Turns Yellow

Aphid

If the foliage on your plants curls, puckers, and turns yellow, and the foliage and blooms become stunted, look for ants. They are a sign that your plants have aphids. Ants are attracted to a sticky honeydew secreted by aphids. These insects are about the size of a pinhead and have soft, pear-shaped bodies. They may be green, brown, or pink. Cabbage aphids also attack turnips. They are green to powdery blue in color and are covered with a fine whitish wax. You will find aphids in clusters on the undersides of young leaves. For light infestations, spray the plants vigorously with water in the early morning three times, once every other day. For heavy infestations, apply a commercial insecticidal soap every 2 to 3 days until aphids are under control.

Small Ragged Holes in Leaves

Cabbage Looper

Small ragged holes in leaves indicate that your plants may be infested with cabbage loopers. The cabbage looper is a 1½-inch-long light green caterpillar with long yellowish stripes on its back. It loops as it walks. Spray *Bacillus thuringiensis* (BT) on plants every 2 weeks until the problem is solved.

Plant Wilts during Heat of Day

Cabbage Maggot

Brown tunnels in the stem just below soil level indicate cabbage maggots. Seedlings become yellow, growth is stunted, and plants lack vigor. The infested plants wilt during the heat of the day, and eventually die. The cabbage maggot is a small, white, legless worm about ¼ inch long. The adult resembles a housefly. Maggots tunnel into plant roots and stems. Bacterial diseases such as black leg, which causes dark patches on leaves, and soft rot, which causes plant decomposition, may result, causing the plants to wilt. To control infestations, mix heaping teaspoonfuls of wood ashes 1 inch into the soil around the plant or pour a cupful of lime drench (1 cup of lime in 1 quart of water; let sit overnight) around the root ball of each plant. The best control is to prevent flies from laying eggs in the first place. Spread a barrier, such as agricultural fleece, over the plants, or place a collar around the stem of each plant. (See chapter 4 for instructions on making these collars.)

Resistant Varieties. Petrosky.

Seedling Stems Severed

Cutworm

Cutworms completely sever the stems of seedlings and transplants at or below the soil surface. They are 1- to 2-inch, dull-colored, plump, soft-bodied larvae that curl up when disturbed. Cutworms feed at night and hide in the soil during the day. To control cutworms, use barriers or traps to deny them access to seedlings. To protect individual plants, surround them with a collar, or make a trap by sprinkling cornmeal or bran meal around each plant. (See chapter 4 for more information on collars and meal traps.)

Tiny Holes in Leaves

Flea Beetle

If you find many little holes or perforations in the leaves of your plants, the plants may have flea beetles. Flea beetles are ¹⁄₁₀ inch long, shiny, and black, and may have yellow or white markings. They are very active and jump like fleas when disturbed. Their feeding can destroy small plants rapidly. Apply pyrethrum to control infestations. Make two applications, 3 to 4 days apart. In the spring, cover plants with a barrier, such as agricultural fleece, to prevent access to your plants.

Wilted Leaves with Black Spots

Harlequin Bug

If the leaves of your plants develop white blotches or black spots, and then wilt and die, suspect the harlequin bug. This insect is ¼ inch long and shaped like a shield, with a triangle on its back. It has patterned markings in black and red. Harlequin bugs emit a foul odor. To control infestations, spray plants every 2 to 3 days for 2 weeks with an insecticidal soap laced with isopropyl alcohol. Apply insecticidal soap twice, 5 to 7 days apart, in early spring to prevent harlequin bugs.

Resistant Varieties. Amber Globe, Purple Top White Globe, and White Egg.

Large Ragged Holes in Leaves

Imported Cabbage Worm

Imported cabbage worms chew large ragged holes in turnip leaves, trailing dark green frass, or excrement, behind them. The worm is light green with one yellow stripe, and measures 1¼ inches long. The adult is a common white butterfly with three to four black spots on its wings that is active during the day. To control infestations, apply *Bacillus thuringiensis* (BT) every 10 to 14 days until the pest is gone. Prevent cabbage worms by spraying transplants with BT every 2 weeks early in the season and covering them with an agricultural fleece barrier.

White or Brown Tunnels in Leaves

Leafminer

White or brown tunnels or blotches on leaves are signs that your turnips have leafminers. The leaves may turn yellow and blotchy and look blistered or curled. Leafminers are small black flies, usually with yellow stripes. The tiny yellowish larvae feed between the upper and lower surfaces of leaves, causing the tunnels or blotches to appear. You may also find stem damage below the soil. Remove the infested leaves before the larvae mature. The best way to control leafminers, though, is to screen out the adult flies by covering seeded areas with agricultural fleece.

Leaves Stippled Yellow

Mite

Leaves of turnip plants infested with mites become stippled, yellow, and dry, and sometimes pale yellow spots or blotches appear. Mites are not insects but arachnids, and are about the size of a grain of black pepper. They may be red, black, or brown. They feed by sucking out the plant's juices. In sucking chlorophyll out of the leaves, they cause small white dots to appear. In addition, they inject toxins into the leaves, which discolors and distorts them. To control infestations, spray plants with a forceful spray of water three times, once every other day, to knock mites from the leaves. If they are still present, spray with insecticidal soap at least three times every 5 to 7 days.

MOST COMMON DISEASES

Yellow, Wedge-shaped Areas on Leaves

Black Rot

Black rot affects young as well as mature plants. Infected seedlings turn yellow and die. On older plants, yellow, wedge-shaped areas develop at the leaf margins and expand toward the center of the leaf. These areas later turn brown and die, and the leaves fall off. The vascular bundles in leaves and stems are black and bad smelling. Black rot cannot be cured. Remove and destroy the infected and surrounding plants. Micronized sulfur helps to control the spread of black rot to other plants. Apply the sulfur to unaffected plants every 7 days until harvest.

Poor Crop Development

Club Root

In general, the aboveground parts of plants exhibit the effects of a malfunctioning root system and show signs of wilting and poor development. The roots become enlarged and misshapen and develop club-shaped swellings. Try to prevent this disease by following clean gardening practices and rotating plants (the fungus persists in the soil for 7 years). Club root is more of a problem with plants growing in acid soil. Test your soil, and if the pH is too low, add lime. Club root can be controlled with approved soil fungicides.

Resistant Varieties. Bruce, Dale's Hybrid, Immuna, and May.

Bluish Black Marks on Leaves

Downy Mildew

Leaf symptoms appear as small yellowish areas that later turn brown and develop bluish black lacelike markings. In moist weather, a whitish downy mold develops on the undersides of leaves. The roots can become discolored internally, sometimes with a netlike brown or black area. In the advanced stages of this disease, the skin develops small cracks, becomes rough, and the root may split. Avoid dense and shaded plantings. If you catch the infection early, apply a copper-based fungicide to diseased and surrounding plants every 7 to 10 days until harvest. Remove and destroy any plants with a serious infection.

Yellow Leaves

Fusarium Wilt

Fusarium wilt (also called yellows or fusarium yellows) causes seedlings to wilt. When older plants contract this disease, they lose vitality; leaves turn yellow, then brown, and then drop off. Lower leaves are affected first. Some plants will produce some fruit, but in most cases you should remove and destroy infected plants. Fusarium wilt is carried in the soil, so using resistant varieties is the best approach to overall control of this disease in your garden. Solarizing the soil also helps. (See chapter 5 for information on solarization.)

HARVEST AND STORAGE

When to Harvest

Turnips should be 2 to 3 inches in diameter or smaller when you harvest them; larger roots have a woody texture. The skin should be uniformly tender and white with a purple tinge.

Yield for 24-Square-Foot Bed   30 to 35 pounds

Yield for 25-Foot Row   25 pounds

Best Fresh Storage Method   Refrigerate turnips in plastic bags; they will keep for 2 to 3 weeks.

Best Long-Term Storage Methods
Turnips can be canned and pickled; they will last for more than 12 months.

Other Long-Term Storage Methods
Turnips will keep in a humid root cellar, or you can mulch plants and leave them in the garden; they will keep for 4 months under both means of storage.

Seed Storage   3 years

CHAPTER 2

Fruits and Berries

Fruits and berries have insect and disease problems just as vegetables do, but gardening literature tends to spend much more time helping to solve problems in the vegetable garden than addressing situations in the mini-orchard and berry patch. One complication with fruits and berries is that, in most cases, they are perennial plants. You can always find a better variety of cabbage for your vegetable garden, but it is not very convenient to change the variety of the apple tree, which is now bearing after 4 years. Consequently, it is very important to learn as much as you can about how to prevent problems in the fruit and berry garden. There are certainly some things you can do if a problem does arise, but with fruits and berries it is much more cost effective to prevent those insect and disease problems in the first place.

Perhaps one of the most discouraging aspects of fruit and berry gardening is the prospect of spraying fruit trees. There are few, if any, serious food gar-

deners in this country who do not use some kind of preventive spray program on their trees. Do I have to spray my fruit trees? If I do spray my fruit trees, when do I do it, and what can I use that will be safe for me, my family, and the neighborhood? How much time does a safe spray program take?

This chapter outlines a basic preventive spray program that is safe and that does not take a great deal of time. If you have the basic problem-solving "medicine kit" discussed in the introduction to this book, you can use these preventive spray programs easily.

The fruits and berries discussed in the following pages are those most commonly grown in the backyard garden and orchard. Follow the management practices given, and implement the prevention strategies outlined for common pests and diseases, and you can successfully grow these fruits and berries in your garden.

General Spray Program

If you use a general preventive spray program on your fruit trees, you will have more fruit, cleaner fruit, and healthier trees. This program, based on a commercial version designed by the Necessary Trading Company in New Castle, Virginia, can be revised if there are specific insects or diseases you need to focus on. However, it serves as a good foundation for any spray program for fruit trees. Steps 1, 2, 3, 6, 7, and 8 are especially important steps that should not be missed.

The supplies you need for this program are a sprayer device (a container with at least 1-gallon capacity), dormant oil spray, lime sulfur fungicide, commercial insecticidal soap, seaweed extract, sulfur-based or Bordeaux mixture fungicide, *Bacillus thuringiensis* (BT) insecticide, and a surfactant (sticker) to help the other materials stick to the leaves.

1. In late winter, at least 3 weeks before the leaf buds begin to show, spray the entire tree with dormant oil (2½ ounces per gallon of water) to suffocate overwintering pests. Do not spray when the temperatures are below 40°F.

2. In spring, when the buds show green tissue, spray lime sulfur (2 ounces per gallon of water) to prevent fungal diseases. (Do not apply lime sulfur within 3 weeks of a dormant oil spray on the same tree.) At the same time that you apply the lime sulfur, spray the tree with insecticidal soap (3 ounces per gallon of water) to control aphids and scale. Also spray with seaweed extract (½ ounce per gallon of water) to stimulate growth; in fact, use liquid kelp in this quantity every time you spray your trees with anything.

3. The following step applies to apple, apricot, cherry, peach, and plum trees: When blossoms begin to show pink (open cluster), apply a sulfur-based spray (1 ounce per gallon of water). Use a surfactant or insecticidal soap with the sulfur-based spray to make it stick to the tree's stems and buds better and to control aphids (add 3 ounces of soap per gallon of spray). Do not apply lime sulfur when the tree is in blossom. In addition, spray trees with BT (1 tablespoon per gallon of water) to kill pest caterpillars. Do not mix a sulfur-based spray with BT.

4. The following step applies to pear trees only: 7 days later, before pink begins to show (called tight cluster), spray with lime sulfur (1 ounce per gallon of water) to prevent apple scab. If precipitation occurs and temperatures are above 60°F, apply lime sulfur at a concentration of 2 ounces per gallon of water. At the same time, apply insecticidal soap (3 ounces per gallon of water) to control aphids, scale, and mites, and spray with BT (1 tablespoon per gallon of water) to kill tent caterpillars. Do not mix lime sulfur with BT.

5. Seven days later (during pink to early bloom), repeat Step 3 for all fruit trees, and repeat yet again 7 days after *that* for pear trees only.

6. During the bloom period, you normally should not spray trees with any fungicide, but if precipitation occurs when temperatures are higher than 60°F, apply a sulfur-based fungicide (½ ounce per gallon of water). You can spray trees with BT (2 ounces per gallon of water) to control pest caterpillars. Use a surfactant with the sulfur but do not mix BT into the sulfur spray.

7. At petal fall, 7 days after full bloom, apply a sulfur-based spray (1 ounce per gallon of water), and spray with BT (*Bacillus thuringiensis*) (2 ounces per gallon of water) for pest caterpillars. Use a spray of insecticidal soap only if there is an obvious infestation of aphids and mites on the plants.

8. Seven days after petal fall (at first cover), repeat Step 6, and repeat again 7 days later (at second cover).

9. Midseason sprays are then made 10 to 14 days apart, using a sulfur spray (1 ounce per gallon of water) or a Bordeaux mixture (2 ounces per gallon of water) to control fungal problems.

10. Halt all sprays 30 days before harvest.

FRUIT Apple *Malus pumila*

DESCRIPTION AND ENVIRONMENT

Height Dwarf, 6 to 12 feet; semidwarf, 12 to 18 feet; standard, 30 to 40 feet.

Spread Dwarf, 6 feet; semidwarf, 15 feet; standard, 40 feet.

Root Depth 10 feet or more. The root spread will be at least half again as far as the dripline

(outside circumference of the spread of the limbs of the tree), and can be as much as twice that distance.

Years to Bearing Dwarf and semidwarf, 3 to 4; standard, 4 to 8.

Shade Tolerance Prefers full sun but can still produce with only 5 to 6 hours of sun a day.

Frost Tolerance Hardy

Preferred Soil pH 6.0 to 6.5

PLANTING AND PROPAGATION

Best Method of Propagation Grafting

When to Propagate Spring

Spring Planting In central and northern areas, plant while dormant; in all other areas, plant in the fall.

Fall Planting Only where winters are mild, and while the tree is dormant.

Planting Depth Keep the graft point 1 inch above the soil line, or the rootstock will start growing.

Spacing between Trees Dwarf, 5 to 20 feet; semidwarf, 20 to 25 feet; standard, 30 to 35 feet.

Pollination Requirements Some types require cross-pollination; all varieties produce better when cross-pollinated. For best cross-pollination, trees should be no more than 50 feet apart. A nearby flowering crabapple will also pollinate with your trees.

Container Varieties Dwarf varieties with Malling 7, 9, and 26 rootstocks grow well in containers. The Garden Delicious is a true dwarf apple tree that grows well in a container.

Container Size At least 24 inches deep.

MANAGEMENT OF FRUIT

Water Requirements

Young trees grow well in the first few years if they get approximately 1 inch of water every week from rain or by watering. Spread at least 2 inches of organic mulch around the trees to hold in moisture. Mature trees need watering only during times of drought. (See chapter 8 for more information on watering.)

Feeding Requirements

Apply compost or a slow-acting general-purpose fertilizer in spring before the leaves begin to pop, and spray foliage with liquid seaweed extract two or three times during the growing season. (See chapter 8 for more information on feeding.)

Season's Growth

On a standard tree, a season's growth of 8 to 15 inches indicates that the tree is receiving adequate nitrogen.

Pruning

Beginners should prune limbs only when the tree is dormant, probably in late winter. General pruning is needed only to remove the vertical branches called water sprouts (no fruit is formed on a vertical branch), any dead material, and any branches that are rubbing together as they cross each other (to avoid possible disease problems). Any further pruning should be done after consulting appropriate references. (One good reference is Lewis Hill's *Pruning Simplified,* listed in the Recommended Reading section at the back of this book.)

Thinning

Many varieties tend to set more apples than the trees can handle. Several weeks after the trees bloom, thin young apples to about 6 to 8 inches apart on the branches. Try to achieve a ratio of leaves to fruit of about 50 leaves for each apple. This provides enough leaves to produce the carbohydrates needed for apples to mature to a full size. In some cases then, there may be enough leaves to support fruit closer than the 6- to 8-inch guideline.

Excess Vegetative Growth

Pruning or Feeding Too Much

Pruning overzealously or providing too much nitrogen can encourage rampant vegetative growth. The trees may not harden off early enough in the fall, which leaves them vulnerable to severe damage if winter comes early. Trees putting out excess vegetative growth will form few fruit buds for the following year.

Less than 6 Inches of Growth

Nitrogen Deficiency

Apple trees should put on 8 to 12 inches of new shoot growth a year, with that growth concentrated in the spring and early summer. If your tree is growing less than 6 inches a year, add more nitrogen by applying manure or compost tea to the soil in early spring. If you don't, the tree will produce a lower number of flowers and set fewer and smaller apples the following year. (See chapter 8 for more information on nitrogen deficiency.)

Pale Leaves, Turning Yellow

Nitrogen Deficiency

If older leaves turn yellowish green, and this yellowing moves toward the leaf tips, especially in the late spring when everything is bursting with new green growth, your trees are probably suffering from a nitrogen deficiency. Sometimes reddish or reddish purple discolorations also appear. The leaves become very small, and the twigs are slender and hard. To remedy the problem quickly, apply a foliar spray of diluted fish emulsion or other liquid fertilizer. (See chapter 8 for more details on nitrogen deficiency.)

Purple Coloring of Stems

Phosphorus Deficiency

If the young twigs of your apple trees develop a greyish hue, and the stems show a purple coloring, your trees are probably suffering from a phosphorus deficiency. Other symptoms include abnormally small and dark green leaves, and old leaves becoming mottled with light and dark green spots. Occasionally, bronze leaves appear on mature branches. To remedy the problem quickly, spray the trees with diluted fish emulsion, or other liquid fertilizer. Spread wood ashes, ½ pound for dwarf trees, 1 pound for full-sized trees, around the soil to help this year's crop. (See chapter 8 for more information on phosphorus deficiency.)

Purplish Tinge on Leaf Edges

Potassium Deficiency

Leaf edges that show scorching and purplish discoloration are a sign of potassium deficiency. Dead spots develop on mature leaves and eventually on younger leaves. The foliage often becomes crinkled, and twigs are slender. Leaf curl generally shows up in late summer about the time the fruit begins to mature. If the deficiency is severe, new shoots may be thin and very susceptible to winter injury. To remedy the problem quickly, apply a foliar spray of fish emulsion, seaweed extract, or other liquid fertilizer. Side-dress plants with wood ashes, ½ pound for dwarf trees, 1 pound for full-sized trees. (See chapter 8 for more information on potassium deficiency.)

MOST COMMON INSECT PESTS

Foliage Curls, Puckers, Turns Yellow

Aphid

If the foliage on your apple trees curls, puckers, and turns yellow, and the foliage and blooms become stunted, look for ants on the trees. They are a sign that your trees have aphids. Ants are attracted to the sticky honeydew secreted by aphids. Look for clusters of aphids on the undersides of young leaves. They are soft-bodied, pear-shaped insects about the size of a pinhead, and may be green, brown, or pink. For light infestations, spray vigorously with water early in the morning, three times, once every other day. For heavy infestations, use a commercial insecticidal soap every 2 to 3 days until aphids are under control.

Apples Have Worms

Apple Maggot

Although they are hard to detect on the outside, if you look inside the apples you will find white worms eating the fruit. These are apple maggots, the larvae of the apple maggot fly. They are white or yellowish, and measure ¼ inch long. The adult fly is also ¼ inch long. It is black with yellow legs, yellow markings across the abdomen, and bands that zigzag across the wings. These flies lay eggs in punctures in apple skin. The best way to control apple maggots is to prevent the adult fly from laying eggs. A sticky trap made from a red ball and yellow rectangle traps the flies, and is available commercially. Clean up all fallen fruit immediately.

Skeletonized Leaves

Cankerworm

Apple trees that have holes in the leaves and eventually become defoliated have been infested by cankerworms, also called inchworms. You might also see silken threads hanging from the branches of trees. When leaves become skeletonized, trees weaken each year, fewer apples mature, and sometimes the tree dies. Cankerworms are 1-inch-long worms. Both species (fall and spring) are colored brown and green, with stripes running along their bodies. To prevent their getting started, apply a dormant oil spray before leaves emerge, and follow with a preventive *Bacillus thuringiensis* (BT) spray from the end of blossoming, continuing every 2 weeks for 1 month. If they do take hold and need controlling, use BT for any further infestations. Apply every 10 to 14 days until cankerworms are removed.

Holes in Skin, Tunnels in Apples

Codling Moth

The larvae of codling moths tunnel their way through apples, eating as they go. You might also spot some cocoons in the bark crevices. The larvae is 1 inch long, pink, and has a brown head. The adult is a grayish brown moth with lacy brown lines on forewings and pale, fringed hind wings. It has a ¾-inch wing span. Adults lay white, flat eggs singly on leaves, twigs, or fruit buds. To control these pests, spray dormant oil on trees prior to leaf budding in late winter or early spring to suffocate the eggs. As apple blossoms are just beginning to open up, set out sticky traps to catch the moths. If there are more than 10 moths caught in a single trap, spray with pyrethrum as the blossom petals begin to fall. Apply preventive sprays of *Bacillus thuringiensis* (BT) and light horticultural oils later in the season in 7- to 10-day intervals to kill newly hatched larvae. Butterfly weed (*Asclepias tuberosa*) hosts parasites of codling moths.

Misshapen Apples with Indented Areas or Cavities

Fruit Worm

Green fruit worms chew on new leaves and flower bud clusters and, when older, bore into and feed on young apples, causing indented areas or cavities. The fruit may be consumed entirely. Severely injured fruit will drop to the ground. Mature apples are often misshapen, with large, indented, corky areas. The caterpillars are active for about a month after bloom. To eliminate them, spray trees with *Bacillus thuringiensis* (BT) at petal fall and every 10 days thereafter until the pests are under control.

Defoliated Tree

Gypsy Moth Caterpillar

Gypsy moths infest many species of trees in the northeastern and Middle Atlantic states. You will see large masses of caterpillars feeding on leaves, and the trees will eventually become defoliated. Newly hatched caterpillars are about 1/16 inch long, and grow to about 2½ inches at maturity. They are gray and have long brown hairs. Eggs are light brown to yellow and are laid in masses on trunks and branches from August through the following April. Scrape them into a bucket of soapy water. To control caterpillars, spray trees with *Bacillus thuringiensis* (BT) every 10 to 14 days from late April to mid-June. In June, switch to trapping the insects with burlap skirts. (See chapter 4 for more information on these traps.)

Weakened Tree

Leafhopper

Both adult leafhoppers and nymphs pierce leaves, buds, and stems and suck the sap and chlorophyll from cells, causing young trees to weaken. Adults are green, wedge-shaped insects, ¼ to ⅓ inch long, that hold their wings in a rooflike position above their bodies. They are very active and move sideways. Nymphs resemble adults. To control serious infestations, apply insecticidal soap laced with isopropyl alcohol every 3 to 4 days. In early spring, apply a preventive spray of insecticidal soap and seaweed extract.

Leaves Stippled Yellow

Mite

Leaves that have become stippled, yellow, and dry, or that have pale yellow spots or blotches, are a sign that spider mites have infested your apple trees. Mites suck chlorophyll out of the leaves, causing small white dots to appear. They also inject toxins into the leaves, which discolors and distorts them. Mites are tiny arachnids about the size of a grain of black pepper. They may be red, black, or brown. Spray trees with a forceful spray of water three times, once every other day, to knock mites from leaves. If that doesn't do the job, spray the undersides of leaves with insecticidal soap at least three times at 5- to 7-day intervals. Be sure to spray the plant from top to bottom.

Apples Fall, Have Cuts in Skin

Plum Curculio

If apples fall to the ground prematurely and are knotted, gnarled, and misshapen, with crescent-shaped marks on the skins, plum curculio beetles have infested your trees. The plum curculio is dark brown and ¼ inch long, with a prominent snout. It can be found on all tree fruit crops from just before bloom to a few weeks after. When disturbed, it curls its legs and antennae and drops to the ground. In feeding, the adult cuts a hole in the skin of the fruit and hollows out a cavity about ⅛ inch deep. Wounds on apples frequently exude sap that dries to a white crust. The beetle lays its eggs in the cuts, and when the eggs hatch, the grayish white larvae bore to the center of the fruit and feed, causing the fruit to drop. To control plum curculios, spread a sheet under each tree and shake the branches. Curculios will drop onto the sheet, and you can collect and destroy them. If curculios are still a problem, apply a pyrethrum spray when petals fall and every 10 to 14 days until September, or until the beetles are under control. Remove and destroy all fallen fruit immediately.

Tree Becomes Defoliated

Tent Caterpillar

Tent caterpillars build large silken nests in the forks of tree branches. These pests grow to be about 2 inches long. They are black and hairy with white stripes and have narrow brown and yellow lines and a row of blue spots along their sides. To control tent caterpillars, remove the tents and destroy the caterpillars by hand, or spray the tree with *Bacillus thuringiensis* (BT) as soon as you notice the tents, continuing to spray every 5 to 7 days until the pest is removed.

Holes in Blossoms, Stunted Tree

Weevil

Larvae and adults may feed on leaves and fruit of apple trees. Larvae make zigzag paths into roots, fruit, or bark. This pest is reddish brown in color with a black snout. It is about ¼ inch long. As weevils appear, spray with pyrethrum twice, 3 to 4 days apart.

Weakened Tree, Yellow Leaves

Whitefly

Trees that are weak, with leaves that turn yellow and die, are probably infested with whiteflies. Honeydew from the whiteflies drops on fruit and encourages fungal growth. As a result, the apples are undersized and poorly colored. Whiteflies are about the size of a pinhead. They are mothlike and have dusty white wings. The yellowish nymphs are legless, somewhat flat, and oval, and they resemble scale at certain stages. If you shake a tree infested with whiteflies, it appears as though dandruff were flying off the leaves. Spray infested trees with an insecticidal soap spray, every 2 to 3 days for 2 weeks. To prevent whiteflies, follow this regimen early in the season, just as leaves are appearing. Spray with pyrethrum as a last resort. Make two applications, 3 to 4 days apart.

Sudden Wilting of Tree

White Grub

A sudden wilting of your young apple trees, when all other conditions seem fine, may indicate the presence of white grubs. These pests are the fat, whitish larvae of the june beetle. They are ¾ to 1½ inches long and they feed on the roots of plants. To control infestations, make one application of beneficial nematodes, which go below the surface of the soil to attack the grubs. (See chapter 4 for more information on parasitic nematodes.) Milky spore disease spread on the soil around the plants will control white grubs, but it takes 3 to 5 years to have a complete effect.

MOST COMMON DISEASES

Olive-Green Spots on Undersides of Leaves

Apple Scab

Pale yellow or olive-green spots that develop on the undersides of leaves and that darken nearly to black indicate scab. Both top and bottom surfaces of leaves may show scab spots. Other symptoms include curling, cracking, and distortion of leaves. The fruit also develops spots, which enlarge and gain a velvety appearance in the center, becoming brown and corky. The fruit of young apple trees drops; growing fruit distorts and cracks. An infection of the twigs will blister and rupture the bark. (To control apple scab, follow the spray program discussed in the entry Apple Scab in chapter 5.)

Resistant Varieties. Akane, Baldwin, Chehalis, Discovery, Dolgo Crab, Florina, Freedom, Gavin, Golden, Gravenstein, Grimes, Jonafree, Jonathan, Liberty, Macfree, Nova Easygro, Novamac, Priam, Prima, Priscilla, Red Baron, Redfree, Sir Prize, State Fair, Transparent, Tydeman's Red, Wealthy, and York Imperial.

Brown Corky Flecks in Apples

Baldwin Spot

Apples infected with baldwin spot develop brown corky flecks in the flesh of the fruit. These flecks usually develop just under the skin but may be scattered through the flesh to the core. The corky tissue has a bitter taste; hence the common name, bitter pit. Baldwin spot is caused by a calcium imbalance. For quick control, spray trees with a solution made from calcium chloride, mixing ⅓ to ½ an ounce in 2 gallons of water. Make two applications, the first 6 weeks before harvest and the second 3 weeks before harvest. Older trees will benefit from ½ pound of borax, spread within the dripline; use ¼ pound for young trees.

Resistant Varieties. McIntosh.

Small Brown Spots on Apples

Black Rot

Black rot does not become evident until a few weeks before fruit maturity, or until later, when it appears as storage rot. Small brown spots develop, usually one to a fruit, which later expand and darken. As these spots expand, they develop concentric zones of alternating shades of brown and black. Minute

black pimples may later appear as the apples shrivel and mummify. During the growing season, the fungus attacks bark, twigs, and fruit, and overwinters in these tissues. Sometimes cankers form on the twigs. Use a sulfur-based fungicide to control the fungus. (See chapter 5 for information on applying fungicides.) In addition, prune infected wood and destroy mummified fruit.

Tiny Pale Yellow Spots on Leaves

Cedar Apple Rust

Pale yellow, pinhead-sized spots on the upper surfaces of leaves, enlarging to bright orange spots on foliage and fruit, indicate cedar apple rust. Apply sulfur fungicides every 5 to 7 days until symptoms disappear. Remove all red cedar trees within 300 yards. Junipers and hawthorns can also spread cedar apple rust to apple trees. Cut down nearby susceptible varieties such as the flowering crabapple.

Resistant Varieties. Baldwin, Delicious, Duchess, Franklin, Golden Delicious, Grimes, Liberty, Melrose, Northwestern Greening, Nova Easygro, Novamac, Priscilla, Red Astrachan, Redfree, Rhode Island, Stayman, Transparent, and Winesap.

Withered and Dead Blossoms

Fire Blight

Infected shoots turn brown or black as though scorched. The blossoms of apple trees infected by fire blight wither and die. Water-soaked bark lesions appear that are reddish in color, and on warm days they ooze an orange-brown liquid. Later they become brown and dry. Prune and destroy blighted branches, and scrape and treat cankers with pruning paint. Disinfect your pruning tool in a bleach solution (one part household bleach to four parts water) after each cut.

Resistant Varieties. Akane, Baldwin, Ben Davis, Delicious, Dolgo Crab, Duchess, Florence Crab, Gano, Haralson, Hibernal, Jerseymac, Jonathan, Liberty, MacFree, McIntosh, Northern Spy, Nova Easygro, Novamac, Prima, Priscilla, Red Delicious, Redfree, Stayman, Winesap, and Winter Banana.

Gray, Velvety Mold

Powdery Mildew

If the terminals of twigs, leaves, and blossoms are covered with white to pearly gray, velvety mold, your apple trees are infected with powdery mildew. Twigs are dwarfed, and the terminal bud is killed, which causes a proliferation of side shoots. Young apples develop russeting or etching. To control powdery mildew, follow the spray program used to control apple scab. (See the entry Apple Scab in chapter 5.) Prune infected terminals for additional control.

Resistant Varieties. Akane, Delicious, Discovery, Golden Delicious, Liberty, Lodi, Macfree, Prima, Priscilla, Red Delicious, Redfree, Sir Prize, Spartan, and Tydeman's Red.

Split Bark

Sunscald

In some parts of the country in January and February, days are often bright and clear, and the warmth of the sun on the southwest side of the tree trunk begins to activate growth cells. Then, when the sun goes down, the temperature plummets, and the cold ruptures those cells and dries them out. To prevent this from happening, wrap the trunks with strips of burlap and secure with twine, or place a wide board several inches away from the tree on the southwest side, which will cast a shadow on the trunk. In March or April, when the weather is milder, remove the sun screen.

HARVEST AND STORAGE

When to Harvest

Except for winter storage varieties, apples should be picked when fully ripe. Winter storage types should be picked while they are slightly underripe. To avoid pulling out the stem when you harvest, cup the apple in your hand, tilt it upward, and twist to separate it from the spur at the point of attachment.

Yield per Tree   Dwarf, 60 to 120 apples (24 to 48 pounds, or ½ to 1 bushel); semidwarf, about 350 apples (144 pounds, or 3 bushels); standard, 1,200 to 1,800 apples (480 to 720 pounds, or 10 to 15 bushels).

Best Fresh Storage Method   Store in a cool place with humidity high enough to prevent shriveling. Storage time will vary greatly depending on the variety.

Best Long-Term Storage Method   Apples can be sliced and dried for storage and will last for 6 to 12 months.

Second-Best Long-Term Storage Method   Any of the many apple products, such as apple sauce.

Apples Spoil in Storage

Bitter Pit from Calcium Deficiency or Excess Nitrogen

Apples with bitter pit have small areas of brownish, corky tissue just under the skin. You can usually spot this easily; the skin over the affected area is sunken into a discolored pit. Apples deficient in calcium have cell membranes that disintegrate prematurely, drastically reducing storage life of fruit. Bitter pit is not necessarily due simply to a lack of calcium; it is actually caused by an imbalance between nitrogen and calcium. Excessive nitrogen prevents trees from getting sufficient calcium. If you have trouble with bitter pit in your apples, cut back on nitrogen, keeping the soil pH at 6.0 to 6.5. Since the fruit accumulates calcium during its early stage of development, make certain the soil is moist around the roots of your apple trees from the time flowers open until the apples appear. This will enable the trees to absorb calcium more readily.

Improper Storage

The reason most home refrigerators don't make good long-term storage areas is that they're not cold enough! Almost all fruit keeps best at temperatures of 30°F to 32°F, with 90 percent humidity (high sugar content keeps fruit from freezing within this temperature range). An old-fashioned root cellar or unheated cellar with a dirt floor make excellent storage areas.

NOTES AND RESEARCH

Studies show that turf suppresses the growth of apple trees; it is better to surround trees with a thick organic mulch.

Apple trees suffer stunting, wilting, or even death when they come in contact with black walnut roots. Allelopathic reactions occur within a circle one and a half times the distance from the trunk of the black walnut to the outermost branches.

Some apple viruses can be spread when roots of an infected tree grow into those of a healthy one. Interplanting with apple varieties resistant to the problem virus, or with other resistant fruit trees, may help.

Potatoes produce toxins that interfere with photosynthesis, protein production, and nitrogen absorption in apple trees, so do not plant them near apples.

Evidence suggests that apples are autoallelopathic: The roots exude a poisonous substance, particularly in waterlogged soil, so do not plant apple seedlings in a place just vacated by the same species.

FRUIT # Apricot *Prunus armeniaca*

DESCRIPTION AND ENVIRONMENT

Height   Dwarf, 6 to 7 feet; semidwarf, 12 to 15 feet; standard, 20 to 30 feet.

Spread   Dwarf, 8 feet; semidwarf, 15 feet; standard, 20 to 24 feet.

Root Spread   The root spread will be at least half again as far as the dripline (the circumference of the branches), and can be as much as twice the dripline.

Years to Bearing   3 to 4

Shade Tolerance   Needs full sun.

Frost Tolerance   Can be grown in Zones 4 through 9. Northern growers should plant trees on north side of a building so they warm up as slowly as possible in the spring.

Preferred Soil pH   6.0 to 6.5

Spring Planting   While dormant

Fall Planting   In areas with mild winters, while the tree is dormant.

Planting Depth   Keep the graft point 1 inch above the soil line, or the rootstock will start growing.

Spacing between Trees   Dwarf, 8 to 12 feet; semidwarf, 15 feet; standard, 25 to 30 feet.

Pollination Requirements   Most apricots self-pollinate, but produce better if cross-pollinated by another variety.

Container Varieties   Dwarf varieties such as Garden Annie can be grown in containers.

Container Size   At least 24 inches deep.

PLANTING AND PROPAGATION

Best Method of Propagation   Grafting

When to Propagate   Spring

MANAGEMENT OF FRUIT

Water Requirements

Apricot trees grow well if they get approximately 1 inch of water every week from rain or by watering.

Spread at least 2 inches of organic mulch around the trees to hold in moisture. Consistency in watering is critical, especially during the heat of the summer. Later in the season, consistent watering is important for good bud set for next year's crop. (See chapter 8 for more information on watering.)

Feeding Requirements

Apply compost or a slow-acting general-purpose fertilizer in spring just before leaves begin to come out. Spray the foliage with liquid seaweed extract two or three times during the growing season. (See chapter 8 for more information on feeding.)

Season's Growth

On a standard tree, a season's growth of 6 to 10 inches indicates that the tree is receiving adequate nitrogen.

Small Apricots

Need Pruning

One way to get larger fruit from your trees is to thin out excess fruit. This also keeps branches from breaking. Thin apricots to 4 to 6 inches apart when they are ½ to ¾ inch in diameter; at that stage, fruit comes off easily.

Excess Vegetative Growth

Pruning or Feeding Too Much

Pruning overzealously or adding too much nitrogen to the soil can encourage rampant vegetative growth. Trees may not harden off early enough in the fall, which leaves them vulnerable to severe damage if winter comes early. Trees putting out excess vegetative growth will form few fruit buds for the following year, and will produce less fruit. Cut back on nitrogen and pruning.

MOST COMMON INSECT PESTS

Foliage Curls, Puckers, Turns Yellow

Aphid

If the foliage on your apricot trees curls, puckers, and turns yellow, and the foliage and blooms become stunted, your trees may have aphids. Look for ants on the trees. They are attracted to a sticky honeydew secreted by aphids. Look for clusters of aphids on the undersides of young leaves. They are soft-bodied, pear-shaped insects about the size of a pinhead, and may be green, brown, or pink. For light infestations, spray vigorously with water early in the morning, three times, once every other day. For heavy infestations, use a commercial insecticidal soap every 2 to 3 days until aphids are under control.

Tunnels in Apricots

Codling Moth
The larvae of codling moths tunnel through apricots. You might also spot some cocoons in bark crevices. The larvae are 1 inch long, pink, and have brown heads. The adult is a grayish brown moth with lacy brown lines on its forewings and pale, fringed hind wings. It has a ¾-inch wing span. Adults lay white, flat eggs singly on leaves, twigs, or fruit buds. To control these pests, spray dormant oil on trees prior to leaf budding in late winter or early spring to suffocate eggs. Set out sticky traps to catch moths just before the blossoms begin to open up. Apply preventive sprays of *Bacillus thuringiensis* (BT) and light horticultural oils later in the season at 7- to 10-day intervals to kill newly hatched larvae. Butterfly weed (*Asclepias tuberosa*) hosts parasites of codling moths.

Defoliated Tree

Gypsy Moth Caterpillar
Gypsy moths infest many species of trees in the northeastern and Middle Atlantic states. You will see large masses of caterpillars feeding on leaves, and the trees will eventually become defoliated. Newly hatched caterpillars are about 1/16 inch long, and grow to about 2½ inches at maturity. They are gray and have long brown hairs. Eggs are light brown to yellow and are laid in masses on trunks and branches from August through the following April. Scrape them into a bucket of soapy water. To control caterpillars, spray trees in early spring with *Bacillus thuringiensis* (BT) every 10 to 14 days. In June, switch to trapping the insects with burlap skirts.

Leaves Stippled Yellow

Mite
Leaves that have become stippled, yellow, and dry, or that have pale yellow spots or blotches, are a sign that spider mites have infested your apricot trees. Mites suck chlorophyll out of the leaves, causing small white dots to appear. They also inject toxins into the leaves, which discolors and distorts them. Mites are tiny arachnids about the size of a grain of black pepper. They may be red, black, or brown. Spray trees with a forceful spray of water three times, once every other day, to knock mites from leaves. If that doesn't do the job, spray the undersides of leaves with insecticidal soap at least three times at 5- to 7-day intervals. Be sure to spray the plant from top to bottom.

Holes in Trunk

Peachtree Borer
Holes in the trunk near the base of the tree from which brown frass (excrement) and gum exude are signs that borers are at work. The adults are wasplike moths. They lay eggs around the base of the trunk in late summer and early fall. These hatch into white, ¼-inch-long caterpillars with brownish heads, which burrow into the trunk as high as a foot above the ground or several inches below the ground. Young trees can be killed during the first season of infestation. Small infestations can be taken care of by inserting a stiff wire into each hole and killing the larva, or *Bacillus thuringiensis* (BT) can be shot into the hole at 10-day intervals until no more frass appears. Remove the soil several inches deep around the trunk to check for borers in the base of the tree. Cultivate shallowly in spring and fall to destroy eggs and pupae.

Apricots Fall, Have Cuts in Skin

Plum Curculio
If apricots fall to the ground prematurely, and have crescent-shaped marks on the skins, plum curculio beetles have infested your trees. The plum curculio is dark brown and ¼ inch long, with a prominent snout. It can be found on all tree fruit crops from just before bloom to a few weeks after. When disturbed, it curls its legs and antennae and drops to the ground. In feeding, the adult cuts a hole in the skin of the fruit, where it lays an egg. When the eggs hatch, the grayish white larvae bore to the center of the fruit and feed, causing the fruit to drop. To

control plum curculios, spread a sheet under each tree and shake the branches. Curculios will drop onto the sheet, and you can collect and destroy them. If plum curculios are still a problem, apply a pyrethrum spray when petals fall, and every 10 to 14 days afterward until September, or until the beetles are under control. Remove and destroy all fallen fruit immediately.

Weakened Tree, Yellow Leaves

Whitefly
Trees that are weak, with leaves that turn yellow and die, are probably infested with whiteflies. Honeydew from the whiteflies drops on fruit and encourages fungal growth. As a result, the apricots are undersized and poorly colored. Whiteflies are about the size of a pinhead. They are mothlike and have dusty white wings. The yellowish nymphs are legless, somewhat flat, and oval, and they resemble scale at certain stages. If you shake a tree infested with whiteflies, it appears as though dandruff were flying off the leaves. Spray infested trees with an insecticidal soap spray, every 2 to 3 days for 2 weeks. To prevent whiteflies, follow this regimen early in the season, just as leaves are appearing. Spray with pyrethrum as a last resort. Make two applications, 3 to 4 days apart.

MOST COMMON DISEASES

Purple Spots on Leaves

Bacterial Canker
Small purple spots on leaves, black lesions on fruit, and cankers on twigs indicate that bacterial canker has infested your trees. This disease cannot be cured. First prune the infected twigs and branches and destroy them. If the canker continues to spread, the entire tree must be destroyed. Try to prevent bacterial canker by following good fall cleanup practices.

Pale Green Spots on Leaves

Bacterial Spot
Small, circular, pale green spots on leaves that later turn light brown indicate that bacterial spot has infected your apricot trees. The tissue around the spots fades to a light yellow-green and then becomes purplish and angular in shape. Small circular sunken spots develop on fruit, and later the fruit cracks. Bacterial spot cannot be cured. First try to control the disease by applying a copper-based fungicide every 7 to 10 days until 3 to 4 weeks before harvest. In addition, prune and destroy the infected parts. If the disease continues to spread, the entire tree must be destroyed.

Brown Spots on Apricots

Brown Rot
If small, round, brown spots appear that spread to cover the whole fruit, your apricot trees are infected with brown rot. The rotted areas develop light gray masses of spores. Destroy the diseased or mummified fruit. Remove dead twigs, and cultivate shallowly around the tree. Do not spray water on ripe fruit. During harvest and storage, handle fruit carefully so as not to damage it, and refrigerate immediately after picking. Try a spray of garlic up to a month before harvest to reduce incidence of brown rot.

Galls on Roots or Crowns

Crown Gall
Crown gall causes galls (swellings) to form on the roots and crowns of apricot trees. The galls occur where bacteria enter the tree through wounds. Remove them with a sharp clean knife, and treat the wound with tree surgeon's paint. To prevent damage to the tree from sunburn, avoid doing this during the hottest part of the summer, and cover the affected part with soil. Clean your hands and tools with bleach solution (one part household bleach to four parts water) afterward to prevent spread of the disease.

Yellowing of New Shoots

Cytospora Canker

The first symptom of cytospora canker is the wilting or yellowing of new shoots and leaves, which later turn brown. The cankers form at the base of a bud in late winter. Cut off the infected branches and burn them. Since the canker infects the trees through wounds, try to protect the tree from winter injury. Paint the trunk and lower limbs with white latex paint to reduce injury from the cold. Delay regular pruning until bud swell.

Dark Greenish Spots on Apricots

Scab

Small, dark, greenish spots that appear about the time fruit is half grown and turn brown as the fruit matures are symptoms of scab. Yellow-brown spots appear on twigs and branches, and the fruit may crack. To control scab, apply a copper-based fungicide 2 to 3 weeks after petals drop. A second application may be needed 2 weeks later. Remove infected fruit, and clean up fallen leaves and fruit. (See the spray program for controlling scab in the entry Apple Scab in chapter 5.)

Wilted Leaves

Verticillium Wilt

When the leaves on your apricot trees wilt and droop during midsummer or later, suspect verticillium wilt. The leaves later turn yellow, curl upward along the midrib, and drop. Leaf damage progresses from the older part of the shoot to the younger growth. Add organic matter to the soil to reduce the fungus. A well-nourished tree has a good chance of recovering.

HARVEST AND STORAGE

When to Harvest

Harvest apricots when they are slightly soft and fully colored. Harvesting peaks in July in mild areas and in August in cooler places. The picking season is short, 1 to 2 weeks.

Yield per Tree   Dwarf, 1 to 2 bushels; standard, 3 to 4 bushels.

BERRY **Blackberry**   *Rubus macropetalus*

DESCRIPTION AND ENVIRONMENT

Height   5 to 26 feet
Root Depth   More than 12 inches.
Years to Bearing   2
Years of Production   10 to 12
Shade Tolerance   Needs some shade (2 to 4 hours) in hot climates, but needs full sun in the northern part of the country.
Frost Tolerance   Can be grown in Zones 5 to 8.
Preferred Soil pH   5.0 to 6.0

PLANTING AND PROPAGATION

Best Method of Propagation   Transplant dormant suckers.

When to Propagate   Spring; fall or winter where winters are very mild.

Planting Depth   Plant 1 inch deeper than planted at the nursery.

Spacing between Plants   For upright plants, 3 feet; for trailing plants, 5 to 8 feet.

MANAGEMENT OF BERRIES

Water Requirements

Make sure the plants get 1 inch of water every week from rain or by watering. When plants start producing fruit, give them 1 to 1½ inches of water each week. (See chapter 8 for more information on watering.)

Feeding Requirements

Apply compost or a slow-acting general-purpose fertilizer in spring as the leaves are beginning to come out. Spray plants with liquid seaweed extract two or three times during the growing season. (See chapter 8 for more information on feeding.)

Excess Vegetative Growth

Pruning or Feeding Too Much

Plants that produce too much vegetation may not harden off early enough in the fall, which leaves them vulnerable to severe damage if winter comes early. In addition, these plants will form few fruit buds for the following year, and will produce less fruit. Cut back on nitrogen and pruning.

MOST COMMON INSECT PESTS

Sudden Wilting of Tips

Caneborer

Sudden wilting of the tips of blackberry or raspberry canes is the first sign that raspberry caneborers have infected your plants. Close examination of canes shows two rows of punctures about 1 inch apart at the tip of the cane. The adult is a bluish black beetle with a red thorax, which lays an egg between the rows of punctures. A small grub hatches from the egg and burrows toward the base of the cane. To destroy this larva, cut off the wilted tips below the lower row of punctures and burn them.

Leaves Stippled Yellow

Mite

Leaves that have become stippled, yellow, and dry, or that have pale yellow spots or blotches, are a sign that spider mites have infested your blackberry plants. Mites suck chlorophyll out of the leaves, causing small white dots to appear. They also inject toxins into the leaves, which discolors and distorts them. Mites are tiny arachnids about the size of a grain of black pepper. They may be red, black, or brown. Spray plants with a forceful spray of water three times, once every other day, to knock mites from the leaves. If that doesn't do the job, spray the undersides of leaves with insecticidal soap at least three times at 5- to 7-day intervals. Be sure to spray the plant from top to bottom.

Weakened Plants, Yellow Leaves

Whitefly

Plants that are weak, and whose leaves turn yellow and die, are probably infested with whiteflies. Honeydew from the whiteflies drops on fruit and encourages fungal growth. As a result, the berries are undersized and poorly colored. Whiteflies are about the size of a pinhead. They are mothlike and have dusty white wings. The yellowish nymphs are legless, somewhat flat, and oval, and they resemble scale at certain stages. If you shake a plant infested with whiteflies, it appears as though dandruff were flying off the leaves. Spray infested plants with an insecticidal soap spray, every 2 to 3 days for 2 weeks. To prevent whiteflies, follow this regimen early in the season, just as leaves are appearing. Spray with pyrethrum as a last resort. Make two applications, 3 to 4 days apart.

Sudden Wilting of Tree

White Grub

A sudden wilting of your blackberry plants, when all other conditions seem fine, may indicate the presence of white grubs. These pests are the fat, whitish larvae of the june beetle. They are ¾ to 1½ inches long and they feed on the roots of plants. To control infestations, make one application of beneficial nematodes, which go below the surface of the soil to attack the grubs. (See chapter 4 for more information on parasitic nematodes.) Milky spore disease spread on the soil around the plants will control white grubs, but it takes 3 to 5 years to have a complete effect.

MOST COMMON DISEASES

Be sure to start out with disease-free plants: It is better to buy new plants than to accept gifts from friends.

Reddish Brown Spots on New Canes

Anthracnose

If new canes show small reddish brown or purplish spots, suspect anthracnose. As the canes grow, these spots enlarge, become round, turn gray in color, develop sunken centers, and grow together. Small, irregular, yellow or purple spots also develop on the leaves. Upon spotting the disease symptoms, apply an approved fungicide such as copper dust or liquid copper spray every 7 to 10 days. To prevent anthracnose, apply a dormant oil spray in late winter before budding.

Grayish Mold on Berries

Botrytis Fruit Rot

Botrytis fruit rot starts as blossom blight, causing discolored petals and wilted fruit stems. If you see grayish mold on the berries, your blackberry plants are infected with this disease. If you spot the disease in early spring, sulfur or fixed copper fungicides provide a good degree of control. Pick the fruit continuously to prevent the accumulation of overripe berries. Handle the berries gently to prevent bruising.

Canes Wilt and Die

Cane Blight

Cane blight causes canes to wilt and die while loaded with fruit. Brownish purple discolorations are visible on the cut or injured part of the cane where the fungus entered. These discolored areas spread along the cane and encircle it. Cane blight cannot be cured. Remove and destroy all affected stalks. Control pest insects such as the caneborer to avoid cane damage, which may encourage cane blight.

Galls on Roots and Stems

Crown Gall

If you find galls (swellings) or knots on roots and stems, sometimes on canes, your blackberry plants have crown gall. The galls occur where bacteria enter the plant through wounds. Remove the infected portion of the plant and destroy. Clean your hands and tools with bleach solution (one part household bleach to four parts water) afterward to prevent spread of the disease.

Yellow Dots on Both Sides of Leaves

Orange Rust

Yellow dots on both sides of leaves indicate orange rust. Two to 3 weeks later, light-colored areas develop on the undersides of leaves; then the surface of the leaves ruptures, exposing large, bright orange-red, powdery masses of spores. Infected plants cannot be saved. Dig them up and destroy them. To prevent orange rust, plant resistant varieties, follow good fall cleanup practices, and remove any wild berries growing nearby, because such plants may carry this disease.

Resistant Varieties. Boysen, Ebony King, Eldorado, Lawton, Orange Evergreen, Russell, and Snyder.

White Powdery Growth on Undersides of Leaves

Powdery Mildew

If the leaves of your blackberry plants become dwarfed and twisted, and a white powdery fungus develops on the undersides, your plants have powdery mildew. Prune and destroy the infected parts and apply a 95 percent wettable sulfur fungicide every 7 to 10 days until symptoms disappear or until 3 to 4 weeks before harvest. Thin plants to let in sun and air. Disinfect your pruning tool in a bleach solution (one part household bleach to four parts water) after each cut.

Small Tan Spots with Purplish Edges

Septoria Leaf Spot

The leaf spots of septoria are small, tan or light brown in the center, and purplish around the edges. When they enlarge, you may see black dots in the center. After discovering the disease, apply copper dust or a liquid copper spray fungicide every 7 to 10 days until symptoms disappear or until 3 to 4 weeks before harvest. Remove and burn all diseased canes after harvest.

Leaves Yellow and Wilt, Canes Die

Verticillium Wilt

At first, the canes grow vigorously; then the leaves yellow and wilt, and the canes die. These symptoms indicate verticillium wilt. Apply a sulfur fungicide every 7 to 10 days until symptoms disappear or until 3 to 4 weeks before harvest. If control is not achieved, destroy infected plants and replant in a new location.

MOST COMMON ANIMAL PESTS

Birds

One way to keep birds away from blackberries is to plant borders of chokecherries, dogwood, mountain ash, mulberries, or other very aromatic types of fruit nearby. Birds seem to prefer them.

For a barrier to succeed at keeping out the birds, it must completely surround the plant. Any opening and the birds are sure to find it. Fabric or plastic netting can't be casually draped over the blackberry plant the way the advertising pictures show. This may save some fruit, but birds will peck right through it and squeeze in under it. Some kind of support is needed to hold the netting out away from the shrub so the birds can't reach any of the fruit.

HARVEST AND STORAGE

When to Harvest

Harvest berries in the early morning just after their color has become dull. Check plants every 2 days for ripe berries.

Yield per Plant   1½ to 2 quarts

Best Fresh Storage Method   Store berries in the refrigerator immediately after picking to maintain flavor.

Best Long-Term Storage Method
Berries freeze well and will last for about 6 months.

Second-Best Long-Term Storage Method   Jams or jellies.

NOTES AND RESEARCH

Blackberries suffer stunting, wilting, or even death when they come in contact with black walnut roots. Allelopathic reactions occur within a circle one and a half times the distance from the trunk of the black walnut to the outermost branches.

Avoid planting blackberries where any plants of the nightshade family (tomatoes, potatoes, eggplants, or peppers) grew within the last 2 years; they can transmit verticillium wilt to blackberry plants.

BERRY **Blueberry**

Vaccinium angustifolium (lowbush);
V. corymbosum (highbush)

DESCRIPTION AND ENVIRONMENT

Height   Lowbush, 2 to 4 feet; highbush, 4 to 10 feet.
Spread   Lowbush, 2 to 4 feet; highbush, 4 to 6 feet.
Root Spread   Roots are very shallow and will spread at least half again as far as the dripline (the circumference of the branches) of the bush.
Years to Bearing   3 to 4 for both lowbush and highbush.
Shade Tolerance   Both types need full sun.
Frost Tolerance   Lowbush blueberries can be grown in Zones 4 to 7; highbush, in Zones 4 to 8, marginal tolerance in Zone 3.
Preferred Soil pH   Lowbush, 4.0 to 5.2; highbush, 4.0 to 6.0.

Yellowish Leaves in Spring

High pH
If the leaves on your plants are yellowish instead of a healthy dark green when they break forth in spring,

check the soil pH. If the level has crept upward, apply a layer of acid mulch to lower the pH to something under 6.0. To increase general soil acidity, apply 1 pound of soil sulfur for every 100 square feet of sandy soil, or 3 to 4 pounds for every 100 square feet of loam. Most blueberry soils will benefit from a yearly addition of generous amounts of peat moss, composted pine needles, or a similar acidic organic material.

PLANTING AND PROPAGATION

Best Method of Propagation   Cuttings
When to Propagate   Spring
Spring Planting   While dormant
Fall Planting   While dormant
Planting Depth   Dig a hole deep enough so that the root mass lies ½ to 1 inch below surface of soil.
Spacing between Plants   Highbush, at least 7 to 8 feet; lowbush, 3 to 4 feet.

Pollination Requirements   Needs cross-pollination from at least one other variety.
Container Varieties   Any variety can be grown in containers.
Container Size   24 inches deep.

MANAGEMENT OF BERRIES

Water Requirements

Make sure the plants get 1 inch of water every week from rain or by watering. When the plants start

producing fruit, give them 1 to 1½ inches of water each week. (See chapter 8 for more information on watering.)

Feeding Requirements

Apply compost or a slow-acting general-purpose fertilizer in spring (avoid straight manure, as it tends to be alkaline). Spray plants with liquid seaweed extract two or three times during growing season. (See chapter 8 for more information on feeding.)

MOST COMMON INSECT PESTS

Berries Have Worms

Apple Maggot
Although they are hard to detect on the outside, if you look inside the berries you will find white worms eating the fruit. These are apple maggots, the larvae of the apple maggot fly. They are white or yellowish, and measure ¼ inch long. The adult fly is also ¼ inch long. It is black with yellow legs, yellow markings across the abdomen, and bands that zigzag across the wings. These flies lay eggs in punctures in berry skin. The best way to control apple maggots is to prevent the adult fly from laying eggs. A sticky trap made from a red ball and yellow rectangle traps the flies, and is available commercially. Clean up all fallen fruit immediately.

Berries Shrivel

Cherry Fruitworm
If you notice shriveled berries or a web woven around a cluster of berries, look for the cherry fruitworm. This green caterpillar eats into the berries near the stem, causing them to shrivel. The adults are gray moths with black spots. They lay their eggs on the berries in mid-July. In small plantings, handpick the caterpillars. You cannot spray anything to kill the worms once they enter the fruit. A good fall cleanup and use of mulch will do as much as anything to keep this pest under control.

Leaves Stippled Yellow

Mite

Leaves that have become stippled, yellow, and dry, or that have pale yellow spots or blotches, are a sign that spider mites have infested your blueberries. Mites suck chlorophyll out of the leaves, causing small white dots to appear. They also inject toxins into the leaves, which discolors and distorts them. Mites are tiny arachnids about the size of a grain of black pepper. They may be red, black, or brown. Spray bushes with a forceful spray of water three times, once every other day, to knock mites from leaves. If that doesn't do the job, spray the undersides of leaves with insecticidal soap at least three times at 5- to 7-day intervals. Be sure to spray the plant from top to bottom.

Berries Fall, Have Cuts in Skin

Plum Curculio

If berries fall to the ground prematurely and have crescent-shaped marks, then your blueberry plants have plum curculios. The plum curculio is dark brown and ¼ inch long, with a prominent snout. When disturbed, it curls its legs and antennae and drops to the ground. The adult beetles feed on the blueberries, causing them to drop. To control plum curculios, spread a sheet underneath each blueberry bush and shake the branches. The plum curculios will drop onto the sheet, enabling you to collect them easily and destroy them. If plum curculios continue to be a problem, apply a pyrethrum spray when petals fall, and again every 10 to 14 days afterward until September, or until the beetles are under control. Remove and destroy all fallen fruit immediately.

Stunted Plants

Weevil

Larvae and adults may feed on leaves and fruit of blueberry bushes. Larvae make zigzag paths into roots, fruit, or stems. This pest is reddish brown in color with a black snout. It is about ¼ inch long. As weevils appear, spray with pyrethrum twice, 3 to 4 days apart.

MOST COMMON DISEASES

Cankers on Stems

Bacterial Canker

Reddish brown or black cankers on stems are a sign of bacterial, or stem, canker. Bacterial canker cannot be cured. Try pruning infected stems. Disinfect pruning tool in a bleach solution (one part household bleach to four parts water) after each cut. If you can't get the disease under control, remove and destroy the plants.

Resistant Varieties. Angola, Croatan, Morrow, Murphy, rabbit-eye varieties, and Walcott.

Galls on Stems

Cane Gall

Galls—rough, irregular, warty growths—on stems of plants indicate cane gall. Older stems are more susceptible. Cane gall cannot be cured. Infected stems should be pruned and destroyed. After each cut, clean hands and tools with a bleach solution (one part household bleach to four parts water) to prevent spread of the disease.

Galls on Roots and Stems

Crown Gall

Galls—rough, irregular, warty growths—or knots on roots and stems indicate crown gall. These occur where bacteria enter the plants through wounds. Remove the infected portions of the plant and destroy them. Clean hands and tools with bleach solution (one part household bleach to four parts water) to prevent spread of the disease.

Whitish Mold on Topsides of Leaves

Powdery Mildew

A whitish mold on the top surfaces of leaves, detected after harvest, indicates powdery mildew. It has no effect on yields. Remove and destroy infected parts, disinfecting tools in a bleach solution (one part household bleach to four parts water) after *each* cut. In addition, apply a 95 percent wettable sulfur fungicide every 7 to 10 days until 3 to 4 weeks before harvest.

MOST COMMON ANIMAL PESTS

Birds

One way to keep birds away from blueberries is to plant borders of chokecherries, dogwood, mulberries, mountain ash, or other very aromatic fruit nearby. Birds seem to prefer them.

For a barrier to succeed at keeping out the birds, it must completely surround the plant. Any opening and the birds are sure to find it. Fabric or plastic netting can't be casually draped over the plant the way advertising pictures show. This may save some fruit, but birds will peck right through it and squeeze in under it. Some kind of support is needed to hold the netting out away from the shrub so the birds can't reach any of the fruit.

HARVEST AND STORAGE

When to Harvest

Harvest berries after they have turned dark blue and only when they come off the bush easily. Taste them to see if they are ripe. Check plants every 2 to 3 days for ripe berries.

Yield per Plant   Lowbush, 5 to 6 pints; highbush, 4 to 8 pints.

Best Fresh Storage Method   Store ripe berries in a covered container in the refrigerator; they will last 1 to 2 weeks.

Best Long-Term Storage Method Blueberries freeze well and will keep for about 6 months.

Second-Best Long-Term Storage Method   Jams, jellies, or preserves.

NOTES AND RESEARCH

Blueberries suffer stunting, wilting, or even death when they come in contact with black walnut roots. Allelopathic reactions occur within a circle one and a half times the distance from the trunk of the black walnut to the outermost branches.

FRUIT
Cherry

Prunus avium (sweet cherry); *P. cerasus* (sour cherry)

DESCRIPTION AND ENVIRONMENT

Height   Sweet cherries: dwarf, 6 to 8 feet; semidwarf, 10 to 15 feet; standard, 25 to 35 feet. Sour cherries: dwarf, 6 to 12 feet; semidwarf, 12 to 18 feet; standard, 15 to 20 feet.

Spread   8 to 40 feet

Root Spread   The root spread will be at least half again as far as the dripline, or maximum circumference of the tree, and can be as much as twice the dripline.

Years to Bearing   Dwarf, 3 to 4; standard, 4 to 6, for sweet and sour.

Years of Production   15 to 30 for both sweet and sour.

Shade Tolerance   Needs full sun.

Frost Tolerance   Sweet cherries can be grown in Zones 5 to 7; sour cherries are generally hardier than sweet and will grow in Zones 4 to 6.

Preferred Soil pH   6.0 to 6.5

Varieties by Use

Fresh Eating   Sweet cherry: Bada, Bing, Compact, Hedelfingen, Lambert, Napoleon, Stark Gold, Stella, Summit, and Van.

Canning or Freezing   Sour cherry: Meteor, Montmorency, North Star, and Suda Hardy.

PLANTING AND PROPAGATION

Best Method of Propagation   Grafting or budding.

When to Propagate   Spring

Spring Planting   While dormant

Planting Depth   Set trees on dwarfing rootstocks with the graft union several inches above soil level. Set trees on standard rootstocks with the graft union a few inches below soil level.

Spacing between Trees   Sweet cherries: dwarf, 5 to 10 feet; standard, 35 to 40 feet. Sour cherries: dwarf, 8 to 10 feet; standard, 20 to 25 feet.

Pollination Requirements   All sweet cherries need a compatible variety for cross-pollination except Compact Stella, Stella, and Starkrimson. Pollinator needs to be within 40 feet of tree. Sour cherries are self-pollinating.

Container Varieties   Sweet cherry varieties include Garden Bing, a self-fertile variety that grows to about 6 feet with a 4-foot spread. Other good dwarf sweet varieties are Black Tartarian, Early Rivers, Gold, Lambert, Napoleon, Schmidt, Seneca, Windsor, and Yellow Spanish.

One sour cherry variety is the North Start sour cherry, a self-fertile tree that grows to about 8 feet. Other good dwarf sour varieties include Early Richmond, English Morello, and Montmorency.

Container Size   At least 24 inches deep.

MANAGEMENT OF FRUIT

Water Requirements

Cherry trees grow well if they get approximately 1 inch of water every week from rain or by watering. Spread at least 2 inches of organic mulch around the tree to hold in the moisture. Consistency of watering is critical, especially in the heat of the summer. Later in the season, consistent watering is important for good bud set for next year's crop. (See chapter 8 for more information on watering.)

Feeding Requirements

Apply compost or a slow-acting general-purpose fertilizer in spring, before the trees start to produce fruit. Fertilize again in the fall. Spray trees with liquid seaweed extract two or three times during the growing season. (See chapter 8 for more information on feeding.)

Season's Growth

On a standard tree, a season's growth of 6 to 10 inches indicates that the tree is receiving adequate nitrogen.

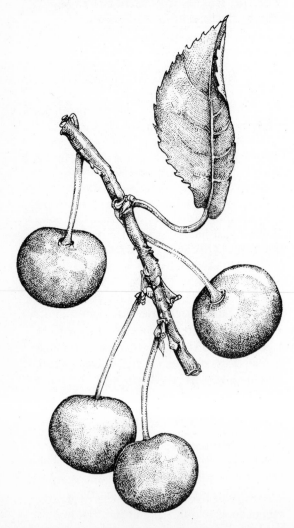

Pruning

Prune cherries to a spreading vase shape for easier care and earlier harvest. Select four main branches for the main framework and prune others off. Cherries only need light, corrective pruning each year. Usually, cutting back the tips of the branches is not necessary. Cut back overly long shoots that don't stay within the general vaselike shape. Prune trees every year in late winter to encourage the growth of new fruiting wood. Do not prune in the fall.

MOST COMMON INSECT PESTS

Foliage Curls, Puckers, Turns Yellow

Aphid

If the foliage on your cherry trees curls, puckers, and turns yellow, and the foliage and blooms become stunted, your trees may have aphids. Look for ants on the trees. They are attracted to a sticky honeydew secreted by aphids. Look for clusters of aphids on the undersides of young leaves. They are soft-bodied, pear-shaped insects about the size of a pinhead, and may be green, brown, or pink. For light infestations, spray vigorously with water early in the morning, three times, once every other day. For heavy infestations, use a commercial insecticidal soap every 2 to 3 days until aphids are under control.

Cherries Have Worms

Apple Maggot

Although they are hard to detect on the outside, you will find white worms inside cherries eating the fruit. These are apple maggots, the larvae of the apple maggot fly. They are white or yellowish, and measure ¼ inch long. The adult fly is also ¼ inch long. It is black with yellow legs, yellow markings across the abdomen, and bands that zigzag across the wings. These flies lay eggs in punctures in the cherries. The best way to control apple maggots is to prevent the adult fly from laying eggs. A sticky trap made from a red ball and yellow rectangle traps the flies and is available commercially. Clean up all fallen fruit immediately.

Skeletonized Leaves

Cankerworm

Cherry trees that have holes in the leaves and eventually become defoliated have been infested by cankerworms, also called inchworms. You might also see silken threads hanging from the branches of trees. When leaves become skeletonized, the tree weakens each year, fewer cherries mature, and sometimes the tree dies. Cankerworms are 1-inch-long worms. Both species (fall and spring) are colored brown and green, with stripes running along their bodies. To prevent their getting started, apply a dormant oil spray before leaves emerge, and follow with a preventive *Bacillus thuringiensis* (BT) spray from the end of blossoming, continuing every 2 weeks for 1 month. If they do take hold and need controlling, use BT for any further infestations. Apply every 10 to 14 days until cankerworms are removed.

Small Misshapen Cherries

Cherry Fruit Fly

If the cherries on your trees are small and misshapen, and you find maggots feeding on rotten flesh in the fruit, cherry fruit flies have infested your trees. The fruit may drop prematurely. The adult fruit flies resemble small houseflies with bars on their wings. They are about ⅕ inch long. They emerge in late spring or early summer. The females lay eggs inside the developing fruit. The maggots that hatch out are yellowish white and legless, with two dark mouth hooks. To control cherry fruit flies, you must control the adults before the eggs are laid. Where infestations are always heavy, hang red or yellow sticky traps in trees, starting in May, to catch females before they lay eggs. Collect and destroy dropped fruit daily.

Cherries Shrivel

Cherry Fruitworm

If you notice shriveled cherries or a web woven around a cluster of cherries, look for the cherry fruitworm. This green caterpillar eats into the cherries, causing them to shrivel. The adults are gray moths with black spots. They lay their eggs on the cherries in mid-July. In small plantings, handpick the caterpillars. You cannot spray anything to kill the worms once they enter the fruit. A good fall cleanup and use of mulch will do as much as anything to keep this pest under control.

Leaves Stippled Yellow

Mite

Leaves that have become stippled, yellow, and dry, or that have pale yellow spots or blotches, are a sign that spider mites have infested your cherry trees. Mites suck chlorophyll out of the leaves, causing small white dots to appear. They also inject toxins into the leaves, which discolors and distorts them. Mites are tiny arachnids about the size of a grain of black pepper. They may be red, black, or brown. Spray trees with a forceful spray of water three times, once every other day, to knock mites from leaves. If that doesn't do the job, spray the undersides of leaves with insecticidal soap at least three times at 5- to 7-day intervals. Be sure to spray the plant from top to bottom.

Holes in Trunk

Peachtree Borer

Holes in the trunk near the base of the tree from which brown frass (excrement) and gum exude are signs that borers are at work. The adults are wasplike moths. They lay eggs around the base of the trunk in late summer and early fall. These hatch into white, ¼-inch-long caterpillars with brownish heads, which burrow into the trunk as high as a foot above the ground or several inches below the ground. Young trees can be killed during the first season of infestation. Small infestations can be taken care of by inserting a stiff wire into each hole and killing the larva, or *Bacillus thuringiensis* (BT) can be shot into the hole at 10-day intervals until no more frass appears. Remove the soil several inches deep around the trunk to check for borers in the base of the tree. Cultivate shallowly in spring and fall to destroy eggs and pupae.

Cherries Fall, Have Cuts in Skin

Plum Curculio

If cherries fall to the ground prematurely and are misshapen, with crescent-shaped marks on the skins, plum curculio beetles have infested your trees. The plum curculio is dark brown and ¼ inch long, with a prominent snout. When disturbed, it curls its legs and antennae and drops to the ground. It can be found on all tree fruit crops from just before bloom to a few weeks after. In feeding, the beetles cut holes in the fruit. They lay their eggs in the cuts, and when the eggs hatch, the larvae feed on the fruit, causing it to drop. To control plum curculios, spread a sheet under each tree and shake the branches. Curculios will drop onto the sheet, and you can collect and destroy them. If curculios are still a problem, apply a pyrethrum spray when petals fall, and every 10 to 14 days until September, or until the beetles are under control. Remove and destroy all fallen fruit immediately.

Large Ragged Holes in Leaves

Slug

Large ragged holes in the leaves, fruit, and stems indicate that slugs have been attacking your trees. Other signs include trails of slime on the leaves and the soil near plants. Slugs look like snails without shells. They are 1 to 2 inches long, and can be brown, gray, white, pale yellow, purple, or nearly black with brown specks. The best way to control them is to set up a barrier of hardware cloth, ashes, or sand to deny them access to the trees. Handpicking works early in the season. There are a number of homemade traps that work as well. (See the entry Slug in chapter 4 for information on making these traps.)

Tree Becomes Defoliated

Tent Caterpillar

Tent caterpillars build large silken nests in the forks of tree branches. These pests grow to be about 2 inches long. They are black and hairy with white stripes and have narrow brown and yellow lines and a row of blue spots along their sides. To control tent caterpillars, remove the tents and destroy the caterpillars by hand, or spray the tree with *Bacillus thuringiensis* (BT) as soon as you notice the tents, continuing to spray every 5 to 7 days until the pest is removed.

Holes in Blossoms, Stunted Tree

Weevil

Larvae and adults may feed on leaves and fruit of cherry trees. Larvae make zigzag paths into roots, fruit, or bark. This pest is reddish brown in color with a black snout. It is about ¼ inch long. As weevils appear, spray with pyrethrum twice, 3 to 4 days apart.

Weakened Tree, Yellow Leaves

Whitefly

Trees that are weak, with leaves that turn yellow and die, are probably infested with whiteflies. Honeydew from the whiteflies drops on fruit and encourages fungal growth. As a result, the cherries are undersized and poorly colored. Whiteflies are about the size of a pinhead. They are mothlike and have dusty white wings. The yellowish nymphs are legless, somewhat flat, and oval, and they resemble scale at certain stages. If you shake a tree infested with whiteflies, it appears as though dandruff were flying off the leaves. Spray infested trees with an insecticidal soap spray, every 2 to 3 days for 2 weeks. To prevent whiteflies, follow this regimen early in the season, just as leaves are appearing. Spray with pyrethrum as a last resort. Make two applications, 3 to 4 days apart.

Sudden Wilting of Tree

White Grub

A sudden wilting of your young cherry trees, when all other conditions seem fine, may indicate the presence of white grubs. These pests are the fat, whitish larvae of the june beetle. They are ¾ to 1½ inches long and they feed on the roots of plants. To control infestations, make one application of bene-ficial nematodes, which go below the surface of the soil to attack the grubs. (See chapter 4 for more information on parasitic nematodes.) Milky spore disease spread on the soil around the plants will control white grubs, but it takes 3 to 5 years to have a complete effect.

MOST COMMON DISEASES

Heavy Oozing from Limbs

Bacterial Canker

If the shoots and limbs of your cherry trees ooze a heavy gum in spring and fall, and the leaves wilt and die in summer, your trees are infected with bacterial canker. Fruit infections are evidenced by a darkened depression on the surface. Bacterial canker cannot be cured. Prune and destroy infected shoots and limbs. After each cut, disinfect hands and tools in a bleach solution (one part household bleach to four parts water). If that doesn't control the disease, the entire tree must be destroyed. To prevent bacterial canker, grow resistant varieties and clean up debris around trees in the fall.
Resistant Varieties. Colt, Corum, Mahaleb *(Prunus mahaleb),* and Stockton Morello *(P. cerasus).*

Black Swellings on Limbs

Black Knot

Hard, coal-black swellings scattered throughout twigs and limbs are a sign that your trees have black knot. These first appear in late summer as olive-green swellings; then they blacken and weaken the limb beyond the knot. Remove all knotted twigs and branches, making cuts at least 4 inches below the beginning of the swelling. Burn pruned branches. If the limb is essential to tree growth, wait until early to midsummer and cut out the knot. Cover wounds with grafting wax or wound paint. Remove all infected wild plum and cherry trees in the area. To prevent the production of spores, apply lime sulfur sprays every 7 to 10 days for 3 to 4 weeks once this disease is spotted.

Brown Spots on Cherries

Brown Rot

Small, round brown spots on cherries may indicate brown rot. They spread to cover the whole fruit. The rotted areas develop light gray masses of spores. Once you have spotted this disease, apply a sulfur- or copper-based fungicide every 7 to 10 days to control the problem. Destroy infected and dropped fruit. Remove dead twigs, and cultivate shallowly around the tree. Do not spray water on ripe fruit. Just before harvesting, apply a sulfur or garlic and onion spray. When harvesting and storing, be careful not to damage fruit. Soak the fruit in water at a temperature of 120°F for 7 minutes and then refrigerate.

Resistant Varieties. Northstar Tart and Stark Gold.

Small Purple Spots on Leaves

Cherry Leaf Spot

Small reddish or purple circular spots appear on the leaves of cherries infected with cherry leaf spot. The dead tissue drops, giving a shothole effect to leaves. Partial to complete defoliation occurs. Spray trees with a 95 percent wettable sulfur fungicide from petal fall until after harvest to reduce this disease.

Galls on Roots or Crowns

Crown Gall

Crown gall causes galls (swellings) on the roots and crowns of cherry trees. The galls occur where bacteria enter the tree through wounds. Remove them with a sharp clean knife, and treat the wound with tree surgeon's paint. To prevent damage to the tree from sunburn, avoid doing this during the hottest part of the summer, and cover the affected part with soil. Clean your hands and tools with bleach solution (one part household bleach to four parts water) to prevent spread of the disease.

Yellowing of New Shoots

Cytospora Canker

The first symptom of cytospora canker is the wilting or yellowing of new shoots and leaves, which later turn brown. Gummy cankers appear at the base of new buds. Cut out infected wood and burn it. Paint the trunk and lower limbs with white latex paint to reduce injury from the cold. Delay pruning until bud swell; you can continue to prune through bloom. Midsummer topping and hedging reduce the need for pruning.

Gray, Velvety Mold

Powdery Mildew

If the terminals of twigs, leaves, and blossoms are covered with white to pearly gray, velvety mold, your cherry trees are infected with powdery mildew. Twigs are dwarfed, and the terminal bud is killed, which causes staghorn growth of side shoots. To control powdery mildew, follow the spray program prescribed for apple scab. (See the entry Apple Scab in chapter 5.) Prune infected terminals for additional control.

Split Bark

Sunscald

In some parts of the country, days are often bright and clear in January and February, and the warmth of the sun on the southwest side of the tree trunk begins to activate growth cells. Then, when the sun goes down, the temperature plummets, and the cold ruptures those cells and dries them out. To prevent this from happening, wrap the trunks with strips of burlap and secure with twine, or place a wide board several inches away from the tree on the southwest side, which will cast a shadow on the trunk. In March or April, when the weather is milder, remove the sun screen.

Wilted Leaves

Verticillium Wilt

When the leaves on your cherry trees wilt and droop during midsummer or later, suspect verticillium wilt. The leaves later turn yellow, curl upward along the midrib, and drop. Leaf damage progresses from the older part of the shoot to the younger growth. A sulfur fungicide used every 7 to 10 days until 3 to 4 weeks before harvest once the symptoms have been noticed has some effect in controlling this disease, but prevention practices will be more effective in the long run. Add organic matter to the soil to reduce the fungus. A well-nourished tree has a good chance of recovering.

MOST COMMON ANIMAL PESTS

Birds

One way to keep birds away from cherries is to plant borders of chokecherries, dogwood, mulberries, mountain ash, or other very aromatic fruit. Birds seem to prefer them.

For a barrier to succeed at keeping out the birds, it must completely surround the plant. Any opening and the birds are sure to find it. Fabric or plastic netting can't be casually draped over the dwarf tree the way the advertising pictures show. Netting draped on a tree may save some fruit, but birds will peck right through it and squeeze in under it. Some kind of support is needed to hold the netting out away from the tree so the birds can't reach any of the fruit. It is difficult to use this method of control on trees over 7 feet tall.

HARVEST AND STORAGE

When to Harvest

Pick cherries with the stems attached, being careful not to tear off the fruit spur that will produce fruit next year. The sugar content of cherries rises dramatically in the last few days of ripening, so wait until they turn fully red, black, or yellow (depending on the variety) before harvesting. Taste them for preferred sweetness. Sour cherries should separate from their pits when pulled. Harvest lasts about a week.

Yield per Tree   Both sweet and sour types: dwarf, 10 to 15 quarts, or 30 to 40 pounds; standard, 30 to 50 quarts, or 80 to 100 pounds.

Best Fresh Storage Method   Pack in tightly closed containers and store in the refrigerator; cherries will keep for 1 to 2 weeks.

Best Long-Term Storage Method Cherries can be frozen for up to 12 months.

Second-Best Long-Term Storage Method   Canning, jellies, jams, or preserves.

FRUIT **Muskmelon** *Cucumis melo*

DESCRIPTION AND ENVIRONMENT

Height and Spread   If grown vertically on a trellis, muskmelons take up little room in the garden. If grown flat on the garden surface, a plant can cover 30 to 40 square feet, depending on the variety. Bush varieties will stand 24 inches tall and spread 36 to 48 inches.

Root Depth   Roots are usually shallow, but some go down 4 feet.

Shade Tolerance   Needs full sun.

Frost Tolerance   Tender

Preferred Soil pH   6.0 to 7.5

PLANTING

Spring Planting   4 weeks after last expected frost.

Fall Planting   16 weeks before first expected frost.

Planting Depth   ½ to 1 inch

Spacing between Plants   48 to 72 inches

Best Soil Temperature for Germination   65°F to 80°F; transplants can be set out when soil temperature reaches 50°F.

Best Soil Temperature for Growing 70°F to 75°F

Best Air Temperature for Growing During the day, 70°F to 80°F; at night, 60°F to 70°F.

Days to Germination   4 to 10

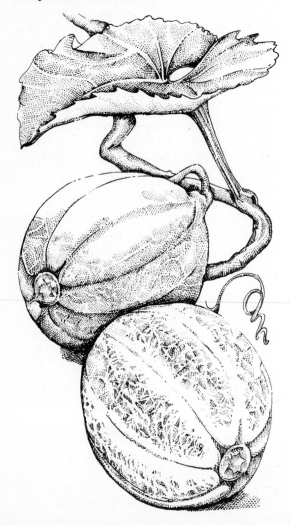

Weeks to Transplanting   3 to 4

Days to Maturity   80 to 100 warm days.

Greenhouse Varieties   Varieties such as New Hampshire Granite and Minnesota Midget can be grown in the greenhouse.

Container Varieties   Special varieties such as Burpee's Sugar Bush, New Hampshire Midget, and Yellow Baby Hybrid do well in containers, as do Muskateer and Bush Star.

Container Size   At least 24 inches deep.

Flat Flavor

Low Air Temperature

If you are having a cold summer, you may have trouble with warm weather crops such as melons. These plants will delay their ripening and will yield flat-flavored crops. In cool summer weather you might cover your melon plants with agricultural fleece to hold in some warmth, especially in the evenings.

MANAGEMENT OF FRUIT

Water Requirements

Make sure the plants get 1 inch of water every week from rain or by watering. Do not overwater, or flavor might be reduced. Uniform watering is important for good root enlargement. When about 4 weeks from harvest—melons will have reached two-thirds their final size—reduce watering. Once the first ripe melon is picked, stop watering altogether. (See chapter 8 for more information on watering.)

Feeding Requirements

Apply compost or slow-acting fertilizer in the spring as you prepare the soil. Spray plants with liquid seaweed extract two or three times during the growing season. If you want, you can give your melons a supplemental light feeding (side-dressing or foliar spray) monthly throughout the growing season, but this is not necessary. Do give plants a supplemental feeding when they are well established and the vines begin to crawl. If you do fertilize during the season, cut back on nitrogen later in the season. (See chapter 8 for more information on feeding.)

MOST COMMON INSECT PESTS

Foliage Curls, Puckers, Turns Yellow

Aphid

The primary problem aphids cause in melons, besides curling and yellowing of leaves, is that they are vectors for viral diseases that can kill the plant. Aphids are soft-bodied, pear-shaped insects about the size of a pinhead, and may be green, brown, or pink. Since they appear earlier in the season than melons do, try to control the aphids on other crops so that by the time the melons come along the aphids are no longer serious. For light infestations, spray the plants vigorously with water in the early morning, three times, once every other day. For heavy infestations, apply a commercial insecticidal soap every 2 to 3 days until aphids are under control. Floating row covers make excellent barriers against aphids and give melons the extra heat they like for growing. Remove covers at flowering.
Resistant Varieties. Cuban Castillian, Georgia 47, Homegarden, Rocky Dew, Smith's Perfect, Texas Resistant 1.

Plants Die from Disease

Cucumber Beetle

Cucumber beetles do minor physical damage to plants. But they spread mosaic and other diseases that quickly kill melon plants. The cucumber beetle is yellow with black stripes or spots. It has an oblong shape and is ¼ inch long. To control them, prevent the beetles from feeding on young plants by covering melons with a floating row cover of agricultural fleece at germination time. Remove the cover when the plants start to bloom.
Resistant Varieties. Hearts of Gold and Gold Cup 55.

Tiny Holes in Leaves

Flea Beetle

Several tiny holes or perforations in leaves can be caused by flea beetles. The beetles are ¹/₁₀ inch long, shiny, and black; they may have yellow or white markings. They are very active. Flea beetles jump like fleas when disturbed. Their feeding can destroy small plants rapidly. To control them, spread barriers, such as agricultural fleece, over plants in the spring as soon as the plants are put into the garden, or when the seedlings sprout. Keep the cover on the plants until the heat under the barrier exceeds 90°F from the summer sun. Spray infested plants with pyrethrum, in two applications, 3 to 4 days apart.

Leaves Stippled Yellow

Mite

Leaves that have become stippled, yellow, and dry, or that have pale yellow spots or blotches, are a sign that spider mites have infested your melons. Mites suck chlorophyll out of the leaves, causing small white dots to appear. They also inject toxins into the leaves, which discolors and distorts them. Mites are tiny arachnids about the size of a grain of black pepper. They may be red, black, or brown. Spray plants with a forceful spray of water three times, once every 5 to 7 days, to knock mites from leaves. If that doesn't do the job, spray the undersides of leaves with insecticidal soap at least three times at 5- to 7-day intervals. Be sure to spray the plant from top to bottom.

Wilted, Dried-up Leaves

Squash Bug

If the leaves of your melon plants wilt, dry up, and turn black, with damage increasing until the vine dies, your plants are infested with squash bugs. Adult squash bugs are flat-backed, shield-shaped, brown to black insects with a light-colored outline on the abdomen. They measure ½ to ¾ inch long. Squash bugs lay brown or red shiny eggs on leaves, which hatch into greenish gray nymphs. Adults and nymphs feed by sucking the juices from leaves. Use a barrier until bloom time to deny the bugs access to young plants. In addition, spray plants with insecticidal soap and seaweed extract. If bugs do get to the melons, handpick pests from the undersides of leaves. If the problem persists, spray plants with insecticidal soap every 2 to 3 days for 2 weeks.

Sudden Wilting of Plants

Squash Vine Borer

Sudden wilting of all or part of a melon vine can be caused by squash vine borers. To determine if squash vine borers are at work, look for moist, sawdustlike debris, called frass, piled up outside their small holes. These fat, white caterpillars with brown heads are about 1 inch long. They tunnel into the stems to feed. The adult is an orange-and-black, clear-winged moth with black stripes around the abdomen. It measures 1 to 1½ inches long. Try to deny the parent moth access to the plant with a fleece or netting barrier, which must be removed when the plant blooms. If the borer does get access to your plants, inject *Bacillus thuringiensis* (BT) into the stem with a hypodermic needle. Remove the borers by slitting the stem, then cover it with soil.

Weakened Plants, Yellow Leaves

Whitefly

Plants that are weak, with leaves that turn yellow and die, are probably infested with whiteflies. Honeydew from the whiteflies drops on fruit and encourages fungal growth. As a result, the melons are undersized and poorly colored. Whiteflies are about the size of a pinhead. They are mothlike and have dusty white wings. The yellowish nymphs are legless, somewhat flat, and oval, and they resemble scale at certain stages. If you shake a plant infested with whiteflies, it appears as though dandruff were flying off the leaves. Spray infested plants with an insecticidal soap spray, every 2 to 3 days for 2 weeks. To prevent whiteflies, follow this regimen early in the season, just as leaves are appearing. Spray with pyrethrum as a last resort. Make two applications, 3 to 4 days apart.

Plants Wilt and Die

Wireworm

If your melon plants wilt and die, suspect the wireworm. Wireworms are the larvae of click beetles. They are ⅓ to 1½ inches long, dark brown to yellowish, jointed, hard shelled, and cylindrical. They chew on the roots of plants. Trap them with pieces of potato speared on the ends of sticks. (See the entry Wireworm in chapter 4 for more information on how to use potato traps.) Plant a cover crop for long-term control.

MOST COMMON DISEASES

Black Sunken Spots on Melons

Anthracnose

Muskmelons infected with anthracnose develop small water-soaked spots on the leaves. These spots enlarge and turn brown, and eventually the leaves shrivel and die. Sunken lesions form on the stems and circular, black, sunken spots appear on the fruit. During moist conditions, these spots become covered with salmon-colored fungus. As soon as you spot the problem, apply a fixed copper or sulfur-based fungicide every 7 to 10 days until 3 to 4 weeks before harvest.

Limp Leaves

Bacterial Wilt

Muskmelons infected with bacterial wilt may wilt so quickly that they are green and dried up at the same time. The vascular system is blocked. This disease is transmitted by spotted and striped cucumber beetles. Try to prevent the beetle from getting access to the garden by covering with a barrier, such as agricultural fleece, until bloom. There is no cure. Remove infected plants immediately and destroy. Wash hands and any tools in a bleach solution (one part household bleach to four parts water) before touching other plants. Prevent bacterial wilt by following clean garden practices and planting seeds that are certifiably wilt-free.

Stunting and Curling of Young Leaves

Curly Top

The young leaves of melons infected with curly top become stunted and curled but may be normal in color. Older leaves are often yellowed. Overall, the plants are stunted and bushy and fail to produce. Curly top cannot be cured. Remove and destroy the infected and surrounding plants. Avoid planting melons near sugar beets, since the disease can be transmitted by beet leafhoppers.

Downy Substance on Leaves

Downy Mildew

Irregularly shaped yellow to brown spots appear on the tops of leaves, usually at the center of the plants, in plants with downy mildew. Under moist conditions, downy purple spots appear on the undersides of leaves. The leaves die as these spots increase in size. Downy mildew spreads rapidly from the crown toward new growth. If you catch the infection early, apply a copper-based fungicide to diseased and surrounding plants every 7 to 10 days until harvest. Remove and destroy any plants with a serious infection.

Brown Discoloration of Stems

Fusarium Wilt

Fusarium wilt occurs primarily in the northern states. In muskmelons it causes stunting, yellowing, wilting, and dying of vines. A water-soaked streak appears at the soil line on one side of the vine. This streak turns yellow, then tan, and finally dark brown. It is diagnostic of the disease in muskmelons. Some plants will produce some fruit, but in most cases you should remove and destroy infected plants. Wilt will live for many years in the soil, so use resistant varieties. Fusarium wilt can be transmitted to young plants by striped cucumber beetles, so to prevent this disease, cover plants with barriers, such as agricultural fleece or netting, which must be removed when the plants bloom.

Resistant Varieties. Charantais, Delicious #51, Golden Gopher, Harvest Queen, Iroquois, and Vedrantais.

Mottled Green or Yellow Leaves

Mosaic

Chlorosis (yellowing of the leaves), stunted plants, and reduced yields are symptoms of mosaic. Leaves appear mottled with dark green, light green, or yellow areas of irregular form. The leaves become irregularly shaped, and portions of the veins may die. Vine tips are stunted or yellowish. Mosaic cannot be cured. Remove and destroy the infected and surrounding plants. Control aphids, because they spread mosaic. Floating row covers make excellent barriers against aphids and give melons the extra heat they like for growing. Remove covers at flowering. Resistant Varieties. Charantais and Vedrantais.

White Powdery Growth on Undersides of Leaves

Powdery Mildew

Circular, whitish spots on the lower surfaces of leaves indicate powdery mildew. These spots increase in number and size, grow together, progress to the upper surface, and finally cover the entire leaf with white, powdery growth. As soon as you discover the disease, remove and destroy the infected parts. Disinfect your pruning tool in a bleach solution (one part household bleach to four parts water) after each cut. In addition to pruning, apply a copper-based fungicide every 7 to 10 days according to the instructions on the package.

Resistant Varieties. Cantaloupes: Dixie Jumbo, Edisto, Magnum 45, Planters Jumbo, Samson Hybrid, and Sweet and Early. Muskmelons: Burpee Ambrosia, Chaca, Dixie Jumbo, Edisto, Magnum 45, Planters Jumbo, Samson Hybrid, Supermarket, and Sweet and Early.

Dark Green Spots on Melons

Scab

In melons with scab, water-soaked spots appear on leaves, which may cause them to wilt. Young melons develop gray, slightly sunken spots. As the plant matures, these spots darken, become more sunken, and are covered with a greenish velvety mold. Remove and destroy infected plants.

HARVEST AND STORAGE

When to Harvest

Pick some fruit before it is fully ripe and take it indoors to complete ripening in a cool spot. This is a preventive measure, which will ensure you some fruit if your garden is hit by heavy rains or animal attack just as the fruit ripens on the vine. Harvest melons when the stem pulls away cleanly from the fruit. Do not wash fruit until just before you eat it. If, after picking, you don't detect a strong perfumelike odor, let the fruit ripen indoors for a few days before eating.

Yield per Plant   The individual fruit can weigh from 1 to 4 pounds, depending on the variety, so a plant can yield 10 to 30 pounds, depending on the variety.

Best Fresh Storage Method   Melons will keep for 1 to 2 weeks in the refrigerator.

Best Long-Term Storage Method Freeze segments of flesh for up to 4 months.

Second-Best Long-Term Storage Method   Pickled or in relish.

NOTES AND RESEARCH

Almost half of a melon's final sugar content is accumulated during the last week of maturation. A plant that is stressed or sick during that time will not manufacture sufficient sugar. Diseases in the melon plant are the greatest cause of flavor loss. When a disease strikes, it weakens the vines and slows the flow of sugars to the fruit, causing the melons to ripen before full sweetness has developed.

Recent work has indicated that you can extend muskmelon storage life with water-impermeable plastic film wraps, which control variations in humidity. Watch for new developments in this area.

FRUIT **Peach**   *Prunus persica*

DESCRIPTION AND ENVIRONMENT

Height   Dwarf, 4 to 10 feet; standard, 15 to 20 feet.

Root Spread   The root spread will be at least half again as far as the dripline, or circumference of the branches, and can be as much as twice the dripline.

Root Depth   Over 90 percent of a peach tree's roots lie within the top 18 inches of soil.

Years to Bearing   Dwarf, 1 to 2; standard, 3.

Years of Production   8 to 20

Shade Tolerance   Needs full sun.

Frost Tolerance   Can be grown in Zones 5 through 9, some in Zone 10; peach buds are very susceptible to cold.

Preferred Soil pH   6.0 to 6.5

PLANTING AND PROPAGATION

Best Method of Propagation   Dwarf, budding; standard, budding or cuttings.

When to Propagate   Spring

Spring Planting While still fully dormant.

Fall Planting In areas with mild winters, plant when dormant.

Planting Depth Keep the graft point 1 inch above the soil line, or the rootstock will start growing.

Spacing between Trees Dwarf, 10 to 12 feet; standard, 15 to 20 feet.

Pollination Requirements Peaches self-pollinate, except for J. H. Hale, Indian Free, and Indian Blood Cling.

Container Varieties Dwarf and semidwarf varieties can be grown in containers. Try Honey Babe, a dwarf variety that grows only 4 to 6 feet tall and bears heavily. Other good dwarf varieties include Garnet Beauty, Glorhaven, Golden East, Golden Jubilee, Halehaven, Marigold, Redhaven, Rich-haven, Triogem, Valiant, and Vedette.

Container Size At least 24 inches deep.

Peaches Are Small

Tree Planted in Grass

Living grass may inhibit the growth of trees, but dead sod can boost tree growth by enriching the soil. Peach trees grown in dead sod produced a heavy yield only 3 years after planting. Another reason for keeping the area around your peach trees free of grass is that grass and weeds increase the chances of peachtree borers infecting the trees.

MANAGEMENT OF FRUIT

Water Requirements

Peach trees grow well if they get approximately 1 inch of water every week from rain or by watering. Spread at least 2 inches of organic mulch around the tree to hold in moisture. Consistency in watering is critical, especially in the heat of the summer. Later in the season, consistent watering is important for good bud set for next year's crop. (See chapter 8 for more information on watering.)

Feeding Requirements

Apply compost or a slow-acting general-purpose fertilizer in spring as the leaves begin to come out. Spray the foliage with liquid seaweed extract two or three times during the growing season. (See chapter 8 for more information on feeding.)

Season's Growth

On a standard tree, a season's growth of 6 to 12 inches indicates that the tree is receiving adequate nitrogen.

Pruning

Prune peach trees to an open center shape for best results.

Thinning

Many varieties tend to set more peaches than the trees can handle. Several weeks after the trees bloom, thin young peaches to about 6 to 8 inches apart on the branches. Try to achieve a ratio of leaves to fruit of about 50 leaves for each peach. This provides enough leaves to produce the carbohydrates needed for peaches to mature to a full size. In some cases, there may be enough leaves to support fruit closer than the 6- to 8-inch guideline.

Pale Leaves, Turning Yellow

Nitrogen Deficiency

If leaves become pale and turn yellow in the late spring, especially the lower leaves, your peach trees are probably suffering from a nitrogen deficiency. The fruit will have a bright blush, and will ripen early. This premature fruit will be watery and will lack full, rich flavor. To remedy the problem quickly, spray the trees with diluted fish emulsion or other liquid fertilizer. (See chapter 8 for more information on nitrogen deficiency.)

Peaches Are Small

Need Thinning

One way to get large fruit from your trees is to thin out the fruit when it is just forming. Thinning also keeps branches from breaking. Thin peaches to 6 to 8 inches apart when they are ½ to ¾ inch in diameter; at that stage, they come off easily. Early peaches especially need to be thinned, or they'll be undersized.

MOST COMMON INSECT PESTS

Foliage Curls, Puckers, Turns Yellow

Aphid

If the foliage on your peach trees curls, puckers, and turns yellow, and the foliage and blooms become stunted, your trees may have aphids. Look for ants on the trees. They are attracted to a sticky honeydew secreted by aphids. Look for clusters of aphids on the undersides of young leaves. They are soft-bodied, pear-shaped insects about the size of a pinhead, and may be green, brown, or pink. For light infestations, spray vigorously with water early in the morning, three times, once every other day. For heavy infestations, use a commercial insecticidal soap every 2 to 3 days until aphids are under control.

Defoliated Tree

Gypsy Moth Caterpillar

Gypsy moths infest many species of trees in the northeastern and Middle Atlantic states. You will see large masses of caterpillars feeding on leaves, and the trees will eventually become defoliated. Newly hatched caterpillars are about $\frac{1}{16}$ inch long, and grow to about 2½ inches at maturity. They are gray and have long brown hairs. Eggs are light brown to yellow and are laid in masses on trunks and branches from August through the following April. Scrape them into a bucket of soapy water. To control caterpillars, spray trees in early spring with *Bacillus thuringiensis* (BT) every 10 to 14 days. In June, switch to trapping the insects with burlap skirts. (See chapter 4 for more information on these traps.)

Skeletonized Leaves

Japanese Beetle

Japanese beetles chew out the leaf tissue between the veins, leaving skeletonized leaves, foliage, and flowers. They are shiny metallic green beetles with copper-brown wings, and are ½ inch long. To control them, set up pheromone traps, making sure traps are no closer than 50 feet from peach trees. Handpick the stragglers. If the infestation is too heavy to be controlled with traps, spray with pyrethrum, making two applications 3 to 4 days apart.

Leaves Stippled Yellow

Mite

Leaves that have become stippled, yellow, and dry, or that have pale yellow spots or blotches, are a sign that spider mites have infested your peach trees. Mites suck chlorophyll out of the leaves, causing small white dots to appear. They also inject toxins into the leaves, which discolors and distorts them. Mites are tiny arachnids about the size of a grain of black pepper. They may be red, black, or brown. Spray trees with a forceful spray of water three times, once every other day, to knock mites from leaves. If that doesn't do the job, spray the undersides of leaves with insecticidal soap at least three times at 5- to 7-day intervals. Be sure to spray the plant from top to bottom.

Holes Low in Trunk

Peachtree Borer

Holes in the trunk near the base of the tree from which brown frass (excrement) and gum exude are signs that borers are at work. The adults are wasplike moths. They lay eggs around the base of the trunk in late summer and early fall. These hatch into white, ¼-inch-long caterpillars with brownish heads, which burrow into the trunk as high as a foot above the ground or several inches below the ground. Young trees can be killed during the first season of infestation. Small infestations can be taken care of by inserting a stiff wire into each hole and killing the larva, or *Bacillus thuringiensis* (BT) can be shot into the hole at 10-day intervals until no more frass appears. Remove the soil several inches deep around the trunk to check for borers in the base of the tree. Cultivate shallowly in spring and fall to destroy eggs and pupae.

Peaches Fall to Ground, Have Cuts in Skin

Plum Curculio

If peaches fall to the ground prematurely, are misshapen, and have crescent-shaped marks on the skins, plum curculio beetles have infested your trees. The plum curculio is dark brown and ¼ inch long, with a prominent snout. It can be found on all tree fruit crops from just before bloom to a few weeks after. When disturbed, it curls its legs and antennae and drops to the ground. In feeding, the adult cuts a hole in the skin of the fruit and hollows out a cavity about ⅛ inch deep. It lays its eggs in the cuts, and when the eggs hatch, the grayish white larvae bore to the center of the fruit and feed, causing the fruit to drop. To control plum curculios, spread a sheet under each tree and shake the branches. Curculios will drop onto the sheet, and you can collect and destroy them. If curculios are still a problem, apply a pyrethrum spray when petals fall, and every 10 to 14 days until September, or until the beetles are under control. Remove and destroy all fallen fruit immediately.

Black Spots and Pitting

Tarnished Plant Bug

Black spots and pitting can be seen on the stem tips, buds, and fruit of infested trees. This pest deforms roots, blackens terminal shoots, and ruins flowers. Only buds that escape feeding will set fruit. The adult tarnished plant bug is a ¼-inch-long, oval, flat, brownish insect, mottled with yellow and black. It sucks on plant parts. Tarnished plant bugs are highly mobile. The nymphs are pale yellow, and the eggs are long and curved and inserted in stems, tips, and leaves. For effective control, sprays must be used early in the morning when bugs are least active. Try three applications of pyrethrum, one every 3 days, to control tarnished plant bug adults and nymphs. The best way to control this pest is by fall and spring cleanup to prevent it from occurring in the first place.

Tree Becomes Defoliated

Tent Caterpillar

Tent caterpillars build large silken nests in the forks of tree branches. These pests grow to be about 2 inches long. They are black and hairy with white stripes and have narrow brown and yellow lines and a row of blue spots along their sides. To control tent caterpillars, remove the tents and destroy the caterpillars by hand, or spray the tree with *Bacillus thuringiensis* (BT) as soon as you notice the tents, continuing to spray every 5 to 7 days until the pest is removed.

Holes in Blossoms, Stunted Tree

Weevil

Larvae and adults may feed on leaves and fruit of peach trees. Larvae make zigzag paths into roots, fruit, or bark. This pest is reddish brown in color with a black snout. It is about ¼ inch long. As weevils appear, spray with pyrethrum twice, 3 to 4 days apart.

Weakened Tree, Yellow Leaves

Whitefly

Trees that are weak, with leaves that turn yellow and die, are probably infested with whiteflies. Honeydew from the whiteflies drops on fruit and encourages fungal growth. As a result, the peaches are undersized and poorly colored. Whiteflies are about the size of a pinhead. They are mothlike and have dusty white wings. The yellowish nymphs are legless, somewhat flat, and oval, and they resemble scale at certain stages. If you shake a tree infested with whiteflies, it appears as though dandruff were flying off the leaves. Spray infested trees with an insecticidal soap spray, every 2 to 3 days for 2 weeks. To prevent whiteflies, follow this regimen early in the season, just as leaves are appearing. Spray with pyrethrum as a last resort. Make two applications, 3 to 4 days apart.

MOST COMMON DISEASES

Purple Spots on Leaves

Bacterial Canker

Small purple spots on leaves, black lesions on fruit, and cankers on twigs indicate that bacterial canker has infested your trees. This disease cannot be cured. First prune the infected twigs and branches and destroy them. If the canker continues to spread, the entire tree must be destroyed.

Pale Green Spots on Leaves

Bacterial Spot

Small, circular, pale green spots on leaves that later turn light brown indicate that bacterial spot has infected your peach trees. The tissue around the spots fades to a light yellow-green and becomes purplish and angular in shape. Small circular sunken spots develop on fruit, and later the fruit cracks. Bacterial spot cannot be cured. First try to control the disease by applying a copper-based fungicide every 7 to 10 days. In addition, prune and destroy the infected parts. If the disease continues to spread, the entire tree must be destroyed.

Resistant Varieties. Belle of Georgia, Bicentennial, Biscoe, Candor, Cardinal, Clayton, Compact Redhaven, Correll, Cumberland, Dixiland, Dixired, Earlired, Early Elberta, Eden, Ellerbe, Emery, Envoy, Hamlet, Harbelle, Harbinger, Harbrite, Harken, Jefferson, Kalhaven, LaGem, LaPremier, Loring, Madison, Marhigh, Newhaven, Norman, Pekin, Polly, Ranger, Rarian, Redhaven, Redkist, Redskin, Reliance, Richhaven, Rose, Royalvee, Sentinel, Southhaven, Summercrest, Sunbrite, Sunhaven, Sunshine, Sweethaven, Wildrose, and Winblo.

Brown Spots on Peaches

Brown Rot

If small, round, brown spots appear that spread to cover the whole fruit, your peach trees are infected with brown rot. The rotted areas develop light gray masses of spores. Apply a sulfur or fixed copper fungicide every 7 to 10 days from the time you spot the disease until 20 days before harvest; then apply a spray of garlic and onion or a sulfur spray once, just before harvest. Destroy the diseased or mummified fruit. Remove dead twigs, and cultivate shallowly around the tree. Do not spray water on ripe fruit. During harvest and storage, handle fruit carefully so as not to damage, and refrigerate immediately after picking.

Resistant Varieties. Carmen, Elberta, Greensbore, Orange Cling, Red Bird, Sneed, and Sunbeam.

Galls on Roots or Crowns

Crown Gall

Crown gall causes galls (swellings) to form on the roots and crowns of peach trees. The galls occur where bacteria enter the tree through wounds. Remove them with a sharp, clean knife, and treat the wound with tree surgeon's paint. To prevent damage to the tree from sunburn, avoid doing this during the hottest part of the summer, and cover the affected part with soil. Clean your hands and tools with bleach solution (one part household bleach to four parts water) to prevent spread of the disease.

Yellowing of New Shoots

Cytospora Canker

The first symptom of cytospora canker is the wilting or yellowing of new shoots and leaves, which later turn brown. Gummy cankers form at the base of a bud in late winter. Cut the infected branches and burn them. Since the canker infects the trees through wounds, try to protect the tree from winter injury. Paint the trunk and lower limbs with white latex paint to reduce injury from the cold. Delay regular pruning until bud swell.

Resistant Varieties. Biscoe, Candor, Carmen, Champion, Comanche, Cumberland, Eden, Emery, Envoy, Harbelle, Jayhaven, Madison, Polly, Raritan Rose, Redqueen, Reliance, Royalvee, and Veteran.

Blistering, Curling of New Leaves

Peach Leaf Curl

The new leaves of peach trees infected with peach leaf curl become blistered and distorted, curl up, turn reddish in color, and then wither and drop. This disease can be controlled by applying lime sulfur or a fixed copper fungicide. Spray the entire tree after all the leaves drop in the fall, and again just before buds open in the spring. Remove and destroy infected leaves as they appear in spring.

Resistant Varieties. Dixigem, Loring, Monroe, Redhaven, Summercrest, and Sunshine.

Dark Greenish Spots on Peaches

Scab

Small, dark greenish spots that appear about the time fruit is half grown and turn brown as the fruit matures are symptoms of scab. Yellow-brown spots appear on twigs and branches, and the fruit may crack. To control scab, apply sulfur spray or dust 2 to 3 weeks after petals drop. A second application may be needed 2 weeks later. Remove infected fruit, and clean up fallen leaves and fruit. (For a full spray program, see the steps for controlling scab in the entry Apple Scab in chapter 5.)

Wilted, Drooping Leaves

Verticillium Wilt

When the leaves on your peach trees wilt and droop during midsummer or later, suspect verticillium wilt. The leaves later turn yellow, curl upward along the midrib, and drop. Leaf damage progresses from the older part of the shoot to the younger growth. Add organic matter to the soil to reduce the fungus. A well-nourished tree has a good chance of recovering.

MOST COMMON ANIMAL PESTS

Birds

To keep birds away from peaches, plant borders of chokecherries, dogwood, mulberries, mountain ash, or other types of very aromatic fruit. Birds seem to prefer them.

HARVEST AND STORAGE

When to Harvest

Harvest peaches when they are fully colored and come off the tree easily; they should give slightly to the touch.

Yield per Tree   Dwarf, 30 to 60 pounds; standard, 60 to 100 pounds.

Best Fresh Storage Method   Peaches will keep for up to 2 weeks in a root cellar or cool cellar.

Best Long-Term Storage Method   Dried peaches will keep for 6 months stored at 70°F, and for up to 2 years at 52°F.

Other Storage Methods   Peaches can be frozen or canned; however, canned peaches are more flavorful.

NOTES AND RESEARCH

Decaying roots of mature peach trees emit substances that cause damage to the roots of young ones, so don't plant new trees where former peach trees grew.

FRUIT **Pear**   *Pyrus communis*

DESCRIPTION AND ENVIRONMENT

Height   Dwarf, less than 15 feet; semidwarf, 15 to 20 feet; standard, 30 to 40 feet.
Spread   Standard, 25 feet.
Root Spread   The root spread will be at least half again as far as the dripline, or circumference of the branches, and can be as much as twice the dripline.
Years to Bearing   Dwarf, 3 to 5; standard, 6 to 8.
Shade Tolerance   Needs full sun.
Frost Tolerance   Can be grown in Zones 5 through 8; some varieties in Zones 4, 9, or 10.
Preferred Soil pH   6.0 to 6.5

Varieties by Use

Fresh Eating   Anjou, Bartlett, Bosc, Conference, Dana Hovey, Gorham, Seckel, Sheldon, and Winter Nelis.

Canning   Bartlett, Gorham, and Seckel.

PLANTING AND PROPAGATION

Best Method of Propagation   Budding or grafting.

When to Propagate   Spring
Spring Planting   While fully dormant.
Planting Depth   Keep the graft point 1 inch above the soil line, or the rootstock will start growing.
Spacing between Trees   Dwarf, 12 to 15 feet; standard, 20 to 25 feet.
Pollination Requirements   Needs cross-pollination, so plant at least two different varieties.
Container Varieties   Dwarf and semidwarf varieties can be grown in containers. Some dwarf varieties include Anjou, Bartlett, Bosc, Clapp Dana Hovey, Duchess, Favorite, Howell, Seckel, Sheldon, Winter Nelis, and Worden Seckel.
Container Size   At least 24 inches deep.

MANAGEMENT OF FRUIT

Water Requirements

Pear trees grow well if they get approximately 1 inch of water every week from rain or by watering. Spread at least 2 inches of organic mulch around the trees to hold in the moisture. Consistency in watering is critical, especially in the heat of summer.

Later in the season, consistent watering is important for good bud set for next year's crop. (See chapter 8 for more information on watering.)

Feeding Requirements

Apply compost or a slow-acting general-purpose fertilizer in spring. Go lightly on the nitrogen, because high nitrogen levels make pear trees much more vulnerable to fire blight. Spray trees with liquid seaweed extract two or three times during the growing season. Pears need boron, which is provided by

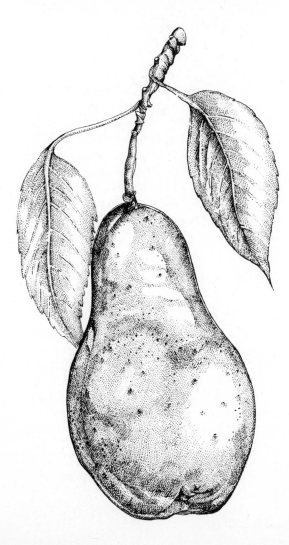

the seaweed extract. (See chapter 8 for more information on feeding.)

Season's Growth

On a standard tree, a season's growth of 12 to 18 inches indicates that the tree is receiving adequate nitrogen.

Pruning

Prune to a central leader for the first few years, then prune to a modified leader; annual light pruning is good.

Thinning

Many varieties tend to set more pears than the trees can handle. Several weeks after the trees bloom, thin young pears to about 6 to 8 inches apart on the branches. Try to achieve a ratio of leaves to fruit of about 50 leaves for each pear. This provides enough leaves to produce the carbohydrates needed for pears to mature to a full size. In some cases then, there may be enough leaves to support fruit spaced more closely than the 6- to 8-inch guideline.

MOST COMMON INSECT PESTS

Foliage Curls, Puckers, Turns Yellow

Aphid

If the foliage on your pear trees curls, puckers, and turns yellow, and the foliage and blooms become stunted, your trees may have aphids. Look for ants on the trees. They are attracted to a sticky honeydew secreted by aphids. Look for clusters of aphids on the undersides of young leaves. They are soft-bodied, pear-shaped insects about the size of a pinhead, and may be green, brown, or pink. For light infestations, spray vigorously with water early in the morning, three times, once every other day. For heavy infestations, use a commercial insecticidal soap every 2 to 3 days until aphids are under control.

Pears Have Worms

Apple Maggot

Although they are hard to detect on the outside, if you look inside the pears you will find white worms eating the fruit. These are apple maggots, the larvae of the apple maggot fly. They are white or yellowish and measure ¼ inch long. The adult fly is also ¼ inch long. It is black with yellow legs, yellow markings across the abdomen, and bands that zigzag across the wings. These flies lay eggs in punctures in pear skin. The best way to control apple maggots is to prevent the adult fly from laying eggs. A sticky trap made from a red ball and yellow rectangle traps the flies, and is available commercially. Clean up all fallen fruit immediately.

Small Misshapen Pears

Cherry Fruit Fly

If the pears on your trees are small and misshapen, and you find maggots feeding on rotten flesh in the fruit, cherry fruit flies have infested your trees. The pears may drop prematurely. The adult fruit flies resemble small houseflies with bars on their wings. They are about ⅕ inch long. They emerge in late spring or early summer. The females lay eggs inside the developing fruit. The maggots that hatch out are yellowish white and legless, with two dark mouth hooks. To control cherry fruit flies, you must control the adults before the eggs are laid. Where infestations are always heavy, hang red or yellow sticky traps in trees, starting in May, to catch females before they lay eggs. Collect and destroy dropped fruit daily.

Tunnels in Pears

Codling Moth

The larvae of codling moths tunnel their way through pears, eating as they go. You might also spot some cocoons in the bark crevices. The larva is 1 inch long, pink, and has a brown head. The adult is a grayish brown moth with lacy brown lines on forewings and pale, fringed hind wings. It has a ¾-inch wingspan. Adults lay white, flat eggs singly on leaves, twigs, or fruit buds. To control these pests, spray dormant oil on trees prior to leaf budding in late winter or early spring to suffocate the eggs. Set out sticky traps to catch the moths just as the blossoms are coming out. Apply preventive sprays of *Bacillus thuringiensis* (BT) and light horticultural oils later in the season to kill newly hatched larvae. Spray trees every 10 to 14 days until 2 weeks before harvest. Butterfly weed *(Asclepias tuberosa)* hosts parasites of codling moths.

Defoliated Tree

Gypsy Moth Caterpillar

Gypsy moths infest many species of trees in the northeastern and Middle Atlantic states. You will see large masses of caterpillars feeding on leaves, and the trees will eventually become defoliated. Newly hatched caterpillars are about $\frac{1}{16}$ inch long, and grow to about 2½ inches at maturity. They are gray and have long brown hairs. Eggs are light brown to yellow and are laid in masses on trunks and branches from August through the following April. Scrape them into a bucket of soapy water. To control caterpillars, spray trees in early spring with *Bacillus thuringiensis* (BT) every 10 to 14 days. In June, switch to trapping the insects with burlap skirts.

Leaves Stippled Yellow

Mite

Leaves that have become stippled, yellow, and dry, or that have pale yellow spots or blotches, are a sign that spider mites have infested your pear trees. Mites suck chlorophyll out of the leaves, causing small white dots to appear. They also inject toxins into the leaves, which discolors and distorts them. Mites are tiny arachnids about the size of a grain of black pepper. They may be red, black, or brown. Spray plants with a forceful spray of water three times, once every other day, to knock mites from the leaves. If that doesn't do the job, spray the undersides of leaves with insecticidal soap at least three times at 5- to 7-day intervals. Be sure to spray the plant from top to bottom.

Leaves Yellow and May Drop

Pear Psylla

Leaf yellowing and a general decline in vigor indicate that your trees have pear psyllids. Severely infected trees may drop their leaves. The pear psylla secretes honeydew that coats leaves and may encourage the growth of a sooty black mold. The adults are reddish brown and emerge in spring and mate. Females begin laying their yellow eggs on twigs in early spring. The immature insects and adults feed by sucking out the plant's juices. To control psyllids, spray with insecticidal soap every 3 to 4 days until the insect is gone. In fall, spray trees with a light horticultural oil, and in early spring, spray with a dormant oil before the leaves emerge. After the leaves emerge, spray insecticidal soap once a week for 3 weeks.

Pears Fall, Have Cuts in Skin

Plum Curculio

If pears fall to the ground prematurely, are knotted, gnarled, and misshapen, and have crescent-shaped marks on the skins, plum curculio beetles have infested your trees. The plum curculio is dark brown and ¼ inch long, with a prominent snout. It can be found on all tree fruit crops from just before bloom to a few weeks after. When disturbed, the plum curculio curls its legs and antennae and drops to the ground. In feeding, the beetles cut holes in the skin of the fruit. They lay their eggs in the cuts, and when the eggs hatch, the larvae feed on the fruit, causing it to drop. To control plum curculios, spread a sheet under each tree and shake the branches. Curculios will drop onto the sheet, and you can collect and destroy them. If curculios are still a problem, apply a pyrethrum spray when petals fall, and every 10 to 14 days until September, or until the beetles are under control. Remove and destroy all fallen fruit immediately.

Large Ragged Holes in Leaves

Slug

Large ragged holes in the leaves, fruit, and stems indicate that slugs have been attacking your trees. Other signs include trails of slime on the leaves and the soil near plants. Slugs look like snails without shells. They are 1 to 2 inches long, and can be brown, gray, white, pale yellow, purple, or nearly black with brown specks. The best way to control them is to set up a barrier of hardware cloth, ashes, or sand to deny them access to the trees. Handpicking works early in the season. There are a number of homemade traps that work as well. (See the entry Slug in chapter 4 for information on making these traps.)

Black Spots and Pitting

Tarnished Plant Bug

Black spots and pitting can be seen on the stem tips, buds, and fruit of infested trees. This pest deforms roots, blackens terminal shoots, and ruins flowers. Only buds that escape feeding will set fruit. The adult tarnished plant bug is a ¼-inch-long, oval, flat, brownish insect, mottled with yellow and black. It sucks on plant parts. Tarnished plant bugs are highly mobile. The nymphs are pale yellow, and the eggs are long and curved and inserted in stems, tips, and leaves. For effective control, sprays must be used early in the morning when bugs are least active. Try three applications of pyrethrum, one every 3 days, to handle adults and nymphs. The best way to control tarnished plant bug damage is by fall and spring cleanup to prevent it from occurring in the first place.

Discolored Leaves, Scarred Fruit

Thrip

Thrips puncture leaves to suck the sap, causing considerable discoloration and disfiguration. Leaves may become bleached and will wilt. Thrips are only ¹⁄₂₅ inch long. What is visible are their dark fecal pellets. To control them, spray with insecticidal soap every 3 days for 2 weeks. For serious infestations, use pyrethrum.

Leaf Buds and Early Bark Eaten

Weevil

If the leaf buds and bark of your young pear trees are eaten in spring, suspect the New York weevil. This pest is gray with dark spots. It is about ⅜ inch long. It feeds at night and hides during the day. As weevils appear, spray with pyrethrum twice, 3 to 4 days apart.

Weakened Tree, Yellow Leaves

Whitefly

Trees that are weak, with leaves that turn yellow and die, are probably infested with whiteflies. Honeydew from the whiteflies drops on fruit and encourages fungal growth. As a result, the pears are undersized and poorly colored. Whiteflies are about the size of a pinhead. They are mothlike and have dusty white wings. The yellowish nymphs are legless, somewhat flat, and oval, and they resemble scale at certain stages. If you shake a tree infested with whiteflies, it appears as though dandruff were flying off the leaves. Spray infested trees with an insecticidal soap spray, every 2 to 3 days for 2 weeks. To prevent whiteflies, follow this regimen early in the season, just as leaves are appearing. Spray with pyrethrum as a last resort. Make two applications, 3 to 4 days apart.

MOST COMMON DISEASES

Velvety Olive-Green Spots on Pears

Apple Scab

Pale yellow or olive-green spots that develop on the undersides of leaves and that darken nearly to black indicate apple scab. Both surfaces of leaves may show scab spots. Other symptoms include curling, cracking, and distortion of leaves. The fruit also develops spots, which enlarge and gain a velvety appearance in the center, becoming brown and corky. The fruit of young pear trees drops; growing fruit distorts and cracks. An infection of the twigs will blister and rupture the bark. (To control scab, follow the spray program discussed in the entry Apple Scab in chapter 5.)

Tiny Pale Yellow Spots on Leaves

Cedar Apple Rust

Pale yellow, pinhead-sized spots on the upper surfaces of leaves, enlarging to bright orange spots on foliage and fruit, indicate cedar apple rust. Use approved fungicides on pears when cedar galls are releasing spores in the early spring. Remove all red cedar trees within 300 yards. Junipers and hawthorns can also spread cedar apple rust to pear trees. Cut down nearby susceptible species, such as the flowering crabapple.

Galls on Roots or Crowns

Crown Gall

Crown gall causes galls (swellings) to form on the roots and crowns of pear trees. The galls occur where bacteria enter the tree through wounds. Remove them with a sharp, clean knife, and treat the wound with tree surgeon's paint. To prevent damage to the tree from sunburn, avoid doing this during the hottest part of the summer, and cover the affected part with soil. Clean your hands and tools with bleach solution (one part household bleach to four parts water) to prevent spread of the disease.

Withered and Dead Blossoms

Fire Blight

Shoots infected with fire blight turn brown or black as though scorched. The blossoms wither and die. Water-soaked bark lesions appear that are reddish in color, and on warm days they ooze an orange-brown liquid. Later they become brown and dry. Prune and destroy blighted branches, and scrape and treat cankers with pruning paint. Disinfect your pruning tool in a bleach solution (one part household bleach to four parts water) after each cut.

Resistant Varieties. Asian varieties and Comice, Dawn, Douglas, Duchess d'Angouleme, El Dorado, Fan-stil, Lincoln, Luscious, Mac, Magness, Maxine,

Moonglow, Orient, Seckel, Starking Delicious, Sugar, Sure Crop, Waite, and Winter Nelis. Disease-resistant rootstocks: Kieffer, Moonglow, Old Home, Oriental *(Pyrus bitulafolis)*, Oriental *(P. communis)*, Oriental harbin pear *(P. ussuriensis)*, Seedling, Stark Honeyseet, and Starking Delicious.

HARVEST AND STORAGE

When to Harvest

Harvest pears when they are green, about 2 weeks before they are ripe, and allow pears to ripen in a cool room (70°F to 75°F) for 5 to 10 days. Tree-ripened pears do not have the quality of flavor and texture as do those ripened indoors.

Yield per Tree   After 5 years, dwarf pear trees will give you 1 bushel of pears each year.

Best Fresh Storage Method   After harvesting, keep pears at temperatures just above freezing for a month, then keep them at room temperature to ripen; they will last for about 3 months.

Best Long-Term Storage Methods   Pears can be canned or pickled and will keep for more than 12 months; dried pears will keep for up to 6 months.

FRUIT **Plum**   *Prunus domestica* (European plum); *P. salicina* (Japanese plum)

DESCRIPTION AND ENVIRONMENT

Height   Dwarf, 3 to 5 feet; semidwarf, 14 feet; standard, 16 to 20 feet.

Spread   Dwarf, 3 to 5 feet; semidwarf, 13 feet; standard, 14 to 18 feet.

Root Spread   The root spread will be at least half again as far as the dripline, or circumference of the branches, and can be as much as twice the dripline.

Years to Bearing   European, 4 to 5; Japanese, 2 to 3.

Shade Tolerance   Needs full sun.

Frost Tolerance   European plums can be grown in Zones 5 to 7, Japanese, in Zones 5 to 9.

Preferred Soil pH   6.0 to 8.0

Varieties by Use

Fresh Eating   Albion, Bavay, Burbank Red Ace, Epineuse, Formosa, Imperial, Ozark Premier, Pearl, and Redheart.

Canning   German Prune, Hall, Italian, Prune, Shropshire, and Stanley Damson.

PLANTING AND PROPAGATION

Best Method of Propagation   Grafting

When to Propagate   Spring

Spring Planting   While dormant

Planting Depth   Keep the graft union 1 inch above the soil line.

Spacing between Trees   Dwarf and semidwarf, 15 to 20 feet; standard, 20 to 25 feet.

Pollination Requirements   European plums self-pollinate; Japanese need cross-pollination.

Container Varieties   Try dwarf varieties such as Albion, Bradshaw, Burbank, Formosa, German Prune, Imperial, Imperial Epineuse, Imperial Gage, Italian Prune, Pearl, President, Santa Rosa, Shiro, Stanley, and Washington.

Container Size   At least 24 inches deep.

MANAGEMENT OF FRUIT

Water Requirements

Young plum trees need 1½ inches of water every week during the first year of growth either from rain or by watering. Mature trees grow well if they get approximately 1 inch of water each week. Spread at least 2 inches of organic mulch around trees to hold in moisture. Consistency in watering is critical, especially in the heat of the summer. Later in the season, consistent watering is important for good bud set for next year's crop. (See chapter 8 for more information about watering.)

Feeding Requirements

Apply compost or a slow-acting general-purpose fertilizer in spring. Spray trees with liquid seaweed extract two or three times during the growing season. (See chapter 8 for more information on feeding.)

Season's Growth

On a standard tree, a season's growth of 12 inches indicates that the tree is receiving adequate nitrogen.

Pruning

European plum trees are best shaped like an apple tree with a more upright form. The Japanese plum should be pruned like a peach tree, with an open center to let in plenty of sunshine. Plum trees need very little pruning while young, and moderate thinning out and heading back as they grow older.

Plums Are Small

Need Thinning

One way to get large fruit from your trees is to thin out excess plums. It also keeps branches from breaking. Thin when fruit are ½ to ¾ inch in diameter; at that stage, they come off easily. Thin Japanese plums until they are 3 to 4 inches apart, but don't thin European plums unless there is an especially heavy crop, when you should thin them to 3 to 4 inches apart.

MOST COMMON INSECT PESTS

Foliage Curls, Puckers, Turns Yellow

Aphid

If the foliage on your plum trees curls, puckers, and turns yellow, and the foliage and blooms become stunted, your trees may have aphids. Look for ants

on the trees. They are attracted to a sticky honey-dew secreted by aphids. Look for clusters of aphids on the undersides of young leaves. They are soft-bodied, pear-shaped insects about the size of a pinhead, and may be green, brown, or pink. For light infestations, spray vigorously with water early in the morning, three times, once every other day. For heavy infestations, use a commercial insecticidal soap every 2 to 3 days until aphids are under control.

Plums Have Worms

Apple Maggot

Although they are hard to detect on the outside, if you look inside the plums you will find white worms eating the fruit. These are apple maggots, the larvae of the apple maggot fly. They are white or yellowish and measure ¼ inch long. The adult fly is also ¼ inch long. It is black with yellow legs, yellow markings across the abdomen, and bands that zigzag across the wings. These flies lay eggs in punctures in the plums. The best way to control apple maggots is to prevent the adult fly from laying eggs. A sticky trap made from a red ball and yellow rectangle traps the flies, and is available commercially. Clean up all fallen fruit immediately.

Small Misshapen Plums

Cherry Fruit Fly

If the plums on your trees are small and misshapen, and you find maggots feeding on rotten flesh in the fruit, cherry fruit flies have infested your trees. The plums may drop prematurely. The adult fruit flies resemble small houseflies with bars on their wings. They are about ⅕ inch long. They emerge in late spring or early summer. The females lay eggs inside the developing fruit. The maggots that hatch out are yellowish white and legless, with two dark mouth hooks. To control cherry fruit flies, you must control the adults before the eggs are laid. Where infestations are always heavy, hang red or yellow sticky traps in trees, starting in May, to catch females before they lay eggs. Collect and destroy dropped fruit daily.

Leaves Stippled Yellow

Mite

Leaves that have become stippled, yellow, and dry, or that have pale yellow spots or blotches, are a sign that spider mites have infested your plum trees. Mites suck chlorophyll out of the leaves, causing small white dots to appear. They also inject toxins into the leaves, which discolors and distorts them. Mites are tiny arachnids about the size of a grain of black pepper. They may be red, black, or brown. Spray trees with a forceful spray of water three times, once every other day, to knock mites from leaves. If that doesn't do the job, spray the undersides of leaves with insecticidal soap at least three times at 5- to 7-day intervals. Be sure to spray the plant from top to bottom.

Holes in Trunk

Peachtree Borer

Holes in the trunk near the base of the tree from which brown frass (excrement) and gum exude are signs that borers are at work. The adults are wasplike moths. They lay eggs around the base of the trunk in late summer and early fall. These hatch into white, ¼-inch-long caterpillars with brownish heads, which burrow into the trunk as high as a foot above the ground or several inches below the ground. Young trees can be killed during the first season of infestation. Small infestations can be taken care of by inserting a stiff wire into each hole and killing the larva, or *Bacillus thuringiensis* (BT) can be shot into the hole at 10-day intervals until no more frass appears. Remove the soil several inches deep around the trunk to check for borers in the base of the tree. Cultivate shallowly in spring and fall to destroy eggs and pupae.

Plums Fall, Have Cuts in Skin

Plum Curculio

If plums fall to the ground prematurely, are misshapen, and have crescent-shaped marks on the skins, plum curculio beetles have infested your trees. The plum curculio beetle is dark brown and ¼ inch long, with a prominent snout. It can be found on all tree fruit crops from just before bloom to a few weeks after. When disturbed, it curls its legs and antennae and drops to the ground. In feeding, the beetles cut holes in the fruit. They lay their eggs in the cuts, and when the eggs hatch, the larvae feed on the fruit, causing it to drop. To control plum curculios, spread a sheet under each tree and shake the branches. Curculios will drop onto the sheet, and you can collect and destroy them. If curculios are still a problem, apply a pyrethrum spray when petals fall, and every 10 to 14 days until September, or until the beetles are under control. Remove and destroy all fallen fruit immediately.

Holes in Blossoms, Stunted Tree

Weevil

Larvae and adults may feed on leaves and fruit of plum trees. Larvae make zigzag paths into roots, fruit, or bark. This pest is reddish brown in color with a black snout. It is about ¼ inch long. As weevils appear, spray with pyrethrum twice, 3 to 4 days apart.

Weakened Tree, Yellow Leaves

Whitefly

Trees that are weak, with leaves that turn yellow and die, are probably infested with whiteflies. Honeydew from the whiteflies drops on fruit and encourages fungal growth. As a result, the plums are undersized and poorly colored. Whiteflies are about the size of a pinhead. They are mothlike and have dusty white wings. The yellowish nymphs are legless, somewhat flat, and oval, and they resemble scale at certain stages. If you shake a tree infested with whiteflies, it appears as though dandruff were flying off the leaves. Spray infested trees with an insecticidal soap spray, every 2 to 3 days for 2 weeks. To prevent whiteflies, follow this regimen early in the season, just as leaves are appearing. Spray with pyrethrum as a last resort. Make two applications, 3 to 4 days apart.

MOST COMMON DISEASES

Green Spots on Leaves

Bacterial Spot

Small, circular, pale green spots on leaves that later turn light brown indicate that bacterial spot has infected your plum trees. The tissue around the spots fades to a light yellow-green and becomes purplish and angular in shape. Infected areas on leaves soon fall. Purplish black, sunken spots develop on green fruit; on some cultivars, small pitlike spots occur. Bacterial spot cannot be cured. The first line of defense, if the disease is identified early in its development, is to apply a copper-based fungicide to the tree every 7 to 10 days as directed on the package. Prune the infected parts immediately, disinfecting tools and hands in a bleach solution (one part household bleach to four parts water) after each cut. If good results don't show up after a second spraying, the plant or tree must be destroyed.

Black Swellings on Limbs

Black Knot

In spring, the bark of twigs and branches infected with black knot cracks, and a light yellow growth develops that later becomes covered with an olive-green layer. In late summer, hard, rough, black swellings develop at these places, weakening the twigs and branches. These swellings are more common on smaller branches, which are often killed by girdling. Remove all knotted twigs and branches, making cuts at least 4 inches below the beginning of the swelling. Burn pruned branches. If the limb is essential to tree growth, wait until early to midsummer and cut out the knot. Cover wounds with grafting wax or wound paint. Remove all infected wild plum and cherry trees in the area. To prevent the production of spores, apply lime sulfur sprays every 7 to 10 days from the time you spotted the problem until 3 to 4 weeks before harvest.
Resistant Varieties. President.

Brown Spots on Plums

Brown Rot

Small round brown spots on plums may indicate brown rot. They spread to cover the whole fruit. The rotted areas develop light gray masses of spores. Once you have spotted this disease, apply a sulfur- or copper-based fungicide every 7 to 10 days to control the problem. Destroy infected and dropped fruit. Remove dead twigs, and cultivate shallowly around the tree. Do not spray water on ripe fruit. Just before harvesting, apply a sulfur or garlic and onion spray. When harvesting and storing, be careful not to damage fruit. Soak the fruit in water at a temperature of 120°F for 7 minutes and then refrigerate.

Galls on Roots or Crowns

Crown Gall

Crown gall causes galls (swellings) to form on the roots and crowns of plum trees. The galls occur where bacteria enter the tree through wounds. Remove them with a sharp, clean knife, and treat the wound with tree surgeon's paint. To prevent damage to the tree from sunburn, avoid doing this during the hottest part of the summer, and cover the affected part with soil. Clean your hands and tools with bleach solution (one part household bleach to four parts water) to prevent spread of the disease.

Yellowing of New Shoots

Cytospora Canker

The first symptom of cytospora canker is the wilting or yellowing of new shoots and leaves, which later turn brown. Gummy cankers appear at the base of new buds. Cut out infected wood and burn it. Paint the trunk and lower limbs with white latex paint to reduce injury from the cold. Delay pruning until bud swell; you can continue to prune through bloom. Midsummer topping and hedging reduce the need for pruning.

Gray, Velvety Mold

Powdery Mildew

If the terminals of twigs, leaves, and blossoms are covered with white to pearly gray, velvety mold, your trees are infected with powdery mildew. Twigs are dwarfed, and the terminal bud is killed, which causes staghorn growth of side shoots. To control powdery mildew, follow the spray program prescribed for apple scab. (See the entry Apple Scab in chapter 5.) Prune infected terminals for additional control.

Wilted Leaves

Verticillium Wilt

When the leaves on your plum trees wilt and droop during midsummer or later, suspect verticillium wilt. The leaves later turn yellow, curl upward along the midrib, and drop. Leaf damage progresses from the older part of the shoot to the younger growth. A sulfur fungicide used every 7 to 10 days once the symptoms have been noticed has some effect in controlling this disease, but prevention practices will be more effective in the long run. Add organic matter to the soil to reduce the fungus. A well-nourished tree has a good chance of recovering.

HARVEST AND STORAGE

When to Harvest

Harvest European plums when they are tree-ripe, which is when they are a little soft and come off easily with a slight twist. Pick Japanese plums slightly early and allow them to ripen in a cool place (65°F to 75°F). For cooking, pick plums somewhat under-ripe, before they are very soft but after they have developed a whitish bloom. For fresh eating, pick when plums are warm from the sun and give slightly to pressure.

Yield per Tree   Dwarf, 30 to 60 pounds; standard, 100 to 120 pounds.

Best Fresh Storage Method   Plums can be stored in the refrigerator for 1 to 2 weeks.
Best Long-Term Storage Methods
Plums can be canned, used in jams or jellies, or dried into prunes; good prune varieties include Aldrich, Earliblue, and Stanley.

NOTES AND RESEARCH

Wild cherries and wild plums can spread black knot to plums, and chokecherries can spread X-disease to plums. Keep peach trees away from plum trees in areas where yellows is a problem.

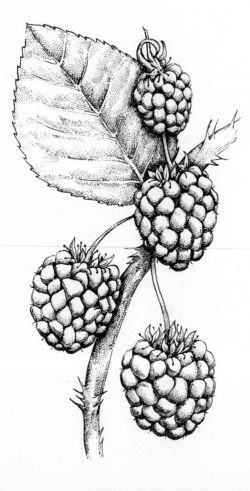

BERRY # Raspberry

Rubus idaeus (red raspberry);
R. occidentalis (black raspberry)

DESCRIPTION AND ENVIRONMENT

Height   5 to 10 feet
Root Depth   12 inches
Years to Bearing   2
Years of Production   8 to 10
Shade Tolerance   Needs full sun.
Frost Tolerance   Hardy up to Zone 2.
Preferred Soil pH   5.5 to 7.0

PLANTING AND PROPAGATION

Best Method of Propagation
Transplanting
When to Propagate   Spring
Spring Planting   Plant in late winter or early spring, while suckers are dormant.
Fall Planting   In Zone 6 and further south, raspberries can be planted in the fall.
Planting Depth   Plant 1 to 2 inches deeper than previously grown; prune new black raspberry transplants back to just above ground level; prune other types down to 8 inches.
Spacing between Plants   24 to 36 inches apart in rows 4 to 6 feet apart.
Mulch   Roots prefer 4 to 8 inches of organic mulch during warm weather to keep them cool. A

4- to 6-inch layer of compost in the fall will protect the roots from heaving and feed the plants in the spring.

Cuttings Didn't Take

Used Wrong Canes

If you take cuttings, and they do not root when planted, you probably took cuttings from canes that bore berries earlier in the season. Canes die back after fruiting, and consequently cannot be used for propagation. Take 4- to 6-inch cuttings from fruitless canes, strip off the bottom leaves, and plant them in a moist rooting medium.

MANAGEMENT OF BERRIES

Water Requirements

Make sure the plants get 1 inch of water every week from rain or by watering. When plants start producing fruit, give them 1 to 1½ inches of water each week. (See chapter 8 for more information on watering.)

Feeding Requirements

Apply compost or a slow-acting general-purpose fertilizer in the spring. Spray plants with liquid seaweed extract two or three times during the growing season. (See chapter 8 for more information on feeding.)

MOST COMMON INSECT PESTS

Foliage Curls, Puckers, Turns Yellow

Aphid

If the foliage on your raspberries curls, puckers, and turns yellow and the foliage and blooms become stunted, your plants may have aphids. Look for ants on the bushes. They are attracted to a sticky honeydew secreted by aphids. Look for clusters of aphids on the undersides of young leaves. They are soft-bodied, pear-shaped insects about the size of a pinhead, and may be green, brown, or pink. The biggest threat aphids pose to raspberries is that they carry a number of viral diseases, such as mosaic, that can kill raspberry plants. For light infestations, spray vigorously with water early in the morning, three times, once every other day. For heavy infestations, use a commercial insecticidal soap every 2 to 3 days until aphids are under control.

Sudden Wilting of Tips

Caneborer

Sudden wilting of the tips of raspberry or blackberry canes is the first sign that raspberry caneborers have infected your plants. Close examination of canes shows two rows of punctures about 1 inch apart at the tip of the cane. The adult is a black-and-yellow beetle, ½ inch long, which lays an egg between the rows of punctures. A small grub hatches from the egg and burrows toward the base of the cane. To destroy this larva, cut off the wilted tips below the lower row of punctures and burn them.

Skeletonized Leaves

Japanese Beetle

If the leaves of your raspberries have been skeletonized, suspect the Japanese beetle. This shiny metallic green beetle is about ½ inch long and has copper-brown wings. Set up pheromone beetle traps, making sure traps are no closer than 50 feet from vulnerable crops. Handpick stragglers or use pyrethrum if traps cannot handle the infestation. If Japanese beetles are a regular problem in your garden, set up the traps a week before emergence.

Leaves Stippled Yellow

Mite

Leaves that have become stippled, yellow, and dry, or that have pale yellow spots or blotches, are a sign that spider mites have infested your raspberry plants. Mites suck chlorophyll out of the leaves, causing small white dots to appear. They also inject toxins into the leaves, which discolors and distorts them.

Mites are tiny arachnids about the size of a grain of black pepper. They may be red, black, or brown. Spray plants with a forceful spray of water three times, once every other day, to knock mites from the leaves. If that doesn't do the job, spray the undersides of leaves with insecticidal soap at least three times at 5- to 7-day intervals. Be sure to spray the plant from top to bottom.

Canes Wilt and Die

Raspberry Root Borer

Canes infested with the raspberry root borer (also called the raspberry crown borer) break off easily at the base and show an overall lack of vigor, or they may wilt and die in the early summer. You can often find the white ½-inch grubs feeding in the crown or the roots. Raspberry root borers can sometimes be killed by probing infected crowns with a wire, but a surer method of control is to cut the infested canes below the soil line and destroy them. Look for rust-colored eggs on leaves in late summer and destroy them. Drench the base of the plants with *Bacillus thuringiensis* (BT) in early spring. Do this for 2 years.

Holes in Blossoms, Stunted Plant

Weevil

Larvae and adults may feed on leaves and fruit of raspberry plants. Larvae make zigzag paths into roots, fruit, or stems. This pest is reddish brown in color with a black snout. It is about ¼ inch long. As weevils appear, spray with pyrethrum twice, 3 to 4 days apart.

Weakened Plants, Yellow Leaves

Whitefly

Plants that are weak, and whose leaves turn yellow and die, are probably infested with whiteflies. Honeydew from the whiteflies drops on fruit and encourages fungal growth. As a result, the berries are undersized and poorly colored. Whiteflies are about the size of a pinhead. They are mothlike and have dusty white wings. The yellowish nymphs are legless, somewhat flat, and oval, and they resemble scale at certain stages. If you shake a plant infested with

whiteflies, it appears as though dandruff were flying off the leaves. Spray infested plants with an insecticidal soap spray, every 2 to 3 days for 2 weeks. To prevent whiteflies, follow this regimen early in the season, just as leaves are appearing. Spray with pyrethrum as a last resort. Make two applications, 3 to 4 days apart.

MOST COMMON DISEASES

Reddish Brown Spots on New Canes

Anthracnose

If new canes show small reddish brown or purplish spots, suspect anthracnose. As the canes grow, these spots enlarge, become round, turn gray in color, develop sunken centers, and grow together. Small, irregular, yellow or purple spots also develop on the leaves. To control anthracnose, apply a dormant oil spray in late winter before budding. Apply an approved fungicide such as copper dust or liquid copper spray every 7 to 10 days after spotting the problem, or when the leaves have come out if you are expecting a problem with anthracnose. Spray the uninfected canes with a light dormant oil to protect them. If the fungicide does not control the disease, remove and destroy infected canes. **Resistant Varieties.** Black Beauty.

Grayish Mold on Berries

Botrytis Fruit Rot

If you see grayish mold on the berries, your raspberry plants probably have botrytis fruit rot. Sulfur or fixed copper fungicides provide a good degree of control, provided the application is properly timed so that it catches the fungus early in its spring development. Pick the fruit continuously to prevent the accumulation of overripe berries. Handle the berries gently to prevent bruising.

Canes Wilt and Die

Cane Blight

Cane blight causes canes to wilt and die while loaded with fruit. Late in the season, brownish purple areas appear on cut or injured parts of the cane. These discolored areas spread down the cane and encircle it. Cane blight cannot be cured. Remove and burn all affected stalks. Control cane-damaging insects, such as caneborers.

Galls on Canes

Cane Gall

Wartlike galls are found on fruiting canes of black and purple raspberries, and on the roots of red raspberries infected with cane gall (also called crown gall). The galls change from white to light brown. Late in the season, they disintegrate. New shoots are not infected. Cut and destroy infected canes.

Small, Tightly Curled Leaves

Leaf Curl

If the leaves on your raspberry bushes are small, tightly curled, and very dark green, suspect the leaf curl virus. This disease attacks all types of raspberries, and it cannot be cured. Remove and destroy infected and surrounding plants.

Dark Reddish Spots on Leaves, Defoliation

Leaf Spot

If dark reddish spots appear on the leaves, and the raspberry plant becomes defoliated, your bushes have leaf spot. Control the disease by thinning and trellising the canes for good air movement. Use approved fungicides. (See fungicides described in chapter 5.)

Pale, Mottled, Puckered, Narrow Leaves

Mosaic

With some strains there are no distinguishing symptoms, but infected plants will be weaker, and will produce fewer canes and berries. Other strains will produce short canes and yellowish, mottled foliage, and the fruit may be dry, seedy, flavorless, and crumbly. On red raspberries, large green blisters develop on the foliage in late spring, with yellowish tissue around them. On black and purple raspberries, canes bend over, turn black, and die. Leaves become mottled and plants are stunted. Mosaic cannot be cured. Remove and destroy infected and surrounding plants. Control aphids, because they spread mosaic.

Resistant Varieties. Indian Summer, Lloyd George, Newburgh, Pyne's Imperial, Pyne's Royal, and Williamette.

Yellow Dots on Both Sides of Leaves

Orange Rust

Yellow dots on both sides of leaves indicate orange rust. Two to 3 weeks later, light-colored areas develop on the undersides of leaves; then the surface of the leaves ruptures, exposing large, bright orange-red, powdery masses of spores. Infected plants cannot be saved. Dig them up and destroy them. To prevent orange rust, follow good fall cleanup practices, mulch with straw and leaf mold, and add a heavy dressing of compost to the garden; malnutrition encourages this disease.

White, Powdery Growth on Undersides of Leaves

Powdery Mildew

If the leaves of your raspberry plants become dwarfed and twisted, and a white powdery fungus develops on the undersides, your plants have powdery mildew. As soon as you discover the disease, remove and destroy the infected parts. Disinfect your pruning tool in a bleach solution (one part household bleach to four parts water) after each cut. In addition to pruning, apply a sulfur- or copper-based fungicide every 7 to 10 days. Limit overhead sprinkling to early in the day, and do not work around plants when they are wet. Thin plants to let in sun and air, and prune mildewed tips.

Lower Leaves Turn Yellowish

Verticillium Wilt

If raspberries are infected with verticillium wilt, the lower leaves develop an off-green or yellowish bronze tinge in June or early July. The leaves curl upward, then turn brown and fall off. Sometimes a sudden wilt occurs in hot, dry weather. Canes show blue or purple streaks. Red raspberry is more resistant, symptoms show up later in the season, and discolored leaves turn upward. It is difficult to see cane streaks in red raspberries because of the natural color in them. Infected plants eventually die. Remove and destroy infected and surrounding plants. For future plantings, avoid heavy, poorly drained soils, and buy disease-free stock.

MOST COMMON ANIMAL PESTS

Birds

A barrier that is to be successful at keeping out raspberry robbers must completely surround the plants. Any opening and the birds are sure to find it. Fabric or plastic netting can't be casually draped over the raspberry bushes the way the advertising pictures show. Draping netting on a bush may save some fruit, but birds will peck right through it and squeeze in under it. Some kind of support is needed to hold the netting out away from the bush so the birds can't reach any of the fruit.

Another way to protect raspberries from birds is to construct a tepee of pipes, pole, or lumber over the berry patch, then drape a net over the structure. You could also build a frame of 2×3's with wire screening; just be sure to leave an access door for yourself.

HARVEST AND STORAGE

When to Harvest

Harvest berries when they slide easily off the small white core. Pick into a small container, so the berries on the bottom don't get crushed.

Yield per Plant   1½ quarts
Best Fresh Storage Method   Raspberries will store in the refrigerator for 4 to 7 days.
Best Long-Term Storage Method Raspberries can be frozen for about 6 months.
Second-Best Long-Term Storage Method   Jams, jellies, or preserves.

NOTES AND RESEARCH

Most raspberry canes are biennial. The first-year primocanes (green stems) bear only leaves. The second-year floricanes (brown stems) produce fruit. To keep plants healthy, remove floricanes after harvest.

A border of raspberries around a garden can be an effective thorny barrier against intruders.

Wild brambles host diseases to which the raspberry might succumb. Himalaya berry *(Rubus procerus)* can spread anthracnose to raspberries. Potatoes and raspberries succumb to verticillium wilt, so do not plant them close together. Raspberries are tolerant of the juglone in black walnut roots.

FRUIT Rhubarb *Rheum rhabarbarum*

DESCRIPTION AND ENVIRONMENT

Height   24 to 36 inches
Spread   36 to 48 inches
Shade Tolerance   Needs 5 to 6 hours of sun a day (partial shade).

Frost Tolerance   Hardy; needs cold winters and is not productive in areas with very hot summers.
Preferred Soil pH   5.5 to 6.8

PLANTING AND PROPAGATION

Best Method of Propagation   Division or seed.

When to Propagate   Fall

Spring Planting   Plant when soil can be worked; spring is the time to divide older plants, after harvest is over.

Fall Planting   Plant seeds 60 days before the first expected frost.

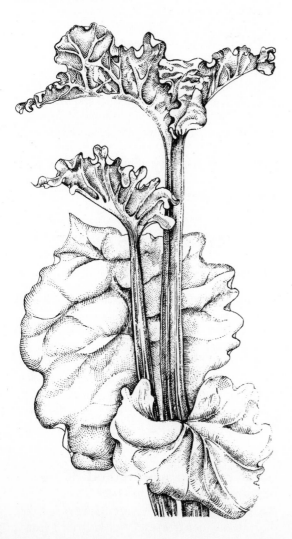

Planting Depth   Seeds, ½ inch; roots 2 to 3 inches over the crown.

Spacing between Plants   30 to 36 inches

Container Varieties   Any variety of rhubarb can be grown in containers.

Container Size   At least 24 inches deep.

MANAGEMENT OF FRUIT

Water Requirements

Rhubarb grows well if it gets approximately 1 inch of water every week from rain or by watering. Spread at least 2 inches of organic mulch around plants to hold in moisture. (See chapter 8 for more information on watering.)

Feeding Requirements

Apply compost or a slow-acting general-purpose fertilizer in spring. Spray plants with liquid seaweed extract two or three times during the growing season. (See chapter 8 for more information on feeding.)

MOST COMMON INSECT PESTS

Leaves Stippled Yellow

Mite

Leaves that have become stippled, yellow, and dry, or that have pale yellow spots or blotches, are a sign that spider mites have infested your rhubarb plants. Mites suck chlorophyll out of the leaves, causing small white dots to appear. They also inject toxins into the leaves, which discolors and distorts them. Mites are tiny arachnids about the size of a grain of black pepper. They may be red, black, or brown. Spray plants with a forceful spray of water three times, once every other day, to knock mites from the leaves. If that doesn't do the job, spray the undersides of leaves with insecticidal soap at least three times at 5- to 7-day intervals. Be sure to spray the plant from top to bottom.

Punctured Stalks

Rhubarb Curculio

The rhubarb curculio punctures the stalks and lays eggs in them. It also bores into the crowns and roots of the plant. The adult is a ½-inch-long black beetle covered with a rusty yellow dust. Handpicking controls them. Remove any dock growing in the area, because it may be infested with this pest.

Weakened Plants, Yellow Leaves

Whitefly

Plants that are weak, and whose leaves turn yellow and die, are probably infested with whiteflies. Honeydew from the whiteflies drops on the stalks and encourages fungal growth. As a result, the stalks are undersized and poorly colored. Whiteflies are about the size of a pinhead. They are mothlike and have dusty white wings. The yellowish nymphs are legless, somewhat flat, and oval, and they resemble scale at certain stages. If you shake a plant infested with whiteflies, it appears as though dandruff were flying off the leaves. Spray infested plants with an insecticidal soap spray, every 2 to 3 days for 2 weeks. To prevent whiteflies, follow this regimen early in the season, just as leaves are appearing. Spray with pyrethrum as a last resort. Make two applications, 3 to 4 days apart.

MOST COMMON DISEASES

Black Leaves

Anthracnose

Anthracnose attacks all parts of the plant above the ground. Examine the leaf stalks for watery spots, which enlarge as the disease progresses. The leaves will wilt and die. As soon as you spot the problem, apply a fixed copper or sulfur-based fungicide every 7 to 10 days until 3 to 4 weeks before harvest.

Leaves Yellow and Collapse

Crown Rot

Crown rot causes leaves to yellow and collapse, leaving the plant wilted. This disease rots the crown and main roots of the rhubarb plant, causing infected crowns to become soft and water soaked. Crown rot cannot be cured. Remove and destroy affected plants.

Water-soaked Spots on Leaves

Leaf Spot

Spots that first appear water soaked and later grow in size and take on a brownish or purplish gray color indicate that your rhubarb has leaf spot. Leaf spot cannot be cured. Remove and destroy infected and surrounding plants.

Wilted, Yellow Leaves

Verticillium Wilt

In rhubarb, verticillium wilt causes leaves to wilt and yellow and results in marginal and interveinal dying of basal leaves. Yellowing alone often occurs early in the season, and may be mistaken for a nutrient deficiency. Remove and destroy infected plants. To prevent verticillium wilt, do not plant rhubarb where other susceptible plants have grown, and use disease-free planting stock.

HARVEST AND STORAGE

When to Harvest

You will have no harvest the first year, and a light harvest the second year. From then on, be sure to leave at least half the plant at each harvest. To harvest rhubarb, pull the stalks rather than cut them. Cutting invites insect and disease attack. Run your thumb down the inside edge of a stalk to its base as you pull with your other hand; the stalk will separate from the crown. Do not eat the leaves (they are poisonous), but only the stalks.

Yield per Plant   3 to 5 pounds
Best Fresh Storage Method   Refrigerate rhubarb; it will keep for 2 to 3 weeks.
Best Long-Term Storage Method   Cook rhubarb and then freeze it; it will keep for 1 year.

BERRY **Strawberry** *Fragaria × ananassa*

DESCRIPTION AND ENVIRONMENT

Height   6 to 12 inches
Spread   6 to 12 inches
Root Depth   8 inches
Root Spread   8 inches
Years to Bearing   June bearing, 2 years; everbearing, 1 year.
Years of Production   June bearing, 3 to 5; everbearing, 2 to 4; proper management results in

new plants and ongoing production for as many years as you take care of the bed.
Shade Tolerance   Needs full sun.
Frost Tolerance   Hardy to Zone 2, depending on variety.
Preferred Soil pH   6.0 to 6.5

PLANTING AND PROPAGATION

Best Method of Propagation   Runners or transplanting.
When to Propagate   Spring
Planting Time   Set the transplants in the soil while they are still dormant, as early as the ground can be worked in the spring.
Planting Depth   Trim roots of new plants so they are no more than 4 to 6 inches long. Soak roots in water (add some liquid kelp to help early growth) for about an hour before planting. Plant with the crown just above soil level.
Spacing between Plants   18 inches
Container Varieties   Try Cyclone, Jerseybelle, Surecrop, or Tioga.
Container Size   At least 12 inches deep, but a 5-gallon pail is best.

Seedlings Rotted

Planted at Wrong Depth
Planting depth is important for strawberries. If planted too high, the roots will dry out and wither; if planted too deep, the plants will rot. For best results, crowns should be right at soil level. When you purchase bare-root strawberries, keep the roots moist until you are ready to plant. Before planting, trim the roots with a pair of scissors to about 4 to 6 inches long.

MANAGEMENT OF BERRIES

Water Requirements

Make sure the plants get 1 inch of water every week from rain or by watering. When the plants start producing fruit, give them 1 to 1½ inches of water each week. (See chapter 8 for more information on watering.)

Feeding Requirements

Apply compost or a slow-acting general-purpose fertilizer in the spring. Spray strawberries with liquid seaweed extract two or three times during the growing season. (See chapter 8 for more information on feeding.)

Strawberries Rot on Ground

No Mulch

Mulched strawberry plants are more likely to bear clean, healthy fruit that is juicier, too, even in drought. Mulch also preserves a bed in winter. Unprotected strawberry roots, which are even shallower than raspberry roots, heave up in a thaw and either rot in excess water or dry out. Pine needles or chopped leaves are good mulches.

MOST COMMON INSECT PESTS

Foliage Curls, Puckers, Turns Yellow

Aphid

If the foliage on your strawberries curls, puckers, and turns yellow, and the foliage and blooms become stunted, your plants may have aphids. Aphids are vectors for certain bacterial diseases, so you need to keep them under control in strawberries. Look for ants. They are attracted to a sticky honeydew secreted by aphids. Look for clusters of aphids on the undersides of young leaves. These insects are soft-bodied, pear-shaped, about the size of a pinhead, and may be green, brown, or pink. For light infestations, spray vigorously with water early in the morning,

three times, once every other day. For heavy infestations, use a commercial insecticidal soap every 2 to 3 days until aphids are under control.

Leaves Stippled Yellow

Mite

Leaves that have become stippled, yellow, and dry, or that have pale yellow spots or blotches, are a sign that spider mites have infested your strawberry plants. Mites suck chlorophyll out of the leaves, causing small white dots to appear. They also inject toxins into the leaves, which discolors and distorts them. Mites are tiny arachnids about the size of a grain of black pepper. They may be red, black, or brown. Spray plants with a forceful spray of water three times, once every other day, to knock mites from leaves. If that doesn't do the job, spray the undersides of leaves with insecticidal soap at least three times at 5- to 7-day intervals. Be sure to spray the plant from top to bottom.

Stunted Plants, Yellow Leaves

Nematode

Plants infected with nematodes are stunted, and the leaves become yellow prematurely. The roots of affected plants have root knots. If they survive to maturity, plants produce low yields. Nematodes are microscopic whitish, translucent worms that are barely visible to the naked eye. They live in the soil and attack plant roots. Replace infected plants with resistant varieties, work 3 to 4 inches of compost (leaf mold compost is especially good) into the soil, fertilize with fish emulsion, and plant strawberries early in the season.

Large Ragged Holes in Leaves

Slug

Large ragged holes in leaves, fruit, and stems indicate slugs have been eating your plants. Other signs that slugs are at work include trails of slime on the leaves and on soil near plants. Slugs look like snails without shells. They are 1 to 2 inches long, and may be brown, gray, white, pale yellow, purple, or nearly black with brown specks. Set up a barrier of hardware cloth, ashes, or sand to deny them access to the garden. Handpicking will work early in the season. There are a number of homemade traps that work as well. (See the entry Slug in chapter 4 for information on making these traps.)

Dwarfed Fruit with Sunken Areas

Tarnished Plant Bug

These pests dwarf and create sunken areas (called catfacing) on fruit of strawberry plants. The adult tarnished plant bug is a ¼-inch-long, oval, flat, brownish insect, mottled with yellow and black. It sucks on plant parts. Tarnished plant bugs are highly mobile. The nymphs are pale yellow, and the eggs are long and curved and inserted into stems, tips, and leaves. For effective control, sprays must be used early in the morning when bugs are least active. Try three applications of pyrethrum, one every 3 days, to handle adults and nymphs. The best way to control tarnished plant bug damage is by fall and spring cleanup to prevent it from occurring in the first place.

Holes in Blossoms, Stunted Plants

Weevil

If the blossoms of your strawberry plants have holes chewed in them and the plants are stunted, suspect the root weevil. This pest is reddish brown in color with a black snout. It is about ¼ inch long. As weevils appear, spray with pyrethrum twice, 3 to 4 days apart.

Sudden Wilting of Plant

White Grub

A sudden wilting of your strawberry plants, when all other conditions seem fine, may indicate the presence of white grubs. These pests are the fat, whitish larvae of the june beetle. They are ¾ to 1½ inches long and they feed on the roots of plants. To control infestations, make one application of beneficial nematodes, which go below the surface of the soil to attack the grubs. (See chapter 4 for more information on parasitic nematodes.) Milky spore disease spread on the soil around the plants will control white grubs, but it takes 3 to 5 years to have a complete effect.

Wireworm

If your strawberry plants wilt and die, suspect the wireworm. Wireworms are the larvae of click beetles. They are ⅓ to 1½ inches long, dark brown to yellowish, jointed, hard shelled, and cylindrical. They chew on the roots of plants. Trap them with pieces of potato speared on the ends of sticks. (See the entry Wireworm in chapter 4 for more information on how to use potato traps.) Plant a cover crop for long-term control.

MOST COMMON DISEASES

Discolored Petals

Botrytis Fruit Rot

Botrytis fruit rot is first seen as blossom blight. Early symptoms are discolored petals and wilted fruit stems. The first symptom on the berry is a small water-soaked spot, which often appears on those berries at the base of the plant. Sulfur or fixed copper fungicides provide a good degree of control, provided the application is properly timed so that it catches the fungus early in its spring development. If control isn't achieved, remove and destroy infected plants. Good sanitation and aeration among the plants are necessary to prevent further spread. Avoid overfertilization so as to prevent excessive plant growth, and cultivate the soil frequently to keep it dry.

White Powder on Leaf Surfaces

Powdery Mildew

Powdery mildew on strawberries is distinguished by upward curling of the leaf margins and the formation of a white, powdery fungus on the upper surface of leaves. As soon as you discover the disease, remove and destroy the infected parts. Disinfect your hands and your pruning tool in a bleach solution (one part household bleach to four parts water) after each cut. In addition to pruning, apply a sulfur- or copper-based fungicide every 7 to 10 days. Limit overhead sprinkling to early in the day, and do not work around plants when they are wet. Thin plants to let in sun and air. Keep weeds down, avoid overgrowth, and rotate or renew plants often.

Reddish Brown Root Discoloration

Red Stele
Red stele is a fungal disease of strawberries, the most common symptoms of which are a reddish brown discoloration in the core of the roots, and the loss of the small white feeder. Plants become stunted and wilted, with a dull, bluish green color. Red stele cannot be controlled. Remove and destroy infected and surrounding plants.

Wilted, Dry Leaf Margins

Verticillium Wilt
Verticillium wilt on strawberry plants causes leaves to wilt and dry at margins and between veins. New growth is retarded; the roots growing from the crown are shortened, with blackened tips. Black streaks appear on leaf stalks and runners. A sulfur fungicide used every 7 to 10 days once the symptoms have been noticed has some effect in controlling this disease, but prevention practices will be more effective in the long run. If control steps aren't effective, pull and destroy affected plants. Do not rotate strawberries with other susceptible crops, such as almonds, apricots, avocados, cane fruit, cherries, cotton, melons, mint, okra, pecans, or roses, and do not plant strawberries where these crops were grown at any time in the last 10 years.
Resistant Varieties. Catskill, Darrow, Earliglow, Guardian, Red Chief, Red Coat, Surecrop, and Veestar.

MOST COMMON ANIMAL PESTS

Birds
A barrier that is to be successful at protecting strawberries from the birds must completely surround the plants. Any opening and the birds are sure to find it. Fabric or plastic netting can't be casually draped over the strawberry plants the way the advertising pictures show. Draping netting on plants may save some fruit, but birds will peck right through it and squeeze in under it. Some kind of support is needed to hold the netting out away from the plants so the birds can't reach any of the fruit.

A floating row cover made of agricultural fleece or slitted polyethylene film keeps pesky birds away from plants. The agricultural fleece is particularly good for protecting strawberries from birds. You can also replace the plastic film panels on row-covering tunnels with agricultural fleece or bird netting as the spring warms up.

HARVEST AND STORAGE

When to Harvest
Berries ripen about 1 month after the plants bloom. You can expect 2 to 3 weeks of harvest. Pick berries every 2 or 3 days. Avoid picking green-tipped berries, because they're not fully ripe. When harvesting, don't leave any berry remnants on the plants. They encourage plant rot.

Yield per Plant   8 to 10 ounces
Best Fresh Storage Method   Strawberries will keep for up to a week in a closed container in the refrigerator.
Best Long-Term Storage Method   Jellies, jams, or preserves.
Second-Best Long-Term Storage Method   Strawberries will keep frozen whole with sugar for about 6 months.

FRUIT *Watermelon*   *Citrullus lanatus*

DESCRIPTION AND ENVIRONMENT

Height   Vining varieties, 12 inches; bush varieties, 12 to 18 inches.

Spread   Vining varieties, 10 to 20 square feet; bush varieties, 36 to 48 inches.

Root Depth   Watermelons usually produce shallow roots, but some go down 4 feet.

Shade Tolerance   Needs full sun.

Frost Tolerance   Tender

Preferred Soil pH   6.0 to 7.0

PLANTING AND PROPAGATION

Best Method of Propagation   Direct seeding

When to Propagate   Spring

Spring Planting   4 weeks after last expected frost.

Fall Planting   16 weeks before first expected frost.

Planting Depth   ½ to 1 inch

Spacing between Plants   4 to 6 feet

Best Soil Temperature for Germination   65°F to 75°F

Best Soil Temperature for Growing   70°F to 85°F

Best Air Temperature for Growing   Day, 70°F to 90°F; night, 60°F to 70°F.

Days to Germination   4 to 10

Weeks to Transplanting   3 to 4

Days to Maturity   80 to 100 warm days.

Greenhouse Varieties   Watermelons cannot be grown in the greenhouse.

Container Varieties   Special varieties such as Sugar Baby can be grown in containers.

Container Size   24 inches deep.

Flat Flavor

Low Air Temperature

If you are having a cold summer, you may have trouble with warm weather crops such as watermelons. These plants will delay their ripening and produce flat-flavored crops. If you cover the plants with agricultural fleece you will preserve some warmth and ease this problem.

MANAGEMENT OF FRUIT

Water Requirements

Make sure the plants get 1 inch of water every week from rain or by watering; be careful not to overwater or flavor might be reduced. Consistency in watering is important for good root enlargement. Reduce watering about 4 weeks before harvest; melons will be about two-thirds their final size. When the first ripe melon is picked, stop watering altogether. (See chapter 8 for more information on watering.)

Feeding Requirements

Apply compost or slow-acting fertilizer in the spring when you prepare the seedbed. Spray plants with liquid seaweed extract two or three times during the growing season. If you want, you can give your melons a supplemental light feeding (side-dressing or foliar spray) monthly throughout the growing season, but this is not necessary. Do give plants a supplemental feeding when they are well established and the vines begin to crawl. If you do fertilize during the season, cut back on nitrogen later in the season. (See chapter 8 for more information on feeding.)

MOST COMMON INSECT PESTS

Foliage Curls, Puckers, Turns Yellow

Aphid

If the foliage on your watermelons curls, puckers, and turns yellow, and the foliage and blooms become stunted, your plants may have aphids. Look for ants. They are attracted to a sticky honeydew secreted by aphids. Look for clusters of aphids on the undersides of young leaves. These insects are soft-bodied, pear-shaped, about the size of a pinhead, and may be green, brown, or pink. For light infestations, spray vigorously with water early in the morning, three times, once every other day. For heavy infestations, use a commercial insecticidal soap every 2 to 3 days until aphids are under control.

Plants Die from Disease

Cucumber Beetle

Cucumber beetles do minor physical damage to plants, but they spread mosaic and other diseases that quickly kill melon plants. The cucumber beetle is yellow with black stripes or spots. It has an oblong shape and is ¼ inch long. To control them, prevent the beetles from feeding on young plants by covering melons with a floating row cover of agricultural fleece at the time of germination. Leave it on until the plants start to bloom. As plants outgrow the barrier, use traps to keep the beetle numbers under control.

Tiny Holes in Leaves

Flea Beetle

Several tiny holes or perforations in leaves can be caused by flea beetles. The beetles are $1/10$ inch long, shiny, and black; they may have yellow or white markings. They are very active, and jump like fleas when disturbed. Their feeding can destroy small plants rapidly. To control them, spread barriers, such as agricultural fleece, over plants in the spring. Remove the fleece when the plant begins to flower. Spray infested plants with pyrethrum, making two applications, 3 to 4 days apart.

Leaves Stippled Yellow

Mite

Leaves that have become stippled, yellow, and dry, or that have pale yellow spots or blotches, are a sign that spider mites have infested your watermelons.

Mites suck chlorophyll out of the leaves, causing small white dots to appear. They also inject toxins into the leaves, which discolors and distorts them. Mites are not insects but arachnids. They are about the size of a grain of black pepper. They may be red, black, or brown. Spray plants with a forceful spray of water three times, once every other day, to knock mites from the leaves. If that doesn't do the job, spray the undersides of leaves with insecticidal soap at least three times at 5- to 7-day intervals. Be sure to spray the plants from top to bottom.

Wilted, Dried-up Leaves

Squash Bug

If the leaves of your melon plants wilt, dry up, and turn black, with damage increasing until the vine dies, your plants are infested with squash bugs. Adult squash bugs are flat-backed, shield-shaped, brown to black bugs with a light-colored outline on their abdomens. They are ½ to ¾ inch long and lay brown or red shiny eggs on leaves, which hatch into greenish gray nymphs. Adults and nymphs feed by sucking the juices from leaves. Use a barrier until bloom time to deny the bugs access to young plants. In addition, spray plants with seaweed extract. If bugs do get to the melons, handpick pests from the undersides of leaves or spray plants with insecticidal soap every 2 to 3 days for 2 weeks.

Sudden Wilting of Plants

Squash Vine Borer

Sudden wilting of all or part of a melon vine can be caused by squash vine borers. To determine if squash vine borers are at work, look for moist, sawdustlike debris, called frass, piled up outside their small holes. These fat, white caterpillars with brown heads are about 1 inch long. They tunnel into the stems to feed. The adult is an orange-and-black, clear-winged moth with black stripes around the abdomen. It measures 1 to 1½ inches long. Try to deny the parent moth access to the plant with an agricultural fleece or netting barrier, which must be removed when the plant blooms. If the borer does get access to your plants, inject *Bacillus thuringiensis* (BT)

into the stem with a hypodermic needle. Remove the borers by slitting the stem, then cover the wound with soil.

MOST COMMON DISEASES

Black Leaves

Anthracnose

Watermelons infected with anthracnose develop small water-soaked spots on the leaves. These spots enlarge and turn black, and eventually the leaves shrivel and die. Sunken lesions form on the stems and circular, black, sunken spots appear on the fruit. During moist conditions, these spots become covered with the salmon-colored fungus. As soon as you spot the problem, apply a fixed copper or sulfur-based fungicide every 7 to 10 days.

Plants Wilt Quickly

Bacterial Wilt

Watermelons infected with bacterial wilt may wilt so quickly that they are green and dried up at the same time. The vascular system is blocked. There is no cure for this disease. Remove infected plants immediately and destroy. Wash hands and any tools in a bleach solution (one part household bleach to four parts water) before touching other plants. The disease is transmitted by spotted and striped cucumber beetles, so try to deny them access to the garden by covering seedlings with a barrier, such as agricultural fleece, until the plant begins to flower.

Stunting and Curling of Young Leaves

Curly Top

The young leaves of melons infected with curly top become stunted and curled but may be normal in color. Older leaves are often yellowed. Overall, the plants are stunted and bushy and fail to produce. Curly top cannot be cured. Remove and destroy the infected and surrounding plants. Avoid planting melons near sugar beets, since the disease can be transmitted by beet leafhoppers.

Downy Purple Spots on Leaves

Downy Mildew

In melons infected with downy mildew, irregularly shaped yellow to brown spots appear on the tops of leaves, usually at the center of the plants. Under moist conditions, downy purple spots appear on the undersides of leaves. The leaves die as these spots increase in size. Downy mildew spreads rapidly from the crown toward new growth. If you catch the infection early, apply a copper-based fungicide to diseased and surrounding plants every 7 to 10 days until harvest. Remove and destroy any plants with a serious infection.

Brown Discoloration of Stem

Fusarium Wilt

Fusarium wilt is evidenced by a brown discoloration of the stem, and wilting of the branches. Some plants will produce some fruit, but in most cases you should remove and destroy infected plants. Striped cucumber beetles will transmit this disease to watermelons, so cover young plants with a barrier, such as agricultural fleece, until bloom time. Fusarium is also carried in the soil, so use resistant varieties. Solarizing the soil also helps. (See chapter 5 for information on soil solarization.)
Resistant Varieties. Black Kleckly, Charleston Gray, Congo, Crimson Sweet, Fairfax, Sweet Princess, Triple Sweet, and Tri-X313.

Mottled Green or Yellow Leaves

Mosaic

Chlorosis (yellowing of leaves), stunted plants, and reduced yields are symptoms of mosaic. Leaves appear mottled with dark green, light green, and yellow areas of irregular form. The leaves become irregularly shaped, and portions of the veins may die. Vine tips are stunted or yellowish. Mosaic cannot be cured. Remove and destroy the infected and surrounding plants. Disinfect hands and tools in a bleach solution (one part household bleach to four parts water) to avoid spreading the disease. Control aphids and cucumber beetles because they spread mosaic. Floating row covers make excellent barriers against these pests and give melons the extra heat they like for growing. Remove covers at flowering.

White Powdery Growth on Undersides of Leaves

Powdery Mildew

Circular whitish spots on the lower surfaces of leaves indicate powdery mildew. These spots increase in number and size, grow together, progress to the upper surfaces of the leaf, and finally cover the entire leaf with white, powdery growth. As soon as you discover the disease, remove and destroy the infected parts. Disinfect your pruning tool in a bleach solution (one part household bleach to four parts water) after each cut. In addition to pruning, apply a copper-based fungicide every 7 to 10 days.

Dark Oozing Spots on Melons

Scab

In melons infected with scab, water-soaked spots appear on the leaves, which may cause them to wilt. Young melons develop gray, slightly sunken spots. As the plant matures, these spots darken, become more sunken, and are covered with a greenish velvety mold. Remove and destroy infected plants. Prevent scab by following good fall cleanup practices and by implementing a 3-year crop rotation plan.

HARVEST AND STORAGE

When to Harvest

Harvest watermelons when the tendril nearest the stem turns dry and brown and two other nearby tendrils die.

Best Fresh Storage Method   Watermelons will keep in the refrigerator for up to 2 weeks.
Best Long-Term Storage Method   Melon balls can be frozen for about 4 months.

NOTES AND RESEARCH

Experiments on watermelon storage, using Sugar Baby, New Hampshire, and other cultivars, have shown that storage in high relative humidity (85 to 95 percent) at warm temperatures (60°F to 65°F) is better than storage at cool temperatures (40°F to 45°F). Sugar Baby maintained good quality after 2 months of storage at 60°F to 65°F. Recent work on extending muskmelon storage life with water-impermeable plastic film wraps might be applicable to watermelons, as an aid in humidity control.

Almost half of a watermelon's final sugar content is accumulated during the last week of maturation. A plant that is stressed or sick during that time will not manufacture sufficient sugar for good flavor.

CHAPTER 3

Herbs

Culinary herbs are considered to be the most problem-free of all the food crops. Many of the herbs, especially the herbaceous, shrublike ones such as rosemary and sage, seem to actually prefer conditions that most vegetable crops would find insufferable. They are more tolerant of drought, often prefer less fertilizer than vegetables, and are vulnerable to fewer insects and diseases than all other food crops. In short, they are a very satisfying collection of plants. Besides being easy to grow, culinary herbs add great beauty to the food garden and provide marvelous variety and zest to any meal in which they are used. Not a bad return for a group of plants that doesn't cause us many problems.

Unfortunately, life is not perfect. There are some problems that can surface in the herb garden. Like many tender seedlings, certain herbs are attractive to small animals like rabbits, cats (our cats love catnip, a member of the mint family that I grow for them), and even deer. Because they require well-drained, almost sandy soil, and can get along on less water than most plants, there is a tendency to neglect their watering needs. Locating these plants near the house, where they are more protected from animals and are convenient to water, minimizes both of these common problems. Also, herbs are more readily used if they are in a sunny spot near the kitchen door.

Most herbs respond well to continuous snipping. In fact, many gardeners, reluctant to reduce their plants in size, or afraid to make a mistake and prune too much, fail to harvest the herbs at their peak tenderness early in the season, and allow them to overgrow and become leggy and tough. Chives, basil, mints, parsley, oregano, and other herbs regenerate quickly and benefit from the cutback, forming fuller, more compact plants. These plants are then sturdier against occasional pest and disease inroads. As a general rule, once the herb has set flowers, it is past peak flavor and tenderness, so when in doubt, prune, prune, and prune.

HERB **Basil** *Ocimum basilicum*

DESCRIPTION AND ENVIRONMENT

There are several varieties of basil, but plants commonly grown as *O. basilicum*—sweet basil and bush basil—are best for kitchen use. Purple-leaved varieties such as dark opal basil are both ornamental and flavorful. The miniature-leaved varieties like Spicy Globe or Green Bouquet make particularly appealing indoor plants.

Height   12 to 24 inches

Spread   20 to 30 inches

Blossoms   White to lavender blossoms in July and August should be pinched off as they are forming to prolong leaf production.

Light Requirements   Full sun

Frost Tolerance   Tender

Soil Preference   Rich, moist, well-drained soil.

Preferred Soil pH   6.0 to 6.5

PLANTING AND PROPAGATION

Best Method of Propagation   Basil is easily grown from seed.

Spring Planting Time   Start basil indoors 2 to 3 weeks before the last expected frost. The best temperatures for germination are between 75°F and 85°F. Transplant seedlings outside 2 to 4 weeks after the last frost. Seeds can be started outdoors 1 to 2 weeks after danger of frost has passed, when the soil temperature is over 50°F.

Fall Planting Time   Basil can be planted again 80 days before the first expected frost. However, a well-pruned plant started in the spring will last all season.

Planting Depth   ⅛ inch

Spacing between Plants   12 inches

Days to Germination   3 to 7

Weeks to Transplanting   4 to 6

Days to Maturity   50 to 60 after direct seeding; 30 after transplanting.

Greenhouse Varieties   Any variety of basil can be grown in the greenhouse.

Container Varieties   Any variety can be grown in containers; the containers should be at least 12 inches deep.

PLANT MANAGEMENT

Water Requirements

Make sure the plants get 1 inch of water every week from rain or by watering. (See chapter 8 for more information on watering.)

Feeding Requirements

This plant is a light feeder, so it needs no supplemental fertilizer over and above one application of slow-acting fertilizer in the spring. Excessive leaf growth reduces basil's flavor. Spray plants with liquid seaweed extract two or three times during the growing season. (See chapter 8 for more information on feeding.)

Pruning

Keep plants pinched back for fuller growth. Pinch off blossoms as they appear, as they will affect leaf growth and the oil content of the leaves. It is best to prune basil before it flowers by cutting the main stem from the top, leaving at least one node with two young shoots. Thereafter, cut the branches every 2 or 3 weeks.

MOST COMMON INSECT PESTS

Skeletonized Leaves

Japanese Beetle

Japanese beetles chew out the leaf tissue between the veins, skeletonizing the leaves. These insect pests are shiny, metallic green beetles, ½ inch long, with copper-brown wings. To control them, set up beetle traps a week prior to emergence in your area, making sure the traps are no closer than 50 feet from vulnerable crops. Handpick stragglers, or use pyrethrum if the traps cannot handle the infestation.

Large Ragged Holes in Leaves

Slug

Slugs chew large ragged holes in leaves and stems. They start at the bottom of the plant and work their way up. Look for trails of slime on the leaves and the soil near plants as further evidence. Slugs look like snails without shells. They are 1 to 2 inches long, and they may be brown, gray, white, pale yellow, purple, or nearly black with brown specks. The best way to control slugs is to set up a barrier, such as hardware cloth, ashes, or sand, to deny them access to the garden. Handpicking will work if you start early in the season. There are a number of homemade or commercial traps that work as well. (See the entry Slug in chapter 4 for information on making traps.)

MOST COMMON DISEASES

Seedlings Die

Damping-Off

Seedlings that have damping-off simply topple over. A watery soft rot at the soil line is another sign of this disease. There is no cure for the disease. Remove and destroy infected plants. When starting seeds indoors, use a commercial potting soil, or pasteurize your own potting soil in an oven. Disinfect tools in heated water or a bleach solution (one part household bleach to four parts water) after each cut. Provide soil with adequate drainage and use a fan near seedlings for better air circulation. For direct seeding, make sure soil is well drained and warm. You might try spreading pasteurized soil or a sterile vermiculite in furrows where you plant your seeds.

HARVEST AND STORAGE

When to Harvest

Basil is ready to pick when it gets to be at least 6 inches tall. Most culinary herbs are best picked early in the morning just as the dew evaporates. Picking the youngest shoots gives best flavor and helps keep the plant pruned. Cut just above a leaf node.

Best Fresh Storage Method   Basil is best when used immediately, but will keep for several days in a jar of water covered with a plastic bag in the refrigerator.

Best Long-Term Storage Method   Basil can be frozen in plastic bags and will keep for 6 months (blanch it first to retain flavor and color); it also freezes well when ground with butter or oil.

Second-Best Long-Term Storage Method   Dry basil by hanging it upside down in a dark, dry, well-ventilated room, and store it in air-tight containers; it will retain its flavor for 1 year.

NOTES AND RESEARCH

Basil's flavor intensifies during cooking. Research has found no evidence to support claims that basil will control various bean, cabbage, or tomato insects, either as an interplant or a spray. Nor is there evidence to support claims that basil enhances the growth and flavor of tomatoes.

HERB *Chervil* *Anthriscus cerefolium*

DESCRIPTION AND ENVIRONMENT

Chervil comes in two varieties, one plain and one curly. The delicate, light green leaves resemble parsley and have a subtle flavor that combines anise and parsley.

Height   24 inches
Spread   12 to 18 inches
Blossoms   Small, white blossoms in umbels, May through July.
Light Requirements   Full sun to partial shade; likes some shade in the afternoon, especially in hot areas.
Frost Tolerance   Tender
Soil Preference   Moist, humusy soil.
Preferred Soil pH   6.5 to 7.0

PLANTING AND PROPAGATION

Best Method of Propagation   Start from seed in its permanent location.

Spring Planting Time   Make the first sowing just after the last expected spring frost. Chervil transplants poorly; sow it directly in the garden. Sow a few seeds every 2 weeks from March or early April until mid-July, or until the weather is hot. Light stimulates germination; sow seeds in furrows an inch deep, but do not cover them. Keep the soil moist with a misting device, or cover the seeds with cheesecloth or agricultural fleece.

Fall Planting Time   Begin sowing again in late summer for the fall crop. Sometimes chervil will self-sow over the winter.

Planting Depth   Sow seeds on the surface.
Spacing between Plants   9 to 12 inches
Days to Germination   10
Days to Maturity   42 to 56
Greenhouse Varieties   Chervil thrives in a cool greenhouse.
Container Varieties   Sow in moderately rich soil with good drainage in containers at least 12 inches deep; because it does not require a lot of sun, chervil can do well in an east window indoors.

PLANT MANAGEMENT

Chervil flowers and goes to seed easily, especially in hot weather. It is better to plant this herb several times through the season than to try to keep it pruned to prevent flowering.

Water Requirements

Make sure the plants get 1 inch of water every week from rain or by watering. (See chapter 8 for more information on watering.)

Feeding Requirements

Chervil is a light feeder, so it needs no supplemental fertilizer over and above one application of slow-acting fertilizer in the spring. Excessive leaf growth reduces the flavor of those leaves. Spray plants with liquid seaweed extract two or three times during the growing season. (See chapter 8 for more information on feeding.)

MOST COMMON INSECT PESTS

Foliage Curls, Puckers, Turns Yellow

Aphid

If the foliage on your plants curls, puckers, and turns yellow, and the foliage and blooms become stunted, look for ants. They are a sign that your plants have aphids. Ants are attracted to a sticky honeydew secreted by aphids. These insects are about the size of a pinhead and have soft, pear-shaped bodies. They may be green, brown, or pink. You will find them in clusters on the undersides of young leaves. For light infestations, spray the plants vigorously with water in the early morning three times, once every other day. For heavy infestations, apply a commercial insecticidal soap every 2 to 3 days.

HARVEST AND STORAGE

When to Harvest

The leaves are ready to harvest 6 to 8 weeks after planting. Most culinary herbs are best picked early in the morning just as the dew evaporates.

Best Fresh Storage Method   Chervil is best when used immediately, but will keep for several days sitting in a jar of water covered with a plastic bag in the refrigerator.

Best Long-Term Storage Method
Chervil can be frozen in plastic bags, and will keep

for 6 months; it also freezes well mixed with butter or oil.

Second-Best Long-Term Storage Method   Dry the leaves rapidly in a commercial dryer or oven (chervil's flavor fades with slow drying), and store in an air-tight container. Dried chervil will keep for 1 year.

NOTES AND RESEARCH

Chervil makes a good ground cover for shady, damp areas.

HERB Chives   *Allium schoenoprasum*

DESCRIPTION AND ENVIRONMENT

A perennial relative of onions, chives are grown for their spiky leaves. Chives usually suffer no problems in the garden. They are very easy to grow.

Height   12 to 18 inches
Spread   6 to 8 inches
Blossoms   Lavender flowers in late spring and early summer; flowers are edible.
Light Requirements   Full sun to partial shade.
Frost Tolerance   Hardy, goes dormant in winter.
Soil Preference   Moderately rich, well-drained soil.
Preferred Soil pH   6.0 to 7.0

PLANTING AND PROPAGATION

Best Method of Propagation   Divide established clumps about every 3 years in early spring.
Spring Planting Time   Start seeds indoors or outside in early spring; the best temperatures for germination are between 60°F and 70°F.

Planting Depth   ½ inch
Spacing between Plants   5 to 8 inches
Days to Germination   10 to 21
Weeks to Transplanting   4
Days to Maturity   60
Greenhouse Varieties   Chives flourish in a cool greenhouse.
Container Varieties   For chives all winter long, start seeds in pots in late summer and grow the plants outdoors to get sizable specimens. Just before frost, move the plants to a sunny windowsill. Alternatively, dig up an established clump in late summer. Leave the potted clump outside until the tops die back and roots freeze. Mature bulbs need a cold dormant period in order to send out new leaves again. Then, after this cooling period, bring the container indoors and set it in a sunny window.

PLANT MANAGEMENT

Water Requirements

Make sure the plants get 1 inch of water every week from rain or by watering. (See chapter 8 for more information on watering.)

Feeding Requirements

This plant is a light feeder, so it needs no supplemental fertilizer over and above one application of slow-acting fertilizer in the spring. Excessive leaf growth reduces the flavor of chives. Spray plants with liquid seaweed extract two or three times during the growing season. (See chapter 8 for more information on feeding.)

Pruning

Cut off the purple flowers as soon as they appear to keep the plant from generating leaves for harvest.

MOST COMMON DISEASES

Soft, Brown Tissue at Neck

Botrytis Rot

The neck tissue on the bulb becomes soft and brownish and may shrivel. Often a gray to brown mold develops on the surface of the bulbs. Leaves may appear water-soaked. Remove any infected plants from the garden to control spread of the disease.

Seedlings Die

Damping-Off

Seedlings that have damping-off simply topple over. You will see a watery soft rot on the stem at the soil line. There is no cure for this disease. Remove and destroy infected plants. When starting seeds indoors, use commercial potting soil, or pasteurize your own potting soil in an oven. Disinfect tools in a bleach solution (one part household bleach to four parts water). Provide soil with adequate drainage and use a fan for better air circulation. For direct seeding, make sure soil is well drained and warm. You might try spreading pasteurized soil or a sterile vermiculite in furrows where you plant your seeds.

Tops Wilted

Pink Root

Chives infected with pink root are stunted, and their tops wilt. The roots are pinkish or red, and eventually rot. Once the soil is infected, do not grow any bulb crops. Remove and destroy infected plants, and make sure your soil is well drained.

HARVEST AND STORAGE

When to Harvest

Begin to harvest chives when the leaves are 6 inches tall. Do not cut the entire clump at one time; the plants need some leaves to continue growing. Instead, snip outer leaves 2 inches from the base of the plant. Stop major harvesting about a month prior to the first expected frost. This reduces the chances of losing the plants from winter-kill.

Best Fresh Storage Method   Chives are best when used immediately, but will keep for several days in a jar of water covered with a plastic bag in the refrigerator.

Best Long-Term Storage Method
Chives freeze well. Snip the leaves into small pieces, spread them on a cookie sheet, and place in the freezer; when frozen, store the pieces in a tightly sealed container in the freezer to use as needed all winter. Frozen chives will keep for 6 months.

Second-Best Long-Term Storage Method   To dry chives, snip the leaves into small pieces, spread them on a screen, and place in a dark, dry, well-ventilated place until they are dry. Store the dried chives in a tightly covered jar. They will keep for 1 year.

NOTES AND RESEARCH

No research has been done on chives and their interaction with other plants, and no data are available to support claims of their insect-repelling power.

HERB **Dill**   *Anethum graveolens*

DESCRIPTION AND ENVIRONMENT

Dill's wispy foliage makes it an attractive as well as tasty plant to add to the herb garden. It is easy to grow, and both leaves and seeds can be used to flavor foods.

Height   3 to 4 feet
Spread   24 inches
Blossoms   Many tiny yellow flowers in flat flower heads or umbels, July through September; multitudinous seeds are flat and brown; seeds and flowers are edible.
Light Requirements   Full sun
Frost Tolerance   Tender
Soil Preference   Moderately rich, moist, well-drained soil.
Preferred Soil pH   6.0 to 6.5

PLANTING AND PROPAGATION

Best Method of Propagation   Direct seeding

Spring Planting Time   Dill is best sown directly in the garden after the last expected spring frost, but the seeds can also be started indoors 2 weeks before the last frost.

Fall Planting Time   Sow seeds in late summer, or allow spring-planted dill to self-sow for a fall crop.

Planting Depth   ¼ to ½ inch
Spacing between Plants   8 to 10 inches if harvesting leaves; 10 to 12 inches if harvesting seeds.
Days to Germination   14
Weeks to Transplanting   4 to 6; dill has a taproot and does not transplant easily once it is past seedling stage.
Days to Maturity   60
Greenhouse Varieties   Given enough root room, dill will produce luxuriant, mild-flavored growth in a cool greenhouse.
Container Varieties   Dill grows well in containers, but bolts quickly; it needs rich soil and large pots (a minimum of 6 to 8 inches in diameter).

PLANT MANAGEMENT

Water Requirements

Make sure the plants get 1 inch of water every week from rain or by watering. (See chapter 8 for more information on watering.)

Feeding Requirements

Dill is a light feeder, so it needs no supplemental fertilizer over and above one application of slow-acting fertilizer in the spring. Spray plants with liquid seaweed extract two or three times during the growing season. (See chapter 8 for more information on feeding.)

Pruning

Pinching off the earliest flower heads will prolong leaf quality for a short time, but to guarantee a constant supply of leaves, sow a small number of seeds every 3 weeks. Dill self-sows vigorously from year to year.

MOST COMMON INSECT PESTS

Leaves Eaten

Parsleyworm

If the leaves of your dill plants are eaten except for the stems, suspect the parsleyworm, or the tomato hornworm discussed below. This larva of the black swallowtail butterfly is about 2 inches long, and green with a yellow-dotted black band across each segment. When upset, it gives off an odor and projects orange horns. Parsleyworms are not usually numerous enough to be damaging, but if they are eating away at your plants, handpick or spray with *Bacillus thuringiensis* (BT) every 2 weeks until caterpillars disappear.

Tomato Hornworm

If your dill plants are defoliated, look for tomato hornworms. The hornworm is a 3- to 5-inch green caterpillar with white stripes and a horn projecting from its rear. Hornworms are easy to see, so handpick the worms. You can also use a *Bacillus thuringiensis* (BT) spray, or, if the infestation gets out of hand, a pyrethrum spray.

HARVEST AND STORAGE

When to Harvest

You can pick the leaves or wait to harvest the seeds. Fresh leaves are picked as soon as they are large

enough to use; clip the leaves close to the stem. Pick them early in the morning or in the late evening.

Collect seeds as the flower heads mature, taking a few seeds each day as the seedpods start to open. Clip the seed heads before they shatter. Those seeds on the lower side of the flower umbel will be ripe; the others will ripen as they dry. Place them in a shallow box and allow them to dry for a day or so. Store them in an air-tight jar.

Best Fresh Storage Method   The foliage is best when used immediately, but will keep for several days in a jar of water covered with a plastic bag in the refrigerator.

Second-Best Fresh Storage Method
Dill leaves can be stored for several months by layering them with pickling salt in a covered jar in the refrigerator; when you are ready to use the leaves, simply wash them and use as if fresh.

Best Long-Term Storage Method   Cut the leaves, long stems and all, into sections short enough to fit into plastic bags (do not chop the leaves into bits or fragrance and flavor will be lost);

dill can be frozen in plastic bags, and will keep for 6 months.

Second-Best Long-Term Storage Method   The foliage can be dried by hanging stems upside down in a dark, airy place; store dried leaves in a tightly sealed jar for 1 year.

NOTES AND RESEARCH

If allowed to blossom, dill supports many kinds of beneficial wasps and other insect predators and parasites, including bees, braconid wasps, ichneumonid wasps, and tachinid flies. When planted in the orchard, it attracts parasites that control codling moths and tent caterpillars. No scientific data are available to prove or disprove the tradition that says that dill helps give flavor to cole crops and is good for onions and lettuce, or that it reduces carrot and tomato growth. No studies have been done to test the traditional belief that dill repels aphids and spider mites, or that it protects cabbage from caterpillars or corn from diseases.

HERB *Garlic*   *Allium sativum*

DESCRIPTION AND ENVIRONMENT

Everyone is familiar with the tangy cloves of garlic. It is one of the best-loved herbs used to season foods.

Height   12 to 24 inches
Spread   6 to 8 inches
Blossoms   Very small, white to pinkish blossoms in terminal globular umbel; sterile; spring and summer.
Light Requirements   Full sun for largest cloves, but will take partial shade.

Frost Tolerance   Hardy
Soil Preference   Rich, deeply cultivated, well-drained soil.
Preferred Soil pH   4.5 to 8.3

PLANTING AND PROPAGATION

Best Method of Propagation   Largest cloves saved from the present season's crop.

Spring Planting Time   Plant cloves up to 6 weeks before the last expected frost (however, in all but the coldest areas, garlic grows best if planted in the fall).

Fall Planting Time   Plant cloves in September, mulching the garlic beds with straw to prevent repeated freezes and thaws from heaving the bulbs. Fall-planted garlic produces bigger cloves than garlic planted in spring. In the spring, if seed stalks appear, pick them off promptly.

Planting Depth   Plant cloves of regular garlic 2 inches deep; elephant garlic, up to 4 inches deep.

Spacing between Plants   6 inches apart; elephant garlic, 12 inches apart.

Days to Maturity   90 to 100 days after spring planting; 8 months after fall planting.

PLANT MANAGEMENT

Water Requirements

Make sure the plants get 1 inch of water every week from rain or by watering. Do not let the soil dry out. Do *not* water garlic as it nears harvest, or you'll produce bulbs with thin wrappers and a shorter storage life. Stop watering once the leaves begin yellowing, about 3 weeks before harvest. (See chapter 8 for more information on watering.)

Feeding Requirements

Garlic needs a rich soil in order to produce big cloves. Add generous amounts of compost to the soil in the spring, and make sure the soil has a proper balance of nitrogen, phosphorus, and potassium. Do not give plants excess nitrogen. In addition to enriching the soil in spring, spray plants with liquid seaweed extract two or three times during the growing season. (See chapter 8 for more information on feeding.)

Pruning

When flower stalks appear in early summer, cut them back so that the plants can devote their energy to developing bulbs.

Garlic Cloves Are Small

Soil Compacted

Garlic needs a very loose soil in order to thrive. Work in at least an inch or more of compost or other organic material before planting.

MOST COMMON INSECT PESTS

Stunted Plants, Yellow Leaves

Nematode

Plants infected with nematodes are stunted; the leaves become yellow prematurely, and if they do survive to maturity, they produce poor yields. Nematodes are microscopic whitish, translucent worms that are barely visible to the naked eye. They live in the soil and attack plant roots. Use resistant varieties, and add 3 to 4 inches of compost (especially leaf mold) to the soil. Fertilize with fish emulsion.

MOST COMMON DISEASES

Soft, Brown Tissue at Neck

Botrytis Rot

The neck tissue on the bulb becomes soft and brownish and may shrivel. Often a gray to brown mold develops on the surface of bulbs. Remove any infected bulbs from the garden to control the spread of the disease. Keep bulbs cool and dry in storage.

White Growth at Neck

White Rot

If you see a white growth on the leaves at the neck of the plant, your garlic may have white rot. This growth is dotted with tiny black spots. White rot cannot be cured. Remove and destroy infected and surrounding plants, and do not plant garlic in the same spot for at least 5 years.

HARVEST AND STORAGE

When to Harvest

Garlic is ready to harvest about 3 weeks after the leaves start to turn yellow. Yellowing will proceed from the bottom up as the leaves dry, fall over, and turn brown. If by midsummer they have not done so, don't wait: Knock them down yourself. Ordinarily, you begin harvesting when approximately one-third of the tops are dry and brown. Pull the plants, clip off the roots to ⅜ inch long, brush off the soil, and let them cure in an airy, rain-free place. The bulbs are cured and ready to store when the leaves are crumbly, the root crown is hard, and the cloves can be cracked apart easily.

Best Storage Method   Store garlic in a cool, dark, dry spot such as a cold attic, hanging in a net bag. Garlic stores best at 50 to 65 percent humidity and at a temperature of around 40°F to 60°F. It will last for about 3 months. Garlic will sprout in the refrigerator, reducing its flavor, so refrigerate only one bulb at a time. Keep garlic in a container with holes in it to allow moisture to drift away, thus increasing shelf life of the cloves.

Split Husks

Late Harvest

If the husks of your garlic are split, you probably waited too long to harvest it. Harvest the garlic by late August, after most of the leaves have yellowed. If bulbs are left in the ground much later, they will continue to fatten and are apt to split their protective husks.

NOTES AND RESEARCH

Although scientists haven't been able to prove its benefits, they have found that garlic contains some fungicides and feeding deterrents. In one study, one application of garlic spray kept aphids away from peas for up to 30 days.

HERB
Marjoram   *Origanum majorana*

DESCRIPTION AND ENVIRONMENT

Marjoram, a low, bushy plant with hairy, gray-green leaves, is a hardy annual in the northern states, and a perennial in the southern states.

Height   12 inches
Spread   6 to 8 inches
Blossoms   Cream-colored, edible blossoms, August to September.
Light Requirements   Full sun
Frost Tolerance   Tender
Soil Preference   Light, well-drained soil.
Preferred Soil pH   6.5 to 7.0

PLANTING AND PROPAGATION

Best Method of Propagation   Seeds sown indoors are best, but outdoor seeding will work; also propagate by division or cuttings.
Spring Planting Time   Plant seeds or transplants outdoors after all danger of frost is past; sow in groups of three seeds.
Planting Depth   ⅛ to ¼ inch
Spacing between Plants   8 to 10 inches
Days to Germination   8 to 14
Weeks to Transplanting   5 to 6
Days to Maturity   60
Greenhouse Varieties   Marjoram can be grown in a cool greenhouse in winter; its flavor will be milder than that of plants grown in the garden.
Container Varieties   Marjoram grows best in large pots, but will produce enough leaves for flavoring if grown in a 4-inch pot on a south windowsill in the winter.

PLANT MANAGEMENT

This plant does not like dampness around its crown, so a summer mulch is not necessarily a benefit. Cultivate the soil to keep down weeds, or use one of the new light, black mulching fabrics that let in air and water but prevent weed growth.

Water Requirements

Make sure marjoram gets about 1 inch of water every week from rain or by watering. Do not overwater. You can let this plant get a bit dry before watering. (See chapter 8 for more information on watering.)

Feeding Requirements

Marjoram is a light feeder, so it needs no supplemental fertilizer over and above one application of slow-acting fertilizer in the spring. Excessive leaf growth reduces the flavor of the leaves. Spray plants with liquid seaweed extract two or three times during the growing season. (See chapter 8 for more information on feeding.)

Pruning

Pinch the plants back just before they bloom to induce bushy growth for harvest; use the prunings in cooking, or dry them for storage.

MOST COMMON INSECT PESTS

Foliage Curls, Puckers, Turns Yellow

Aphid

If the foliage on your plants curls, puckers, and turns yellow, and the foliage and blooms become stunted, look for ants. They are a sign that your plants have aphids. Ants are attracted to a sticky honeydew secreted by aphids. These insects are about the size of a pinhead and have soft, pear-shaped bodies. They may be green, brown, or pink. You will find them in clusters on the undersides of young leaves. For light infestations, spray the plants vigorously with water in the early morning three times, once every other day. For heavy infestations, apply a commercial insecticidal soap every 2 to 3 days.

Leaves Stippled Yellow

Spider Mite

The leaves of plants that have mites become stippled, yellow, and dry, and sometimes have pale yellow spots or blotches. Mites are tiny arachnids about the size of a grain of black pepper, and may be red, black, or brown. They feed by sucking out plant juices, including the chlorophyll, leaving small white dots on the leaves. They also inject toxins into the leaves, causing discoloration and distortion. Spray plants forcefully with water three times, once every other day, to knock mites off the leaves. If they persist, spray with insecticidal soap.

MOST COMMON DISEASES

Rotting of Older Leaves

Botrytis Rot

If older leaves in the center of the plant near the base are rotted, your marjoram may be infected with botrytis rot. This disease is encouraged by damp conditions. Remove infected plants to control spread of the disease.

Seedlings Die

Damping-Off

Seedlings that have damping-off simply topple over. You will find a watery soft rot on the stem at the soil line. There is no cure for this disease. Remove and destroy infected plants. When starting seeds indoors, use a commercial potting soil, or pasteurize your own potting soil in an oven. Disinfect tools in heated water or a bleach solution (one part household bleach to four parts water). Provide soil with adequate drainage and use a fan near seedlings for better air circulation. For direct seeding, make sure soil is well drained and warm. You might try spreading pasteurized soil or a sterile vermiculite in furrows where you plant your seeds.

Gradual Wilting of Plants

Rhizoctonia

A slow wilting of the plants may be a sign that your marjoram has rhizoctonia. Roots and the base of stems are yellowish brown to black, and rotted. This occurs in wet, heavy soils. Remove and destroy infected plants. Provide good drainage, and rotate plants every 3 years. Compost discourages this fungus.

HARVEST AND STORAGE

When to Harvest

Pinch a sprig for flavoring anytime after the plants are 3 inches tall. To get a large number of stems for drying, pinch the plants just before the first bloom to induce bushiness. When the plants are ready to bloom again, cut them back to within an inch of the ground. You may get two harvests a season. Like most culinary herbs, marjoram is best picked early in the morning just as the dew evaporates. Picking the youngest shoots gives the best flavor and helps keep the plant pruned. Cut just above a leaf node.

Best Long-Term Storage Method   Use freshly picked marjoram, or dry it for long-term storage. To dry, cut the stems anytime before frost, rinse clean, and dry carefully; then hang bunches of the herb upside down or lay it on screens and place in an airy, dark place until dry. Store in air-tight containers. It will retain its flavor for 1 year.

HERB **Mint**   *Mentha spp.*

DESCRIPTION AND ENVIRONMENT

Mint is a square-stemmed perennial whose aromatic, opposite leaves may be smooth, hairy, crinkled or variegated. Most varieties spread rapidly in the garden.

Height   1 to 3 feet
Spread   8 to 12 inches
Blossoms   Small, purple, pink, or white blossoms in whorls on terminal spikes, July and August.
Light Requirements   Full sun to partial shade.
Frost Tolerance   Hardy to −20°F.
Soil Preference   Moist, well-drained soil; do not top-dress with manure or too much compost.
Preferred Soil pH   6.0 to 7.0

PLANTING AND PROPAGATION

Best Method of Propagation   Root divisions, stem cuttings, or layering. Mint varieties hybridize so readily that mint seeds, even when offered by reputable dealers, often fail to be true to name. If you just want mint and don't mind whether it's curly mint, apple mint, or peppermint, go ahead and plant mint seeds. For specific mint cultivars, however, it's best to buy plants.
Spring Planting Time   Divide established clumps before growth starts; later, root stem tip cuttings in water or moist soil.
Fall Planting Time   Divide and replant established stands in early fall.
Planting Depth   Set plants so the roots are just beneath the surface of the soil. If planting seeds, sow them ¼ inch deep.
Spacing between Plants   12 to 18 inches

Greenhouse Varieties Mint grows well in a cool greenhouse.

Container Varieties Mint will grow in containers of rich, moist soil that are at least 10 inches deep; it needs to be divided and repotted every year to stay healthy.

PLANT MANAGEMENT

Mint can be invasive in a garden. It is often controlled by planting in a roofing tile, bottomless pail, or other bottomless container sunk into the soil at least 10 inches to prevent plants from spreading.

Water Requirements

Make sure the plants get 1 inch of water every week from rain or by watering. (See chapter 8 for more information on watering.)

Feeding Requirements

This plant is a light feeder, so it needs no supplemental fertilizer over and above one application of slow-acting fertilizer in the spring. Too much fertilizer encourages rust in mint. Excessive leaf growth reduces the flavor of the leaves. Spray plants with liquid seaweed extract two or three times during the growing season. (See chapter 8 for more information on feeding.)

Pruning

Keep mints pinched back for fuller growth. Avoid letting the flowers bloom, as blossoming affects the oil content of the leaves. Prune back the whole top half or more of plants in the late spring and again in midsummer. It is difficult to over-prune your mint. In the late fall, after your final harvest, cut the plants back to the ground. This eliminates overwintering sites for mint insect pests.

MOST COMMON INSECT PESTS

Foliage Curls, Puckers, Turns Yellow

Aphid

If the foliage on your plants curls, puckers, and turns yellow, and the foliage and blooms become stunted, look for ants. They are a sign that your plants have aphids. Ants are attracted to a sticky honeydew secreted by aphids. These insects are about the size of a pinhead and have soft, pear-shaped bodies. They may be green, brown, or pink. You will find them in clusters on the undersides of young leaves. For light infestations, spray the plants vigorously with water in the early morning three times, once every other day. For heavy infestations, apply a commercial insecticidal soap every 2 to 3 days.

Small Ragged Holes in Leaves

Cabbage Looper

Small ragged holes in leaves are signs of cabbage loopers. The cabbage looper is a light green caterpillar with long yellowish stripes on its back. It loops as it walks. Spray *Bacillus thuringiensis* (BT) on plants every 2 weeks until the pests disappear.

Seedling Stems Severed

Cutworm

Cutworms sever the stems of seedlings and transplants at or below the soil surface. These pests are plump, dull-colored, soft-bodied caterpillars that curl up when disturbed. They feed at night and hide in the soil during the day. The best way to control a cutworm problem is to use a barrier or trap of some kind. Protect individual plants with a collar. Or a trap can be made by sprinkling cornmeal or bran meal around each plant. (See chapter 4 for more information on collars and meal traps.)

Tiny Holes in Leaves

Flea Beetle

Lots of tiny holes in the leaves can be caused by mint flea beetles. They can destroy small plants rapidly with their feeding. Mint flea beetles are about the size of a pinhead. They are shiny, black, and may have yellow or white markings. Flea beetles are very active and jump like a flea when disturbed. Cover plants in spring with barriers, such as agricultural

fleece, to prevent access to plants. If your mint does become infected, apply pyrethrum every 2 to 3 days until infestation is under control.

Leaves Stippled Yellow

Spider Mite

Leaves of mint infested with spider mites become stippled, yellow, and dry, and sometimes have pale yellow spots or blotches. Mites are tiny arachnids about the size of a grain of black pepper, and may be red, black, or brown. They feed by sucking out the plant's juices, including the chlorophyll, causing small white dots to appear. They also inject toxins into the leaves, causing discoloration and distortion. Spray plants with a forceful spray of water three times, once every other day, to knock mites from the leaves. If that doesn't control them, spray with commercial insecticidal soap.

MOST COMMON DISEASES

Water-soaked Spots on Leaves

Anthracnose

Small, water-soaked spots develop on the above-ground parts of mint infected with anthracnose. These spots turn a light color and may drop out. Elongated tan cankers may develop on the stems. Remove and destroy infected plants. Try to prevent anthracnose by following good fall cleanup practices.

Brown Spore Masses on Undersides of Leaves

Mint Rust

Initially, mint infected with mint rust develops small, whitish, slightly raised spots, which after a few days turn to many small, reddish orange to brown spore masses, mostly on undersides of leaves and possibly on the stem. The leaves rapidly yellow, dry up, and drop. Dust leaves with a sulfur fungicide every 7 to 10 days until 3 to 4 weeks before harvest. Avoid wetting the foliage or handling wet plants. Use mulch and drip irrigation to keep soil moist, or water overhead before noon so plants will dry before nightfall. Remove diseased plant matter at the end of the season.

Wilted, Drooping Leaves

Verticillium Wilt

Wilting and drooping of leaves during midsummer or later is a sign of verticillium wilt. The leaves turn yellow, curl upward along the midrib, and drop. The disease progresses from the older part of the plant to the younger growth. Soils high in organic matter reduce the fungus. Remove infected and surrounding mint plants and destroy them. Plant mint in a new location.

HARVEST AND STORAGE

When to Harvest

Mint can be harvested almost as soon as it comes up in the spring. It is best when picked early in the morning just as the dew evaporates. Picking the youngest shoots gives best flavor and helps keep the plant pruned. Cut just above a leaf node.

Best Fresh Storage Method   Mint is best used when as fresh as possible, but will keep for several days in the refrigerator in a jar of water covered with a plastic bag.

Best Long-Term Storage Methods   Dry by hanging stems or laying them on screens in an airy place out of direct sun; store dried mint in air-tight containers; it will retain its flavor for 1 year. Mint leaves can also be frozen in ice cubes.

VARIETIES

There are many varieties of mint, and they are all grown the same way.

Apple Mint. *(Mentha suaveolens)* 20 to 30 inches tall; purplish white flowers in 2- to 3-inch spikes; round, toothed, stalkless, hairy leaves 1 to 4 inches long.

Bergamot Mint. *(M. ×piperita* var. *citrata)* Also called orange mint; 24 inches tall; lavender blossoms; 2-inch leaves have little yellow dots, wavy edges, and smell of oranges and mint.

Pennyroyal. *(M. pulegium)* Prostrate, branching; small rosy lilac blossoms; roundish leaves 1 inch long.

Peppermint. *(M. ×piperita)* 3 feet tall; small purple flowers in 1- to 3-inch spikes; purple stems and strongly scented leaves.

Spearmint. *(M. spicata)* Most familiar mint, used in mint jelly; 18 to 24 inches tall; small purple flowers; leaves shorter stalked, hairier than peppermint.

NOTES AND RESEARCH

Field tests have not confirmed that interplanting mints with vegetables repels insect pests. However, menthol is an effective repellent, and some mint species contain fungicides and feeding deterrents as well.

HERB **Oregano** *Origanum vulgare* subspecies *hirtum*

DESCRIPTION AND ENVIRONMENT

O. heracleoticum is the preferred Greek oregano, properly pungent smelling and peppery on the tongue. Oregano grown from seeds labeled *O. vulgare,* wild oregano, is likely to be sprawling and scentless.

Height   12 to 24 inches

Spread   12 inches

Blossoms   White to purple, depending on variety, in terminal spikes, July through September.

Light Requirements   Full sun

Frost Tolerance   Hardy to −30°F. Greek oregano is said to be only half-hardy; it may be kept outside if located where conditions are appropriate to its Mediterranean origins—in the hottest, driest corner available. Mulch it with gravel or small pebbles, and if it lacks a snow cover during winter, protect it with evergreen boughs.

Soil Preference   Average, well-drained soil.

Preferred Soil pH   6.5 to 7.0

PLANTING AND PROPAGATION

Best Method of Propagation   Cuttings taken in the summer or division in the spring; since plants vary greatly in flavor, taste a leaf first and propagate only the most flavorful plants.

Spring Planting Time   In early spring, scatter seeds on the surface of a flat of soil (they germinate better in light) and keep them at 70°F; plant more than you will need to be sure of getting plants with good flavor.

Planting Depth   Surface of soil.

Spacing between Plants   18 to 24 inches

Days to Germination   About 4

Weeks to Transplanting   5

Days to Maturity   50

Greenhouse Varieties   Any variety of oregano can be grown in the greenhouse.

Container Varieties   Plants grow well in containers that are at least 6 inches deep.

PLANT MANAGEMENT

Water Requirements

Oregano tolerates dryness well, but try to make sure plants get 1 inch of water every week from rain or by watering. Do not overwater, or you will reduce flavor. (See chapter 8 for more information on watering.)

Feeding Requirements

This plant is a light feeder, so it needs no supplemental fertilizer over and above one application of slow-acting fertilizer in the spring. Excessive fertilizer reduces the herb's flavor. Spray plants with liquid seaweed extract two or three times during the growing season. (See chapter 8 for more information on feeding.)

Pruning

Keep oregano pruned or picked to avoid letting the flowers develop, which would reduce or at least change the flavor of the leaves. Radically cut back the top half of the plant in summer before flowering, and then again in early fall.

MOST COMMON INSECT PESTS

Foliage Curls, Puckers, Turns Yellow

Aphid

If the foliage on your plants curls, puckers, and turns yellow, and the foliage and blooms become stunted, look for ants. They are a sign that your plants have aphids. Ants are attracted to a sticky honeydew secreted by aphids. These insects are about the size of a pinhead and have soft, pear-shaped bodies. They may be green, brown, or pink. You will find them in clusters on the undersides of young leaves. For light infestations, spray the plants vigorously with water in the early morning three times, once every other day. For heavy infestations, apply a commercial insecticidal soap every 2 to 3 days.

White or Brown Tunnels in Leaves

Leafminer

White or brown tunnels or blotches on the leaves of plants are signs that your oregano has leafminers. Leaves can turn yellow and look blistered or curled. Leafminers are small black flies, usually with yellow stripes. It is the tiny, yellowish maggots that do the damage, by feeding between the upper and lower surfaces of leaves. There may be stem damage below the soil. Protect plants from the flies by covering seedlings with cheesecloth or agricultural fleece. If leafminers get to the plants, try to remove the infested leaves before the larvae mature.

Leaves Stippled Yellow

Spider Mite

Leaves of oregano plants infested with spider mites become stippled, yellow, and dry, and sometimes have pale yellow spots or blotches. Mites are tiny arachnids about the size of a grain of black pepper, and may be red, black, or brown. They feed by sucking out the plant's juices, including the chlorophyll, causing small white dots to appear. They also inject toxins into the leaves, causing discoloration and distortion. Spray plants with a forceful spray of water three times, once every other day, to knock mites from the leaves. If that doesn't control them, spray with commercial insecticidal soap.

MOST COMMON DISEASES

Rotting of Older Leaves

Botrytis Rot

If older leaves in the center of the plant near the base are rotted, your oregano may be infected with botrytis rot. This disease is encouraged by damp conditions. Remove infected plants to control the spread of the disease.

Gradual Wilting of Plants

Rhizoctonia
A slow wilting of the plants may be a sign that your oregano has rhizoctonia. Roots and the base of stems are yellowish brown to black, and rotted. This occurs in wet, heavy soils. Remove and destroy infected plants. Provide good drainage, and rotate plants every 3 years. Compost discourages this fungus.

HARVEST AND STORAGE

When to Harvest

Sprigs of oregano can be snipped when the plant is only 6 inches high. Oregano is best picked early in the morning just as the dew evaporates. Picking the youngest shoots gives best flavor and helps keep the plant pruned. Pick as needed, stripping the plants of the outermost stems and leaves. Stop major harvesting about 1 month prior to the first expected frost date. This reduces chances of losing this perennial plant from winter-kill.

Best Fresh Storage Method Oregano tastes best when cut as needed, but it will keep for several days in the refrigerator in a jar of water covered with a plastic bag.

Best Long-Term Storage Method Dry stems of oregano by hanging them upside down or laying them on screens in an airy place out of the sun; store dried oregano in air-tight containers; it will retain its flavor for 1 year.

NOTES AND RESEARCH

There is no scientific evidence to support claims about oregano's pest-repellent powers.

HERB *Parsley* *Petroselinum crispum*

DESCRIPTION AND ENVIRONMENT

Both curly and flat-leaved varieties are grown for flavoring and garnishes, but the flat-leaved variety is said to have the best flavor. Parsley is a biennial, but is usually planted annually.

Height 9 to 18 inches
Spread 6 to 9 inches
Blossoms Tiny, greenish yellow blossoms, borne in umbels the second year in early summer.
Light Requirements Full sun to partial shade.

Frost Tolerance Very hardy
Soil Preference Moderately rich, moist, well-drained soil.
Preferred Soil pH 6.0 to 7.0

PLANTING AND PROPAGATION

Best Method of Propagation Direct seeding

Spring Planting Time　Sow seeds indoors 4 to 6 weeks before the last frost and keep them at 60°F to 85°F for germination. Transplant seedlings outside after danger of frost has passed. Direct-seed parsley outdoors when the soil temperature reaches 50°F.

Fall Planting Time　Parsley is a hardy biennial and will often winter over with some protection, and then set seed in spring.

Planting Depth　¼ inch

Spacing between Plants　6 to 8 inches

Days to Germination　Slow to germinate; soak seeds for 24 hours before planting. Chilling in the freezer for a day before planting also helps. Will germinate in 11 to 27 days.

Weeks to Transplanting　8 to 10

Days to Maturity　70 to 90

Greenhouse Varieties　Parsley thrives in a cool greenhouse.

Container Varieties　Parsley can be transplanted from the garden into containers for winter harvesting. Parsley has a taproot, so it is best to transplant a full-grown plant into a large container that is at least 12 inches deep. You can also start seeds in mid- to late summer and grow the plants in pots outdoors to get large plants for winter harvest indoors.

PLANT MANAGEMENT

Water Requirements

Make sure the plants get 1 inch of water every week from rain or by watering. (See chapter 8 for more information on watering.)

Feeding Requirements

Parsley is a heavy feeder and likes some supplemental fertilizer. In addition to one application of slow-acting fertilizer in the spring, a monthly supplement will ensure healthy growth. Spray plants with liquid seaweed extract two or three times during the growing season. (See chapter 8 for more information on feeding.)

MOST COMMON INSECT PESTS

Defoliated Plants

Cabbage Looper

If parsley plants are defoliated, suspect the cabbage looper. This light green caterpillar has long yellowish stripes on its back, and it loops as it walks. Spray

Bacillus thuringiensis (BT) on plants every 2 weeks until loopers disappear.

Carrot Weevil

Defoliated plants may be a sign of carrot weevils. The larvae tunnel into the tops and roots of parsley, destroying most of the plant's tissue and leaving only stems and ribs. The carrot weevil is ⅕ inch long and brownish, with a hard shell. The larvae are pale and legless, with brown heads. Use pyrethrum sprays as soon as adult beetles appear in spring. Try to deny weevils access by covering the seedlings with agricultural fleece early in the season.

Parsleyworm

If the leaves are eaten and only the stems remain, suspect the parsleyworm. The larva of the black swallowtail butterfly, this pest is about 2 inches long, and is green with a yellow-dotted black band across each segment. When upset, it gives off an odor and projects orange horns. Usually parsleyworms are not numerous enough to threaten the crop, but if much damage occurs, handpick the worms or spray plants with *Bacillus thuringiensis* (BT) every 2 weeks until the caterpillars disappear.

Rotting or Dwarfing of Plants

Carrot Rust Fly

The maggots of the carrot rust fly chew roots, causing plants to be dwarfed. Soft-rot bacteria may infect plants damaged by carrot rust flies, and the entire plant may quickly decompose. The carrot rust fly is a black fly with long yellow hairs and a yellow head and legs. The maggots are yellow to white and ⅓ inch long. The flies lay their eggs in the plants near the soil line. Prevent access to the crop by covering the ground with agricultural fleece or fine nylon mesh when the seeds are planted.

Stunted Plants, Yellow Leaves

Nematode

Plants infected with nematodes show stunted growth. The leaves become yellow prematurely, and if the plants do survive to maturity, they will produce low yields. Roots of affected plants have root knots. Nematodes are microscopic whitish, translucent worms that are barely visible to the naked eye. They live in the soil and attack the roots of the plant. Use resistant varieties if available. Add 3 to 4 inches of compost (especially leaf mold) to the soil, fertilize with fish emulsion, and plant early in the season.

Leaves Stippled Yellow

Spider Mite

The leaves of parsley infested with spider mites become stippled, yellow, and dry, and sometimes have pale yellow spots or blotches. Mites are tiny arachnids about the size of a grain of black pepper, and may be red, black, or brown. They feed by sucking out the plant's juices, including the chlorophyll, causing small white dots to appear. They also inject toxins into the leaves, causing discoloration and distortion. Spray plants with a forceful spray of water three times, once every other day, to knock mites from the leaves. If that doesn't control them, spray with commercial insecticidal soap.

MOST COMMON DISEASES

Small Yellow Specks on Leaves

Septoria Leaf Spot

The leaf spots of septoria begin as small yellow specks, which later enlarge, becoming brown with a yellow border. They can be either circular or irregular in shape, and often have a black dot in the center. Make two applications of copper dust or a liquid copper spray fungicide every 7 to 10 days after discovering the disease. If that doesn't solve the problem, pull the infected plants.

Resistant Varieties. Paramount.

HARVEST AND STORAGE

When to Harvest

You can begin harvesting parsley when it begins to produce leaves with three branches.

Best Fresh Storage Method

Store fresh sprigs of parsley upright in a jar of water covered with a plastic bag in the refrigerator, or sprinkle the leaves with water, slip them into a plastic bag, and refrigerate; both techniques give you fresh parsley for 2 weeks.

Best Long-Term Storage Method

Parsley freezes well chopped up and stored in plastic bags or blended in water or stock and frozen in an ice cube tray. Remove cubes when frozen and store in sealed plastic freezer bags. Frozen parsley will keep for 6 months.

Second-Best Long-Term Storage Method

Parsley also dries well, although it loses much of its flavor. One technique is to place parsley on a cookie tray, set it in an oven preheated to 400°F, turn off the oven, and leave it undisturbed overnight. This is best done on a day with low humidity. Store dried parsley in an air-tight jar. It will retain its flavor for 1 year.

HERB Rosemary   *Rosmarinus officinalis*

DESCRIPTION AND ENVIRONMENT

Rosemary is neither a hardy perennial nor a tender annual, but rather a tender perennial shrub that can overwinter only in Zone 6 and south of this zone. Rosemary adapts well to pot culture.

Height   1 to 4 feet
Spread   12 to 24 inches
Blossoms   Lavender to blue blooms in clusters along branches, December through spring.
Light Requirements   Full sun
Frost Tolerance   Withstands light frosts, but not hard freezes; in cold climates, winter potted plants in a cool, sunny window indoors.
Soil Preference   Well-drained soil.
Preferred Soil pH   6.5 to 7.0

PLANTING AND PROPAGATION

Best Method of Propagation   Propagate rosemary from softwood cuttings. In summer, snip a 3-inch cutting from the tops of several branches and remove the leaves from the lower third of each piece. Plant three to six cuttings firmly in a 4-inch pot of very light, moist soil; then slip a clear plastic bag, punctured with a few tiny holes, over the pot, fastening the bag with a rubber band. Keep the pot in a bright place out of direct sun. The roots should form within 3 weeks, after which the new plants should be potted singly. To root cuttings in winter, provide them with a bottom heat of 70°F and good light.

Spring Planting Time   Set rooted cuttings or overwintered plants outdoors after the last frost.
Planting Depth   ¼ inch
Spacing between Plants   12 to 18 inches
Days to Germination   21
Weeks to Transplanting   5
Days to Maturity   60
Greenhouse Varieties   Greenhouse conditions produce impressive specimens of rosemary.
Container Varieties   Set a small starter plant directly into an oversized pot (12 inches in

diameter or larger) of fertile soil. If a potted rosemary on the patio or porch dries out too quickly, sink the pot into the ground up to the rim. Potted rosemary should thrive for 3 to 4 years if you keep both the foliage and roots pruned. Rosemary roots do not mind being crowded, so occasional root pruning is preferred to transplanting to a bigger pot. Use a well-drained potting mix to prevent root rot.

PLANT MANAGEMENT

Water Requirements

Make sure the plants get 1 inch of water every week from rain or by watering, but do not overwater. With rosemary grown in pots, let the soil surface dry out between waterings. Whether indoors or outdoors, mist the foliage occasionally in hot weather. (See chapter 8 for more information on watering.)

Feeding Requirements

This plant is a light feeder and needs no supplemental fertilizer over and above one application of slow-acting fertilizer in the spring. Excessive leaf growth reduces the flavor of those leaves. Apply foliar spray of liquid seaweed or kelp extract two or three times during the growing season. (See chapter 8 for more information on feeding.)

Pruning

An annual pruning just before rosemary goes outdoors for the summer keeps the shrub shapely and leafy. Shorten the winter-spindly stems by at least one-half. Wait until flowering is over before pruning.

MOST COMMON INSECT PESTS

Leaves Stippled Yellow

Spider Mite

The leaves of rosemary infested with spider mites become dry and stippled with tiny yellow dots. Mites are tiny arachnids about the size of a grain of black pepper, and may be red, black, or brown. They feed by sucking out the plant's juices, including the chlorophyll, causing small white dots to appear. They also inject toxins into the leaves, causing discoloration and distortion. Spray plants with a forceful spray of water three times, once every other day, to knock mites from the leaves. If that doesn't control them, spray with commercial insecticidal soap.

Weakened Plants, Yellow Leaves

Whitefly

Plants that have whiteflies weaken, their leaves turn yellow, and they die. Honeydew secreted by whiteflies encourages fungus. Molds often develop following an attack. Adults are about the size of a pinhead and mothlike, with dusty white wings. When an infested plant is shaken, it appears as if dandruff were flying off the leaves. Nymphs are yellowish, legless, flat, and oval, resembling scale at certain stages. To control infestations, spray plants with insecticidal soap spray every 2 to 3 days for 2 weeks. Use it also early in the season to prevent whiteflies. Pyrethrum may be used as a last resort. Make two applications, 3 to 4 days apart.

MOST COMMON DISEASES

Rotting of Older Leaves

Botrytis Rot

If the center of the plant near the base is rotted, your rosemary may be infected with botrytis rot. This disease is encouraged by damp conditions. Remove infected plants to control spread of the disease.

Gradual Wilting of Plants

Rhizoctonia

A slow wilting of the plants may be a sign that your rosemary has rhizoctonia. Roots and the base of stems are yellowish brown to black, and rotted. This occurs in wet, heavy soils. Remove and destroy infected plants. Provide good drainage, and rotate plants every 3 years. Compost discourages this fungus.

HARVEST AND STORAGE

When to Harvest

Pick rosemary leaves as you need them throughout the year. Pick in the morning for best flavor. Cut 3 to 4 inches from one branch rather than cutting ½ inch from a number of branches.

Best Storage Method   Rosemary can be dried. Cut as many shoots as you wish to dry, rinse and dry them carefully, and then tie them in bunches and hang them upside down in a dark, airy place. Store the dried leaves in an air-tight jar.

NOTES AND RESEARCH

No data are available on the power of rosemary as an insect repellent.

HERB **Sage**   *Salvia officinalis*

DESCRIPTION AND ENVIRONMENT

Height   24 inches

Spread   12 to 18 inches

Blossoms   Violet-blue, in terminal spikes, June.

Light Requirements   Full sun

Frost Tolerance   Hardy to −30°F if covered

with a loose mulch such as hay or evergreen boughs; though shriveled, the leaves taste fresher than dried sage kept inside.

Soil Preference   Well-drained, moderately rich soil.

Preferred Soil pH   6.0 to 7.0

PLANTING AND PROPAGATION

Best Method of Propagation Direct seeding or cuttings; the woody crowns of old sage plants can seldom be divided successfully.

Spring Planting Time Sow seeds indoors at 60°F to 70°F in late winter or early spring, and set the plants out after the last expected frost.

Fall Planting Time Root 3- to 4-inch tip cuttings from established plants in late summer, winter them in a sunny window or a protected cold frame, and plant them in the garden in spring.

Planting Depth ¼ inch
Spacing between Plants 20 inches
Days to Germination 14 to 21
Weeks to Transplanting 4
Days to Maturity 50
Greenhouse Varieties Any variety of sage can be grown in the greenhouse.
Container Varieties Any variety of sage can be grown in containers of at least 12-inch depth.

PLANT MANAGEMENT

Water Requirements

Make sure the plants get 1 inch of water every week from rain or by watering. Do not overwater; it causes mildew. (See chapter 8 for more information on watering.)

Feeding Requirements

Sage is a light feeder, so it needs no supplemental fertilizer over and above one application of slow-acting fertilizer in the spring. Excessive leaf growth reduces the flavor of the leaves. Spray plants with liquid seaweed extract two or three times during the growing season. (See chapter 8 for more information on feeding.)

Pruning

In early spring, clip the straggling, winter-worn branches back by about half, but not to the woody portions. New growth soon sprouts, and the plants stay compact. Then, in midseason, cut plants back to encourage bushiness. Even given this treatment, sage will need replacing after three or four seasons.

MOST COMMON INSECT PESTS

Large Ragged Holes in Leaves

Slug
Slugs chew large ragged holes in leaves and stems. They start at the bottom of the plant and work their

way up. Look for trails of slime on the leaves and the soil near plants as further evidence of slugs. Slugs look like snails without shells. They are 1 to 2 inches long, and may be brown, gray, white, pale yellow, purple, or nearly black with brown specks. The best way to control slugs is to set up a barrier, such as hardware cloth, ashes, or sand, to deny them access to the garden. Handpicking will work if you start early in the season. There are a number of homemade or commercial traps that work as well. (See the entry Slug in chapter 4 for information on making traps.)

Leaves Stippled Yellow

Spider Mite

The leaves of plants that have mites become stippled, yellow, and dry, and sometimes have pale yellow spots or blotches. Mites are tiny arachnids about the size of a grain of black pepper, and may be red, black, or brown. They feed by sucking out plant juices, including the chlorophyll, leaving small white dots on the leaves. They also inject toxins into the leaves, causing discoloration and distortion. Spray plants forcefully with water three times, once every other day, to knock mites off the leaves. If they persist, spray with insecticidal soap.

MOST COMMON DISEASES

White Powdery Spots on Leaves

Powdery Mildew

In plants with powdery mildew, the upper surfaces of leaves become covered with a white powdery mold. The foliage wilts, browns, and then drops. Remove and destroy infected plants. Try to prevent powdery mildew by following good fall cleanup practices. If you water plants from overhead, do this in the morning so that the plants will dry before evening. Moist conditions encourage the growth of this disease.

Gradual Wilting of Plants

Rhizoctonia

A slow wilting of the plants may be a sign that your sage has rhizoctonia. Roots and the base of stems are yellowish brown to black, and rotted. This occurs in wet, heavy soils. Remove and destroy infected plants. Provide good drainage, and rotate plants every 3 years. Compost discourages this fungus.

Wilted, Drooping Leaves

Verticillium Wilt

Wilting and drooping of the leaves during midsummer or later is a sign of verticillium wilt. The leaves turn yellow, curl upward along the midrib, and drop. The disease progresses from the older part of the plant to the younger growth. Soils high in organic matter reduce the fungus. Remove infected and surrounding plants and destroy them. Plant sage in a new location.

HARVEST AND STORAGE

When to Harvest

Strip leaves from the stem as needed. Stop major harvesting about 1 month prior to the first expected frost. This reduces the chance of losing this perennial plant from winter-kill.

Best Fresh Storage Method   Sage is best when used immediately, but will keep for several days in a jar of water covered with a plastic bag in the refrigerator.

Best Long-Term Storage Method   Dry sage by snipping leaves from stems and drying them on screens in an airy place out of the sun. Store in air-tight jars. Dried sage has a stronger and somewhat different flavor than fresh sage. It will retain its flavor for about a year.

HERB Savory

Satureja hortensis (summer savory); *S. montana* (winter savory)

DESCRIPTION AND ENVIRONMENT

Summer savory is a bushy, upright annual with linear gray-green leaves. Winter savory is a dense, compact, short-lived perennial with glossy evergreen leaves.

Height   Summer savory, 12 to 18 inches; winter savory, 6 to 12 inches.

Spread   12 to 18 inches, summer and winter.

Blossoms   White or pinkish lavender; summer savory blooms in midsummer, winter savory from July through mid-September.

Light Requirements   Full sun

Frost Tolerance   Winter savory is hardy to Zone 6.

Soil Preference   Average, well-drained soil.

Preferred Soil pH   6.5 to 7.0

PLANTING AND PROPAGATION

Best Method of Propagation   Both kinds of savory are easy to grow from seeds or cuttings. Use fresh seeds, because they do not store well for more than a year. Winter savory tends to die out after 2 or 3 years. Root vigorous tip cuttings in summer to keep replacements coming.

Spring Planting Time   Sow seeds of both species indoors in early spring. Do not cover the seeds with soil, and germinate at 60°F to 70°F. Transplant seedlings outdoors after the last expected frost. Summer savory can also be direct-seeded in the garden after the last frost date.

Planting Depth   Surface of the soil.

Spacing between Plants   Summer savory, 10 inches apart; winter savory, 10 to 12 inches apart.

Days to Germination   10 to 15 or more.
Weeks to Transplanting   6
Days to Maturity   60

Greenhouse Varieties   Either species of savory can be grown in the greenhouse.

Container Varieties   Either species of savory can be grown in containers at least 6 inches deep.

PLANT MANAGEMENT

To make sure that winter savory survives northern winters, plant it on a very well drained site and cover it loosely with straw or evergreen boughs as soon as the ground freezes. Remove the mulch after the last hard freeze in spring. (Summer savory is an annual.)

Water Requirements

Make sure savory gets 1 inch of water every week from rain or by watering. Don't overwater winter savory or it may rot. Cultivate rather than mulch these plants to avoid soggy conditions. (See chapter 8 for more information on watering.)

Feeding Requirements

These herbs are light feeders, so they need no supplemental fertilizer over and above one application of slow-acting fertilizer in the spring. Excessive leaf growth reduces the flavor of the leaves. Spray plants with liquid seaweed extract two or three times during the growing season. (See chapter 8 for more information on feeding.)

Pruning

If growth becomes leggy, prune back the top half of the plant in midsummer or early fall before flowering.

MOST COMMON DISEASES

Seedlings Die

Damping-Off
Seedlings that have damping-off simply topple over. You will find a watery soft rot on the stem at the soil line. There is no cure for this disease. Remove and destroy infected plants. When starting seeds indoors, use a commercial potting soil, or pasteurize your own potting soil in an oven. Disinfect tools in heated water or a bleach solution (one part household bleach to four parts water). Provide soil with adequate drainage and use a fan near seedlings for better air circulation. For direct seeding, make sure soil is well drained and warm. You might try spreading pasteurized soil or a sterile vermiculite in furrows where you plant your seeds.

Gradual Wilting of Plants

Rhizoctonia
A slow wilting of the plants may be a sign that your savory has rhizoctonia. Roots and the base of stems are yellowish brown to black, and rotted. This occurs in wet, heavy soils. Remove and destroy infected plants. Provide good drainage, and rotate plants every 3 years. Compost discourages this fungus.

HARVEST AND STORAGE

When to Harvest

Harvest sprigs for fresh use anytime. Frequent snipping of branch tips stimulates growth of side shoots, extending the harvest. The youngest shoots have the best flavor. Try to prevent flowering; it affects the oil content and flavor of the leaves.

Best Fresh Storage Method   Both types of savory are best when picked fresh, but will keep for several days in the refrigerator in a jar of water covered with a plastic bag.

Best Long-Term Storage Method   Both types of savory dry well. Cut stems of winter savory, or whole plants of summer savory, just before flowering, and dry by hanging them upside down or laying them on screens in a shady, airy place. Store the dried leaves in air-tight containers. They will retain their flavor for 1 year.

HERB *Tarragon* *Artemisia dracunculus*

DESCRIPTION AND ENVIRONMENT

To get the right tarragon for cooking, buy rooted cuttings specifically marked "French tarragon" or "culinary tarragon." "Russian tarragon," which can be grown from seeds, has little or no flavor.

Height　30 inches

Spread　24 inches

Blossoms　Yellow or whitish green; may not bloom in all climates. French tarragon is sterile; do not let Russian tarragon self-sow.

Light Requirements　Full sun to partial shade.

Frost Tolerance　Hardy perennial; apply winter mulch in colder climates to prevent heaving.

Soil Preference　Prefers a rich, sandy, well-drained loam; never plant tarragon in a wet or acid soil.

Preferred Soil pH　6.5 to 7.0

PLANTING AND PROPAGATION

Best Method of Propagation　True tarragon produces no seeds. Divide mature plants in spring or root tip cuttings anytime during the growing season.

Spring Planting Time　Plant rooted cuttings outdoors after all danger of frost is past. Divide old clumps before growth starts.

Planting Depth　Deep enough to cover roots.

Spacing between Plants　2 feet

Greenhouse Varieties　French tarragon can be a year-round greenhouse crop in the northern states if the plants are given 16-hour days with supplementary artificial lighting, after providing a 6-week cool period at 40°F.

Container Varieties　Tarragon likes a pot at least 10 inches in diameter. It can be forced for winter use. Pot a large division in late summer, cut the stems off at the base, wrap the pot in plastic, and place it in the refrigerator until fall to provide a cool dormant period. Then unwrap the pot and set it in a sunny window to induce sprouting. Harvest leaves sparingly all winter.

PLANT MANAGEMENT

Divide tarragon every 2 or 3 years to assure vigor and flavor. The shallow roots spread out in a 2-foot radius around the plant, so be careful not to cultivate too deeply. Tarragon benefits from a light summer mulch.

Water Requirements

Make sure the plants get 1 inch of water every week from rain or by watering. (See chapter 8 for more information on watering.)

Feeding Requirements

Tarragon is a light feeder, so it needs no supplemental fertilizer over and above one application of slow-acting fertilizer in the spring. Excessive leaf growth reduces the flavor of the leaves. Spray plants with liquid seaweed extract two or three times during the growing season. (See chapter 8 for more information on feeding.)

Pruning

Remove flowers if any appear. Cut tips often to keep plants bushy.

MOST COMMON DISEASES

Yellow Spots, Downy Mold on Leaves

Downy Mildew

Light green or pale yellow areas on the upper surfaces of leaves and discolored spots with downy growth on the undersides are symptoms of downy mildew in tarragon. The leaves wither and die. If you catch the infection early, apply a copper-based fungicide to diseased and surrounding plants every 7 to 10 days until harvest. Remove and destroy any plants with a serious infection.

White Powdery Spots on Leaves

Powdery Mildew

In plants with powdery mildew, the upper surfaces of leaves become covered with a white powdery mold. The foliage wilts, browns, and then drops. Remove and destroy infected plants.

Gradual Wilting of Plants

Rhizoctonia

A slow wilting of the plants may be a sign that your tarragon has rhizoctonia. Roots and the base of stems are yellowish brown to black, and rotted. This occurs in wet, heavy soils. Remove and destroy infected plants. Provide good drainage, and rotate plants every 3 years. Compost discourages this fungus.

HARVEST AND STORAGE

When to Harvest

Pick leaves needed for fresh use anytime. Handle the leaves gently, as they bruise easily. You can take two major cuttings from tarragon, the first 6 to 8 weeks after setting out plants, the second 1 month prior to first fall frost. Stop major harvesting about 1 month prior to the first expected fall frost date. This reduces chances of losing this perennial from winter-kill.

Best Fresh Storage Method   The sprigs will keep for several days in the refrigerator in a jar of water covered with a plastic bag.

Best Long-Term Storage Method   Preserve sprigs in white vinegar for 1 year.

Second-Best Long-Term Storage Method   Dry stems by hanging them in a shady, airy place at about 85°F. Drying browns the leaves and substantially mellows the flavor of tarragon. Dried tarragon will keep for 1 year.

HERB *Thyme*   *Thymus vulgaris*

DESCRIPTION AND ENVIRONMENT

Many varieties of thyme are available, including lemon-flavored types. The plants are low growing and can be used ornamentally. They are perennial in warm and moderate climates.

Height   2 to 12 inches

Spread   18 inches or more

Blossoms   White, lavender, or pink blooms, June and July; flowers are edible.

Light Requirements   Full sun to partial shade.

Frost Tolerance   Thyme is not reliably hardy in cold climates unless it is mulched in winter.

Soil Preference   Light, well-drained soil.

Preferred Soil pH   5.5 to 7.0

PLANTING AND PROPAGATION

Best Method of Propagation   Direct seeding, division, or layering. You can divide or take cuttings from established plants anytime from midspring to early summer, but preferably in the spring.

Spring Planting Time   Thyme grows easily from seeds started indoors at 70°F to 80°F about a month before the last frost date.

Planting Depth   Don't cover seeds; sow them in a little furrow, and enough soil will wash over them when they're watered.

Spacing between Plants   8 to 12 inches

Days to Germination   8 to 21

Weeks to Transplanting   4

Days to Maturity   Thyme reaches a usable size by midsummer.

Greenhouse Varieties   Thyme grows well in a cool greenhouse if the matted foliage is kept dry to prevent rot.

Container Varieties   You can keep thyme in the same pot for years by pruning roots and harvesting the foliage. When the plant starts growing out in all directions and the tiny leaves on the bottom begin to dry up, clip it down to the main stems to make it bushy again. Dry the leaves for seasoning. After a year of this treatment, remove the plant from its pot, trim off the roots along the sides and bottom, and transplant to a larger pot. If the plant has grown large, divide it.

PLANT MANAGEMENT

Plant all types of thyme in well-drained soil in a location with good air circulation. Wet, heavy soil causes root rot and winter-kill, and dampness around the dense foliage leads to fungal diseases. Cultivate to control weeds, or use one of the new black mulching fabrics that exclude weeds but still allow air and water to reach the soil. In winter, mulch with an airy material such as straw or evergreen boughs as soon as the ground freezes. Remove the mulch after the last hard frost in spring.

Water Requirements

Make sure the plants get 1 inch of water every week from rain or by watering. Be careful not to overwater. (See chapter 8 for more information on watering.)

Feeding Requirements

Thyme benefits from some supplemental fertilizer once a month over and above the one application of slow-acting fertilizer in the spring. In addition, spray plants with liquid seaweed extract two or three times during the growing season. (See chapter 8 for more information on feeding.)

Pruning

In areas with long growing seasons, you can prevent excessive woody growth and extend the productive life of thyme by pruning it heavily in the spring, or more lightly three times during the growing season. If, however, the last pruning is made too late, you run the risk of winter-kill.

MOST COMMON INSECT PESTS

Foliage Curls, Puckers, Turns Yellow

Aphid
If the foliage on your plants curls, puckers, and turns yellow, and the foliage and blooms become stunted, look for ants. They are a sign that your plants have aphids. Ants are attracted to a sticky honeydew secreted by aphids. These insects are about the size of a pinhead and have soft, pear-shaped bodies. They may be green, brown, or pink. You will find them in clusters on the undersides of young leaves. For light infestations, spray the plants vigorously with water in the early morning three times, once every other day. For heavy infestations, apply a commercial insecticidal soap every 2 to 3 days.

Leaves Stippled Yellow

Spider Mite
The leaves of thyme infested with spider mites become stippled, yellow, and dry, and sometimes have pale yellow spots or blotches. Mites are tiny arachnids about the size of a grain of black pepper, and may be red, black, or brown. They feed by sucking out the plant's juices, including the chlorophyll, causing small white dots to appear. They also inject toxins into the leaves, causing discoloration and distortion. Spray plants with a forceful spray of water three times, once every other day, to knock mites from the leaves. If that doesn't control them, spray with commercial insecticidal soap.

MOST COMMON DISEASES

Rotting of Older Leaves

Botrytis Rot
If the center of the plant near the base is rotted, your thyme may be infected with botrytis rot. This disease is encouraged by damp conditions. Remove infected plants to control spread of the disease.

Gradual Wilting of Plants

Rhizoctonia
A slow wilting of the plants may be a sign that your thyme has rhizoctonia. Roots and the base of stems are yellowish brown to black, and rotted. This occurs in wet, heavy soils. Remove and destroy infected plants. Provide good drainage, and rotate plants every 3 years. Compost discourages this fungus.

HARVEST AND STORAGE

When to Harvest

Cut leaves and shoots as needed all season. For a major harvest, cut back the entire plant in midsummer to about 2 inches from the ground. It will grow back before winter. Stop major harvesting about a month prior to the first expected frost date. This reduces chances of losing this perennial plant from winter-kill.

Best Fresh Storage Method   Sprigs will keep for several days in a plastic bag in the refrigerator.

Best Long-Term Storage Method   Dry thyme by hanging bunches or laying it on screens in a warm, shady, airy place. Store dried thyme in an air-tight container. It will retain its flavor for a year.

Other Long-Term Storage Methods

Freeze sprigs in an air-tight container, or mix leaves with oil or butter before freezing. Frozen thyme will keep for 6 months.

PART 2

Pests and Diseases

CHAPTER 4

Insects

The goal of backyard pest management (BPM) is to control insect pests in the garden. Rather than completely eradicating the pests, BPM focuses on effectively limiting their numbers while causing minimal harm to the rest of the garden's environment and ecosystem. A few pests in a garden generally cause no measurable harm to the fruit and vegetables. They provide food for natural predators, allowing those friends to hang around the garden and help keep things under control. The goal of BPM is to keep pest populations below a level that interferes with plant growth and crop yields.

There are two distinct ways of implementing a BPM program in your garden: Keep pests under control when they show up, and prevent pest problems from showing up in the first place.

Typically, gardeners use both approaches. Most of us wait until we have a pest problem and then take the control steps needed to minimize the damage; then we become interested in ways to prevent that particular pest from ever becoming a problem again.

CONTROLLING INSECT PESTS

Identify the Pest

Your first task is to learn how to spot, and then identify, insect pests that invade your garden sanc-

tuary. Learn to recognize the signs of insect damage for each vegetable or fruit, and which insect is likely to be the cause of each symptom. Such symptoms might be holes in the leaves, wilted plants, or a shiny coating on the leaves. It's important to identify the symptoms before taking action, because most of the insects in your garden are harmless or beneficial insects, not pests.

Use Early Warning Devices

The sooner you note the presence of an insect pest in your garden, the easier it will be to control it. You can expect a much higher rate of control if you begin when pest populations are small. One trick is to set a trap that attracts the particular pest you are expecting. Keep an eye on the trap, and as soon as you see some of the culprits in question, immediately begin control measures.

Traps and Manual Control Techniques

Once the presence of an insect pest has been detected, you have several options for controlling that pest before it causes any serious harm to the food crop. Cover traps, sticky traps, handpicking, or spraying forcefully with water will remove most of the pests from the vulnerable plants.

Natural Sprays and Dusts

If handpicking and mechanical controls don't work, you may need a spray or dust to get rid of the pests. Some insects can be controlled by feeding them to death. For example, if you dust plants threatened by Colorado potato beetles with dry wheat bran early in the morning, the beetles will eat the bran, drink dew to satisfy their thirst, and then later burst from the water-expanded bran. Cornmeal can be used as a dust to control cutworms: They eat the cornmeal but can't metabolize it, and eventually it kills them. Some gardeners report that a dusting of one part salt to two parts flour is fatal to the cabbage worm.

Sometimes, on certain plants or with certain pests, a spray is better than dust. Sprays usually give a more even coverage. You can use virtually any type of sprayer for applying sprays to insects in your garden. The primary concern is size. A small hand-held 1-pint or 1-quart sprayer is handy for the small garden, but it's a nuisance if you have a big garden that requires a number of refills to cover the whole territory. Also, be sure your garden sprayer is easy to

Certain insects, such as codling moths, are attracted to red, spherical sticky traps.

fill, easy to operate, and easy to clean. (See the source list at the back of this book for a number of companies that produce quality sprayers.)

Bug Juice Spray

Bug juice is a spray made from the crushed insect pests and applied to the infested plants. It is not clear whether bug juice is effective, but some gardeners have had success. Bug juice may indeed be a good control, since grinding up the insects could release their "alarm pheromone" or warning scent, which would frighten other bugs away. Or, maybe a few sick or disease-carrying bugs, when whizzed up and sprayed on crops, quickly spread the disease to others. Or, finally, it may be that the smell of chopped-up insects attracts the pest's natural enemies. In any case, do your own experiments to see whether bug juice is a successful control technique in your garden.

To make bug juice, collect half a cup of the specific problem insect. Place the pests in a blender with 2 cups of lukewarm water, and liquefy them. Strain the liquid through cheesecloth or a fine sieve to prevent particles from clogging your sprayer. Dilute about ¼ cup of the strained liquid with 1 or 2 cups of water in a small hand sprayer (the leftover liquid can be frozen for a year or more). Spray both sides of your vegetables' leaves, along with stems and runners. If it rains, spray again. For obvious reasons, don't use your household blender to make this juice! If you don't have an old blender jar, just mash the insects up with a mortar and pestle, add water, and proceed.

Commercial Insecticidal Soap

The fatty acid salts in certain kinds of soaps kill a large percentage of common insect pests, including aphids, mites, and whiteflies. Do not confuse homemade kitchen soap sprays with the commercial insecticidal soap sprays. The commercial brands have been especially formulated to be lethal to specific pests, and to avoid damage to plants and beneficial insects. Only commercial soap sprays are recommended for uniform performance. Insecticidal soap is biodegradable within 7 to 14 days, and,

Pheromone traps work by emitting an odor based on an insect's sex hormones. Several different types and sizes of these traps are available.

ticidal soap is a contact insecticide, so it must have direct contact with the insect to be effective.

Insecticidal Soap and Alcohol
When you add isopropyl alcohol to a spray of commercial insecticidal soap (about ½ cup alcohol to each quart of insecticidal soap mixture), you increase the effectiveness of the insecticidal soap immensely. The alcohol alone might burn a few of your plants, but with another pesticide it becomes an effective wetting agent or surfactant that penetrates the insect's waxy protective coating and carries the pesticide into contact with the insect's body.

Garlic Spray
Garlic, onion, or chive sprays can also be effective insect controls. They don't actually kill insects, but seem to discourage them from attacking plants. To make the garlic spray, chop peeled garlic cloves, onions, or chives into fine particles. Mix ½ cup of the ground-up material with 1 pint of water; then strain out the particles to form a clear solution.

A more potent brew is still in the research stage, but promises effective control of many common pests. Pack 10 to 15 finely minced garlic cloves in a pint of mineral oil and let stand for at least 24 hours. Strain the oil. Add 2 teaspoons of the strained oil to a quart of insecticidal soap spray and use. In some tests, the soap spray's effectiveness has been greatly improved by the added garlic oil, even on pests not normally killed by the soap alone.

Horticultural Oil Sprays
There are two grades of horticultural oil—the traditional heavier grade oil, which is often used as a preventive spray on fruit trees in early spring, and the newer light horticultural oils, which are very effective insect controls because they can be used on foliage without harming trees, even in the summer months.

Traditional heavy horticultural spray oils have a viscosity of 100 to 200. If used indiscriminately on plant foliage, they can clog the pores on leaves and buds, cutting off respiration and killing the plant. These dormant oil sprays were designed to be used

for the most part, attacks only problem insects. It will not harm beneficial insects, animals, or people. The spray is easy to use and is effective, especially in the early part of the season before predator insects take over.

Spray plants every 2 to 3 days for 2 weeks for bad infestations. Use a strong pressure with medium droplet size to thoroughly wet all surfaces of the plant top to bottom. It is especially important to spray the undersides of leaves, where you'll find most of the pests. Cover the plant thoroughly; insec-

in fall through early spring on plants that have lost their leaves during the winter, primarily fruit trees. Applied to branches and stems while trees are leafless, the oil smothers insect eggs hidden in the bark.

The newer type of oil, called superior horticultural spray oil, is lighter and less viscous (viscosity 60 to 70) than heavy oil and evaporates much more quickly from leaves and stems. Any common woody ornamental plant can tolerate a spray using a 2 percent solution of this oil, as long as the plant is healthy, soil moisture is adequate, and the relative humidity creates conditions for fairly rapid evaporation of the oil. Two to 3 percent solutions can be very effective against mites and other soft-bodied sucking insects, and they have minimal impact on beneficial insects.

Light horticultural oil works by thinly coating the insect and suffocating it. Use a lower concentration of oil on plants with hairy leaves. Never spray a plant in full leaf when soil is dry. If you are uncertain about using the oil on a particular plant, test it on a few leaves. Damage will show up within several days as yellowing leaf tips and margins.

Light horticultural oils may be used in spring, summer, or winter, up to 1 month before harvest. Horticultural oils are extremely low in toxicity to man, pets, and wildlife, due in part to their lack of residual life on vegetation. They pose little threat to any natural enemies of your target pests.

Horticultural Oils and Alcohol

Just as with insecticidal soap, when you add isopropyl alcohol to a horticultural oil mixture, you increase its effectiveness. Combine 1 cup of alcohol and ½ teaspoon of Volck oil in 1 quart of water. The alcohol kills insects on contact, and the Volck oil stays on the plant to smother unseen young and eggs. This mixture can be sprayed daily or every 2 days until the pest population is reduced to a nondestructive level.

Hot Pepper Spray

A hot pepper spray can be an effective insect control. This spray is made by chopping or grinding hot peppers into fine particles and mixing ½ cup of them with 1 pint of water, then straining out the particles to form a clear solution. Avoid getting this solution near your eyes. Hot pepper powder can also be used to make a spray.

A forceful spray of water knocks aphids off of plants, and, if used repeatedly, can effectively control aphid populations.

New Developments in Sprays

A number of new products still in the research stages promise to be effective pest controls while causing little harm to the surrounding environment. Watch garden magazines for their introduction in the next few years.

Antifeedant Sprays. Antifeedants are chemicals produced by plants that, when sprayed on another plant, deter insects from eating that other plant. Researchers have begun extracting antifeedants by distilling, boiling, or grinding plants and applying the substances to infested plants. Many plants contain antifeedant substances: Peppermint contains a substance effective against Colorado potato beetles. The Japanese *Clerodendron tricotomum* inhibits feeding of European corn borers. Chemicals in *Artemisia tridentata* work against Colorado potato beetles.

Current research probably will lead to the introduction of a number of commercial antifeedant products in the next few years. One product already available is Green Ban, which is made in Australia from kelp, English ivy, sage, garlic, and eucalyptus.

Caffeine. Research has indicated that the caffeine in powdered tea or coffee kills or disrupts the behavior of numerous insects, from the tobacco budworm to the mosquito. When combined with other insecticides, caffeine multiplies their killing power many times. Mosquito larvae can't swim, mealworms can't reproduce, and tobacco budworms lose their appetites, develop tremors, and die. Researchers found that when given a choice, most insects will avoid foods treated with caffeine.

Citrus Peel. Research has revealed that citrus peels have insecticidal qualities. The effective substance in citrus peel is called limonene and is concentrated in the outer part of the peel. Limonene is used in very low concentrations to avoid harming the leaves of plants. This insecticide has been used in research as a contact poison and a fumigant. Watch for future insect control products having citrus peel in them.

Neem Products. Derived from a tree native to Asia and Africa, neem products are extremely effective as insecticides or, in some cases, as antifeedants.

A wide range of sprayers is available. When selecting one, keep in mind the size of your garden. A hand-held spray bottle is easy to use, but will need to be refilled several times if your garden is very large.

The active chemicals in neem repel or kill insects. Unlike synthetic pesticides or botanical poisons, the neem molecules do not act as a nerve or stomach poison. Instead, neem disrupts the insects' hormonal systems. Insects cannot molt properly, so they die trapped in their own skins. Neem's dual role as a repellent and a pesticide may make it doubly difficult for insects to develop resistance to it.

Neem-based products are now available for both food crops and ornamental crops. Mixed according to label directions, neem solution can be either poured on the soil around a plant or sprayed on the leaves. Neem repels or kills 80 different insect pests. In tests, it killed 95 percent of leafminers and was also effective against Colorado potato beetle and Mexican bean beetle. At the same time, beneficial insects like ladybugs and honeybees seem to be unaffected.

Biological Controls

The best known form of biological control is predatory and parasitic insects (beneficials), which attack and destroy pest insects. Predatory insects are discussed later in this chaper. Here we consider pest control products that make use of beneficial bacteria, viruses, and other microscopic creatures. Like natural sprays, these biological controls are harmless to the rest of the environment.

Bacillus Thuringiensis (BT)

BT is a type of bacterium that comes in powder form to be used as a dust or, when diluted with water, as a foliar spray. It kills leaf-eating caterpillars by invading the caterpillars' digestive system. You can purchase BT under a number of trade names, including Bactur, Biotrol, Dipel, Safer, and Thuricide. BT does not reproduce or overwinter in nature, so it must be applied each year as the pest caterpillar emerges. BT breaks down in sunlight. The powdered form remains viable for only 7 days after application, and the liquid spray for just 24 hours. Stored in the container in a cool, dark place, dry BT has a shelf life of at least 3 years. Once it has been mixed with water, it lasts just 1 year. It can be used indefinitely when stored at 40°F to 50°F.

The timing of BT applications is critical. BT has little residual effect, so you must be sure to apply it when feeding larvae are actually present. It must be eaten by the caterpillars to be effective. All parts of plant leaves, especially the undersides, should be thoroughly covered.

Observe your plants closely, and apply BT when you see worms or caterpillars beginning to feed. BT is most effective in the spring and again in the late summer, when caterpillar feeding activity is greatest. In using the powdered form of BT, wet plants before you dust them. Dusting the undersurfaces as well as the top surfaces of leaves keeps the BT spores active, because they survive longer when not hit by direct sunlight. Reapply the dust after rain.

To make a foliar spray from powdered BT, follow the directions on the container. Spray on affected plants every 10 to 14 days until the pest is under control. To help the diluted powder adhere to plant leaves, add 1 tablespoon of fish emulsion to each gallon of spray. A little commercial insecticidal soap or light horticultural oil also works as an adherent.

The liquid concentrate formulation of BT adheres well to plants.

Milky Spore Disease

This bacterial disease comes in powder form and is spread around the base of plants to control insect pests. The pests ingest the bacteria and eventually die.

New Developments in Biological Controls

Avermectin Insecticides. The new avermectin insecticides, such as abamectic (Avid), are fermentation products of a soil-inhabiting streptomyces organism. They are very potent against mites, thrips, loopers, beetles, and other insects.

Viral Insecticide. There is now a viral insecticide for control of codling moths. It is currently being developed and marketed under the trade name Decyde viral insecticide. Decyde is a highly selective, safe insect virus that controls codling moths without affecting beneficial insects or the environment. It does not affect soil, water, or the atmosphere. Decyde is a water-soluble concentrate, which can be applied as a foliar spray. It requires no special protective clothing or special handling during application.

The Last Resort, Botanical Poisons

If the types of controls already discussed do not effectively solve a particular pest problem in your garden, then you may need to bring in the "big bangers"—the botanical poisons. These are the plant-derived insecticides: pyrethrum and neem. The most important thing to remember about botanical poisons is that even though they are wholly natural, they may knock off as many good guys in your garden as bad guys. They should be used as your control weapon of last resort. (Neem is less harmful to beneficials than pyrethrum.)

If a botanical poison must be used while honeybees are pollinating, spray at dusk, when bees are least active. Pyrethrum usually breaks down within 6 hours if the temperature is 55°F or higher. However, if a heavy dew is predicted, don't spray at all; it won't break down before the bees begin feeding in the morning. Foliar sprays of pyrethrum are less toxic to bees than are dusts.

To minimize damage to all beneficials, apply these pesticides only to plants that are infested with pests; don't use them as preventive sprays.

PREVENTING INSECT PESTS

While the techniques described earlier may control any insect pest that appears in your garden, you should be interested in finding ways to prevent that same pest from ever becoming a problem again. Here are some suggestions.

Garden Cleanup

Fall garden cleanup may be the single most important pest control step you take all season long. It is absolutely critical that you reduce overwintering pests if you want to ease your problems next year.

Research for this book has led to the design of a fall/spring pest cleanup. Each of the steps in this process is related to the other, and it is their combined impact that gives the best insect protection.

Fall Cleanup

As soon as you finish the harvest for each crop, and before most insects have left host plants, remove all old plants and weeds. Leave a completely bare soil—no blades of straw, no stems and roots left in the ground to decompose, no exceptions. And remember, it is very important during the harvest period never to let overripe or spoiled fruit just fall to the ground and lie there.

If you have late fall crops, try to plan them so they are in one specific area of your garden, allowing the rest of the garden to get this thorough housecleaning.

When a good portion of your garden is cleared, cultivate the soil thoroughly 6 to 8 inches deep, using a hand tool or a rotary tiller. This fall cultiva-

Aphids often carry viruses from one row of vegetables to another.

To What Depths Will They Go?

Insect pests can be found at various levels in the vegetable garden.

On or Near the Host Plant. The eggs of aphids, gypsy moths, and thrips can be found on host plants. Carrot weevils, leafhoppers, Mexican bean beetles, and pear psyllids overwinter as adults. Those pest insects that overwinter as pupae on host plants and nearby objects include cabbage worms, cabbage loopers, and imported cabbage worms. The larvae of European corn borers overwinter inside the host plant.

In Crop Debris. Adult insects and some larvae that overwinter under crop residues and debris on the surface and in the top 1 or 2 inches of soil near the host plant include harlequin bugs, squash bugs, flea beetles, cucumber beetles, Mexican bean beetles, and asparagus beetles. Apple maggots, asparagus beetles, cherry fruit flies, Colorado potato beetles, harlequin bugs, plum curculios, squash bugs, and tarnished plant bugs overwinter as pupae.

In the Soil. Larvae that can be found 3 to 6 inches down in the soil include cutworms, white grubs, and wireworms. The pupae of corn earworms, root maggots, squash vine borers, and tomato hornworms overwinter in the soil near the host plant.

---

tion buries those insects that normally overwinter on the surface of the soil, and it exposes those that prefer to winter below the surface.

This is a good time to add some soil amendments to your garden, such as lime or compost.

About 2 to 3 weeks after that first deep cultivation, give the garden a shallow, 2-inch-deep cultivation with a rotary tiller or garden rake. This brings up more larvae already in the soil.

At this point you may leave the soil bare to freeze and thaw during the winter. While a winter mulch has value for a perennial flower garden or for a raspberry or strawberry patch, it is a waste of time for a vegetable garden. If you leave the soil bare, it is more likely to be affected by the heaving and shifting caused by freezing, which is a form of natural cultivation. One exception of course is when you wish to leave root crops, such as carrots, in the ground.

You may also choose to grow a winter cover crop. Plant winter rye or other green manure crops after the first cultivation.

Spring Cleanup

Since you have already deeply cultivated the ground during the previous fall, spring soil preparation is minimal. About 2 weeks before planting, give the garden a shallow cultivation. Just dig down about 2 inches. This step is designed to disturb, surface, and even kill any larvae that overwintered in the soil, and to remove early weed seedlings, which hatching larvae like to eat. Leave the soil fallow for 2 weeks before planting, letting the robins and starlings feed on the larvae.

At planting, give the soil one final shallow cultivation to bring up a few more grubs for your bird colleagues and to snag the annual weeds that have germinated in that time.

Barriers

For centuries, gardeners have been inventing ingenious methods for protecting plants from invading insects. The success of these barriers depends on how completely they protect plants and when they are set up. Set up the barrier before pests emerge and seal the edges well. Such barriers will keep out *all* flying insects—the beneficial predators and parasites, as well as the pests. If pests do sneak in, they may find it easy to destroy the crop. Keep this in mind as you decide whether to use barriers on certain crops.

Plastic or Fleece Row Covers

Plastic row covers, supported on frames or floating directly on plants, are usually used to extend the growing season. They also help protect crops against flying insects. The key is to be sure that the edges of the row cover are well anchored so insects can't sneak under them. Because plastic must have ventilation slits, it is a less effective barrier than agricultural fleece.

Netting Barriers

Later in the season, when the danger of frost is gone, you can use a nylon netting or other fine screening. Use material having at least 20 to 30 threads per inch, such as fine nylon netting, cheesecloth, or agricultural fleece. You can also use the ⅛-inch mesh nylon netting that's sold in fabric shops. It's very light and nonbinding, and can be used as a floating cover, placed directly over the plants. It will keep out most flying pests, and will last for about three seasons.

Cover vulnerable transplants or a newly seeded bed immediately after planting. Seal all the edges to the ground. Leave the cover in place until the particular moths or flies you are worried about have ceased to lay eggs. This may be a few weeks or most of the summer, depending on the pest. Consult your County Extension agent for emergence dates and egg laying time of the problem insect.

Use netting to protect chard, spinach, and turnip greens from leafminers; cole crops, onions, carrots, and turnips from various maggots; broccoli, brussels sprouts, cabbage, cauliflower, Chinese cabbage, lettuce, and turnip greens from cabbage loopers and imported cabbage worms; and asparagus, beans, cucumbers, eggplants, melons, peas, rhubarb, squash, tomatoes, and other vulnerable crops from cucumber beetles, leafhoppers, and squash bugs.

Keep in mind that netting won't keep out insects already present in the soil. Leafminers and other

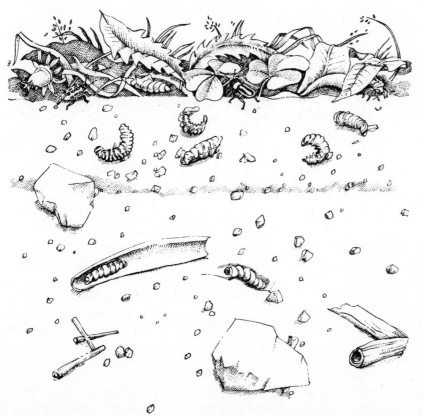

Insect pests overwinter in the garden under debris and down as far as 6 to 10 inches in the soil. During the fall cleanup process, cultivate your garden deeply to expose those pests that prefer the depths of the soil and to bury those that live on the surface.

Agricultural fleece works well as a barrier to insects. It is more effective than plastic because it does not require slits.

pests may overwinter in the garden soil and emerge in early spring. If they emerge beneath the netting, your plants will be an easy mark.

Mulch Barrier

In some cases, mulch can be an effective barrier to insect pests, especially the ones overwintering in the soil. At the very least, it controls weeds, which may harbor pests. Black plastic mulch laid on bare soil keeps some larvae that have overwintered in the soil from escaping and attacking your plants. If your plants are thoroughly surrounded by black plastic, the flies that lay eggs at the stems of the plants at soil level may have trouble getting to the stems. (See chapter 7 for information on how to use black plastic in the vegetable garden.)

Sawdust Mulch. Aged sawdust mulch also makes an effective barrier against some insect pests. Be sure that the sawdust has been aged for at least a year, and pile it about 4 inches deep around plant stems. This will discourage flies from laying eggs, and eggs already laid will be less likely to survive.

Diatomaceous Earth Barrier

Another effective barrier is diatomaceous earth (D.E.), sold as Perma-Guard and under other trade names. The kind intended for garden use is a fine powdery material, made of the 30-million-year-old shells of microscopic sea creatures called diatoms. D.E. acts like tiny razor blades on soft-bodied pests such as caterpillars. It does not kill instantly. The insect is scratched when it crawls over the material or eats some. Once injured, the insect dries out and dies. D.E. works against most pests only when they are in their larval, maggot, or grub stage, and it won't harm earthworms. It is less effective in humid weather because the pest won't dry up.

To use D.E., dust it around the base of the plant in the late evening or at night. The application works best after a light rain or after plants have been sprayed with a fine mist of water. Dusting should progress upward from the ground, covering all stems and leaves, especially the undersides. Reapply D.E. after every rain.

By dusting seeds before planting, you can also protect your crops against weevils.

Diatomaceous earth can also be applied wet. Using a 5-gallon sprayer, place 1 teaspoon of flax soap (available from paint supply stores) or insecticidal soap concentrate in a quart of warm water. Put ¼ pound of D.E. in the sprayer and add the soap mixture. Add enough water to make 5 gallons of mix. Be sure to keep the solution well mixed. Reapply after rainstorms if insects are still a problem.

To protect fruit trees, paint the trunks with this mixture. Also sprinkle a liberal amount of D.E. on the ground around the trees.

A diatomaceous earth barrier is worth trying against aphids, cabbage loopers, codling moths, Colorado potato beetles, cucumber beetles, cutworms, some fruit maggots, Mexican bean beetles, various root maggots, slugs, snails, thrips, and tomato hornworms.

Wood-Ash Barrier

Wood ashes can be effective against root maggots and other pests. You can change the pH of the pest's environment by sprinkling two handfuls of wood ashes around each vulnerable plant when it is 4 to 5 inches tall. For best results raise plants in a protected cold frame until they are this size, and then transplant them to the garden, working the ashes into the soil around the plants. Another approach is to surround each plant with a shallow, 3- to 4-inch-wide trench filled with wood ashes. Aboveground pests may avoid crawling over them, and underground pests will avoid the area because the pH has changed. Care should be taken not to get ashes on the plant or allow them to touch the stem. Vegetables that may benefit from this protection are cabbage and other brassicas susceptible to root maggots, and crops such as asparagus, beans, and cucumbers, which are bothered by cucumber beetles, cutworms, slugs, and snails.

Collars or Mats

Individual collars or mats can be placed around the base of vulnerable transplants to keep flies from laying eggs there. One type of mat barrier is a disk made from foam rubber carpet paddings. The disk should be 5 to 10 inches in diameter, with a small hole punched in the middle and a slit along the radius. A disk is fitted carefully around the stem of each vulnerable plant, on top of the soil. These disks prevent adult flies from laying eggs near the plant stems, and at the same time they harbor beneficial ground beetles that eat many pests. They also keep soil moist so plants stay healthy and able to tolerate maggot damage.

Tar paper also makes an effective cover. Cut squares 5 or 6 inches wide and slit them halfway. Place a square around the base of each transplanted seedling. Press the squares firmly against the soil.

Wax paper cups work even better than tar paper. Cut a hole in the bottom of each cup, then cut a radial slit outward from the hole, and fit the cup upside down into the soil and around the plant stem.

For cutworm control, be sure collars extend 1 or 2 inches into the soil. A bottomless, topless tin can or an aluminum foil collar will discourage these pests.

Barrier Bands for Trees

Barrier bands placed around the trunks discourage insects that must climb the tree to do their damage. Bands of cotton quilt batting are effective against caterpillars of the gypsy moth and cankerworm. A greasy or sticky substance stops some other wingless

Diatomaceous earth prevents grubs and maggots from getting to seedlings by scratching the insects as they crawl over the material. The injured pests eventually die.

A collar placed around a seedling prevents flies from laying their eggs around the base of the plant.

Learn Insect Emergence Times

Each species of insect has its own fairly predictable pattern of birth, feeding, maturity, reproduction, wintering, and death. If you can learn these patterns and how they coincide with your garden calendar, you'll be able to predict when problems might arise. It is especially important to know when overwintering pests emerge in your garden. This varies from place to place, and depends on temperature, moisture, and the availability of food. Check with your County Extension agent for a rough idea of when the problem insect typically emerges, and then keep your own records from year to year.

Insect emergence usually coincides with some stage of the flowering perennials in your yard. Lilacs are good standards against which to track insect emergence, since they blossom early in the season. Check the status of your lilac when you spot the first aphids, for example. Is it budding, or blossoming, or are the leaves just coming out? Next year, look for the pest when the lilac approaches the same stage.

Armed with this emergence information, you can juggle planting dates so that crops are too old or too young or not there at all when the pest is active. You can plant early or plant a fall crop only. You can sometimes sidestep much of a pest insect's threat simply by not sowing or transplanting the plants during the insect's egg-laying peaks. Maggot populations are usually highest in early summer and late summer. Mature plants are less susceptible to maggot damage; thus, sowing carrots in June, after the spring maggot population has peaked, will help to reduce your losses. If you must plant early, protect carrot seedlings with a fine screen to prevent the flies from laying eggs on the carrot crowns.

insects. Tack or wire a strip of paper or cloth around the trunk before smearing on Tanglefoot, Ant-Bar, or other sticky materials, to prevent injury to the bark. Apply barriers at the end of September at the very latest, because the tree-climbing pests enter trees in fall to overwinter. If bands are not placed in time, the wingless form of the codling moth and other fruit tree pests will calmly climb up the trees to lay their eggs in the treetops, where they will hatch the following spring.

A special barrier can be made to prevent ants from entering the crowns of fruit trees where they can exacerbate aphid problems. Use a 4-inch-wide strip of polyester fiber matting to snugly surround the trunk, covered by a 4-inch-wide strip of household plastic wrap. Smear this with a sticky material such as Ant-Bar. The barrier will stretch as the tree trunk grows, but when it splits, replace it.

BENEFICIAL INSECT PREDATORS AND PARASITES

You are not alone in fighting off pests in your garden. Garden residents such as songbirds and toads are constantly waging war against plant-eating insects. In addition, there are many different species of

---

Host Plants for Beneficial Insects

To attract these beneficial insects to your garden and encourage them to stay, grow the plants they seem to prefer.

Lacewings. Members of the carrot family, oleander, and wild lettuce.

Lady Bugs. Alfalfa, angelica, coffeeberry, evergreen euonymous, goldenrod, Mexican tea, morning-glory, oleander, and yarrow. Lady bugs also like ragweed, but you probably don't want to plant that in your garden!

Parasitic Wasps. Members of the carrot family, and members of the daisy family, including buckwheat, buttercup, goldenrod, oleander, strawberries, and white clover.

Syrphid Flies and Hover Flies. Members of the daisy family.

---

beneficial insects devouring thousands of insects each day. The wise gardener knows these "good" insects and also knows how to keep them in the garden. There are two groups of beneficial insects: predators, which hunt and kill other insects, and parasites, which lay their eggs on other insects so that, upon hatching, their young eat the host.

Many of these natural enemies appear later in the season than the coming of warmer temperatures. Some gardeners find they have more pest problems early in the season than they do later on when the beneficials have set up housekeeping. Don't be tempted to eradicate all your pests at this early stage, for the beneficials will only stay in your garden if there is something for them to eat. Your goal should be to maintain a balance of "bad" and "good" insects, not to have a sterile environment for your plants. Use pesticides sparingly, and preferably only early in the season, before beneficials come on the scene.

Create the Best Environment

Encourage beneficial species by creating the kind of environment they like. The more diverse the plantings in and around your garden, the more attractive the site is going to be for sheltering and holding beneficial insects. Set aside a special "nursery" patch where weeds, brambles, and wildflowers make a haven, making sure not to include those plants that are primary hosts for pests that could become problems in your garden. Plantings may be effective up to 150 feet away from the garden, but within 25 to 50 feet is best. Hedgerows, windbreaks, and wooded patches also serve as nurseries for the beneficials that keep many of your yard and garden pests under control.

Beneficial insects need food, shelter, water, and access to their particular prey. The parasites, especially, depend on nectar for fuel as they fly around seeking suitable hosts for their eggs. In the wild, parasitic wasps choose the flowers of Queen Anne's lace and other members of the carrot family. These plants, along with daisies and related flowers, and some evergreens, will be a haven for all sorts of beneficials throughout the gardening season. (See the box Host Plants for Beneficial Insects for suggestions on specific plants to host beneficials.)

Beneficial Insects Available Commercially

There are lots of beneficial insects available commercially for release into your own little ecosystem. However, they are expensive, and if you don't know what you are doing, they may fly away before doing their job.

The best time to introduce predators and parasites is before pests get out of hand, but when there are enough of them to keep the beneficials busy and well fed. This is a complicated, little-understood balancing act, and one that gardeners often can't manage. Both populations (good bugs and bad bugs) must be able to grow concurrently, so control develops as the beneficials begin to outnumber the pests.

Unless the beneficials find pests to eat and the kinds of plants they prefer, they will either starve or go elsewhere. If you plan to buy and release beneficials, be sure you have a garden they'll want to call home. Follow the guidelines already given for attracting beneficial insects to your garden.

Beneficial Fungus

Special fungi attack harmful root-knot nematodes in distinctly different ways. For example, one fungus forms rings that close around nematodes when they enter the ring openings. Another is a parasite of nematode eggs. The fungi are sold by the pound; 3 pounds cover 100 square feet of garden; 10 pounds cover 350 square feet.

Beneficial Nematode

Beneficial nematodes are tiny soil-dwelling worms that burrow inside maggots and reproduce. The pests are killed by bacteria that the nematodes release.

Nematodes will overwinter as far north as Minnesota, but their survival rate is not high enough to provide effective insect control the following season. Only the infective juvenile stage of the nematode is effective as an insect control.

The nematode *Neoaplectana carpocapsae* attacks cutworms and other insects that live in the soil, including wireworms, black vine weevils, codling moth larvae, strawberry weevils, pine weevils, gypsy moth larvae, corn earworms, cabbage root maggots, onion maggots, white grubs, Japanese beetle grubs, cutworms, wireworms, cabbage maggots, and the larvae of cucumber beetles, flea beetles, squash vine borers, and Japanese beetles. It will not harm beneficials or earthworms. You kill squash vine borers when a liquid preparation is injected into the stem.

Beneficial nematodes come in groups of 1,000,000 to 10,000,000. They can be stored in your refrigerator for up to 3 months. Apply the nematodes using an ordinary sprayer or sprinkling can. For borers or other hard-to-reach pests, you may need to use a syringe. Apply 5,000 nematodes per 1 gallon container, and apply 50,000 per row foot, or per large plant, such as a tomato. (Follow label instructions to attain the correct number of nematodes in an application.) Apply in the early spring around the base of your plants. You should see an effect within 5 days, but allow 2 months for maximum control.

Green Lacewing Larva

Of all the bugs you can buy through the mail, lacewings are probably the most effective. There are various species throughout North America, but all have a slender body and delicate long green wings. They are ½ to ¾ inch long. The adults eat pollen, nectar, and honeydew. It is the larvae that feed on the pest insects. They are yellowish gray with brown marks and tufts of long hair, and they grow to about ⅜ inch long. The most distinctive feature is a pair of long, thin jaws, which curve together like ice tongs. Three to four generations are produced per year. Lacewings pass the winter in the pupal stage in cocoons.

Lacewing larvae feed on aphids, young corn earworms, mites, scale insects, whiteflies, and the eggs of caterpillars, mites, thrips, and other small pests. They can eat up to 60 aphids an hour. By boosting your garden's natural lacewing population in the early summer, you can get a jump on these insect pests. However, lacewings can't bear cold weather, so wait until the average air temperature is at least 70°F.

Lacewings come in egg or larval form. Eggs are hard to handle and not generally recommended. Approximately 1,000 lacewing larvae cover a garden of about 1,000 square feet. The lacewing eggs may hatch in shipment, and the larvae will be hungry and ready for action in a container packed with moth eggs or rice hulls for food. The larvae like to eat each other, so release them as quickly as possible after you receive them, and spread them apart from each other.

The eggs, as said, may be difficult to handle. If possible, lodge them gently in crevices, in spaces between petals, or in flowers. Otherwise, try folding corners of a 1-by-1½-inch square of facial tissue to create a small sling for holding an egg. Tape, pin, or tie the sling near the aphids. Sprinkle the larvae around the garden, and they will stay put.

You will probably not see evidence of the lacewing larvae's work immediately, as you would with a chemical insecticide. The insects do most of their hunting in their last larval phase, just before adulthood. Expect the younger, smaller larvae to attack the younger, smaller pests, and the larger, older larvae to attack the larger, older pests.

To maintain a large lacewing population, place "Wheast" in the garden or orchard. This is a sweetened dairy product sold as food for beneficial insects. Lacewing adults will also eat an artificial diet made of one part sugar and one part brewer's yeast in water. Try setting this mixture near vulnerable plants to encourage adult lacewings to remain in your garden and reproduce. Also be sure to grow plenty of wild carrot, oleander, and other plants these insects prefer.

Lady Bug

Found throughout North America, lady bugs are the most widely recognized beneficial insects, yet the larval stage is not well understood. Larvae are black grubs with orange spots. They are about ½ inch long and are usually covered with spines. Eggs are yellow. Lady bugs will migrate if the food supply is low. One generation occurs per year. In the East and Midwest, lady bugs overwinter in weedy areas or garden trash.

Both larvae and adults eat small insects. They consume up to 40 aphids an hour and also eat bean thrips, small larvae, beetle grubs, scales, spider mites, whiteflies, and other soft-bodied pests, as well as insect eggs. You'll need 3,000 individuals, or about 2 ounces, to control aphids in 1 acre of crops. For 5,000 to 7,000 square feet, 500 lady bugs are enough.

Don't release lady bugs too early in the season: They will either fly away or starve because of lack of food. Instead, release a few (if the pest population is not large), and store the rest in the refrigerator for up to 3 weeks. Release in late evening during the dew period. If there is no dew, then spray the garden before you release the beetles. Don't toss them into the air. Gently place them on the ground and immediately cover them with straw or hay. Beetles tend to climb the nearest plants and begin hunting. Gently

place handfuls at the base of pest-ridden plants. Leave about 20 to 30 paces between each release. Handle them as calmly as possible since rough handling, especially in the warmer months, may excite the beetles to flight. Under normal conditions, they will mate within 48 hours and produce offspring in 2 weeks.

To encourage lady bugs to stay in your garden, grow pollen and nectar plants such as yarrow, evergreen euonymus, coffeeberry, angelica, alfalfa, goldenrod, Mexican tea, morning-glory, and oleander.

Parasitic (Non-stinging) Wasp

Braconid Wasp. The adult braconid wasp is just ¹⁄₁₆ to ⅝ inch long. It lays its eggs in the body of grubs and caterpillars. Larvae hatch and grow inside the host, weakening and often killing it. The larvae pupate on the back of the host.

The wasps attack aphids, codling moths, cucumber beetles, cutworms, gypsy moths, imported cabbage worms, tent caterpillars, tomato hornworms, and various other larvae.

Braconids prefer humid, warm conditions, above 59°F. They come commercially as eggs.

Chalcid Wasp. The adult chalcid is just ¹⁄₁₆ to ⅜ inch long, so you'll probably not see them unless you are determined to do so. Eggs are laid in or on the pest. Larvae weaken and eventually kill the host. Some adults also feed directly on the host. Chalcid wasps are found throughout North America. They attack aphids, asparagus beetles, leafhoppers, scale, whiteflies, various caterpillars, and beetles.

Ichneumonid Wasp. The ichneumonid ranges in size from ⅛ inch to 3 inches long. Adults lay eggs in the hosts, which include eastern tent caterpillar, cutworms, European corn borers, and other larvae.

Release parasitic wasps when there are plenty of pest eggs around, but before any of them have hatched. Some eggs will survive; after they hatch, the larvae will chew a bit on the plant leaves for a couple of days. The release of ichneumonid wasps is more effective when coupled with a spray of *Bacillus thuringiensis* (BT) on infested plant leaves. A sequence of three smaller releases is preferable to just one large release. It is important to make the three releases at 2-week intervals in order to catch the pests in the most vulnerable stages of their life cycle.

Trichogramma Wasp. The tiny trichogramma wasp kills pests in their egg stage, long before they can damage plants. The female wasp lays her eggs in the pest egg, and when the trichogramma egg hatches into a larva, it consumes its host. Adult trichogramma parasites feed on nectar, which they obtain from weeds and wildflowers, mostly in the daisy and carrot families.

Among the pests which trichogramma wasps parasitize are aphids, cabbage loopers, corn earworms, gypsy moths, imported cabbage worms, whiteflies, spring cankerworms, and various beetle larvae.

Praying Mantid

Various species of these large insects are found throughout North America. They are green or brownish, and about 2 inches long. They have long bodies with papery wings and enlarged front legs adapted for grasping. Mantids overwinter in the egg stage. Eggs are deposited on twigs and grass stems in a papier-mâchélike egg case, with each case containing 200 or more eggs. One generation of mantids is produced per year.

Buying praying mantid egg cases is less of a bargain than with some of the other good guys. For one thing, the mantids prey on all insects, including their brothers and sisters. They will eat lady bugs as well as cabbage loopers. Each egg case may produce a couple hundred hungry little mantids, but they'll eat each other before they start working on your pest problem. The few that survive will establish territories and drive off others of their kind. No matter how many egg cases you set out, you'll probably find only two or three mantids in a 20-by-40-foot garden by midsummer. You'll wind up paying a couple of dollars each for those few insects, when you probably had some occurring naturally in your own backyard.

If you must purchase mantid eggs, try about three egg cases for 2,000 to 3,000 square feet of garden. To increase the young mantids' survival rate, put the egg cases in a screen-covered box. Check them every day after the trees begin to leaf out. Provide water and, 2 days after they hatch, separate them before they start eyeing one another. Scatter them around the garden, orchard, and flower beds. They will still drive their brothers and sisters off, but you will be sure of having good coverage and may even have a generation reproducing for next year.

Predatory Mite

Predatory mites are used to control Mexican bean beetles, spider mites, and greenhouse mites. One release per season should be adequate. (Follow label instructions for number of mites to apply.) After control is gained, the predatory mites remain in low numbers, providing effective control through the growing season. Mites like warm weather with temperatures averaging between 68°F and 86°F. If daytime temperatures are too low, their reproductive rate slows.

Beneficial Insects in Nature

Here are some beneficial insects to look for in your garden. Get to know them so you won't mistakenly kill these natural friends.

Assassin Bug

Generally brown or black, the assassin or "kissing" bug has a slender head with protruding eyes, and legs armed with sharp spines. Various species range from ⅜ inch to 2 inches long. The bug moves rather clumsily and flies slowly, relying on its lightning fast front legs to snatch prey. Piercing its catch with a powerful beak, it injects a paralyzing venom. It feeds mostly on larvae. Eggs are laid in the soil. Assassin bugs overwinter as adults, nymphs, or eggs. Do not pick them up, as their bite is a bit painful. Assassin bugs prey on aphids, various caterpillars, Colorado potato beetles, Japanese beetles, leafhoppers, and Mexican bean beetles. They'll also catch bees and butterflies. Look for assassin bugs on alfalfa, camphorweed, plants in the carrot family, goldenrod, Mexican tea, and oleander.

Bigeyed Bug

Found in western North America, this bug is grayish, with tiny black spots on the head and thorax, and huge eyes. Several generations are produced each year. In winter, adults hibernate in garden trash. Bigeyed bugs prey on aphids, leafhoppers, spider mites, and most immature bugs. Attract the bugs with alfalfa, plants in the carrot family, goldenrod, Mexican tea, and oleander.

Damselfly

The damselfly has a small, slender body about ⅜ inch long. It likes to hide in flowers, but prowls on other plant parts as well. The damselfly attacks a large variety of pests, including aphids, leafhoppers, treehoppers, and many caterpillars and other immature insects. Attract damselflies with alfalfa and many wildflowers. This insect is common throughout North America.

European Earwig

Although it can be a pest in its own right, some species of earwig are beneficial predators. Earwigs are reddish brown with short, leathery forewings and pincers on the tip of the abdomen. They are about ¾ inch long. One to two generations are produced per year. Earwigs help control the common aphid as well as *Aphis pomi,* the aphid that attacks apple, plum, pear, spirea, dogwood, flowering crabapple, and flowering quince, among others. Earwigs are attracted to wild lettuce, among other wild plants. They are widespread throughout North America.

Firefly

The firefly is well known for its light show. The adults eat insects, but the larvae are more important predators. Larvae look like flat beetles with jaws. They emerge from eggs laid in the soil. Firefly larvae feed on slugs, mites, and small crawling insects.

Ground Beetle

Ground beetles are typically black to purplish, although there are many different species. They produce just one generation per year, and adults hibernate in the soil. Ground beetles like the shade of low vegetation such as clovers and low growing weeds. They feed at night on caterpillars, grubs, and slugs. Ground beetles also eat eggs or larvae of ants, aphids, Colorado potato beetles, flea beetles, nematodes, spider mites, and thrips. They only occasionally dine on some beneficial. Attract and hold the beetles with camphorweed, evening primrose, pigweed, and any long-growing weeds and grasses.

Praying Mantid

Mantids are discussed in the preceding section on beneficial insects available commercially. They are not uncommon in and around the garden.

Robber Fly

Found throughout North America, the adult fly is gray and ¼ to 1⅛ inch long, with long legs and a hairy mouth. Some species have slender, tapering abdomens; others are so stocky they look like bumblebees. The robber flies overwinter in the soil as larvae. Larvae and adult flies are useful predators. They attack bees, beetles, flies, grasshoppers, grubs, leafhoppers, and wasps.

Rove Beetle

Rove beetles are small (⅛ to ½ inch long) and very active. They have unusually slender bodies and extremely short wing covers. Various species are found throughout North America. Rove beetles are common scavengers in decaying plant and animal material, including piles of manure and compost. They overwinter as larvae, pupae, or adults. Several generations are produced each year. Rove beetles are one of the most important natural enemies of the cabbage maggot. As many as 80 percent of cabbage maggots in the field may be destroyed by rove beetles. Adult beetles feast on eggs, and larvae attack the pupae in the soil. The rove beetle also goes after mites, beetle larvae, aphids, and small worms.

Soldier Beetle

This beetle is black with a white thorax and head. It resembles a firefly that doesn't glow. It is ½ inch long. Soldier beetles are found in most of the United States, and produce one or two generations per year. Mature larvae overwinter in the soil. Soldier beetles feed on aphids, various small beetles and caterpillars, slugs, and spider mites. Attract soldier beetles with wild lettuce, milkweed, hydrangea, and goldenrod.

Spider

Spiders aren't insects, but they are "beneficial" since they eat all sorts of pest insects. Most spiders overwinter as eggs, although some hibernate as adults.

They are one of the first predators to emerge in the spring. Any insect can be a target for spiders. Plant camphorweed, goldenrod, or asters to bring in spiders to catch pest flies and many other pests that get stuck in their webs.

Syrphid Fly

Syrphid or hover flies resemble small wasps. Like hummingbirds, they can remain motionless in flight.

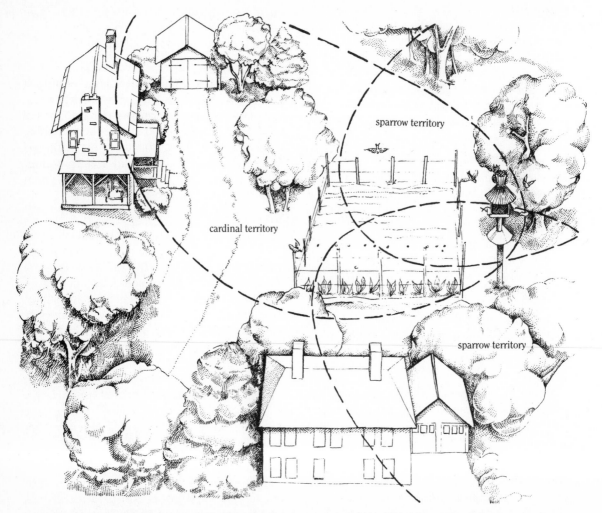

By filling your bird feeder in the summer, you can increase the population of birds in your yard. Although territories will overlap, the availability of food will allow more birds to coexist. This means increased control of insect pests in your garden.

The adult is ½ inch long with short antennae and one pair of wings. The larva is a sightless green or brown maggot. Syrphids spend the winter as larvae. Adults feed on nectar and other sweet fluids and are important pollinators. Larvae are the predators, eating aphids, leafhoppers, thrips, and a number of other soft-bodied pests. Plant buckwheat to attract and to serve as a host for the syrphid fly. Also plant coreopsis, baby blue eyes, candytuft, morning-glory, and oleander in your flower garden to attract syrphid flies.

Tachinid Fly

The tachinid is the most beneficial of all flies. The adult is often mistaken for a housefly, but it is larger, nearly ½ inch long. Tachinids overwinter as yellow larvae. These parasitize adult beetles, grasshoppers, caterpillars, sawflies, and various other bugs.

Tiger Beetle

The adult tiger beetle is ⅜ inch to ⅝ inch long, with big eyes, long antennae, and long, thin legs for running swiftly. Its metallic colors range from green, blue, and purple to black and bronze and are sometimes iridescent. The tiger beetle overwinters as an adult or larva. Tiger beetle larvae trap and eat ants, aphids, caterpillars, and other crawling insects.

ANIMAL PREDATORS

There are a number of animals, including bats, birds, frogs, lizards, skunks, snakes, and toads, that sometimes can be pests in your garden, but which, if kept under control, can actually serve as allies in your fight against pest insects. The odoriferous skunk, for example, is a voracious eater of grubs and larvae. The only problem is that he can tear up your seedlings in the process of getting to the grubs. This is one good reason for cultivating your garden and leaving it fallow for a few weeks to let birds, skunks, and even moles clean out the grub and larva population without harming plants.

Guide to Insect Pests

In spite of how tiny some insects are, they can ravage the garden, some severing plants right at ground level. However, you have many options available for controlling and preventing insect pests. One of the keys to effective control is preparation. Study the life cycles of the insects that frequent your garden—the beneficials as well as the pests. Learn the emergence times; then you will be prepared to use the right tools at the right time for the most effective control of insect pests in your garden.

Following are some of the most common insect pests that attack vegetables, fruits, and herbs. Several options for control and prevention are given. Some are recommendations from gardeners that have not undergone extensive research and testing but might be effective in your garden. Insect control is both an art and a science.

INSECT *Aphid*

DESCRIPTION

Aphids are less than 1/10 inch long. They are soft-bodied, pear-shaped, green, brown, black, or pinkish insects with long antennae and two tubelike projections from the rear of the abdomen. They may have wings. Aphids suck leaves, fruit, and stems, causing foliage to curl, pucker, and yellow, and reducing the plant's vigor. Aphids also transmit many viral diseases, such as mosaic. They excrete excess sugars and sap known as honeydew, which will support growth of black, sooty mold. Aphids are very injurious to seedlings and young trees. They overwinter in the egg stage. They are found throughout the United States.

Aphid problems may be a symptom of too much nitrogen fertilizer, excessive pruning of fruit trees (which causes succulent sucker growth), or extravagant use of pesticides that kill off aphid predators and parasitoids.

MOST OBVIOUS SYMPTOMS

Foliage curls, puckers, and turns yellow. The foliage and blooms may be stunted or misshapen. Ants,

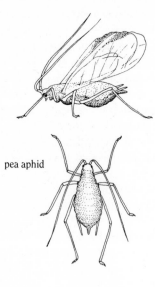

pea aphid

bean aphid

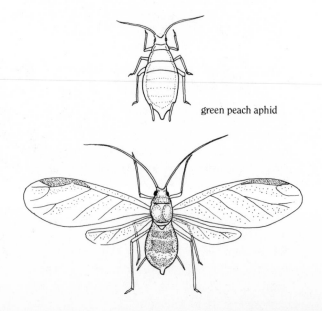

green peach aphid

attracted to the honeydew, are probably present. Check the undersides of new leaves, and around buds and tender stems. Cottony masses may appear on twigs of infested trees and shrubs.

VULNERABLE PLANTS

All garden fruits and vegetables may be bothered by one or more kinds of aphid.

Emergence Time

Aphids overwinter in the northern states as eggs on bark or on ground litter, emerging at the end of May or June. In warmer climates, they reproduce continually. They are a serious threat mostly to young plants, although they can be a problem throughout the growing season. They can be particularly bad during a cold spring, when they multiply faster than their predators.

BEST CONTROL STRATEGY

For light infestations, spray vigorously with water three times, once every other day, in the early morning. Use insecticidal soap every 2 to 3 days for heavier infestations. As a last resort, use pyrethrum spray.

OPTIONS FOR CONTROLLING APHID

Early Warning Devices

Sticky Trap
Early warning traps may be made from boards painted yellow and covered with a sticky material, such as Tanglefoot. Rig one or two traps in or about your target crop a week or two before you expect aphids to appear.

Trap Crop
Nasturtiums can be used as a trap crop to spot early infestations of aphid. Grow them in the garden, or within 10 to 15 feet of it.

Natural Sprays

See the beginning of this chapter for more information on making natural sprays.

Bug Juice
Crush some aphids and blend with water to make a liquid repellent spray. Gardeners report that the bug juice kills the aphids, or at least repels them.

Garlic Spray
Chop or grind garlic, onions, or chives into fine particles. Mix the ground-up material with water, then strain to form a clear solution. Spray in two applications, 2 or 3 days apart. Make sure the spray makes contact with the aphids.

Horticultural Oil Spray
Where aphids are a persistent problem in orchards, use a heavy horticultural spray oil (viscosity 100 to 200) during the dormant season. Coat the entire tree evenly.

A lighter, less viscous (viscosity 60 to 70) oil, called superior horticultural spray oil, can be used during the growing season to control aphids. Spray a 2 to 3 percent solution and make sure the spray contacts the aphids, because oil works by suffocation.

Hot Pepper Spray
Chop or grind hot peppers into fine particles. Mix the ground-up peppers with water, then strain out the particles to form a clear solution. Spray twice, 2 or 3 days apart. Make sure contact is made with the aphids.

Insecticidal Soap
Commercial insecticidal soap is effective in controlling aphids. Spray every 2 to 3 days for 2 weeks for bad infestations. Cover the plant thoroughly. Soap sprays are contact insecticides, so spray the plant top to bottom, especially under the leaves, where you'll find most aphids.

Other Sprays
Coriander and Anise Oil. Coriander and anise oil, mixed to form an emulsion, will kill aphids.

Lime and Water. Spray with a strong lime and water mixture.

Oxalic Acid. Found in spinach and rhubarb leaves, oxalic acid is poisonous in high concentrations. Mix a simple rhubarb spray by first cutting up 1 pound of leaves and boiling them in 1 quart of water for 30 minutes. Strain and bottle the liquid. To help it stick to leaves, add a touch of soap, not detergent.

Tomato-Leaf Spray. Tomato-leaf spray may also kill aphids. Pack 1 quart of leaves into a crock or bucket; pour 1 quart of boiling water over them. Let steep 1 hour, then strain through a cloth, squeezing leaves to extract as much liquid as possible. Refrigerate in a capped jar until needed. Before using, dilute with a gallon of water.

Traps and Mechanical Controls

Sticky Trap

If these cover a large enough area, sticky traps can be used as control devices for aphids. Bright yellow panels about 10 by 10 inches in size should be coated with sticky material such as Tack Trap, motor oil, or petroleum jelly. Place traps adjacent to, not above, susceptible plants. Do not leave these traps out for more than 3 or 4 weeks, or beneficial insects, as well as pests, may be trapped.

Water Spray

A forceful spray of water can knock many aphids from plants. This is best done in the early morning. Use a nozzle that will give a fine spray of water, and thoroughly wash off the undersides of affected leaves. Repeat three times, once every other day.

Handpicking

Actually, you don't pick as much as squeeze them between thumb and finger. Try to get the first generation, before eggs are laid.

Botanical Poisons

Neem

Purchase a commercial neem product and mix it according to label instructions. Apply the spray to aphid-infested plants twice, at weekly or longer intervals, until pests are under control. Spray carefully to thoroughly cover all plant parts. The spray will be most effective if you apply it in early morning or late afternoon. Neem is generally fairly harmless to beneficials, but it may have an effect with repeated use. Save it for use against serious infestations, when milder measures such as handpicking or water sprays don't work.

Pyrethrum

Apply pyrethrum directly to aphids in a spray form. Coat the undersides of the leaves as well as the tops. Two applications are recommended, 3 to 4 days apart. Remember, pyrethrum also harms beneficial insects, so use it only as a last resort.

STEPS TO PREVENT APHID

Fall Cleanup

The fall garden cleanup is the best way to prevent aphid problems. Get rid of aphids overwintering as eggs on bark or garden litter. As soon as you harvest each crop, remove all old plants and overgrown weeds, leaving soil completely bare. Cultivate soil 6 to 8 inches deep, using a hand tool or a rotary tiller. About 2 to 3 weeks later, cultivate just 2 inches deep. In early spring, about 2 weeks before planting, give the garden another 2-inch cultivation, and cultivate again at planting time.

Preventive Spray Programs

There are a number of preventive sprays you can use to reduce aphid numbers early in the season. Don't spray much past a month after last frost, or you will be killing a lot of beneficial insects.

Combination Preventive Spray Program

Make a spray with *Bacillus thuringiensis* (BT), insecticidal soap, and seaweed spray. Apply to the whole garden a week after your first transplants are set out, again 2 weeks later, and then again 2 weeks after that. That routine puts you about a month into the normal growing season, when beneficials are starting to emerge, and you will want to avoid hurting them with any unnecessary generalized spraying.

Horticultural Oil Spray

In late winter, before any leaf buds open, spray heavy horticultural oil (viscosity 100 to 200) on fruit trees to control aphids. Make sure the entire surface of the tree is covered.

Insecticidal Soap

Spray commercial insecticidal soap on the undersides of all new growth. Make 2 or 3 applications every 2 weeks in the beginning of the growing season, followed by a monthly application just on plants most vulnerable to aphids.

Seaweed Spray

Treat crops with liquid seaweed extract to minimize aphid damage. Spray plants at transplant time and every 2 weeks.

Barriers

Aluminum Foil Mulch

Aluminum foil used as a mulch repels aphids very effectively, but light-colored mulch materials such as straw are also useful for this purpose. A mulch of aluminum foil or white plastic may confuse the aphids flying overhead so they can't tell where to land. The mulch must extend at least 6 inches beyond the diameter of the plant.

Diatomaceous Earth (D.E.)

Dust the whole plant with D.E. to destroy aphids. Dusting should progress upward from the ground, covering all stems and leaves, especially the undersides. (For details on how to apply diatomaceous earth, see the beginning of this chapter.) Dust in late evening or at night, and predator insect destruction will be low.

Dusting

Aphids may be slowed down if the undersides of leaves are dusted with flour or baking powder. Dust leaves frequently and repeat after rain.

Netting or Fleece Cover

Tunnels or floating covers are very effective for keeping aphids away from vulnerable plants. Be sure edges are firmly anchored. Very fine screening and agricultural fleece are also effective barriers. Immediately after transplanting or seeding, cover the area with the preferred material. (See the beginning of this chapter for more information on these covers.)

Sticky Band

On apple trees, control ants (which protect aphids) by ringing the tree trunk with a nontoxic sticky band. Apply the band early in spring before the rise in ant activity.

Resistant Varieties

Check the seed catalogs to locate possible varieties resistant to the diseases aphids carry, and where possible, to aphids themselves. In addition to those listed below, there are varieties of tomatoes and cabbages resistant to aphids.

Lettuce

Avoncrisp and Avondefiance.

Pea

Champion of England, Laurier, Melting Sugar, and Prince of Wales.

Potato

British Queen, De Soto, Early Pinkeye, Houma, Irish Daisy, and LaSalle.

Intercropping or Companions

Some gardeners recommend interplanting vegetables with chives, garlic, mints, onions, and petunias to repel aphids. Anise, coriander, nasturtiums, pennyroyal, petunias, and southernwood are mentioned for controlling aphids in the orchard. Some clover species support parasites of woolly apple aphid. Studies have shown that collards intercropped with beans had more wasp parasites, four times fewer aphids, and less aphid damage than when planted alone.

Cover Crops

Cover cropping apple orchards with rye, vetch, and clover creates a haven for aphid predators.

Crop Rotation

Make sure that you never plant the same kind of vegetable in the same place 2 years in a row. By rotating or shifting the location of your crops each year, you prevent the aphid larvae from finding the host plant next year. Rotating a distance of over 10 feet each year is desirable, but simply moving a plant 4 or 5 feet from last year's location is better than planting it in exactly the same place. Ideally, a plant should not be set in the same place more frequently than every 3 to 5 years.

Animal Predators

Chickadees, nuthatches, purple finches, warblers, chipping sparrows, and toads are some of the common aphid eaters.

Insect Predators and Parasites Available Commercially

See the beginning of this chapter for more information on each of these beneficial insects.

Lacewing
Of all the bugs you can buy through the mail to control aphids, lacewings are probably the best.

Lady Bug
Lady bugs are voracious eaters of aphids, but they are only worth importing if you have a tremendous aphid population and can provide the plants and alternate hosts they need.

Parasitic (Non-stinging) Wasp
Braconid and chalcid wasps can be used to control aphids.

Insect Predators Found in the Garden

The following beneficial insects are commonly found in and around healthy, well-balanced gardens in many parts of the country. They all prey on aphids: Assassin bugs, bigeyed bugs, chalcid wasps, damselflies, ground beetles, hoverflies, minute pirate bugs, predatory thrips, soldier beetles, and spiders.

Other Preventive Steps

Make sure there is good air circulation around vulnerable crops. Stagnant air around plants creates a more attractive environment for aphids.

NOTES AND RESEARCH

Recent research indicates that aphids, among other insects, are attracted by electrical fields, such as the one surrounding an electric fence. If the voltage is high enough, it can paralyze and even kill insects, while still being harmless to everything else. In the future, we may see an electric fence that can be adjusted to be made selective enough so that, although aphids would be killed by it, bees and other beneficials would coast through safely.

INSECT **Apple Maggot**

DESCRIPTION

Apple maggots hatch from the eggs of a fly slightly smaller than the common housefly. These flies are black with yellow legs, yellow-striped abdomen, and zigzag bands across the wings. The eggs are laid singly in the apple skin. The maggot itself is white or yellowish and measures ¼ inch long. This is a major pest in the northeastern United States and Canada. One to two generations occur a year. It is also known as the apple fruit fly or the railroad worm.

MOST OBVIOUS SYMPTOMS

Female flies wander over the fruit inserting eggs into it. The maggots are hard to detect until the fruit is opened or bitten into. They cause slight depressions and tiny holes where they emerge. The greatest damage occurs after a cold spring.

VULNERABLE PLANTS

Apples, blueberries, cherries, pears, and plums.

BEST CONTROL STRATEGY

Trap the adult flies with a commercial trap made from a red ball and yellow rectangle. Clean up all fallen fruit immediately.

OPTIONS FOR CONTROLLING APPLE MAGGOT

Emergence Time

Apple maggots overwinter as pupae in the top 2 or 3 inches of the soil. The adult flies emerge anytime between May and mid-August, depending on your location.

Early Warning Devices

Red, 3½-inch wooden balls coated with Tack Trap and hung in open areas of apple trees capture adult females as they search for egg-laying sites. For trees less than 9 feet, use two traps per tree; six to eight traps may be needed for full-sized trees. Once hung in the trees, the traps should be recoated every 2 weeks. These traps can be used for actual control as well as early warning.

Traps and Mechanical Controls

Sticky Trap

A sticky trap combining a red ball and yellow rectangle is available to control apple maggot flies. The trap has an apple-sized red hemisphere in the middle of an 8-by-10-inch yellow rectangle, all smeared with Tangle Trap adhesive, and baited with a volatile lure. Use one trap for each dwarf tree or three to four for each standard tree to reduce maggot populations by up to 98 percent. Do not leave these traps out for more than 3 or 4 weeks, or beneficial insects, as well as pests, may be trapped.

A trap bait called Nu-lure is designed to attract clear-winged flies such as apple maggots. When mixed with a suitable insecticide, Nu-lure leads such flies to their deaths.

Botanical Poisons

Sprays are generally not effective against apple maggots. The adult flies are not out very long, so sprays are more likely to affect lingering beneficial insects than the pests. And after the flies lay their eggs, the larvae develop within the fruit, so they're out of reach of sprays. You'll get better results from cleaning up and destroying dropped fruit.

STEPS TO PREVENT APPLE MAGGOT

Fall Cleanup

Remove and destroy all fallen fruit every week or two. Clean up weeds, leaving a lightly cultivated bare soil for at least 2 weeks. Plant a cover crop, or cultivate again and lay a thick winter mulch.

INSECT # *Asparagus Beetle*

DESCRIPTION

The asparagus beetle is blue-black with four white spots and reddish margins. It has an oblong shape and is ¼ inch long. It chews on leaves, fruit, and spears. The larvae are greenish gray, hump-backed grubs with dark heads. This insect is found throughout the United States.

The spotted asparagus beetle is red or brownish with 12 black spots on the back. Its eggs are dark brown and are laid on leaves. The larvae are orange with a black head and legs.

MOST OBVIOUS SYMPTOMS

Plants are defoliated, and young spears are misshapen.

VULNERABLE PLANTS

Asparagus.

BEST CONTROL STRATEGY

Handpicking may be adequate for the home asparagus patch. Clean up garden debris. For serious infestations, apply pyrethrum.

OPTIONS FOR CONTROLLING ASPARAGUS BEETLE

Emergence Time

Adult beetles overwinter in garden trash and emerge in spring to lay eggs on spears. The eggs hatch in about a week. The larvae feed for 2 weeks, then burrow into the soil to pupate. Adults emerge in 10 days. There are usually 2 or 3 generations per year.

Traps and Mechanical Controls

Handpicking

Handpick asparagus beetle adults and nymphs as they appear, to set back their egg-laying activities. Careful, regular handpicking, especially in early spring, can go a long way to reducing spear and frond damage from the second generation of pests.

Botanical Poisons

Pyrethrum

Spray the entire plant with pyrethrum when asparagus beetles get out of hand. Usually two applications 3 or 4 days apart will control the problem. Remember that pyrethrum sprays also harm beneficial insects, so save them for use as a last resort when milder measures aren't effective.

STEPS TO PREVENT ASPARAGUS BEETLE

Fall Cleanup

In the fall, cut off the drying plants an inch above the soil and remove any overgrown weeds. Cultivate the soil 2 inches deep around plants. After a week or two, lay a 4- to 6-inch layer of straw, leaves, or other clean organic mulch over the garden.

In early spring, about 2 weeks before spears are expected, remove the mulch and cultivate the first 1 or 2 inches of soil again. Leave the soil bare during harvest and then mulch for the summer.

Preventive Spray Programs

Seaweed Extract Spray

Asparagus beetles are less likely to cause unacceptable damage to crops treated with seaweed extract.

Barriers

Netting or Fleece Cover

Protect emerging spears with a row cover that allows sun, air, and rain to get through. Cheesecloth or netting are fine, as long as they completely cover the plants. If you choose agricultural fleece, be sure to remove it before temperatures around the spears get above 65°F.

Intercropping or Companions

The beetle supposedly dislikes tomatoes, nasturtiums, and calendula, so you might try growing these near the asparagus bed.

Animal Predators

Chickens, ducks, and other fowl will do a good job of controlling asparagus beetles if allowed in the asparagus bed before the spears surface. Songbirds, including Baltimore orioles, bluebirds, cardinals, and chickadees, all feed on asparagus beetles.

Insect Predators and Parasites Found in the Garden

Lady bugs and the parasitic and predatory flies help control beetles.

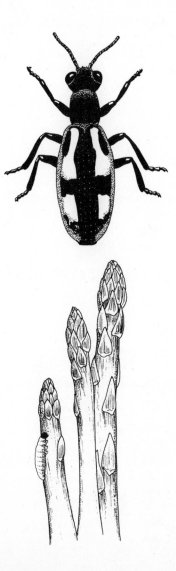

Cabbage Looper

DESCRIPTION

The cabbage looper is a light green caterpillar with yellowish stripes running down its back. It loops as it walks. The adult is a brownish night-flying moth with a silver spot in the middle of each forewing, and a 1½-inch wingspan. Eggs are greenish white, round, and laid singly on leaves. This pest is widespread throughout North America.

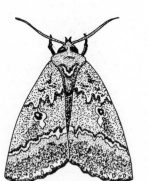

MOST OBVIOUS SYMPTOMS

Small to large ragged holes are eaten in leaves. Later in the season, the worms bore into developing heads of cabbage family crops. Seedlings can be wiped out.

VULNERABLE PLANTS

Beans (lima and snap), broccoli, brussels sprouts, cabbage, cauliflower, Chinese cabbage, collards, kale, kohlrabi, lettuce, parsley, radishes, rutabagas, and turnips.

BEST CONTROL STRATEGY

Spray plants with *Bacillus thuringiensis* (BT) every 2 weeks until loopers are under control. In the case of cabbage family members, stop spraying when heads form.

OPTIONS FOR CONTROLLING CABBAGE LOOPER

Emergence Time

Several broods occur each year. Pupae overwinter on garden litter except in the extreme north, where the moths migrate south during the cold months.

Early Warning Devices

Trap Crop

Celery can be used as a trap crop to spot early infestations of cabbage loopers. Locate it within 10 to 15 feet of the crop threatened by the cabbage looper. Amaranth is also attacked by this pest and is another option for a trap crop.

Natural Sprays

See the beginning of this chapter for more information on making natural sprays.

Bug Juice

Try crushing some cabbage loopers and liquefying them with some water. Strain and spray on infested plants.

Hot Pepper Spray

Chop or grind hot peppers into fine particles. Mix ½ cup of the ground-up peppers with 1 pint of water, then strain out the particles to form a clear solution. Spray twice, 2 or 3 days apart. Make sure contact is made with the cabbage loopers.

Biological Controls

Bacillus Thuringiensis (BT)

BT, especially the strain kurstaki (B.t.k.) kills cabbage loopers. Thoroughly dust all parts of the leaves, especially the undersides. Repeat after a rain. To use as a foliar spray, apply BT in liquid form to the affected plants at 10- to 14-day intervals until the pest is removed.

Traps and Mechanical Controls

Handpicking

Handpicking makes a sizable dent in the cabbage looper infestation right away. It is best to attend to the very first worms and eggs that appear.

Botanical Poisons

Neem

Purchase a commercial neem product and mix according to label instructions. Apply twice at weekly or longer intervals until pests are under control.

Pyrethrum

If pests get out of control, spray all sides of the leaves with pyrethrum. Usually two applications, 3 to 4 days apart, are sufficient.

STEPS TO PREVENT CABBAGE LOOPER

Fall Cleanup

Clean up debris after harvest to eliminate overwintering sites for larvae and pupae. Compost debris only if the pile is very hot.

Preventive Spray Programs

Bacillus Thuringiensis (BT)

If loopers have been a chronic problem in previous years, try making a spray with BT, insecticidal soap, and seaweed extract. Apply this spray on the whole garden a week after first transplants are set out, again 2 weeks later, and then again 2 weeks after that. You can also try a BT spray, applied every 2 weeks from transplanting until heads form.

Barriers

Diatomaceous Earth (D.E.)

Dust plants with D.E., covering all stems and leaves, especially the undersides. Apply in the late evening or at night, and predator insect destruction will be minimized.

Netting or Fleece Cover

Covers or tunnels of nylon netting, fine screening, or agricultural fleece prevent cabbage looper moths from flying in to lay eggs. Cover transplants immediately. Seal all the edges to the ground. Leave it on all season, or until the summer heat becomes a problem. Provide lots of extra material so when the plants grow larger they don't strain against the covering.

Resistant Varieties

Cabbage

Market Prize cabbage may have some resistance to the imported cabbage worm but not to the cabbage looper, at least not in comparison to Abbott and Cobb No. 5, Green Winter, Rioverdi, Savoy, and Savoy Chieftain, which do exhibit some resistance. Red cabbages, like Red Danish, Mammoth Red Rock, and Red Acre, are less attractive to the cabbage looper moth than green cultivars, so fewer eggs are laid on them, resulting in fewer hungry loopers.

Intercropping or Companions

Marigolds seem to reduce cabbage pests, but harvested heads may be smaller than usual. The cabbage looper is reportedly repelled by garlic, hot peppers, hyssop, onions, rosemary, sage, tansy, and thyme. Research has not confirmed the value of these interplantings. Weeds host various predators and parasites of cabbage loopers, so a naturalized area near the garden would seem a good idea.

Crop Rotation

A 3- to 5-year rotation is best. Rotating a distance of over 10 feet each year is desirable, but simply moving a plant 4 or 5 feet from last year's location is better than planting it in exactly the same place.

Planting Date

You can avoid a looper infestation simply by not sowing or transplanting susceptible plants during the pest's peaks. Stagger your planting dates. Start some seedlings indoors very early so plants are big enough to withstand some looper feeding. Sow small groups of plants every 10 days so they won't all be at their most vulnerable stage at the same time.

Animal Predators

Baltimore orioles, bluebirds, chickadees, cowbirds, flickers, redwing blackbirds, robins, sparrows, and starlings, as well as skunks and toads, all like to eat cabbage loopers.

Insect Predators and Parasites Available Commercially

See the beginning of this chapter for more information on each of these beneficial insects.

Lacewing

Of all the bugs you can buy through the mail to control cabbage loopers, lacewings are probably the best.

Lady Bug

Lady bugs are voracious eaters of cabbage loopers, but they are only worth importing if you have a tremendous looper population and can provide the plants and alternate hosts the lady bugs need.

Trichogramma Wasp

Trichogramma wasps are also effective controls for cabbage loopers.

Insect Predators and Parasites Found in the Garden

Any of the beneficials that attack soft-bodied insects destroy cabbage loopers. Among these are the parasitic wasps, lady bugs, yellow jackets, and lacewings.

NOTES AND RESEARCH

If you find cabbage loopers that have turned chalky white and appear nearly dead, they may have been infected with nuclear polyhedrosis virus (NPV). They might be lying motionless on top of leaves or even hanging from the underside of a leaf. You can make your own form of viral insecticide if you can find a dozen or so loopers infected with NPV. NPV is slower acting but longer lasting than *Bacillus thuringiensis* (BT). It takes 5 to 6 days to kill the loopers, but a single application of bug juice made from the infected insects may last the whole season. (See the beginning of this chapter for more information on homemade bug juice.) A commercial version of NPV is being researched and is expected on the market in the next year or two.

INSET # Cabbage Maggot

DESCRIPTION

The cabbage maggot is a small, white, legless worm with a blunt end. It is about ¼ to ⅓ inch long. The adult resembles a housefly. Flies lay eggs in the soil at the base of the stem of plants. The maggots tunnel into plant roots and stems and cause wilting. Bacterial diseases, such as black leg or soft rot, may result. The cabbage maggot overwinters as a pupa in garden soil. It is widespread throughout the western United States.

MOST OBVIOUS SYMPTOMS

Brown, sometimes slimy, tunnels develop in stems and roots. These tunnels can serve as entryways for bacterial and fungal diseases. Seedlings become yellow, and the plant is stunted and lacks vigor. The plant wilts during the heat of the day, and eventually dies.

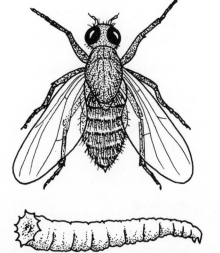

VULNERABLE PLANTS

Broccoli, brussels sprouts, cabbage, cauliflower, Chinese cabbage, collards, kohlrabi, peas, radishes, rutabagas, and turnips, especially seedlings.

BEST CONTROL STRATEGY

Use juvenile stage parasitic nematodes at transplanting time, and use a barrier, such as agricultural fleece, or place a collar around the stem of each plant. If pests still appear, use wood ashes or a lime drench around the base of plants.

OPTIONS FOR CONTROLLING CABBAGE MAGGOT

Emergence Time

Several generations appear from early spring to fall.

Early Warning Devices

Trap Crop

Radishes and turnips are good trap crops for observing the early flies as they emerge. They also serve as decoy crops, so once they are heavily infested, you must pull and destroy all parts of the plants.

Biological Controls

Parasitic nematodes, chalcid wasps, and trichogramma wasps are the best choices here. However, time and habitat are so tricky that you might not have much luck controlling this pest with biological controls.

STEPS TO PREVENT
CABBAGE MAGGOT

Barriers

Alkaline Barrier

Cabbage maggots may be discouraged by a strongly alkaline environment, so use wood ashes or powdered limestone to raise the soil pH. Mix four parts wood ashes to one part powdered limestone and one part rock phosphate. Lightly rake ½ to 1 cup of this mixture into the soil in a 6-inch radius around each seedling, or mix a heaping teaspoonful of wood ashes into soil about 1 inch deep around the stems of vulnerable seedlings and plants. Firm the soil around each plant, and water.

A drench has the same effect. Place 2 pounds of lime in a 5-gallon can. Fill the can with water and let it stand for 24 hours. Pour off the clear water into another container, and in the afternoon, water with this clear water, about a cupful at the base of each plant. Do not soak the entire garden, or you will harm earthworms.

Collar or Mat

An impenetrable barrier around the base of transplants prevents flies from laying eggs there. Make 5- to 10-inch disks from carpet padding or tar paper. Cut a slit along the radius and place a disk around the base of each transplanted seedling. Press the slits flat against the soil.

Wax paper cups, inverted, work well too. Cut a hole in the bottom, then cut a radial slit, and fit the cup upside down into the soil and around the plant stem. Make sure the rim of the cup is set into the soil.

Netting or Fleece Cover

Nylon netting, fine screening, agricultural fleece, or a similar covering prevents flies from laying eggs at the base of plants. No eggs means no cabbage maggot. Cover transplants or a newly seeded area with the netting immediately after planting. Lay the barrier material directly on the plants or on supports, but be sure to seal it firmly to the ground.

Resistant Varieties

Cabbage
Early Jersey.

Intercropping or Companions

Mint, rosemary, sage, and tomatoes may repel the cabbage maggot, but research has not confirmed the reports. Intercropping cabbage and related plants with any plants belonging to a different family is bound to reduce predators.

Planting Date

Plant very early, or plant a fall crop only. You can sidestep much of the maggot threat simply by not sowing or transplanting the plants during the pest's egg-laying peaks. Maggot populations are typically highest in May and early June and again during late summer. If you use shading devices in summer and soil-warming mulches in spring and fall, you can shift planting times so cabbages are not at their weakest stage when maggots are strongest. An early June sowing and July transplanting, after the spring maggot population has peaked, will help to reduce losses.

Animal Predators

Starlings, sparrows, wrens, and toads all feast on cabbage maggots when they can find them.

Insect Predators and Parasites Available Commercially

See the beginning of this chapter for more information on these beneficial insects.

Beneficial Nematode
Beneficial nematodes help control this and other cabbage pests. Use about 50,000 per transplant.

Green Lacewing
Of all the bugs you can buy through the mail, lacewings are probably the most effective in controlling cabbage maggots.

Parasitic (Non-stinging) Wasp

Chalcid and trichogramma wasps parasitize the eggs of cabbage maggots.

Insect Predators and Parasites Found in the Garden

Because the maggots spend most of their lives inside plant stems and roots, they are protected from most predators and parasites. Robber flies, spiders, and other predators probably help control the adults, however, and beetles feast on the maggot pupae in the soil. It has been estimated that as many as 80 percent of the cabbage maggots in a field may be destroyed by rove beetles.

INSECT Caneborer

DESCRIPTION

The caneborer is a bluish black beetle with a red thorax. The adults lay eggs in the spring in older blackberry canes. White grubs bore into the canes, causing the bark to swell. This pest is widespread throughout the northeastern United States, with similar species occurring elsewhere in North America.

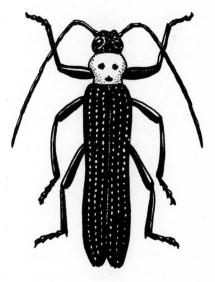

MOST OBVIOUS SYMPTOMS

Watch for large, cigar-shaped swellings on blackberry or raspberry canes.

VULNERABLE PLANTS

Blackberries and raspberries.

BEST CONTROL STRATEGY

Control borers by cutting off and destroying infested canes.

Cankerworm

DESCRIPTION

Also known as inchworms, these are striped brown and green worms about 1 inch long. They may drop from trees on fine silken threads when the branch is jarred. Adults are grayish moths. Eggs of fall cankerworms are brown or grayish, shaped like flowerpots, and laid in compact masses on tree trunks or branches. Spring cankerworm eggs are brownish purple and laid in groups beneath the bark. Fall cankerworms lay their eggs in late fall, after frost, and spring cankerworms lay their eggs in very early spring while trees are still dormant. The fall cankerworm is widespread throughout most of the United States, and the spring cankerworm is found throughout North America.

MOST OBVIOUS SYMPTOMS

Cankerworms skeletonize leaves, causing trees to weaken each year. Not much fruit will mature, and sometimes trees will become defoliated and die. You might see the inchworms hanging from branches on threads.

VULNERABLE PLANTS

Apples and cherries.

BEST CONTROL STRATEGY

A preventive spray of *Bacillus thuringiensis* (BT) in spring, and a band of Tanglefoot or other sticky material around the trunk, help keep the cankerworm numbers down. Prevention is the most effective control in this case.

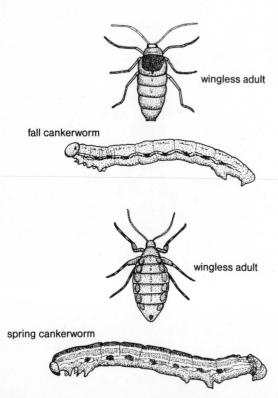

wingless adult

fall cankerworm

wingless adult

spring cankerworm

OPTIONS FOR CONTROLLING CANKERWORM

Emergence Time

The larvae emerge in spring or early summer to feed for 3 to 4 weeks on new leaves.

Biological Controls

Bacillus Thuringiensis (BT)
BT dust or spray controls the larvae. Apply BT when pests appear, being sure to thoroughly coat

all the leaves. Repeat after a rain. When using the foliar spray, apply every 10 to 14 days until the pest is removed.

STEPS TO PREVENT CANKERWORM

Fall Cleanup

Pupae of fall cankerworms lay in the soil before the adult emerges to lay eggs after the frost. A thorough fall cleanup, including tilling the first several inches of soil, may help predators find these pests.

Preventive Spray Programs

Horticultural Oil Spray
Spray trees with a heavy dormant oil before leaves emerge in spring. If the tree's surface is thoroughly covered, overwintering eggs will be suffocated. Later in the season, spray infested trees with *Bacillus thuringiensis* (BT) every 2 weeks, beginning at the end of blossoming and ending 1 month later.

Barriers

Sticky Band
Sticky bands used around the trunk from mid-October to December and again in February will help foil wingless females crawling up to lay eggs. Wrap a band of cotton batting or heavy paper around each tree trunk and coat it with Tanglefoot or some other sticky material.

Animal Predators

Bluebirds, chickadees, nuthatches, tufted titmice, and other birds are terrific controls for cankerworm because they eat the eggs in the bark.

Insect Predators and Parasites Available Commercially

See the beginning of this chapter for more information on these beneficial insects.

Parasitic (Non-stinging) Wasp
Chalcid and trichogramma wasps are likely to control cankerworms.

Insect Predators and Parasites Found in the Garden

Among the naturally occurring beneficials that kill cankerworms are the predatory beetles, stinkbugs, tachinid flies, and a predatory mite, *Nothrus ovivorus*.

INSECT *Carrot Rust Fly*

DESCRIPTION

The carrot rust fly is a black fly, $\frac{1}{5}$ inch long, with yellow hairs and yellow head and legs. The maggots are yellow to white and are about $\frac{1}{3}$ inch long. The flies lay eggs in the crown of plants. Larvae hatch and burrow down into root crops, creating tunnels that are rust-colored from the maggots' excrement. Several generations occur each year. The winters are spent in the maggot or pupa stage. This pest is found throughout North America, but is most common in the northern United States.

MOST OBVIOUS SYMPTOMS

The maggots chew roots, causing plants to be dwarfed; soft-rot bacteria may become a problem.

VULNERABLE PLANTS

Carrots, celery, parsley, and parsnips.

BEST CONTROL STRATEGY

Once plants have been attacked, there is little the gardener can do. Destroy infested plants, rotate crops, and protect new plantings with netting or a similar barrier. Try adjusting planting dates to avoid the pest at its peak.

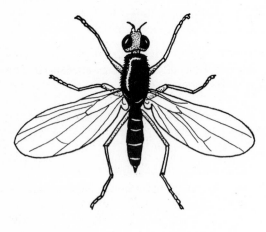

STEPS TO PREVENT
CARROT RUST FLY

Fall Cleanup

Maggots or pupae hibernate in the soil, so a thorough fall cleanup goes a long way to keep this pest under control.

Barriers

Netting or Fleece Cover

Fine nylon netting, fine screening, or agricultural fleece are all effective barriers, preventing the fly from laying eggs at the plant's stem. Set up the covers at planting time.

Wood Ashes

Spreading ashes around the crowns of plants may discourage the flies from laying eggs.

Intercropping or Companions

Onions and leeks interplanted with the carrots release volatile substances which affect the fly so it can't find the crop. Gardeners also report that coriander, pennyroyal, rosemary, salsify, sage, and wormwood repel the carrot rust fly.

Planting Date

If you must plant early, protect seedlings with fine screening or agricultural fleece. The best approach is to plant later, so carrots will mature in fall and miss the height of the carrot rust fly season.

INSECT Carrot Weevil

DESCRIPTION

The legless white grub of the carrot weevil chews celery hearts and tunnels into the tops and roots of carrots and other plants, destroying most of the plant tissue. The adult weevil is brownish with a hard shell and is about ⅕ inch long. This pest overwinters as an adult in garden litter and hedgerows. It is found east of the Rockies.

MOST OBVIOUS SYMPTOMS

Zigzag tunnels can be seen in the tops and roots of infested plants. In celery, the hearts are chewed. The plants may be defoliated with just the stems remaining.

VULNERABLE PLANTS

Carrots, celery, parsley, and parsnips.

BEST CONTROL STRATEGY

Use juvenile stage parasitic nematodes to prevent infestation, and use netting or other barriers to keep out adults throughout the season. To control infestations, apply pyrethrum.

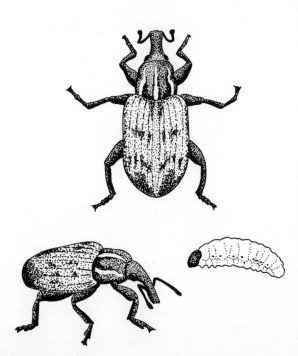

OPTIONS FOR CONTROLLING CARROT WEEVIL

Emergence Time

Overwintering adults emerge in May and lay eggs on plant stems. Larvae enter stems and bore downward into the roots, then pupate in the soil by late June. A second generation of adults emerges in July.

Traps and Mechanical Controls

Handpicking

The weevil can be handpicked in the larval stage.

Botanical Poisons

Pyrethrum

Spray with pyrethrum when carrot weevils get out of hand. Use two applications 3 to 4 days apart. Pyrethrum also harms beneficials, so use as a last resort.

STEPS TO PREVENT CARROT WEEVIL

Fall Cleanup

Adult carrot weevils overwinter in grass and garden litter, so clear away all weeds and dead plants in the fall. Cultivate the garden thoroughly 6 to 8 inches deep, using a hand tool or a rotary tiller. Leave the garden bare for a week or two, cultivate 2 inches deep, and plant a cover crop, or lay 4 to 6 inches of winter mulch.

Barriers

Netting or Fleece Cover

Keep out carrot weevils with agricultural fleece, fine screening, cheesecloth, or other barriers. A floating row cover laid directly on the plants or a tunnel-type row cover is fine.

Animal Predators

Chickadees, juncos, bluebirds, and warblers are some of the common songbirds that eat carrot weevils. Toads and turtles do their share as well.

Insect Predators Available Commercially

See the beginning of this chapter for more information on these beneficial insects.

Beneficial Nematode
The only commercially available beneficial insects worth using for weevil control are beneficial nematodes.

Insect Predators and Parasites Found in the Garden

Spiders.

Other Preventive Steps

Keep Queen Anne's lace and other weeds in the carrot family away from the garden if the carrot weevil is a particularly bad problem.

INSECT # *Cherry Fruit Fly*

DESCRIPTION

Adult fruit flies resemble small houseflies with barred wings. They lay eggs in developing fruit. The maggots are yellowish white and legless, with two dark mouth hooks. The insects overwinter as pupae in the soil, and adults emerge in early summer. Cherry fruit flies are found throughout the United States, except the extreme Southwest and Florida.

MOST OBVIOUS SYMPTOMS

Fruit is small and misshapen, with rotten flesh, in which maggots are found feeding. Cherries may drop prematurely.

VULNERABLE PLANTS

Cherries, pears, and plums.

BEST CONTROL STRATEGY

Sprays are generally not effective against cherry fruit flies. The adult flies are not out for a very long time and the larvae develop within the fruit, so they're out of reach of sprays. You'll get better results by using traps and by cleaning up and destroying dropped fruit.

OPTIONS FOR CONTROLLING CHERRY FRUIT FLY

Traps and Mechanical Controls

Red spherical sticky traps and yellow sticky cards can help against cherry fruit flies. Buy commercial traps or make your own, then cover them with a sticky coating, such as Tangle-Trap. From early to late May, hang four to eight traps in each full-size tree at eye level, about 2 feet back from the stem tips, near the fruit but not completely hidden by leaves. Clean traps every few days and reapply the sticky coating. Do not leave sticky trap out for more than 3 or 4 weeks.

STEPS TO PREVENT CHERRY FRUIT FLY

Fall Cleanup

Regular raking and destroying dropped fruit can help to reduce cherry fruit fly damage in following years. Clean up dropped fruit every few days: the more often, the better. Getting the fruit off the ground quickly will help to keep maggots from leaving the fruit and entering the ground to pupate.

Also cultivate the top 2 inches of soil under trees in very late fall, after several frosts. This exposes overwintering pupae to the cold and predators and may reduce numbers next year.

INSECT *Codling Moth*

DESCRIPTION

The larva of the codling moth is pink with a brown head, and is about 1 inch long. The adult is a grayish brown moth with lacy brown lines on the forewings and pale, fringed hind wings. It has a ¾-inch wingspan. The eggs are white, flat, and laid singly on leaves, twigs, or fruit buds. Two generations occur every year and are common in much of the country; the first generation attacks immature fruit, the second hits mature fruit. Codling moths overwinter as pupae in bark or debris. They are common throughout North America.

MOST OBVIOUS SYMPTOMS

Symptoms of infestation include holes in the fruit skin, tunnels through the fruit, and fecal wastes in the core. The larvae push brown excrement pellets out their tunnel entrance. This produces a characteristic brown mound at the opening. You might also spot some cocoons in the bark crevices.

VULNERABLE PLANTS

Apples, apricots, and pears.

BEST CONTROL STRATEGY

Set out sticky traps to catch the moths. Use a preventive spray of *Bacillus thuringiensis* (BT) and light horticultural oil later in the season to get the newly hatched larvae before they bore into the fruit.

OPTIONS FOR CONTROLLING CODLING MOTH

Emergence Time

First adults appear at petal fall and continue to emerge for several weeks. Since this is a major orchard pest, local growers will have a good sense of emergence times in your area.

Early Warning Devices

Homemade Trap

Some growers report that codling moths flock to a pot containing a mixture of two parts vinegar to one part molasses. Hang it about 8 inches below a limb. Three to four traps take care of a whole tree. Clean out moths daily and replenish the liquid.

Pheromone Trap

Codling moths can be monitored and trapped with a pheromone bait. This bait gives off an odor that attracts the moth, which gets stuck in the trap. As soon as a moth appears, you can take other control steps. These traps are available commercially.

Sticky Trap

Early warning sticky traps are available for codling moths. They use red spheres covered with very sticky material, such as Tanglefoot.

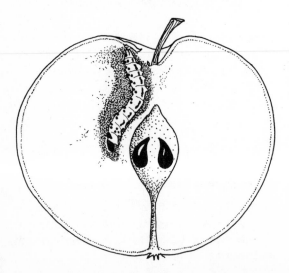

Natural Sprays

See the beginning of this chapter for more information on making natural sprays.

Horticultural Oil Spray

Traditional heavier horticultural spray oils (viscosity 100 to 200) are designed to be used in fall through early spring to smother codling moth pupae when the winter host plants are leafless.

Biological Controls

Bacillus Thuringiensis (BT)

BT are bacteria that come in powder form. A BT spray perfectly timed to hit larvae while they are still outside the fruit will reduce codling moth damage to some extent. To use as a foliar spray, apply BT in liquid form to the plants just at egg hatching. Field trials using BT mixed with light oils at low concentrations (0.25 percent) showed that the first and second generations of codlings could be controlled successfully if populations were not dense. Apply BT with oil at the time of mass egg laying, determined by monitoring the damage and trapping male moths.

Traps and Mechanical Controls

Bagging

You can produce blemish-free fruit, even in areas where codling moths are a serious problem, by tying a lunch-size paper bag over each developing fruit in June. (Cut a small slit in the base of the bag, slip it over the fruit, then staple shut the open end.) Besides keeping adult moths from laying eggs in the fruit, the bag also helps protect the fruit from damage caused by birds or bad weather.

Burlap Strip Trap

After they leave the fruit, the larvae crawl down the trunk and look for a place to spin their cocoons. To stop them, wrap a 6-inch-wide burlap strip around the trunk and cover it with a sticky substance like Tanglefoot. Then, remove the burlap bands and destroy the larvae.

Corrugated Cardboard Trap

About 5 weeks after petal fall, wrap 6-inch-wide corrugated paper around tree trunks to provide a substitute location for larvae to spin cocoons. Remove and burn the bands in the fall.

Pheromone Trap

You can use commercial pheromone traps for codling moth control, particularly if you have only a few apple trees to protect. Use one trap per tree. Clean out moths every 2 weeks and replace pheromones bimonthly. To catch the most moths, place traps near the tops of tree canopies. Results are best if the traps are oriented so the openings are parallel to the prevailing wind direction. Traps positioned behind trees in rows perpendicular to the prevailing wind might not be very efficient. In orchards with widely varying wind directions, attach traps to a vane so their openings remain facing the wind.

Sticky Trap

If a sufficient number are used, sticky traps can be used to control codling moths as well as to monitor their numbers. Hang spherical traps coated with sticky material, such as Tack Trap, motor oil, or petroleum jelly, in susceptible trees. Don't leave traps out for more than 3 or 4 weeks, or beneficial insects, as well as pests, will be trapped.

STEPS TO PREVENT CODLING MOTH

Fall Cleanup

As soon as you finish the harvest, remove all overgrown weeds and other debris, leaving the area around the fruit trees bare; then cultivate the soil thoroughly to a depth of 2 inches, and leave the soil bare for a week or two. Plant a cover crop or a 4- to 6-inch layer of winter mulch, leaving space around the trunks to prevent rodent damage over the winter.

Preventive Spray Programs

Bacillus Thuringiensis (BT)

Spraying with the bacteria known as BT effectively controls codling moth larvae just after they've hatched, but sprayings must be done before the larvae burrow into the fruit. Researchers have discovered that BT mixed with light horticultural oil can penetrate codling moth eggs and kill larvae before they hatch. Applied during mass egg laying, the BT and oil mixture controls first and second generation moths, if populations aren't too dense.

Horticultural Oil Spray

Late winter, before any leaf buds begin to open, is the best time to spray heavy oil on fruit trees to control codling moths. Make sure the entire surface of the tree is covered, because the oil works by suffocating the pupae.

Animal Predators

Woodpeckers and other bark cleaning birds relish codling moth eggs. One of the best codling moth controls is a block of suet in the trees to attract woodpeckers during the winter.

Insect Predators and Parasites Available Commercially

See the beginning of this chapter for more information on these beneficial insects.

Beneficial Nematode

Beneficial nematodes are tiny soil-dwelling worms that find their way to the codling moths, burrow inside them, and reproduce. The codling moths are killed by bacteria released by the nematodes.

Parasitic (Non-stinging) Wasp

Braconid, chalcid, and trichogramma wasps parasitize the eggs of the codling moth. Set out trichogramma wasps in June when moths lay eggs and again in midsummer when second generation moths appear.

Insect Predators and Parasites Found in the Garden

Ground beetles and spiders are the important predators of this pest. Parasitic wasps also attack codling moths.

INSEСT Colorado Potato Beetle

DESCRIPTION

Adults are yellow convex beetles, about ⅓ inch long. They are marked with black stripes and an orange head covering. The eggs are bright yellow and are laid on the undersides of leaves. Grubs are plump and red, with black spots and a black head. Both adults and larvae chew foliage. One or two generations occur every year. The beetles overwinter in the adult stage. Colorado potato beetles are found in most parts of the United States and Canada, but especially in the eastern areas.

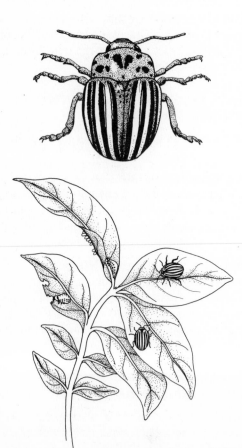

MOST OBVIOUS SYMPTOMS

Defoliated plants with skeletonized leaves are signs of the Colorado potato beetle.

VULNERABLE PLANTS

Eggplants, potatoes, and tomatoes.

BEST CONTROL STRATEGY

Handpick the first arrivals in spring and use pyrethrum spray if they get out of hand. In addition, apply a heavy organic mulch; potato beetles cannot emerge through the mulch.

OPTIONS FOR CONTROLLING COLORADO POTATO BEETLE

Emergence Times

Adults emerge from soil in late April to early May.

Early Warning Devices

Trap Crop

Black nightshade *(Solanum nigrum)* can be used as a trap crop to spot early infestations of Colorado potato beetles. Locate it in or within 10 to 15 feet of the crop threatened by the beetles. Once the trap crop is heavily infested, you must pull and destroy it before it begins to create more pest problems itself.

Natural Sprays

Bug Juice

Do not use bug juice against Colorado potato beetles since it can be toxic to potato plants.

Biological Controls

Bacillus Thuringiensis (BT)

BT are bacteria that come in powder form (used as a dust or a foliar spray) and kill only leaf-eating caterpillars. However, there is a new metabolite form of BT that achieves excellent control of the Colorado potato beetle when the beetle is in its larval stage.

Traps and Mechanical Controls

Cornmeal or Bran Trap

Sprinkle plants with cornmeal or wheat bran meal. The beetles eat the meal, it expands inside them, and they explode.

Handpicking

Handpicking makes a sizable dent in the beetle infestation right away. It is best to attend to the very first adults that appear to set back their egg-laying activities.

Botanical Poisons

Neem

Neem spray is most effective against the larval stage of Colorado potato beetles. Purchase a commercial neem product and mix it according to label instructions. Apply the spray to beetle-infested plants twice, at weekly or longer intervals, until pests are under control. Be sure to spray carefully to thoroughly cover all plant parts.

Pyrethrum

Usually two applications of pyrethrum, applied 3 to 4 days apart, will control the beetles.

STEPS TO PREVENT COLORADO POTATO BEETLE

Fall Cleanup

As soon as you finish the harvest for each crop, remove all old plants and overgrown weeds, leaving completely bare soil for a few days. Then cultivate the soil thoroughly to a depth of 6 to 8 inches. About 2 to 3 weeks after that deep cultivation, shallowly rake the soil and leave it bare for a few more days. This allows the birds to work on the beetles that are looking for a place to overwinter. Plant a cover crop, or lay a 4- to 6-inch layer of winter mulch.

In the early spring, about 2 weeks before planting, give the garden another shallow cultivation, to a depth of about 2 inches, and leave it bare for the birds to work over.

Barriers

Diatomaceous Earth (D.E.)

Dust the whole plant with D.E. to destroy the larvae. Dusting should progress upward from the ground, covering all stems and leaves, especially the undersides. Apply in the late evening or at night, when beneficial insects are less likely to be on the plants.

Netting or Fleece Cover

Nylon netting, fine screening, or agricultural fleece row covers are all effective barriers that prevent beetles from flying in to lay eggs on the crop's leaves. Lay the barrier material directly on the plants and seal all the edges to the ground. Provide lots of extra material so that the plants don't strain against the covering when they grow larger. Don't use a row cover if you grew infested potatoes in that spot the previous season, or if you have seen beetles in the soil. You will be trapping them on the crop, not keeping them off it.

Resistant Varieties

Potato

Sequoia and Katahdin.

Intercropping or Companions

In research studies, interplanted catnip, coriander, and tansy all showed promise in reducing Colorado potato beetles on potatoes. The volatiles emitted by the tansy and catnip are repellent to the beetles.

It has been determined that Colorado potato beetles find their food by smell, so an intercrop of an aromatic herb, such as basil, that would mask the smell of potatoes would help.

Animal Predators

Birds, including Baltimore orioles, bluebirds, cardinals, chickadees, grosbeaks, juncos, purple finches, and robins, all eat Colorado potato beetles.

Insect Predators and Parasites Available Commercially

See the beginning of this chapter for more infortion on these beneficial insects.

Beneficial Nematode

Nematodes burrow inside beetles and reproduce. Once inside, they release bacteria, which kill the beetles. Apply beneficial nematodes on either side of potatoes at the rate of 100,000 per running foot of row.

Parasitic (Non-stinging) Wasp

Chalcid, trichogramma, and Colombian wasps parasitize the eggs of Colorado potato beetles.

Insect Predators Found in the Garden

Assassin bugs, ground beetles, lady bugs, and stinkbugs are important predators. Naturally occurring parasitic wasps also help keep Colorado potato beetles in check.

Other Preventive Steps

Grow potatoes on top of the ground with heavy mulch. The thick organic mulch makes it hard for emerging beetles to reach plants in the spring.

Keeping the weeds cut around your garden is a good cultural practice to discourage early Colorado potato beetles.

NOTES AND RESEARCH

Researchers have found that peppermint marc, the material left after oils are distilled from the peppermint plant, is effective against Colorado potato beetles.

INSECT Corn Earworm

DESCRIPTION

The corn earworm is a white, green, or red caterpillar with spines. It measures about 1½ inches long. The adult is a brown moth. The first generation chews the buds and leaves; later generations feed on silks and kernels at the tip of the ear just inside the husk. The corn earworm overwinters as a pupa in the soil. It is found throughout the United States, but occurs most often in southern and central states.

MOST OBVIOUS SYMPTOMS

Signs of corn earworms are damage to buds and young plants. The plants may be stunted. In corn, the ears are destroyed from the tip down. Damp castings may be seen near the silk. Green tomatoes are destroyed from the stem end.

VULNERABLE PLANTS

Beans (lima and snap), corn, okra, squash (summer and winter), and tomatoes.

BEST CONTROL STRATEGY

The best strategy is to spray young plants with light horticultural oil mixed with *Bacillus thuringiensis*

(BT) every 2 weeks. Spray from the time corn is knee-high until ears begin to form. Next, apply a drop of mineral oil to the silks of each ear, after the silk has dried. If the earworm does get access to the ear of corn, inject BT into the ear with a hypodermic needle or garden syringe.

OPTIONS FOR CONTROLLING CORN EARWORM

Emergence Time

The pupae overwinter in the soil, emerging in late spring.

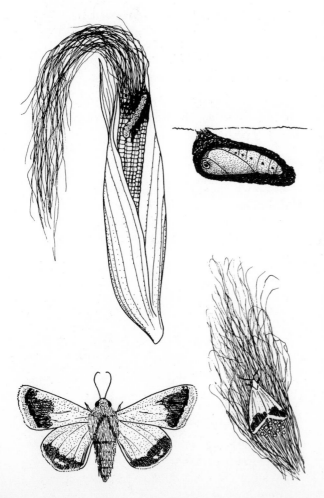

Early Warning Devices

Pheromone Trap

Adults can be monitored and trapped with a pheromone bait. This warning allows you to take other control steps immediately. If you use enough traps, you may actually control the pest with these devices. Three traps are adequate for up to 5,000 square feet of corn.

Trap Crop

Smartweed has been found to attract corn earworms and can be used as a trap crop. Locate plants within 10 to 15 feet of the crop threatened by the corn earworm. Remember, once the trap crop is heavily infested, you must pull and destroy it before it begins to create more pest problems itself.

Natural Sprays

See the beginning of this chapter for more information on making natural sprays.

Light Horticultural Oil Spray

Light horticultural oil (viscosity 60 to 70) can be used during the growing season to control corn earworms. Spray with a 2 to 3 percent solution, and make sure contact is made with the pest because the oil works by suffocation. If you add *Bacillus thuringiensis* (BT) to this light oil spray, you increase its effectiveness significantly.

Biological Controls

Bacillus Thuringiensis (BT)

BT are bacteria that kill corn earworms on contact. To use BT as a dust, apply every 10 to 14 days until the pest is under control. Thoroughly cover all parts of the leaves, especially the undersides. To use as a foliar spray, apply BT in liquid form to the affected plants at 10- to 14-day intervals until the pest is removed. Once the earworm has entered the ear of corn, you can inject a couple of squirts of the BT solution into the top of the ear with a syringe. Allow at least 3 to 5 days before harvesting injected ears.

Traps and Mechanical Controls

Handpicking

You can handpick the earworm by gently pulling back the husk at the tip of each ear and removing the worm. Do this only after the silks begin to brown, indicating that pollination has already occurred.

Mineral Oil

Apply half a medicine dropperful of mineral oil to the silk on each ear of corn after the silks have wilted and begun to turn brown; this will suffocate the worms but will not affect the flavor of the corn. Any earlier application may interfere with the corn's pollination. Red pepper, pyrethrum, or *Bacillus thuringiensis* (BT) can be added to the mineral oil. Make two follow-up applications spaced 1 week apart.

Botanical Poisons

Neem

Spray neem when pheromone traps indicate that adult moths have appeared. Apply the material twice at weekly or longer intervals to control larvae hatching from the eggs.

Pyrethrum

Pyrethrum paralyzes corn earworms on contact. It must be applied directly to the worm to work, so spray the undersides of the leaves as well as the tops, since the worm is usually on the underside if it is on the leaf at all. Usually two applications, 3 to 4 days apart, will control the problem.

STEPS TO PREVENT CORN EARWORM

Fall Cleanup

The earworms overwinter as pupae 2 inches or more below the soil surface right near the host plant. Rotary tilling kills some of these pupae and exposes them to weather, birds, and other predators. As soon as you finish harvesting crops, remove all old plants and overgrown weeds. After a few days, cultivate the bare soil 6 to 8 inches deep, using a hand tool or a rotary tiller. About 2 to 3 weeks after that deep cultivation, give the garden a shallow cultivation to about 2 inches, again leaving it bare for the birds to work over. Then you can plant a cover crop or lay a 4- to 6-inch layer of winter mulch. About 2 weeks before planting, give the soil another shallow cultivation, down about 2 inches, to expose any pupae that made it through the winter.

Resistant Varieties

Plant resistant or tolerant varieties of sweet corn. Resistance is associated with tighter husks, harder kernels, and lower concentrations of amino acids.

Corn

Aristogold, Calumet, Country Gentleman, Dixie 18, Iona, Seneca Chief, Seneca Scout, Silver Cross Bantam, Staygold, and Victory Golden.

Intercropping or Companions

There tend to be fewer corn earworms if corn is intercropped with soybeans, which encourage the activity of trichogramma wasps.

Planting Date

Plant early to avoid hot weather. In the northern states, it's best to plant corn as early as possible, to miss the summer earworm populations. In the southern states, both early and late plantings will encounter the pests, so the planting date is not so critical.

Animal Predators

Flycatchers, barn swallows, downy woodpeckers, sparrows, blackbirds, grackles, and phoebes relish eating corn earworms. Moles and toads eat their share as well.

Insect Predators and Parasites Available Commercially

See the beginning of this chapter for more infortion on these beneficials.

Beneficial Nematode

Beneficial nematodes are tiny soil-dwelling worms that must be injected into the infested ears to find their way to the corn earworms, burrow inside them, and reproduce. The earworms are killed by bacteria released by the nematodes. Use a garden syringe for this task. All the corn in a 50-by-100-foot plot can be injected in 20 minutes.

Green Lacewing

Of all the bugs you can buy through the mail, lacewings are probably the best to choose.

Parasitic (Non-stinging) Wasp

Braconid, chalcid, ichneumonid, and trichogramma wasps parasitize earworm larvae. Release of trichogramma wasps is more effective when coupled with a spray of *Bacillus thuringiensis* (BT). Release the insects just before the corn silks.

Insect Predators Found in the Garden

Assassin bugs, green lacewings, ground beetles, minute pirate bugs, parasitic wasps, soldier beetles, and tachinid flies all prey on corn earworms.

Other Preventive Steps

Some gardeners have reported reduced earworm damage by turning lights on in their garden at night. The light supposedly repels the egg-laying moth.

NOTES AND RESEARCH

If you find corn earworms that have turned chalky white and appear nearly dead, they have probably been infected with nuclear polyhedrosis virus (NPV). They might be lying motionless on top of leaves or even hanging from the underside of a leaf. You can make your own form of viral insecticide by making bug juice from a dozen or more earworms infected with NPV. (See the beginning of this chapter for more information on homemade bug juice.) NPV is slower acting but longer lasting than *Bacillus thuringiensis* (BT). It takes 5 to 6 days to kill the corn earworm, but a single application may last the whole season. A commercial version of NPV is being researched and is expected on the market in the next year or two.

INSECT *Cucumber Beetle*

DESCRIPTION

Also called the southern corn rootworm, the adult is an oblong yellow beetle about ¼ inch long, with black stripes or spots. The eggs are orange and are usually laid in the soil near host plants. The whitish larvae are found near the base of the plant and feed underground on the roots. The adult beetle chews leaves and flowers. The beetles can carry the bacillus *Erwinia tracheiphila*, which causes bacterial wilt, and which overwinters in the beetles' intestines. If the beetle has eaten a cucumber plant infected with cucumber mosaic, it can transfer that disease to healthy plants. Once a plant gets bacterial wilt or mosaic, there's no cure. This pest is found throughout the United States but is especially serious in the southern states, particularly where soils are heavy. One or two generations occur every year.

The most destructive type is the striped cucumber beetle, a species that feeds mainly on members of the cucurbit family. Other wilt-carrying beetles include the spotted cucumber beetle, the western spotted cucumber beetle, and the banded cucumber beetle.

MOST OBVIOUS SYMPTOMS

Beetles do minor physical damage to crops, but can spread cucumber wilt, cucumber mosaic virus, bacterial wilt, or other serious plant diseases. Young cucumber plants are especially vulnerable to attacks by cucumber beetles. Beetles can burrow right into the soil and eat the germinated seedling before it even breaks the soil surface. Larvae attack roots of corn and other young vegetable plants, causing them to wilt and collapse.

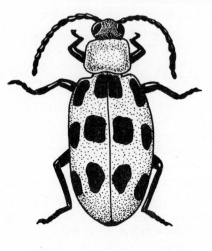

spotted cucumber beetle

VULNERABLE PLANTS

Asparagus, early beans (lima and snap), corn, cucumbers, eggplants, muskmelons, peas, potatoes, pumpkins, squash (summer and winter), tomatoes, and watermelons.

BEST CONTROL STRATEGY

Prevent the beetles from feeding on young plants. From germination until the plants start to bloom is the critical period. Use some type of barrier, such as agricultural fleece, to keep beetles from flying in to lay eggs near plants. Pyrethrum works well on adult beetles.

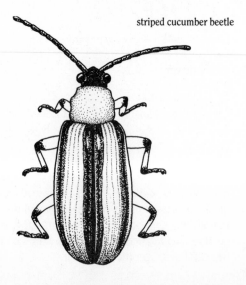

striped cucumber beetle

OPTIONS FOR CONTROLLING CUCUMBER BEETLE

Emergence Time

Both striped and spotted cucumber beetles overwinter as adults in ground debris or dense grass. They emerge in spring when temperatures reach about 65°F to feed on leaves, new shoots, and seedlings. They also lay eggs in the soil at the base of plants. Eggs hatch in about 10 days. Cucumber beetle larvae feed in roots and crowns of plants for several weeks, often stunting or even killing young plants. The larvae then pupate for several weeks. Emerging adult beetles feed on blossoms and maturing fruit. Both kinds of cucumber beetles usually have only 1 or 2 generations per year. Spotted cucumber beetles may have a third generation in southern areas.

Early Warning Devices

Cucumber Trap
Cucumber peelings and the rinds of most cantaloupes contain enough cucurbitacin, a chemical that attracts the beetles, to serve as early warning beetle traps. Coat rinds with rotenone and place them where cucumber beetles are expected. If many beetles are caught, you will know that full-scale emergence is underway. Using cucurbitacin traps may have one major flaw. The traps may attract beetles feeding on wild plants and actually increase the beetle population in the garden.

Gourd Trap
Powdering the dried fruit of bitter varieties of gourds and mixing specific insecticides such as pyrethrum with the powder can stop beetles and also serve as an early warning device. Only cucumber beetles will ingest the bait, but they will consume enough to kill them. The technique is still in the experimental stage, and the desperate gardener might want to experiment with a home version of the gourd trap. One particular cucurbit that holds fatal sway over the beetles is the buffalo gourd, *Cucurbita foetidissima,* a weed vine that grows wild throughout the Southwest.

Trap Crop
Trap crops can be used to spot early infestations of pests. This is particularly important for the cucumber beetle, since it is a disease carrier. Try radishes or a potted miniature rose bush as a trap crop among the cucumber plants.

Beetles seem to attack weaker plants first. Grow a cucumber plant indoors so that it is quite a bit larger than your normal plants at transplant time. Pull the large plant out of the soil and let it wilt lying in the garden near the new transplants. The early beetles will be attracted to the weak and dying plant while leaving the crop plants alone. Pick the bugs off the bait plant and cover your good plants with netting or other barriers.

Traps and Mechanical Controls

Blossom Trap
If your plants are in the blooming stage, you can trap some beetles inside the spent blossoms. They gather there after the blooms have been pollinated and have begun to wither and close. Check the blossoms in late evening. If you see any beetles inside, pick the flowers and drop them into a bucket of ammonia water to dispose of them.

Cover Trap
A simple device can be used to protect cucumber beetles from the hot sun during the day, and therefore can become a cover trap. Use wilted and dead squash leaves for this purpose. It is best to visit these cover traps twice a day to drown or crush the pests under the leaves.

Gourd Blossom Trap
A natural trap for the beetles are the blossoms of large gourds *(Cucurbita lagenaria).* They have large white flowers that open in the evening, then close and wither the next morning. In the morning you can find many beetles, both the striped and the spotted kind, males and females.

Pheromone Trap
There is on the market a new trap for the cucumber beetle. The bait contains three basic ingredients: a synthetic version of a sex pheromone, a compound made from certain plants of the cucumber family that stimulates the beetles to stop moving and start feeding, and an insecticide.

Botanical Poisons

Pyrethrum
Pyrethrum appears to possess some beetle-repellent as well as insecticidal qualities. Apply it when you see adult cucumber beetles feeding on pollen in flowers. Two applications, made 3 or 4 days apart, will control the problem.

STEPS TO PREVENT CUCUMBER BEETLE

Fall Cleanup

Fall cleanup is critical to preventing a serious infestation the next year. Disposal of spent cucurbit plants will destroy a potential habitat for striped beetles and their larvae.

Barriers

From germination until the plants start to bloom is the critical period for preventing the beetles from feeding on the young plants and from laying their eggs at the stems of host plants. By the time the plants outgrow the barriers, they will have outgrown the danger of a systemic infection.

Diatomaceous Earth (D.E.)

Dust D.E. around the base of the plant to create a barrier to egg laying, or dust the infested plant with D.E. Dust in the late evening or at night to minimize destruction of predator insects.

Netting or Fleece Cover

Unless plants are trained to a trellis, you can easily protect them with barriers that allow sun, air, and rain to get through while keeping out the cucumber beetle. Nylon netting, fine screening, or agricultural fleece are all effective covers, as long as the entire plant is covered. Cover transplants or a newly seeded area with the preferred material immediately to prevent both insect disease-transfer and insect egg laying, which can lead to later damage. Lay the barrier material directly on the plants, or on tunnel braces. Seal all the edges to the ground, and leave the barrier on until the crop is harvested.

Seedling Barrier

To avoid losing seedlings in spring, set out cucurbit transplants in mid-April under cloches made of plastic milk jugs. When the plants outgrow the hotcaps or jugs, replace them with a larger piece of agricultural fleece.

Wood Ashes

Sprinkle two handfuls of wood ashes around the base of each plant when the vines are 4 to 5 inches tall, or encircle them with a 3- to 4-inch-wide trench, a few inches deep, filled with wood ashes. Care should be taken to avoid getting ashes on the plant or the stems.

Resistant Varieties

A 2-year study of hundreds of squash species, varieties, and breeding lines turned up several with resistance to cucumber beetles. Beetles were less attracted to scallop-type squash than to zucchini. The researchers also found that the yellow squash varieties Slendergold and Early Prolific Yellow Straightneck, as well as the winter squash Table King, Table Ace, Table Queen, and Royal Acorn, showed some resistance.

Squash, Summer

Varieties resistant to the spotted cucumber beetle include Bennings Green Tint Scallop, Black Zucchini, Early Golden Bush Scallop, Long Cozella, Seneca Prolific, Summer Crookneck, and Summer Straightneck.

Those resistant to the striped cucumber beetle include Bennings Green Tint Scallop, Cozella Hybrid, Early Golden Bush Scallop, Early Prolific Straightneck, Early Yellow Summer Crookneck, Long Cocozelle, Marine Black Zucchini, Short Cocozelle, Summer Crookneck, U Conn, White Bush Scallop, and Zucchini.

Squash, Winter

Varieties resistant to the spotted cucumber beetle include Blue Hubbard, Green Hubbard, and Royal Acorn.

Those resistant to the striped cucumber beetle include Butternut and Royal Acorn.

Cucumber

Ashley, Chipper, Fletcher, Niagara, and Stono.

Pumpkin

Dickinson Field, King of the Mammoth, and Mammoth Chili.

Intercropping or Companions

Broccoli, catnip, corn, and radishes are sometimes suggested as interplants for discouraging cucumber beetles from feeding on cucumbers.

Planting Date

Plant susceptible crops late, for the fall harvest when possible, since the pest disappears by late June in many areas of the northern United States. Stagger your planting dates. Start some seedlings early indoors and set them out at normal planting time. If the plants are covered with barriers for the first month or so, they will avoid much damage. Sow new hills every week so your plants won't all be at the most vulnerable stage at the same time.

Animal Predators

Baltimore orioles, bluebirds, brown thrashers, chickadees, juncos, phoebes, purple finches, sparrows, towhees, and warblers relish eating cucumber beetles.

Insect Predators and Parasites Available Commercially

See the beginning of this chapter for more infor-

mation on these beneficial insects.

Beneficial Nematode

The cucumber beetle larvae are killed by beneficial nematodes. Apply juvenile-stage nematodes in an 18-inch circle around the base of vine crops at a rate of 50,000 per vine, or at the rate of 50,000 per foot on row crops like beans.

Parasitic (Non-stinging) Wasp

Braconid, chalcid, and trichogramma wasps parasitize the eggs of the cucumber beetle.

Insect Predators and Parasites Found in the Garden

The most effective beneficials are soldier beetles and tachinid flies, which lay eggs and develop inside the bodies of adult cucumber beetles.

Other Preventive Steps

Mulch your garden well. A thick straw mulch can reduce the number of adult beetles laying eggs at the base of the plants.

INSECT *Cutworm*

DESCRIPTION

The cutworm is a plump, soft-bodied, dull grayish or brownish caterpillar that measures 1 to 2 inches long and curls up when disturbed. It feeds at night and hides in the soil during the day. The adult is a night-flying moth. Eggs are laid in the soil, and the cutworm overwinters as a larva or pupa. Various species are found throughout the United States. Up to five generations can occur in 1 year.

MOST OBVIOUS SYMPTOMS

Cutworms sever the stems of seedlings at or below the soil surface. They are most active at night. If the plants look as though they have been leveled by a lawn mower, you may have cutworms. (If the base looks like it has been cut at an angle, it could be rabbits.) Cutworms can also harm the root system, so that the plant wilts and collapses.

VULNERABLE PLANTS

Beans (lima and snap), broccoli, brussels sprouts, cabbage, cauliflower, Chinese cabbage, collards, corn, eggplants, kohlrabi, lettuce, radishes, rutabagas, peppers, potatoes, tomatoes, and turnips.

BEST CONTROL STRATEGY

Protect individual seedlings with a 3-inch collar made from stiff paper or plastic. Push the collar an inch or so into the ground. Or make a trap by sprinkling ½ teaspoon of cornmeal or bran meal around each plant. Apply it in a circle leading away from the stem of the plant. The cutworm eats the meal and dies. Juvenile nematodes are also an excellent control.

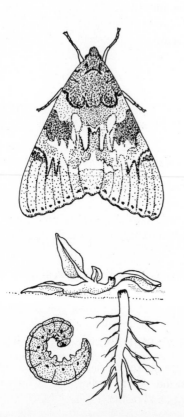

OPTIONS FOR CONTROLLING CUTWORM

Emergence Time

Cutworms seem to do most of their damage in early spring. However, many species produce new generations throughout the year.

Biological Controls

Bacillus Thuringiensis (BT)
The bacteria known as BT are effective on some species. Dust seedlings and transplants at the soil level.

Traps and Mechanical Controls

Cornmeal or Bran Trap
After putting out transplants, sprinkle ½ teaspoon of cornmeal or bran meal around each plant. Apply it in a circle leading away from the stem of the plant. The cutworm will eat the meal, which will swell inside the worm's body and kill it.

Molasses Trap
Immobilize cutworms with molasses. Mix equal parts hardwood sawdust and bran. Add anough molasses to make the mixture sticky and enough water to moisten it. Scatter a few spoonfuls around each plant at dusk. The cutworms should leave your plants and get caught in the sticky molasses. The bait clings to their bodies and hardens. By morning they are completely helpless, and exposed to wind, sun, and birds.

Handpicking
Cutworms can be handpicked at night. Check near the base of plants, and just under the soil surface. Destroy any cutworms you see at planting time.

STEPS TO PREVENT CUTWORM

Fall Cleanup

In the fall, as soon as you finish the harvest for each crop, remove all old plants and overgrown weeds, leaving completely bare soil. Then cultivate the soil thoroughly to a depth of 6 to 8 inches, using a hand tool or a rotary tiller. About 2 to 3 weeks after that deep cultivation, give the garden a shallow cultivation to about 2 inches in order to expose cutworm larvae for the birds to devour.

In spring, about 2 weeks before planting, give the garden another shallow cultivation to a depth of about 2 inches. The first generation of cutworms, which is the most troublesome, can be checked by a light cultivation as soon as the soil can be worked in spring, and then by waiting 10 to 14 days to plant.

Barriers

Placement of matchsticks or toothpicks alongside plants is based on the erroneous belief that cutworms must curl their bodies around the stem in order to cut through it. These barriers will not stop cutworms from feeding.

Diatomaceous Earth (D.E.)

Dust diatomaceous earth around the base of your plants to create a barrier to the pest.

Milk Carton Barrier

To defeat really pesky cutworms and help vulnerable transplants, plant the transplants in half-gallon paper milk cartons. When you transplant them outside, merely cut out the bottom of the carton and plant the whole carton with its edge sticking out of the soil about an inch. Cutworms will be unable to get to the plants.

Paper Cup

Cut a hole in the bottom of the cup, then cut a radial slit and fit the cup upside down into the soil and around the plant stem. Make sure the rim of the cup is set 1 to 2 inches deep in the soil.

Paper Collar

Protect individual plants by putting a 3-inch collar made from stiff paper or plastic around them. Push the collar 1 to 2 inches into the ground.

Wood Ashes

Sprinkle two handfuls of wood ashes around the base of each plant when the transplants are put out, or encircle them with a 3- to 4-inch-wide trench, a few inches deep, filled with wood ashes. The pests will avoid crawling over them. Care should be taken not to let ashes touch the plants.

Resistant Varieties

Bean, Lima and Snap

The Fordhook and Baby White varieties of lima bean and the Gold Crop, Idaho Refugee, Regal, and Wade varieties of snap bean are all resistant to cutworms.

Animal Predators

Swallows and bats eat the adult moths. Blackbirds, bluejays, brown thrashers, meadowlarks, poultry fowl, robins, sparrows, and wrens, as well as moles, shrews, snakes, and toads, eat cutworms.

Insect Predators and Parasites Available Commercially

See the beginning of this chapter for more information on these beneficial insects.

Beneficial Nematode

Beneficial nematodes can be used to control cutworms. Apply nematodes to the ground around your seedlings or transplants using 50,000 around each plant.

Parasitic (Non-stinging) Wasp

Braconid and trichogramma wasps prey on cutworms.

Insect Predators Found in the Garden

Any of the caterpillar eaters prey upon cutworms. These include ground beetles, fireflies, soldier beetles, stinkbugs, and tachinid flies.

INSECT *European Corn Borer*

DESCRIPTION

The European corn borer is a grayish to pink caterpillar with a darker head and spots on each segment. White eggs are laid in groups on the undersides of foliage. The adult is a yellowish nocturnal moth with ½-inch wings that have dark bands. The corn borer chews leaves and tassels of corn and the foliage of other plants. It overwinters as larva in corn stubble. It is common throughout North America except in the far West and Southwest. Several generations occur in a year.

MOST OBVIOUS SYMPTOMS

The first symptom is "shotgun" holes in the funnel-like new growth of corn. Shortly thereafter, the borers move into the stalk or into the ears. A sawdust trail can be seen around the stalk. The plant gradually wilts. On potatoes, borers invade the stalks.

VULNERABLE PLANTS

Chard, corn, peppers, potatoes, and tomatoes.

BEST CONTROL STRATEGY

Corn borers are difficult to control and easier to prevent. The bacteria known as *Bacillus thuringiensis* (BT), especially the new granular form, are effective controls if used at proper times. Fall cleanup, crop rotation, and a healthy crowd of predators keep borers under control in the long run.

OPTIONS FOR CONTROLLING EUROPEAN CORN BORER

Emergence Time

After overwintering as caterpillars in old corn stalks, adult moths emerge in early summer. One or two more generations may follow.

Early Warning Devices

Trap Crop
Sunflowers can be planted as a trap crop.

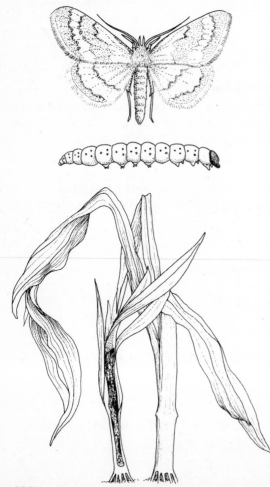

Biological Controls

Bacillus Thuringiensis (BT)

To use BT, bacteria that come in powder form, on borers, apply it immediately after the first eggs are laid. Repeat the application every 7 to 10 days until that egg-laying period has run its course. In corn, direct the first-generation sprayings at the whorl, and the second-generation sprayings at the leaf axils, the tassels, and the ear area. Granular BT formulations, such as Dipel G, have proved to be more effective against first-generation borer invasions than liquid or wettable powder mixes. The opposite is true for second-generation borer problems in sweet corn—the liquid is more effective than the granular version.

Traps and Mechanical Controls

Handpicking

If you see telltale holes and "sawdust" castings (excrement), slit the stalk just below the hole and pluck out the worm with tweezers.

Botanical Poisons

Neem

Neem sprays can help to control larvae feeding on leaves. Purchase a commercial neem product and mix it according to label instructions. Apply the spray to beetle-infested plants twice, at weekly or longer intervals, until pests are under control.

Pyrethrum

Spray plants with pyrethrum if you see larvae feeding on leaves. Usually two applications 3 or 4 days apart will control the problem.

STEPS TO PREVENT EUROPEAN CORN BORER

Fall Cleanup

The European corn borer overwinters as a caterpillar in the garden debris, especially in corn stalks, so destroy all plant debris by burning.

Barriers

Pantyhose Barrier

Old pantyhose can be used to cover corn ears. It dries off quickly after rain and doesn't hold heat.

Resistant Varieties

Corn

Apache, Bellringer, Burgundy Delight, Butter & Sugar, Calumet, Country Gentleman, Quicksilver, Stowell's Evergreen, Sweet Sue, and Tablevee show some resistance to borers.

Intercropping or Companions

Intercropping with peanut or soybean seems to reduce corn borer numbers, possibly by encouraging predators and making it harder for the borers to locate the corn plants.

Planting Date

The moths do most of their egg laying early in the season, so delay your corn planting if you expect problems. Borers in each multigeneration area follow a similar life cycle; between generations there is a gap of about 3 weeks when virtually no egg laying occurs. Refer to your records of the previous season's insect activity for the best planting date. You should plant so that your crop ripens during this midsummer gap.

Animal Predators

Barn swallows, blackbirds, downy woodpeckers, flycatchers, grackles, phoebes, and sparrows, as well as moles and toads, all eat corn borers.

Insect Predators and Parasites Available Commercially

See the beginning of this chapter for more information on these beneficial insects.

Beneficial Nematode

Beneficial nematodes are recommended for use against these borers.

Green Lacewing

These larvae eat borer eggs.

Lady Bug

Lady bugs are voracious eaters of corn borers.

Parasitic (Non-stinging) Wasp

Braconid wasps parasitize the eggs of corn borers.

Insect Predators Found in the Garden

Assassin bugs and tachinid flies help control the European corn borer.

Other Preventive Steps

If your soil pH isn't too alkaline, mix in wood ashes at planting time.

INSECT *Flea Beetle*

DESCRIPTION

Flea beetles are shiny, black beetles about the size of a pinhead. Some species have yellow or white markings. They are very active and jump like fleas when disturbed. Flea beetles chew tiny holes in the foliage. They transmit viral and bacterial diseases, including early blight, to potatoes, and bacterial wilt to corn. The larvae feed on roots of plants. Flea beetles are widespread throughout the United States.

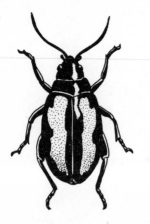

MOST OBVIOUS SYMPTOMS

Lots of tiny holes in the leaves are signs of flea beetles. These insects can destroy small plants rapidly with their feeding. The larvae attack the roots and weaken the plant.

VULNERABLE PLANTS

Beans (lima and snap), beets, broccoli, brussels sprouts, cabbage, cauliflower, chard, Chinese cabbage, collards, corn, eggplants, kohlrabi, muskmelons, peppers, potatoes, radishes, rutabagas, spinach, tomatoes, turnips, and watermelons.

BEST CONTROL STRATEGY

Use barriers, such as agricultural fleece, to prevent access to target plants in spring. Use pyrethrum for any infestations. Juvenile nematodes take care of the flea beetle larvae.

OPTIONS FOR CONTROLLING FLEA BEETLE

Emergence Time

Adults overwinter in the soil and in garden debris, emerging in early spring.

Early Warning Devices

Sticky Trap
White sticky traps provide early warning of flea beetle infestation.

Trap Crop
Bok Choy and other varieties of Chinese cabbage, as well as radishes, can be used as trap crops to spot early infestations of flea beetles. Locate them in or within 10 to 15 feet of the crop threatened by the beetles.

Natural Sprays

See the beginning of this chapter for more information on making natural sprays.

Garlic Spray
Chop or grind garlic, onions, or chives into fine particles, mix with water, then strain out the particles to form a clear solution. Spray infested plants, making sure the spray makes contact with the pest.

Hot Pepper Spray
Chop or grind hot peppers into fine particles, mix with water, then strain out the particles to form a clear solution. Spray the solution on the plants, making sure contact is made with the pest.

Traps and Mechanical Controls

Sticky Trap
White sticky traps, which are constructed and hung like yellow sticky traps, are effective controls for flea beetles. Do not leave traps out for more than 3 or 4 weeks, or they will trap beneficial as well as pest insects.

Botanical Poisons

Neem
Purchase a commercial neem product and mix it according to label instructions. Apply the spray to infested plants twice, at weekly or longer intervals, until pests are under control. Spray carefully to thoroughly cover all plant parts.

Pyrethrum
Pyrethrum must be applied directly to the beetles to work, so spray the undersides of the leaves as well as the tops. Usually two applications, made 3 or 4 days apart, will control the problem.

STEPS TO PREVENT FLEA BEETLE

Fall Cleanup

Flea beetles overwinter in the soil, in garden debris, on trees, or in nearby brush. In other words, they can be all over the place, so fall cleanup may not have a great effect on next year's flea beetle populations. The most important action is to get rid of weeds that are related to problem crops.

Barriers

Diatomaceous Earth (D.E.)
Dust D.E. around the base of the plant to create a barrier to the pest, or dust the whole plant with D.E. Dusting should progress upward from the ground, covering all stems and leaves, especially the undersides. Dust in the late evening or at night to minimize predator insect destruction. Other materials used by gardeners to repel flea beetles include lime and used coffee grounds. Spread them in a circle around each plant.

Netting or Fleece Cover
Cover vulnerable plants with netting, agricultural fleece, cheesecloth, or a similar cover as soon as the seedlings are placed in the garden. These materials prevent the flea beetles from getting to the plant. Later in the season, as the plants get larger and more difficult to keep entirely covered, simply lay the cover over the top of the plant to shade them a bit. The flea beetle dislikes shade, so the cover does two jobs—it cools the plant under the hot summer sun and creates an unpleasant environment for the flea beetle.

Resistant Varieties

Broccoli
Atlantic, Coastal, De Cicco, Gem, and Italian Green Sprouting.

Cabbage
Copenhagen Market 86, Early Jersey Wakefield, Ferry's Round Dutch, Mammoth Red Rock, Savoy Perfection Drumhead, and Stein's Early Flat Dutch.

Cauliflower
Early Snowball A and Early Snowball X.

Collard
Georgia, Georgia LS, and Vates.

Potato
Sequoia.

Radish
Champion and Sparkler.

Intercropping or Companions

Experiments with cole crops indicated that even the slight increase in plant variety produced, for example, by interplanting collards with tomatoes, seems to reduce the flea beetle population. One study indicated that a catnip border reduced cabbage flea beetles on collards.

Animal Predators

Chickadees, purple finches, titmice, vireos, and warblers, as well as toads, relish eating flea beetles or their pupae.

Insect Predators and Parasites Available Commercially

See the beginning of this chapter for more information on these beneficial insects.

Beneficial Nematode
Beneficial nematodes are recommended against flea beetles.

Insect Predators and Parasites Found in the Garden

Beneficial insects that prey on flea beetles include ground beetles and parasitic wasps.

Other Preventive Steps

Flea beetles like it hot and dry, so make the microclimate around the vulnerable plants somewhat cool and moist. Sprinkle the plants during the hottest part of the day. Space plants close together so that the leaves touch.

INSECT # Gypsy Moth

DESCRIPTION

Gypsy moth caterpillars grow from about 1/16 inch long at hatching to about 2½ inches long by the time they become pupae. In July, they encase themselves in brown shells to pupate. The adult male is a brown-colored moth; the female is white. Their wingspan measures about 1½ inches. Female moths cannot fly. Eggs are light brown or yellowish and are laid in hairy masses. They can survive temperatures down to −25°F. Gypsy moths are found in the eastern United States.

MOST OBVIOUS SYMPTOMS

Trees infested with gypsy moths become defoliated. You can see masses of caterpillars feeding. Damage will not be immediately noticeable, since the young larvae feed only around leaf edges. When larvae are about 1 inch long, large holes begin to appear in the leaves. A serious infestation can completely defoliate a tree.

VULNERABLE PLANTS

Apples, apricots, peaches, and pears.

BEST CONTROL STRATEGY

Spray trees with *Bacillus thuringiensis* (BT) every 10 to 14 days from late April to mid-June. In June,

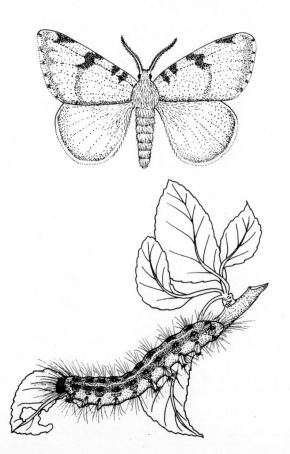

switch to trapping with the burlap skirts described on the next page.

OPTIONS FOR CONTROLLING GYPSY MOTH

Emergence Time

Eggs begin hatching by late April or early May. Not all the larvae emerge at the same time. The crucial control period is late April to early June, after the larvae reach ¾ inch long and have begun to eat leaves. Pupation occurs for 2 weeks in midsummer.

Early Warning Devices

Pheromone Trap

Adult gypsy moths can be monitored and caught with pheromone, or sex lure, traps. Pheromones attract the moths into traps and prevent them from mating. Use them to locate gypsy moths, estimate their numbers, and give you time to plan for controls. The trap usually contains a sticky substance that traps the moths on contact. Lures are placed in the yard in and around the garden 2 to 3 weeks before the expected emergence of the adult gypsy moths, usually sometime in July. Gypsy moth catches are highest when traps are placed near the tops of trees and oriented so the openings are facing the prevailing wind direction. These traps will not control the moths, but only alert you to their presence and give you an indication of the severity of the infestation.

Biological Controls

Bacillus Thuringiensis (BT)

BT, a form of bacteria, is a good control for leaf-eating caterpillars, including gypsy moths. Make a foliar spray from powdered BT according to instructions on the container, and apply it to affected trees at 10- to 14-day intervals until the caterpillars are about an inch long. At that point, the BT is no longer effective.

Traps and Mechanical Controls

Burlap Trap

When larvae are an inch long, they become night feeders and come down from the tree each morning. Wrap a piece of burlap a foot wide around the tree trunk, about chest high. Tie it at the center with heavy twine, letting the top fold over to form a skirt. Descending caterpillars will hide under the fold. In the late afternoon, put on garden gloves and sweep the caterpillars off into a container of detergent and water.

Sticky Trap

Sticky bands around tree trunks also stop the caterpillars. Wrap a 4-inch-wide piece of cotton batting around the trunk of the tree, about chest high. Over this, tie a 6- to 12-inch-wide piece of tar paper smeared with a sticky material like Tanglefoot. Replace the band whenever needed until mid-July, at which time you should remove it. The U.S. Department of Agriculture (USDA) cautions against applying any sticky substance, especially grease, tar, or other petroleum products, directly to the bark of trees; the practice can cause swelling and cankering. Furthermore, the underlayment of cotton keeps caterpillars from crawling under the band.

Botanical Poisons

Neem

Purchase a commercial neem product and mix it according to label instructions. Apply the spray to infested plants twice, at weekly or longer intervals, until pests are under control. Spray carefully to thoroughly cover all plant parts.

STEPS TO PREVENT GYPSY MOTH

Fall and Winter Cleanup

Carefully check lawn furniture for egg masses before putting it away in fall. During the winter, check stone walls, woodpiles, fences, garages, and outbuildings. All of these objects serve as homes for the gypsy moth's egg clusters. Debris on the ground can serve as protection for egg masses, larvae, and pupae. Egg masses can be destroyed by scraping them into a can of soapy water, or by burning them. Simply knocking the eggs to the ground does not kill the eggs.

Barriers

Tree Barrier

Just wrapping cotton batting around tree trunks can stop some gypsy moths from climbing the tree to do their damage.

Animal Predators

The more birds living and breeding in and around your garden, the fewer gypsy moth problems you'll have. Gypsy moths are part of the diet of 45 species of birds, including blue jays, chipping sparrows, crows, cuckoos, grackles, robins, starlings, towhees, and vireos. Chickadees, nuthatches, and titmice work on the egg cases attached to the bark of trees over winter. Chipmunks, moles, shrews, squirrels, voles, white-footed mice, and other rodents eat gypsy moth caterpillars.

Insect Predators and Parasites Available Commercially

See the beginning of this chapter for more information on these beneficial insects.

Beneficial Nematode

Beneficial nematodes are tiny soil-dwelling worms that find their way to the gypsy moth caterpillar, burrow inside it, and reproduce. The caterpillars are killed by bacteria released by the nematodes.

Parasitic (Non-stinging) Wasp

Chalcid and trichogramma wasps parasitize the eggs of gypsy moths.

Insect Predators and Parasites Found in the Garden

Among the important beneficial insects that prey upon gypsy moths are assassin bugs, ground beetles, two species of flies, soldier beetles, tachinid flies, and several types of wasps. Grow sweet white clover and most flowering plants of the carrot family, such as celery, dill, and Queen Anne's lace, to attract them.

Other Preventive Steps

Maintain good growing conditions for trees. The healthier the tree, the better its chances of surviving defoliation. Keep soil conditions favorable for the tree's roots; fertilize, water, and prune regularly. Don't use lime or weed killers around the base of the trees, as they can damage shallow root systems, and never use de-icing salts nearby. Grasses tend to be heavy competitors for water, so replace them with a less thirsty ground cover or simply mulch with leaves or other material. Avoid compacting the soil around the base of trees with heavy equipment or paths. Diversify plant species. Replace dead or dying trees with ones that are less favored by gypsy moths, such as ash, the conifers, hickory, honey locust, maple, and tulip poplar. Consult your local nurseryman and County Extension agents on trees most compatible with your climate and soil.

NOTES AND RESEARCH

An extract from the neem tree, a large East Indian tree, marketed as Margosan, has just been registered for control of gypsy moths. Also, a fungus may be the final end for the gypsy moth's march across North America. *Entomophaga aulicae*, a fungus strain imported from Japan, has been shown to kill moths at a rate of 90 percent.

INSECT *Harlequin Bug*

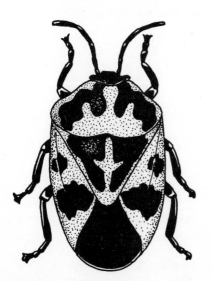

DESCRIPTION

Harlequin bugs are ¼ inch long and patterned in shiny black and red. They are shield-shaped insects with large triangles on their backs. They give off a foul odor. Harlequin bugs suck leaves, causing them to wilt and die; white blotches may appear. Females lay rows of black-ringed eggs on the undersides of leaves. This insect is found mostly in the southern states. It may produce many generations, even breeding throughout the year, in the warmest regions.

MOST OBVIOUS SYMPTOMS

Wilting of plants is seen, especially on young seedlings, and yellowish or black spots develop on leaves.

VULNERABLE PLANTS

Broccoli, brussels sprouts, cabbage, cauliflower, Chinese cabbage, collards, eggplants, kohlrabi, radishs, rutabagas, and turnips.

BEST CONTROL STRATEGY

Use a preventive insecticidal soap spray in early spring; then use insecticidal soap laced with isopropyl alcohol if pests get out of hand.

OPTIONS FOR CONTROLLING HARLEQUIN BUG

Emergence Time

Adults overwinter under garden debris and in weeds in waste areas. They emerge as soon as the weather begins to warm in the spring. They begin laying eggs at about the time the earliest garden plants are set out. Females can lay up to 500 eggs each. The eggs hatch in about a week, and nymphs develop into adults in about 5 weeks. There are usually two or more generations per year.

Early Warning Devices

Trap Crop

Plant trap crops of turnips or mustard greens about 10 to 15 feet from the main crop.

Natural Sprays

See the beginning of this chapter for more information on making natural sprays.

Insecticidal Soap

Commercial insecticidal soap effectively controls harlequin bugs. For bad infestations, spray every 2 or 3 days for 2 weeks. Soap sprays are contact insecticides, so spray the plant top to bottom, espe-cially under the leaves, where you'll find most pest insects.

Insecticidal soap sprays can be even more effective if isopropyl alcohol is added. The alcohol helps the soap penetrate the insect's outer skin. Add about ½ cup of alcohol to each quart of insecticidal soap mixture.

Traps and Mechanical Controls

Handpicking

Handpicking makes a sizable dent in the harlequin bug infestation right away. Try to get rid of the very first adults and their eggs as they appear. Crush egg masses on the undersides of leaves or shake plants over a tray of soapy water.

Botanical Poisons

Pyrethrum

Pyrethrum paralyzes harlequin bugs on contact. It must be applied directly to the bugs to work, so spray the undersides of leaves as well as the tops. Usually two applications, made 3 or 4 days apart, will control the problem. Pyrethrum sprays tend to work best in cool weather, when temperatures are below 80°F. Also remember that pyrethrum sprays also harm beneficial insects, so use them as a last resort when milder measures, such as handpicking or soap sprays, aren't effective.

STEPS TO PREVENT HARLEQUIN BUG

Fall Cleanup

In fall, as soon as you finish harvesting each crop, remove all old plants and overgrown weeds in which bugs might hibernate. Leave the soil completely bare. Then cultivate the top 6 to 8 inches, using a hand tool or a rotary tiller. Leave the soil bare to allow birds to work on any bugs they find. About 2 to 3 weeks after that deep cultivation, give the garden a shallow cultivation to a depth of about 2 inches, using a rotary tiller or garden rake. Wait another few days before planting your winter cover crop or laying down 4 to 6 inches of winter mulch.

Resistant Varieties

Broccoli
Atlantic, Coastal, Gem, and Grande.

Cabbage
Copenhagen Market 86, Early Jersey Wakefield, Headstart, Savoy Perfection Drumhead, and Stein's Early Flat Dutch. (Michihli Chinese cabbage is quite susceptible to the harlequin bug.)

Cauliflower
Early Snowball X or Snowball Y.

Collard
Green Glaze, Morris Improved Heady, and Vates.

Kale
Vates (Dwarf Siberian is susceptible).

Radish
Champion, Cherry Belle, Globemaster, Red Devil, and White Icicle.

Animal Predators

English sparrows and mockingbirds, as well as turtles, are important predators to encourage in your garden.

INSECT *Imported Cabbage Worm*

DESCRIPTION

Also known as the cabbage worm and the European cabbage worm, this pest is a 1¼-inch light green caterpillar with one yellow stripe. It chews foliage, and produces soft green excrement. Its bullet-shaped whitish yellow eggs are laid singly on leaves. The adult is a white, day-flying butterfly with three to four black spots on its wings. Several generations occur each year. Imported cabbage worms are found throughout the United States.

MOST OBVIOUS SYMPTOMS

Ragged holes in the leaves and bits of green excrement are signs of imported cabbage worms. The female butterfly zips about from plant to plant, depositing her eggs at the base of the leaves. In about a week, tiny green caterpillars hatch and begin to chomp the leaves. Larvae eventually bore their way into the main head of the vegetable, turning it into mush.

VULNERABLE PLANTS

Broccoli, brussels sprouts, cabbage, cauliflower, Chinese cabbage, collards, kale, kohlrabi, radishes, rutabagas, and turnips.

BEST CONTROL STRATEGY

Use an agricultural fleece or net barrier and a preventive *Bacillus thuringiensis* (BT) spray early in the season; then use more BT for later infestations.

OPTIONS FOR CONTROLLING IMPORTED CABBAGE WORM

Emergence Time

Imported cabbage worms overwinter in the ground on or near the plant as larvae or pupae, and emerge in late spring.

Biological Controls

Bacillus Thuringiensis (BT)

BT are bacteria that kill only leaf-eating caterpillars, including imported cabbage worms. Dust all parts of the leaves, especially the undersides, and dust again after rains, or make a BT foliar spray and apply it to infested plants every 10 to 14 days until the pest is removed.

Traps and Mechanical Controls

Dusting Plants

Sprinkle damp leaves with rye flour. Cabbage worms that eat this coating will bloat and die.

Handpicking

Handpicking in the early morning makes a sizable dent in the worm infestation right away.

STEPS TO PREVENT IMPORTED CABBAGE WORM

Fall Cleanup

Imported cabbage worms overwinter as larvae or pupae in the soil or on garden litter. In the fall, as soon as you finish harvesting each crop, remove all old plants and overgrown weeds, leaving a completely bare soil. Then cultivate the soil thoroughly to a depth of 6 to 8 inches, using a hand tool or a rotary tiller. Either actively compost those old plants or destroy them. Too cold a compost pile will simply serve as the pest's winter quarters.

Preventive Spray Programs

Bacillus Thuringiensis (BT)

Dust or spray with BT early in spring, every 2 weeks from transplanting until heads form.

Combination Preventive Spray

An effective preventive spray program for imported cabbage worms includes a combination of natural sprays that work together to prevent the imported cabbage worm from establishing itself in the garden for very long. Make a spray with *Bacillus thuringiensis* (BT), insecticidal soap, and kelp extract. Use this spray three times at 2-week intervals. First, spray the whole garden a week after your first transplants are set out. Repeat 2 weeks later and then again 2 weeks after that. That routine puts you about a month into the normal growing season, when beneficials are starting to emerge and you will want to avoid hurting them with any unnecessary generalized spraying.

Barriers

Netting or Fleece Cover
You can make barriers from a material that allows sun, air, and rain to get through but prevents the adult, white butterfly from getting access to your plants. Nylon netting, fine screening, or agricultural fleece are all effective barriers, preventing the butterfly from laying eggs at the plant's stem. Cover transplants or a newly seeded area with the preferred material immediately so the moth can never get to plants and lay eggs on them. Drape the barrier material directly over the plants and seal all the edges to the ground. Provide lots of extra material so when the plants grow larger they don't strain against the covering.

Pantyhose Cover
Use the stocking part of pantyhose or a regular nylon stocking to cover cabbage heads as soon as they start to form. The nylon stretches as the cabbage grows, allowing air, sun, and moisture in but keeping the cabbage butterfly out.

Resistant Varieties

Cabbage
Mammoth Red Rock, Savoy, and Savoy Chieftain.

Intercropping or Companions

In experiments done with cabbage, all interplants or companions tested seemed to attract more moths of the imported cabbage worm into the plots for egg laying than if no interplants had been used. Catnip and tansy were most attractive. These companion plantings also increased imported cabbage worm on broccoli. Nasturtiums demonstrated no effect on imported cabbage worms on collards, although gardeners often recommend them. Other research is now in progress, but it appears that many of the customary companion plantings designed to reduce imported cabbage worm have no scientific basis.

Animal Predators

Bluebirds, chickadees, and English sparrows.

Insect Predators and Parasites Available Commercially

See the beginning of this chapter for more information on these beneficial insects.

Parasitic (Non-stinging) Wasp
Braconid and trichogramma wasps parasitize the eggs of imported cabbage worms.

Insect Predators and Parasites Found in the Garden

Lacewings, lady bugs, ground beetles, parasitic wasps, and yellow jackets all prey upon imported cabbage worms. The butterfly milkweed *(Asclepias tuberosa)* hosts a parasite of cabbage worms, but a substance in the plant's leaves may harm some garden crops.

Other Preventive Steps

Put cornmeal around cabbage family plants and you may not need an insecticide. The imported cabbage worm eats the cornmeal, becomes bloated, and dies.

NOTES AND RESEARCH

If you find cabbage worms that have turned chalky white and appear nearly dead they have probably been infected with nuclear polyhedrosis virus (NPV). You can make your own form of viral insecticide by turning a dozen or more infected cabbage worms into bug juice. (See the beginning of this chapter for more information on homemade bug juice.) NPV is slower-acting but longer-lasting than *Bacillus thuringiensis* (BT). It takes 3 to 4 days to kill the cabbage worm, but a single application of this bug juice may last the whole season. A commercial version of NPV is being researched and is expected on the market in the next year or two.

INSECT *Japanese Beetle*

DESCRIPTION

The adult Japanese beetle is about ½ inch long. It is shiny metallic green, with copper-brown wings. The grub is grayish white with a dark brown head and two rows of spines that form a V on the underside of the last abdominal segment. The eggs are white and spherical, and are laid in the soil. The adult eats foliage and fruit, flying only in daytime. The beetles can fly a distance of up to 5 miles. Larvae feed on grass roots. Japanese beetles have a 1 or 2-year life cycle with larvae overwintering in soil. They are found primarily in the eastern half of the United States, but are moving westward.

MOST OBVIOUS SYMPTOMS

Leaf tissue between the veins is chewed away, leaving foliage and flowers of infested plants skeletonized. The grub chews on plant roots, especially those of lawn grasses.

VULNERABLE PLANTS

Adults feed on asparagus, beans (lima and snap), okra, peaches, raspberries, rhubarb, and leaves and silks of sweet corn. The larvae will chew on onions and potatoes, and on the roots of beans, sweet corn, and tomatoes.

BEST CONTROL STRATEGY

Set up pheromone beetle traps a week before expected emergence in your area, making sure traps are no closer than 50 feet from vulnerable crops. Handpick stragglers, or use pyrethrum if traps cannot handle the infestation. Juvenile stage nematodes are effective against the larvae. (See the beginning of this chapter for more information on beneficial nematodes.)

OPTIONS FOR CONTROLLING JAPANESE BEETLE

Emergence Time

Females lay eggs in early August. Upon hatching, the larvae burrow through the soil, feeding on decaying vegetation initially, then progressing to grass and other lawn roots. They stay underground all winter. They pupate in spring and early summer, and adult beetles emerge in June or early July.

Early Warning Devices

Trap Crop
Borage is a common trap crop. White geraniums, grape vines, and zinnias, especially white or light-colored ones, can be used as trap crops to spot early infestations of Japanese beetles. Japanese beetles also love to feed on the evening primrose (*Oenothera*), which grows as a weed everywhere. Locate trap crops within 10 to 15 feet of the plants threatened by the beetles.

Other Early Warning Devices

Japanese beetles can be monitored and trapped with a commercially available pheromone bag trap. The bait gives off an odor that attracts the beetles, which then fall into the bag. Do not locate these traps closer than 50 feet to the vulnerable crops, as not all of the beetles attracted to the devices are caught. The traps can also be used to control a beetle infestation (see below).

Biological Controls

Milky Spore Disease

Milky spore (*Bacillus popilliae*) infects larvae and kills them within several years. Apply the granular form with a regular fertilizer spreader to mowed areas of the yard. It infects grubs anytime they start to feed, when they hatch, or in the fall before they burrow deeper into the soil to overwinter. The milky spore bacillus remains in the soil, where it will infect the next crop of beetle grubs. Its limitations are that it takes 3 to 5 years to have a major impact on a beetle population, and it is relatively expensive.

Traps and Mechanical Controls

Pheromone Trap

Another control for the Japanese beetle is the commercially available pheromone trap with dual lures (food and sex attractant). Lures are attached to a slick plastic bag that the beetles cannot climb out of. These traps work best when used throughout a wide area, such as a whole neighborhood. Never place the traps any closer than 50 feet to a vulnerable crop, since some beetles do miss the trap bag. Hang the traps about 5 feet off the ground. Set them up a week or so prior to the emergence of adults in late spring or early summer. Note the date you first see the beetles one year and relate it to the flowering of some perennial on your property. The beetles will come around again next year within a day or two of that plant's flowering.

Handpicking

Handpicking makes a sizable dent in the Japanese beetle infestation right away. It is best to attend to the very first adults that appear, to set back their egg laying activities. Do it in the morning when the dew is still on their wings and they are less likely to fly. You can shake groups onto tarps laid on the ground around the plant or actually pick each beetle and drop it into a can of kerosene or detergent and water.

Botanical Poisons

Neem

Purchase a commercial neem product and mix it according to label instructions. Apply the spray to infested plants twice, at weekly or longer intervals, until pests are under control. Spray carefully to thoroughly cover all plant parts.

Pyrethrum

Pyrethrum paralyzes Japanese beetles on contact. It must be applied directly to the beetles to work, so spray the undersides of the leaves as well as the tops. Its effectiveness can be increased by adding some isopropyl alcohol to the spray; it helps the pyrethrum penetrate the Japanese beetle shell. Usually two applications, 3 to 4 days apart, will control the problem.

STEPS TO PREVENT JAPANESE BEETLE

Barriers

Diatomaceous Earth (D.E.)

Dust the whole plant with D.E. Dusting should progress upward from the ground, covering all stems and leaves, especially the undersides. Dust in the late evening or at night to minimize destruction of predator insects.

Animal Predators

Starlings are the only birds willing to eat adult beetles. Robins, starlings, and other grub eaters will work on the larvae in the spring.

Insect Predators and Parasites Available Commercially

See the beginning of this chapter for more information on these beneficial insects.

Beneficial Nematode

If grubs are a particular problem in your garden, you should consider making one application of beneficial nematodes (available commercially), which attack the grub population below the surface of the soil. Beneficial nematodes are tiny soil-dwelling worms that find their way to the Japanese beetle grubs, burrow inside them and reproduce. The beetle grubs are killed by bacteria released by the nematodes.

Insect Predators and Parasites Found in the Garden

Assassin bugs as well as two parasites, spring and fall tiphia wasps, attack larvae.

Other Preventive Steps

Fallen fruit left rotting on the ground is an invitation to all nearby beetles, so keep it picked up.

NOTES AND RESEARCH

Neem is an effective repellent against this beetle, but hasn't been approved for food crops yet.

INSECT # *Leafhopper*

DESCRIPTION

Leafhoppers may be green, brown, or yellow, and often have colorful markings. They are ¼ to ⅓ inch long. Their wedge-shaped wings are held in a rooflike position over their bodies. Leafhoppers are very active and move sideways. Eggs are laid on the undersides of vegetable leaves and nearby perennial weeds. Many species can be found all over the United States.

The beet leafhopper is pale green or yellow, about ⅛ inch long, with slender, long hind legs that enable it to jump quickly into the air. When flying, it looks like a tiny white fly. It winters as an adult in hedgerows.

MOST OBVIOUS SYMPTOMS

Nymphs and adults suck juices from plant leaves, buds, and stems. They pierce tissue on the undersides of the leaves, sucking sap and removing chlorophyll from the cells. Plants weaken. Leafhoppers may spread viral diseases. The foliage may be covered with white or yellow mottling and may drop. The large amounts of honeydew excreted by leafhoppers gives plants a glazed appearance. Black sooty mold may grow on this honeydew.

The beet leafhopper carries a tomato virus from infected weeds or other vegetables. There are no controls for the disease once a plant has become infected. Tomato plants infected by the virus have a pronounced upward rolling of fully developed leaves. The leaves then become yellowish with purple veins, and foliage gets stiff and brittle. Soon the plants die.

The potato leafhopper slows down production. When they feed, they secrete substances that decrease the plant's photosynthesis. Just one leafhopper for every three potato leaves occurring after blooming can reduce potato yields by as much as 42 percent.

VULNERABLE PLANTS

Beans (lima and snap), beets, carrots, celery, chard, citrus, eggplants, lettuce, potatoes, raspberries, rhubarb, spinach, squash (summer and winter), tomatoes, and most fruit trees.

BEST CONTROL STRATEGY

Use an agricultural fleece barrier over early spring crops, and apply a preventive spray of insecticidal soap and seaweed extract to vulnerable crops during the first month of growth. Later, use insecticidal soap laced with isopropyl alcohol to control any serious infestations.

OPTIONS FOR CONTROLLING LEAFHOPPER

Early Warning Devices

Trap Crop
A trap crop of early corn, planted nearby, may help you keep an eye on some leafhoppers.

Natural Sprays

See the beginning of this chapter for more information on making natural sprays.

Insecticidal Soap
Commercial insecticidal soap effectively controls leafhoppers. Spray every 2 to 3 days for 2 weeks for bad infestations. Soap sprays are contact insecticides, so spray the plant top to bottom, especially under the leaves, where you'll find most pest insects. The soap's effectiveness with leafhoppers is greatly improved if you add 1 tablespoon of isopropyl alcohol to 1 quart of the mixture. It helps the soap penetrate the bug's outer shell.

Botanical Poisons

Neem
Neem sprays can help to control leafhopper nymphs. Purchase a commercial neem product and mix it according to label instructions. Apply the spray to

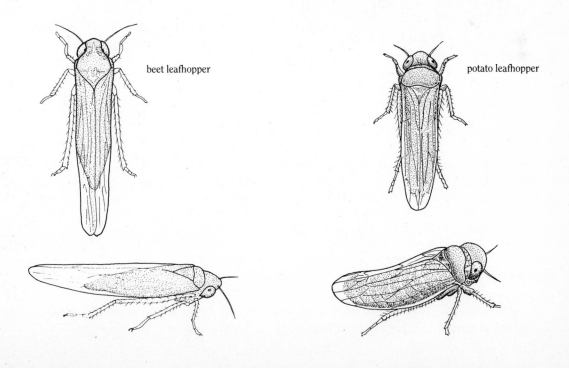

beet leafhopper

potato leafhopper

infested plants twice, at weekly or longer intervals, until pests are under control. Spray carefully to thoroughly cover all plant parts. The spray will be most effective if you apply it in early morning or late afternoon. Neem is generally fairly harmless to beneficials, but it may have an effect with repeated use. Save it for use against serious infestations.

Pyrethrum

Pyrethrum paralyzes leafhoppers on contact. It must be applied directly to the leafhopper to work, so spray the undersides of leaves as well as the tops. Usually two applications, 3 to 4 days apart, will control the problem.

STEPS TO PREVENT LEAFHOPPER

Fall Cleanup

Adults like to hibernate in weeds, but dislike perennial grasses. By keeping the winter garden clean, using cover crops, and having turf around your vegetable beds, you discourage this pest.

Preventive Spray Programs

Combination Preventive Spray

An effective preventive spray program for leafhoppers includes a combination of natural sprays that work together to prevent the leafhoppers from appearing in the garden for very long. Make a spray with *Bacillus thuringiensis* (BT), insecticidal soap, and seaweed extract. Use this spray three times at 2-week intervals. Apply over the whole garden, a week after the first transplants are set out, again 2 weeks later, and then again 2 weeks after that. That routine puts you about a month into the normal growing season, when beneficials are starting to emerge, and you will want to avoid hurting them with any unnecessary generalized spraying.

Barriers

Diatomaceous Earth (D.E.)

Dust the whole plant with D.E. Start from the ground and move upward to cover all stems and leaves, especially the undersides. Dust in the late evening or at night to minimize destruction of beneficial insects.

Netting or Fleece Cover

You can make barriers from a material that allows the sun, air, and rain to get through, but prevents the leafhopper from getting to your plants. Nylon netting, fine screening, or agricultural fleece are all effective barriers, preventing leafhoppers from laying eggs at the plant's stem. Use floating covers that rest directly on plants, or tunnels supported by braces. Set up the barrier immediately after planting to prevent any leafhoppers from infecting the crop. Seal all the edges to the ground.

Repellent Mulch

Aluminum foil and aluminum polyethylene mulches reduce the number of leafhoppers coming into the garden. The reflections from the aluminum confuse the leafhopper's system for identifying its target plants.

Resistant Varieties

Bean, Lima

Fordhook. In the West, Great Northern, Red Mexican, and University of Idaho beans resist leafhoppers.

Potato

Delus, Plymouth Pungus, Sebago, and Sequoia. Remember, Sequoia is susceptible to aphids.

Intercropping or Companions

The Extension Service at the University of Colorado recommends that gardeners not plant beets or spinach near their tomatoes. The beet leafhopper carries with it a viral disease that, when spread to tomatoes, may kill the plants.

Nearby blackberry bushes help control grape leafhopper, since they provide alternate winter hosts for *Anagrus epos,* a parasite of grape leafhopper.

Animal Predators

Chickadees, purple finches, sparrows, swallows, titmice, and wrens eat leafhoppers.

Insect Predators and Parasites Available Commercially

See the beginning of this chapter for more information on these beneficial insects.

Green Lacewing

Lacewings will attack leafhoppers, and if you can keep them in your garden, they may be worth purchasing.

Parasitic (Non-stinging) Wasp

Braconid, ichneumonid, and trichogramma wasps attack leafhoppers.

Insect Predators and Parasites Found in the Garden

Assassin bugs, bigeyed bugs, damselflies, and syrphid flies are important predators. Parasitic wasps, which occur naturally, are also valuable in controlling these pests.

Other Preventive Steps

Weed control is effective in reducing egg-laying sites. Get rid of thistles, plantains, and dandelions especially.

NOTES AND RESEARCH

Organic apple orchards cover-cropped with rye, vetch, and clover were compared with cultivated orchards for insect populations and fruit damage. Researchers found fewer leafhoppers, as well as fewer codling moths and aphids, among cover-cropped orchards due to greater numbers of natural predators inhabiting the ground cover.

INSECT *Leafminer*

DESCRIPTION

Adult leafminers are minute black flies, about 1/10 inch long, usually with yellow stripes. They lay eggs on the undersides of leaves. Yellowish larvae hatch and tunnel inside the leaves and feed between the upper and lower surfaces, causing white to brown tunnels or blotches. There can be stem damage below the soil. Leafminers carry black leg and soft rot diseases. Several generations develop each summer. Winters are passed in a cocoon in the soil. Many species occur throughout North America.

MOST OBVIOUS SYMPTOMS

White to brown tunnels or blotches appear on the leaves of plants infested with leafminers. The leaves can turn yellow and blotched and look blistered or curled.

VULNERABLE PLANTS

Beans (lima and snap), beets, cabbage, chard, lettuce, peppers, radishes, spinach, and turnips.

BEST CONTROL STRATEGY

Screening out the fly is the best technique to control it. Use a barrier such as agricultural fleece. If flies get to the plants, try to remove and destroy infested leaves before the larvae mature.

OPTIONS FOR CONTROLLING LEAFMINER

Emergence Time

Leafminers emerge from the soil in early spring. Egg laying continues throughout the summer as new generations mature.

Early Warning Devices

Trap Crop

Radishes or the weed lamb's-quarters can be used as a trap crop to spot early infestations of leafminers. Locate them within 10 to 15 feet of the crop threatened by the miners and be sure to remove and destroy them as soon as the larvae start work-

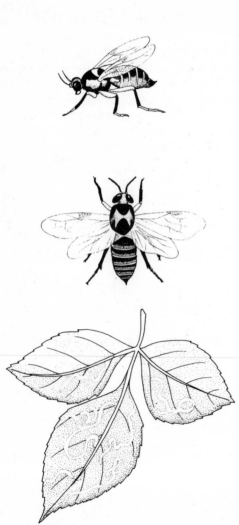

ing on the trap crop. If you don't want a trap crop, make sure lamb's-quarters are kept out of the garden.

Natural Sprays

Light Horticultural Oil Spray

The newer horticultural oils, called "superior horticultural spray oil," are lighter and less viscous (viscosity 60 to 70) than traditional oils, and evaporate much more quickly from leaves and stems. They can be used during the growing season to control leafminers. Use a spray made up of about a 2 to 3 percent solution, and make sure contact is made with the pest, because the oil works by suffocating it.

Traps and Mechanical Controls

Handpicking

Handpick the eggs. Leafminer eggs are dry and unbreakable. Learn to spot them on the undersides of the leaves. Turn the leaves over and look for the eggs, which are chalky white and $1/16$ to $1/8$ inch long. Three, four, or even five of them will be lined up next to each other. Not all leaves will be affected. Scratch off the cluster with your fingernail. Flies continue to lay eggs; repeat this process once a week for 3 or 4 weeks. If the eggs have already hatched, the upper surface of the leaves will have grayish blisters. Cut off the blisters. Cut the damaged part out of the leaves; it's not necessary to cut off the entire leaf. The plants will survive and grow quickly if you leave as much healthy tissue as possible. Destroy all the damaged leaf parts that you cut from the plant.

STEPS TO PREVENT LEAFMINER

Fall Cleanup

Leafminers overwinter in the soil and emerge in early spring; consequently, a thorough fall cleanup helps control them. Remove weeds, especially lamb's-quarters, unless you want to use this weed as a trap crop.

Barriers

Netting or Fleece Cover

The best way to prevent leafminers is with screening. Make a barrier from a material that allows sun, air, and rain to get through but prevents the leafminer from getting to your plants. Nylon netting, fine screening, or agricultural fleece are all effective barriers, preventing leafminers from laying eggs at the plant's stem. Cover transplants or newly seeded areas with the preferred material immediately to prevent both insect damage and insect egg laying, which can lead to later damage. Lay the barrier material directly on the plants and seal all the edges to the ground. Provide lots of extra material so that when the plants grow larger they don't strain against the covering.

Planting Time

Plant early or grow only a fall crop. Beets and chard planted after mid-June don't have much of a problem.

Spinach sown in late August is never bothered. The easiest way to avoid this insect is to plant these vegetables late.

Animal Predators

Chickadees, purple finches, and robins are some common songbirds that eat leafminers.

NOTES AND RESEARCH

Neem tree seed solutions repel adult leafminers and kill eggs and larvae on lima bean and chrysanthemum leaves, according to U.S. Department of Agriculture (USDA) researchers at Beltsville, Maryland. The extract achieved up to 100 percent mortality of miner eggs and larvae, even at solutions as low as 0.05 percent. One neem product is already available for use on gypsy moths, and new products for use on food crops may be approved in the next few years.

INSECT *Mexican Bean Beetle*

DESCRIPTION

The adult is about ¼ inch long. It is a yellow- to copper-colored round beetle with 16 black dots in three rows down its back. It looks something like a lady bug. The yellow eggs are laid in clusters on the leaves. The orange or yellow, hump-backed, fuzzy larvae are about ⅓ inch long. Both adults and larvae chew holes in leaves. Winters are passed as an adult. Mexican bean beetles are found throughout the United States, especially in the East and portions of the Southwest. Four generations a year may occur in warmer regions.

MOST OBVIOUS SYMPTOMS

Adults and larvae feed on the lower surfaces of

foliage, skeletonizing the leaves. When in high numbers, they also feed on bean pods and stems.

VULNERABLE PLANTS

Beans (lima and snap), and squash (summer and winter).

BEST CONTROL STRATEGY

Handpick early arrivals with special attention to the easy-to-spot bright yellow eggs laid in groups of 40 to 60 on the undersides of bean leaves. If the infestation gets out of control, use pyrethrum.

OPTIONS FOR CONTROLLING MEXICAN BEAN BEETLE

Crop Cleanup

To significantly reduce your garden's Mexican bean beetle populations over a 2- to 3-year period, use fall cleanup. Immediately pull up infested plants as soon as they finish bearing and stuff the vines into a plastic bag (preferably a big clear one, if you can find such a bag). It is important that you don't wait till the very last bean has been picked. Pull those plants when the main harvest is over and the plants still have a population of the pest beetles. After tying the bag, leave it in the sun for a week or so. Nothing will survive that treatment, and you will have disposed of the major source of next year's beetle population. Repeat the cleanup for every crop vulnerable to bean beetle attack.

Emergence Time

Adults emerge from neighboring plants in late spring or early summer, when temperatures are between 58°F and 69°F.

Early Warning Devices

Trap Crop
Burpee's Improved bush lima plants are good trap crops, since beetles are particularly attracted to this variety.

Traps and Mechanical Controls

Handpicking
Check leaves frequently and pick off beetles, larvae, and the yellow egg clusters first. Handpicking means actually plucking the beetles from the vegetables and killing them between your fingers or by dropping them into a can half full of kerosene or soapy water.

Botanical Poisons

Pyrethrum
Pyrethrum paralyzes Mexican bean beetles on contact. It must be applied directly to the beetles to work, so spray the undersides of the leaves as well as the tops. Usually two applications, 3 to 4 days apart, will control the problem.

Neem
Neem sprays can help to control Mexican bean beetles. Purchase a commercial neem product and mix it according to label instructions. Apply the spray to infested plants twice, at weekly or longer intervals, until pests are under control.

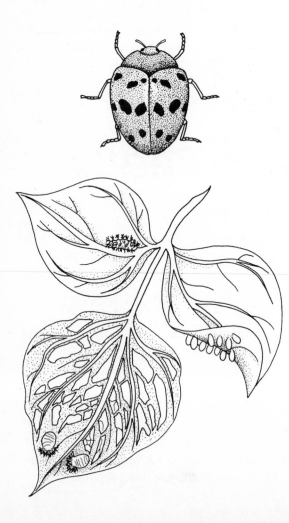

STEPS TO PREVENT MEXICAN BEAN BEETLE

Fall Cleanup

Fall garden cleanup is important for preventing Mexican bean beetles. In fall, as soon as you finish the harvest for each crop, remove all old plants and overgrown weeds, leaving bare soil for a few weeks to give the birds a chance to clean up any beetles they might find looking for winter quarters; then you can plant your cover crop or lay a 4- to 6-inch layer of winter mulch.

Barriers

Diatomaceous Earth (D.E.)

Dust D.E. around the base of each plant to create a barrier to the pest, or dust the whole plant with D.E. Dusting should progress upward from the ground, covering all stems and leaves, especially the undersides. Apply D.E. in the late evening or at night, and predator insect destruction will be low.

Netting or Fleece Cover

You can make barriers from a material that allows sun, air, and rain to get through but prevents the Mexican bean beetle from getting to your plants. Fine nylon netting, fine screening, or agricultural fleece are all effective barriers, preventing Mexican bean beetles from laying eggs on the plant's leaves. Cover transplants or newly seeded areas with the preferred material immediately to prevent both insect damage and insect egg laying, which can lead to later damage. Lay the barrier material directly on the plants, and seal all the edges to the ground. Provide lots of extra material so when the plants grow larger they don't strain against the covering.

Reflective Mulch Barrier

Aluminum foil and aluminum polyethylene mulches reduce the number of Mexican bean beetles coming into your garden. These mulches work because they reflect the sky, and beetles looking for the right color green, which would signal a green bean plant, will instead see the blue of the sky and fly on into your neighbor's garden. This technique does not work as well in beds that are intensively planted and have little soil showing. In a row garden with wide paths it can be effective in the early part of the season.

Resistant Varieties

Bean, Snap

Black Valentine, Idaho Refugee, Logan, Supergreen, and Wade. (Varieties particularly susceptible include Bountiful, Burpee Improved, Dwarf Horticultural, and State.)

Intercropping or Companions

French marigolds rid the soil of nematodes and may repel Mexican bean beetles, but seem to have an allelopathic effect that stunts beans.

Planting Time

Beetles tend to be more active in midsummer, so plant your biggest crop early in the season or much later. In general, earlier crops are less troubled than later crops.

Animal Predators

Many songbirds eat Mexican bean beetles, as do toads.

Insect Predators and Parasites Available Commercially

See the beginning of this chapter for more information on these beneficial insects.

Lady Bug

Lady bugs are voracious eaters of Mexican bean beetles. Be sure you have very large pest populations that can support the lady bugs before you order and release these beneficials.

Predatory Mite

Predatory mites are very effective against bean beetles.

Predatory Wasp

A small predatory wasp, *Pediobus foveolatus*, is best against Mexican bean beetles. The wasp is not native to the United States and can't live through the winter in most areas, so you need to release them each season. The primary purpose of *P. foveolatus* is to reduce overwintering beetles, not to reduce immediate damage to crops.

Insect Predators and Parasites Found in the Garden

Anchor bugs, assassin bugs, bigeyed bugs, centipedes, pirate bugs, spiders, spined soldier beetles, tachinid flies, and wasps prey upon Mexican bean beetles. Sweet white clover, most flowering plants of the carrot family (celery, coriander, dill, ginseng, parsnips, and Queen Anne's lace), stinging nettle, and a generally diverse range of wild plants attract these beneficials.

NOTES AND RESEARCH

Scientists at the U.S. Department of Agriculture's (USDA) Agricultural Research Center in Beltsville, Maryland, are using pheromones to lure beneficials to feed on Mexican bean beetles and other pests.

Dr. Jerry McLaughlin, professor of pharmacognosy at Purdue University, is patenting a new insecticide derived from the pawpaw tree. He says the new broad-spectrum botanical, especially effective against nematodes, Mexican bean beetles, and mosquito larvae, is environmentally safe and comparable to pyrethrum in action and toxicity.

INSECT **Mite**

DESCRIPTION

Mites are not true insects; rather, they are closely related to spiders. They are minute red, black, or brown arachnids that attack many kinds of plants, feeding on leaf undersides, flowers, and at the blossom ends of fruit. They feed by sucking out plant juices, causing leaves to become stippled, yellow, and dry, sometimes leaving pale yellow spots or blotches. They suck chlorophyll out of the leaves, causing small white dots to appear; they also inject toxins into the leaves, which discolors and distorts them.

Mites are encouraged by hot, dry conditions. The hotter the temperature, the more rapidly they develop from egg to adult, and the more eggs they lay. They reproduce rapidly, producing many generations each year. They are found throughout the United States.

MOST OBVIOUS SYMPTOMS

Leaves become stippled, yellow, and dry. Sometimes pale yellow or white spots or dots appear. The leaves may begin to yellow first along the veins and then over the entire leaf surface, and they become mealy underneath. Fine webbing may run between leaves and across leaf undersides. Fruit trees will have small, poorly colored fruit that drops early. The leaves of the tree dry and curl slightly upward, a copper color develops on the bottom of the leaf, and it is covered with a fine web.

Look at the undersides of plant leaves weekly with a magnifying glass to check for mites and mite damage. Simply tap two or three leaves or a small branch tip against a sheet of white paper. Look for dislodged mites crawling on the paper. If you see five or more, consider spraying.

VULNERABLE PLANTS

All fruit and vegetable crops are susceptible to mites.

BEST CONTROL STRATEGY

Spray plants with a forceful spray of water to knock mites from the leaves. If that doesn't do the job, spray with insecticidal soap. On fruit trees, a spray of insecticidal soap mixed with a light horticultural oil is effective.

OPTIONS FOR CONTROLLING MITE

Natural Sprays

See the beginning of this chapter for more information on making natural sprays.

Insecticidal Soap

Commercial insecticidal soap is effective in controlling mites. Spray it on the undersides of leaves at least three times at 5- to 7-day intervals. Cover the plant thoroughly. Soap sprays are contact insecticides, so spray the plant top to bottom, especially under the leaves, where you'll find most mites.

Light Horticultural Oil Spray

The newer horticultural oils, called "superior horticultural spray oil," are lighter and less viscous (viscosity 60 to 70) than traditional oils, and evaporate much more quickly from leaves and stems. They can be used during the growing season to control mites. Spray with a 2 to 3 percent solution and make sure contact is made with the pest, because the oil works by suffocation.

Misting and Shading

Mites prefer a warm, dry environment. Discourage them by misting daily with water and shading plants. This creates a cooler microclimate around plants and helps keep mite populations from exploding.

Water Spray

Spraying plants with a forceful jet of water knocks mites from the leaves. This is best done in early morning. Use a nozzle that produces a fine spray of water, and thoroughly wash off the undersides of the affected leaves. It is important to do this at least three times—3 days in a row or every other day. This gets rid of the pests that will hatch from eggs already laid when you began spraying.

Traps and Mechanical Controls

Glue Trap for Fruit Trees

Try a glue trap designed to imprison small insects like mites. Dissolve ¼ pound of glue in a gallon of warm water and let it stand overnight. Apply this mixture with a sprayer to twigs and leaves of fruit trees. When the mixture dries, it will flake off, taking the trapped bugs with it. In midseason, several applications, 7 to 10 days apart, are needed to halt consecutive generations of mites.

Botanical Poisons

Neem

Purchase a commercial neem product and mix it according to label instructions. Apply the spray to

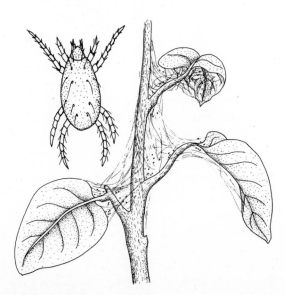

infested plants twice, at weekly or longer intervals, until pests are under control.

Pyrethrum

Pyrethrum must be applied directly to the mites to work, so spray the undersides of leaves as well as the tops. Usually two applications, 3 or 4 days apart, will control the problem.

STEPS TO PREVENT MITE

Preventive Spray Programs

Combination Preventive Spray

On plants most vulnerable to mites, begin a biweekly preventive spray program using commercial insecticidal soap mixed with very dilute seaweed extract on the undersides of all new growth. Make two or three applications every 2 weeks in the beginning of the growing season, followed by a monthly application just on those plants most vulnerable to mites. For fruit trees, add a light horticultural oil to this mixture for best effect.

Dormant Oil Spray

Traditional heavier horticultural spray oils, with a viscosity of 100 to 200, can be used in fall through early spring to smother mites when the trees in which they winter over are leafless. Make sure you get an even coat over the entire tree.

Barriers

Diatomaceous Earth (D.E.)

Spread D.E. around the base of plants, or dust the whole plant with D.E. Dusting should progress upward from the ground, covering all stems and leaves, especially the undersides. Dust in late evening or at night to minimize predator insect destruction.

Resistant Varieties

Tomato

Try Better Boy, Champion, Romas, and Super Fantastic.

Planting Time

Plant before hot weather to minimize or avoid mite damage.

Insect Predators and Parasites Available Commercially

See the beginning of this chapter for more information on these beneficial insects.

Lacewing

Of the bugs you can buy through the mail to control mites, lacewings are one of the best.

Lady Bug

Lady bugs are effective controls for spider mites.

Predatory Mite

One release of predatory mites per season should provide adequate control of mites.

Insect Predators and Parasites Found in the Garden

Firefly larvae, lacewings, lady bugs, and predatory thrips attack mites.

Wild brambles are a nursery for beneficial bugs. The beneficials that prey on red spider mites in orchards are particularly plentiful where blackberries are growing nearby. Hedgerows, windbreaks, and wooded patches are also nurseries for the beneficials that control mites on apple and other fruit trees.

Other Preventive Steps

Make sure there is good air circulation around vulnerable crops.

INSECT *Nematode*

DESCRIPTION

Nematodes are whitish, translucent worms, smaller than $\frac{1}{16}$ inch. They are barely visible to the naked eye. The nematode enters plant roots soon after hatching from its egg. It injects toxins and bacteria into the plant, causing tissue to rot and knots to form. Nematodes prefer warm areas and are serious problems on sandy or loamy soils; they can also cause damage on heavy soils. The root-knot nematode inhabits soil, and can live for many years, even when susceptible crops are avoided. Many different species of nematode exist.

MOST OBVIOUS SYMPTOMS

Plants infected with nematodes are stunted, and the leaves yellow. If plants do survive to maturity, they produce low yields. Cells on the roots enlarge grotesquely, forming a protective and nourishing gall known as the root knot. This renders the roots useless in the absorption and translocation of water and nutrients.

VULNERABLE PLANTS

Beans (snap), carrots, okra, potatoes, sweet potatoes, tomatoes, and strawberries.

BEST CONTROL STRATEGY

Use resistant varieties. Add 3 or 4 inches of compost (especially leaf mold) and kelp meal to the soil. This encourages the growth of fungi that attack nematodes. Fertilize with fish emulsion, and plant early in the season. Fish emulsion repels nematodes.

OPTIONS FOR CONTROLLING NEMATODE

Early Warning Devices

Trap Crop
Castor beans (*Ricinus* spp.) act as a decoy crop for some nematodes.

Natural Sprays

See the beginning of this chapter for more information on making natural sprays.

Fish Emulsion
Crops fertilized with fish emulsion suffer less nematode damage than those fertilized in other ways. It is suspected that some component of the fish oil may be toxic or offensive to the nematodes. A combination of fish emulsion and a by-product of the yucca cactus is even more effective at knocking out nematodes. In tests with citrus trees, a mixture of 70 percent fish emulsion and 30 percent yucca extract reduced root-knot and pin nematode populations by up to 90 percent.

Seaweed Extract Drench or Spray
Whether used as a foliar spray or as a soil flush, seaweed extract will reduce root-knot nematode infestations of tomatoes. Natural hormones in the seaweed, called cytokinins, help the plants increase their resistance to nematode invasion. Fewer larvae penetrate the roots, and those that do are inhibited in their development. As a side benefit, the seaweed extract produces bigger roots and stems and better yields. Mix 1 tablespoon of liquid seaweed in 2 gallons of water.

Yucca Drench
An effective, nontoxic soil drench can be made with ordinary corn oil and an extract of the yucca plant (the latter is available commercially as Pent-A-Vate).

The oil is thought to act as a nematocide. The Pent-A-Vate acts as a wetting agent, allowing the oil to penetrate the soil. To make the drench, mix one part Pent-A-Vate with ten parts water. Mix four parts of this with one part corn oil, and sprinkle it on the soil around the plants. Then water it in with a hose.

Traps and Mechanical Controls

Kelp Meal
Certain soil fungi that kill root-knot nematodes will be stimulated by the presence of kelp meal in the infested soil. That stimulation will increase the fungi's lethal effectiveness against the nematodes. Add about 1 pound of meal for every 100 square feet of garden. This treatment is particularly effective if combined with the addition of compost.

Leaf Mold Compost
Extensive research at the Connecticut Agricultural Experiment Station has shown that leaf mold composts can suppress populations of harmful nematodes. Fatty acids, similar to those used as pest control agents, are produced by the compost and regulate nematode populations. For example, decomposing rye and timothy grasses have been shown to release the fatty acids that control some species of parasitic nematodes. For best results, the compost should be mixed into the garden soil. Many plant leaves are toxic to nematodes, and laboratory tests have shown pine needles to be particularly potent.

STEPS TO PREVENT NEMATODE

Fall Cleanup
Sowing rye in the fall and tilling it under in the early spring has proved very satisfactory in reducing root-knot nematode populations. Nematodes enter the roots and die because they cannot develop further. When the rye is tilled under, an organic acid is produced that is toxic to nematodes. The rye provides a cover for the soil in winter, adds green matter when tilled in, and conditions the soil.

Soil Solarization

Solarization has been effective in controlling nematodes in the warmer southern and western states. This is a matter of plowing or tilling deeply during hot weather, super-soaking the soil, covering the area with clear plastic, and leaving it on until the soil temperature heats up enough to destroy the nematodes, as well as many weed seeds. (See chapter 5 for more information on solarization.)

Resistant Varieties

The most satisfactory control is the use of resistant varieties.

Tomato
Beefmaster, Better Boy, Big Pick, Celebrity, Lemon Boy, Park's Whopper, and Supersteak Hybrid VFN (the initials indicate resistance to verticillium and fusarium wilts, as well as to nematodes).

Intercropping or Companions

You can grow repellent plants to discourage nematodes. Certain French marigold *(Tagetes patula)* cultivars are effective in controlling harmful root-knot nematodes. The marigolds act as a trap crop, allowing the nematodes to enter their roots, where the nematodes appear to be trapped without being able to reproduce. Marigolds effectively suppress nematodes by releasing a nematocidal substance from their roots. French marigold varieties, such as Tangerine and Park's Nemagold, work best.

Plant the nematode-infested area of the garden with nothing but marigolds. Let them grow, and then turn them under at season's end. The roots will decay in the soil. Once the plant matter has broken down, you can plant the usual crops again. The larvae that do penetrate the roots can't lay eggs. Keep weeds under control so the impact of the marigolds is not diluted.

Roots of plants such as asparagus, some mustards and grasses, rattlebox, smartweed, and wild chicory are also toxic to some nematodes. Some species of chrysanthemum (in particular, *Chrysan-*

themum coccineum and *C. pyrethrum*) reduce harmful nematodes in the soil.

Planting Time

Plant early in the season: Low soil temperatures restrict nematode development. If your crop gets a head start, it will be better able to withstand a nematode attack. Make sure the soil has plenty of organic matter, which encourages nematode predators. Rich soil may also stimulate root growth, which lessens the effect of nematode damage. Decomposing organic matter may generate nematode-toxic compounds. Soil amendments such as leaf mold, grass clippings, castor pomace (a by-product of castor oil production), and manure have been known to suppress nematodes under the right conditions.

Crop Rotation

Crop rotation can greatly reduce nematode populations in the soil, but does not eliminate them. To control them, plant your crops in a new location every 3 to 4 years if possible. Pull up and burn all affected plant roots, and keep infested soil tilled to prevent weeds from gaining hold. The nematodes will starve from lack of food.

Insect Predators and Parasites Found in the Garden

Mites are important controllers of harmful nematodes. Springtails are also nematode controllers.

Other Preventive Steps

Fallow Soil

If you garden in an area that has hot, dry summers, you can control nematodes cheaply and easily by letting the infested area lie fallow and by withholding water during the hottest months. Turning the soil occasionally during this time exposes nematode eggs, many of which die in the sun.

Garden Hygiene

Using a bleach solution (one part household bleach to four parts water), clean all tools and garden shoes that have been in contact with infested soil, or you will carry worms to new garden sites.

Heavy Mulch

Heavy mulching of the soil provides a rapid increase in soil bacteria and soil fungi, which are antagonistic to nematodes.

NOTES AND RESEARCH

Dr. Jerry McLaughlin, professor of pharmacognosy at Purdue University, is patenting a new insecticide derived from the pawpaw tree. He says the new broad-spectrum botanical, especially effective against Mexican bean beetles, mosquito larvae, and nematodes, is environmentally safe and comparable to pyrethrum in action and toxicity.

In other research, bacteria that control nematodes have been found. Watch for new information on this development.

INSECT *Onion Maggot*

DESCRIPTION

Adult onion maggots resemble brown, hairy, humpbacked houseflies. They lay eggs at the base of plants. The maggots are ⅓ inch long and legless. They are found near the plant bulb or neck; they also burrow into the underground part of the stem of young onion plants or into the developing bulb of larger onions in spring and early summer. Onion maggots overwinter as pupae in the soil. They are found especially in the northern and coastal areas. Three generations may occur in a year. Cool, wet weather favors these maggots.

Two species of maggots commonly attack onions: the onion maggot, which seldom attacks any crop except onions, and the seed-corn maggot, which damages seedling onions. In northern regions, the onion maggot is the worst pest that bothers onions.

MOST OBVIOUS SYMPTOMS

The lower stem of onions near the bulb will be destroyed, and the neck will be damaged. The last generation often attacks onions just before they are harvested, causing many to rot in storage.

VULNERABLE PLANTS

Onions and radishes.

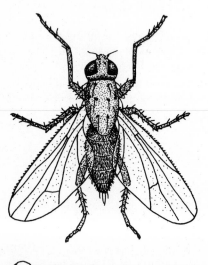

BEST CONTROL STRATEGY

Avoid close spacing of onions in the garden. Don't plant onions in rows, since this helps the maggot move from plant to plant.

OPTIONS FOR CONTROLLING ONION MAGGOT

Emergence Time

Adult flies emerge in late spring to lay eggs at the base of young onion plants.

Early Warning Devices

Trap Crop
Use culled onions to attract maggots, and destroy them. Spread the culled onions amongst the young onions 1 week before the onion heads begin to form.

STEPS TO PREVENT ONION MAGGOT

Fall Cleanup

Remove any unharvested onions to reduce maggot infestations. Research suggests that maggot infestations can be greatly reduced if damaged onions are removed at harvest. Damaged bulbs left in the field over winter provide the main source of food for overwintering maggots. Harvest all your onions—perfect and damaged—in order to reduce the maggot population next year. Go ahead and throw the damaged onions in a compost pile, for maggots will not survive the winter there.

Barriers

Diatomaceous Earth (D.E.)
Dust with D.E. early in the season to discourage adults from laying eggs.

Wood Ashes

Spread wood ashes on the soil around bulbs to discourage adults from laying eggs.

Resistant Varieties

Onion

Yellow or bunching varieties are generally more tolerant of maggots than other onions. Another option is to plant Japanese bunching onions, which are resistant.

Intercropping or Companions

Scatter onion plants throughout the garden, intercropping with plants that aren't susceptible.

Crop Rotation

The maggots live, mate, eat, and die in a very small area, so move the onion patch every other year. Maggots will die out in the off-years.

Animal Predators

Crows, robins, starlings, and other birds eat onion maggots.

Insect Predators and Parasites Available Commercially

See the beginning of this chapter for more information on these beneficial insects.

Beneficial Nematode

Beneficial nematodes are tiny soil-dwelling worms that find their way to onion maggots, burrow inside them, and reproduce. The onion maggots are killed by bacteria released by the nematodes.

Insect Predators and Parasites Found in the Garden

Some beetles, predatory flies, spiders, and ichneumonid wasps are important in keeping this pest under control.

Other Preventive Steps

Some gardeners report that used tea leaves worked into the soil where radishes or onions are to be planted will keep the crop free of maggots.

INSECT # *Parsleyworm*

DESCRIPTION

The parsleyworm is a 2-inch caterpillar that is green with a yellow-dotted black band across each body segment. It gives off an odor and projects orange horns when upset. The adult is the black swallowtail butterfly. It lays white eggs on leaves. The parsleyworm overwinters as a pupa or adult. Several generations occur in a year. This pest is found throughout the United States.

MOST OBVIOUS SYMPTOMS

The leaves of plants infested with parsleyworms are chewed; often only the bare stems remain.

VULNERABLE PLANTS

Members of the parsley family, including carrots, celery, dill, and parsnips.

BEST CONTROL STRATEGY

Handpick worms or use *Bacillus thuringiensis* (BT).

OPTIONS FOR CONTROLLING PARSLEYWORM

Biological Controls

Bacillus Thuringiensis (BT)

BT, a bacterium available in powder or liquid form, will kill parsleyworms. Dust all parts of the leaves, especially the undersides, or spray thoroughly with the liquid form. Although the pests may live several more days, they will stop feeding, darken in color, and eventually drop to the soil. Reapply every 10 to 14 days until the pests are gone.

Traps and Mechanical Controls

Handpicking

These bright, large caterpillars are easy to hand-pick in the early morning. Keep in mind that parsleyworms are the larval form of the beautiful black swallowtail butterfly. If you want to enjoy the adults in your garden, set aside a few parsley or carrot plants as food for these larvae, and move any parsleyworms that you find to these plants.

STEPS TO PREVENT PARSLEYWORM

Animal Predators

Baltimore orioles, barn swallows, bluebirds, chickadees, flycatchers, and kinglets, as well as snakes and toads, usually keep parsleyworms under control in the home garden.

Insect Predators and Parasites Found in the Garden

All the insects that prey upon caterpillars help control parsleyworms. These include assassin bugs, lacewing larvae, parasitic wasps, and predatory flies.

INSECT # Peachtree Borer

DESCRIPTION

Adult peachtree borers are blue, clear-winged moths that resemble wasps. The males have narrow yellow rings about the abdomen; females have wide orange bands. Brown or gray eggs are laid on the trunk of a fruit tree, usually near the base, in late summer and early fall. The larvae are yellowish-white caterpillars with brown heads, about 1¼ inch long. They bore into the tree as high as a foot above ground down to several inches below and may girdle young trees. Larvae overwinter in the trunk, pupate in their tunnels from late spring to early summer, and then emerge in midsummer to lay eggs. If they are not controlled, borers can kill a tree. At best, productivity is down and the tree is more vulnerable to diseases and weather damage. One generation occurs in a year. Peachtree borers are found throughout the United States, wherever vulnerable plants are grown.

MOST OBVIOUS SYMPTOMS

Gummy sawdust (frass) can be seen at the feeding sites. The tree is weakened and becomes less resistant to heat, drought, and diseases.

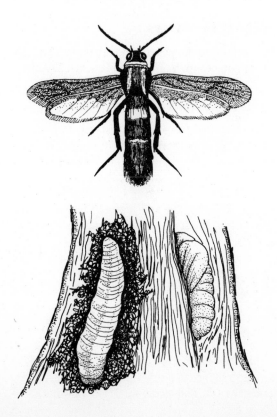

VULNERABLE PLANTS

Apricots, cherries, peaches, and plums.

BEST CONTROL STRATEGY

Small infestations can be taken care of by inserting a stiff wire into each hole and killing the larvae. *Bacillus thuringiensis* (BT) can be shot into each hole at 10-day intervals until no more frass appears. Cultivate shallowly around the trunk to destroy peachtree borer pupae.

OPTIONS FOR CONTROLLING PEACHTREE BORER

Emergence Time

Timing of controls is especially critical for this pest. Consult your County Extension agent and keep your own records of the moth's summer emergence and egg-laying periods.

Early Warning Devices

Pheromone Trap

Pheromone traps with the appropriate lures will catch male peachtree borers. They are useful in tracking emergence times. Traps may also be used to control these pests if you only have a few trees.

Commercial traps are relatively inexpensive and easy to use, and they come in several shapes and sizes. The bottoms of the traps are covered with a sticky coating that catches the insects and holds them tight. Plastic traps can last for several growing seasons. Disposable cardboard traps will last through one growing season if you clean them periodically.

You can also make your own traps from 1-quart ice cream containers. Cut three large holes in the sides of the container, and fill the bottom half with soapy water. Hang the pheromone capsule from the lid using string or wire, then snap the trap closed.

Hang traps in fruit trees in early spring, about 6 feet from the ground and away from the trunk.

Use two traps in each large tree; hang one trap in each dwarf tree.

When pests are most active, check traps twice a week, and remove collected insects and debris. When the traps get full, replace disposable traps, and follow the manufacturer's directions for renewing reusable traps. If needed, replace pheromone lures according to the directions on the package.

Biological Controls

Bacillus Thuringiensis (BT)

BT bacteria kill the peachtree borer if you can get contact with the pest. One technique is to use a garden syringe and squirt BT into each of the borer holes. Repeat every 10 days until evidence of the borer has ceased.

Traps and Mechanical Controls

Sticky Trap

You can catch the male peachtree borer moth with a pheromone trap, but you'll need more to thwart the egg-laying female. Wrap heavy paper around the trunk, from 2 inches below ground to at least 6 inches above. Coat it with Tangle Trap or another sticky material. Destroy the wrap weekly, and keep replacing it until no more larvae are trapped.

Wire Insert

If the infestation is not too extensive, you can try killing the larvae by poking a thin, flexible wire into the hole and working it around to impale the borers in their tunnels. To find the borer holes in late summer and early fall, check tree trunks from 1 foot or so aboveground to just below the soil surface. You may need to remove the soil a few inches deep around the base of the trunk to check for borer holes there. Do not remove the gummy exudate that forms around the holes, as it helps to seal the injury.

STEPS TO PREVENT PEACHTREE BORER

Fall Cleanup

Remove litter from around the tree and do not damage the bark in cultivation. Do not scrape off the gummy exudate produced by the borer, as it helps to seal the opening.

Barriers

Tightly wrap the trunks with cotton batting, beginning 1 inch below the soil surface and extending 1 foot above. Cover this with black plastic and secure with string. Apply a coat of Tanglefoot to the barrier. This prevents the adults from laying eggs on the trunk and catches some larvae before they begin boring. The bands should be removed in early fall and replaced every spring.

Animal Predators

Sapsuckers, woodpeckers, and other birds are able to penetrate bark to prey upon peachtree borers.

Other Preventive Steps

Injured or weak trees are the first targets of borers, so keep trees well fertilized and properly pruned. Use mowers, string trimmers, and other lawn care equipment carefully around trees to avoid damaging the bark and creating easy entry points for borers. Cultivate the soil around the base of the trunk in fall and spring to expose and destroy larvae and pupae.

Hang bags of yellow or other soft soaps in the crotch of the tree. The rain washes the soap down the trunk, supposedly making it taste bad to the borer.

INSECT *Pear Psylla*

DESCRIPTION

Adult psyllids are reddish brown and 1/10 inch long. They lay yellowish eggs on twigs, on the base of buds, or on leaves. The immature insects are very active. Nymphs and adults feed by sucking out the plant's juices. Adults spend winter on or near host plants. There are usually three to four generations per year. Pear psylla causes damage from feeding and spreads fire blight. It is found mostly in eastern and western parts of the country, rather than the central states.

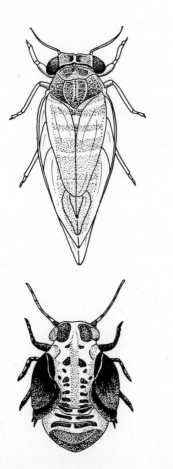

MOST OBVIOUS SYMPTOMS

Plants infested with psyllids show leaf yellowing and general decline in vigor. Severely infected trees may drop their leaves. These pests secrete honeydew, a sticky, sugary substance that coats leaves and fruit and may encourage the growth of a sooty black mold. Fruit is scarred and possibly misshapen. Yellow jackets may congregate around the black fungus caused by the honeydew.

VULNERABLE PLANTS

Pears.

BEST CONTROL STRATEGY

During the growing season, spray the tree with insecticidal soap. In fall, spray with light horticultural oil, and in early spring, before the leaves emerge, spray with dormant oil.

OPTIONS FOR CONTROLLING PEAR PSYLLA

Emergence Time

Adults emerge in spring and mate. They lay eggs when temperatures reach 70°F, or a bit lower if there is no wind.

Natural Sprays

See the beginning of this chapter for more information on making natural sprays.

Insecticidal Soap

Commercial insecticidal soap is effective in controlling pear psyllids during the growing season.

Spray every 2 to 3 days for 2 weeks for bad infestations. Cover the plant thoroughly. Soap sprays are contact insecticides, so spray the plant top to bottom, especially under the leaves, where you'll find most psyllids.

Light Horticultural Oil Spray

Control psyllids with a light horticultural oil spray in the fall. Spray again in the spring; spray at the green tip stage, when you first see eggs (use a magnifying glass to find them). Then spray again 7 days later, and keep spraying every 7 days until the leaves start to emerge. The insects don't seem to like laying eggs on this oily surface.

STEPS TO PREVENT PEAR PSYLLA

Fall Cleanup

Pick up damaged fruit and rake away infested leaves throughout the season. In fall, clear away weeds, and burn or otherwise destroy all of this debris, for it harbors psyllids.

Preventive Spray Programs

Insecticidal Soap

Use an insecticidal soap spray to kill females before they lay eggs. Apply in early spring, as soon as the females emerge, and when leaf buds are just beginning to turn green.

Insect Predators and Parasites Available Commercially

See the beginning of this chapter for more information on these beneficial insects.

Lady Bug

If the psylla population is extremely high, it may be worth your while to release lady bugs.

Lacewing

Again, lacewing larvae are useful only if psylla population is very large.

INSECT *Plum Curculio*

DESCRIPTION

The adult curculio is a hard-shelled brown beetle, about ¼ inch long. Its snout curves downward. When disturbed, the beetle retracts its legs and antennae and drops to the ground. It lays its eggs in crescent-shaped wounds in fruit. The larvae are grayish white, legless grubs with brown heads. They bore to the center of the fruit and feed near the core. They emerge after the fruit drops to the ground. The adults overwinter in soil and hedgerows. One to two generations occur in a year. Plum curculios are found in the eastern United States and Canada.

MOST OBVIOUS SYMPTOMS

In feeding, the adult cuts a hole in the skin of the fruit and hollows out a tiny, crescent-shaped cavity.

Signs of infestation first appear when the fruit is about ½ inch in diameter. Wounds on apples frequently exude sap that dries to a white crust. Larval injury inside the fruit is extensive and usually results in misshapen fruit that falls to the ground prematurely. Fruit may develop brown rot disease.

VULNERABLE PLANTS

Apples, apricots, blueberries, cherries, peaches, pears, and plums.

BEST CONTROL STRATEGY

Spray with a pyrethrum solution at petal fall and every 10 to 14 days until September, or until curculios are under control. Be sure to remove and destroy all fallen fruit immediately.

OPTIONS FOR CONTROLLING PLUM CURCULIO

Emergence Time
Adults emerge at the same time that blossoms are out on the apple trees.

Early Warning Devices

Sticky Trap
Hang white 8-by-10-inch sticky cards in trees. Place one card in each tree; hung chest high, they will catch the first immigrants. If you catch just one beetle every other day, you obviously don't need to bother with sprays.

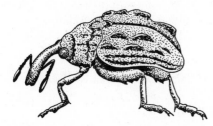

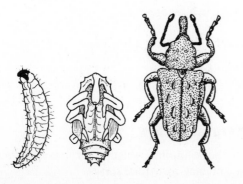

Traps and Mechanical Controls

Sticky Trap
The sticky traps used for early warning also can be used to control curculios. You will need several traps per tree. Hang them in early spring. Do not leave these traps out for longer than 3 or 4 weeks, or they will trap beneficial insects as well as pests.

A sticky band of Tanglefoot, applied to heavy paper wrapped around the trunk, will also help trap some curculios.

Handpicking
Using a padded bat or similar tool, knock curculios from trees onto a sheet placed under the tree. Shake curculios into a bucket of kerosene. Do this early every morning for about 6 weeks, beginning at blossom time. Pick up and destroy dropped fruit daily.

Botanical Poisons

Pyrethrum
Spray with pyrethrum if plum curculios can't be controlled by handpicking or traps. Usually two applications 3 or 4 days apart will control the problem. Remember that pyrethrum sprays can also be harmful to beneficial insects, so save them for use as a last resort.

STEPS TO PREVENT PLUM CURCULIO

Fall Cleanup
Remove all fallen and diseased fruit from the tree and the area around it. Burn the fruit, since it contains curculio larvae. Clean up weeds.

Animal Predators
Domestic fowl and many garden birds, including bluebirds, chickadees, flycatchers, and juncos, eat curculios.

Other Preventive Steps
Avoid planting vulnerable trees near wooded areas.

Slug

DESCRIPTION

Slugs are not true insects; rather, they are mollusks. They are 1 to 2 inches long, and look like brown, gray, white, purple, black, or yellow snails without shells. They feed on a wide variety of plants. Slugs feed only at night and hide in moist, dark places during the day. They are most active from 2 hours after sunset until 2 hours before sunrise, and are attracted to well-mulched gardens. Slugs are very vulnerable to dehydration. They prefer temperatures under 75°F. They overwinter in the soil. Several years may be required before they reach maturity. Slugs are found throughout the United States.

MOST OBVIOUS SYMPTOMS

Plants attacked by slugs suffer large ragged holes in leaves, fruit, and stems. Slugs like damaged plants and will start at the bottom of the plant. Other signs that slugs are at work include trails of shiny, silvery slime on leaves and soil.

VULNERABLE PLANTS

Almost all garden vegetables and some fruit trees are vulnerable to slug attack.

BEST CONTROL STRATEGY

The best way to control slugs is to set up a barrier to keep them out of the garden. Handpicking will work if you get them early in the season. There are a number of traps that work as well.

OPTIONS FOR CONTROLLING SLUG

Emergence Time

Slugs like cool temperatures. They surface in early spring in most areas.

Early Warning Devices

Trap Crop

Grow plantain weed or hosta nearby as a decoy plant. Collect and destroy slugs every evening.

Natural Sprays

See the beginning of this chapter for more information on making natural sprays.

Bug Juice

Bug juice is made by crushing some of the slugs, mixing them with water, and spraying the strained liquid back onto the affected plants. Some gardeners claim that the bug juice kills or repels the slugs.

Traps and Mechanical Controls

Beer Trap

Shallow pans of stale beer attract slugs, which fall in and drown. The yeast in the beer is the attractant. Replace the beer every few days or after a rain. Sink the pan into the soil so the slugs have easy access to the trap. Some gardeners have found that 1 teaspoon of baking yeast in 3 ounces of water is even more effective than beer.

Cover Trap

Anything that produces a cool, shady environment may become a cover trap for slugs. Use pieces of old board, carpet, stones, plantain, or cabbage leaves laid in the garden. It is best to visit these cover traps twice a day to drown or crush the pests.

Grapefruit Rind

Place the rinds, hollow side down, in the garden and check them several times a day to remove the slugs. The attraction of each shell lasts about 2 or 3 days. Cantaloupe shells work just as well.

Slug Bar Trap

These commercial traps are small rectangular boxes that are filled with beer or slug poison and placed in the garden. They are covered so the rain does not dilute the beer. They can be used for early warning or for control.

Handpicking

Handpicking makes a sizable dent in the slug infestation right away, particularly if combined with trapping. Go out at night, armed with a flashlight and a can half full of kerosene or soapy water. Check plants, boards, mulched areas, and walkways for the slimy creatures. Sprinkle table salt on slugs and snails if you want to kill them without picking them up.

STEPS TO PREVENT SLUG

Fall Cleanup

Keep your eyes open for slugs when you do your fall cleanup. Don't expect cold temperatures to destroy them for you.

Preventive Spray Programs

Horsetail Spray

The primitive plant horsetail *(Equisitum arvense),* which grows wild throughout most of North America, makes a fine spray. Put 1 to 2 ounces of the dried herb into an enamel pan and pour in 1 gallon of water. Bring to a boil and allow to simmer for 20 minutes. Cayenne peppers may be added to the pot. Cool and strain. The high silica content of the horsetail and the aconitic acid it is said to contain make it a spray that effectively repels slugs.

Barriers

Aluminum Screening

Fence slugs out of raised beds with strips of aluminum screening about 3 inches high. Unweave the top two horizontal strands from one long edge of the screening and bend the exposed vertical strands to face outward. Push the bottom edge about 1 inch into the soil.

Aluminum Sulfate Dusting

Aluminum sulfate is used to acidify soil, but research in England indicates that it also is a very effective repellent for slugs. Work about ½ pound of aluminum sulfate into 100 square feet of the garden. At this rate, it will not effect the pH of the soil very much but will effectively repel slugs. You can also sprinkle a small handful around the base of a vulnerable plant to repel the slugs. You may have to redust after a heavy rain.

Cedar Sawdust

Some gardeners have reported success with using cedar sawdust barriers to repel slugs and snails. Sprinkle a thick layer around the plants or beds you want to protect. Renew the barrier frequently, especially after a rain, to keep it effective.

Copper Flashing

Another development in the battle against slugs is the use of a strip of copper flashing material. (A commercial version is called Snail Barr.) Tack a 2-inch strip of copper flashing material around the outside of boxed raised beds, about 1 inch from the top of the bed. Copper is apparently a successful slug barrier because it always carries a very mild electric charge. Humans can't detect it, but slugs can, and they don't cross into the bed.

Diatomaceous Earth (D.E.)

Slugs don't like rough surfaces, so D.E. spread around vulnerable plants prevents slugs from getting up into the plant. Cover the plant as well, dusting the stems and the undersides of leaves. If it rains, the slugs will be able to crawl over the rough barrier, so dust again after rain.

Eggshells

Spread crushed eggshells thickly around each plant. Slugs won't go over the sharp shells. Scatter shells in the rows as you plant seeds.

Hardware Cloth

Hardware cloth with sharp points along one edge, tacked onto the top outside edge of a boxed raised bed, discourages slugs from reaching the plant. Make sure the hardware cloth extends 2 inches above boards.

Salt

Salt is lethal to slugs. Petroleum jelly coated with salt is a champion slug stopper. Surround the entire garden with old boards propped up with rocks at 35- to 40-degree angles to the ground; then cover the undersides of these planks and their supporting stones with a layer of the jelly followed by a coating of salt.

Sand

Baby slugs make a very thin layer of slime and are easily discouraged by a texture that wouldn't deter their big parents. When peas are planted early in spring, most of the slugs are tiny. They don't like to crawl through sharp river sand, so you can use it as a barrier around pea vines.

Seaweed Mulch

Try a seaweed mulch. Rinse it with fresh water and pile it on the garden and around the outside of flower beds. Slugs won't go over or under the seaweed, it's effective until it decomposes, and it adds nutrients to the soil.

Wood Ashes

Sprinkle two handfuls of wood ashes around the base of each plant when the plants or vines are 4 to 5 inches tall, or you can encircle them with a 3- to 4-inch-wide trench, a few inches deep, filled with wood ashes. Care should be taken not to get ashes on the plant.

Planting Time

Slugs are not active when air temperatures exceed 75°F. Late planting, when possible, can help you avoid peak slug seasons.

Animal Predators

Downy woodpeckers, robins, and other garden birds relish eating slugs. Garter snakes are also important predators. They like to live under black plastic. If you mulch with plastic, they will hang around there and eat up all the slugs and all the slug eggs. Other slug enemies include grass snakes, salamanders, shrews, toads, and turtles. Chickens don't usually care for slugs, but ducks will eat them.

Insect Predators and Parasites Found in the Garden

Black rove beetles, centipedes, firefly larvae, ground beetles, and soldier beetles all prey on slugs or slug eggs. You can encourage these predatory beetles to make their homes in your garden by maintaining permanent walkways of clover, sod, or stone mulch.

Other Preventive Steps

Avoid Nitrogen Deficiency

Slugs prefer to eat soft, slightly rotting plant debris.

When plants are deficient in nitrogen, their lower leaves turn yellow and gradually decay. Nitrogen-deficient plants have a hard time making the enzymes that slugs don't like to taste. Feed plants liquid manure or some form of readily available nitrogen, and they will withstand mild slug damage and eventually get too big to be seriously injured by the pests.

Eliminate Hiding Places
If slugs are a problem, eliminate leafy ground covers, weedy patches, rubble, and other likely breeding areas near the garden. Consider removing the mulch on garden paths, and the boards around raised beds. The fewer hiding places you provide slugs, the fewer slugs there will be invading the garden.

Mulch Later
Some gardeners don't use mulch because slugs like to hide under mulch during the day. Slugs don't like warm weather over 75°F, so don't lay organic mulch until the average temperature is above 75°F.

INSECT Squash Bug

DESCRIPTION

Adult squash bugs are flat-backed, shield-shaped, brown to black insects with a triangle on the back. They have a light-colored outline on their abdomens and are ½ to ¾ inch long. They lay brown or red shiny eggs on leaves. Young squash bugs are greenish gray with reddish legs. Adults and young feed by sucking out the juices from leaves, causing leaves to wilt, dry up, and turn black. You will find the adults near the main stem and the shiny red egg masses. The nymphs can be found on the undersides of the upper leaves. Usually only one generation occurs in a year. The adult hibernates in garden trash. Squash bugs are found throughout North America.

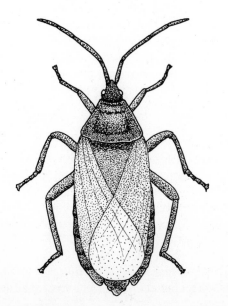

MOST OBVIOUS SYMPTOMS

The leaves of infested plants wilt, dry up, and turn black.

VULNERABLE PLANTS

Cucumbers, muskmelons, pumpkins, squash (summer and winter), and watermelons.

BEST CONTROL STRATEGY

Use a barrier to keep the bug off young plants. Also apply a preventive spray of insecticidal soap and seaweed extract. If bugs do get to the plant, use insecticidal soap. If the problem persists, spray plants with neem.

OPTIONS FOR CONTROLLING SQUASH BUG

Emergence Time

Adults emerge about the time vines begin to "run," or extend beyond the hill.

Early Warning Devices

Trap Crop

Plant radishes near cucurbit plants and handpick or spray the bugs as they show up.

Natural Sprays

See the beginning of this chapter for more information on making natural sprays.

Insecticidal Soap

Commercial insecticidal soap is an effective control. Check plants daily, and spray adults every 2 to 3 days for 2 weeks during their first appearance in spring. Continue watching for and spraying adults and nymphs through the season. Eggs won't be affected by the soap, so pinch them between two hard surfaces. For bad infestations, cover the plant thoroughly. Soap sprays are contact insecticides, so spray the plant top to bottom, especially under the leaves.

Traps and Mechanical Controls

Cover Trap

Boards can be used as traps. Bugs will hide under them during the day. Collect and destroy the pests every morning.

Handpicking

Handpicking is an effective line of defense, if it is done regularly. Keep a bucket of ammonia water or kerosene handy to dispose of the bugs. Mash the eggs, or if the whole leaf is infested with eggs and nymphs, cut it off and immerse it in ammonia. To locate bugs, grasp each vine at the growing tip and hold it straight up. The bugs will try to run up the plant, or they will drop off and run for shelter. Act quickly to catch and destroy them.

Botanical Poisons

Neem

Purchase a commercial neem product and mix it according to label instructions. Apply the spray to infested plants twice, at weekly or longer intervals, until pests are under control. Spray carefully to thoroughly cover all plant parts. The spray will be most effective if you apply it in early morning or late afternoon. Neem is generally fairly harmless to beneficials, but it may have an effect with repeated use. Save it for use against serious infestations, when milder measures such as handpicking or soap sprays don't work.

STEPS TO PREVENT SQUASH BUG

Crop Cleanup Trick

To significantly reduce your garden's squash bug population over a 2- to 3-year period, use the crop cleanup trick. Pull up plants vulnerable to the squash bug as soon as they finish bearing and put them into a large plastic bag, preferably a big clear one.

Tie the bag, and leave it in direct sun for a week or so. Nothing will survive that treatment, and a major source of next year's squash bug population will have been destroyed.

Fall Cleanup

To further reduce the bug population, remove and destroy all squash vines and other trash at the end of the season, leaving only a few immature squash in the patch. Wandering squash bugs in search of winter quarters zero in on the fruit, sometimes completely covering it. Exposed like this, the pests are easy to destroy. The squash continues to attract bugs for several weeks. The fruit can be put in plastic bags and set in the sun as described above.

Preventive Spray Program

Combination Preventive Spray

An effective preventive spray program for the squash bug includes a combination of natural sprays that work together to prevent the squash bug from appearing for over a month. Make a spray with insecticidal soap and seaweed extract, mixed in equal parts. Apply it to the whole garden, beginning a week after seeds have germinated. Repeat 2 weeks later, and then again 2 weeks after that. This routine puts you about a month into the normal growing season, when beneficial insects begin to emerge, and you will want to avoid hurting them with any unnecessary general spraying.

Barriers

Netting or Fleece Cover

Later in the season, when the danger of frost has passed, you can use a material for barriers that allows the sun, air, and rain to get through but prevents squash bugs from getting to your plants. Nylon netting, cheesecloth, fine screening, and agricultural fleece all keep out squash bugs. Cover transplants or a newly seeded area with the preferred material immediately. Lay the material directly on the plants and seal all the edges to the ground by laying soil over the edges. Provide lots of extra material to prevent plants from straining against the covering as they grow. Remove the fleece when plants begin to flower.

Wood Ashes

When the plants or vines are 4 to 5 inches tall, sprinkle two handfuls of wood ashes around each plant, but not up to the stem. Take care not to get ashes on the plant. You can also make a trench around the plant that is 3 to 4 inches wide and a few inches deep and fill it with wood ashes. The pests will avoid crawling over the ashes.

For best results, raise plants in a cold frame, transplant to the garden when the plants are about 4 inches high, and then spread ashes around the plants.

Resistant Varieties

Squash, Summer

Early Golden Bush Scallop, Early Prolific Straightneck, Early Summer Crookneck, and Sweet Cheese.

Squash, Winter

Butternut, Improved Green Hubbard, Royal Acorn, and Table Queen.

Intercropping or Companions

Nasturtiums are grown among squash to deter squash bugs. Give them a head start over the squash. Catnip is also said to deter squash bugs from squash.

Planting Time

Plant early, since mature plants are better able to withstand the pests. A late fall crop can often escape attack as well.

Animal Predators

Bluebirds, mockingbirds, and other birds, as well as turtles, eat squash bugs.

Insect Predators and Parasites Found in the Garden

Parasitic wasps prey upon the eggs of the squash bug.

Other Preventive Steps

Avoid deep loose mulches like straw and hay; they provide a refuge for the insects. Instead, use black plastic, compost, or some other compact matter, such as sawdust.

NOTES AND RESEARCH

The squash bug, biting into a leaf, causes the plant to rush insect-repellent substances to the damaged region within 40 minutes, but the bug has adapted by cutting a circular trench in the leaf within 10 minutes of alighting on it. The repellent compounds can't cross the trench, so the beetle can enjoy the island of leaf at its leisure.

Squash Vine Borer

DESCRIPTION

The adult squash vine borer is a moth with a 1½-inch wingspan. Its abdomen has red, black, and copper rings. The front wings are dark, and the rear wings are transparent. The pest is active in the morning. Its eggs are ¹⁄₁₀ inch long, brown or reddish brown, and disk shaped, and are laid in rows or clusters on the main stem near the base of the plant. Fat, white caterpillars with brown heads hatch and tunnel into the stems to feed. Winter is spent as a larva or pupa in the soil. One generation occurs per year in the northern states and two in the deep South. This insect pest is widespread east of the Rockies.

MOST OBVIOUS SYMPTOMS

Sudden wilting of all or part of a vine is a sign that your plant has squash vine borers. You can tell borers are at work by the moist, sawdustlike debris

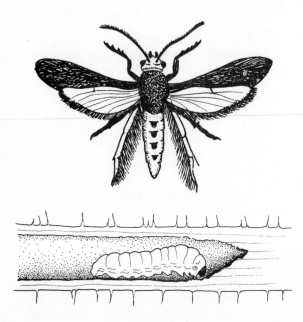

(frass) piled outside their small holes. If you cut open the stem of the wilted vine lengthwise, you will find the frass and often one or more caterpillars. It only takes two or three larvae to knock a plant back. Inspect each vine carefully for a hole and a little pile of sawdust excrement near the base.

VULNERABLE PLANTS

Cucumbers, muskmelons, pumpkins, squash (summer and winter), and watermelons.

BEST CONTROL STRATEGY

Try to deny the moth access to the plant in the first place with an agricultural fleece or netting barrier. If the borer does get access, use *Bacillus thuringiensis* (BT) injected into the stem with a hypodermic needle or garden syringe. Slit the stem to remove the borers, and then cover it with soil.

OPTIONS FOR CONTROLLING SQUASH VINE BORER

Emergence Time

In late spring, adults emerge from the pupal stage and lay eggs. Larvae hatch in 1 to 2 weeks and tunnel into the stem. They feed for 4 to 6 weeks, then burrow into the soil and make cocoons.

Biological Controls

Bacillus Thuringiensis (BT)

Squash borers can be controlled by injecting the squash vine with BT. You can use a disposable syringe from the pharmacy or, even better, a glue injector used in wood working. Timing is critical to the success of the injection method. It is crucial to infect the borers just after they hatch, but before they harm the stem. Give plants their first inoculation just after the first blossoms appear. Inject the plants again in a week to 10 days. The liquid form of BT works best. Mix it in normal solution, according to package directions, just before you're ready to use it. Gardeners also recommend preparing a bowl of disinfectant, such as chlorine bleach, mixed with an equal amount of water, and using that solution and clean water to clean and rinse the syringe between injections. Cleaning the syringe between injections reduces the possibility of spreading any diseases from one plant to another.

Insert the syringe right into the center of the stem, about 1½ inches above the soil line. This is approximately where the borers will feed first after hatching. The idea is to bathe the hollow interior of the stem with BT so that the tiny borers eat it as they feed. Use about 1 cubic centimeter (cc) of BT per injection. (If you inject too much, it will overflow out of the stem.) It's also fine to inject the BT into the holes left by borers that have already entered the stem, but since the borers are feeding above this hole, they may avoid the bacteria.

Parasitic Nematodes

You can also inject a solution of beneficial, parasitic nematodes into plant stems to control squash vine borers. Use the same timing and technique guidelines given above for BT.

Traps and Mechanical Controls

Trap Crop

Plant early summer squash around late winter varieties. Since the summer squash will mature first, borers tend to infest these plants. As soon as you harvest a few summer squash, burn and destroy plants to control borers. Don't wait for the second and third harvests from these plants. For more summer squash, plant a fall crop.

Handpicking

Try handpicking the eggs: They're easy to see.

Slitting the Stem

At the first sign of light yellow, sawdustlike deposits on the main stalk or at its base, get out a small sharp knife. At the opening, make a vertical slit as long as is necessary to find and remove the larvae. Kill the worms with the knife blade or a piece of wire. Do not cut horizontally across the stalk. The wound may be left open, or soil may be mounded up over it to encourage the plant to put out roots above the wound.

There may also be larvae in the leaf stems. Remove and destroy all badly damaged leaf stems.

Botanical Poisons

Pyrethrum

Pyrethrum paralyzes squash vine borer moths on contact. It must be applied directly to the moth to work, so it is not a terribly effective technique unless you can spot those particular moths. Remember that pyrethrum sprays can also be harmful to beneficial insects. For these reasons, you're better off using more effective controls such as barriers and handpicking.

STEPS TO PREVENT SQUASH VINE BORER

Crop Cleanup Trick

To significantly reduce your garden's squash vine borer population over a 2- to 3-year period, use the crop cleanup trick. Pull up crops vulnerable to squash vine borer as soon as they finish bearing and put them into a large plastic bag, preferably a big clear one. After tying the bag, leave it in direct sun for a week or so. Nothing will survive that treatment, and a major source of next year's squash vine borer population will have been destroyed.

Fall Cleanup

The fall garden cleanup is another important step in preventing squash vine borers. As soon as you finish harvesting your crops, remove all old plants and overgrown weeds, leaving a garden of completely bare soil for a day or two to give the birds an opportunity to pick out the pupae and larvae. Next, cultivate the soil thoroughly to a depth of 6 to 8 inches, using a hand tool or a rotary tiller, and again leave it bare for a few days. Then you can plant your winter cover crop or lay down a 4- to 6-inch winter mulch.

In the spring, about 2 weeks before planting, cultivate the garden about 2 inches deep. Leave it bare for a week or so to again give the birds a chance to eat the overwintering pests.

Barriers

Aluminum Foil Mulch

An aluminum foil mulch around vulnerable seedlings is an excellent deterrant to the moths that lay eggs on the vine. It reflects the sky, disorienting the moths as they attempt to locate the vulnerable plants by their green color. The moths move on to other locations.

Collar or Mat

Some form of matting can be placed around the base of transplants to keep moths away from the stems. These are excellent alternatives to chemical controls. Use foam-rubber carpet underlay or tar paper cut in 5- to 10-inch disks. Punch a small hole in the center, and slit along one radius. Place a disk around the base of each susceptible plant. Press the slits flat to the soil.

Diatomaceous Earth (D.E.)

Try sprinkling D.E. around the base of the plant to create a barrier to the pest, or over the whole plant. Dust in late evening so predator insect destruction will be low.

Mothballs

Mothballs reportedly repel the moth. Place several of these around the seedling and cover them lightly with soil. Naphthalene mothballs are advised for vegetable gardens, since the paradichlorobenzene type are suspected of being carcinogenic.

Netting or Fleece Cover

You can use a material for barriers that allows the sun, air, and rain to get through, but prevents the squash vine borer moth from getting to your plants. Nylon netting, fine screening, or agricultural fleece all prevent squash vine borer moths from laying eggs on the plant's stem. Cover transplants or a newly seeded area immediately after planting to prevent both insect damage and insect egg laying. Lay the barrier material directly on the plants and seal all the edges to the ground with loose soil. Provide lots of extra material so that the plants don't strain against the covering when they grow larger. Be sure to remove the covers by bloom time to allow for pollination.

Stem Cover

Wrap strips of aluminum foil or pieces of nylon stocking around the stems of vulnerable plants. Beginning at soil level, cover at least 6 inches of the stems.

Wax Paper Cups

Cut a hole in the bottom; then cut a radial slit on the bottom and on one side so the cup can be split apart to place around the seedling. Fit the cup upside down into the soil and around the plant stem. Make sure the rim of the cup is set into the soil.

Wood Ashes

When plants are about 5 inches tall, sprinkle two handfuls of wood ashes around each. Do not pile them against the stem or get them on the plant. Wood ashes can have a dramatic effect on soil pH and nutrients, so use sparingly.

Resistant Varieties

Winter squash varieties, like Hubbard, and most summer squash varieties are severely damaged by attack.

Squash, Winter

Baby Blue and Butternut are somewhat resistant.

Pumpkin

Dickson, Green Striped Cushaw, Kentucky Field, Large Sweet Cheese, and Sweet Potato.

Intercropping or Companions

Some gardeners plant radishes in the hill with vulnerable plants to repel borers.

Planting Date

Earlier plantings under cloches are a good idea, because the adult borer doesn't begin laying eggs until July, by which time the plants are larger and much more tolerant of attacks. Just be sure to destroy any larvae that do infest the plant, and to also destroy all squash plants after harvest so that no borers overwinter. See Crop Cleanup Trick, earlier.

Animal Predators

Barn swallows, blackbirds, downy woodpeckers, flycatchers, grackles, phoebes, and sparrows are some of the common birds that relish eating this pest.

Insect Predators and Parasites Available Commercially

See the beginning of this chapter for more information on these beneficial insects.

Green Lacewing

Lacewings eat borer eggs, but you need very large numbers of the pest in order to encourage the beneficials to stay in your garden.

Insect Predators and Parasites Found in the Garden

Since the borer spends most of its life safe within its host, it is not well controlled by any insect. Assassin bugs, however, have been known to prey upon the borer moths, and undoubtedly other predators occasionally destroy them.

Other Preventive Steps

Pinch off the growing tip while the plant is young and before the borers attack. This causes the plant to branch out, becoming multistemmed. During the growing season, bury every fifth leaf node on the trailing squash stems. The vine will root at those leaf nodes. Then, if the plant begins to die from borer attack, the infected section of the plant can be cut off, leaving the unaffected section to continue growing.

INSECT *Tarnished Plant Bug*

DESCRIPTION

The adult tarnished plant bug is a ¼-inch-long, oval, flat, brownish insect, mottled with yellow and black. It sucks on blossom stems and other plant parts. Tarnished plant bugs are highly mobile. The nymphs are pale yellow and the eggs long and curved, and inserted in stems, tips, and leaves. Adults and nymphs inject poison into young shoots, flower buds, and fruit when puncturing cells to suck juices. The tarnished plant bug also carries fire blight disease, infecting trees as it feeds. Winter is spent as an adult or a nymph in garden trash. Several generations occur in a year.

MOST OBVIOUS SYMPTOMS

Black spots and pitting can be seen on the stem tips, buds, and fruit of infested plants. This pest deforms roots, blackens terminal shoots, and ruins flowers. Adults fly to fruit trees in the first warm days of spring. They feed on developing buds, immediately halting fruit development. Only buds that escape feeding will set fruit. On dwarf trees, this can totally eliminate fruit production. Later feeding damage usually appears as a dimple or a scab. Tarnished plant bugs cause leaves and shoots to die on trees. On strawberries, pears, and peaches, they dwarf fruit and create sunken areas (called catfacing).

VULNERABLE PLANTS

Most vegetables, strawberries, and some fruit trees, including peaches and pears.

BEST CONTROL STRATEGY

Sprays must be used early in the morning when bugs are least active. Try three applications of pyrethrum, one every 3 days, to control adults and nymphs. The best way to control this pest is by fall and spring cleanup to prevent it from occurring in the first place.

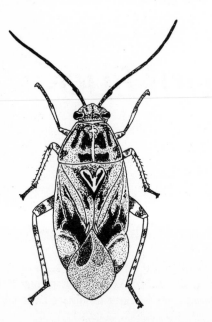

OPTIONS FOR CONTROLLING TARNISHED PLANT BUG

Emergence Time

Adult tarnished plant bugs overwinter under bark or in leaf litter. They emerge in early spring to begin feeding on budding trees and young seedlings. They also lay eggs in leaf tissue; eggs hatch in 10 days. Nymphs feed for 3 to 4 weeks, then molt to the adult stage. There may be up to 5 generations per year.

Early Warning Devices

Sticky Trap

One type of early warning trap is made from an 8-by-10-inch white panel covered with a sticky substance such as Tack Trap. These are available commercially or can be made at home. At blossom time, hang the panels from the outer branches of fruit trees, 2½ feet above the ground. Clear any foliage within 18 inches of the panel to increase visibility. If you make your own traps, use a glossy white paint, which will reflect light in the same way that an apple blossom does. In the vegetable garden, place them adjacent to, not above, susceptible plants.

Traps and Mechanical Controls

Sticky Trap

If several are used in each tree, sticky traps can be used as control devices for tarnished plant bugs. Make 10-inch square panels from a bright white material such as Masonite and coat them with sticky material such as Tack Trap, motor oil, or petroleum jelly. In the vegetable garden place them adjacent to, not above, susceptible plants. In the orchard hang them 2½ feet above the ground. Do not leave sticky traps out for over 3 or 4 weeks, as they may trap beneficial insects as well as pests.

Botanical Poisons

Pyrethrum

Pyrethrum will kill tarnished plant bugs, but when there is an abundance of bugs, spraying has little effect on the population. Try three applications of pyrethrum, 2 or 3 days apart. Remember that pyrethrum sprays can also be harmful to beneficial insects, so use the poison only as a last resort.

STEPS TO PREVENT TARNISHED PLANT BUG

Fall Cleanup

Be sure to clean up crop residues and any fallen fruit in fall and destroy all bugs that are ready to overwinter there.

Barriers

Netting or Fleece Cover

Netting, agricultural fleece, or other material that keeps out insects, but lets in air, light, and water, will protect vegetables. Lay it over crops at planting time. Floating covers placed directly over plants, or tunnels supported on braces, are also effective.

Insect Predators and Parasites Found in the Garden

Bigeyed bugs, damsel bugs, and pirate bugs prey on tarnished plant bugs. Encourage these beneficials with plantings of groundcovers and pollen plants.

INSECT *Tent Caterpillar*

DESCRIPTION

In the eastern and central United States, the caterpillar is hairy and black, with white stripes. Along its sides it displays narrow brown and yellow lines and a row of blue spots. In the west, the caterpillar is orange-brown, with blue dots on the back and sides. The caterpillar will grow to about 2 inches long. The adult moth has beige to brown wings with a wingspan of about 1¼ inches. It lays its eggs in a ring around twigs, and covers them with a shiny, hard substance.

MOST OBVIOUS SYMPTOMS

On some fruit trees, especially cherry and apple, you will see large, tentlike, silken nests filled with small caterpillars in the forks of branches. The tree will become defoliated.

VULNERABLE PLANTS

Apples, cherries, and pears.

BEST CONTROL STRATEGY

Remove the nests and destroy the caterpillars by hand. Spray the tree with *Bacillus thuringiensis* (BT) as soon as you see the nests begin to reappear, and repeat every 5 to 7 days until the pest is gone.

OPTIONS FOR CONTROLLING TENT CATERPILLAR

Emergence Time

Soon after hatching in the early spring, the larvae spin their "tents," or nests, in tree crotches. They venture out to eat leaves during the day and return to their nests at night.

Traps and Mechanical Controls

Burlap
Burlap wrapped around the trunk will trap mature

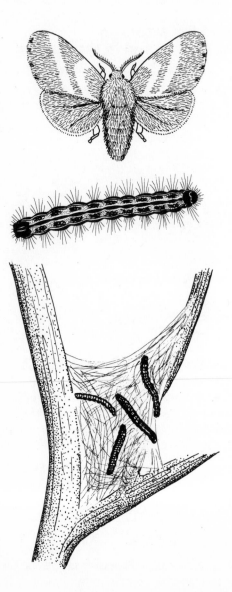

larvae as they crawl down the tree seeking a place to pupate. Check the burlap daily to collect the pests.

Handpicking
Remove the nests and their occupants as soon as you spot them. Wearing gloves, pull the nests out early in the day, and step on the worms or drop them into a can of kerosene.

Biological Controls

Bacillus Thuringiensis (BT)
Spray BT on affected trees every 10 to 14 days until the pest is removed. Be sure to spray the undersides of leaves.

STEPS TO PREVENT TENT CATERPILLAR

Animal Predators

Baltimore orioles, bluebirds, and chickadees eat tent caterpillars.

Insect Predators and Parasites Found in the Garden

Ground beetles and praying mantids prey on tent caterpillars. Digger wasps, *Podalonia occidentalis*, attack a western species—the Rocky Mountain tent caterpillar.

Intercropping or Companions

Butterfly milkweed (*Asclepias tuberosa*) hosts parasites of tent caterpillars, as do plants of the carrot family: celery, dill, parsnips, and queen anne's lace.

Other Preventive Steps

In the winter, look for the egg bands on tree trunks, fences, and house siding; scrape off these egg bands and destroy them.

<small>INSECT</small> *Thrips*

DESCRIPTION

Only ¹⁄₂₅ inch long, thrips are very difficult to see. What is visible are their dark fecal pellets and the whitened, desiccated tissue that results from mass feedings. Eggs are inserted into leaves, fruit, or stems. Nymphs and adults scrape the surface of flower buds, leaves, and stems to suck the sap. In cold regions, winters are passed as eggs. Many species are found throughout North America.

MOST OBVIOUS SYMPTOMS

Thrips attack flowers, especially white, yellow, and other light-colored blooms. They scrape and puncture petals causing considerable discoloration and disfiguration. Leaves and onion foliage become bleached or silver, then wither; flowers and fruit become scarred. Where heavy infestation occurs, foliage appears scorched and blossoms destroyed.

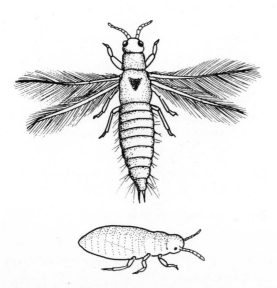

VULNERABLE PLANTS

Beans (lima and snap), corn, onions, pears, and squash (summer and winter).

BEST CONTROL STRATEGY

A spray of insecticidal soap every 3 days for 2 weeks should stop most infestations before they get out of control. For serious problems, use pyrethrum.

OPTIONS FOR CONTROLLING THRIPS

Natural Sprays

See the beginning of this chapter for more information on making natural sprays.

Garlic Spray

For a spray that repels thrips, finely chop or grind garlic, onions, or chives. Mix with water and then strain to form a clear solution. Spray the solution directly on the pests.

Insecticidal Soap

Commercial insecticidal soap effectively controls thrips. Spray every 2 to 3 days for 2 weeks for bad infestations. Soap sprays are contact insecticides, so spray the plant from top to bottom, especially under the leaves, where you'll find most thrips.

Light Horticultural Oil Spray

The newer horticultural oils, called "superior horticultural spray oil," are lighter and less viscous (viscosity 60 to 70) than traditional oils, and evaporate much more quickly from leaves and stems. They can be used during the growing season. Make up a 2 to 3 percent solution and spray directly on the thrips, because the oil works by suffocating them.

Spray in the morning. Two applications, 3 to 4 days apart, should do the job if you get good coverage.

Water Spray

If you spray plants with a forceful spray of water, you can knock many thrips from the leaves. This is best done in the early morning. Use a nozzle that will give you a fine spray of water, and thoroughly wash off the undersides of the affected leaves. It is important to do this at least three times—3 days in a row, or every other day—to get the thrips that will hatch from eggs that were laid before you began spraying.

Botanical Poisons

Neem

Purchase a commercial neem product and mix it according to label instructions. Apply the spray to thrips-infested plants twice, at weekly or longer intervals, until pests are under control. Spray carefully to thoroughly cover all plant parts. The spray will be most effective if you apply it in early morning or late afternoon.

Pyrethrum

Pyrethrum paralyzes thrips on contact. It must be applied directly to the thrips to work, so spray the undersides of the leaves as well as the tops. Usually two applications, 3 to 4 days apart, will be successful in controlling the problem.

STEPS TO PREVENT THRIPS

Preventive Spray Program

Horticultural Oil Spray

In late winter, before any leaf buds begin to open, spray dormant oil on fruit trees to control thrips. Make sure the entire surface of the tree is covered.

Barriers

Aluminum Mulch

Aluminum paper and aluminum polyethylene mulches reduce the number of thrips.

Diatomaceous Earth (D.E.)

On vegetable plants or very small trees, try D.E. Dust around the base of plants to create a barrier for the pest, or dust the whole plant with D.E. Dusting should progress upward from the ground, covering all stems and leaves, especially the undersides of leaves. Apply in the late evening or at night to minimize injury to predator insects.

Resistant Varieties

Use resistant varieties where possible. Spanish-type onions seem to tolerate or resist thrips damage better than globe onions.

Planting Date

Start plants early, monitor them regularly, and provide infested plants with supplemental feeding.

Insect Predators and Parasites Available Commercially

See the beginning of this chapter for more information on these beneficial insects.

Green Lacewing

Of all the bugs you can buy through the mail, lacewings are the most effective at controlling thrips.

Lady Bug

Lady bugs are voracious eaters of thrips.

Predatory Mite

The predatory mite *Amblyseius mackenziei* controls thrips on cucumbers and beans.

Insect Predators and Parasites Found in the Garden

Some species of thrips are actually beneficial insects, preying upon other thrips and small insect pests. Other naturally occurring beneficials that control thrips include ground beetles, lacewings, lady bugs, and syrphid flies.

Other Preventive Steps

A heavy mulch can keep adults from emerging from the ground in early spring. Make sure plants are adequately watered. Weed control is important. Pulling all weeds eliminates some winter hiding places.

NOTES AND RESEARCH

The new avermectin insecticides such as abamectic (Avid), which are fermentation products of a soil-inhabiting streptomyces organism, are very potent defenses against thrips.

INSECT *Tomato Hornworm*

DESCRIPTION

The tomato hornworm is a green caterpillar, 3 to 5 inches long, with white stripes. A horn projects from its rear. The horn cannot sting, contrary to what is sometimes thought. This pest chews leaves and fruit. The adult is a large, mottled, gray or brown moth with five orange spots along each side of the body. Its wingspan is 4 to 5 inches. The moths fly quickly and are able to hover like hummingbirds. They lay round, greenish yellow eggs singly on undersides of leaves. The pupae are 2 inches long and have a curved "handle." They overwinter 3 to 4 inches underground. One generation occurs every year in the northern states and two or more in the southern states. Tomato hornworms are found throughout North America.

MOST OBVIOUS SYMPTOMS

Plants injured by these pests have holes in their leaves and sometimes on the fruit. To spot the larvae before they have reached full size, look for dark-colored droppings on the foliage and spray the plants with water. The caterpillars will thrash about and give away their location.

VULNERABLE PLANTS

Dill, eggplants, peppers, potatoes, and tomatoes.

BEST CONTROL STRATEGY

They are easy to see, so handpick early. Use a *Bacillus thuringiensis* (BT) spray, or if the infestation gets out of hand, a pyrethrum spray.

OPTIONS FOR CONTROLLING TOMATO HORNWORM

Emergence Time

After overwintering in the soil in 2-inch, brown, spindle-shaped pupal cases, moths emerge in late spring to early summer to lay greenish yellow eggs on leaf undersides. Look for moths at dusk, when they visit flowers. Larvae feed for about 1 month before pupating.

Early Warning Devices

Trap Crop
Dill is a good trap crop.

Natural Sprays

See the beginning of this chapter for more information on making natural sprays.

Hot Pepper Spray
To repel tomato hornworms, try a hot pepper spray. Finely chop or grind hot peppers. Mix them with

water and then strain to form a clear solution. Spray the solution directly on the pest.

Biological Controls

Bacillus Thuringiensis (BT)
BT are bacteria that kill tomato hornworms. The

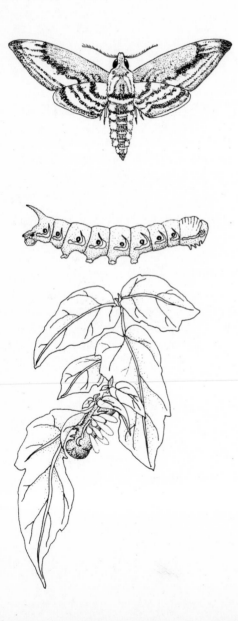

bacteria are most effective when worms are small. Apply as a dust, covering the leaves entirely, especially the undersides, or spray the affected plants every 10 to 14 days until the pests are gone.

Traps and Mechanical Controls

Handpicking
Handpicking is a way to make a sizable dent in the tomato hornworm infestation right away. It is best to attend to the very first adults that appear, to set back their egg-laying activities. If your garden is healthy, you may find small, white, elliptical braconid wasp eggs attached to the hornworm's back. Transport the hornworm away from your crops to allow these parasitic wasps to mature. If no wasp eggs are present, drop the worms into a can of water and kerosene.

Botanical Poisons

Neem
Purchase a commercial neem product and mix it according to label instructions. Apply the spray twice, at weekly or longer intervals, until pests are under control. Spray carefully to thoroughly cover all plant parts. The spray will be most effective if you apply it in early morning or late afternoon.

Pyrethrum
Pyrethrum paralyzes tomato hornworms on contact. It must be applied directly to the tomato hornworm to work, so spray the undersides of the leaves as well as the tops. Usually two applications, 3 to 4 days apart, will be successful.

STEPS TO PREVENT TOMATO HORNWORM

Fall Cleanup

It is absolutely critical to reduce overwintering tomato hornworms if you want to ease your problems next year. Look for the pupae buried 3 to 5 inches down in the soil as you cultivate in fall.

In the fall, as soon as you finish harvesting, remove all old plants and overgrown weeds, leaving soil completely bare; then cultivate the soil thoroughly to a depth of 6 to 8 inches, using a hand tool or a rotary tiller. About 2 to 3 weeks later, give the garden a shallow cultivation to a depth of about 2 inches with a rotary tiller or garden rake; then you can plant your winter cover crop, or lay down 4 to 6 inches of winter mulch.

In early spring, about 2 weeks before planting, give the garden another shallow cultivation, to a depth of about 2 inches. When planting, give the soil one final shallow cultivation.

Preventive Spray Programs

Bacillus Thuringiensis (BT)
If hornworms have been a severe problem in past seasons, spray BT on vulnerable plants every 2 weeks from transplant until blossoms form. This will keep tomato hornworms from establishing themselves on crops.

Barriers

Diatomaceous Earth (D.E.)
Dust D.E. around the base of vulnerable plants to create a barrier to the pest, or dust the whole plant with D.E. Dusting should progress upward from the ground, covering all stems and leaves, especially the undersides of leaves. Apply D.E. in late evening or at night, and fewer beneficial insects will be harmed.

Resistant Varieties

Tomato
Peron is said to be immune to hornworms.

Animal Predators

Baltimore orioles, barn swallows, blackbirds, bluebirds, downy woodpeckers, flycatchers, grackles, phoebes, and sparrows are some of the common songbirds that relish eating tomato hornworms. Moles, skunks, and toads eat their share as well.

Insect Predators and Parasites Available Commercially

See the beginning of this chapter for more information on these beneficial insects.

Parasitic (Non-stinging) Wasp
Braconid and trichogramma wasps are very small, almost microscopic, wasps that parasitize the eggs of tomato hornworms.

Insect Predators Found in the Garden

If a tomato hornworm has papery cocoons (braconid wasp eggs) on its back, natural parasites have already doomed it. Remove the hornworms from the garden but allow them to live so their parasites can reproduce. Other natural predators include assassin bugs and praying mantids.

INSECT *Weevil*

DESCRIPTION

Weevils are a whole family of small beetles. Most of the common pest weevils are brown or black and tear-shaped. They have hard-shelled bodies and long snouts. They feed at night and hide in the soil during the day. The larvae are small whitish grubs, which feed within the fruit, stem, or roots of plants. Eggs are typically laid on susceptible plants, or even injected into them. Winter may be passed as an adult or grub. Often, many generations occur a year.

MOST OBVIOUS SYMPTOMS

Larvae and adults may feed on leaves and fruit. Larvae make zigzag paths into roots, fruit, or stems. The bean weevil does most of its damage with the dried seeds.

VULNERABLE PLANTS

Most garden vegetables, as well as apples, blueberries, cherries, peaches, pears, plums, raspberries, rhubarb, and strawberries, are susceptible to weevil damage.

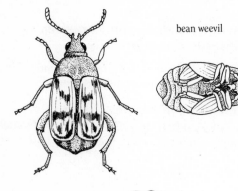

bean weevil

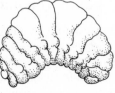

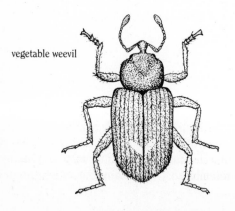

vegetable weevil

BEST CONTROL STRATEGY

Inspect garden plants regularly, and as soon as weevils appear, begin spraying weekly with pyrethrum, making sure to thoroughly cover all leaf surfaces. Treat the soil around susceptible crops with a solution of predatory nematodes to stop the reproduction of weevils.

OPTIONS FOR CONTROLLING WEEVIL

Traps and Mechanical Controls

Handpicking

Knock weevils from trees or shrubs using a padded stick, and let them fall onto a sheet spread below. Gather and destroy the weevils. Collect infested fruit, especially early drops.

Botanical Poisons

Pyrethrum

Pyrethrum paralyzes weevils on contact. It must be applied directly to the weevils to work, so spray the undersides of the leaves as well as the tops. Usually two applications, 3 to 4 days apart, will successfully control the problem.

STEPS TO PREVENT WEEVIL

Fall Cleanup

Clean up and destroy dead plants, and control weeds, especially wild relatives of the infested crops, in order to deprive the weevils of alternate hosts. Remove and destroy any tree fruit that falls prematurely.

Crop Rotation

Don't grow the same crop in the same place 2 years in a row. After a particularly bad infestation, wait a year or two before growing the same crop in that bed, or at all.

Barriers

Diatomaceous Earth (D.E.)

Dust D.E. around the base of the plant to create a barrier for the pest, or dust the whole plant with D.E. Dusting should progress upward from the ground, covering all stems and leaves, especially the undersides of leaves. Apply D.E. in late evening or at night, and predator insect destruction will be low.

Netting or Fleece Cover

Nylon netting, fine screening, or agricultural fleece can help to keep weevils off your crops. Cover transplants or newly seeded areas with the preferred material immediately. Lay the material directly on the plants and seal all the edges to the ground by laying soil over the edges. Provide lots of extra material to prevent plants from straining against the cover as they grow. Remove the fleece when plants begin to flower.

Resistant Varieties

Sweet Potato

Regal is resistant to the sweet potato weevil and is available in limited supply from Webber Produce Company. Though the roots of Regal are about 80 percent resistant, you'll still find weevils in the vines. Inspect the plants regularly.

Animal Predators

Bluebirds, warblers, wrens, and other birds eat weevils.

Insect Predators and Parasites Available Commercially

See the beginning of this chapter for more information on these beneficial insects.

Beneficial Nematode

One of the best techniques for preventing a weevil attack or controlling a bad infestation is to introduce predatory nematodes to the garden. Release them early in the season, around planting time if possible.

Insect Predators and Parasites Found in the Garden

Spiders catch adult weevils.

NOTES AND RESEARCH

Scientists have discovered that hairs on the lower sides of the leaves of the wild beach strawberry *(Fragaria chiloensis)* repel black vine weevils, which are responsible for huge losses of commercially grown strawberries. The next step is to breed strawberry cultivars that have this trait.

 INSECT **Whitefly**

DESCRIPTION

Adult whiteflies are about the size of a pinhead, mothlike, dusty, and white winged. When shaken off a plant, they look like flying dandruff. The yellowish nymphs are legless, flat, and oval, and may resemble scale at certain stages. Eggs are yellow and cone shaped, and are laid on the undersides of leaves. Nymphs and adults suck juices from plant leaves, buds, and stems. The plants weaken. Whiteflies are found throughout the United States. Many generations occur in a year.

MOST OBVIOUS SYMPTOMS

Whiteflies are clearly visible on the plants. The plants themselves weaken, and the leaves turn yellow and die. Fruit and leaves may be covered with shiny, sticky honeydew secreted by whiteflies, and a black fungus that is encouraged by the honeydew. Plants and fruit are undersized and poorly colored.

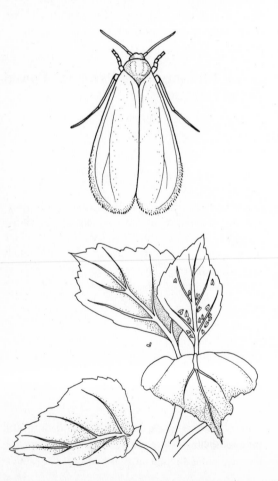

VULNERABLE PLANTS

Most fruits and vegetables are susceptible to whitefly attack. In western states, the name "whitefly" is also used to refer to leafhoppers.

BEST CONTROL STRATEGY

Use a preventive insecticidal soap spray early in the season, and then use the soap spray again if there is any noticeable infestation. Pyrethrum is used as a last resort.

OPTIONS FOR CONTROLLING WHITEFLY

Emergence Time

Whiteflies appear as soon as weather warms in the spring. They are most prolific during moist, hot summers.

Early Warning Devices

Sticky Trap
Some early warning traps on the market (which can also be made at home) are colored yellow to attract whiteflies, and they are covered with a very sticky material such as Tack Trap.

Trap Crop
Ornamental flowering tobacco, nicotiana, can be planted as a trap crop for whiteflies, which are attracted to the plant's sticky leaves.

Natural Sprays

See the beginning of this chapter for more information on making natural sprays.

Alcohol
Alcohol mixed with water and Volck oil can be completely effective in controlling whiteflies. Two applications with a trigger sprayer, a week apart,

saturating the plants to the point of runoff, gives total control with no injury to the plants. The mixture is 1 cup alcohol and ½ teaspoon Volck oil in 1 quart water. The Volck oil helps the alcohol to stick. Insecticidal soap may be used instead of Volck oil. It too helps the alcohol adhere, and doubles the chances of killing the whiteflies. Never use alcohol alone, without the oil and water, because it can burn some plants, especially young ones.

Insecticidal Soap

Commercial insecticidal soap effectively controls whiteflies. Spray every 2 to 3 days for 2 weeks. Soap sprays are contact insecticides, so spray the plant from top to bottom, especially under the leaves, where you'll find most whiteflies.

Light Horticultural Oil Spray

The newer horticultural oils, called "superior horticultural spray oil," are lighter and less viscous (viscosity 60 to 70) than traditional oils, and evaporate much more quickly from leaves and stems. Use them during the growing season to control whiteflies. Make a 2 to 3 percent solution and spray directly on the whiteflies, because the oil works by suffocation. Spray anytime there is an infestation, using two applications, 3 to 4 days apart, for best control.

Water Spray

If you spray plants forcefully with water, you can knock many whiteflies from the leaves. This is best done early in the morning. Use a nozzle that will give a fine spray of water, and thoroughly wash off the undersides of the affected leaves. It is important that you do this at least three times—3 days in a row or every other day—to get the whiteflies that will hatch from eggs that were laid before you began spraying.

Traps and Mechanical Controls

Sticky Trap

To make an effective trap, take a 10-by-10-inch piece of material such as Masonite and paint it bright, school-bus yellow. Coat it with sticky material such as Tack Trap, motor oil, or petroleum jelly.

Place the traps adjacent to, not above, susceptible plants, where they will catch enormous numbers of whiteflies. A single trap will attract whiteflies from plants that are 4 to 5 feet away. Do not leave traps out for over 3 to 4 weeks, as they may trap beneficial as well as harmful insects.

Botanical Poisons

Neem

Purchase a commercial neem product and mix it according to label instructions. Apply the spray twice, at weekly or longer intervals, until pests are under control. Spray carefully in early morning or late afternoon to thoroughly cover all plant parts.

Pyrethrum

Pyrethrum paralyzes whiteflies on contact. Apply it directly to the whiteflies, spraying the undersides of the leaves as well as the tops. Usually two applications, 3 to 4 days apart, will be successful in controlling the problem.

STEPS TO PREVENT WHITEFLY

Preventive Spray Programs

Horticultural Oil Spray

In late winter, before any leaf buds begin to open, spray dormant oil on fruit trees to control whiteflies. Make sure the entire surface of the tree is covered.

Insecticidal Soap

On plants most vulnerable to soft-bodied pests such as whiteflies, you can follow a biweekly preventive spray program using commercial insecticidal soap on the undersides of all new growth. Start by spraying seedlings you are starting indoors. Spray plants every 2 weeks, continuing for the first months of the plant's life in the garden.

Seaweed Spray

Liquid seaweed extract is neither an insecticide nor a fungicide, but its effect in minimizing or even eliminating insect damage is remarkable. Whiteflies are less likely to cause unacceptable damage to crops treated with seaweed or kelp extract. It seems that, once sprayed, the leaves of such crops become unsuitable for the reproduction of the pest.

Intercropping or Companions

Some research has indicated that from mid-July up to late September, onions or chives planted in and around the garden may repel whiteflies. Gardeners often recommend nasturtiums and savory, but no studies confirm that these plants are effective repellents.

Animal Predators

Gnatcatchers, kinglets, phoebes, and swallows are some of the common songbirds that relish eating whiteflies.

Insect Predators and Parasites Available Commercially

See the beginning of this chapter for more information on these beneficial insects.

Green Lacewing

Of all the bugs you can buy through the mail, lace-

wings are the most effective at controlling whiteflies.

Lady Bug

Lady bugs are voracious eaters of whiteflies.

Parasitic (Non-stinging) Wasp

Chalcid and trichogramma wasps are very small, almost microscopic, wasps that parasitize the eggs of whiteflies. The parasitic wasp *Encarsia formosa* can be used to control whiteflies in the greenhouse, but is not effective outdoors.

Insect Predators and Parasites Found in the Garden

Spiders eat whiteflies.

Other Preventive Steps

Make certain that the phosphorus and magnesium content of the soil is at the proper level. Apply magnesium as a soil drench while plants are growing. Make the drench by dissolving ½ cup of Epsom salts in 1 gallon of water. Thoroughly soak the soil surrounding the plants with the solution.

Good air circulation around plants will help to prevent whiteflies from becoming a serious problem. Humid, stale air encourages them.

INSECT # White Grub

DESCRIPTION

White grubs are fat, whitish larvae, ¾ to 1½ inches long. The adult is the may beetle or june beetle. These larvae feed on roots and seldom cause noticeable damage unless they get very numerous. Winters are spent as grubs in the soil. The pests are found throughout North America, and are especially common in new gardens just built on former

lawns. Damaged sections of lawn appear burned and can be lifted up with ease, exposing the grubs. After working on the grass, the grubs can move into the food garden and eat roots and the bases of plants. They can cripple or ruin plants without ever being detected. Their life cycle requires several years to complete.

MOST OBVIOUS SYMPTOMS

Infestations of white grubs may cause sudden wilting of plants, usually in early summer. White-grub damage begins in early fall, as eggs laid in July and August begin to hatch. The white grub feeds on the roots of grass until the ground freezes in late fall; then it burrows deeply into the ground to stay warm. In the spring, the grub returns to the surface and again feeds on roots.

VULNERABLE PLANTS

Young apple trees, blackberries, corn, onions, potatoes, and strawberries.

BEST CONTROL STRATEGY

Juvenile stage nematodes are effective against white grubs. Apply milky spore disease for long-term control.

OPTIONS FOR CONTROLLING WHITE GRUB

Biological Controls

Milky Spore Disease
Milky spore *(Bacillus popilliae)* affects the grub. Spread the dry powder on mowed areas of the yard using a fertilizer spreader. It infects grubs anytime they start to feed, when they hatch or in the fall before they burrow more deeply into the soil to overwinter. The disease stays in the soil, where it will infect the next population of beetle grubs. It takes 3 to 5 years to have major impact on the population, and it is very expensive, but it does work.

STEPS TO PREVENT WHITE GRUB

Fall Cleanup

White grubs winter over in soil near the host plant, so the fall garden cleanup may be the most important white grub control step you take all season long. It is absolutely critical to reduce overwintering white grubs if you want to ease your problems next year.

In fall, as soon as you finish harvesting each crop, remove all old plants and overgrown weeds, leaving the soil completely bare; then cultivate the soil thoroughly to a depth of 6 to 8 inches, using a hand tool or a rotary tiller. About 2 to 3 weeks after that deep cultivation, give the garden a shallow cultivation to a depth of about 2 inches with a rotary tiller or garden rake; then you can plant your winter cover crop, or lay down 4 to 6 inches of winter mulch.

In early spring, about 2 weeks before planting, give the garden another shallow cultivation to a depth of about 2 inches. When planting, give the soil one final shallow cultivation.

Animal Predators

Crows, robins, and starlings are among the best grub eaters in the yard.

Insect Predators and Parasites Available Commercially

See the beginning of this chapter for more information on these beneficial insects.

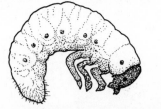

Beneficial Nematode

If grubs are a particular problem in your garden, you should consider making one application of beneficial nematodes, which attack the grub population below the surface of the soil. Beneficial nematodes are tiny soil-dwelling worms that find their way to the white grub, burrow inside, and reproduce. The white grub is killed by bacteria released by the nematodes.

Insect Predators and Parasites Found in the Garden

Ground beetles help control the grubs.

INSECT *Wireworm*

DESCRIPTION

Wireworms are the larvae of click beetles. They are ⅓ to 1½ inches long, dark brown to yellowish, jointed, hard shelled, and cylindrical. Do not confuse wireworms with millipedes, which have many pairs of legs; wireworms have only three pairs directly behind the head. They chew on underground stems, roots, seeds, and tubers of a wide variety of plants. Eggs are laid in the soil. Eggs, larvae, and adults overwinter in the soil. Wireworms are found throughout the United States and are especially common on land that is poorly drained or has recently been in sod. One generation occurs in a year. Some species in some locations may require several years to mature.

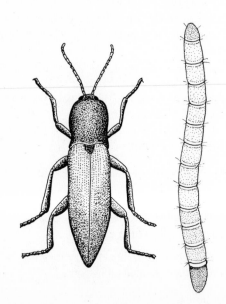

MOST OBVIOUS SYMPTOMS

Plants wilt and may die.

VULNERABLE PLANTS

Most garden fruits and vegetables, including beets, beans (snap), carrots, corn, lettuce, muskmelons, onions, peas, potatoes, strawberries, and sweet potatoes, are attacked by wireworms.

BEST CONTROL STRATEGY

Trap them with pieces of potato, as described on the next page, and plant a cover crop for long-term control.

OPTIONS FOR CONTROLLING WIREWORM

Emergence Time

Adult beetles lay eggs in the soil in the spring. The

worms, or larvae, may take from 2 to 6 years to reach adulthood, depending on the species.

Early Warning Devices

Potato Trap

Trap wireworms in pieces of potato. Spear pieces of potato with sticks and bury them 2 to 4 inches deep in the garden, leaving a portion of the stick above ground. Set the potato traps at 3- to 10-foot intervals. The wireworms will burrow into the potato pieces to feed. After a week, dig up the pieces and destroy them, along with the wireworms that are inside.

Natural Sprays

See the beginning of this chapter for more information on making natural sprays.

Bug Juice

Try a bug juice spray made by crushing some of the wireworms themselves and adding water. Strain, and spray on affected plants. Gardeners report that the bug juice kills or repels the wireworms.

STEPS TO PREVENT WIREWORM

Fall Cleanup

Adults, larvae, and eggs overwinter in soil near the host plant, so the fall garden cleanup may be the most important wireworm control step you take all season long. It is absolutely critical to reduce overwintering wireworms if you want to ease your problems next year.

In fall, as soon as you finish harvesting each crop, remove all old plants and overgrown weeds, leaving the soil completely bare; then cultivate the soil thoroughly to a depth of 6 to 8 inches, using a hand tool or a rotary tiller. About 2 to 3 weeks after that deep cultivation, give the garden a shallow cultivation, about 2 inches deep, with a rotary tiller or garden rake. Then plant your winter cover crop, or lay down 4 to 6 inches of winter mulch.

In early spring, about 2 weeks before planting, give the garden another shallow cultivation to a depth of about 2 inches. When planting, give the soil one final shallow cultivation.

Cover Crops

Alfalfa and clover cover crops repel wireworms. A cover crop of alfalfa repeated every year will gradually reduce wireworms on corn.

Insect Predators and Parasites Available Commercially

See the beginning of this chapter for more information on these beneficial insects.

Beneficial Nematode

Beneficial nematodes are tiny soil-dwelling worms that find their way to the wireworm, burrow inside, and reproduce. The wireworm is killed by bacteria released by the nematodes.

NOTES AND RESEARCH

Wireworms don't seem to like a chemical in butterfly milkweed *(Asclepias tuberosa)*. In a laboratory test, wireworms lost their appetites when seeds and seedlings were coated with an extract of butterfly milkweed juice. The pests even avoided soil that had been treated with the extract.

CHAPTER 5

Diseases

You have fewer tools for fighting diseases in the food garden than you have available for use against insect and animal pests. In many cases, once the disease appears, effective or practical control steps for individual plants do not exist, and you must consign the sick plant to the trash. However, removal of infected plants does control diseases in your garden as a whole.

Remember, a number of fungal diseases can occur that cause spots or some yellowing but are not lethal to the plant or seriously detrimental to the quality of the harvest. So do not panic at first sight of a single yellow leaf on your bush beans. Look at the general vigor of the plant. If it looks otherwise healthy, wait for a few days or even weeks to see if in fact you have a serious problem. Fungal diseases occur slowly. If your plants are deteriorating very rapidly, it is a sign of a viral or bacterial disease, and the infected plants should be immediately removed and destroyed.

CONTROLLING DISEASES

The first step in controlling diseases in the garden is to spot and identify them. Look for symptoms. Examine plants for any changes in their general appearance. Many, if not most, of the problem symptoms you will find on your plants are caused by insects rather than disease, but by reading the descriptions given for diseases and insect pest prob-

lems in this book, and with experience, you will learn the differences. (See chapter 4 to become familiar with the symptoms of insect problems.)

Once you've decided that the problem is caused by a disease rather than an insect pest, you will need to determine the exact disease that has infected your plants. Unfortunately, not every disease exhibits its own specific pattern of symptoms. Many symptoms can be caused by more than one disease.

Diseases in the food garden can be divided into five broad categories: environmental, fungal, bacterial, viral, and nematode. Unfortunately, it is not always easy to distinguish symptoms among the categories, since many of the symptoms can be a result of two or three different types of disease. Nevertheless, some problems are more common than others, and gardeners learn to diagnose disease problems from their experience of what has happened in their gardens in previous years. Although there is some overlap, each type of disease—environmental, fungal, bacterial, and so forth—can be recognized by a general set of symptoms.

There are a number of good books for identifying diseases; Rodale's *Encyclopedia of Natural Insect and Disease Control,* the National Garden Association's *Gardening,* and Penn State's *Identifying Diseases of Vegetables* are particularly easy to use.

If you have just begun to garden, most of your disease problems in the early years will be environmental. The next to attack your garden will most likely be fungal diseases, with bacterial, viral, and

Symptoms of Diseases

1. Chlorosis (yellowing) of leaves.
   All leaves.
   Youngest leaves only.
   Older leaves only.
   Leaf edges.
   Between leaf veins.
   Round spots, all leaves.
   Irregular spots, all leaves.
   Small dots, all leaves.
   Mosaic patterns, all leaves.
2. Dead or brownish areas on leaves.
   Leaf edges or tips.
   Spots or sections, all leaves.
   Edge and inner sections, all leaves.
3. Water-soaked or greasy appearance.
4. Premature defoliation.
5. Wilting plant.
6. Abnormal plant growth.
7. Rotten spots on leaves or fruit.
8. Plant dies mysteriously.

nematode diseases occurring least often on the average.

ENVIRONMENTAL DISEASES

The environment surrounding a plant above and below the ground can be the cause of certain disorders. Above the surface of the soil, the vagaries of wind, rain, sunlight, and temperature cause such problems as dieback, blasting, leaf scorch, hollow heart, and sunscald. Environmental conditions below the surface of the soil, such as tilth of the soil, nutrient deficiencies or excesses, moisture content, and an inappropriate pH reading, cause other disorders. (See chapter 7 for more information on soil problems.) Environmental disorders can weaken a plant and lead to real pathogenic diseases. For example, smut and anthracnose in corn, fusarium in cabbage and muskmelons, and powdery mildew in cucumbers are all fungal diseases encouraged by hot, dry summer weather.

Of the five groups of plant diseases, environmental disorders are the easiest to correct once they have been properly diagnosed. Getting a proper diagnosis, however, takes some skill and experience. Any of the symptoms listed in the box Symptoms of Diseases may be the result of an environmental disease; however, the most common are general weakening of the whole plant or some color change in the leaves, such as yellowing or reddening.

Control of Environmental Diseases

Environmental disorders can usually be quickly remedied by applying the appropriate foliar spray to a weakening plant. However, you can also take long-term measures to control environmental problems without ever knowing the specific cause. Simply follow these steps:

1. Make sure the soil is healthy, and has the proper pH level and nutrient balance, sufficient drainage, and sufficient water-holding capability.
2. Make sure the plant gets the appropriate amount of water.
3. Make sure the plant gets the appropriate amount of fertilizer.

For example, if you add an inch of compost to the garden every year, you will be correcting many of the soil deficiencies most commonly found in the new garden. If you spray your plants once or twice a season with a kelp extract, your plants will get the necessary micronutrients, even if there are some deficiencies in the soil. If you make sure that the plants get a consistent level of water (about 1 inch a week), you eliminate over- or underwatering. And finally, if you add an appropriate amount of slow-acting fertilizer (roughly 1 cup per 25 square feet of garden) once a season, you will eliminate most nutritional problems. So even though it may be difficult to identify the environmental cause of a problem, these easy steps will help to remedy and prevent the problem and any other environmental diseases that could occur.

FUNGAL DISEASES

Disease fungi are microscopic plants that take their energy from the plants on which they live—they parasitize food crops. Fungal diseases exhibit a number of distinct symptoms, often indicated by their names. Downy mildew and powdery mildew create pale patches on the leaves of the plants. Rusts can be identified by their rusty color on leaves. Leaf spot causes round, yellow spots on the leaves that darken over time. Many fungal diseases can be controlled or even eliminated by proper garden practices. Not all fungal diseases are found in all parts of the country. When you spot a problem in a plant, rule out possible environmental problems before looking for a fungal cause.

Fungal diseases tend to spread over the entire plant somewhat slowly, occurring over weeks rather than days, whereas problems caused by viruses or bacteria spread quite quickly. This does not mean you can wait to confirm that you have a fungal problem, because the low toxic fungicides are not very effective in controlling the disease if it is well established in the plant.

Control of Fungal Diseases

Treatment of fungal diseases varies depending on the disease. In some cases, you should simply remove the affected leaves. However, in most cases, you should leave the plant alone and begin some control strategy using fungicidal sprays or dusts. Discussions of the diseases later in this chapter offer specific control steps, but in general, once you've decided your plant has one of the fungal diseases, such as rust or black spot, it often can be arrested by the application of an appropriate fungicide.

How to Use Fungicides

Fungicides are much less effective once diseases have become well established, so, for best results, apply them early in the season, even before there is evidence of plant damage, if a particular disease has consistently been a problem in your garden. This means, of course, remembering when a fungal disease struck a particular crop last year so you can anticipate its arriving at about the same time this year. Generally you will repeat fungicide treatments every week or 10 days through the growing season to either prevent a disease from developing or to keep a fungal disease controlled. Stop treatments about 3 to 4 weeks before harvest.

Remember, whether you use a dust or a spray, only those parts of the plant that are actually coated with the fungicide are protected; that is why some kind of "sticker" material should be included in any spray mixture. With fruit trees you will need to use about 1 gallon of spray for dwarf and semidwarf trees and up to 2 gallons for mature, full-sized trees to get complete coverage. Vegetable crops require varying amounts of fungicide, depending on the size of the crop.

The fungicides listed on the next page are safe to use in the food garden, but they should be handled carefully. You should wash your hands thoroughly after using these materials, and you should thoroughly wash any fruit or vegetables that have been sprayed with these products before eating them.

A single fungicide will not control all fungal diseases. Fortunately, your food garden will not experience large numbers of different fungal diseases, requiring a shelf full of different control products. All food gardeners should have a sulfur-based fungicide on their shelves, since it does control several fungal problems. You can add other products to your store as they become necessary.

Types of Fungicides

Although there are many powerful fungicides on the market that will control most fungal diseases, only a few are considered totally safe to the environment, and are recommended here for safe application in the home ecosystem.

Bordeaux Mixture. This fungicide is a mixture of certain salts of copper and hydrated lime and has a very low level of toxicity. It works by burning the spores of fungal diseases. Do not mix it with other materials, except oil. When combined with BT, it makes the BT ineffective. Do not use a Bordeaux mixture during cool, wet weather or it will damage plants. It can be used to control anthracnose, apple scab, black knot, black rot, brown rot, cherry leaf spot, fire blight, leaf spot, peach leaf curl, and other fungal diseases. For control of brown rot, peach leaf curl, and apple scab, apply Bordeaux mixture when the plants are dormant. Wherever Bordeaux mixture is recommended you may safely substitute one of the fixed copper fungicides (see below). Bordeaux mixture is corrosive to iron and steel.

Copper Sulfate. The fixed copper compounds, such as basic copper sulfate, copper oxychloride, and cuprous oxide, are effective in controlling various fungal and bacterial diseases. These compounds are sold under various trade names and should be used only as directed on the labels. Do not use them during cool, wet weather, or they may damage the plants. They help to control anthracnose, apple scab, bacterial spot, black leg, botrytis fruit rot, brown rots, downy mildew, early blight and late blight, leaf blight of celery, leaf spot, powdery mildew, scab, septoria leaf spot, and other fungal diseases.

Among the fixed copper fungicides on the market are Basic Copper Sulfate, Basi-Cop, Microcop, Copper 53 Fungicide, Tribasic Copper Sulfate, and T B-C-S 53. Others include Bordo, Bordo-Mix, C-O-C-S, Coprantol, Kocide 101, Miller 658, and Ortho Copper Fungicide.

Lime Sulfur. A fungicide that is somewhat caustic and works by burning the germinating fungal spores, lime sulfur helps to control apple scab, black knot, brown rot, powdery mildew, and other fungal diseases. To use, make a dilution of 1 part lime sulfur to 50 parts water. Spray plants right after a rain, before the leaves dry. Lime sulfur is also available as a dust. Neither the spray nor the dust should be used when temperatures climb above 80°F. Do not spray fruit trees when they are in blossom. Lime sulfur will stain buildings, walls, and trellises.

Sulfur. Sulfur is one of the best natural fungicides available, and it is very low in toxicity. Applied to the surface of leaves, ground-up sulfur rock will prevent the germination of certain fungal spores that fall on a treated leaf. Sulfur is also available in liquid form, combined with a soap-base material as the carrier. The liquid sticks to the undersides of leaves better than the powder. Use sulfur in 2-week intervals as a preventive method during periods when you expect certain fungal infections to occur. Do not apply it when air temperatures are over 80°F.

Sulfur fungicides will help control the following fungal diseases: anthracnose, black knot, black rot, brown rot on stone fruit, cedar apple rust, cherry leaf spot, common scab, leaf spot, powdery mildew, rust, scab on peaches, and other fungal diseases. Do not use sulfur on D'Anjou pears or cucurbits.

BACTERIAL DISEASES

The bacteria that attack food crops are carried to those plants in flowing or splashing water or in transported soil. They can enter a plant through wounds or through the tiny natural openings in the epidermis. Once inside, bacteria travel short distances in the sap of the plant. Generally, they cause rotting and wilting.

Control of Bacterial Diseases

Bacterial diseases cannot be cured. Infected plants must be immediately removed from the garden. *All the affected plants must be removed to the trash can, even if they have only slight symptoms of a bacterial disease.* Do not place diseased plants in your compost pile, even if you maintain an active pile that heats up.

To prevent the spread of a bacterial disease, clean your pruning tools after cutting a diseased plant. Use a bleach solution made up of one part common household bleach and four parts water. After disinfecting your tools, coat them with oil to avoid any rusting. Wash your hands after handling infected plants, not because they are dangerous to you, but because you can transmit the disease to healthy plants.

VIRAL DISEASES

It is not yet clear whether viruses are living organisms or nonliving chemicals. In any case, they damage the plant by destroying the chlorophyll in cells, causing yellowing of leaves. Typical symptoms of viral diseases include smaller than normal yields and poor fruit or vegetable quality. If a plant becomes sick and dies within just a few days, suspect a virus.

Viruses are spread from plant to plant in a number of ways. Insects often carry them, especially aphids, leafhoppers, mealybugs, and whiteflies. Aphids are the worst offenders; the green peach aphid can carry more than 50 different plant viruses. Viruses can also be carried on your hands or on garden tools.

Control of Viral Diseases

Viral diseases cannot be cured. Remove and destroy the infected plants. As with bacterial diseases, *remove all the affected plants,* even if symptoms are mild. Do not place diseased plants in your compost pile, and clean hands and tools with a bleach solution made up of one part household bleach to four parts water.

NEMATODE DISEASES

Nematodes are tiny parasitic worms that either stick their heads in a plant to suck the sap or actually spend their lives inside the plant. Although they are actually pests, the problems they cause are included with diseases, because those problems continue for the life of the plant as do pathogenic diseases.

Generally, it is difficult to diagnose nematodes by just looking at the plant. Very often a nematode problem will show up with the plant weakening and not looking healthy and vigorous. What usually happens is that you leave nematodes as the last diagnosis of the problem: If no other explanation seems to fit, check the possibility that your plants have nematodes.

PREVENTING DISEASES

Usually we wait until we have a disease problem and then take control steps to minimize the damage. It's at this time that we become interested in how to prevent that particular disease from ever becoming a problem again. This approach works fairly well, but the best way to fight diseases is to prevent their occurrence in the first place, and fortunately that is not a complicated task: A few simple garden maintenance steps will go a long way in achieving it. For example, by spreading compost, using seaweed extract sprays, and watering properly, you can significantly reduce the incidence of environmental diseases. Using mulch reduces the spread of fungal and bacterial diseases that are often transported to the plant in rain splashing up from the soil. Bacteria can live in the soil for years; consequently, rotation of crops within the garden helps reduce the incidence of bacterial diseases. Viral diseases can be prevented by controlling insect pests such as aphids, which carry these diseases. These and many other general garden practices can keep your garden disease-free.

Garden Management Practices

Rather than worry about preventing a specific disease from recurring in your garden, follow some general garden practices that help to prevent *all* diseases from showing up. You might think building healthy soil with compost or adding mulch around your plants is simply extra effort, but such practices expend less energy than trying to combat a disease once it has gotten a foothold in the garden. In addition, many of these garden management practices prevent all sorts of other possible problems—soil deficiencies, pest infestations, poor drainage. Remember, an initially healthy garden has a better

Disease Prevention Steps

1. Build healthy soil.
2. Use compost.
3. Use resistant varieties.
4. Rotate crops. (See page 379 for information on crop rotation.)
5. Use a foliar spray.
6. Use mulch.
7. Eliminate the method of transmission.
8. Water plants before noon.
9. Keep tools clean.
10. Clean up the garden in fall. (See chapter 4 for information on fall cleanup practices.)
11. Solarize the soil. (See page 379 for information on soil solarization.)
12. Use drip irrigation to prevent fungal diseases.
13. Don't work with plants when they are wet, to avoid spreading fungal diseases.
14. Mow under fruit trees and remove clippings and leaves to the compost pile.

chance of combating occasional diseases on its own, without your efforts.

Build Healthy Soil

A garden soil that has a minimum of 5 percent humus content (more than 10 percent is even better), has a pH of around 6.5, contains at least five earthworms per cubic foot, and gets an annual 1-inch layer of compost, will prevent diseases as effectively as any other disease-fighting tool you might use. A healthy soil maintains a balance between the beneficial bacteria, viruses, and other microorganisms and those pathogens that can cause diseases if allowed to multiply. The most common disease viruses, bacteria, and spores in your neighborhood are usually present in the soil. However, beneficial microorganisms keep those diseases under control

as long as the soil is healthy. (See chapter 7 for more information on soil management.)

Use Compost

Compost benefits the garden in many ways, and one of the benefits it offers is disease control. Recent research by Safer Agro-Chem Ltd., of Victoria, British Columbia, has shown that compost produces certain fatty acids that are toxic to fungal diseases and to certain bacterial diseases of plants. Decomposing rye and timothy grasses, for example, release fatty acids that control parasitic nematodes.

Research by the Ohio Agricultural Research and Development Center has shown that compost, especially the kind that is made the passive way (by simply piling compost materials and leaving them to decompose), suppresses harmful root-invading fungi, which can cause such diseases as root rot and damping-off. Certain beneficial bacteria, for example, are present in compost that produce substances called siderophores, which tie up iron, depriving harmful organisms of this necessary element. Beneficial fungi found in compost, particularly species of trichoderma and pythium, are antagonistic to pathogenic fungi. For example, they will attack rhizoctonia root rot fungi and some water mold fungi. The more of these beneficial bacteria and fungi that are present in the soil, the fewer the disease problems that will occur.

Compost produced using the active method (by chopping and turning the materials in your compost pile), with its high temperatures, has less disease-suppressive ability than a low-temperature compost made using the passive method, because beneficial microorganisms are killed by the high heat. "Seeding" high-temperature compost with small amounts of mature compost made at moderate temperatures (about 80°F) restores its ability to fight disease-causing organisms. (See chapter 7 for more information about compost.)

Use Resistant Varieties

Planting resistant varieties of vegetables and fruit is, of course, one of the most effective ways to avoid disease problems. In the past 25 years, seed companies and plant breeders have put a lot of effort into developing disease-resistant varieties of plants.

Resistance is not the same as immunity. Resistance refers to the plant's ability to overcome, to a degree, the effect of the pathogen. Varieties of plants listed in a seed catalog as resistant are resistant under certain growing conditions and may not necessarily be resistant in your area. However, it is still advisable to try these resistant varieties if you know you have a particular disease problem to contend with.

Varieties of plants have been developed to resist viral, bacterial, and fungal diseases and certain insects. Environmental diseases are really disorders caused by unhealthy soil and poor gardening practices, and must be controlled by garden management rather than by the use of certain seed varieties.

No variety of plant is resistant to all diseases. If a catalog lists a variety as disease-resistant without listing the specific disease, you have no way of knowing whether the plant is protected against a specific problem. Many of the individual descriptions of vegetables, fruit, and herbs in chapters 1 through 3 contain lists of the most common resistant and tolerant varieties available from seed companies and nurseries. Only the most common varieties are listed, so if you are struggling with a particularly difficult problem, you may wish to dig deeper into the gardening literature for a variety that is best for your situation. Your local County Extension Office is probably the best place to begin that search. They try to keep close track of all the new resistant and tolerant varieties of vegetables and fruit that are particularly useful in your area.

Rotate Crops

A very important technique in preventing all but the environmental diseases is crop rotation. Many diseases are caused by spores or bacteria that live in the soil right on into the next season. However, these bacteria or spores often do not travel very far from where their host plant was grown. So by making sure that you never plant the same kind of vegetable in the same place 2 years in a row, you can avoid many disease problems.

Crop rotation in a small garden may seem to be a bit difficult. However, if you have four beds, for example, and you rotate your crops to different beds each year, that will assure that some crops will not be planted in the same place for 3 years. That is often sufficient time to control certain diseases. Even moving a crop from one side of a 4-foot-wide bed 3 feet over to the other side of the bed can be helpful in many cases.

One of the problems with crop rotation is keeping track of where you planted things the previous year. You probably think you will remember where you put the lettuce, the cabbage, and the tomatoes, but sometimes it all seems the same and gets blurred as the years go by. There are a number of different schemes for labeling a garden so you can keep track. The best way of course, and the one guaranteed to work, is to make a diagram of the garden on paper with the location of the different vegetables carefully marked.

The system that is the easiest and most effective is to keep track of which vegetables have been planted in each bed, without worrying about exactly where in the bed they were located. This means that the rotation plan will be set up to shift vegetables from bed to bed each year, trying to avoid planting a variety in a bed more than once every 3 to 5 years. This approach makes for a cleaner record; in fact, you can put 3 or 4 years of rotation records on one sheet of paper. And in the final analysis, moving plant families from bed to bed will give you better disease prevention than simply moving them around within a single bed, assuming you have that extra space.

Use a Foliar Spray

In chapter 4, the use of seaweed extract to prevent insect problems was discussed. Seaweed extract can also help to prevent diseases in the garden. A disease may still appear on a plant that has been sprayed with seaweed extract, but it does little or no damage, and the disease never seems to spread to the whole crop. It is thought that the leaves of plants sprayed with seaweed extract are unsuitable for spore reproduction.

A number of natural fungicides made from sulfur suspended in liquid soaps are available commercially; they can be used to prevent as well as control diseases. When mixed with a seaweed extract, these fungicides can be especially effective in preventing fungal diseases from being a problem. They can be used as a preventive spray every 2 weeks during the early part of the growing season on those crops that are vulnerable to fungal diseases. Wait at least 4 days after applying any insect spray before using these fungicides, to avoid any conflict between the two products.

Use Mulch

Organic mulches also demonstrate certain disease prevention capabilities. For example, research is beginning to suggest that organic mulches such as chopped leaves may mitigate the harmful effects of certain soil fungi and nematodes by creating a chemical environment which either repels those disease-carriers or kills them outright. Backyard gardeners might consider using straw as an allelopathic mulch. Research in Michigan has shown that root rots of peas and beans are reduced by wheat-straw mulching. (See chapter 7 for more information about mulch and mulching systems.)

Eliminate the Method of Transmission

If you know your garden is vulnerable to certain diseases, or if you simply want to take all measures to prevent diseases in your garden, consider the ways in which diseases are transmitted to plants and remove those means of transmission.

Virtually all of the fungal diseases are transmitted by the movement of microscopic spores that travel to the plant by wind or water. Water splashing up from the ground during rains or while watering commonly carries fungal diseases up to the plant from the ground. One way to prevent this is to spread black plastic mulch over the soil early in the season, even before the soil thaws from the winter freeze. Most fungal spores do not emerge from the soil until air temperatures are in the 70's, so if you use black plastic mulch on all your beds, or at least on those beds with crops vulnerable to fungal diseases, you prevent spores from bouncing up onto the plants.

Using drip irrigation to water your food garden instead of an overhead sprinkler or hose is another way to eliminate the splashing of water that carries spores and bacteria with it. The drip irrigation system, under the black plastic mulch, benefits the plants in many ways, while reducing fungal disease problems.

Another good practice is to avoid handling any plants that are wet. You are much more likely to transfer pathogens from plant to plant when plants are wet.

Water Plants before Noon

One of the easiest ways to prevent the incidence of diseases, especially the bacterial and fungal diseases, is to water your garden in the morning. This allows plants to dry thoroughly before nightfall. Diseases thrive in moist, damp conditions, and the cooler temperatures of night prevent drying.

Keep Tools Clean

If diseases are a problem in your garden, it is especially important to keep your gardening tools cleaner than you normally might. Hoes, rakes, shovels, trowels, and other tools can carry fungal spores, bacteria, and viruses and spread those pathogens to other plants in your garden. An easy practice is to keep a 5-gallon pail containing bleach solution (one part household bleach to four parts water) handy. Then, as a matter of routine, you can dip your tools in the solution to disinfect them.

Clean Up the Garden in Fall

Fall cleanup is one of the most important steps you can take to reduce both insect and disease problems in your garden. It is essential that all debris from infected plants be removed from the garden and placed in the trash. Be certain to remove all fallen fruit as well. It might not be carrying a disease, but removing it to the trash is an important disease-prevention step. Diseases overwinter on plant

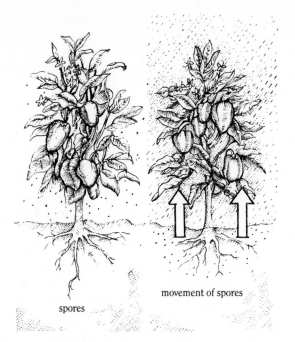

movement of spores

spores

Disease spores drop from an infected plant to the soil. There they overwinter, and in the next growing season, the splash of rain can carry them up to your new plants.

residues, and even if your season's crops were healthy, plants left in the garden provide a good environment for any diseases that might be carried into the garden by air, water, insects, or animals. (See chapter 4 for a detailed discussion about fall cleanup of the food garden.)

Solarize the Soil

In the past, it has been assumed that if certain disease pathogens, such as verticillium wilt and fusarium wilt, were present in the soil, they would remain there, and you would always have problems with those diseases. Over the past 10 years, a technique called solarization has been developed that may solve many garden disease problems. Solariza-

tion was developed in Israel and has been tested at a number of universities across this country. It is a process that produces very high levels of heat and humidity in the soil, which pasteurizes the soil, destroying harmful bacteria, fungi, some nematodes, virtually every type of insect larva, and the stock of weed seeds near the surface. Solarization has been found to be an effective control against such pesky disease problems as verticillium wilt in tomatoes, potatoes, and eggplants. It knocks out fusarium wilt in tomatoes and onions. It is effective against rhizoctonia in potatos and onions, and eliminates a variety of nematodes that attack potatoes and other crops.

An unexpected and unexplained benefit of solarization is that it also enhances the soil's ability to grow especially robust and healthy plants. Greater yields have been seen in beds that have been solarized. Solarization destroys harmful organisms, but it seems that certain beneficial organisms are not harmed. Jim DeVay, chairman of the plant pathology department at the University of California at Davis, is quoted as saying: "While many fungi, bacteria and other pathogens are killed, certain fungi that play an important role in utilization of plant nutrients and crop development withstand the heat and survive."

The best time to solarize soil is during July and August when temperatures are highest and days are sunny. The procedure for solarizing all or part of a bed is fairly straightforward. Simply follow these steps:

1. Loosen up the top foot or so of soil with a fork, U-bar digger, or tiller.

2. Water the soil heavily so that it is soaking wet—wetter than if you were simply watering your plants. Then let the bed sit overnight.

3. The next day, cover the bed, or part of the bed, with 3- to 6-mil clear plastic film. Don't use black plastic because it will not produce the greenhouse effect.

To solarize the soil, clear plastic is spread over an empty bed. The high heat and humidity produced under the plastic effectively destroy harmful fungi and bacteria that are in the soil.

4. Seal the plastic film along all edges with soil, and keep the soil covered for 4 to 6 weeks.

It is likely to rain during the 4-to-6-week solarization period, leaving puddles on the plastic. Take a broom and wipe the puddles away, because they reduce the effect of the sunlight striking the film.

Do not punch holes in the plastic to drain the water, because that will let the heat escape.

After the solarization process is finished, you can plant a vegetable crop for late fall harvest or a cover crop. Try not to disturb the soil very much when you put in the new crop. The weed seeds near the surface have been killed, but the seeds 4 or more inches down could still germinate if brought to the surface.

Solarization offers a wonderful opportunity to strike back at some of the soil diseases that have foiled gardeners up until now. Although research has not definitively determined how long the effects of solarization last, 4 to 5 years is a good estimate.

New Developments

Immunizing Plants

Disease-resistant varieties of plants have disease-fighting capabilities genetically built into the seed or plant. What is being studied now is the possibility of spraying a plant to give it those same qualities of resistance or tolerance, without having to go to the trouble of breeding them into the gene structure of the particular plant.

It has been learned that disease-resistant plants often do not have special genes for specific resistance mechanisms, but instead are able to recognize and combat pathogens more quickly than disease-susceptible plants. All plants have some ability to combat diseases, but resistant varieties are more able to combat them. Researchers have recently found certain compounds that are able to enhance the immune system responses of plants. These compounds can be injected into the plants, or in some cases sprayed on them, to provide disease immunity for up to 6 weeks. In one study, after inoculating the leaf of a cucumber plant with these new immunizing compounds, 4 to 6 weeks of protection was provided against 13 different fungi, viruses, and bacteria. Immunizing compounds promise excellent disease protection if they can be successfully developed for the commercial market.

Guide to Diseases

Diseases are more worrisome for the gardener than insect pests and animal pests, perhaps because we can't really see them. They can sneak up and take hold of a plant, and in the case of viral and bacterial diseases, once a plant falls ill, death is inevitable. But there are more measures of control available to the gardener now than ever, and when you come right down to it, preventing disease problems in the garden is fairly simple. Good sanitation practices and careful cleanup will go a long way in controlling diseases. The following entries include the most common diseases of the food garden with specific strategies for the control and prevention of each.

DISEASE Anthracnose

TYPE OF DISEASE

Anthracnose is a fungal disease generally found in the eastern part of North America. Cool wet weather promotes its development, and the optimum temperatures for continued growth of the spores are between 78°F and 86°F.

VULNERABLE PLANTS

Beans (lima and snap), blackberries, cucumbers, mint, muskmelons, peppers, pumpkins, raspberries, rhubarb (anthracnose is also called stalk rot on rhubarb), squash (summer and winter), tomatoes, and watermelons.

MOST OBVIOUS SYMPTOMS

In general, plants infected with anthracnose develop dark lesions on stems, leaves, or fruit. These lesions often become covered with pink spore masses. Dieback often occurs.

Bean, Lima and Snap

Look for round, black, sunken spots on the pods and stems. These spots are about ½ inch in diameter and usually are covered by a salmon-colored ooze during moist conditions. The spots on the pods are most conspicuous. In addition, the veins on the undersides of leaves turn black.

Blackberry

New canes of infected blackberries have small reddish brown or purplish spots. As the canes grow, these spots enlarge, become round, turn gray in color, develop sunken centers, and grow together. Small, irregular yellow or purple spots also develop on the leaves.

Cucumber

Small water-soaked spots develop on the leaves. They enlarge and turn brown, and eventually the leaves shrivel and die. Sunken lesions form on the stems and circular, black, sunken spots appear on the fruit. During moist conditions, these spots become covered with the salmon-colored fungus.

Mint

Small, water-soaked spots develop on the aboveground parts of mints infected with anthracnose. These spots turn a light color and may drop out.

Muskmelon

The symptoms are the same as those seen in cucumbers.

Pepper

Sometimes dark watery spots develop on the leaves, but usually anthracnose affects the fruit. Dark sunken spots form on the fruit, which becomes covered with pink spore masses.

Pumpkin

The fungus attacks all parts of the plant above the ground. The oldest leaves develop black specks, and eventually shrivel. Dark red, sunken spots appear on leaves and stems. Fruit may have round, sunken lesions, in which pink spore masses may be seen.

Raspberry

In the spring, new canes infected with anthracnose exhibit small reddish brown or purplish spots. As the cane grows, these spots enlarge, become round, turn gray in color, develop sunken centers, and grow together. Small, irregular yellow or purple spots appear on the leaves. Only young plants are susceptible to infection. Wild blackberry can spread anthracnose to raspberries. Gatineau (red) and Bristol (black) varieties are particularly susceptible.

Rhubarb

Look for watery spots on the leaf stalks, which enlarge as the disease progresses. The leaves will wilt and die.

Squash, Summer

The symptoms are the same as those seen in cucumbers.

Tomato

Look for depressed, circular, water-soaked spots on ripe or ripening fruit. These spots look as if they were made with a pencil eraser. They darken from the center outward as the fungus develops and enlarge to about ¼ inch. Anthracnose spreads internally to produce soft rot.

Watermelon

The symptoms are the same as those seen in cucumbers, except the leaf spots are black instead of brown.

METHOD OF TRANSMISSION

Anthracnose overwinters in the garden soil and on residues from diseased plants. It is spread by wind or rain, animals, gardeners, and tools.

CONTROL STRATEGY

As soon as you spot the problem, apply a fixed copper- or sulfur-based fungicide every 7 to 10 days. If this does not control the disease, remove and discard infected plants.

Bean, Lima and Snap

If you save seeds, don't plant any seeds that are discolored or that come from spotted pods.

Raspberry

Use a copper-based fungicide rather than a sulfur-based fungicide. Spray the uninfected canes with a light dormant oil to protect them.

STEPS TO PREVENT ANTHRACNOSE

Resistant Varieties

Use disease-free western-grown seeds, which have not been exposed to the fungus.

Bean
Charlevoix Dark Red Kidney and Seafarer (navy bean).

Cucumber
Bounty, Calypso, Carolina, County Fair, Dasher II, Flurry, Gemini Hybrid, Lucky Strike, Marketsett, Monarch, Pik-Rite, Pioneer Hybrid, Poinsett, Score, Spear-it, Sprint 440, Stokes Early Hybrid, Victory Hybrid, and many more.

Raspberry
Black Beauty.

Watermelon
Allsweet, Blackstone, Bush Jubilee, Charleston Gray, Charleston Gray #5, Congo, Fairfax, Madera, Oasis, Seedless Hybrid 313, and Sweet Favorite.

Garden Management Practices

Critical to preventing any fungal diseases is a thorough garden cleanup in the fall. (See chapter 4 for a detailed description of fall cleanup.) To avoid spreading anthracnose, do not work near plants when they are wet.

Blackberry
To prevent anthracnose, make one application of a dormant oil spray in late winter before budding.

Raspberry
Treat as blackberries.

DISEASE ## *Apple Scab*

TYPE OF DISEASE

Apple scab is a fungal disease found throughout North America, particularly in northern areas. It is difficult to control once it infests your fruit trees, so follow the 9-step spray program outlined on page 384 to prevent this disease from occurring in the first place.

VULNERABLE PLANTS

Apples and pears.

MOST OBVIOUS SYMPTOMS

Apple

Look for pale yellow or olive-green spots on leaves. These spots darken nearly to black. Curling, cracking, and distortion of the leaves may occur. Spots also develop on the fruit, and as these spots enlarge and become older, the velvety appearance in the center turns brown and corky. Fruit becomes distorted and cracked as it grows, and young fruit drops. An infection of the twigs causes the bark to blister and rupture. Scab results in a heavy reduction in yield, and may result in defoliation or the eventual loss of the tree.

Pear

Velvety olive-green spots develop on the fruit, becoming black and scabby at maturity. Black spots appear on the leaves, and the fungus will infect twigs.

METHOD OF TRANSMISSION

Scab overwinters in fallen leaves and in the soil. It is picked up and transmitted to plants by the wind in early spring. During damp periods in the spring, the opening leaves of the apple or pear tree are easily infected. The longer the leaves are wet, the more severe the infection will be.

STEPS TO PREVENT APPLE SCAB

Preventive Sprays

The time to begin controlling scab is in early spring when it is just beginning to infect the new leaves. Apple scab is difficult to control. If you haven't been following the preventive spray program outlined below (an effective scab control program developed by the Necessary Trading Company, in Newcastle, Virginia), and you discover symptoms of apple scab on your trees, use sprays according to the directions given below for the particular stage of development your trees have reached in the growing season. You will need a sprayer device (of at least 1-gallon capacity), lime sulfur, a wettable sulfur spray, a surfactant (sticker) or insecticidal soap, and Bordeaux mixture.

1. When the buds begin to show green tissue, spray trees with a lime sulfur solution made with 2 ounces of lime sulfur for each gallon of water. Do not apply the lime sulfur within 3 weeks of applying a dormant oil spray on the same tree.

2. Seven days later, before the buds begin to show pink (tight cluster), again spray the trees with a lime sulfur solution, this time made with 1 ounce of lime sulfur for each gallon of water. If precipitation occurs and temperatures are warmer than 60°F, apply the lime sulfur solution described in Step 1 as soon as possible. For best results, use lime sulfur alone. Do not mix it with BT.

3. Seven days later, when blossoms begin to show pink (open cluster), apply a wettable sulfur spray (1 ounce of sulfur per gallon of water). Use a surfactant or insecticidal soap mixed in equal amounts with the wettable sulfur spray to make it stick better. Do not apply lime sulfur when the tree is in blossom.

4. Seven days later, during pink to early bloom, make another application of the wettable sulfur spray.

5. Usually you do not spray during the bloom period, but if precipitation occurs and temperatures are above 60°F, apply the wettable sulfur at a concentration of ½ ounce of sulfur per gallon of water. Use a surfactant, but do not mix BT into the sulfur spray.

6. At petal-fall (7 days after full bloom), spray trees with a wettable sulfur solution (1 ounce of sulfur per gallon of water). You can substitute standard Bordeaux mixture (1 ounce per gallon of water) if black rot has been a problem in the past; however, do not apply Bordeaux mixture in cool, damp weather. Do not apply wettable sulfur or lime sulfur if temperatures are higher than 80°F.

7. Seven days later (at first cover), repeat Step 6, and repeat again in another 7 days (at second cover).

8. Midseason sprays are then applied 10 to 14 days apart, using a Bordeaux mixture (2 ounces of the mixture per gallon of water).

9. Stop spraying 30 days before harvest.

Resistant Varieties

Apple
Freedom (3 through 7), Jonafree (5 through 8), Liberty (4 through 7), Macfree (3 through 6), Nova Easygro (3 through 6), Prima (4 through 7), Priscilla (5 through 8), and Redfree (5 through 8). The numbers indicate Hardiness Zones.

Garden Management Practices

Remove and destroy all diseased and fallen fruit, and rake up all fallen leaves. Mow the area under the trees to remove grass, which might harbor spores. Prune trees to allow air and light into the trees' canopy to promote faster drying after rain.

DISEASE # *Asparagus Rust*

TYPE OF DISEASE

Asparagus rust is a fungal disease, found throughout North America. It is most severe during moist seasons.

VULNERABLE PLANTS

Asparagus.

MOST OBVIOUS SYMPTOMS

Seen after the cutting season, the spores of the rust disease create reddish brown masses on the ferns of the plant. When these areas are touched, they give off a dusty cloud. In late summer, black masses of spores may be produced. The disease retards fern growth, causes early maturity, and reduces food storage in the crown of the plant.

METHOD OF TRANSMISSION

The spores overwinter on old asparagus stems and stubble. Heavy dews favor the development of this disease.

CONTROL STRATEGY

Cut the diseased tops to the ground and burn them. Try applying a sulfur spray every 10 days until 3 to 4 weeks before harvest to reduce spread of the disease.

STEPS TO PREVENT ASPARAGUS RUST

Preventive Sprays

In the early spring, after the foliage begins to form, apply a sulfur spray every 10 days until 3 to 4 weeks before harvest to prevent the disease from becoming a problem.

Resistant Varieties

Asparagus
California 500, Martha Washington, Mary Washington, Seneca Washington, Viking, and Waltham Washington.

Garden Management Practices

Use mulch and drip irrigation to reduce moisture on asparagus plants. In the fall, cut all foliage down to the ground and remove it to the compost pile or trash. (See chapter 4 for detailed information on fall cleanup.)

Bacterial Blight

TYPE OF DISEASE

This is a bacterial disease that is most severe in areas where relative humidity remains high for long periods of time. It is found throughout the United States, but seldom west of the Rockies.

VULNERABLE PLANTS

Beans (lima and snap) and peas.

MOST OBVIOUS SYMPTOMS

Bean, Lima and Snap

Look for large brown blotches on the leaves; they may be bordered with yellow or red. Water-soaked spots develop on pods, and the seeds may be discolored. One species of bacterial blight causes a yellow halo to form around spots and is called halo blight.

Pea

The stems of peas infected with bacterial blight turn purplish or nearly black near the ground and show discolored areas on the nodes. Small water-soaked spots appear on the leaves, and yellow to brown water-soaked spots form on the pods.

METHOD OF TRANSMISSION

Bacterial blight enters plants through the tiny openings in their epidermis or through wounds. Bacteria are carried by wind, and they also infect seeds. This disease overwinters in plant refuse.

CONTROL STRATEGY

Bacterial blight cannot be cured. Pull infected and surrounding plants and discard them in the trash.

STEPS TO PREVENT BACTERIAL BLIGHT

Resistant Varieties

Bean, Snap
Seafarer (navy bean) and Tendergreen (some types).

Garden Management Practices

Use only certified seeds, preferably western-grown, since these bacteria are seldom found west of the Rockies. It is particularly important not to work around peas and beans when they are wet because that is the best way to spread this incurable disease.

Planting
Delay and plant beans for a fall crop to avoid blight.

Bacterial Canker

TYPE OF DISEASE

This is a bacterial disease whose growth on cherries is encouraged by prolonged periods of cool, windy, moist weather.

VULNERABLE PLANTS

Apricots, blueberries (in blueberries, bacterial canker is also known as stem canker), cherries, peaches, and tomatoes.

MOST OBVIOUS SYMPTOMS

Apricot

Look for small purple spots on the leaves, black lesions on the fruit, and cankers on twigs.

Blueberry

Reddish brown or black cankers appear on the stems. The plant will die.

Cherry

The shoots and limbs exhibit heavy oozing of gum in spring and fall. The leaves wilt and die in the summer, and infected fruit has a darkened depression on its surface.

Peach

The symptoms are the same as those seen on apricots.

Tomato

On plants of all sizes, the first symptom is wilting of the margins of the leaflets and lower leaves. Wilting begins on one side of the leaf; the margins become dry, and eventually entire leaves curl upward, turn brown, wither, and die. Diseased plants may wilt and die early, but many survive, though stunted and wilted. As the disease progresses, cankers form on the stem. Small, raised, snowy dots appear on the surface of the fruit, and the centers of those dots break open and become brown and rough, with the white color persisting as a halo. Fruit that is small, stunted, and deformed has been affected internally.

METHOD OF TRANSMISSION

The bacteria overwinter in the soil and can be carried to plants by wind and rain. They also overwinter in the buds, cankers, and sap of cherry trees, and are carried in tomato seeds.

CONTROL STRATEGY

Bacterial canker cannot be cured, so if pruning doesn't stop the disease, the tree or plant must be destroyed. When pruning, clean tools in a bleach solution (one part household bleach to four parts water) after each cut.

Tomato

Destroy the plants, and, assuming the soil is infected, grow a different crop in that spot for at least 3 years.

STEPS TO PREVENT BACTERIAL CANKER

Resistant Varieties

Blueberry
Angola, Croatan, Morrow, Murphy, rabbit-eye varieties, and Walcott.

Cherry
Colt, Corum, Mahaleb *(Prunus maheleb)*, and Stockton Morello *(P. cerasus)*.

Garden Management Practices

Destroy all tomato vines after harvest and remove and clean up any plant debris around apricot and cherry trees and blueberries. (See chapter 4 for a detailed description of fall cleanup.)

Crop Rotation
Maintain at least a 3- to 4-year crop rotation policy for tomatoes in the garden.

Bacterial Spot

TYPE OF DISEASE

This is a bacterial disease that affects tomatoes and peppers most seriously in midwestern, southern Atlantic, central, and Gulf states. Peaches are most severely infected during warm, wet spring weather.

VULNERABLE PLANTS

Apricots, peaches, peppers, plums, and tomatoes.

MOST OBVIOUS SYMPTOMS

Apricot

Check leaves for small, circular, pale green spots, which later turn light brown. The tissue around the spots fades to a light yellow-green and becomes purplish and angular in shape. On the fruit, small circular sunken spots develop, and cracking eventually occurs.

Peach

Bacterial spot produces the same symptoms in peaches as it does in apricots.

Pepper

The young leaves develop small yellow-green spots; older leaves show larger spots with dead, straw-colored centers and dark margins.

Plum

Infected areas on the leaves fall out, giving a shothole effect. Purplish black, sunken spots develop on green fruit; on some cultivars, these spots are small and pitlike.

Tomato

Small, dark, raised spots, sometimes surrounded by water-soaked margins, appear on green fruit. These spots enlarge up to ¼ inch in diameter and become brown and scabby.

METHOD OF TRANSMISSION

Bacterial spot overwinters in the soil around infected tomatoes and peppers as well as on plant debris. It is carried in tomato seeds. It also remains in the twig cankers, leaves, stems, and fruit of infected fruit trees. Wind and rain transmit the disease to plants.

CONTROL STRATEGY

Bacterial spot cannot be cured. The first line of defense, if the disease is identified early in its development, is to apply a copper-based fungicide every 7 to 10 days. Prune the infected parts immediately, disinfecting tools and hands in a bleach solution (one part household bleach to four parts water) between each cut. If good results don't show up after a second spraying, the plant or tree must be destroyed.

STEPS TO PREVENT BACTERIAL SPOT

Resistant Varieties

Peach

Belle of Georgia, Bicentennial, Biscoe, Candor, Cardinal, Clayton, Compact Redhaven, Correll, Cumberland, Dixiland, Dixired, Earlired, Early Elberta, Eden, Ellerbe, Emery, Envoy, Hamlet, Harbelle, Harbinger, Harbrite, Harken, Jefferson, Kalhaven, LaGem, LaPremier, Loring, Madison,

Marhigh, Newhaven, Norman, Pekin, Polly, Ranger, Rarian, Redhaven, Redkist, Redskin, Reliance, Richhaven, Rose, Royalvee, Sentinel, Southhaven, Summercrest, Sunbrite, Sunhaven, Sunshine, Sweethaven, Wildrose, and Winblo.

Pepper
Early Calwonder, Long Red Cheyenne, Red Chili, and Sunnybrook.

Plum
Bradshaw and President.

Garden Management Practices
Thoroughly clean the garden in the fall. (See chapter 4 for detailed information on fall cleanup.)

DISEASE *Bacterial Wilt*

TYPE OF DISEASE

This is a bacterial disease common in moist soils and active at temperatures above 75°F. It infects corn grown in central, southern, and eastern states; cucumbers grown in north central and northeastern states; and tomatoes grown in southern states.

VULNERABLE PLANTS

Beans (lima and snap), corn (in corn, bacterial wilt is also known as Stewart's wilt; sweet corn is most susceptible, especially the early, yellow, and sweeter varieties), cucumbers, muskmelons, pumpkins, squash (summer and winter), tomatoes, and watermelons.

MOST OBVIOUS SYMPTOMS

Bean, Lima and Snap
Bacterial wilt usually kills bean seedlings. If they survive to grow higher than 3 inches, the disease will cause the leaves to become limp, wilt, and die.

Wilting occurs especially during the warm part of the day.

Corn
The leaves of infected corn plants wilt on dry days and develop long pale streaks. Bacterial wilt blocks the vascular system.

Cucumber
Infected plants may wilt so quickly that they may be dried up but still green. White, sticky material oozes from cut stems. Bacterial wilt blocks the vascular system of cucumbers.

Muskmelon
The symptoms are the same as those seen in cucumbers.

Pumpkin
The symptoms are the same as those seen in cucumbers.

Squash, Summer and Winter

Usually a single leaf gradually wilts and dies, followed by the vine and then the whole plant. Plants often show stunted growth.

Tomato

Infected plants wilt rapidly and die without showing any signs of yellowing or leaf spotting.

Watermelon

The symptoms are the same as those seen in cucumbers.

METHOD OF TRANSMISSION

Bean, Bush and Lima

Bacterial wilt is carried in the seeds, and overwinters there and in diseased plant debris.

Corn

Flea beetles transmit the disease to corn.

Cucumber

Cucumbers may pick up bacterial wilt from spotted and striped cucumber beetles.

Squash, Summer and Winter

Squash may pick up the disease from spotted and striped cucumber beetles.

Tomato

Bacterial wilt in the soil infects tomatoes through the roots and stem. It can be carried by infected seedlings and by water.

Watermelon

Watermelons may pick up bacterial wilt from spotted and striped cucumber beetles.

CONTROL STRATEGY

Bacterial wilt cannot be cured. Remove and destroy infected plants immediately, and wash hands and any tools in a bleach solution (one part household bleach to four parts water) before touching other plants.

STEPS TO PREVENT BACTERIAL WILT

Resistant Varieties

Bean, Snap
Tendergreen.

Corn
Bantam, Carmelcross, Country Gentleman, F-M Cross, Golden Beauty, Golden Cross Bantam, Ioana, Iochief, Marcross, N.K. 199, Seneca Chief, Silver Queen, and most white, late-maturing varieties.

Cucumber
Saladin.

Squash, Winter
Buttercup, Butternut, and Table Queen.

Tomato
Saturn and Venus.

Garden Management Practices

Clean up all plant debris in the fall. (See chapter 4 for more information on fall cleanup.)

Bean, Bush and Lima
Plant seeds that are certified wilt-free.

Corn
Protect young plants from flea beetles by covering them in the spring with agricultural fleece.

Cucumber

Protect plants from cucumber beetles. Mulch heavily, and if your growing season permits, plant late, after cucumber beetles lay their eggs. Dust seedlings with pyrethrin early in the season, before beetles reproduce.

Squash, Summer and Winter

Treat as cucumbers.

Watermelon

Treat as cucumbers.

DISEASE *Baldwin Spot*

TYPE OF DISEASE

Baldwin spot is also known as bitter pit. It is an environmental disease caused by a calcium deficiency in the soil coupled with optimum temperature and humidity.

VULNERABLE PLANTS

Apples. Varieties that are most susceptible include Baldwin, Greening, Red Delicious, York, Stayman, and Northern Spy.

MOST OBVIOUS SYMPTOMS

Brown corky flecks can be seen in the flesh of the fruit. They usually develop just under the skin but may be scattered through the flesh to the core. The corky tissue has a bitter taste; hence the common name bitter pit.

CONTROL STRATEGY

Add calcium to the soil. The best sources are natural ground limestone, dolomite limestone, wood ashes, bone meal, or oyster shells, in the amount of two or three 1-pound coffee canfuls per 100 square feet. Check pH levels so that you don't add so much material that it creates a pH imbalance. In addition, spray trees with a solution made from calcium chloride, mixing $\frac{1}{3}$ to $\frac{1}{2}$ of an ounce in 2 gallons of water. Make two applications, the first 6 weeks before harvest and the second 3 weeks before harvest. Older trees will benefit from $\frac{1}{2}$ pound of borax, spread within the drip line (a circumference determined by the ends of the branches); use less for young trees.

STEPS TO PREVENT BALDWIN SPOT

Resistant Varieties

Apple

The McIntosh group is seldom affected.

Garden Management Practices

Pruning

Prune trees lightly; heavy pruning of vigorous trees stimulates growth and increases the chances of baldwin spot. Encourage heavy cropping of fruit by delaying thinning of the blossoms or fruit as long as possible.

Feeding
Cut down on fertilizers particularly rich in nitrogen and potassium, keeping the proportions of each below 10 percent. Maintain uniform soil moisture throughout the growing season. When planting apple trees, apply lime as called for by a soil test. Since the fruit accumulates calcium during its early stage of development, make certain the soil is moist around the roots of apple trees from the time flowers open until the apples appear. This will enable the trees to absorb calcium more readily.

Harvesting
Harvest fruit from overly vigorous or lightly cropped trees early, segregate it, and use as soon as possible, especially if it is large, since the disease is progressive in the fruit.

DISEASE *Bean Rust*

TYPE OF DISEASE

Bean rust is a fungal disease found in most areas where high relative humidity prevails for 8 to 10 hours a day. It is a serious problem in several eastern seaboard states, and in irrigated sections of the western states.

VULNERABLE PLANTS

Beans (lima and snap).

MOST OBVIOUS SYMPTOMS

It is most common on mature plants, and symptoms can be seen primarily on the surfaces of lower leaves. Initially, look for small, whitish, slightly raised spots on the undersides of leaves and sometimes on the stems. After a few days, these spots become covered with many small, reddish orange to brown spore masses. The leaves yellow rapidly, dry up, and drop.

METHOD OF TRANSMISSION

Bean rust spores are blown by the wind or can be carried on animals, tools, insects, or gardeners. The spores overwinter on stakes or in debris.

CONTROL STRATEGY

Apply a sulfur spray or undiluted sulfur dust every 7 to 10 days until the disease is controlled.

STEPS TO PREVENT BEAN RUST

Resistant Varieties

Bean, Snap
Cherokee Wax (yellow), Dade, Harvester, Kentucky Wonder, some types of Tendergreen, U.S. No. 3 Kentucky Wonder, and White Kentucky Wonder 191.

Garden Management Practices

Critical to preventing any fungal disease is a very thorough garden cleanup in the fall, which reduces the overwintering sites for the fungal spores. (See chapter 4 for more information on fall cleanup.) In addition, use new stakes each year; last year's stakes can be used with other vegetables not affected by bean rust.

Mulching and Drip Irrigation
Using mulch and drip irrigation in the garden eliminates splashing water, which can carry fungal spores from the ground to your plants.

DISEASE *Black Heart*

TYPE OF DISEASE

Black heart is an environmental disease. In celery, it is caused by calcium levels within the plant that are low in relation to the potassium levels. In potatoes, the disease is caused by insufficient oxygen in the center of the potato tuber that results when soil is waterlogged or temperatures are too high. Black heart also occurs in storage if ventilation is poor or if potatoes are stored for a long time at temperatures near freezing.

VULNERABLE PLANTS

Celery and potatoes.

MOST OBVIOUS SYMPTOMS

Celery

The tips of the youngest leaves develop water-soaked areas, which turn brown and may spread until all the leaves are affected.

Potato

The inside of the tubers have dark gray, purple, or black areas.

CONTROL STRATEGY

Celery

Add calcium to the soil. The best sources are natural ground limestone, dolomite limestone, wood ashes, bone meal, or oyster shells. Check pH levels so that you don't add so much material that it creates a pH imbalance. Spray celery with kelp or seaweed extract.

Potato

Once it occurs, black heart cannot be eliminated from potatoes.

STEPS TO PREVENT BLACK HEART

Garden Management Practices

Celery
Test the soil to determine that the calcium levels are balanced, and adjust by adding calcium as described above.

Potato
Make sure that soil drainage is good throughout the garden. Do not leave tubers in or on hot soil (over 90°F).

DISEASE *Black Knot*

TYPE OF DISEASE

A widespread fungal disease that occurs in spring, but does not become evident until the following spring.

VULNERABLE PLANTS

Cherries and plums.

MOST OBVIOUS SYMPTOMS

In spring, the bark of infected twigs and branches cracks, and a light yellow growth develops that later becomes covered with an olive-green layer. In late summer, hard, rough, black swellings develop at these places, weakening the twigs and branches. These swellings are more common on smaller branches, which are often killed by girdling.

METHOD OF TRANSMISSION

The fungus produces spores in both summer and winter. In the summer, black knot spores are released in moderate to warm weather and are carried by air currents. They overwinter in the knotlike swellings of infected twigs and limbs. It is the winter spores that begin new infections just before full bloom in the spring. Wild cherries and wild plums can spread black knot to cultivated cherries and plums, so remove all wild trees that have the disease and burn them.

CONTROL STRATEGY

It is very important to remove potential sources of infection. In late winter, remove all knotted twigs and branches and burn them, making cuts at least 4 inches below the beginning of the swelling on the branch. If the limb is essential to tree growth, wait until early to midsummer and cut out the knot. Cover wounds with grafting wax or wound paint. Burn all prunings.

Fungicides such as Bordeaux mixture have some effect in controlling the disease, and lime sulfur sprays prevent the production of spores, but true control is only achieved by using fungicides in addition to pruning.

STEPS TO PREVENT BLACK KNOT

Resistant Varieties

Plum
President.

Garden Management Practices

Remove and burn all infected wild plum and cherry trees in the area.

DISEASE **Black Leg**

TYPE OF DISEASE

Black leg is a fungal disease characterized by dry rot. It produces its most severe damage during humid or rainy weather. Black leg occurs in central, southern, and eastern states.

VULNERABLE PLANTS

The whole cabbage family: broccoli, brussels sprouts, cabbage, cauliflower, Chinese cabbage, collards, kale, kohlrabi, and potatoes.

MOST OBVIOUS SYMPTOMS

Plants infected with black leg develop sunken areas on the stem near the ground, which girdle the stem. Gray spots speckled with black dots appear on the leaves and stems. The edges of leaves wilt and turn bluish or red, and the entire plant may wilt or topple over.

Potato

On older plants infected with black leg, yellowing occurs between leaf veins, and the leaf margins brown and curl upward. When young plants are affected, stunting and erratic growth may occur. Infected plants may wilt during hot weather. The stems may turn an inky black and become soft and mushy just above and below the soil line.

METHOD OF TRANSMISSION

Black leg is carried in the seeds of infected plants. The spores overwinter for 1 to 2 years in plant debris and can be carried on tools. Dew and rain can spread this disease also.

CONTROL STRATEGY

Fixed copper fungicides are sometimes effective. If this treatment does not halt the disease, remove and destroy the infected plants.

STEPS TO PREVENT BLACK LEG

Use seeds from the Pacific coast states, since black leg fungus does not occur there.

Garden Management Practices

A thorough cleanup in the fall will help to prevent this disease. (See chapter 4 for more information on fall cleanup.) Clean garden tools in a bleach solution (one part household bleach to four parts water), and do not work around plants when they are wet.

Crop Rotation

Rotate crops so that for at least 2 years a noncruciferous plant (that is, not a member of the cabbage family) is grown where any of the vulnerable plants had been planted.

DISEASE **Black Rot**

TYPE OF DISEASE

Black rot is a bacterial disease, the growth of which is encouraged by wet weather. It occurs in the central, southern, and eastern states.

VULNERABLE PLANTS

Broccoli, brussels sprouts, cabbage, cauliflower, Chinese cabbage, collards, kohlrabi, and turnips.

MOST OBVIOUS SYMPTOMS

Black rot affects young as well as mature plants. Infected seedlings turn yellow and die. On older plants, yellow, wedge-shaped areas develop at the leaf margins and expand toward the center of the leaf. These areas later turn brown and die, and the leaves fall off. The vascular bundles in leaves and stems are black and bad smelling. Young plants may not produce heads, and the heads on older plants that become infected will rot.

METHOD OF TRANSMISSION

Insects, rain, and surface water carry the disease to plants. The bacteria overwinter in soil, plant refuse, and seeds.

CONTROL STRATEGY

Bacterial black rot cannot be cured. Remove and destroy the infected and surrounding plants. Micronized sulfur helps to control the spread of black rot to other plants. Apply the sulfur to unaffected plants every 7 days until harvest.

STEPS TO PREVENT BLACK ROT

Resistant Varieties

Broccoli
Emperor Hybrid.

Cabbage
Bravo, Custodian, Hancock, Jadekeeper, Lariat, Regalia, Safekeeper Hybrid, and Survivor Hybrid.

Kohlrabi
Grand Duke Hybrid.

Garden Management Practices

Clean up the garden thoroughly in the fall. (See chapter 4 for detailed information on fall cleanup.) Do not handle plants when they are wet.

DISEASE **Black Rot**

TYPE OF DISEASE

A fungal disease that affects apples in the eastern United States. Sweet potato black rot is also a fungus that occurs throughout the United States; its growth is encouraged by moist soil conditions.

VULNERABLE PLANTS

Apples and sweet potatoes.

MOST OBVIOUS SYMPTOMS

Apple

Black rot isn't evident in apple trees until a few weeks before maturity. It may not even appear until later, as storage rot. When it does appear, you will find small brown spots, usually one to a fruit. As these spots expand, they develop concentric zones of brown and black. Minute black pimples later appear, and the fruit eventually shrivels. Sometimes cankers form on the twigs.

Sweet Potato

Symptoms of black rot in sweet potatoes appear on the foliage and on the fleshy roots. The foliage becomes yellowish and sickly. On roots, depressed circular spots of various sizes develop. These spots appear grayish black when dry and greenish black when moist. The entire plant turns yellow and often develops black cankers on the subsurface portions of the stem.

METHOD OF TRANSMISSION

Apple

Rain and wind transmit the spores, which overwinter in bark, twigs, and fruit.

Sweet Potato

The black rot of sweet potatoes lives in the soil and moves from plant to plant by wind and rain. The spores survive in the soil for several years and from season to season on stored tubers.

CONTROL STRATEGY

Sulfur-based fungicides will control fungal black rot. (See the beginning of this chapter for details on using these fungicides.)

STEPS TO PREVENT BLACK ROT

Resistant Varieties

Sweet Potato
Allgold.

Garden Management Practices

In general, clean up plant debris in the fall, and do not work around wet plants. (See chapter 4 for detailed information on fall cleanup.)

Apple
Prune infected wood and destroy the fruit.

Sweet Potato
Use sweet potato plants with clean, white roots, and start plants from cuttings rather than sprouts.

Crop Rotation
Maintain a 3- to 4-year rotation with sweet potatoes.

DISEASE *Blossom Drop*

TYPE OF DISEASE

An environmental disorder. Any type of stress can cause this disorder, but it is most likely to occur during hot, dry conditions when soil moisture is low, or with a quick change from hot to cool, wet weather.

VULNERABLE PLANTS

Tomatoes. Early-bearing tomatoes and varieties with smaller fruit are less susceptible; large beefsteak types are more susceptible.

MOST OBVIOUS SYMPTOMS

Plants do not set fruit.

CONTROL STRATEGY

Spraying plants with seaweed extract sometimes eases the problem. One application should help.

STEPS TO PREVENT BLOSSOM DROP

Growing resistant varieties is the best way to prevent this disorder.

Resistant Varieties

Tomato
Burpee's Big Early Hybrid, Floramerica, Hot-set, New Yorker, Porter, Red Cherry, Tiny Tim, and Walter.

Garden Management Practices

Water tomatoes in hot, dry weather. If blossom drop is a common problem in your garden, place plants closer together to provide some shade to the blossoms. Be careful not to overfertilize the crop because that, too, causes stress.

Blossom End Rot

TYPE OF DISEASE

An environmental disease often caused by improper watering or by a calcium deficiency when fruit is forming. Blossom end rot can be caused by several other factors as well. It most often occurs when plants have been grown under favorable conditions in the early part of the season and are then subjected to a long period of drought while the fruit is in the early stages of development. Under such circumstances, the cells at the end of the blossom fail to receive sufficient water to grow. Blossom end rot can also occur after a period of heavy rain, because many small rootlets die from lack of aeration in the soil. Overdoses of nitrogen hinder the uptake of calcium, a situation which aggravates the problem. Blossom end rot can also be caused by excessive root pruning, which results from heavy cultivation near the plants.

VULNERABLE PLANTS

Peppers and tomatoes.

MOST OBVIOUS SYMPTOMS

Pepper

Light-colored, sunken, water-soaked spots develop near the blossom end of the fruit. A third of the fruit may become shriveled.

Tomato

Sunken, dry, brown to black leathery spots develop near the blossom end of tomatoes.

CONTROL STRATEGY

Water plants evenly (consistently) and only as needed. Check the pH of the soil: It should be between 6.0 and 7.0. If it's below 6.0, add limestone, which contains calcium.

STEPS TO PREVENT BLOSSOM END ROT

Resistant Varieties

Tomato
Flora-Dade, Manalucie, and Olympic.

Garden Management Practices

Pepper
Avoid adding surplus nitrogen, and be sure to apply ample amounts of phosphate rock and ground limestone. Water plants consistently and evenly throughout the growing season. Cultivate the soil as little as possible in dry weather to avoid further drying of the soil, and be careful not to damage roots during cultivation. Test for and correct calcium deficiency. (See chapter 7 for information on soil management.)

Tomato
Treat as peppers.

DISEASE *Botrytis Fruit Rot*

TYPE OF DISEASE

This fungal disease, also called gray mold, affects strawberries in regions where rainfall or dews occur frequently. Bruised or overripe berries are more susceptible. The disease is spurred on by cool temperatures and high humidity.

VULNERABLE PLANTS

Blackberries, raspberries, strawberries, and tomatoes.

MOST OBVIOUS SYMPTOMS

Botrytis fruit rot starts as blossom blight, causing discolored petals and wilted fruit stems. Small water-soaked spots, most often seen at the base, develop on fruit. These spots enlarge and eventually become covered with a grayish mold.

METHOD OF TRANSMISSION

The spores overwinter in garden trash and debris. Wet weather encourages spread of the disease.

CONTROL STRATEGY

Sulfur or fixed copper fungicides provide a good degree of control, provided the application is properly timed so that it catches the fungus early in its spring development. (See the beginning of this chapter for details on using fungicides.)

STEPS TO PREVENT BOTRYTIS FRUIT ROT

Garden Management Practices

Remove all plant debris from the garden in the fall. (See chapter 4 for details on fall cleanup.) Space plants in the garden so that air circulates freely, and cultivate the soil to dry it.

Harvesting

Pick fruit continuously to prevent the accumulation of overripe berries, and handle fruit gently to prevent bruising.

DISEASE *Botrytis Rot*

TYPE OF DISEASE

Also called neck rot, this fungal disease is seldom seen in the garden; symptoms are usually seen after harvest.

VULNERABLE PLANTS

Chives, garlic, marjoram, onions, oregano, rosemary, and thyme.

MOST OBVIOUS SYMPTOMS

Garlic

The neck tissue on the bulb becomes soft and brownish and may shrivel. Leaves may appear water-soaked. Often a gray to brown mold develops on the surface of bulbs.

Marjoram

Leaves in the center of the plant near the base rot.

Onion

The symptoms are the same as those seen in garlic.

Oregano

The symptoms are the same as those seen in marjoram.

Thyme

The symptoms are the same as those seen in marjoram.

METHOD OF TRANSMISSION

Botrytis rot overwinters in plant residue and is present wherever plants are grown. Infection is promoted by prolonged wet conditions.

CONTROL STRATEGY

Remove any infected plants from the garden to control spread of the disease.

Garlic

Keep bulbs cool and dry in storage.

Onions

Keep bulbs cool and dry in storage.

STEPS TO CONTROL BOTRYTIS ROT

Garden Management Practices

Maintain a healthy soil rich in organic nutrients, and plants will be less likely to develop this disease. Remove all plant debris from the garden in fall. (See chapter 4 for details on fall cleanup.) When watering, direct water at the soil to keep plants dry. An application of compost reduces problems.

DISEASE # Brown Rot

TYPE OF DISEASE

Brown rot is a fungal disease that can cause blossom blight if warm weather occurs when flowers begin to bloom. From the blossoms, the fungus grows back into the twigs to cause cankers that can girdle and kill twigs. The two species of this fungus cause problems throughout the United States, except in very dry areas.

VULNERABLE PLANTS

Apricots, cherries, peaches, and plums.

MOST OBVIOUS SYMPTOMS

A small, round, brown spot develops on the fruit and spreads to cover the whole fruit. Light gray masses of spores cover these rotted areas.

METHOD OF TRANSMISSION

Brown rot overwinters in rotted fruit and in cankers on infected twigs. The spores are carried by wind and rain.

CONTROL STRATEGY

Apply an approved fungicide (sulfur, lime sulfur, copper, or Bordeaux mixture) to infected trees late in spring, and continue applications every 7 to 10 days until 20 days before harvest. Apply a sulfur spray or a spray of garlic just before harvesting and be careful not to damage the fruit when picking. (See chapter 4 for information on garlic spray.) Soak fruit in water at a temperature of 120°F for 7 minutes to kill any fungi, and then refrigerate the fruit.

STEPS TO PREVENT BROWN ROT

Resistant Varieties

Cherry
Northstart Tart and Stark Gold.

Peach
Carmen, Elberta, Greensbore, Orange Cling, Red Bird, Sneed, and Sunbeam.

Garden Management Practices

Destroy diseased or mummified and dropped fruit, and remove and destroy dead and infected twigs. (See chapter 4 for details on fall cleanup.) Do not spray water on ripe fruit, as it can spread the disease spores.

Pruning
Proper pruning creates good air circulation, which allows faster drying and reduces spore development.

DISEASE *Cane Blight*

TYPE OF DISEASE

Cane blight is a fungal disease that primarily attacks weak or injured brambles.

VULNERABLE PLANTS

Blackberries and raspberries.

MOST OBVIOUS SYMPTOMS

The infection is not apparent until late in the season, when brownish purple areas appear on cut or broken parts of canes, spreading down the canes and encircling them. The canes wilt and die while loaded with fruit.

METHOD OF TRANSMISSION

Spores will continue to live on dead infected canes for 2 or more years. Wind and rain carry the spores to plants.

CONTROL STRATEGY

Remove all affected stalks and burn them.

STEPS TO PREVENT CANE BLIGHT

Garden Management Practices

Remove all plant debris from the garden, and do not handle plants when they are wet. (See chapter 4 for details on fall cleanup.) Control pests such as the caneborer, which damage the canes and provide an entryway for the disease, by cutting off and burning the wilted tips of plants.

Cane Gall

TYPE OF DISEASE

Cane gall is a bacterial disease of brambles.

VULNERABLE PLANTS

Blueberries (in blueberries, cane gall is also known as stem gall; older stems are more susceptible) and raspberries (black).

MOST OBVIOUS SYMPTOMS

Blueberry

Look for rough, irregular, warty growths on the stems of plants.

Raspberry

Galls develop on the fruiting canes. They change from white to light brown and disintegrate late in the season. Roots and new shoots do not become infected.

METHOD OF TRANSMISSION

The bacteria overwinter in the soil, and will enter a plant through wounds. Cane gall is transmitted by wind, rain, tools, and people.

CONTROL STRATEGY

Cane gall cannot be cured. Immediately prune and destroy infected canes. Clean the pruning tool between each cut by dipping it in a bleach solution (one part household bleach to four parts water).

STEPS TO PREVENT CANE GALL

Garden Management Practices

Remove all plant debris from the garden in fall. (See chapter 4 for details on fall cleanup.) Do not handle plants while they are wet, and keep hands and tools clean.

Cedar Apple Rust

TYPE OF DISEASE

Cedar apple rust is a fungal disease that has a 2-year life cycle. Spores from infected red cedars are carried to fruit trees one year, then the spores that develop there reinfect the cedar tree the next year. Cedar apple rust occurs in the eastern and central United States and Alaska.

VULNERABLE PLANTS

Apples and pears.

MOST OBVIOUS SYMPTOMS

Look for pale yellow pinhead-sized spots on the upper surface of the leaves. These enlarge to bright orange spots. Orange spots may develop on the fruit as well.

METHOD OF TRANSMISSION

The spores are carried by the wind. Cedar apple rust can also be transmitted from juniper trees to apples.

CONTROL STRATEGY

Apply sulfur fungicides every 5 to 7 days until symptoms disappear.

STEPS TO PREVENT CEDAR APPLE RUST

Resistant Varieties

Apple
Baldwin, Delicious, Duchess, Franklin, Golden Delicious, Grimes, Liberty, Melrose, Northwestern Greening, Nova Easygro, Novamac, Priscilla, Red Astrachan, Redfree, Rhode Island, Stayman, Transparent, and Winesap.

Garden Management Practices

Remove all red cedar trees and junipers within 300 yards. Cut down nearby susceptible varieties such as flowering crabapple. Clean up fallen fruit, leaves, and twigs. (See chapter 4 for details on fall cleanup.)

DISEASE *Cherry Leaf Spot*

TYPE OF DISEASE

Also known as yellow leaf, this fungal disease is considered the most important disease of sour cherries. It also affects sweet cherries. Cherry leaf spot is common east of the Rockies.

VULNERABLE PLANTS

Cherries.

MOST OBVIOUS SYMPTOMS

When the spores germinate on a leaf, they leave small reddish or purple circular spots. These enlarge, turn brown, and drop out of the leaf, giving it a shothole effect. Cherry leaf spot causes partial to complete defoliation of the tree.

METHOD OF TRANSMISSION

The spores overwinter in fallen leaves and are spread in the spring by the wind. Rain or high humidity encourage the spread of an infection.

STEPS TO CONTROL CHERRY LEAF SPOT

Spray trees with a 95 percent wettable sulfur fungicide from petal fall through post harvest for partial control. Bordeaux mixture works, but will tend to decrease the fruit size if used frequently or in high concentrations. Lime sulfur may discolor the fruit.

STEPS TO PREVENT CHERRY LEAF SPOT

Garden Management Practices

Remove and destroy fallen fruit and leaves. (See chapter 4 for details on fall cleanup.) Rotary-mow around trees after leaf drop.

DISEASE *Club Root*

TYPE OF DISEASE

Club root is a fungal disease found throughout the United States. It prefers a soil with a pH below 7.2.

VULNERABLE PLANTS

Broccoli, brussels sprouts, cabbage, cauliflower, Chinese cabbage, collards, kohlrabi, and turnips.

MOST OBVIOUS SYMPTOMS

In general, the aboveground parts of plants exhibit the effects of a malfunctioning root system and show signs of wilting, poor development, and small heads. The roots become enlarged and misshapen and develop club-shaped swellings.

METHOD OF TRANSMISSION

The spores can be carried by infected plants, by tools, or by water and wind. They survive in the soil for at least 7 years.

CONTROL STRATEGY

Try to prevent this disease by following clean gardening practices and rotating plants (the fungus persists in the soil for 7 years). Club root is more of a problem with plants growing in acid soil. Test your soil: If the pH is too low, add lime.

STEPS TO PREVENT CLUB ROOT

Resistant Varieties

Turnip
Bruce, Dale's Hybrid, Immuna, and May.

Garden Management Practices

If club root is a problem in your garden, raise the pH of the soil to 7.2 (using limestone). Keep hands clean and disinfect tools in a bleach solution (one part household bleach to four parts water). Do not work around plants when they are wet.

Planting
Grow your own seedlings in a sterile soil mix.

Crop Rotation
A 3- to 4-year crop rotation plan helps prevent this disease.

DISEASE Common Mosaic

TYPE OF DISEASE

Common mosaic is a viral disease that occurs throughout the United States.

VULNERABLE PLANTS

Beans (lima and snap).

MOST OBVIOUS SYMPTOMS

The first sign of common mosaic is a puckering of the leaflets along the midrib. Leaves will become elongated and will develop a mottled, light and dark green appearance. Dwarfing may occur in a few leaves or over the entire plant, and the plant might die.

METHOD OF TRANSMISSION

Common mosaic overwinters in perennial weeds, such as Canadian thistle and crab grass, and even in the flower garden. It is spread by aphids and by people handling the plants.

CONTROL STRATEGY

Common mosaic cannot be cured. Remove and destroy the infected and surrounding plants.

STEPS TO PREVENT COMMON MOSAIC

Resistant Varieties

Bean, Snap
Blue Lake (pole), Contender, Golden Wax Improved, Great Northern, Greensleeves, Idaho Refugee, Robust, Roma II, Tendercrop, Topcrop, U.S. No. 5, and Wisconsin Refugee.

Garden Management Practices

Control aphids in the garden. Wash hands and clean garden tools in a bleach solution (one part household bleach to four parts water).

DISEASE Crown Gall

TYPE OF DISEASE

Crown gall is a bacterial disease that is common throughout the United States.

VULNERABLE PLANTS

Apricots, blackberries, blueberries, cherries, peaches, and plums.

MOST OBVIOUS SYMPTOMS

Apricot

Plant weakens and produces small fruit. Galls girdle the roots and crown. These swellings occur where bacteria enter the tree.

Blackberry

Plant weakens and produces small fruit, which may be deformed. Galls or knots develop on the roots and stems and sometimes on the canes.

Blueberry

The symptoms are the same as those seen on blackberries.

Cherry

The symptoms are the same as those seen on apricots.

Peach

The symptoms are the same as those seen on apricots.

Plum

The symptoms are the same as those seen on apricots.

METHOD OF TRANSMISSION

Bacteria enter the plant through wounds. They are carried in contaminated tools and in infected soil.

CONTROL STRATEGY

Fruit Trees

Remove galls with a sharp, clean knife, and treat the wound with tree surgeon's paint. To prevent damage from sunburn, avoid doing this in the hottest part of the summer, and cover the affected part with soil after painting it. If the tree does not recover, remove and destroy it.

Berries

Remove the infected portion of the plant and destroy it. Clean hands and tools with a bleach solution (one part household bleach to four parts water) between each cut.

STEPS TO PREVENT CROWN GALL

Resistant Varieties

Apricot
Japanese apricots are resistant to crown gall.

Plum
Somewhat resistant rootstocks are Marianna 2623, Marianna 2624, and Myrobylan 29.

Garden Management Practices

Do not buy trees or plants that show swellings. When propagating fruit trees, budding is safer; grafting can allow bacteria access to the tree. Disinfect tools in an alcohol or bleach solution (one part household bleach to four parts water).

Other Preventive Steps

A strain of bacterium that will not cause disease is registered for use in preventing crown gall. The product is called Gall-trol. It occupies the same ecological niche as the crown gall bacterium and serves to prevent the pathogen from developing. To use Gall-trol, dip seedlings in the solution (made according to package instructions) before planting.

DISEASE *Curly Top*

TYPE OF DISEASE

Curly top is a viral disease found throughout the United States.

VULNERABLE PLANTS

Beans (lima and snap), muskmelons, pumpkins, tomatoes (in tomatoes, curly top is also known as western yellow blight), and watermelons.

MOST OBVIOUS SYMPTOMS

Bean, Lima and Snap

Curly top generally affects young plants. The leaves pucker and curl downward; they may be cupped or look like small green balls. Growth is stunted and the young plants die. Mature plants do not usually show symptoms, and usually live.

Muskmelon

The young leaves of diseased melons are stunted and curled, but may be normal in color. Older leaves are often yellowed. Overall, the plants show stunted growth, become bushy, and fail to produce fruit.

Pumpkin

The symptoms are the same as those seen in muskmelons.

Tomato

The foliage of infected seedlings yellows, curls, and twists, and the seedlings usually die. Leaflets of older plants that become infected twist and roll upward, exposing their undersides. The foliage becomes stiff and leathery, and the entire plant assumes a dull yellow appearance. The branches and stems are abnormally erect. The leaf stalks bend downward and the veins in the leaflets turn purple. Plant growth is stunted, and either no fruit sets, or the fruit that is produced ripens prematurely.

Watermelon

The symptoms are the same as those seen in muskmelons.

METHOD OF TRANSMISSION

Whiteflies and beet leafhoppers carry curly top to bean plants. Beet leafhoppers also transmit this disease to melons and tomatoes.

CONTROL STRATEGY

Curly top cannot be cured. Remove and destroy infected and surrounding plants.

STEPS TO PREVENT CURLY TOP

Resistant Varieties

Bean, Bush and Lima
Cape, Great Northern, Red Mexican, and University of Idaho.

Tomato
Owyhee and Payette.

Garden Management Practices

Try to control whiteflies on beans by spraying seedlings with insecticidal soap. If beet leafhoppers are a problem in your garden, cover melon and tomato seedlings with agricultural fleece, removing the fleece when the plants begin to flower.

Muskmelon

Avoid planting melons near sugar beets, since the disease can be transmitted by beet leafhoppers.

Watermelon

Treat the same as muskmelons.

DISEASE Cytospora Canker

TYPE OF DISEASE

A fungal disease, cytospora canker is also known as peach or perennial canker.

VULNERABLE PLANTS

Apricots, cherries, peaches, and plums.

MOST OBVIOUS SYMPTOMS

The first symptom to look for is wilting or yellowing of new shoots and leaves, which later turn brown. Gummy cankers develop in the bark.

METHOD OF TRANSMISSION

Cytospora canker infects the woody parts of stone fruit trees through bark injuries, pruning cuts, dead buds, and winter injury.

CONTROL STRATEGY

Cut out and remove infected wood and burn it.

STEPS TO PREVENT CYTOSPORA CANKER

Resistant Varieties

Peach
Biscoe, Candor, Carmen, Champion, Comanche, Cumberland, Eden, Emery, Envoy, Harbelle, Jayhaven, Madison, Polly, Raritan Rose, Redqueen, Reliance, Royalvee, and Veteran.

Garden Management Practices

Since the disease enters trees through wounds, try to avoid winter injury. Plant trees in a well-drained soil; trees planted in wet areas suffer more winter injury. Avoid planting fruit trees on ridge tops and in open areas, as winter winds can dessicate dormant buds. Select winter-hardy cultivars. Adjust nitrogen levels in soil, and follow cultivation practices to induce terminal bud set by September. Paint the trunk and lower scaffold limbs with white latex paint to reduce cold injury.

Pruning
Delay pruning until bud swell; you can continue to prune through bloom. Midsummer topping and hedging reduces the need for pruning.

DISEASE Damping-Off

TYPE OF DISEASE

Damping-off is a fungal disease that strikes many plants. It occurs throughout North America. Warm temperatures and high humidity encourage its growth.

VULNERABLE PLANTS

Basil, beans (lima and snap), broccoli, brussels sprouts, cabbage, carrots, cauliflower, celery, Chinese cabbage, chives, collards, kohlrabi, lettuce, marjoram, onions, savory, spinach, and tomatoes.

MOST OBVIOUS SYMPTOMS

Seedlings infected by damping-off simply topple over. A watery soft rot can be seen at the soil line. This disease will attack stored carrots, producing a white, cottony fungal growth.

METHOD OF TRANSMISSION

The sclerotinia fungus (damping-off) lives in the soil, and is primarily a problem in seedbeds. It can be transported on garden tools and in garden soils taken into the house or greenhouse.

CONTROL STRATEGY

Nothing can be done to control damping-off once it attacks, since it immediately kills a plant. However, you can prevent it from infecting other seedlings.

STEPS TO PREVENT DAMPING-OFF

Garden Management Practices

Disinfect tools in a household bleach solution (one part household bleach to four parts water).

Planting

When starting seedlings indoors, use commercial potting soil, or pasteurize your own potting soil in an oven. Make sure your soil mix drains very well. When seedlings sprout, place them near a fan turned on low to keep air moving around the seedlings and to reduce humidity. Plant seedlings so that the soil surface is not more than ¼ inch below the level of the top of the container to be sure that air can circulate freely around the stems of the plants. For direct seeding, make sure soil is well drained and warm. You might try spreading pasteurized soil or a sterile vermiculite in furrows where you plant your seeds.

Watering

Watering systems that give seedlings water from below are preferred to overhead watering if damping-off is a problem. Never water past noon so that the soil surface and the plants are dry by dark.

DISEASE Downy Mildew

TYPE OF DISEASE

Downy mildew is a fungal disease whose growth is favored by cool wet nights and warm humid days.

Infestations of lima beans are most common in the mid- and northern Atlantic states, and infestations of cucumbers are most common in Atlantic and Gulf States. Downy mildew is prevalent in spinach growing in coastal areas. Spore production is favored by temperatures cooler than 65°F and by relative humidities approaching 100 percent.

VULNERABLE PLANTS

Beans (lima), broccoli, cauliflower, chard (in chard, downy mildew is known as chard blue mold), cucumbers, lettuce, muskmelons, onions, pumpkins, radishes, spinach (in spinach, downy mildew is known as chard blue mold), squash (summer and winter), tarragon, turnips, and watermelons.

MOST OBVIOUS SYMPTOMS

In general, look for yellowish or light green areas on the upper surfaces of older leaves. Seedlings develop purplish lesions on the leaves and stems, which become covered with the white downy fungus. Plants die very rapidly after contracting downy mildew.

Bean, Lima

White, cottony patches develop on infected bean pods; some may have a purple border. The infected pods shrivel, turn black, and die. The upper surfaces of older leaves will have yellowish or light green areas. Downy mildew may also infect young shoots, flowers, and leaves, causing leaf veins to become purplish and distorted. Infected plants can die in a few days.

Broccoli

In broccoli, downy mildew appears as small leaf spots, which first are yellow and later turn brown with bluish black, lacelike markings. In moist weather, a white downy mold develops on the leaf spots. Broccoli heads become uneven and shaggy. Downy mildew can predispose plants to bacterial soft rot.

Cucumber

Irregularly shaped yellow to brown spots appear on the tops of leaves, usually at the center of the plants. Under moist conditions, downy purple spots appear on the undersides of leaves. The leaves die as these spots increase in size. Downy mildew spreads rapidly from the crown toward new growth.

Lettuce

Downy mildew affects both seedlings and mature lettuce plants. The symptoms appear first on the oldest leaves. Look for light green or pale yellow areas on the upper surfaces of leaves, and spots with downy white growth on the undersides.

Muskmelon

The symptoms are the same as those seen in cucumbers.

Onion

Symptoms usually appear after leaves are 6 inches long. The oldest leaves are affected first. Yellow or grayish elongated leaf spots appear on these leaves, which later become covered with a white to purplish mold during cool moist weather. As the leaves are affected down to the leaf sheath, they drop over and dry up.

Pumpkin

The symptoms are the same as those seen in cucumbers.

Radish

Leaf symptoms appear as small yellowish areas that later turn brown and develop bluish black, lacelike markings. In moist weather, a whitish downy mold develops on the undersides of leaves. The roots can become discolored internally, sometimes with a netlike brown or black area. In the advanced stages of this disease, the skin develops small cracks and becomes rough, and the root may split. Avoid dense and shaded plantings.

Spinach

Yellow leaf spots with fuzzy purple growth develop on the undersides of leaves. The affected areas turn black and die. The disease may affect entire leaves and plants. In severe attacks, all plants in a garden may be destroyed within a few days. Most prevalent in coastal areas.

Squash, Summer and Winter

The symptoms are the same as those seen in cucumbers.

Tarragon

The upper surfaces of leaves become covered with a white powdery mold, and the leaves wilt, brown, and then drop.

Turnip

The symptoms in turnips are similar to those described for radishes.

Watermelon

The symptoms are similar to those described for cucumbers.

METHOD OF TRANSMISSION

Downy mildew overwinters on diseased plant debris and in the soil. The spores can be carried by insects, wind, rain, or tools.

CONTROL STRATEGY

If you catch the infection early, apply a copper-based fungicide to diseased and surrounding plants every 7 to 10 days until harvest. Remove and destroy any plants with a serious infection.

STEPS TO PREVENT DOWNY MILDEW

Resistant Varieties

Bean, Lima
Eastland and Thaxter.

Broccoli
Citation, Emperor, Futura, Green Dwarf, and Orion.

Cucumber
Ashley, Burpee Hybrid, Cherokee 7, Comanche, County Fair, Dublin, Fletcher, Gemini Hybrid, High Mark II, Burpee's M & M Hybrid, Marketmore 76, Palmetto, Palomar, Pioneer, Poinsett, Poinsett 76, Salty, Santee, Saticoy, Slicemaster, Smoothie, Stono, Streamliner Hybrid, and Suyo Long.

Lettuce
Crisp Mint (romaine); Grand Rapids (looseleaf); Hot Weather (butterhead); Salinas (butterhead); Tania (butterhead); Valmaine Cos (romaine); and Valverde (head).

Muskmelon
Delta Gold, Edisto 47, Georgia 47, Gulfstream, Home Garden, and Perlita.

Spinach
Califlay, Dixie Market, Dixie Savoy, High Pack, Hybrid No. 7, Hybrid No. 424, Hybrid No. 425, Indian Summer Hybrid, Kent, Marathon, Melody Hybrid, and Texas Early Hybrid 7.

Garden Management Practices

Remove plant debris from the garden in the fall. (See chapter 4 for details on fall cleanup.) Disinfect tools by dipping them in a bleach solution (one part household bleach to four parts water.) Keep hands clean, and do not handle plants when they are wet.

Crop Rotation

Maintaining at least a 3-year crop rotation is an important preventive tool in fighting downy mildew.

Early Blight

TYPE OF DISEASE

Early blight is a fungal disease whose spread is encouraged by heavy dew, rainfall, and warm temperatures. It occurs throughout North America.

VULNERABLE PLANTS

Celery, potatoes, and tomatoes.

MOST OBVIOUS SYMPTOMS

Celery

Look for circular, small, yellow spots on the leaves of seedlings. These rapidly enlarge to up to ½ inch, and the color changes from yellow to brown with a grayish cast in the center. The spots can grow together and kill the leaves. In addition, sunken lesions may develop on the stalks, and growth of the plant is stunted.

Potato

The symptoms are similar to those seen on tomatoes. In potatoes, early blight also affects the tubers, causing shallow decay and small circular lesions surrounded by puckered skin. This disease is most severe in alternately wet and dry conditions.

Tomato

Tomatoes infected by early blight develop collar rot—dark, girdling lesions on the stem at the soil line. The foliage infection appears first as circular or irregular dark spots on older leaves. As these spots enlarge, a series of concentric rings develops, forming a target pattern. Often these spots grow together. Cankers develop on fruit stems, branches, and large stems. Both green and ripe fruit cracks at the stem.

METHOD OF TRANSMISSION

The spores of early blight are carried by wind and insects. They overwinter on diseased plant refuse.

CONTROL STRATEGY

As soon as you spot symptoms, begin applying a copper-based fungicide every 7 to 10 days.

STEPS TO PREVENT EARLY BLIGHT

Resistant Varieties

Celery
Emerson Pascal and Green Giant Hybrid.

Potato
Chieftain and Norgold Russet.

Tomato
Floradel, Manahill, Manalucie, and Southland.

Garden Management Practices

Clean all plant debris from the garden in the fall. (See chapter 4 for detailed information on fall cleanup.)

Celery
Plant 3-year-old seeds, because the fungus cannot survive that long, whereas celery seeds are viable for 6 years.

Potato
Proper management of soil moisture and soil fertility greatly decreases the severity of early blight in potatoes. (See chapters 7 and 8 for more information on watering and fertilizing.)

DISEASE *Fire Blight*

TYPE OF DISEASE

Fire blight is a bacterial disease that spreads rapidly in moist weather.

VULNERABLE PLANTS

Apples and pears. Susceptible varieties of apples include Hopa Crab, Hyslop Crab, Ida Red, Transcendant Crab, Wealthy, Whitney Crab, and Yellow Transparent. Susceptible varieties of pears include Aurora, Bartlett, Bosc, Clapp's Favorite, Flemish Beauty, Gorham, Highland, Howell, Idaho, Packer, Packham's Triumph, Patton, and Sheldon.

MOST OBVIOUS SYMPTOMS

The blossoms wither and die, and reddish, water-soaked lesions develop on the bark. On a warm day, the lesions on the tree ooze an orange-brown liquid. They later become brown and dry. Infected shoots turn brown or black as though scorched. Most branch tips, once infected, wilt rapidly, taking on the characteristic shape of a cane.

METHOD OF TRANSMISSION

Fire blight is carried by rain, dew, insects (bees, aphids, psylla), and wind. It overwinters in infected bark. The bacteria gain entry to the tree through blossoms or lush new growth, and once inside, begin to work toward the roots. Fire blight spreads rapidly in periods of warm, humid weather, and so it is during such times that you should check the trees for symptoms.

CONTROL STRATEGY

As soon as you discover fire blight, remove all suckers and any infected branches and burn them before the bacteria attack the tree further. Cut off the infected branches at least 12 inches below the point of last visible wilt. After each cut, dip your pruning tool in a bleach solution (one part household bleach to four parts water) to avoid transmitting the disease from one branch to another. Some antibiotic sprays are used in commercial settings, but they are not yet available to the home gardener.

STEPS TO PREVENT FIRE BLIGHT

Resistant Varieties

Apple

Akane, Baldwin, Ben Davis, Delicious, Dolgo Crab, Duchess, Florence Crab, Gano, Haralson, Hibernal, Jerseymac, Jonathan, Liberty, MacFree, McIntosh, Northern Spy, Nova Easygro, Novamac, Prima, Priscilla, Red Delicious, Redfree, Stayman, Winesap, and Winter Banana.

Pear

Asian varieties and Comice, Dawn, Douglas, Duchess d'Angouleme, El Dorado, Fan-stil, Lincoln, Luscious, Mac, Magness, Maxine, Moonglow, Orient, Seckel, Starking Delicious, Sugar, Sure Crop, Waite, Winter Nelis. Disease-resistant rootstocks: Kieffer, Moonglow, Old Home, Oriental (*Pyrus communis*), Oriental *(P. bitulafolis)*, Oriental harbin pear *(P. ussuriensis)*, Stark Honeyset, and Starking Delicious.

A variety's resistance depends to some extent on local weather conditions during bloom, the proximity of trees that have cankers, and the number of insect carriers in the area.

Garden Management Practices

Very rigorous garden sanitation is absolutely essential to prevent the spread of fire blight bacteria. Clean up any fallen fruit, leaves, and branches, and mow around the base of the tree. (See chapter 4 for details on fall cleanup.) Sod cover crops such as grass, clover, or alfalfa reduce the chances of fire blight and increase populations of beneficials.

Removing Hosts

Remove possible hosts for fire blight, including cotoneaster hedges, hawthorns, mountain ash, saskatoons, and wild apples, all of which harbor the bacteria and can pass the disease along to apple and pear trees. Control aphids and pear psylla by spraying plants with insecticidal soap every 2 to 3 days for 2 weeks.

Feeding

Avoid fast, lush growth, especially in pears, by being careful not to overfertilize.

DISEASE *Fusarium Wilt*

TYPE OF DISEASE

Fusarium wilt is a fungal disease that likes warm, dry weather. Soil temperatures below 60°F or above 90°F retard the disease. It is found throughout the United States, but occurs most often from Long Island to Colorado.

VULNERABLE PLANTS

Cabbage (in cabbage, fusarium wilt is known as fusarium yellows), celery (in celery, fusarium wilt is known as yellows), muskmelons, peas (green and snap; in peas, fusarium wilt is also known as pea wilt), potatoes, spinach, tomatoes, turnips, and watermelons.

MOST OBVIOUS SYMPTOMS

Asparagus

Asparagus infected by fusarium wilt produces weak, spindly spears in the spring. As the season progresses, shoots from severely infected crowns may turn bright yellow.

Cabbage

Affected plants have a sickly, dwarfed, yellow appearance. The seedlings wilt, and older plants lose vitality. The leaves turn yellow, then brown; then they drop off. Lower leaves are affected first.

Celery

Look for stunted, one-sided growth and yellowing. Infected plants tend to be brittle and taste bitter. The vascular strands become reddish brown from the roots to the leaves. As the disease progresses, the crowns and roots may rot.

Muskmelon

Fusarium wilt in muskmelons causes stunting, yellowing, wilting, and dying of vines. A water-soaked streak appears at the soil line on one side of the vine. This streak turns yellow, then tan, and finally dark brown. It is diagnostic of the disease in muskmelons.

Pea

Lower leaves yellow and the plants wilt. A cross-section of the stems would show a lemon-yellow discoloration. The wilted plants may eventually die.

Potato

Look for yellowing of the foliage, brown discoloration of the vascular system, and wilting of the leaves and stems. The tubers will show internal browning of the vascular ring. Fusarium wilt also affects tubers in storage; blue or white swellings develop on the decayed areas.

Radish

Plants become stunted and roots are discolored. Most young radish plants infected with fusarium wilt turn yellow and die.

Spinach

The plant will turn yellow; lower leaves lose their firmness and wilt; and water channels turn brown.

Tomato

Yellowing of the leaves occurs, which spreads upward from the base of the plant as the disease progresses. The yellowing may occur on only one side of a leaf midrib or on one side of a plant. These leaves wilt noticeably before they die. The whole plant will eventually die.

Watermelon

Fusarium wilt in watermelons causes stunting, wilting, and death of established plants. Look for a brown discoloration of the stem and wilting of the branches.

METHOD OF TRANSMISSION

The spores can be transmitted by water or by striped cucumber beetles. Fusarium wilt can live in the soil for as long as 20 years.

CONTROL STRATEGY

Some plants will produce some fruit, but in most cases you should remove and destroy infected plants. Fungicides are not effective against fusarium fungi.

STEPS TO PREVENT FUSARIUM WILT

Resistant Varieties

Fusarium wilt is generally carried in the soil, so using resistant varieties is the best way to prevent the disease.

Cabbage
Charleton Wakefield, Globe, Harvester Queen, Hercules, Hybrid Blueboy, Jersey Queen, Marion Market, Resistant Detroit, Stonehead, Wisconsin All Season, and Wisconsin Golden Acre.

Celery
Green petiole varieties, or Ornell 19; Emerson Pascal; Florida Golden; Forbes Golden Plume; Golden Pascal; Michigan Golden; and Tall Golden Plume.

Muskmelon
Charantais, Delicious #51, Golden Gopher, Harvest Queen, Iroquois, and Vedrantais.

Pea
Alaska, Alderman, Bolero, Dwarf Gray Sugar, Freezonian, Frosty, Greater Progress, Green Arrow, Little Marvel, Mars, Novella, Perfection, Pride, Sparkle, Thomas Laxton, Venus, Wando, and Wisconsin Early Sweet.

Radish
Red Prince.

Tomato

Ace 55, Beefeater Hybrid, Beefmaster, Better Boy, Better Girl, Burpee's Big Girl, Campbell's 17, Floradel, Homestead, H 1350, KC 146, Kokomo, Manalucie, Manapal, Marion, and Supersonic.

Watermelon

Black Kleckly, Charleston Gray, Congo, Crimson Sweet, Fairfax, Sweet Princess, Triple Sweet, and Tri-X313.

Garden Management Practices

Remove all plant debris from the garden in the fall and destroy. (See chapter 4 for details on fall cleanup.) Do not work around plants when they are wet. Protect young plants from striped cucumber beetles by covering them with agricultural fleece or fine nylon netting until bloom time. Solarizing the soil helps to eliminate fusarium wilt. (See page 379 for more information on solarizing soil.)

DISEASE *Late Blight*

TYPE OF DISEASE

Late blight is a fungal disease that attacks plants after they blossom. It is most common in north central, northeastern, and Atlantic states. Rainy, foggy weather and temperatures of 40°F to 60°F at night and 70°F to 80°F during the day are favorable conditions for late blight.

VULNERABLE PLANTS

Celery, potatoes, and tomatoes.

MOST OBVIOUS SYMPTOMS

Celery

Late blight first appears on seedlings as small, round, yellow spots on the leaves. The spots turn almost black in 2 weeks.

Potato

Purplish or brownish black areas develop on the blade of the leaflet, on the leaf stalk, or on the stem. Lower leaves are the first to be affected. Pale halos form around the blackened areas.

Tomato

Greenish black, water-soaked patches develop on the older leaves of tomatoes infected with late blight. These spots enlarge, and in moist weather may show white, downy growth of the fungus on their surface. On the fruit, you will see large dark-colored spots that are firm and have a rough surface.

METHOD OF TRANSMISSION

Wind, water, and seeds carry this disease. Late blight overwinters in crop debris.

CONTROL STRATEGY

Once you spot the symptoms, apply a copper-based fungicide every 7 to 10 days until harvest.

STEPS TO PREVENT LATE BLIGHT

Resistant Varieties

Celery
Emerson Pascal and Green Giant Hybrid.

Potato
Essex, Kennebec, Ona, Pungo, Saco, and Sebago.

Garden Management Practices

Clean up all plant debris from the garden in the fall. (See chapter 4 for details on fall cleanup.) Do not work around plants when they are wet.

DISEASE **Mosaic**

TYPE OF DISEASE

Mosaic is a viral disease found throughout the United States.

VULNERABLE PLANTS

Cucumbers, lettuce, muskmelons, peppers, potatoes, raspberries, squash (summer and winter), tomatoes, and watermelons.

MOST OBVIOUS SYMPTOMS

Cucumber

Look for yellow-green mottling of the leaves near the growing terminals and a similar mottling of the fruit. Plant growth is stunted.

Lettuce

Leaves of infected plants are mottled yellow and green. The whole plant takes on an overall yellowish cast. Growth is stunted, and no head forms.

Muskmelon

Leaves become mottled with dark green, light green, or yellow areas of irregular form. They grow to an irregular shape, and portions of the veins may die. Vine tips are stunted or yellowish, overall growth is stunted, and yields are low.

Pepper

Look for mottled green and yellow leaves. The growth of infected plants is stunted.

Potato

Look for a mottled light and dark green pattern on curled or crinkled leaves. Brown specks may appear on tubers. The plant yellows, droops, and dies.

Raspberry

Some strains show no distinct symptoms, but the infected plants will be weaker and will produce fewer canes and berries. Other strains will show short canes and yellowish, mottled foliage, and the fruit may be dry, seedy, flavorless, and crumbly. Red raspberries develop large green blisters surrounded by yellowish tissue on the foliage in the late spring. Black and purple raspberries show mottled leaves, and their growth is stunted. Canes bend over, turn black, and die.

Squash, Summer

Mosaic is most common on straightneck and crookneck summer squash. Yellow spots appear on the leaves and sometimes on the fruit. Plant growth is stunted.

Tomato

Infected plants are yellow and bushy; growth is stunted. The leaves develop a shoestring appearance.

Watermelon

Look for mottled leaves. Plants are stunted, and they produce misshapen fruit.

METHOD OF TRANSMISSION

Aphids and spotted or striped cucumber beetles spread mosaic to vulnerable plants. The mosaic virus overwinters on perennial weeds, such as bittersweet, chickweed, ground cherry, horse nettle, jimson weed, mints, nightshade, pokeweed, ragweed, and wild cucurbits. Aphids often transmit the virus from these weeds to garden plants. The virus also can be spread by gardeners working around infected plants, especially when they are wet.

CONTROL STRATEGY

Mosaic cannot be cured. Remove and destroy the infected and surrounding plants.

STEPS TO PREVENT MOSAIC

Resistant Varieties

Cucumber

Burpee Hybrid, Burpee Pickler, Bush Champion, Challenger, China, Comanche, Dublin, Early Set, Gemini Hybrid, High Mark II, Marketmore 70, Pacer, Pot Luck, Saladin, Salty, Slicemaster, SMR, Spacemaster, Spartan Dawn, Tablegreen 65, and Victory.

Lettuce
Nancy and Parris Island Cos.

Muskmelon
Charantais and Vedrantais.

Pepper
Bellringer, Giant, Keystone Resistant, and Yolo Wonder.

Potato
Cherokee, Chippewa, Earlaine, Houma, Katahdin, Kennebec, Ona, Penobscot, Pungo, Saco, and Sebago.

Raspberry
Indian Summer, Lloyd George, Newburgh, Pyne's Imperial, Pyne's Royal, and Williamette.

Tomato
Beefmaster, Moto-red, Ohio M-12, Ohio M-39, Park's Whopper, Quick Pick, Tropic, Vendor, and others.

Garden Management Practices

Deny aphids and cucumber beetles access to your plants by covering plants with agricultural fleece until bloom time. In addition, remove all perennial weeds within at least 100 yards of the garden. In the fall, remove all plant debris. (See chapter 4 for details on fall cleanup.) Do not work around plants while they are wet, or you may spread the disease.

DISEASE *Orange Rust*

TYPE OF DISEASE

Orange rust is a fungal disease.

VULNERABLE PLANTS

Blackberries and raspberries.

MOST OBVIOUS SYMPTOMS

Yellow dots appear on both sides of the leaves of infected plants. Two to 3 weeks later, light-colored areas develop on the undersides of leaves; then the epidermis (surface layer of cells) ruptures, exposing large, bright orange-red powdery masses of spores.

METHOD OF TRANSMISSION

Orange rust overwinters in roots and stems of old plants. It is also a disease of wild berries. The spores are carried by wind and water.

CONTROL STRATEGY

Infected plants cannot be saved. Dig them up and destroy them.

STEPS TO PREVENT ORANGE RUST

Resistant Varieties

Blackberry
Boysen, Ebony King, Eldorado, Lawton, Orange Evergreen, Russell, and Snyder.

Garden Management Practices

Eliminate nearby wild plants that are infected, and in the fall thoroughly clean the garden. (See chapter 4 for details on fall cleanup.) Do not work around plants when they are wet.

Mulching and Feeding
Mulch heavily with straw and leaf mold, and when the season is finished, apply a heavy dressing of compost with extra potash and phosphate to prevent malnutrition, which encourages this disease.

DISEASE *Powdery Mildew*

TYPE OF DISEASE

Powdery mildew is a fungal disease found throughout North America. It causes severe problems in irrigated regions. Low soil moisture combined with high humidity at the plant surface favors this disease. It affects peas in rainy seasons.

VULNERABLE PLANTS

Apples, blackberries, blueberries, cherries, cucumbers, muskmelons, peas (green and snap), plums, pumpkins, raspberries (red), sage, squash (summer and winter), strawberries, tarragon, and watermelons.

MOST OBVIOUS SYMPTOMS

Apple

The infected terminals of twigs, leaves, and blossoms are covered with a white to pearly gray, velvety mold. Twigs become dwarfed and rosetted, and the terminal bud is killed, which causes staghorn growth of side shoots. Young fruit develops russeting or etching.

Bean, Lima and Snap

Powdery mildew usually develops on mature plants late in the season. It begins as faint discolored leaf spots that become covered with a grayish white, talcumlike powdery growth. This growth spreads to all aboveground parts of the plant. Young leaves are dwarfed and curled and may turn yellow and drop. The pods are dwarfed and distorted.

Blackberry

Dwarfing and twisting of leaf tips occurs, followed by the growth of the white, powdery fungus on the undersides of leaves.

Blueberry

Blueberries infected with powdery mildew develop a whitish mold on the upper surfaces of leaves after harvest. Yield is not affected.

Cherry

The symptoms are the same as those seen in apples.

Cucumber

Look for circular, whitish spots on the lower surfaces of leaves. These spots increase in number and size and grow together. They progress to the upper surfaces and finally cover entire leaves with a white, powdery growth. Powdery mildew is encouraged in cucumbers by temperatures higher than 80°F.

Muskmelon

The symptoms are the same as those seen in cucumbers.

Pea

The leaves, stems, and pods of infected plants are covered by white, talcumlike powdery mold. When pods are affected, the seeds may turn gray or brown.

Plum

The symptoms are the same as those seen in apples.

Pumpkin

The symptoms are the same as those seen in cucumbers.

Raspberry, Red

Powdery mildew affects red raspberries. The symptoms are the same as those seen in blackberries.

Sage

The upper surfaces of leaves become covered with a white powdery mold. The foliage wilts, browns, and then drops.

Squash, Summer

The symptoms are the same as those seen in cucumbers.

Strawberry

Look for upward curling of the leaf margins and the growth of the white powdery fungus on the upper surfaces of leaves.

Tarragon

The symptoms are the same as those seen in sage.

Watermelon

The symptoms are the same as those seen in cucumbers.

METHOD OF TRANSMISSION

Powdery mildew overwinters in apple and plum buds and in other plant debris. It also lives on wild or cultivated cucurbits and other plants. Wind and water transmit the spores to plants.

CONTROL STRATEGY

Fruit Trees

To control powdery mildew, follow the spray program prescribed for apple scab. (See the entry Apple

Scab earlier in this chapter.) Prune infected terminals for additional control.

Berries and Vegetables

As soon as you discover the disease, remove and destroy the infected parts. Disinfect your pruning tool in a bleach solution (one part household bleach to four parts water) after each cut. In addition to pruning, apply a sulfur- or copper-based fungicide every 7 to 10 days. Limit overhead sprinkling to early in the day, and do not work around plants when they are wet. Thin plants to let in sun and air.

STEPS TO PREVENT POWDERY MILDEW

Resistant Varieties

Apple
Akane, Delicious, Discovery, Golden Delicious, Liberty, Lodi, Macfree, Prima, Priscilla, Red Delicious, Redfree, Sir Prize, Spartan, and Tydeman's Red.

Bean, Snap
Contender, Greencrop, Provider, and Tendercrop.

Blueberry
Berkeley, Earliblue, and Ivanhoe.

Cucumber
Bounty, Burpee's M & M Hybrid, Burpless Hybrid, Calypso, County Fair, Gemini Hybrid, Liberty Hybrid, Marketmore 76, Park's Comanche Hybrid, Patio Pik, Pik-Rite, Premier, Royal, Sprint 440, Supersett, Sweet Success, Ultraslice Early, and Victory.

Muskmelon
Muskmelons: Burpee Ambrosia, Chaca, Dixie Jumbo, Edisto, Magnum 45, Planters Jumbo, Samson Hybrid, Supermarket, and Sweet and Early. Cantaloupes: Dixie Jumbo, Edisto, Magnum 45, Planters Jumbo, Samson Hybrid, and Sweet and Early.

Pea
Grenadier, Knight, Maestro, Olympia, Oregon Sugar Pod, Snappy, Snowflake, Sugar Bon, and Sugar Daddy.

Strawberry
Redcoat and Surecrop.

Garden Management Practices

Be sure to remove all plant debris and fallen fruit from the garden in the fall, and mow around trees. (See chapter 4 for details on fall cleanup.) Pull up all nearby wild relatives of the vulnerable plants that can also become infected with powdery mildew.

Watering
If you water your plants from overhead, try to do this earlier in the day so the plants will dry before evening.

Pea
Train your peas along tall supports so the air can circulate freely. When watering, don't wet the foliage unnecessarily, especially in the afternoon.

Strawberry
Keep weeds down, avoid overgrowth, and rotate or renew plants often.

DISEASE *Rhizoctonia*

TYPE OF DISEASE

Also known as wirestem rot, bottom rot, and head rot, this fungal disease occurs throughout the United States. Its growth is encouraged by moderately cool, wet weather, and moist, heavy soil conditions.

VULNERABLE PLANTS

Broccoli, brussels sprouts, cabbage, cauliflower, Chinese cabbage, collards, kohlrabi, marjoram, oregano, potatoes (in potatoes, rhizoctonia is known as black scurf), rosemary, sage, savory, tarragon, and thyme.

MOST OBVIOUS SYMPTOMS

In general, plants become weak or wilted. Rot occurs on the stem near the soil and in the roots.

Crucifers

Rhizoctonia in crucifers is characterized by darkened and girdled areas on the stem near the soil line. Affected plants are weak, produce small heads, and sometimes wilt and die. Bottom rot develops on plants after they have been transplanted to the garden. Dark, slightly sunken spots develop on basal leaves near the soil. In moist conditions, the rot spreads to adjacent leaves and causes the head to rot. Rhizoctonia also commonly causes damping-off.

Potato

Look for brown cankers that "burn off" young potato sprouts as they emerge, causing uneven stands. Cankers and girdling develop on infected roots, stolons, and stems. Stem cankers prevent the normal functioning of the plants, and they become stunted. Brown, sunken, dead areas appear on mature stalks, rosettes and purple discoloration occur on foliage, and aerial tubers form. Infected tubers have black or brown sclerotia on the skin.

METHOD OF TRANSMISSION

Rhizoctonia lives on plant refuse and in the soil indefinitely. It is transmitted by wind and water.

CONTROL STRATEGY

Rhizoctonia cannot be controlled. Remove and destroy infected plants.

STEPS TO PREVENT RHIZOCTONIA

Garden Management Practices

Remove and destroy all plant debris in the fall. (See chapter 4 for details on fall cleanup.) Do not work around plants when they are wet. Provide good drainage. Compost discourages this fungus.

Crop Rotation
Follow a 3-year crop rotation plan.

Solarization
Pasteurizing the soil used to raise seedlings and solarizing the garden soil also help to control rhizoctonia. (See page 379 for information on soil pasteurization and solarization.)

Potato
Shallow planting gives some control by encouraging rapid emergence. Avoid planting potatoes in heavy, poorly drained soils, and delay planting until warm weather sets in.

DISEASE  **Scab**

TYPE OF DISEASE

Scab is a fungal disease found throughout North America. Humid conditions favor the growth of scab on cucumbers, watermelons, and peaches.

VULNERABLE PLANTS

Apricots, beets, cucumbers, muskmelons, peaches, potatoes, pumpkins, squash (summer and winter), and watermelons.

MOST OBVIOUS SYMPTOMS

Apricot

Small, dark, greenish spots appear about the time the fruit is half grown; these spots turn brown as the fruit continues to mature. (In peaches, they turn black.) The fruit may crack. Yellow-brown spots also may appear on twigs and branches.

Beet

Corky spots develop on the surfaces of infected roots.

Cucumber

Water-soaked spots appear on leaves, which may cause them to wilt. Stems may develop small cankers. Young fruit develops gray, slightly sunken spots. As the plant matures, these spots darken, become more sunken, and develop a greenish velvety mold.

Muskmelon

The symptoms are the same as those seen in cucumbers.

Peach

The symptoms are the same as those seen in apricots.

Potato

The surfaces of tubers have brown, roughened, irregularly shaped areas that may be raised and warty, level with the surface, or sunken. These lesions may affect just a small part of the tuber surface, or may completely cover it.

Pumpkin

The symptoms are the same as those seen in cucumbers.

Squash, Summer

The symptoms are the same as those seen in cucumbers.

Watermelon

The symptoms are the same as those seen in cucumbers.

METHOD OF TRANSMISSION

Scab overwinters in fallen leaves and in the soil. It is picked up and transmitted to plants by the winds in early spring.

CONTROL STRATEGY

Apricot

Apply a sulfur spray or dust 2 to 3 weeks after petals drop from apricots. Make a second application 2 weeks later if needed.

Beet

Maintain uniform soil moisture for beets, and lower the soil pH to 5.3 or less.

Cucumber

Remove and destroy infected plants.

Muskmelon

Treat as cucumbers.

Peach

Apply a sulfur spray or dust 3 to 4 weeks after the petals have dropped from peach trees. Make a second application 2 weeks later if needed.

Potato

Treat as beets.

Pumpkin

Treat as cucumbers.

Squash, Summer

Treat as cucumbers.

Watermelon

Treat as cucumbers.

STEPS TO PREVENT SCAB

Garden Management Practices

Remove and destroy all diseased and fallen fruit, and rake up all fallen leaves. Mow the area under the trees to remove grass, which might harbor spores. Prune trees to allow air and light into the trees' canopy to promote faster drying after rain.

Crop Rotation

Do not grow beets, cucumbers, muskmelons, potatoes, or watermelons in the same soil more than once every 3 years.

Resistant Varieties

Cucumber

Highmoor, Maine No. 2, Marketmore 70, Northern Pickling, Pacer, Salty, Slicemaster, Spacemaster, Victory, Wisconsin SR 6, and Wisconsin SR 10. All cucumber plants will be more resistant to scab if grown on a trellis.

Potato

Cayuga, Cherokee, Early Gem, Menominee, Norchip, Norgold Russet, Norland, Ontario Rhine Red, Seneca, and Superior.

DISEASE *Septoria Leaf Spot*

TYPE OF DISEASE

This fungal disease, also known as septoria blight, requires high moisture levels for germination. Infestation of tomatoes occurs frequently in Atlantic and central states.

VULNERABLE PLANTS

Blackberries, parsley, and tomatoes.

MOST OBVIOUS SYMPTOMS

Blackberry

Look for small dots on leaves that are purplish on the edge and tan or light brown in the center. When they enlarge, you may be able to see black dots in the center.

Parsley

Small, tan leaf spots occur.

Tomato

Numerous small, gray, circular spots appear scattered all over older leaves.

METHOD OF TRANSMISSION

Rain, wind, and seeds carry the disease. It is also easily transmitted by brushing against wet plants.

CONTROL STRATEGY

Apply copper dust or a liquid copper spray fungicide every 7 to 10 days after discovering the disease.

STEPS TO PREVENT
SEPTORIA LEAF SPOT

Resistant Varieties

Parsley
Paramount.

Garden Management Practices

Control perennial weeds, since they carry this fungus. Remove all plant debris from the garden in fall. (See chapter 4 for details on fall cleanup.) Do not work around plants when they are wet.

Watering
Septoria spores require a high moisture level for germination. Water the plants at ground level rather than overhead to avoid wetting the leaves. In addition, water early in the day so plants will dry by evening.

Blackberry
Train canes to allow for good air circulation. Remove old leaves and cultivate early.

DISEASE *Sunscald*

TYPE OF DISEASE

Sunscald is an environmental disorder. Sunscald in apples and cherries occurs in winter on days when the warmth of the sun on the southwest side of the tree trunk begins to activate growth cells. Then, when the sun goes down, the temperature plummets, and the cold ruptures those cells and dries them out. Sunscald occurs whenever green tomatoes are exposed to the sun; most frequently in hot, dry weather. It is aggravated in plants that have been subject to premature foliage loss due to disease or some other problem.

VULNERABLE PLANTS

Apples, cherries, and tomatoes.

MOST OBVIOUS SYMPTOMS

Apple

Sunscald in apples causes the bark to split in winter.

Cherry

The symptoms are the same as those seen in apples.

Tomato

Sunscald most commonly appears on green fruit. A whitish or yellowish patch develops on the side of the fruit facing the sun. In severe cases, the affected area shrinks and forms a large flattened grayish white spot with a paperlike surface.

STEPS TO PREVENT SUNSCALD

Resistant Varieties

Tomato
Use varieties like Humaya and Pirate, which are resistant to any disease that might cause defoliation.

Garden Management Practices

Apple
To prevent sunscald in apples, wrap the trunks with

strips of burlap and secure with twine, or place a wide board several inches away from the tree on the southwest side, to cast a shadow on the trunk. In March or April, when the weather is milder, remove the sun screen.

Tomato
When you prune suckers from the tomato plant, prune above the first group of leaves on the sucker rather than at the base. This will provide more foliage to shade tomatoes and prevent sunscald.

DISEASE # Tobacco Mosaic

TYPE OF DISEASE

Tobacco mosaic is a viral disease that occurs throughout the United States.

VULNERABLE PLANTS

Eggplants, peppers, and tomatoes.

MOST OBVIOUS SYMPTOMS

Symptoms vary. Young plants have malformed leaflets. Older plants exhibit mottling (dark green), and the leaflets tend to be stringy and fernlike or pointed. Overall, the plants exhibit a grayish appearance, and the fruit may be mottled, or it may ripen unevenly.

METHOD OF TRANSMISSION

Anything that comes in contact with the plants can spread tobacco mosaic. Users of tobacco products can spread the disease, which can be carried in tobacco.

CONTROL STRATEGY

Tobacco mosaic cannot be cured. Remove and destroy the infected and surrounding plants.

STEPS TO PREVENT TOBACCO MOSAIC

Resistant Varieties

Eggplant
Black Bell, Blacknite, Dusky, French Imperial, and Midnite.

Pepper
Annabell, Bell Captain, Big Bertha, California Wonder, Emerald Giant, Gypsy Hybrid, Lady Bell, Ma Belle, Melody, Ringer, and Yolo Wonder.

Tomato
Big Pick, Buffalo, Celebrity, Dombello, Park's Extra Early Hybrid, Sierra, and Vendor.

Garden Management Practices

Clean up the garden in the fall. (See chapter 4 for details on fall cleanup.) Wash hands, disinfect garden tools in a bleach solution (one part household bleach to four parts water), and keep tobacco users away from your garden.

DISEASE *Verticillium Wilt*

TYPE OF DISEASE

A fungal disease, verticillium wilt is most severe during cool, humid seasons.

VULNERABLE PLANTS

Apricots, blackberries, cherries, eggplants, mint, peaches, plums, potatoes, raspberries, rhubarb, sage, and strawberries.

MOST OBVIOUS SYMPTOMS

Apricot

Look for wilting of the leaves during midsummer or later. The leaves later turn yellow, curl upward along the midrib, and drop. This progresses from the older part of the shoot to the younger growth.

Blackberry

At first the canes grow vigorously; then the leaves yellow and wilt, and the canes die.

Cherry

The symptoms are the same as those seen in apricots.

Eggplant

Leaves wilt in the heat of the day and recover toward night. They eventually die and fall off. The inside of the stem becomes discolored.

Mint

Leaves wilt and droop in midsummer or later. The leaves later turn yellow, curl upward along the midrib, and drop.

Peach

The symptoms are the same as those seen in apricots.

Pepper

The leaves of infected plants turn yellow, dry up (often without evidence of wilting), and drop prematurely. The shoot tips wilt slightly during the day. As defoliation progresses, the leaves at the tips may curl inward at the margin, but they usually remain alive. Leaf symptoms appear on oldest leaves first and later develop on younger leaves.

Plum

The symptoms are the same as those seen in apricots.

Potato

Late in the season, the older leaves of infected potato plants become yellow and die. Leaflets may curl, and tipburn may occur. The inside of the stem turns yellow or brown.

Raspberry

In black raspberries, the lower leaves develop an off-green or yellowish bronze tinge in June or early July. They curl upward, then turn brown and fall off. Blue or purple streaks can be seen in the canes.

In red raspberries, which are more resistant, the same symptoms occur, but they show up later in the season. The streaks in the canes are difficult to see because of the coloring in red raspberry canes. Plants will eventually die.

Rhubarb

Look for wilting and pronounced yellowing and dying of basal leaves at the margins and between the veins.

Sage

Yellow splotches appear on the leaves, which gradually turn brown. The entire plant wilts during midday, and leaves drop, beginning at the bottom of the plant.

Strawberry

The leaves wilt and dry at the margins and between the veins. New growth is retarded. Roots growing from the crown are shortened, with blackened tips, and black streaks appear on leaf stalks and runners.

Tomato

The symptoms are the same as those seen in peppers.

METHOD OF TRANSMISSION

Verticillium wilt overwinters in plant debris and fallen fruit, and lives in the soil. It can be transmitted during cultivation or in flowing water. Bittersweet, chickweed, ground-cherry, horse nettle, jimson weed, mints, nightshade, pokeweed, ragweed, and wild cucurbits can spread verticillium wilt to cucumbers, peppers, and tomatoes.

CONTROL STRATEGY

A sulfur fungicide used every 7 to 10 days once the symptoms have been noticed has some effect in controlling this disease, but prevention practices will be more effective in the long run.

Raspberry

Remove and destroy infected plants.

STEPS TO PREVENT VERTICILLIUM WILT

Resistant Varieties

Pepper
Giant Szegedi.

Potato
Green Mountain, Katahdin, Ona, Pontiac, Rhinered, and Shoshoni.

Strawberry
Catskill, Darrow, Earliglow, Guardian, Red Chief, Red Coat, Surecrop, and Veestar.

Tomato
Ace 55, Beefeater Hybrid, Beefmaster, Better Boy, Better Girl, Flora-Dade, Quick Pick, Small Fry Hybrid, Star Pak, Toy Boy Hybrid, and many others.

Garden Management Practices

In general, do not plant vulnerable crops where other susceptible plants have grown, including all the plants mentioned above in the vulnerable plants section, as well as almonds, avocados, cotton, okra, pecans, and roses. Maintain a healthy soil high in organic matter. Remove nearby weeds, and clean the garden of all plant debris in the fall. (See chapter 4 for details on fall cleanup.)

Apricot
When planting, these should never follow other susceptible plants. Soils high in organic matter reduce this fungus, and well-nourished trees have a good chance of recovering from the disease.

Cherry
Treat as apricots.

Eggplant
Avoid growing eggplants in soil that has recently grown tomatoes or potatoes.

Mint
Remove and destroy infected plants and plant in a new location.

Peach
Treat as apricots.

Plum
Treat as apricots.

Raspberry
Avoid planting raspberries in heavy, poorly drained soils. Use disease-free stock.

Rhubarb
Do not plant where other susceptible plants have grown. Use disease-free stock.

Sage
Treat as mint.

CHAPTER 6

Animal Pests

Animal pests, such as moles, gophers, and deer, can discourage gardeners to the point where they consider giving up their gardens completely. Unfortunately, there are no quick, surefire solutions to any serious animal pest invasion. You have two basic choices in almost all cases: You can trap the pest and kill it, or set up a barrier of some kind that will deny the pest access to your garden. Over the years you spend tending a garden, you come to realize that there are few shortcuts to preventing animal pest problems. In this chapter, we'll focus first on the most effective control measures you can use, and then discuss the various preventive measures available. The chapter ends with a pest-by-pest description of the most effective management methods.

CONTROLLING ANIMAL PESTS

Effective control of animal pests depends on three prime factors: timing, persistence, and diversification.

Timing. In managing animal pests, it is certainly true that timing is crucial. Install barriers *before* you expect an animal pest to make an appearance, and start control measures at the very first indication of damage. Unlike most insects, animals can wipe out an entire crop or even the whole garden in a very short time if the problem is left unattended.

Persistence. Some animals, such as the raccoon and the crow, are ingenious in foiling your attempts to thwart them. A single try at establishing a barrier may not be sufficient to do the job. You'll have to keep trying until you come up with the control that outsmarts the wily predators.

Diversification. No single control method or preventive step is always satisfactory, even if it worked last year. Various devices often need to be used in combination, and their placement must be shifted frequently to be certain of success against persistent pests.

In most cases, the only alternative you can consider in controlling a pest after it has discovered your garden is fencing. Biological controls have limited effectiveness, and poisons are not recommended because of the hazards they pose to pets and children. In this section, we present the control steps in order of least to most impact on the environment.

Traps

Many gardeners are unhappy about having to kill a living creature, and prefer to use "live" traps, which catch the animal but do not harm or kill it. This approach to pest control assumes that you can take the trapped animal to a park or out into the country and release it so it will continue to live—but no longer be a pest in your garden. This "happy ending" turns out to be a terribly naive belief. It does not take into account some basic laws of nature. When you release a squirrel or raccoon in a park, or even out in the country where space seems limitless, you are almost certainly condemning that animal or another of the same species to death by starvation and/or disease.

All the animals that are pests in the garden and orchard can be found in cities and suburbs, as well as in the country. They have been in all of those places for many years, and their population is directly related to the availability of appropriate food, water, and cover. Their territories will depend on those variables. When you introduce just one more member of a particular species into any territory, you have just reduced the available food supply for all the members of that same species already present in that territory. A reduced food supply weakens all the members of the species and makes them more vulnerable to diseases. On top of that, you are probably releasing the animal near enough to someone else's garden so that that person is going to experience the damage you are trying to avoid.

Live traps are not recommended for controlling animal pests in the food garden unless you intend to kill the culprit as humanely as you can after you have trapped it. If you are not willing to trap and kill the animal pest, your only recourse is to establish some kind of barrier that denies the pest access to your garden in the first place.

Box traps are the safest design for live-trapping garden pests. The leg-hold design and the snare design are nonspecific, can maim the animal instead of kill it, and will trap and maim or kill pets as well as pests. Box traps are available for many of the most troublesome animal pests, including chipmunks, gophers, mice, rabbits, and squirrels. (See the box The Best Traps for the Worst Pests for recommended sizes.)

Using Traps

Set the trap in some sheltered area near or around where you have spotted a pest in action. Don't set the trap out in the open. Conceal it with leaves, sticks, and/or grass clippings so that it looks a bit

---

The Best Traps for the Worst Pests

Birds

$12'' \times 16'' \times 24''$ starling trap.

$10'' \times 24'' \times 24''$ pigeon trap.

Bait with corn, birdseed, or pieces of fruit.

Gopher

Regular wooden-based rat traps, two-pronged pincher trap (called the Macabee trap), or a squeeze-type box trap.

Bait with a large amount of grain, sunflower seeds, peanuts, or other nut meats.

Groundhog (woodchuck)

$12'' \times 12'' \times 36''$ box trap.

Bait with nut meats or pieces of fruit.

Mole

Choker or harpoon-type trap.

No bait needed.

Mouse

$5'' \times 5'' \times 15''$ box trap, or glue boards especially for mice.

Bait with nut meats, dried fruit, or bacon.

Rabbit

$10'' \times 12'' \times 30''$ box trap.

Bait with fresh greens, carrots, or fresh clover.

Raccoon

$12'' \times 12'' \times 36''$ box trap.

Bait with cut-up fruit or nut meats.

---

more natural. To avoid giving the animals any clues, it is best not to leave your own scent around any more than you have to. Of course your scent is naturally all around the garden, so it is the trap you want to keep as clean as possible. You can boil traps with pine cones, dried leaves, or other natural materials to mask your scent. Handle the traps and the bait with gloves, preferably rubber gloves just out of the package. Follow the directions that come with the trap to set it up correctly with bait in place. Check the trap every day to renew the bait and see whether you have trapped the culprit.

Once you have trapped the animal, how do you kill it as humanely as possible? We all have our own definitions of "humane." For most of us, it means a method that is as quick and painless as possible. Keep in mind that you must take great care in handling any animal that is trapped, especially those prone to carrying rabies, such as raccoons, opossums, and bats. Consult a veterinarian or the local Society for the Prevention of Cruelty to Animals (SPCA) for advice on the best way to handle the pest in question.

Biological Controls

Compared to the insect world, there are few biological controls available for animal pests. While badgers eat gophers and mountain lions eat deer, we do not generally have those kinds of natural predators in our backyard ecosystem. However, a couple of possibilities for biological control may be present in your yard already.

Many people keep dogs or cats as pets and often allow them to roam around the yard. Gardeners have found that animal pests tend to be less of a problem when there are dogs or cats outside much of the time. Most rabbits, for example, do not feel very comfortable eating while a dog or cat roams the yard. Cats and male dogs will mark their territory with some scent, and that can serve to deter rabbits from even entering your property.

Look up into the sky for another helper—the wren. Wrens are very small birds, but they are also fearless and absolutely dominating within 50 feet of their nest when there are babies in residence. They eat only insects and no fruit or berries. One very effective method of protecting your fruit and berries from birds is to erect a wren house in the middle of the plot. The wren will chase away any birds interested in the fruit. This approach is not advised within 50 feet of the vegetable garden, because that same wren will keep all the other insect-eating birds away from your plants.

PREVENTING ANIMAL PESTS

Barriers

Over the years, desperate gardeners have resorted to a number of ingenious tactics in the battle against animal pests. Here are some of the most successful preventive measures, from electrified fences to sticks of chewing gum.

If you know, from past experience, that one or more animal pests are likely to attack your garden, then the best approach to controlling them is to deny them access in the first place. There are a number of techniques for preventing access, some more effective than others. If you want to use a barrier, that usually means using some kind of fence.

Fence

Here you have a choice: You can have a temporary fence that is designed to be movable and easily erected, or you can take the time and go to the expense of building a permanent fence to solve the problem once and for all. There are a number of fence designs in both categories meant to keep animals out of the garden, and there are just as many stories about how some of those animals, especially raccoons and deer, overcame the barrier and still entered the garden sanctuary.

Fencing off the area is relatively easy for a small garden, but the time and materials required for a large one may be prohibitive. Always calculate your costs before starting any fencing project, to avoid any surprises. If you do try fencing, remember various animals can jump, dig, and squeeze through small places. The size of the fence may vary depending on which pest you are trying to thwart: Make sure your fence is high enough to be effective (see table 1 on page 434). Even if burrowing pests are not currently a problem, if you are going to the trouble of erecting a permanent fence, it's a good idea to bury it at least 6 inches in the ground to stall any future subterranean invasions. Finally, be sure to use a fencing material with mesh spacing of less than 2 inches. The actual design of your fence and the materials you use will ultimately depend on how much time and money you wish to spend.

There are many designs and materials on the market for garden fences, but the most effective barrier for most animal pests, including the peskiest ones, like raccoons and deer, is an electric fence.

There are very few backyard gardeners in this country who think of an electric fence as an option to use in fighting pests in their average-sized vegetable gardens. However, if you are being plagued by animal pests season after season and have tried everything else with no success, perhaps you are among those gardeners who should consider "going electric." If your garden is ravaged by skunks, rabbits, or raccoons, your very best line of defense is to use the electric fence as a barrier. You can try all the other remedies, such as moth balls, radios, and even chicken-wire fences, but when you decide you

want a sure thing that is safe and that takes no time to manage, install an electric fence.

First, let's clear up some myths about electric fences. They are not designed to hurt anyone or anything. They are designed to surprise anything that touches the fence. Birds don't get shocked by sitting on an electric fence. You have to be in contact with the ground when you touch an electric fence to receive the shock. The shock of an electric fence is not really painful. It is best described as a very strong buzzing feeling that definitely makes you want to let go. This is in no way comparable to the dangerous shock you can receive from your home's electrical system. The zap of an electric fence is designed to be more of a psychological barrier to animals than a physical one. Few animals that touch an electric fence two or three times will ever touch it, much less go near it, again. Some gardeners can turn the power off in their fences after a few weeks because all the deer have learned about its zap and wouldn't go near that fence even if you dangled the garden's best produce in front of them.

Most gardens need only two strands of wire,

TABLE 1.

Fencing to Outsmart Hungry Animals

Animal	Height	Depth	Mesh
Deer	7–8 ft.	On surface of soil	Woven mesh wire, 12½-ga. or larger, with 6- by 6-in. mesh
Gopher	2 ft.	2 ft.	½-in. mesh
Groundhog	2 ft.	3 ft., with bottom 2 ft. turned outward and buried 1 ft. deep	½-in. mesh
Rabbit	2½–3 ft.	1 ft., with bottom 6 in. turned outward and buried 6 in. deep	1-in. mesh, no larger
Raccoon	3 ft., with top 2 ft. unattached, making "floppy" fence	6 in.	1-in. mesh

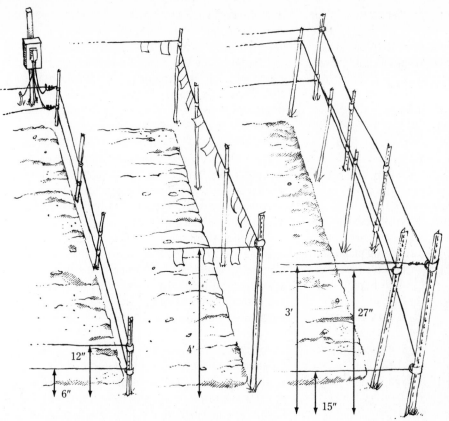

The type of electric fence you will need depends on the pests you want to keep out of your garden. Most animals will be repelled by a low fence with two strands of wire. To teach deer a lesson, construct a 4-foot fence and bait it with strips of aluminum smeared with peanut butter. While taking a sniff of the peanut butter, the deer will be shocked by the fence and won't return to the garden again. A third option, the New Hampshire three-wire fence, uses strands at different levels to repel deer and small animals.

one set 6 inches above the ground and the second 12 inches (deer need a higher configuration of 15 and 36 inches). Raccoons can climb wooden posts holding electric fencing, so PVC (polyvinyl chloride, a plastic) poles are better if you have very smart raccoons lurking around your garden. In most cases, the animal pests are only a problem when your plants are young and small and at their tastiest, so that is when you should have your fence. If you give it juice for 2 or 3 weeks and then turn off the power, the fence alone will continue to repel your furry nuisances and you don't have to worry about anything shorting out.

The only real problem with an electric fence in a vegetable garden is that it can be shorted out if it is touched by a wet leaf of a plant tall enough to reach the strand. Shorting out does not permanently

damage the fence, just keeps it from operating. It is difficult to know if your fence is shorted out unless you touch it briefly. If it isn't keeping the pests out of the garden, inspect the fence for any material that might be touching it; then all you have to do is find and remove the material that is touching the fence and it will function again.

The size of your fence depends a lot on the layout of your garden. You can use your fence selectively around only a few beds at a time as needed and plant crops that are vulnerable to animal pests in those protected beds. It is handy to have a source of electric power from your house available near your garden so you don't have to worry about using a battery. Whether you use an outlet from the house or a car battery, you will need a device called a "controller," which is a transformer that reduces the power of the electricity in your fence so that it will not harm anything. Electric fence kits are now available from many home gardening mail-order houses. They will cost anywhere

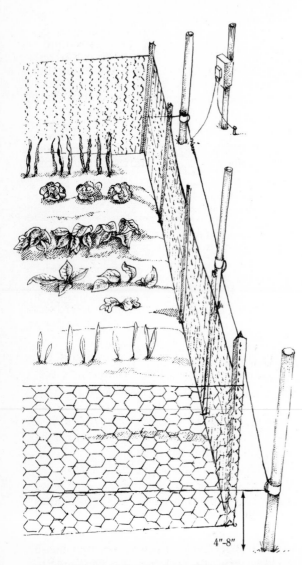

4"–8"

If your chicken-wire fence isn't keeping all the animals out of your vegetable garden, surround it with a single-strand electric fence for double protection.

from $75 to $150, depending on the size of your garden. You can install these kits yourself, without need for special tools or knowledge of electricity.

If you already have a chicken-wire fence around your garden but still have pest problems, consider adding a single-strand electric fence. Set up the single strand of wire 6 inches outside the chicken wire and 4 to 8 inches off the ground, using PVC posts as supports. This combination fence has been nearly 100 percent effective in excluding raccoons, groundhogs, rabbits, and surprisingly, even deer, though some deer will beat that system (see the discussion about deer later in this chapter for more information on using fences).

Some gardeners only charge their fence at night to avoid surprising children during the day and because their animal pests generally do their damage at night. In any case, the electric fence might mean the difference between having a good crop or not having any crop at all, if your furry pests are persistent.

Netting and Screening Material

There are forms of barriers other than the traditional fence. Various materials, including clear plastic film, fine-meshed nylon netting, and agricultural fleece, can be rigged to be effective barriers to many pesky animals.

One good barrier is the row cover that is used by many gardeners to extend their growing season in the spring and fall. The easiest device to set up is the floating row cover, using a new material called agricultural fleece. It is made of spun polypropylene and is extremely light, so it lies softly over the plants, allowing them to push up the material as they grow. By covering a row or bed of plants with this fleece, you protect the plants from birds and other animals that may like to nibble on seedlings. This material is usually removed as the weather warms up and the temperatures under the fleece begin to get too high for the plants.

Another form of season-extending row cover, the plastic tunnel, is also effective in protecting young spring seedlings from animal pests. These tunnels can be purchased from mail-order houses or can be homemade. (Details on and directions for making tunnels can be found in the book *Jeff Ball's 60-Minute Garden,* cited in the Recommended Reading list at the end of this book.) In either case, they offer excellent protection, at least until the warm weather arrives and the tunnel is no longer needed.

One way to lengthen the value of this sort of tunnel as a pest barrier is to replace the clear plastic film used in the early spring with pieces of agricultural fleece or fine-meshed nylon netting. These materials allow the air to circulate, eliminating overheating, while still protecting the plants from all animals and most insects. The fleece also provides some degree of shading, allowing the growth of heat-sensitive plants such as lettuce, Chinese cabbage, and peas further into the summer season.

Netting used over the berry patch prevents birds from eating the fruit.

It simultaneously discourages the rabbits who love these crops. Keep an eye on air temperatures under these devices in case they get too high. Sometimes all you need to do is open the ends during the day to get sufficient ventilation and then cover the ends at night to give you nighttime pest protection.

To prevent birds from devouring your fruit and berries before you have a chance to enjoy them, use plastic netting with a 1-inch mesh. This netting can be laid over an entire dwarf fruit tree or a berry patch, and is quite effective as long as you make sure there are no bird-sized openings. Anchor the edges securely by burying them or using rocks as weights. On trees, gather the loose netting around the trunk and tie it together. One trick is to rig a set of tunnel ribs over a strawberry bed, and then use the plastic netting to cover the ribs.

Repellents

For many years, gardeners have been trying to find substances that will repel animals from their gardens. There are on the market a number of products to ward off various animal pests such as birds, rabbits, raccoons, and deer. In addition, there are dozens of home remedies invented by frustrated gardeners under siege by some troublesome animal. These products work better for some gardeners than others, so no one product seems to be foolproof all of the time in all places in the country. If you prefer not to rig a barrier, then you may wish to experiment with one or more of these repellent products. However, you must not be too confident about their effectiveness in your particular garden.

Repellents come in two general forms: those that repel by odor and those that repel by some visual, tactile, or audio characteristic.

Using Odor to Repel

Various animal repellents are sold commercially in many garden centers and through mail-order catalogs. The success of the odor repellents is quite spotty. Some gardeners swear by them; others find that they don't work. As mentioned earlier, no single method of animal pest control works well in all situations. Through experimentation, you will find out which repellents work for you.

Using Audio, Visual, and Tactile Tricks

Although there are many success stories reported in the popular gardening literature, there are few, if any, tactics that are certain to work in all situations. Nevertheless, the methods listed below tend to be popular and have a fair number of gardeners reporting that they're effective. There is no scientific research to support these claims, but their popularity suggests that in some cases they are worth a try.

Audio Trick. You might want to give this technique a try to beat the birds to the blueberries. Stretch a piece of audio recording tape tightly between two stakes. Position the stakes so the tape passes over the plants. It is thought that the vibrations set up by the wind blowing over the tape scare the birds. A commercial version called Scareaway Bird Line is being offered for sale to commercial fruit growers after tests in California showed bird-loss reductions of 60 to 70 percent in strawberries, nuts, and grapes. Hopefully, it will be available to gardeners soon.

Flashing or Moving Devices. Aluminum pie tins tied to stakes so they flash and clatter in the wind are a popular way to scare away raccoons, birds, and squirrels. The trouble is, they have a limited lifespan. They may work for a few days, but then the animal gets used to them and they lose their scariness.

To keep birds from devouring seedlings, strawberries, and other fruit, some gardeners create a sort of garden sculpture with moving parts. They take a pair of 3-foot-tall stakes and push them into the ground about 10 feet apart, across the area of the garden to be protected. Then they stretch fishing line between the stakes. Attached to this line are strips of plastic ribbon spaced 3 feet apart. The strips should hang down to almost touch the plants, where they will twist in the slightest breeze. This constant motion is reputed to keep the birds away.

High-Tech Vibrations. This commercial device might fall under the category, "for the gardener who has everything." The Rodent-Repelling Garden Stake comes from West Germany and is battery-powered, vibrating at 60-second intervals to repel burrowing rodents and moles over as much as $1/3$ acre, depending on soil conditions. This gadget carries a hefty price tag (over $75).

Juicy Fruit Trick. Although it sounds a bit strange, moles have been reported to be controlled with sticks of Juicy Fruit chewing gum. Moles are fatally attracted to the flavor of the gum. The key to success is that there be absolutely no human scent on the gum at all. To plant a gum trap, don gloves and remove a stick of Juicy Fruit from the paper and foil. Roll up the gum like a cigarette. With a stick or rod, punch a hole through the roof of a freshly made mole tunnel. Then, with a gloved hand, drop in the gum, depositing sticks 4 to 6 inches apart along the mole runs. The moles eat the gum but cannot digest it. Within days, the moles' activity should cease.

Lights. Raccoons generally prefer to operate in the dark, so gardeners sometimes deter them by hanging a few lights around the garden. The more movement the lights have, the better the deterrence, report some folks. A commercial product called Bye Light, a flashing light, is designed to keep raccoons out of the corn patch. There's also a flash mechanism available for do-it-yourselfers.

Pepper Technique. Pepper is organic, so it doesn't harm the soil, and it's very inexpensive. Sprinkle the black or hot kind all over and around plants. It is reported to repel rabbits and squirrels. Black pepper sprinkled liberally around the ripening ears on a corn plant is claimed to repel raccoons. Do this before the corn is ripe and repeat the process after rain.

These schemes just scratch the surface of the long list of home remedies for animal pests. If you don't have the time or the inclination to experiment, or the patience to try multiple approaches, then your most reliable control device is a trap, and the best prevention is an effective barrier. The rest of this chapter will discuss individual animal pests and the best prevention and control measures for each.

Guide to Animal Pests

As long as there are gardens and animals that want their share of the harvest, gardeners will be trying ways to keep the furry and feathered bandits out. What follows in this section are profiles of the eight most troublesome pests and options for controlling and preventing problems. Some of these solutions have been proven more effective than others: Try them and see how they work in *your* garden.

ANIMAL PEST *Birds*

The key to keeping birds from becoming pests is to use a number of different approaches at the same time. Your goal is to prevent them from even getting access to the vulnerable crops. No single method is always satisfactory. Various devices and techniques must be used in combination and their placement frequently shifted to be sure of success.

Various species of birds will bother the vulnerable plants in the garden at certain times and in certain areas of the country. Blackbirds, crows, grackles, quail, robins, sparrows, and starlings are considered particularly pesky birds, although most species at one time or another have been accused, rightly or wrongly, of causing some harm in the food garden.

MOST OBVIOUS SYMPTOMS

Suspect your local songbird population if any of these signs appear in the garden: most of a patch of young seedlings completely disappear; the tops of the young plants are bitten off; chunks are taken out of the snap peas, tomatoes, or strawberries; raspberries and blackberries disappear just as they become ripe.

VULNERABLE PLANTS

At various times songbirds are known to bother apples, apricots, blackberries, blueberries, broccoli, cherries, corn, currants, garden peas, grapes, peaches, pears, plums, raspberries, snap peas, and strawberries.

BEST CONTROL STRATEGY

A cover or barrier, if that is feasible, is the best method for preventing bird damage to any crop.

OPTIONS FOR CONTROLLING BIRDS

As mentioned earlier, wrens will keep all other birds away from their nest when there are babies present. Since they eat only insects and leave your fruit and berries alone, you can use them as "watch birds" to keep other hungry birds from your harvest.

STEPS TO PREVENT BIRDS

Barriers

For a barrier to succeed at keeping out the birds, it must completely surround the plant. Any opening

439

and the birds are sure to find it. To be covered completely, trees and bushes must be reasonably small; it is difficult to screen plants taller than 7 feet. Bush fruit and dwarf trees, because of their size, make perfect candidates for barrier protection.

Netting
If you're interested in using fabric or plastic netting, you should know that it can't be casually draped over the dwarf tree or bush the way the advertising pictures show. Draping netting on a tree may save a few fruit, but birds will peck right through it and squeeze in under it. Some kind of support is needed to hold the netting out away from the tree or bush so the birds can't reach any of the fruit. If you must drape, cheesecloth is a better deterrent than the wider-meshed fabrics.

Row Cover
A floating row cover made of agricultural fleece or slitted polyethylene film keeps pesky birds away from plants. The agricultural fleece is particularly good for protecting corn seedlings from birds. You can also replace the plastic film panels on row-covering tunnels with fleece or bird netting as the spring warms up. This is especially good for young corn plants and strawberries, which are vulnerable to bird attack.

Screen Box
A reliable way to protect plants is to build a screen box around them using stout, rot-resistant posts. Stretch and nail a fine-meshed wire fence around the posts. Nail 2-by-4-inch stretchers from post to post at the tops, and spread more fencing over the stretchers to form a roof. A screen door makes a handy entrance for you to get in and out.

An even better way to protect the plants is to make up 4-by-8-foot panels of wire mesh, using 1-by-4-inch boards for frames, and affix these panels to the posts and over the stretchers. The panels can be taken down and put up again after the fruiting season, then stored indoors for the rest of the year. It will take time and money to build these panels, but they should last a lifetime.

Tepee
To protect raspberries from birds, construct a tepee of pipes, poles, or lumber over the berry patch, then drape a net over the structure.

Repellents
As mentioned earlier, repellents have varying effectiveness, depending on the time of the year and the area of the country. However, many of these measures have been successful, and so are worth considering. In addition to using plastic strips and audio recording tape stretched over plants as mentioned earlier, there are a couple more tricks you can employ.

Scare Device
Look through most garden supply catalogs, and you'll find several models of fake owls or hawks that are made from inflatable plastic material. These fake predators can be mounted on a fence at the edge of the garden. It's a good idea to move them around every week or so to keep the birds from catching on that they're fakes.

Seed Coating
Coating seeds with the malodorous mixture of tar and kerosene will keep birds away. And to foil crows intent on eating sprouting corn, soak the seeds in turpentine before planting. For every ½ pound of seeds, use 1 tablespoon of turpentine. Let the seeds soak for 3 days. A commercial product, Ro-Pel, can be used to coat seeds, and is supposed to repel birds.

TECHNIQUES TO PROTECT TARGET PLANTS

Since corn and fruit and berries are special favorites of birds, here are some specific tips on how to protect these crops.

Corn

Planting Techniques
To protect seedlings, scatter extra corn seeds along the edges of a newly planted corn patch or in an

adjoining area or bed. The corn on top of the soil will sprout first, tending to distract the birds until the main crop of garden corn is too big to be of interest. A similar technique is to plant a few oats with your corn. The oats germinate a day or so before the corn. Birds do not seem to like oat sprouts, and this early, less desirable crop of seedlings seems to divert the birds' attention from the newly sprouting corn. This "decoy" crop allows most of the corn to grow past the crucial bird-hunting time.

Mulch
Use mulch to trick the birds. Put fresh green grass clippings down the rows of young corn so the birds are confused about which shoots are coming up. To be successful, this must be done as shoots emerge, using bright green grass clippings.

Planting Time
Time plantings to foil the birds. Avoid the earliest corn varieties. The first extra-early corn is what the birds attack most greedily. Plant the later-maturing corn. When there is a lot of corn sprouting in the neighborhood, the birds are less likely to completely wipe out your crop.

Resistant Varieties
Plant bird-resistant varieties. Research indicates that there appear to be significant correlations between resistance to bird damage and certain physical characteristics of sweet corn ears. Ears with heavy husks or husks that extend far past the kernels appear less susceptible to bird damage. Growers in blackbird-infested areas might try planting 'Gold Dust' and 'Advance', both of which have those characteristics.

Other Techniques
Set up a feeding station of purchased feed corn next to the corn patch so the birds will eat that instead of the newly planted seeds. And finally, for mature corn, tie small rubber bands over the end of each ear when the silks turn brown. This will keep corn safe from hungry beaks.

Fruit and Berries

Decoy Plants
Sometimes if you have other crops of berries available at the same time as your favored crops, the birds will be attracted to those "trap" crops and leave your fruit alone. For example, Juneberries will draw birds away from cherries; mulberries will attract them away from raspberries; and wild cherries and elderberries will lure birds away from blackberries.

To keep birds away from peaches and cherries, plant borders of chokecherries, dogwood, mountain ash, mulberries, or other bushes with very aromatic fruit and berries. Place them within 10 feet of the fruit trees. Birds seem to prefer these over the peaches and cherries. Autumn olive, bittersweet, crabapple, elderberry, firethorn, hawthorn, highbush cranberry, holly, honeysuckle, sunflower, and Virginia creeper are other good decoy plants birds love. The trick is to find a plant that has an attractive fruit or berry at the same time in the season that your bird-vulnerable food crop is ripe.

NOTES AND RESEARCH

The insect control section in this book recommends using red spheres covered with sticky material to control apple maggot flies. There have been some reports that birds are also attracted to these sticky spheres and can become fatally trapped. If you use these traps in your yard, you'll want to keep an eye on them.

Deer

Deer can be a disaster to a food garden. They usually feed in the late evening or early morning when no one is around. One or two deer can virtually destroy a vegetable garden in one night. Far from finicky eaters, they devour almost everything found in the food garden. Various species of deer are found throughout the United States and Canada.

MOST OBVIOUS SYMPTOMS

You'll know that deer have been to your vegetable garden when you find that entire plants have disappeared. On fruit trees, deer will eat leaves, fruit, and young limbs.

VULNERABLE PLANTS

Special favorites include corn, fruit, and leafy crops. Deer especially relish the growing tips on fruit trees in summer and the buds in winter.

BEST CONTROL STRATEGY

A fence is the best method for preventing deer from ravaging the garden.

STEPS TO PREVENT DEER

Fences

The most effective way to control deer is with a very high fence, or one that's electrified. Unfortunately, both approaches become quite expensive as the size of your garden increases.

Electric Fence

There are a number of different designs for electric fences. The one you choose depends on how much money you're willing to spend and on the type of fencing that's already in place.

Bait and Shock. The bait and shock electric fence is a relatively inexpensive approach to deer control. It involves rigging a temporary 4-foot-high single-strand electric fence with flaps of aluminum foil attached with adhesive tape. The flaps should measure 3 by 4 inches. Smear peanut butter on the backing of the adhesive tape. When the deer smell the peanut butter, they come closer to investigate and their noses touch the flaps. One shock can be enough to deter them.

Another version of this same design is to use aluminum foil pouches, each containing ¼ teaspoon of salt, spaced every 6 feet along the wire. The deer are attracted to the salt and get their noses buzzed. Gardeners who use this approach turn on the fence for about 4 weeks in the spring and again for about 4 weeks in the fall. This bait and shock technique can "train" the deer to stay away from the food garden for the entire season without having to have the electricity on for that whole period.

Chicken Wire. If you already have a chicken-wire fence around your garden, but the deer ignore it as they leap over on their way to graze, it's a relatively easy matter to add a single-strand electric fence in front. To be effective, the chicken-wire fence should be at least 4 feet high. Using PVC (polyvinyl chloride, a plastic) posts, set up a single strand of wire 3 feet from the chicken wire and 2½ feet off the ground. The assumption in this design is that the deer will have trouble leaping high enough from a standing position to clear the mesh fence with a single strand of wire in the way. You can place a single-strand electric fence in front of a permanent stone wall or fence as well.

New Hampshire Three-Wire Fence. If your garden or orchard occupies only a small area and there are relatively few deer around, consider the New Hampshire three-wire electric fence. This consists of an outer and inner fence with a total of three electrified wires. The strands on the outer fence are set 15 and 36 inches high. The inner fence is 36 inches inside with a strand set 27 inches high.

A variation on this fence that guards against small mammals as well as deer uses the same type of outer fence with the inner fence having strands placed at 5, 11, 17, 27, and 38 inches.

Seven-Wire Fence. For gardeners whose deer problems require a serious electric fence, try a seven-wire fence. This works best to protect small- to medium-sized areas. This model is a vertical fence with strands at 8, 16, 24, 32, 40, 50, and 60 inches.

A slanted seven-wire fence works well for moderate to high deer infestation on moderate to large areas. This is a slanted seven-wire electric fence with 12-inch intervals between each wire. The rails or posts slant 6 feet out and 4 feet above the ground.

Wall

A 6-foot solid wood or masonry wall will deter deer even though they can actually jump that high because they are less likely to bother a garden they can't see. For small areas, gardeners have had success with a double woven wire fence 8 to 10 feet tall. Don't skimp on fence height, it must be that high to be effective.

Repellents

The gardening literature is filled with dozens of schemes for repelling deer from the food garden. Some of these work in some places but not in others. As mentioned at the head of this chapter, you should try these remedies remembering that they are not uniformly effective across the country.

If odor is the repelling agent, then it must be kept fresh to be effective. One handy trick is to mix your repellent with an antidesiccant such as Wiltpruf, Pro-Tec, or VaporGard to give it season-long effectiveness.

Commercial Repellent

If home remedies don't seem to work, there are many commercial products that may be worth a try.

Bonide Rabbit-Deer Repellent and Bulb Saver. Repels by taste; spray, brush, or dip branches; for shrubs, evergreens, trees, and fruit trees; when this product is mixed with an antidesiccant, it is said to prevent basal rot and decay on bulbs as well as deter animal pests; will last 3 to 6 months.

BGR. (Big Game Repellent) Made from eggs; repels by smell; apply according to package directions; use on any plant.

Chew-Not. Repels by taste; spray, brush, or dip branches; for fruit trees and some varieties of evergreen.

Gustafson 42-S. Repels by taste; spray, brush, or dip branches; for fruit trees and shrubs.

Hinder. Repels by odor; spray; for fruit trees, vines, and vegetables.

Hot Sauce. Repels by taste; concocted from hot peppers; brush thickly on branches; for trees and shrubs.

Magic Circle. Repels by taste; used for perimeter spraying, not direct application to edible plants; use around all plants.

MGK Big Game Repellent. Repels by odor and taste; apply according to package directions; can be used on all plants.

Mountain Lion Deer Repellent. Repels by odor; apply around the perimeter of plants; can be used on all plants.

Raw Egg Spray

Make an egg spray by whipping together 2 eggs and 1 quart of water in a blender at high speed for a few seconds. To this mixture, add enough water to make 1 gallon of spray. A large batch can be made by mixing together 18 eggs and 5 gallons of water. Spray this mixture on plants or trees. The eggs in these recipes will decompose and release an odor that is undetectable to humans but that is effective at repelling deer.

Hair

You might try human hair hung in nylon stockings from trees in the orchard.

Hot Sauce Spray

Whip up a homemade hot sauce or repellent spray of Tabasco sauce. Mix 1 to 2 tablespoons of Tabasco sauce plus 2 tablespoons of an antidesiccant in 1 gallon of water. Spray plants with this mixture. Be sure to respray after it rains.

Soap

There are any number of home remedies you can try, but the following one is the most effective. For the orchard, use pieces of deodorant soap hung in cheesecloth bags from tree branches. The strong-smelling soap provides protection from late winter until the following winter.

ANIMAL PEST # Gopher

Gophers range in length from 6 to 12 inches. They have a thick body with small eyes and ears. Their sense of smell is excellent. They seldom are found aboveground. Once gophers arrive on the scene, they can appear to be a small invasion force. There may be 16 to 20 living in a single acre, so it's easy to see how gophers can become a very serious problem. Gophers range from Indiana west to the Pacific Ocean.

MOST OBVIOUS SYMPTOMS

Gophers push soil out of their hole, creating a diagnostic fan-shaped or crescent-shaped mound. After digging, they may close up the hole with a soil plug. One gopher can create several mounds a day. Gopher tunnels, about 2 inches in diameter, follow no pattern, running from a few inches to 2 feet below the soil. You know you have gophers when your plants are damaged in areas where you have the fan-shaped mounds.

VULNERABLE PLANTS

Gophers eat the underground parts of garden crops and a wide variety of roots, bulbs, tubers, grasses, and seeds. They can damage lawns, flowers, vegetables, vines, and trees. Their mounds sometimes smother small plants, and they can girdle and kill young fruit trees.

BEST CONTROL STRATEGY

One way to drive the pest away, if not kill it, is to determine the location of all the entrances to its tunnel system and then fumigate the tunnel. To do this, find a piece of hose material that can be attached to the exhaust of a power lawn mower. Stick one end of the hose into the gopher's tunnel and seal it with soil. Then drop some oil onto the inside of the hot exhaust pipe to create smoke and attach the other end of the hose. After a few minutes you should see smoke coming from all other entrances to the tunnel system. You may see some gophers emerging as well.

Now that you know the entrances to the tunnel system, you have several choices. You can seal all the entrances with piles of soil and continue to blow exhaust from the power mower into the tunnel, killing the inhabitants with carbon monoxide poison. An alternative is to put a sulfur product into the holes and seal all the entrances. The cheapest source of sulfur is the emergency highway candle. Cut through the emergency flare with a sharp knife (not a saw), and sprinkle the material into one of the "runs" or holes. Dig into the runway so you're able to apply the flare powder directly into the tunnel, then cover this hole as well as the exit holes that you discovered. The more airtight the tunnel system is, the more anxious the gophers will be to leave. Once you're sure that the gophers are gone, seal the tunnels with soil as best you can. You know the gophers are gone when the mounds do not begin to reappear.

Another option is to place a small ammonia-soaked sponge into each gopher hole and then seal them all. This will cause the gophers to dig out of the burrow in a hurry. The best time to do this is in early spring.

OPTIONS FOR CONTROLLING GOPHERS

Trapping is also an effective method for eliminating gophers. Place regular wooden-based rat traps in shallow pits near burrow entrances. Lure your victims to the traps by sprinkling small amounts of grain on the thin layer of dirt covering the trap trigger.

STEPS TO PREVENT GOPHERS

Barriers

A fence of small-mesh wire, sheet metal, or concrete extending about 24 inches below ground and 10 to 12 inches above will give a measure of protection. In lighter soils, it's desirable to sink a fence deeper than 24 inches.

Line the inside of boxed raised beds with aviary wire, which is strong and finely meshed. This wire should reach down at least 1 to 2 feet into the soil.

NOTES AND RESEARCH

The gopher has a number of natural predators that may help you in your battle to rid the yard of these persistent pests. Certain snakes of the *Pituophis* genus (bull snakes, gopher snakes, and pine snakes) relish gophers. Other predators include cats, dogs, king snakes, skunks, barn owls, badgers, hawks, and coyotes.

ANIMAL PEST # *Groundhog*

The groundhog, also called the woodchuck, is a voracious vegetarian. Its burrows can go down as deep as 5 feet and extend over 60 feet long. A widespread pest, it is found from the Atlantic to the Great Plains, and from northern Alabama up into parts of Alaska. Groundhogs emerge from their winter dens in March and can be a problem in the garden until fall.

MOST OBVIOUS SYMPTOMS

Groundhogs work fast. One day the garden will be fine, and the next it will be completely devastated.

Young plants are pulled and partly eaten, and older plants are partly eaten.

VULNERABLE PLANTS

Groundhogs feast on alfalfa, beans, carrots, grass, peas, sweet corn, weeds, and many more plants.

BEST CONTROL STRATEGY

The best way to keep groundhogs from the food garden is to fence them out.

OPTIONS FOR
CONTROLLING GROUNDHOGS

Fumigating the groundhog's tunnel system can be one way to solve the problem. (For directions on how to do this, see the entry Gopher in this chapter.)

Barriers

Surround the garden with 5-foot pieces of chicken-wire fencing that is rigged so that the vertical part is about 24 inches high. Bend the fencing into the shape of an L. Position the fence around the garden with the short arm of the L standing up (24 inches) and the long arm (about 36 inches) resting at least 1 foot below ground level. Completely cover the long arm with soil. The vertical arm of the fence will stop the groundhog above the ground, and if he decides to dig his way in, he'll run into the wire buried in soil. You can also electrify a chicken-wire fence for effective protection. (See the discussion on fences at the beginning of this chapter for more information.)

Traps

You can try setting traps. Commercial groundhog traps are available. Box traps that measure 12″ × 12″ × 36″ are recommended.

Trap Crops

Plant a trap crop. Raise a patch of alfalfa and clover at least 50 feet away from the food garden. These should attract the groundhog away from the vegetables.

Other Options

It does help to keep a swath of grass mowed all the way around the garden. This short grass deprives the groundhog of shelter for at least a few seconds on his way to the garden, so he is less likely to take the chance to make himself vulnerable to his predators, such as cats, dogs, and hawks.

ANIMAL PEST **Mole**

Moles don't eat plants, but they do eat lots of grubs, beetles, and other soil dwellers. Their favorite food is earthworms, friends in any garden's soil. Moles can harm the root systems of young plants simply by tunneling through the soil in search of food. This damage is compounded by the fact that they can spread diseases from plant to plant. In addition, other more harmful pests like field mice use mole runs. There are several species, including the Eastern mole and the California mole, so they are found throughout the United States.

MOST OBVIOUS SYMPTOMS

In their search for food, moles make an extensive network of tunnels, many of which are used only once. They are solitary animals, and it's likely that only one or two moles are responsible for the damage to your lawn or garden. Moles are active all year long. When cold weather comes, they follow earthworms deep below the frost.

VULNERABLE PLANTS

Young seedlings in the early spring can be affected by moles tunneling in search of grubs and other insects.

BEST CONTROL STRATEGY

Traps can be effective, but you have to be persistent. The best time to use them is in early spring when the first mole ridges appear. To find out which runs are being actively used, step lightly on a small section of several tunnels so that you disturb but don't completely collapse them. Mark these sections with stones or garden stakes. In 2 days, note which ones are raised—those are active runs and good locations for setting traps. You can restore the turf over unused tunnels with a lawn roller or by treading on them.

Choker traps and harpoon traps have proven adequate for the task of trapping a mole. Install either type of trap according to instructions that come with the devices.

OPTIONS FOR CONTROLLING MOLES

Digging

Besides trapping, you can try digging out moles. A mole may be active at any time of the day. It is often possible to see the soil ridging up as the mole moves along. Put a shovel into the soil right behind the mole, and flip him out into a bucket.

Juicy Fruit Gum

Although it sounds a bit strange, moles have been reported to be controlled with sticks of Juicy Fruit chewing gum. Moles are fatally attracted to the flavor of the gum. The key to success is that there be absolutely no human scent on the gum at all. To plant a gum trap, don gloves and remove a stick of Juicy Fruit from the paper and foil. Roll up the gum like a cigarette. With a stick or rod, punch a hole

through the roof of a freshly made mole tunnel. Then, with a gloved hand, drop in the gum, depositing sticks 4 to 6 inches apart along the mole runs. The moles eat the gum but cannot digest it. Within days, the moles' activity should cease.

STEPS TO PREVENT MOLES

Repellents

Cat Box Litter

Dump several scoops of litter right into the mole's burrow, as long as the opening isn't in the food garden. The strong odor will repel them.

Windmills

Another trick is to set windmills (available commercially through garden supply catalogs) in mole runs. These windmills create vibrations that seem to deter moles. A less expensive alternative is to insert a child's pinwheel into the ridge. Empty glass soda bottles work along the same principle. Set a bottle in the mole run open end up. The wind blowing across the opening of the bottle creates vibrations.

NOTES AND RESEARCH

Cats are natural predators. They'll kill the moles, but won't eat them because of their bad taste.

There is no evidence to support or refute claims that castor beans (sometimes called mole plants) keep moles away or that daffodil bulbs or dandelions work either.

ANIMAL PEST **Mouse**

There are a number of different mice that can nibble on your garden plants. The field mouse (also called a vole) is white underneath and gray-brown

on top, while the house mouse is uniformly gray all over. The white-footed mouse, or deer mouse, ranges over most of the continent in many species and subspecies. It has whitish underparts like the field mouse, as well as whitish legs and feet. It is found throughout the United States.

MOST OBVIOUS SYMPTOMS

Mice are known to move into mole tunnels and use them to gain access to crop roots. They can also gnaw the ground level bark of fruit trees, sometimes girdling and killing the trees. Orchardists report that voles can kill scores of fruit trees in an orchard during a single winter. Tree-girdling usually occurs between October and April. Mice may overwinter in the mulch placed around strawberries or other perennials, where they chew on the roots. These pests are generally active all year round.

VULNERABLE PLANTS

Roots of vegetable plants in the garden are fair game for mice. These rodents also gnaw on roots of trees and bark buried under the snow.

BEST CONTROL STRATEGY

The traditional mousetrap still works. The most effective way to reduce mice through trapping is to buy a large number of snap-traps and set them all out at once for a 1- or 2-night period. Buying a few traps and expecting to catch mice over a long period of time doesn't work as well. Bait the traps with a tiny dab of peanut butter or bacon. A good technique is to bait the traps for 2 or 3 nights without setting them. Then when you finally do set the traps, you'll catch the mice by surprise.

OPTIONS FOR CONTROLLING MICE

Glue Boards

Besides the basic mousetrap, there is a product on the market called glue boards. This is a sheet of extremely sticky material that stops mice in their tracks when they try to cross the boards.

STEPS TO PREVENT MICE

Barriers

Gravel
Gravel barriers around garden plots are an effective and easy means of protection. The gravel should be 6 to 8 inches deep and 1 foot or more wide. No rodent will tunnel through that, and if the gravel border is kept clear of weeds and compost, mice will be discouraged from running across it.

Tree Guards
Commercial plastic guards or a piece of chicken wire or small mesh wrapped around the base of trees and extending at least 6 inches below the soil will prevent damage to bark.

Other Options

Good sanitation is one way to keep from attracting mice to your yard. Clean up all possible food sources, such as vegetables left in the garden at season's end. Be sure to use rodent-proof containers of metal or glass to store seeds and bird feed.

Always pull mulch away from the base of fruit trees in the winter and use plastic tree guard strips if mice are a threat. Don't mulch strawberries or other perennials until the ground freezes hard. Putting mulch down early invites the mice to set up housekeeping and gives them easy access to roots in unfrozen soil.

Keep an area of at least 3 feet around trees clear of tall grass and other growth. Mice do not like to come out in the open, and will hesitate to cross that bare space to gnaw on the trees.

NOTES AND RESEARCH

Natural predators of mice, which include cats, owls, and snakes, can help keep down the population.

ANIMAL PEST *Rabbit*

Rabbits have shown themselves to be extremely adaptable to human environments. Cottontails are active mainly from dusk until midmorning and spend the warmer part of the day in a shaded area. They may hide under thick shrubs or beneath garden sheds. The Eastern cottontail rabbit is most likely the species found nibbling around in the vegetable garden. Various species of rabbits are found throughout the United States.

MOST OBVIOUS SYMPTOMS

The plants, especially young ones, will be nibbled down to the base.

VULNERABLE PLANTS

Rabbits' favorite foods include beans, carrots, grasses, lettuce, peas, strawberries, weeds, and the bark of fruit trees and raspberries. They especially relish young bean growth and the bark of young fruit trees, namely apples. Rabbits don't like squash, cucumbers, or corn.

BEST CONTROL STRATEGY

Trapping is the most effective way to contol rabbits. Commercial box traps measuring 10″ × 12″ × 30″ are recommended.

STEPS TO PREVENT RABBITS

Barriers

Fence
Ordinary chicken-wire fence can rabbit-proof the garden. The wire fencing should be buried 6 inches into the soil and extend at least 2 feet above the ground. Make sure the holes or mesh are smaller than 2 inches. You can electrify a chicken-wire fence by following the directions found in the discussion on fences at the beginning of this chapter. When using an electric fence to bar rabbits, most gardens need only two strands of wire, one set at 6 inches and the second at 12 inches.

Milk Jugs
In the spring, protect young seedlings in the food garden with plastic milk jugs. Remove the bottoms and anchor them so the wind doesn't carry them away or a pushy rabbit doesn't knock them over. You can also cover plastic ribs with agricultural fleece or fine-meshed nylon netting to create an anti-rabbit tunnel cover.

Tree Guards
Tree guards are an essential piece of equipment in the war against rabbits. In preparing the orchard for the winter, wrap the lower portion of small tree trunks with commercial tree wrap, burlap, aluminum foil, or a piece of metal window screen. The wrapping should be at least 18 inches above the height of the deepest expected snow cover (rabbits can walk on top of the snow). Then, in the winter, tramp down the snow around the trees so rabbits can't chew on low limbs.

Wire Guards
Wire guards can be established around individual plants or trees if you have the room. Hardware cloth—a stiff, fine-meshed wire fencing material—is set up around the plant. Stakes are used to keep it upright. Make the guards high enough so that a rabbit can't stand up on its hind legs and reach its lunch: about 18 inches.

Repellents

Repellents may help you reduce rabbit damage. As mentioned at the beginning of this chapter, these techniques vary in their effectiveness. In the case of rabbit control, the odor repellents are often not as effective as the taste repellents.

Taste Repellent

You can try either homemade or commercially prepared repellents. During the growing season, you might spray or dust plants and the soil around them with dried blood (available from garden supply stores or mail-order sources). Another repellent involves sprinkling black or hot pepper all over and around plants.

Commercially prepared taste repellents include No Nib'l, which can be dusted or sprayed on plants. The can has a shaker top for dusting. To spray, mix the contents of the 6-ounce can with 2½ gallons of water.

A combination antidesiccant and pest repellent is Bonide Rabbit-Deer Repellent and Bulb Saver. It is said to deter mice and moles and will last 3 to 6 months. You have your choice of spraying, brushing, or dipping the branches of shrubs and fruit trees.

Other Options

One way to reduce the rabbit population in the yard is to remove one of their favorite daytime resting places—brush piles. The lack of cover will discourage them from hanging around. Anything you can do to eliminate sanctuaries will help solve the rabbit problem. If you live next to a wooded area, there may be too many hiding places to deal with in this manner.

NOTES AND RESEARCH

A dog or cat roaming the yard appears to bar most rabbits from coming onto the property. Cats and male dogs will mark their territory with urine and serve to establish an invisible fence for rabbits.

ANIMAL PEST *Raccoon*

Raccoons have become particularly comfortable in urban and suburban areas, feeding at night at man's garbage can restaurants. They range across most of the United States. They eat both plant and animal material of a wide variety and are active all year long in most parts of the country.

MOST OBVIOUS SYMPTOMS

Ears of corn, just ripe, will be either gone or lying on the ground, chewed up. Corn stalks are knocked down. Melons will be broken and partially eaten.

VULNERABLE PLANTS

Raccoons go after sweet corn, melons, and other fruit.

BEST CONTROL STRATEGY

Raccoons are easy to catch with box traps. Use the 12″ × 12″ × 36″ trap, available from many garden supply mail-order houses. Bait the traps with meat scraps, fish, or moist dog food. Other baits include honey-soaked bread, pieces of fruit, marshmallows, and peanut butter.

STEPS TO PREVENT RACCOONS

Barriers

Normal fencing will not keep raccoons from your garden. If they can't go under it or through it, they'll wiggle themselves over it. It takes a special fence to stand in the way of a hungry raccoon intent on getting into your garden.

Electric Fence

Electric fencing is particularly effective against raccoons. Most gardens need only two strands of wire—one at 6 inches and the second at 12 inches. Use PVC (polyvinyl chloride, a plastic) poles, since raccoons can climb wooden posts holding electric fencing. A combination of chicken wire and electric fence is an effective deterrent. (For directions, see the discussion on fences at the beginning of this chapter.)

Floppy Wire Fence

A floppy wire fence is another option. Attach chicken-wire fencing to stakes, leaving the top foot free. When the raccoon tries to climb the fence, this loose section will bend so far backward that the masked bandit can't make it over.

Plastic Fence

A slippery plastic fence may also offer some measure of deterrence. Staple sheets of black plastic (use 6-mil thickness) to stakes spaced about every 10 feet. Make sure the stakes are on the inside of the plastic, toward the garden; otherwise raccoons will climb the stakes and jump into the garden. The plastic should be 30 to 36 inches wide and the lowermost 3 to 6 inches should rest on the ground. Raccoons trying to climb the slippery plastic soon give up in defeat.

Other Options

Black Pepper

Sprinkling black pepper on ripening corn ears is reputed to keep raccoons at bay. Apply before the corn is ripe, and repeat after a rain.

Lights

Raccoons prefer the cover of darkness to do their dirty work. You can sometimes deter them by hanging some lights around the garden. Flashing lights seem to bother them the most. (For more on this, see the discussion on lights at the beginning of this chapter.)

Radios

A radio left on in the garden has worked for some gardeners. This ploy is most successful when the radio is connected to a timer so that it goes on and off. Dusk and dawn are key times when you want to pipe in the sound of music and human voices.

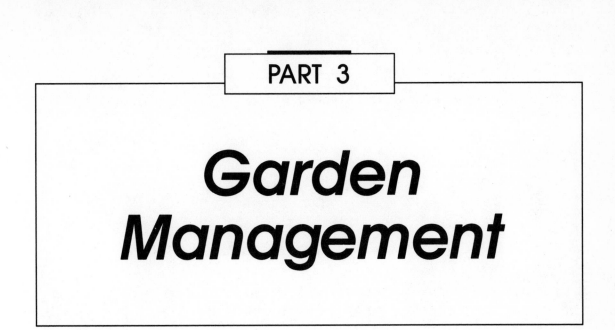

PART 3

Garden Management

CHAPTER 7

Managing the Environment

Many garden problems could be avoided if gardeners took a plant's eye view of the environment. Plants need light, water, air, nutrients, and warmth in order to grow and develop. Just how adequately the garden supplies these needs depends on its microclimate, or specific conditions of wind and weather. Sunlight, soil, wind, temperature, and other factors interact to create the microclimate. A garden in an open field has very different conditions from one surrounded by trees. The microclimate of your garden changes throughout the day, and it changes as the seasons change. It might even be different in different areas of the garden.

If you don't adjust your gardening practices to accommodate the changes in the microclimate, you may have some serious problems with your food crops.

SUN AND LIGHT

A critical variable in the vegetable garden is the amount of sunlight available to plants during the growing season. Remember, trees are leafless in early spring, and what may seem like a lovely sunny space will be shaded in summer and fall. Shadows will also fall around a house or city terrace at different times of the year and at different times of the day within the growing season. Plants not getting sufficient sunlight tent to be stunted, pale, or leggy. They are more vulnerable to insects and diseases, and will produce smaller and less fruit.

In order to avoid such problems, choose a vegetable garden site that has full sun from sunrise to about 3:00 P.M. Morning sun is generally better than late afternoon sun because it warms the plants faster. Many gardeners succeed with shadier sites, however. As long as your garden receives 6 hours of sun at some time of the day, you'll be able to grow most vegetables. Lettuce, onions, parsley, radishes, spinach, and other plants can even produce well, with less light. Keep tall plants and those needing less light to the north, or shadier side of the garden, leaving the sunniest spots for plants that require the most direct light.

One other caution is to watch out for possible problems when locating a garden next to a fence or the wall of a building that is light in color. Intense sunlight and heat are reflected from such structures and can harm vegetable plants in the middle of summer. Although that same reflected heat may be helpful to the early season crops, it can wilt the more tender summer vegetables such as melon and squash (see shading materials, later in this chapter).

SOIL TEMPERATURE

Most gardeners keep a close eye on air temperature around their property. They dutifully wait until temperatures climb well above freezing before they plant tender crops. Yet by relying on air temperature alone, they are asking for trouble. They should be watching the temperature of the soil too. This is far more critical to plant growth than air temperature.

Soil temperature is important because the microlife of the soil, which is responsible for creating food for plants, doesn't really become active until the soil reaches a temperature of about 40°F to 45°F. For example, the bacteria needed to make nitrogen available to plant roots in a form they can use do not become active until the soil temperature is about 40°F, and they don't reach the height of their activity until it climbs to 80°F. Plants themselves also have critical soil temperatures below which they won't germinate or grow. These range from 35°F for chard, to 65°F for pepper. By the same token, extremely high soil temperatures (above 85°F) will slow down some plants' growing. Consequently, your gardening season doesn't really start with the last spring frost and end with the first fall frost. It starts when the soil temperature reaches 35°F and it ends when the soil temperature falls again to 35°F.

To keep track of soil temperatures, buy a standard soil thermometer at your local hardware store or garden center. You can also order one from many mail-order garden catalogs. There is now even a device that allows you to read your soil temperature remotely in your kitchen, via sensors on the end of wires. These sensors can be placed in the soil, in the middle of the compost pile, and any other site in which you would like to monitor temperatures. They keep track of the temperatures in up to nine different sites and take a lot of the guesswork out of gardening.

With a soil thermometer, you will soon realize that air temperature is only a rough indicator of soil temperature. The nip may be out of the spring air a few weeks before the soil has warmed enough for planting.

There is little to be gained from sowing or setting out plants before the soil warms to their critical level. If set out too early, they will be vulnerable to rot, fungal diseases, and insect attack. At the very least, they will not grow until conditions improve. Before sowing seeds and setting out transplants, check the soil and air temperature guidelines in tables 2 and 3.

On the other hand, too hot a soil is also threatening to plants. When the soil temperature exceeds 85°F, most food plants simply stop growing. They won't usually die—they just sit there.

Another concern is to minimize any rapid swings in soil temperature that might occur once the plants are in the ground. Plants are not happy when there is a fluctuation in the temperature around roots.

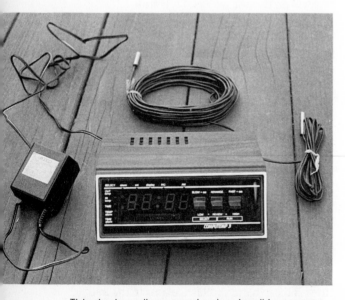

This device allows you to check soil temperatures in several different locations at once. The sensors at the ends of the wires are pushed into the soil or into a compost pile, and the temperatures are displayed on the monitor.

Mulch

There are several ways mulch can be used to manage and change soil temperatures. Mulch helps buffer the changes in soil temperature: Whereas the air temperature may be swinging radically up and down, the temperature of the soil under mulch will change much more slowly. Plastic mulches can be used to warm the soil in spring and fall. Organic mulches of straw, hay, chopped leaves, or similar materials can cool the soil during the summer and help minimize drastic shifts in temperature. You can combine these materials to create the best soil temperatures over the longest period.

Plastic Mulch

Both clear and black plastic film are excellent materials for warming the soil. Their main drawback is a tendency to make soil too warm during the main part of the growing season. Don't let this keep you from taking advantage of these materials. Start off with a plastic film and, when soil temperatures get too high, cover it with straw, hay, or other organic mulch. When fall comes, take off the straw so the plastic film can do its warming trick again.

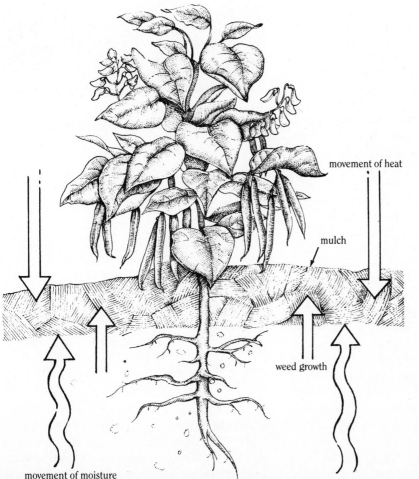

movement of heat

mulch

weed growth

movement of moisture

Organic mulch offers three important benefits: It keeps the soil cool during hot summer months, prevents weed growth, and slows the evaporation of moisture from the soil.

Black plastic film is the most popular warming mulch. It absorbs most of the solar radiation striking it, and radiates heat to the soil. Clear plastic film transmits sunlight directly into the soil and holds the heat there, just like a greenhouse traps and holds heat. The clear plastic mulch heats up the ground very quickly. In Wisconsin, experiments with clear plastic increased soil temperatures 20°F above the surrounding open soil. However, that same clear plastic might take the soil up 30°F or 40°F in Virginia, and do more harm than good. As discussed in chapter 5, clear plastic can even be used to sterilize the soil. Use clear plastic only if you live in the far north, where the angle of the sun is low and soil temperatures need a big boost.

If you live in Hardiness Zones 1 to 4, you will probably be able to use clear plastic with success. In Zone 5, it's best to try both in your garden in the first season and watch the soil temperatures carefully. Black plastic works best in Zones 6 and above.

Clear plastic does not give off the radiant heat at night that black plastic does. However, if you use the mulch along with a plastic tunnel, the plants won't need that extra heat as much. Clear plastic mulch, unlike the black plastic, does not prevent weed seeds from sprouting, but the physical barrier provided by the layer of plastic film keeps the weeds from seriously competing with your vegetables. In addition, when you add the layer of straw or hay in the early summer, those weeds will die.

Plastic mulch is most effective if it covers all of the growing area of the row or bed. Generally, it is laid over the surface of the growing bed and held down with handfuls of soil, bricks, rocks, or homemade "hairpins" made from coat hangers cut in two. Make properly spaced planting holes in the plastic. For massed vegetables such as onions, beets, and carrots, make a plywood pattern with holes cut at the appropriate spacing. Fold up the plastic so that the holes can be cut through the pattern. For larger plants such as broccoli, cutting an X into the plastic with a sharp knife is the easiest method. After the plant is placed, the flaps of the plastic fall back closely around the stem of the plant, continuing to

Pins made from wire coat hangers effectively hold down plastic mulch in the garden.

give protection from weeds, water evaporation, and drops in soil temperature.

Plastic mulch is often criticized for cutting off the rain supply from the soil. This problem can be solved by placing a drip irrigation system *under* the mulch. You can also buy plastic mulches with thousands of little holes punched in them so water can seep into the soil.

Generally, plastic mulch will last for only one season. If the film itself doesn't break down, the holes from two or three successions of plants get ragged enough to make the material difficult to work with in the second year. Plastic is inexpensive, though, so an annual replacement won't break the garden budget.

Organic Mulch

Organic mulches, such as chopped leaves or straw, cool the soil. Chopped leaves cool it down as much as 18°F. Only use leaves that have aged for 6 months or so. Otherwise, some natural chemicals might leach from the decaying leaves and harm plants. Place the organic mulch on top of plastic mulch rather than directly on the open soil. The layer of plastic keeps the decomposing leaves from depleting nitrogen in the top inch or so of soil. The big advantage of leaves, of course, is that they are free. Only use them chopped, since whole leaves mat down and cut off air and water to the soil.

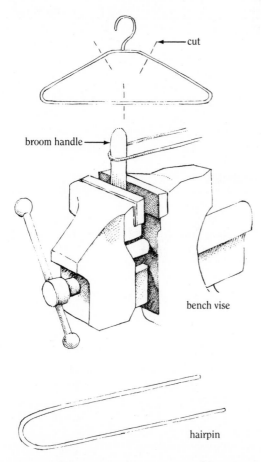

Homemade "hairpins" work well to hold plastic mulch in place in the garden. Use wire cutters to clip pieces from a wire coat hanger. Clamp a broom handle into a bench vise and use pliers to bend the wire pieces around the broom handle and into the shape of hairpins.

Follow the soil temperature guidelines given in tables 2 and 3 on pages 460 and 461 when applying organic mulch to plants. At about 65°F, cool season crops such as peas, lettuce, spinach, and Chinese cabbage will benefit from a thick blanket of organic mulch. This, in combination with drip irrigation, can keep the soil cool enough to gain as much as a week or two of additional harvest from your crops. Heat-loving plants such as peppers and tomatoes won't benefit from the organic mulch until the soil temperature hits about 75°F.

Watch soil temperatures carefully as fall approaches. Take the straw mulch off the beds when the average soil temperature is about 65°F, allowing the black plastic mulch to begin doing its warming job again.

AIR TEMPERATURE

Air temperatures that are too hot or too cold can also cause problems. A blast of cold air can wipe out an early garden. Frost damage occurs when the liquid in plant cells freezes. As the cells freeze, they expand and burst, causing irrevocable damage.

Colder temperatures tend to slow and then stop plant growth. At that point, the plant produces more natural sugars within the leaf to help depress the freezing point of the water within the leaf. This tends to protect the leaf from the damage caused by 'reezing, which bursts the plant's cells. Vegetables, such as cabbage, spinach, and peas, that can handle such conditions are called *frost hardy* or *cold hardy*. They have this sugar-producing capacity to protect themselves from some frost exposure and survive colder temperatures.

Spinach, cabbage, peas, and other cool season crops tolerate mild frosts quite nicely. Some, such as carrots and cabbage, even thrive on cold weather, getting sweeter after a heavy frost. Yet most of our favorite garden crops are quite tender, and gardeners who want to extend their harvests must protect them from the freezing temperatures of spring and fall.

Fortunately, controlling air temperatures around your plants is relatively easy. The most effective way is with temporary covers. Such devices include cold frames, cloches, plastic film tunnels, and row covers or blankets.

Season-Extending Devices

Gardeners have been using cloches and cold frames to extend the gardening season for centuries. More recently, tunnels, agricultural fleece, and black plastic have offered attractive methods of season extension.

Cloches

Cloches are coverings placed over an individual plant at night to protect it from frost damage. They are usually removed in the morning unless they are well ventilated or the day is quite cloudy. Cloches are available commercially from mail-order houses, or they can be made at home. One effective cloche is a gallon glass jug with its bottom cut out. You can leave it on during most spring days, as long as you take off the top. Cloches make particular sense if you have a very small garden, or if you have just a few extra plants that can't fit under the tunnel or in the cold frame.

Plastic 2-liter soft drink bottles can be used as cloches to protect plants. Cut off the colored bottoms, and use an awl or heated nail to punch ventilation holes in the lower 2 to 3 inches of the bottles. Put the cloches over the plants, and leave the caps off for air circulation.

TABLE 2.

Soil and Air Temperature Ranges for Crops
(Early Spring Season)

Crop	Soil Germination Temperature (°F)	Ideal Soil Temperature (°F)	Ideal Daytime Air Temperature (°F)
Beet	40-85	65-75	40-75
Broccoli	45-85	65-75	40-75
Cabbage	50-85	65-75	40-75
Carrot	40-80	65-75	45-75
Cauliflower	50-85	65-75	45-75
Celery	50-70	60-70	45-75
Chinese cabbage	40-85	60-70	45-75
Kale	40-70	60-70	40-75
Kohlrabi	50-85	65-75	40-75
Leek	40-75	65-75	45-85
Lettuce	40-80	65-75	45-75
Onion	40-85	65-75	45-85
Parsley	50-85	65-75	45-75
Pea	40-85	65-75	45-75
Radish	40-85	65-75	40-75
Spinach	40-85	60-70	40-75
Swiss chard	35-70	60-70	40-75

TABLE 3.

Soil and Air Temperature Ranges for Crops
(Spring Season)

Crop	Soil Germination Temperature (°F)	Ideal Soil Temperature (°F)	Ideal Daytime Air Temperature (°F)
Bean	60–85	70–80	50–80
Corn	55–85	75–85	50–95
Cucumber	60–85	70–80	60–80
Eggplant	60–85	75–85	65–95
Melon	65–85	70–80	60–80
Pepper	65–85	70–80	65–80
Squash, summer	60–85	75–85	50–90
Squash, winter	60–85	75–85	50–90
Sweet potato	60–85	75–85	65–95
Tomato	60–85	70–80	65–80

Cold Frames

Cold frames are simply boxes with some kind of cover made of glass or clear plastic. Commercial models are usually not much bigger than 3 by 4 feet, but you can build one as large as you wish. A bottomless wooden box covered with an old storm window has been a popular homemade design for many years. There is some heat retention inside a cold frame at night, but its primary purpose is to protect plants from frost. Cold frames can be very handy for hardening off seedlings before they go into the garden.

One trick which involves using a cold frame is to plant some spinach in the late fall, and as soon as it germinates, cover it with a piece of agricultural fleece. Leave the fleece over the small plants during the winter. About 2 months before the expected last frost, place a portable cold frame over the spinach patch, leaving the fleece in place. Don't forget to water it every so often, and you'll be harvesting spinach a month earlier than normal for your area.

Tunnels

The polyethylene tunnel can turn an entire bed or several rows into a temporary greenhouse. Made from plastic film and some metal or plastic supports, it can extend the growing season from 1 to 2 months at both ends of the season, or a total of 2 to 4 months each year!

Whereas a cold frame is used primarily to start or harden off a few spring seedlings, plastic tunnels can be used in many other ways.

First, because the tunnel protects the rows or beds themselves, it makes direct planting possible much earlier in spring. Come fall, the tunnel can be used again to keep these same crops producing as the temperatures dip. During the summer months, when the plastic is folded back, the tunnel frame can be covered with cheesecloth to shade heat-sensitive crops, or with netting to protect vulnerable crops from birds or insect pests.

Garden supply houses sell plastic tunnels, but you can easily make your own, customized to fit your own garden. Use 4- to 6-mil polyethylene plastic film. Make supporting ribs from heavy gauge wire or flexible PVC (polyvinyl chloride) pipes. Cut ventilation openings (6 inches long and 4 inches apart along the length of the tunnel, high on both sides, about 6 inches from the peak) in the clear plastic film to allow excess heat to escape so you don't have to closely supervise the conditions inside the tunnels every day.

Tests show that slit plastic tunnels provide about 2°F to 3°F of frost protection, and they increase daytime growing temperatures from 10°F to 20°F.

Jugs of water placed under tunnels help to control temperatures. The water warms up during the day and releases its heat during the cold hours of the night.

Used in conjunction with black plastic mulch, tunnels allow the soil to gain heat slowly but steadily and retain it for several days, even after the air temperature has fallen.

If, in addition to using black plastic mulch, you add water storage devices, the tunnels are even more effective. Place 1-gallon cider jugs filled with water at 2-foot intervals down the middle of the tunnel. As the temperature inside the tunnel increases during the day, the water heats up. When the air cools at night, the water releases its heat, raising the temperature inside the tunnel slightly above that outside. This trick can add up to a week of season extension to your tunnel system.

Don't get so intent on frost protection that you let temperatures get too high inside the tunnels. On sunny, late-spring days, temperatures inside slit tunnels may exceed outside temperatures by 30°F. Such a buildup of heat can wither plants. Roll back the plastic covers and use them only at night. When the soil temperature reaches 60°F, it is time to remove the plastic altogether.

Row Covers

Agricultural fleece is a lightweight material that can be safely draped directly onto plants. It may extend the vegetable growing season up to 2 weeks in the spring and a month in the fall, by giving up to 5°F of frost protection. Made of soft polypropylene or spunbonded polyester, fleece weighs just 0.6 ounces per square yard, so it can be laid right on top of the tenderest plants, such as lettuce seedlings, and they will push it up as they grow. It lets in 75 to 80 percent of outside light, and it "breathes," so no special ventilation is required. Water seeps right through. The material is ultraviolet-stabilized and won't rot, shrink, or sag in wet weather. With careful removal and storage it can be used for at least two seasons.

This floating row cover is ideal for getting cool season crops off to an extra early start, or for delaying that killing frost in fall. When air temperatures fall below freezing, dew drops freeze between the fleece fibers to create an insulating ice barrier. Plants beneath the fleece are safe at outside air temperatures as low as 28°F in the spring and 25°F in the fall. Plant leaves touching the material may suffer minor frost damage.

Spread out the fleece over the crop at planting time, or later if you like. Drape it loosely over the beds or rows, leaving enough slack for plant growth. The material needs to be weighted down along the edges to keep it from flapping in the wind and to ensure that no insects get inside. Remember to remove fleece from plants such as strawberries, cucumbers, and melons when they begin to flower, to allow for natural pollination of those plants. If it is kept on lettuce, celery, and Chinese cabbage as they become mature plants, the shading it provides will slow down their bolting to seed in the late spring.

When you are ready to stop using the fleece, remove it from the crop on a cloudy day, or in the evening, to reduce the transition shock to the plants. Remove fleece when the temperature under the covers reaches 86°F and is likely to remain that high for several hours.

In the fall, you can extend the growing season by covering your vegetable crops with two layers of fleece. Pepper and tomato fruit on mature plants has been protected when the temperature has dropped as low as 21°F. This trick will permit harvesting of tomatoes, peppers, and eggplants 2 to 4 weeks past the first light frost, which usually signals the end of the harvest.

Shading in the Summer

There are some vegetables, such as lettuce, Chinese cabbage, and spinach, that prefer to grow in cooler temperatures. In fact, as the air temperatures rise with the coming of summer, those vegetables may bolt and go to seed, making them bitter and generally inedible. One way to extend the harvest period of cool-loving vegetables is to use organic mulch to cool the soil temperatures (see earlier) and to rig some kind of shading material to keep the air temperatures down, to give you a week or two more of harvesting time.

Agricultural fleece or cheesecloth make excellent shading materials. They can be laid over tunnel ribs. The fleece is so light, it can be laid directly on top of the plants without harming them; however, if the fleece is mounted above the plants a bit, there will be better air circulation and more opportunity for cooling breezes to keep the air temperature down.

WIND AND AIR CIRCULATION

Wind is no friend of the gardener. Together with the sun, wind can severely desiccate, or dehydrate, plants. In the spring, it can stunt seedlings and prevent peas from attaching themselves to a trellis. In the summer, wind can dry out plants, toughen or wither fruit, and cause blemishes such as "catfacing" on the skins of tomatoes. If protected from the wind, a tomato plant at 68°F will grow better than a similar plant will grow at 77°F in the open, exposed to even moderate winds. Any area routinely buffeted by winds over 10 to 15 mph will benefit from some kind of protective barrier.

There are a number of ways to protect your plants from wind. Ideally, your garden is already located in the most protected place available. On a hilly site, the garden should be near the top of the slope, with free movement of the air to lower levels. Such a location is more likely to escape late spring and early autumn frost damage than a spot at the bottom of the hill. In the early spring and late fall, the polyethylene tunnel is an excellent wind protector. You can also rig a windbreak for your garden.

Windbreaks

Traditionally, gardeners have established shrub or tree barriers to shield their gardens from the wind. Now, instead of having to wait years for a natural windbreak to grow, you can buy a special netting that serves as an instant windbreak. Made of tightly knitted polyethylene threads, it is easily attached to any kind of fence post. It comes in widths of 3½ or 6 feet and in lengths of 25 feet or 50 feet.

Before setting up a wind fence, be certain you know the direction of the prevailing winds. Attach a ribbon or windsock to a pole in your garden and watch it for a few weeks. Or purchase an inexpensive plastic wind indicator, which will give you a rough reading of wind velocity as well as direction. Set up the wind netting perpendicular to the direction of the prevailing winds. It can be off perpendicular by as much as 20 degrees and still be helpful. You can run this fabric fence right along the edge of the garden or set it back as much as 10 feet from the garden.

It is better to slow or filter the wind rather than try to completely block it. A natural windbreak of

You can extend your growing season in the fall by covering plants with agricultural fleece.

pines is better than a stone wall, since the wind comes faster over and around the wall. The wind netting reduces wind speed by 60 percent so that a 20 mph gust passing through it becomes a mere 8 mph breeze.

The windbreak will protect an area six to ten times the area of the fence. Therefore, the 25-foot netting that is 3 feet tall can protect a 300- to 500-square-foot garden, and the 50-foot netting that is 3 feet tall protects a 1,000- to 1,500-square-foot garden. The 3-foot-high fence is good for gardens with few tall plants. However, if you have tomatoes on poles or pole beans, then the 6-foot fence is needed for best protection.

Antidesiccant Sprays

Another way to protect your plants from harsh wind is by spraying with an antidesiccant spray. These sprays are organic, biodegradable materials, which form a clear, flexible film over the surface of the plant without interfering with plant growth. This film helps hold in the plant's moisture, which would otherwise evaporate in heavy wind.

Antidesiccant sprays are used primarily to protect fruit trees and shrubs. Use the spray in late fall to prepare blueberry bushes and young fruit trees for the winter winds. Simply spray the entire surface of the plant when the air temperature is above 40°F. Spray also before transplanting berry bushes or small fruit trees. The antidesiccant spray helps the plant retain water, giving it a chance to recover from the shock of transplanting. One application of an antidesiccant spray is all that is needed.

SOIL

Soil supports plants mechanically, provides nutrients and water, and permits the gas exchanges necessary for root respiration. Compaction, inadequate drainage, and infertility can interfere with these functions. In most cases, such problems can be solved. The following discussion deals with the overall condition and structure of the soil and how to make it desirable for food gardening. For information on periodic fertilizing, see chapter 8.

Long before you plant your first crop, assess the quality of the soil. Once the plants are in the ground, soil development is much more difficult. You need to know whether you must take certain steps to improve the soil conditions even before you plant your first seed. First you need to understand how the roots function in that soil. Then you can evaluate your soil's ability to provide nutrients and water, to mechanically support plants, and to promote the necessary gas exchange.

How Roots Work in the Soil

Roots are the bridge from soil to plant. They anchor the plant; they store food and water; and they take in and transport water and nutrients from the soil to the rest of the plant. They also improve soil conditions. Roots are valuable even after the plant has died. Channels left by dead roots bring water and oxygen down to the microorganisms living in the soil. They penetrate the subsoil, bringing up minerals that are not normally available in the topsoil.

The looser the garden's soil is, the better it drains and the more readily the root systems can spread. A plant with an expansive root system has a greater ability to absorb water, oxygen, and nutrients from the soil. You can't see healthy roots, but their vigor is reflected in the hardiness of the plants in your garden.

As a general rule, a vegetable plant's root system penetrates as deeply into the soil as its leaves rise above the soil. So a 24-inch-tall broccoli plant probably has roots that go down at least 24 inches. Fruit trees can have roots that are two to three times wider and deeper than the height and breadth of the tree. However, it is very important to note that about 85 percent of a plant's roots are found in the first 6 inches of soil. The ones that go deeper are mainly in search of water. This means that you don't have to work organic material into the soil very deeply to get it to the place where it is most needed.

Managing the Microclimate Throughout the Year

Here is a brief calendar of climate-controlling practices for the garden. Let it be a kind of checklist as you plan your garden year.

Late Winter. Six to 8 weeks before the last expected frost, set up a plastic mulch and a tunnel to warm soil above freezing in at least part of the garden. Erect a wind barrier if needed.

Early Spring. After about 2 weeks under the plastic and the tunnel, the soil should be thawed and dried out sufficiently to be worked. When the soil temperature is above 40°F, remove the tunnel and plastic mulch and prepare the seedbed. Lay out the drip irrigation lines on the bed. Replace the plastic mulch. Then rebuild the tunnel over all.

When the soil reaches 45°F, plant peas and onion sets. You can also direct-seed Chinese cabbage, lettuce, beets, and spinach. At 50°F, set out cool weather transplants, such as cabbage, broccoli, Chinese cabbage, spinach, and lettuce.

Late Spring. As soon as air temperatures stay above 40°F at night and the soil temperature averages around 60°F, take off the plastic tunnel, but leave the framework in place.

Early Summer. When the soil reaches 75°F, lay 4 to 6 inches of organic mulch on top of the plastic mulch. If necessary, shade cool weather crops by draping cheesecloth over the tunnel frame.

Summer. On the hottest days, water with the drip system at noon to cool down plants' root systems. Continue to drape shading material over cool-loving crops.

Fall. Rake away the organic mulch when soil temperatures fall to 65°F. When night air temperatures are in the 30's, put up the plastic tunnel.

Early Winter. When the last protected crops have been harvested, remove the tunnel and plastic mulch, and follow the recommended fall garden cleanup procedure described in chapter 4; then you may plant a cover crop, lay a layer of winter mulch, or leave the soil bare. Spray blueberry bushes and young fruit trees in exposed areas with antidesiccant spray. Wrap the trunks of fruit trees with a commercial tree wrap to prevent sunscald.

Late Winter. Six to 8 weeks before the last expected frost, start the cycle all over again.

Soil Structure

A good garden soil is made up of almost 25 percent water and 25 percent air. Minerals, organic matter, and animal life make up the rest. Air and water are essential resources in the soil for growing healthy plants.

Microorganisms

Soil, especially in that first 6 inches where most roots reside, is a constantly changing, living environment. Microscopic creatures such as fungi, yeasts, and bacteria live on and around the roots. They help create the environment plants need to grow. Their respirations and excretions create the materials that roots absorb. For example, *Rhizobia* bacteria live in the root nodules of legumes. These microorganisms transform nitrogen into a form that can be utilized by plants.

Organic materials provide much of the source matter for this microscopic transformation. The higher the percentage of organic matter you have in your soil, the more complete will be the mix of nutrients these microscopic creatures are able to produce for your plants. This is one reason why the addition of organic matter to soil is valuable to the food garden. Without the proper environment to host such beneficial microbes, plants do not thrive, because reduced microbial populations produce fewer nutrients for the plant itself.

Compaction

If plants appear to be stunted, the cause may be compacted soil. Compaction is caused by pressure from equipment, frequent foot traffic, or even from the weight of a single footstep. Such compressed soil cuts off water and oxygen to roots, hindering their growth. This shortage of water and oxygen also means that organic matter cannot decompose properly. No matter how much organic material is piled on the surface, it won't bring any benefit if the top foot or more of soil is compacted. As if that weren't enough, compaction discourages the good work done by earthworms.

Limit the areas in your garden where you allow yourself (or anyone else) to walk. It doesn't take much compaction to affect plant growth. Research completed by Al Trouse, of the United States Department of Agriculture's National Tillage Machinery Laboratory, has demonstrated that normal, everyday compaction caused by just stepping on the beds can reduce plant growth by at least 10 percent.

Never work wet soil, particularly a heavy clay one. Tilling or spading breaks down a wet soil's physical structure, forming clods that are hard as rocks when they dry. This condition may take years to correct. To determine if the ground is dry enough to work, squeeze some tightly in your fist. If it sticks together in a ball, it is too wet to work. If it crumbles easily after it has been squeezed, then the soil is dry enough to work.

The best way to solve a compaction problem that already exists is to break up the compacted soil by adding lots of organic material, as is discussed later in this chapter.

Poor Drainage

The health of plants in the garden depends on the soil's ability to quickly drain away excess water. If water fills all the pores in the soil, there is no room for oxygen and the plants drown.

A garden that has long-standing puddles after a rainstorm or snow that melts away slowly may have a drainage problem. To be sure, use this drainage test. Dig a hole in the garden about the size of a gallon jug. Fill that hole with water and let it drain. As soon as the water has completely drained, immediately fill it again and keep track of how much time it takes to drain. If it takes more than 8 hours to drain, you have a drainage problem that needs attention.

To solve the problem, you can move the garden to a better site, get professional advice on laying a drainage system, or add a great deal of organic material to the top 24 inches of your soil. Adding organic material will usually solve the problem, although results may be slow in coming.

Poor Water Retention

Plants sometimes suffer because the soil is composed mostly of sand. The problem is not usually one of drainage, but rather failure to retain enough water. The solution is to get the soil to hold onto water long enough for roots to absorb it. Here again, as with compaction and drainage problems, adding organic matter can correct the situation.

Soil Fertility

With a little practice, the home gardener can see and feel soil structure, but overall fertility is not as easily analyzed. To assess your soil's ability to support a food garden, you first need to understand

---

The Makings of Good Garden Soil

A healthy, well-structured soil should have the following components. These estimates are for 100 cubic feet of soil.

Minerals. 3,900 pounds

Organic Matter. 250 pounds

Live Organisms. 4 to 6 pounds

Water. 844 pounds

Air. 20 to 25 percent by volume

The gross weight for this soil is 5,000 pounds.

something about the role soil nutrients play in plant growth.

The Ideal Soil

Plants do not get their food from the soil. They make their own food (protein and carbohydrate) using air, water, sunlight, and ingredients from the soil such as nitrogen, phosphorus, and many other compounds and elements that are called plant nutrients. There are several essential nutrients: nitrogen, phosphorus, potassium, calcium, magnesium, and sulfur are needed in large quantities. Minor ones such as cobalt and sodium are required in much smaller doses.

All these nutrients are important; however, what is equally important is that they are available to the plant in certain balanced amounts—not too much and not too little. This somewhat complex state of affairs is further complicated by the fact that the pH level of the soil (acid or alkaline) affects the plants' ability to absorb certain of these critical nutrients. Therefore, problems can arise from having a surplus or a deficiency of a certain nutrient, or from having an improper pH level that chemically locks up certain nutrients, making them unavailable for use by the plant. All this may seem terribly complicated, but remember, you do not need to be a soil scientist to have healthy, well-balanced garden soil.

A primary objective for successful gardening is to create soil conditions in which soil microorganisms will release the balance of nutrients that each crop requires. In a fertile, well-kept soil containing at least 5 percent organic matter and having a near neutral pH (6.2 to 6.5), natural biological processes can provide as much as 3 pounds of actual nitrogen for every 1,000 square feet of garden area each season. This is equivalent to a 50-pound bag of 6-10-4 commercial fertilizer. About half of this annual nitrogen supply comes from decomposition of organic matter, such as manure, plant residues, and compost. The other half is captured from the air by nitrogen-fixing organisms.

Soils differ widely throughout the country in their content of plant nutrients. This is because soils differ greatly in their origins and histories. Different rocks produce different types of soil. Plants and other living things add to and take away from the soil's stock of nutrients. Erosion, leaching, and harvesting further change the soil's makeup.

Much of a plant's needs are met from the minerals in the soil. However, organic matter is equally vital to a soil's fertility. Nearly all of the nitrogen and sulfur, and more than one-third of the phosphorus, is supplied by organic matter. Smaller quantities of the other nutrients also come from this source. Organic matter must decompose to make specific plant nutrients available to plant roots. Therefore, an increase in the rate of organic matter decomposition increases the quantities of nitrogen, phosphorus, potassium, calcium, magnesium, and other plant nutrients in the soil solution.

So what is needed is not only lots of organic material, but an active microbiotic life in the garden's soil that is constantly breaking down or decomposing that organic matter so it will be in a form useful to the plants.

Taking a Soil Test

If you are building a garden for the first time or using a garden that doesn't seem to be performing as well as you expected, you should definitely take a soil test. Testing is inexpensive, quick, and gives accurate results. Even experienced gardeners are advised to take a soil test every 5 to 10 years to be sure no nutrient imbalances have developed. If there has been a slow buildup of potassium in your soil, for example, you will want to avoid adding manure and potassium-rich powders for a few years. With a soil test you can discover an excess or deficient nutrient before its effects show up in your plants.

Soil test kits are available commercially, but you can get a more thorough and accurate report from the County Extension Service (CES) in your county. You'll find the address listed in the phone book under state or local government offices. You can purchase one of these soil test packets from your local CES for only a few dollars. The packet will probably consist of a plastic or cloth bag, a preaddressed envelope, and a questionnaire to fill out about your garden. Take your soil sample properly so it will accurately represent the soil in your garden. Follow the directions that come with the packet.

A good soil test requires the following steps:

1. Take 1 tablespoon of soil from at least ten locations around your garden.

2. Do not sample from the surface of the soil. Remove a trowelful of soil and set it aside; then take the soil sample from inside that hole, at a depth of 4 to 6 inches.

3. Let the collected soil samples dry out enough so they can be easily mixed.

4. From this mixture take the final soil sample for mailing to the CES laboratories or to test with your home test kit.

The CES soil test report will tell you whether the levels of nitrogen, phosphorus, and potassium are low, medium, high, or excessive. Food crops do best in soils where the nutrients are in balance at the medium to high levels. The soil analysis will also report your soil's pH level and may indicate the levels of critical minerals like calcium and magnesium. Finally, most reports will indicate the percentage of organic material found in your soil.

TABLE 4.

Lab Report for a Fertile Soil

Soil Component	Amount of Component (lb./100 sq. ft.)
Nitrate nitrogen	(0.114)
Phosphorus	(0.36)
Potassium	(0.8)
Magnesium	(0.64)
Organic matter	1 in.
pH	6.0 to 6.5

Soil pH

The pH reading is a measure of the acidity or alkalinity of your soil. The pH scale goes from 0 (very acid) to 14 (very alkaline), with 7 being neutral. Problems in growing most food crops will occur only when pH readings are in the extremes—below 5 or above 8. A moderate pH level provides the best environment for the soil-dwelling microorganisms that release nutrients, especially nitrogen, to the roots of the plants. If soil pH is too low or too high, nutrients needed by plants to make food will not dissolve quickly and may turn into insoluble forms that the plant cannot use. For best plant growth you should try to keep the food garden's pH between 6 and 7, a slightly acidic level. Many soils naturally fall within this range, but some need to be corrected. (See the individual plant entries in chapters 1 to 3 for their specific pH preferences.)

Taking a pH Reading

Some gardeners like to check just the pH of their soil, without having to take an entire soil test. For this purpose, you can use plastic strips with pH-sensitive dyes. These are commercially available, often in a good drug store. You can also buy a meter that measures the soil's pH from electrodes inserted into the soil, but the strips are almost as accurate as the meters and a whole lot less expensive. The only disadvantage is that they require distilled water to function.

To use the strip, make a slurry of your soil and some distilled water in a clean dish. It should be the consistency of molasses, and slide slowly off a spoon or spatula. Let it stand for an hour or so. If it has thickened too much, add a little more water to get to the right consistency again. Place the pH strip directly into the slurry and leave it there for at least a full minute (6 minutes is best for accuracy). Remove the strip and rinse it with distilled water. You can then match its color to a chart that comes with the pH kit. Each color represents a different pH level.

Correcting an Acid Soil

When soil pH is below 6.0, there is a marked drop in the solubility of certain soil nutrients, making them

Enter the Twilight Zone

Many gardening books recommend that you have two different soil management strategies—one for your acid-loving plants like blueberries and one for the majority of food plants, which prefer a more neutral pH. There is increasing evidence that you don't need to worry about such things once your plants are established, assuming you add at least 1 inch of compost to your entire garden every year.

A recent study was done by the Department of Agriculture at the University of Connecticut, on a property that had soil with a nearly neutral pH. The gardener had planted some rhododendrons and azaleas many years previously without taking any special steps to prepare the soil for these acid-loving plants. For years, this gardener had put 1 inch of compost around each plant annually (compost is almost always nearly neutral in pH). When a researcher went around the property and took soil samples, he found that the soil around the rhododendrons and azaleas was *acidic*, whereas soil on the rest of the property was still *neutral*. Scientists haven't figured out how, but the plants seem to have created their own acidic environment.

It is still a good idea to add lots of peat moss or other acidic material to a neutral soil when planting an acid-loving plant such as blueberries. This helps the plant get off to a good start. But after that you needn't worry about the pH of the soil as long as you add compost every year.

less available to the plants. Nitrogen, phosphorus, and other major nutrients are locked into more complex compounds that don't readily break down and become available to plants below a pH of 6.0. The excessive acidity also allows toxic aluminum to be more readily absorbed by plant roots, and further, low pH contributes to excessive availability of other trace elements, especially manganese. These complications limit the plants' ability to produce their own food, and at worst, can sicken plants in the food garden. If your soil is too acid, you need to do something to lessen its acidity. Once the pH level is raised and stabilizes between 6.0 and 7.0, "locked up" nitrogen and phosphorus will gradually unbond and become available for uptake by the roots of the plants.

Limestone. Adding lime to the garden will both reduce the acidity (raise the pH) and improve soil structure and fertility. Limestone comes in several forms. Hydrate of lime is fast acting, but it tends to leach away quickly. Ground limestone is available to plants over a longer period. There are two types of ground limestone: calcitic and dolomitic. Choose the dolomitic type, since it contains magnesium as well as calcium, both necessary nutrients. Because ground limestone breaks down very slowly in the soil, you should always apply it to the garden in the fall. That way you can assure its impact on the spring plants.

Lime not only increases pH, but also increases the bacterial activity in the soil, thereby speeding up the decomposition of organic matter. Consequently, if you add lime, but not organic material, to your soil, you will only get the best results in the first season. In subsequent years, productivity will fall unless you add some organic material also.

A 1-pound coffee can holds about 3 pounds of limestone, or 3¾ cups. For sandy soils, add less lime, and for clay soils, add more. A general guideline for most soils that tend to be a bit acidic, under 6.0, is an annual application of 5 to 10 pounds for each 100 square feet, or two to three full coffee cans.

Wood Ashes. Wood ashes may be used in place of limestone, although they are a stronger, faster-acting alkaline material and so must be used with

TABLE 5.

Adding Lime to a Loam Soil

Change in pH	Amount of Lime (lb./100 sq. ft.)
From 4.0 to 6.5	16.1
From 5.0 to 6.5	10.6
From 6.0 to 6.5	4.1

caution. Ashes are 20 to 50 percent calcium carbonate (a form of lime), depending on the type of wood. The highest percentages are in the hardwoods, especially young trees and twigs. Wood ashes also contain two of the basic components of a complete fertilizer, 3 to 7 percent potassium carbonate (potash) and 8 to 20 percent phosphorus pentoxide (phosphorus). In addition, they contain the trace elements sodium, magnesium, iron, copper, zinc, manganese, boron, silicon, and sulfur.

Because wood ashes are twice as high in acid-neutralizing power as ground limestone, use them sparingly. Don't apply them year after year without measuring soil pH every season. Wood ashes may be spread on the soil at any time of the year, although late winter or early spring is probably the best time.

Mixed with water, wood ashes produce lye, which burns. Therefore, keep the ashes away from germinating seeds and seedling roots. Spread about 5 to 15 pounds of ashes for every 100 square feet, depending on how acid your soil is.

A 1-pound coffee can holds about 1 pound of sifted wood ashes. For sandy soil add fewer ashes, and for clay soil, add slightly more.

Organic Matter. Organic matter, used along with lime, also helps neutralize soil acidity. If you add well-rotted compost in sufficient quantities, you help stabilize the soil at a pH level somewhere below 7.0. The more organic matter you add to the garden, the less lime you are going to need to add. It is probably better to add the compost to the garden in the spring, so that nutrients in the material are not leached out as much by the rain and snow.

Correcting an Alkaline Soil

A pH reading of over 7.0 indicates an alkaline soil. For the food garden, you will need to add materials that lower the pH level to the desired 6.0 to 7.0 range. Gypsum (calcium sulfate), aluminum sulphate, and powdered sulfur all lower the pH.

Organic Matter. Organic matter in the form of well-rotted manure, compost, or other material also helps lower pH. Ample humus in the form of finished compost buffers soil alkalinity, just as it does

TABLE 6.

Adding Wood Ashes to a Loam Soil

Change in pH	Amount of Wood Ashes (lb./100 sq. ft)
From 4.0 to 6.5	15
From 5.0 to 6.5	10
From 6.0 to 6.5	5

acidity, pulling it closer to neutral. Normally, you should try to add about 1 inch of compost to your garden every year, just as a matter of routine. If your soil is too alkaline, add 2 to 3 inches of compost to bring the garden soil down to a healthy pH level. After a few years of adding extra compost and organic matter, the alkalinity problem will be solved.

SOIL IMPROVEMENT

The next chapter gives you the information you need to correct specific nutrient deficiencies in your soil; however, you can solve most of your soil problems without ever taking a soil test or paying attention to whether you have a particular deficiency. If you take the following steps over a 2- to 3-year period, you will almost assuredly have well-balanced, highly fertile soil, no matter what the condition of the original soil.

1. In the spring, use a tiller or a hand tool to break up the subsoil layer, and till 2 to 4 inches of compost, rotted manure, mushroom soil, or other organic material into the top 6 inches of soil.

2. Cover the entire garden surface around the plants with 4 to 6 inches of organic mulch from May or early June until the end of the growing season.

3. In the fall, till under the organic mulch and plant a cover crop, preferably a legume such as alfalfa or vetch. This cover crop will provide

additional nitrogen to compensate for the nitrogen lost when the organic materials decompose in the soil.

4. In the spring, till in the cover crop. Spread 1 to 2 inches of compost over the entire garden, and add mulch when the soil warms up. Repeat the entire cycle each year. If you use black plastic to heat up your early spring soil, simply lay it right on top of the cover crop to thaw the soil, remove it to do your tilling and compost amending, and then replace for spring planting.

It takes only 2 or 3 years for this annual soil-building cycle to create a soil that is very fertile, and balanced with all the major and minor nutrients. The mulch and cover crops are critical to slowing down the decomposition rate of the buried organic material, allowing for a slow buildup of humus. If your garden is smaller than 100 square feet, this soil-building process is not terribly difficult work. If you have a garden larger than 400 square feet, this process represents a great deal of hard work, but is almost guaranteed to solve all your soil problems.

Organic Matter

Organic material includes all those things that, when left to nature, will decompose and become humus. Humus is that fine dark brown or black material you find underneath the dead leaves on the floor of the forest. Topsoil is usually darker than subsoil because it contains more decomposed plants, sticks, animals, and other organic materials.

TABLE 7.

Adding Sulfur to a Loam Soil

Change in pH	Amount of Sulfur (lb./100 sq. ft.)
From 9.0 to 6.5	5-6
From 8.0 to 6.5	2-3
From 7.5 to 6.5	1-1½

Virtually all soil structure and nutrition problems can be solved with organic matter. The question is, what should you add, and how much do you need?

The accepted standard for a healthy soil for food gardens is at least 5 percent humus in the first foot of soil, but a higher humus content will produce healthier plants. For comparison, consider that roses do best in a soil with 20 to 25 percent humus, and lawns are easiest to care for if their soil has a 25 percent humus content. Therefore, the 5 percent humus recommended for food gardens is actually a minimum standard.

There is a catch here, unfortunately. Soil organisms consume humus at varying rates, depending on the environmental conditions in and around the soil. For example, in the southern states it is very difficult to maintain humus in a clay soil because of the increased density of microorganisms found in the clay (as opposed to the lower density in sand) and the higher average temperatures, which cause the organic material to be consumed faster. On the other hand, there is a limit to how much humus can be efficiently processed by the microbiotic population in your soil, and that limit depends a lot on your gardening practices. The microorganisms in your soil will consume humus at a higher rate when it is tilled excessively (several times a year in seed preparation and for weed control) or when it is left exposed to the elements. A soil that is lightly cultivated, mulched during the growing season, and covered with a mulch or a cover crop during the winter will gradually increase its humus content.

One inch of compost or fine organic material spread over the surface of the garden equals about 5 percent of the volume in the first foot of soil. Consequently, if you add about 1 inch of organic matter to the garden every year, and follow the humus-preserving guidelines, in a few years you will surely have at least 5 percent humus in your soil.

Compost

The best inexpensive organic amendment to soil is compost. Finished compost is essentially pure, homemade humus. When mixed into the soil, it resists compaction and drains quickly, yet still retains an enormous amount of water. Compost will retain ten times its weight in water. (See the instructions for making compost later in this chapter.)

Moss, Leaves, and Manure

Other satisfactory organic soil amendments include peat moss, sphagnum moss, chopped leaves, and dried animal manures. Neither peat moss nor sphagnum moss are cheap, so they are best used to condition smaller gardens. Like compost, peat moss and sphagnum moss are great water-retainers, holding up to 20 times their weight in water. However, they are biologically sterile and add no microorganisms or nutrients to the soil. For a soil amendment closer to compost, mix the peat moss or sphagnum moss with about 25 percent dried cow manure.

Sawdust

Sawdust has a bad reputation, but if handled properly it can be a soil amendment. Weathered or unweathered, from hardwood or softwood, sawdusts other than black walnut are not toxic in any way. Like other carbon-rich materials, sawdust will sometimes turn plants yellow, but that is only when it is used alone and without proper curing. Soil bacteria and fungi need nitrogen to decompose sawdust. They may take it from the soil, leaving little for the plants. This can be prevented by enriching the fresh sawdust with any of the nitrogenous organic fertilizers, such as compost, manure, blood meal, fish emulsion, or cottonseed meal. You may also let the sawdust age outside for a few years before using it in the garden. If exposed to the weather for about 2 years, sawdust will turn black from slow decomposition. When added to the soil, this aged compost steals little nitrogen.

Amounts to Use

If you use a garden cart, you can measure its dimensions to calculate how many cubic feet it will carry, or you can use the ubiquitous 30-gallon garbage can to measure out your organic amendments. Each can holds about 4 cubic feet of material. Table

TABLE 8.

Organic Material Needed to Cover 100 Square Feet

Depth (in.)	% in First Foot of Soil	Amount of Organic Matter (cu. yd.; cu. ft.)
6	50	2; 54
4	33	1.3; 35
3	25	1; 27
2	16	0.66; 18
1	8	0.33; 9

8, above, shows that you will need more than two full garbage cans of compost to cover your 100-square-foot bed with about 1 inch of compost (giving you about 8 percent humus content).

Working It into the Soil

There are several methods for getting the organic material down into the soil where it will do the most good. The fastest method is to use a rotary tiller. Equally effective, but more demanding, is hand digging or double-digging. Finally, if the soil has lots of earthworms, you can simply lay the material on the surface and earthworms will work it down below the surface for you.

There are many rotary tillers available to backyard gardeners. Some are designed for large gardens and others are designed especially for the modest garden. In any case, most tillers allow you to till at variable depths, usually from 2 inches to 6 to 8 inches. Such equipment loosens compacted soil and works organic materials and fertilizers down into the soil. Tillers do this job very well, as long as they are handled properly. However, gardeners should remember two important points: Never till when the soil is wet, and never till so much that the soil structure is broken down to a fine powder. Both practices can seriously harm soil structure and tilth.

Working organic materials down into the soil by hand spading takes more time and energy, but it does the job just as well. You can just loosen up the soil with a U-bar digger, a tool designed specifically for loosening the soil without putting extra strain on your back. If you wish to mix the material thoroughly, double-dig your garden. Remember, even with the innocuous spading fork, you must still resist working your soil if it is too wet.

Using a tiller is the fastest method of working the soil before planting.

Cover Crops

A valuable method of building soil fertility is to plant a cover crop or green manure. A cover crop is a plant, such as winter rye, that is sown in the garden in the fall, after the harvest is completed. It is allowed to grow through the winter, covering the bare soil in the empty garden beds. In the spring the cover crop is tilled into the soil. As the cover crop breaks down, it gives the soil the nutrients it has stored. All cover crops will add nitrogen to the soil, but if a legume is used, nitrogen levels will truly be boosted. For example, Austrian winter pea fixes $\frac{1}{10}$ pound of nitrogen for every 100 square feet. Crimson clover fixes $\frac{2}{10}$ pound, and white clover fixes up to $\frac{3}{10}$ pound of nitrogen for every 100 square feet.

Besides providing fertilizer, the benefits of cover cropping to the garden are numerous. In the first place, it adds organic matter, thereby improving the physical structure of the garden soil. Soil that is left uncovered during the winter loses much of its humus because the nutrients produced by the microorganisms in the soil are leached away by rain and snow. The cover crop's roots aerate clay soils, providing drainage channels as the plants decay. A clay soil that is cover-cropped is much less likely to be hard and impervious come spring planting time. Cover crops also help minimize or even eliminate erosion problems by holding the rain and snow until they have time to soak more slowly into the earth. During the cold winter months in the northern states, cover crops serve as an extra protection against deep frost by retaining soil moisture and moderating temperature fluctuations, and protecting earthworms and soil-building microbes from sudden freezes and thaws.

Sow cover crops whenever you have finished harvesting a food crop in the garden. When you pull the food crop, sprinkle some cover crop seeds in the same spot. If you use winter rye (annual rye), you'll see a green mat in a week or so. Even if you don't plant a cover crop until the day after the first frost has wiped out your tender crops, you will have a month to a month and a half for those plants to spread roots and produce some foliage. In many cases, the winter stops their growth, but they will come back in the very early spring as the ground begins to thaw.

Plants used for green manures are of two classes: nitrogen gatherers (legumes), those that work atmospheric nitrogen from the air into the soil, and nitrogen consumers (nonlegumes), those that cannot perform this function but use what nitrogenous compounds are already in the soil. The former are generally most recommended because they increase the supply of this essential element. The latter are used for short-term production of organic matter. In any case, you should avoid using any perennial plant, such as perennial rye, since perennials are more likely to be popping up again later, even after a good tilling. Use only annual plants in your cover crop so the tilling cleans them up once and for all.

One good cover cropping approach is to blend the two types of green manures. A blend of legume and grain adds extra nitrogen while also providing valuable organic matter. Seeded together, the fast-growing grain protects the dawdling legume so it can make a good stand. For best germination, treat the seeds of the legumes with a nitrogen-fixing bacteria inoculant before sowing.

Legumes

Alfalfa. *Medicago sativa* roots deeply in the soil. It does well in all but sandy, clay, acid, or poorly drained soils. Broadcast seeds.

Austrian Winter Pea. *Pisum arvense,* also commonly known as Canadian field pea, grows all over the United States and Canada, but winter kills it in the northern states. It must have cool, moist conditions, and prefers loamy soils high in lime. Inoculate seeds with *Rhizobium leguminosarum,* and sow them 1½ inches deep, at a rate of 4 ounces for every 100 square feet.

Crimson Clover. *Trifolium incarnatum* will grow through the winter from New Jersey south. It must have adequate soil moisture for good germination and growth. It prefers loam soils that are high in humus, but will grow on almost any well-drained soil. It will not do well in extremely acid soils, but will withstand shade and low fertility. Inoculate seeds with *Rhizobium trifoli,* and sow ½ to ⅔ ounce for every 100 square feet, covering seeds with ½ inch of soil.

White Clover. *Trifolium repens* is a hardy perennial legume that grows throughout Canada and the United States south to the Gulf of Mexico. It thrives in cool, moist climates, and prefers humus-rich, well-drained clay, clay loam, and loam soils. It grows well in shade. It needs soil with a high content of lime, phosphorus, and potash. Inoculate seeds with *Rhizobium trifoli,* and sow ¼ ounce for every 100 square feet, covering seeds with ½ inch of soil.

White Lupine. *Lupine albus* is an annual that grows best in the Deep South and northeastern and northern central states. It prefers acid, sandy loam soils. It is an excellent soil-builder for barren, sandy, and wornout soil, and is also good for opening up heavy clay. Inoculate seeds with *Rhizobium lupini,* and sow 6½ ounces for every 100 square feet, covering seeds with 1 inch of soil.

Yellow Lupine. *Lupinus luteus* var. *sativus* (fragrant lupine) is an annual legume. It grows best in Florida and is the least winter-hardy of the lupines. It prefers sandy loam and acid soils, and it must have good drainage. Inoculate seeds with *Rhizobium lupini,* and sow 2 ounces for every 100 square feet, covering the seeds with 1 inch of soil.

Others. Cowpeas, *Vigna unguiculata,* grow quickly and are a good soil-builder. Velvet beans, *Gynura aurantiaca,* are grown in the southern states and are one of the best crops for poor, sandy soils. There are varieties of vetches for all climates; they will grow in any reasonably fertile soil with ample moisture. Finally, soybeans, *Glycine max,* will grow well in all soils and all climates.

Nonlegumes

Annual ryegrass. *Lolium multiflorum,* also known as Italian ryegrass, grows all over the United States, but is best adapted to the areas where crimson clover thrives. It prefers loam or sandy loam soils, but will grow on any soil. Annual ryegrass grows rapidly and holds soil well with its heavy, fibrous roots. Sow 1½ ounces for every 100 square feet, covering seeds with ¾ inch of soil.

Oats. *Avena sativa,* also called winter barley oats, is an annual grass that grows all over the United States and makes an especially good cover crop in the southern states, where it overwinters. It prefers cool, moist climates. It does not need a soil high in lime and will grow on many soils, except heavy clay. Provide a firm seedbed to prevent frost heaving in winter. Sow 4 ounces of seeds for every 100 square feet, covering the seeds with 1 inch of soil.

Rye. *Secale cereale* (winter wheat, rape, winter rye, cereal rye) is an annual grass that grows all over the United States, but is especially well suited to the northern states because of its ability to tolerate extreme cold. It grows best on well-drained loams, but will grow on any soil. It likes plenty of moisture, but has low lime and fertility requirements. Sow 4 ounces of seeds for every 100 square feet, covering the seeds with ¾ inch of soil.

Winter Barley. *Hordeum vulgare* is an annual grass that grows all over the United States and overwinters in mild climates. It is well adapted to high altitudes and semiarid regions. It prefers well-drained loam soils and is tolerant of saline and alkaline soils. Winter barley does not grow well on sandy or acid soils. Sow 4 ounces of seeds for every 100 square feet, covering the seeds with ¾ inch of soil.

Winter Rape. *Brassica napus* grows all over the United States, preferring a cool growing season and mild winters like those along the Pacific Coast. It grows quickly and densely, and matures in 8 to 10 weeks, crowding out weeds. Winter rape likes fertile loam soils with plenty of moisture, and needs a firm seedbed. It has a low lime requirement. Sow ½ ounce for every 100 square feet, covering the seeds with ¼ inch of soil.

Winter Wheat. *Triticum aestivum* is an annual grass that grows all over the United States. It does well at high elevations. It prefers loam soils and grows best in a fertile soil, but it does not require

high amounts of lime. Sow 4 ounces of seeds for every 100 square feet, covering the seeds with ¾ inch of soil.

Others. Buckwheat, *Fagopyrum esculentum,* is one of the best crops for rebuilding poor or acid soils and is mostly grown in the northeastern states. Millet, *Panicum miliaceum,* does well in poor soils, and can be grown in the arid regions of the southern and southwestern states.

Earthworms

Often ignored by gardeners, earthworms are Nature's own tillers and soil conditioners. Their favorite food is the dried leaves and other organic materials gardeners want to incorporate into the soil. Worms drag these materials down into their burrows and break them down. If you have a healthy population of earthworms in your garden, that inch of organic matter laid over the surface of the soil in the spring will be gone by fall without your having to do anything but spread the stuff in the first place; the worms take care of the rest of the job. In turn, earthworms also work in the subsoil, bringing mineral-rich soil from below up to the garden's surface. This adds to the plant's nutrient store. Research shows that earthworms in 100 square feet of garden soil will bring to the surface between 4 to 8 pounds of dirt each year.

Besides integrating organic material into your soil, earthworms manufacture great fertilizer. Every day, they produce nitrogen, phosphorus, potassium, and many micronutrients in a form all plants can use. In a 200-square-foot garden, for example, with a low worm population of only five worms per cubic foot, earthworms provide over 35 pounds (about ⅓ pound per worm) of top-grade fertilizer each gardening year. They not only produce this valuable fertilizer, but also spread it evenly throughout the top 12 inches of soil. In many cases, they incorporate it much deeper, sometimes as far down as 6 feet. A well-managed soil rich in humus might easily support 25 worms per cubic foot, which, in that same 200-square-foot garden, means at least 175 pounds of fertilizer a year!

Worms make other very significant contributions to your garden soil. They secrete calcium carbonate, a compound that helps to moderate soil pH. Earthworms can help change acid or alkaline soils toward a neutral pH over time. Also, the rearrangement and loosening of the soil by earthworms enhances aeration, which allows more oxygen to penetrate the soil. This not only helps the plant directly, but also improves conditions for certain beneficial soil bacteria. Finally, by their tunneling, earthworms create access to deeper soil levels for countless smaller organisms that contribute to the health of the soil.

You can add earthworms to your soil to increase the worm population. Be sure you get the variety *(Lumbricus terrestris)* that will survive in garden soil. Many worms sold commercially are naturally adapted to live in the heat of a compost pile and will die when left in the garden soil. When you add new worms, spread them around the garden so that there are only a few introduced in every square foot.

COMPOST

Properly made compost looks just like the dark, almost black material you find in the forest just under the layer of leaves on the forest floor. It looks and feels much like a potting soil mix you might buy from your local gardening store, and it has little

odor. Compost is the by-product of the decomposition of organic materials such as leaves, tree bark, weeds, and anything else organic that will decompose over time.

Making Compost

Compost is produced when billions of microorganisms break down raw organic material into humus, which looks and feels like soil. These microorganisms require a certain environment in which to multiply and to continue the breakdown process. If you create that environment, you produce beautiful compost. If you don't create and maintain that environment, you don't get compost. Fortunately, the microorganisms aren't that fussy, and you have a great deal of leeway in how you build your pile. The main requirements for good compost are some carbon-containing materials (such as straw or dried leaves), some nitrogen-containing materials (such as fresh grass clippings or kitchen garbage), oxygen, and moisture.

Making compost is a very simple process. Many books and articles describe precise formulas and ratios of materials. All of those formulas produce compost, but they are unnecessarily complicated. If you definitely don't want to do any work on the compost, you can simply make a pile of stuff and let it sit in a corner of your yard for a few years. This "passive" method does produce compost, but it takes a long time and a lot of yard space. Simply by chopping the materials before they are dumped in the pile, and by turning or mixing the compost a few times during the year, you can speed up the decomposition and make more compost. Chopping and turning of the compost are the "active" parts of making compost.

Research has revealed that compost made the slow, passive way has some benefits over the compost made the fast, active way. Low-temperature compost, made the passive way, appears to have better disease-resisting capacity than that made by the hot method. However, you can mix the two together for a compost that has good disease resistance and that doesn't take years and years to make. If you make compost by the high-temperature method, also make some slower, low-temperature compost in a corner of your yard and mix a little in with your high-temperature material whenever you add it to the soil.

The Materials

Woody plant materials (wood chips, pine cones, and brush), even when shredded, take a long time to decompose. Consider composting them separately. You can let them rot completely without tying up your regular compost pile. Stiff materials such as peanut hulls, cotton burrs, corn cobs, and corn stalks won't take quite as long as wood chips, but they'll outlast the softer stuff. Most dry and woody plant materials are high in carbon, which means they will actually use up some of the nitrogen in your compost pile as they decompose. If you use a heavy duty shredder, you can incorporate sticks and limbs into a normal pile. Your compost will be a bit more lumpy, but it will be fine to use in all situations. Keep sticks and limbs that are not shredded out of the compost pile.

A properly made compost pile shouldn't smell. Never include any meat products, bones, or grease in your compost pile, because they will not only cause the compost pile to smell bad, but will also attract rodents. If you add too much green stuff, or allow the pile to get too wet, it may develop an odor.

A compost pile needs to have much more carbon material (straw, leaves, and other dried organic material) than nitrogen material (grass clippings, freshly picked weeds, and kitchen garbage). Many gardening books recommend a ratio of about 30 to 1, carbon to nitrogen. My experience indicates that you can cut down that ratio to 10 to 1 if you turn the pile frequently. If the pile smells bad, add more carbon material. If the pile is not heating up, add more nitrogenous material. You can tell if your pile is heating well by sticking your fist into the pile about a foot deep. If it is almost uncomfortably warm, the pile is decomposing nicely.

Although water is necessary for the decomposition process, you can have too much of a good thing. The material in the pile should feel damp but not

TABLE 9.

Common Composting Materials

Carbon Materials	Nitrogen Materials
Aged sawdust	Fresh grass clippings
Dry leaves	Kitchen scraps
Seaweed	Manure
Straw	Weeds and garden waste

moist—like a sponge that has been thoroughly soaked and then wrung out. Once you have built your compost pile, cover it to keep the rain from soaking it and cooling it down. If you let finished compost sit out in the weather uncovered, much of its nitrogen will be leached away by the rain before you ever use it. Use a piece of polyethylene plastic or an old shower curtain, anchored by a couple of bricks, as a cover for the pile.

Speeding Up the Process

There are three tricks that will speed up the composting process. If you put your compost materials through a shredder or chop them with a rotary lawn mower first, they will decompose much more quickly than material that is not chopped. If you turn the pile every 4 to 6 days, you will be providing optimum oxygen to the pile, which serves as fuel for the bacteria that are actually breaking down the organic materials. Finally, you can add a composting catalyst. This is usually a powder that contains billions of composting bacteria. It is best used as a quick start for a new pile than as an ongoing fuel for the composting process. If the pile is properly constructed, the bacteria should reproduce.

To really speed things up, shred material as you build the pile, and shred everything in the pile thoroughly every 5 days. In addition, use a compost activator to get things going. Such a process should give you finished compost in about 3 weeks. Normally, if you don't shred the material, and turn the pile only once a month, you will have finished compost in 3 to 4 months.

Applying Compost

There are as many ways to apply compost as there are to make it. You can place a layer across the surface of each bed in spring and work it into the soil by hand or with a rotary tiller. You can place a 1-inch layer of it across your entire garden, ideally in the spring, and just leave it there. The worms and microorganisms will take care of moving your compost down into the soil. Finally, you can use it as a side-dressing, laying it between rows or placing a circle of compost around each plant at any time during the year. Just how you apply the compost depends on what you hope to accomplish.

Using Compost to Improve Soil Conditions

Compost can cure soil problems such as bad drainage and a soil pH that is too acid.

Soils containing high percentages of gray clay often drain very poorly. They also tend to compact and turn hard in the middle of the hot summer. The best way to solve the problem is to add large volumes of organic materials, and compost is the very best supplement of all. Adding organic matter such as chopped leaves, chopped straw, or peat moss will ease the compaction and drainage problems, but such material takes nitrogen from the soil as it decomposes, and over time, it reduces the amount of nitrogen available to your food crops. Finished compost, however, does not deplete soil nitrogen, since it has already decomposed completely.

Soil is considered good for food crops if it contains at least 5 percent humus (1 inch of compost equals 5 percent of the volume of the first cubic foot of soil). In situations where drainage is poor and compaction may be a problem, you are advised to add at least 25 percent organic material in the beginning to overcome those soil problems. It takes 5 to 7 inches of organic matter (5 inches of finished compost) to raise the soil's organic matter content to 25 percent. Work the material down into the soil at least 10 to 16 inches. In subsequent years, add just 1 inch of compost to keep the garden well drained.

Every gardener should have a good supply of compost. The benefits it offers are numerous: It improves drainage, adds nutrients, corrects pH, and encourages earthworms.

Another soil problem compost solves is low pH. The ideal vegetable garden soil has a pH level of between 6.0 and 7.0. Virtually all finished compost has a pH of around 6.8 to 7.0, regardless of what materials were used to make it. Oak leaves, which are acidic in their natural form, turn into neutral compost. Consequently, when you add large volumes of compost to an acidic soil, its pH will rise to 6.0 to 6.8. Annual supplements of compost will keep that soil within the preferred level for food crops. If the addition of compost is not enough to do the job, add the necessary amount of ground limestone.

The addition of compost to the soil improves overall fertility and cures some soil mineral deficiencies. Compost itself is not a direct fertilizer for the plants. It is a food for the billions of microorganisms in the soil that transform the compost into the soluble compounds that can then be absorbed by the roots of plants. Compost, with its many oxygen-containing compounds, brings oxygen to these microorganisms, which is essential to their reproduction. As compost is created (during its decomposition process), certain acids are formed, which help to break down some of the rock particles in the soil, releasing nutrients to the plants that would otherwise not be available to them. When compost is freshly applied to the garden, it provides nitrogen, some potassium, and many of the trace minerals needed by your garden during the entire season. Finished compost is generally low in phosphorus, so you should add rock phosphate to the compost or directly to the soil.

Stay away from super phosphate fertilizers. They do make phosphate available immediately in water-soluble form. But the phosphate becomes bound with iron or aluminum in acidic soil, or with calcium in alkaline soil, and thus is unavailable for plant uptake. Rock powder forms of phosphorus, on the other hand, become mineralized slowly and are available to plants over a longer time period. Add about 3 to 5 pounds of rock phosphate or some other phosphorus source to a pile 4 by 4 by 4 feet in size.

About half of the nutrients that are present in your compost are released for plant use during the first year. Half of the remaining nutrients are released during the second year, and so on after that. Most vegetable crops require about ½ pound of nitrogen for every 100 square feet. Since many gardeners have two and sometimes three successions of crops in their garden, you want to have at least 1 pound of nitrogen available for every 100 square feet, or 2 pounds for an intensively planted garden with two or three successions.

The amount of nitrogen in finished compost depends on the raw materials used to make the compost. Compost made from hay is higher in nitrogen than compost made from straw. Leaves have about half the nitrogen that manure has. Varieties of leaves differ, but studies have shown that about 75 pounds of leaves produce compost with about as much nitrogen as a 5-pound bag of blood meal. For comparison, aged cow manure is about 1.4 percent nitrogen, and aged chicken manure is about 2.8 percent nitrogen. If your compost is made of leaves and grass it will probably have about 0.8 to 1 per-

cent nitrogen. That percentage is sufficient to give you the amount of nitrogen most average gardens will need, about 0.6 pound for 100 square feet. This means you can supply your garden's nitrogen demands by adding a 1-inch layer of compost each spring.

Compost can be used as a side-dressing for plants, though its availability as a fertilizer is so slow that this technique is not terribly practical. Foliar feeding with a liquid fertilizer is preferred to side-dressing with anything. Nevertheless, a couple of handfuls of compost sprinkled around each plant early in the season will provide a continuous source of nutrients for the whole season.

Using Compost to Reduce Watering Needs

If you find that your garden seems to need watering very frequently, compost can be used to reduce watering needs. Compost has the capacity to store a tremendous amount of water. On the surface of your vegetable garden bed, a layer of compost will help to soak up water rather than letting it puddle and run off, washing away nutrients and eroding the soil. Mixed into the soil, compost has this effect, too. As the soil's humus content increases, its ability to hold water increases. Particles of organic

---

Solving Problems with Compost

Here's what compost can do for the soil:

  change pH

  improve drainage

  improve fertility

  reduce watering needs

  reduce insect problems

  reduce disease problems

  reduce weed problems as a mulch and killer of weed
    seeds

matter act like microscopic sponges, soaking up and holding water in sandy soil and opening up spaces in clay soils through which water can move more easily. Increasing your soil's humus content from 2 to 5 percent can quadruple its water-holding capacity.

Using Compost to Reduce Insects and Diseases

Plants sometimes sicken even though soil and growing conditions are excellent. One cause is root-knot nematodes, a problem in many parts of the South. These nematodes live deep in the soil, and form nodules on the roots of your plants.

Compost is an indirect pest control. Recent research by Safer Agro-Chem Ltd., of Victoria, British Columbia, has shown that compost produces fatty acids similar to those that are the basis for the commercial insecticidal soap sprays. Such fatty acids control pests without harming beneficial insects.

Studies have shown that decomposing rye and timothy grasses release fatty acids that control parasitic nematodes. Since no chemical nematocide is registered for use in home gardens, compost or leaf mold is the only available control method for nematodes at present. Many different leaves are toxic to nematodes, but laboratory tests have shown compost made from pine leaves to be particularly potent. Work this material down 6 to 8 inches into the soil if you suspect nematodes.

Soil may also harbor fungal spores and sources of other plant diseases. It turns out that other fatty acids produced in the making of compost are toxic to fungal diseases and to certain bacterial diseases of plants. Although this relationship is still very much under study, it is clear that a soil rich in compost is likely to encourage fewer disease problems.

Using Compost to Reduce Weed Problems

Healthy soil produces healthy plants. It also has a disconcerting tendency to produce healthy weeds. Compost made using the active method will reach temperatures of around 150°F, which is sufficient to kill most annual weed seeds, and a 1-inch layer of finished compost is usually sufficient to prevent the germination of most annual weed seeds residing in the top inch of garden soil.

How Much Compost?

One inch of *finished* compost spread evenly over 200 square feet is about 16 cubic feet, or a pile 2 by 4 by 2 feet in size. Since organic materials decompose to about one-third their original volume, you'll need to start with a compost pile 4 by 4 by 3 feet in size. Table 8, on page 473, will help you determine the amounts of compost you would need to cover your garden with a 1-inch layer.

Compost Substitutes

If you choose not to make compost, you have several alternatives for providing the inch of humus to your garden each year. Some communities have their own large-scale composting programs for handling various solid waste products, formerly placed in expensive landfills. This compost is often made available to the public for free or for a very reasonable fee. The only concern you should have in using this community compost is its heavy metal content. Sludge or compost high in heavy metals is safe for flower beds but should never be used in a food garden. The officials at the composting site will know whether the material is safe or not. Some communities also compost leaves (passive method), producing enormous amounts of leaf mold, which is a great humus additive for your vegetables. Either way, you not only save yourself some work, but you are recycling city waste.

A good substitute for compost, at least on the modest scale found in most gardens of America, is a mixture of peat humus and processed cow manure, which can be purchased at most garden centers. A large bale of peat humus mixed with one or two 50-pound bags of processed cow manure will give you the layer of humus you need each year. Be aware that peat moss is different from peat humus. Peat moss is more acidic than peat humus and is not as desirable as a compost substitute. The pH of peat moss is about 3.2 to 4.5, whereas peat humus is anywhere between 4.0 and 7.5. However, lime should be added if either is used as a compost substitute (5 to 10 pounds per bale of peat).

Another excellent source of humus is composted mushroom soil. Mushrooms are grown in composting straw and manure. After the composting process is over, the material is no longer any good for growing mushrooms. This "spent" mushroom soil is an excellent soil conditioner and is usually sold by the mushroom farmers at a very reasonable price. Let the mushroom soil age for at least 6 weeks before using it in your garden, because the manure may not be sufficiently aged to be safe for the food crops.

MANAGING MULCH

Mulch is one of the most important tools available to the gardener. Most gardeners mulch to cut down on watering and weeding tasks, but there are lots of other good reasons for covering the soil. Mulch can be used to reduce soil compaction and moderate soil temperatures. It also works to control insects and diseases. Your reasons for using mulch determine what material you choose. Mulch comes in many different forms and often can be acquired at no cost. The best mulches are easy to lay down and require little maintenance during the growing season.

Using Mulch to Hold Water

Mulching is a great way to conserve soil moisture. Soil exposed to the harsh influence of sun, air, and wind will dry out rapidly. Even with frequent watering, plants don't seem to get the moisture they need. Mulch is such an obvious solution that many gardeners never think of it. A good mulch can reduce the rate at which soil moisture evaporates by as much as 50 percent, depending on what material is used.

Using Mulch to Control Weeds

Gardeners who have mulched their garden spend little time weeding. If mulch is thick enough (at least 2 inches, preferably 4 inches), it will prevent most annual weeds from growing. Those few that do get through are easily pulled, since the soil under the mulch, if it has been properly prepared, never gets hard and compacted. A good mulch virtually eliminates the onerous task of weeding the garden.

Using Mulch to Control Insects and Diseases

The right mulch can help protect some plants from insect pests. If your plants are being attacked by cucumber beetles, a thick straw mulch may reduce the number of adult beetles laying eggs at the base of the plants. In most areas you'll get more than one generation of cucumber beetles hitting the garden, so keep the mulch on all season long.

An aluminum foil or white plastic film mulch repels aphids very effectively, but other light-colored mulch materials are also useful for this purpose. The mulch seems to blind aphids so they can't see the plants and aren't able to land. Some gardeners report similar success in thwarting potato aphids and bean beetles. Aluminum foil is also an excellent deterrant to the squash borer, for the same reason. It reflects the sky and disorients the moths as they attempt to fly under the plant leaves to lay their eggs at the base of the stem. Make sure the aluminum mulch extends beyond the perimeter of the plant by at least 6 inches.

Organic mulch has been known to encourage slugs. They like the cool darkness and will hide under straw or hay mulch during the heat of a summer day. If you have problems with slugs, that should not deter you from using mulch, because its benefits by far outweigh that one liability. There are many tips for controlling slugs in chapter 4, and they do not include abandoning mulch.

Fungal diseases often spread to plants as water splashes off the hard ground. Mulch reduces or even eliminates splashing of the fungal spores up onto the plants.

Although mulch is not used primarily as a preventor of diseases, research has shown that certain organic materials may have some chemical reaction to the soil when used as a mulch. Some of these reactions might be harmful (allelopathic), but others are definitely beneficial. Research is beginning to suggest that organic mulches may reduce the harmful effects of certain soil fungi and nematodes.

Using Mulch to Protect the Soil

Nutrients in the soil can be leached down out of reach of the roots by the rain that hits the soil directly, and this can render your soil infertile. Because mulch slows down the rate of the rain entering the soil, it gives the soil a chance to absorb the water, rather than letting it drain off the soil surface or flow down into the subsoil past the roots. A mulch also encourages microorganisms to work nearer the surface of the soil, since the soil there stays moist and friable. Furthermore, the mulch itself is slowly decomposing, creating an ongoing nutrient supplement to your garden. Some people worry about the fact that the decomposing mulch can tie up nitrogen in the top few inches of the soil; however, this is unimportant. Nitrogen lost from decomposing mulch is irrelevant to the total nitrogen available in a healthy soil.

Another advantage mulch offers is reduced soil compaction. Even black plastic film protects the soil to a certain degree. Bare soil tends to be compacted over time by the beating of the rain, and by drying out of the soil particles in the blazing sun. Any mulch protects the surface of the soil from the impact of rain and sun, thus reducing the compacting process. Less compaction means healthier roots and a more active microlife below the surface of the soil.

A winter mulch over your entire bed, although it does not prevent soil freezing, helps stabilize the winter temperature of the soil, avoiding the rapid fluctuations that occur in unprotected soil. The soil bacteria and fungi come back the next spring, and you can speed that process by protecting the soil from the cold. A rapid fluctuation in temperature is more harmful to soil microorganisms than a steady cold period. Winter mulch also reduces freeze damage to roots of permanent crops such as berries, asparagus, and rhubarb, and prevents further soil compaction.

Kinds of Mulch

The best garden mulch is easy to work with, allows air to pass through it, is relatively windproof, holds some moisture, and is attractive to the eye. Ideally, it will not cost very much. The following list includes the most popular materials used for mulching in the food garden. Some materials are more available than others, and some have advantages over others. However, any kind of mulch is better than no mulch at all!

Agricultural Fleece

Spunbonded polyester, or agricultural fleece, is a rather new winter mulching material. Tests in New Hampshire showed strawberry yields were increased by 76 percent in 1983 and 37 percent in 1984 by using fleece. This was applied in mid-September and removed just before blooming in the spring. The fleece covering increased fruit numbers but didn't affect fruit size or quality.

Black Plastic

As already discussed, black plastic mulch is a valuable tool for warming the soil early in the growing season and again in late fall, at the tail end of the growing season. The earlier the soil warms up, the earlier the plants begin to grow. Black plastic mulch will raise soil temperature 6°F to 8°F. In northern parts of the country, clear plastic mulch works even better, but be careful to avoid overheating the soil with the clear material.

Black plastic mulch now comes in handy rolls 3 or 4 feet wide. Thickness of the plastic ranges from 2 to 4 mil. The thicker the material, the higher the cost. Most black plastic mulch is good for only one season, not so much because it breaks down from the sunlight, but because it gets so many holes cut in it for placing plants that it is not very practical for the second season.

The mulch can be held down by handfuls of soil, rocks, bricks, or homemade "hairpins" made by cutting coat hangers in half. If there are no holes cut in the material to let water through, a drip irrigation system should be placed on the bed before laying the plastic.

Recent research has revealed that you will get better initial fruit yields from apple trees that have been mulched with black plastic mulch while young, compared to fruit yields of trees grown in sod. Use 4-by-5-foot black plastic sheets to mulch newly planted apple and pear trees.

Chopped Leaves

Leaves are free, generally available in most areas, and attractive when chopped up. They will cool the soil by 10°F to 18°F. You should not use whole leaves as a mulch because they will mat and prevent the even draining of water into the soil. There are a number of ways to chop the leaves for mulch. The easiest way is to use a shredder designed for handling leaves. Be careful: Some shredders work well with dry leaves but will jam when the leaves are wet. Another way is to shred the leaves with a rotary lawn mower. You can chop the leaves as you mow the lawn, controlling the pattern of mowing so that you are always blowing the leaves and grass into the middle of the lawn. That way the leaves go through a few times and end up well shredded. Some people have had success shredding leaves with a snow blower set in slow-slow drive. Another way to shred leaves when you don't have a shredder is to put them in a large garbage can and use your string trimmer. This shreds dry leaves very finely, but it doesn't work too well with wet leaves.

You might want to avoid using fresh maple leaves in the vegetable garden. Maple leaves con-

tain chemicals called phenols that reduce the growth and yields of cole crops and other vegetables by inhibiting root elongation. Early crops are most vulnerable because the phenols are quickly released when the leaves begin to decompose in spring. Fall crops are usually not affected because most of the phenols have leached by midseason.

Compost

If you have a large compost pile, you can top-dress the soil with partially decomposed compost and accomplish several things with this one technique. Feed, weed, warm, and protect simultaneously!

Geotextile Mulch

There are a number of new synthetic fabrics, made of polyester, nylon, or polypropylene, that can be used as warming mulches in the food garden. Unlike plastic mulches, these geotextiles let water and air penetrate to the soil. They are more expensive than black plastic, but last longer: They are tough enough to last for several seasons, even with lots of holes cut in them, and they resist decomposition. Geotextiles are well suited for fruit trees and berry patches, but might not be as easy to work with in the vegetable garden because they are so tough and difficult to cut.

Grass Clippings

Grass clippings make an excellent organic mulch, but should be applied in a thin layer of no more than an inch at a time or they will decompose and become putrid. They must be dry to serve as an effective mulch. Be sure never to use grass clippings that have herbicide residue on them or you may harm your vegetable plants.

Hortopaper

Hortopaper is made from paper and peat moss, so it can be composted or tilled into the soil at the end of the growing season. This material comes in rolls (50 or 400 feet long and 32 feet wide), squares (32 feet by 24 feet, 32 feet by 32 feet, or 32 feet by 48 feet), and fertilizer-impregnated 8-foot diameter disks.

To apply this mulch, level the growing area, thoroughly soak it with water, and roll out the Hortopaper onto the soil surface. Secure the edges with earth or bricks and cut holes for plants. Water soaks through the paper without breaking it. At the end of the season, turn the paper into the soil, where it will break down and add to the soil structure.

Newspapers

Newspapers make a good mulch. The new colored inks used by newspapers are water-based and non-toxic, so they can be used safely in the garden. However, other paper products should not be used as a mulch.

Place the newspapers down whole, with a light covering of soil to anchor them. You may want to shred the papers so they will allow water through more easily. One gardener uses six hamsters to shred her newspapers. They produce an enormous amount of valuable mulch for her!

Peat Moss

Peat is another popular organic mulch. It is acidic and will lower soil pH. It tends to dry out, however. A serious drought can cause it to form a dry crust that repels water instead of absorbing it.

Pine Needles

Pine needles make an attractive mulch and have some beneficial effects in controlling several harmful soil fungi, including fusarium. However, they do tend to make your soil more acid, so they might not be advisable in the vegetable garden. They are especially good around blueberries, which prefer an acid soil. Pine needles can also be used on straw-berries.

Sawdust

Sawdust should be aged in a pile exposed to the elements for at least a year before it is used as a mulch. Unlike chopped leaves, fresh sawdust will leach enough nitrogen from the top few inches of your soil to cause your plants to require additional nitrogen supplements.

Seaweed Mulch

Seaweed, eelgrass, and other marine plants make a practical, effective mulch, where they are available.

Trace mineral values are usually higher in the marine plant wastes. Salt does indeed wash out of marine mulch pretty quickly. However, be sure the salt levels are safe (wet some and taste it with your tongue to detect the salt level: you should not taste any). Marine vegetation should be composted or allowed to stand in the rain for several months before using it in the garden.

Shredded Bark

Shredded bark or wood chips, at least 2 inches thick, make a good mulch around fruit trees and berry patches. Spread these materials thickly for good weed control. You can use either wood chips, shredded pine bark, or nugget pine bark. For appearance, the shredded pine bark is a good choice because it's the most natural looking. Nugget pine bark is the most expensive of these materials, but it has the advantage of being available in many different sizes. Wood chips are the least expensive of the three. Tree trimming companies will often give you an entire truckload of fresh shredded wood chips.

Stone Mulch

Stones are a fine mulch around trees and berry plants. Like all good mulches, they discourage weeds, protect the plants' roots, retain moisture, and encourage essential soil aeration. They also hold midday heat and release it gradually during the cooler nights. Some stone mulches are made from 8-inch or 9-inch flat stones set closely together, at least an inch from the tree trunk. You can also angle the stones so that rain water runs down the roots. They protect dwarf trees from the power mower and provide favorable conditions for soil bacteria and earthworms.

Straw or Hay

Straw or hay makes an excellent organic mulch, which will cool the soil by 8°F to 12°F. Some gardeners are concerned about weed seeds in the bales of straw or hay. These can be a problem if you don't use black plastic mulch underneath the straw. Even if plastic mulch is not used, a thick layer of straw itself will keep most annual weed seeds from germinating.

CHAPTER 8

Managing the Garden

Once you have taken charge of the wide physical environment of the garden, you can begin to focus your efforts on the heart of gardening: the planting, watering, and fertilizing of vegetables, fruit, and herbs. At this level, too, you can develop techniques and follow certain practices that will help you to grow your finest crops ever.

PLANTING SEEDS

Seeds are living embryos. Given the right conditions, they will germinate and grow into healthy, productive plants. Given the wrong conditions, they will rot or shrivel up without becoming anything at all.

Improving Germination Rates

Low germination rates may be due to improper soil conditions when the seeds are planted. Remember that each plant has a critical temperature for seed germination. If the ground is too wet, the seeds will rot before they germinate. If the soil is too cold, the seeds will not germinate, no matter how warm the air temperature might be. Wait until the soil temperature and moisture content are optimal for each type of vegetable or herb. The soil should be lightly cultivated with a rake or tiller and raked fairly smooth. The soil may feel cold, but it should

not feel wet or lumpy. (See the entries for each vegetable, fruit, and herb in chapters 1 through 3 for appropriate times and temperatures for planting seeds in the garden.)

Presoaking Seeds

In some cases, germination rates can be improved by soaking your vegetable, flower, or herb seeds before they are actually planted. You can soak them in a dilute solution of seaweed extract, or in plain water.

Virtually all seeds presoaked in a dilute seaweed extract solution for 30 minutes have a better germination rate than untreated seeds. Research suggests that something in the seaweed may increase the respiratory activity of the seeds. To treat seeds and transplants, stir ¼ teaspoon of extract into 1 quart of lukewarm water. Don't use a more concentrated solution, and don't soak seeds for more than 30 minutes, or the benefits will be lost.

Soaking seeds in plain water can also help germination rates, especially for plants that have hard seed coats, like parsley, beets, and carrots. These seeds may be soaked overnight. Mix the wet seeds with sand or coffee grounds to make planting easier. Soak softcoated seeds such as beans and peas for no more than 1 hour. Then drain the water and plant the seeds right away.

While presoaking can be quite beneficial for

some kinds of seeds, it isn't necessarily a good idea for seeds you'll sow outdoors in early spring. At that time, the soil tends to be rather wet and cold, which can inhibit germination. If the seeds are already full of moisture, they may rot in the ground before temperatures warm up enough for germination. Save presoaking for garden seeds that you'll sow indoors, or for those you plan to sow outdoors once the soil warms up a bit.

Sowing Seeds

It is important to sow seeds at the right depth. Some seeds need light to germinate and will never sprout if below the soil surface. Other seeds need no light, but require a particular combination of air and moisture and must be planted deeply enough so that the young plant roots have adequate support from the soil. Planting at the wrong depth can cause poor seed germination and poor seedling development. The general rule of thumb for sowing seeds is to cover them with soil at a depth of only three to four times a seed's thickness. Firm the soil to make sure that contact is made between the seeds and the damp soil.

Spacing and Thinning

A common mistake of beginning gardeners is planting too closely. Seeds are so small that it is hard to believe they'll ever grow into the large plants described on their packets. Could that squash plant really require 6 feet of space? Gardeners try to squeeze more plants into the garden than conditions can support. The result is undersized plants and harvests and possibly some diseases and pest problems as well.

Beginning gardeners should follow the spacing instructions on the seed packet. Only plant vegetables more closely than is usually recommended if the soil is very rich and well prepared. Typical planting distances are very conservative because they are intended for vegetables planted in rows and periodically tilled. If you use well-prepared beds instead of rows, you can plant more closely.

Intensive Planting

Intensive planting means planting vegetables in beds at equal distances from each other so that when they are fully grown, their leaves will just touch, and the entire bed will be covered by foliage. This creates a kind of canopy that helps to keep the garden soil cooler. When you space vegetables intensively, you get less fruit from each individual vegetable, but more per square foot of growing space. If you want the biggest eggplant at the county fair, don't plant intensively. If you want the most eggplants for your table from the available space in your garden, use intensive planting techniques.

Closely spaced plants will generally require more fertilizer and water than normally spaced plants. You must also be more diligent about pest control, since the close spacing makes it easier for the pests to spread from plant to plant.

There is a limit to how tightly you can arrange plants in a bed, even when soil is quite rich. If you plant vegetables more closely than conditions allow, you will get too much competition between the plants, and productivity will suffer considerably. Begin conservatively, and as you gain experience and improve soil conditions, you can gradually plant more closely. A safe guideline for planting in beds is to space vegetables 75 percent closer than recommended on the seed packet.

STARTING YOUR OWN TRANSPLANTS

A problem for some gardeners, particularly those who wish to extend their growing season, is the lack of early transplants at the garden center. Raising your own seedlings gives you much more control over your garden. You can have the plants when you want them and need them rather than when the garden center stocks them. You can choose from dozens of varieties of each vegetable rather than from just a few at the nursery. Finally, once you've learned the tricks, you can grow healthier and stronger seedlings than you can purchase from the store.

When to Start Seedings

A common mistake is to start seedlings too early in the spring prior to planting time, or too late in the summer to mature in time for the fall harvest. You should time seed sowing against the dates of the last frost in the spring and the first frost in the fall.

Soil temperature is the best guide for planting time, but it is usually safe to set out cool weather plants such as cabbage 1 or 2 weeks before expected last frost. Seedlings should be just 6 to 8 weeks old at transplant time. Estimate seed-starting time by subtracting 8 weeks from the last expected frost. If you start the seeds later, no harm is done and the plants are sure to thrive. If you start too early and the roots start to outgrow their container, transplant seedlings into bigger containers so they can continue to grow before being moved outdoors.

Put warm weather vegetables into the garden 2 or more weeks after the last expected frost. Start tomatoes, peppers, and eggplants 4 weeks before the last frost so that they will be 6 weeks old at transplant time. Remember, these are the conservative timings. As you gain experience with tunnels, cloches, and other tricks, planting dates can become more flexible.

Timing is a bit more complicated for fall crops. Not only is the temperature an important factor, but day length becomes critical also. There are fewer daylight hours in the fall, thereby slowing down the growing rate of the vegetables. If you don't compensate for this, you may be disappointed in the harvest. Calculate fall seeding dates by starting with the date of the first expected frost. Back up 2 weeks for harvest period, then back up the number of days it takes for the particular crop to mature, as indicated on the seed packet. Add 2 to 3 additional weeks to compensate for the slower growth rate in fall. The total number of days from those three figures subtracted from the first frost date gives you the date the seeds should germinate. Subtract the number of days it takes the seeds to germinate, as indicated on the seed packet, and you have the planting date for starting fall seedlings.

Providing a Healthy Environment

Like plants in the garden, seedlings started indoors need just the right amount of light, nutrients, and water. Indoors, where the environment is designed to please people, not plants, providing these essentials can be challenging.

Light

Seedlings grown indoors often get spindly because they don't get enough light. You can start seedlings on a windowsill of a south-facing window or in a greenhouse, but in late winter, the days are still relatively short, so there is not really enough light to produce compact, healthy transplants. Seedlings raised on the windowsill will be spindly compared to those grown in the South someplace and shipped north for sale in a garden center.

The best seedlings are grown under fluorescent lights. Use lights all year long for seedling production. They give enough light to produce healthy strong seedlings with very little trouble. For most gardeners, just one shop light fixture with two 48-inch fluorescent tubes is sufficient to get started raising seedlings. Be sure the fluorescent light fixture is adjustable so that you can move it either up or down, or move the plants up and down. You'll need to maintain the proper distance between plants and light as the plants grow.

The basement is an ideal location for setting up a fluorescent light for starting seedlings. The temperatures are usually more constant in a basement, keeping between 60°F and 75°F throughout the whole year. Most basements have water available, which makes caring for the seedlings convenient. Folks without basements might consider building a seedling bench that harmonizes comfortably with the other houseplants in the living room.

The keys to successfully growing seedlings under lights are the duration of light and the distance the light sits from the top leaf of the plant. Have your lights on for 14 to 16 hours a day, every day. Anything less will not produce the best growth. Use an automatic timer to turn the lights on and off.

When seedlings are just little sprouts, hang the lights no more than 3 inches above. As the plants get their first true leaves, move the lights up to about 4 inches. You can set the lights at 6 inches when the seedlings are several inches tall so that the light shines evenly on all the plants, even those on the edge of the shelf.

Growing Medium and Containers

In choosing a container for your seedlings, consider not only convenience but also how much damage might occur to seedling roots at transplant time. If roots are torn or broken during transplanting, otherwise healthy seedlings may stop growing while they recover from their injuries. Flats of seedlings that must be untangled or cut apart may take more than a week to recover. To make transplanting less of a shock to plants, choose individual containers for seed starting. Seedlings can be started in Styrofoam coffee cups, egg cartons, peat pots, and dozens of other containers. The coffee cups are fine, but they do take a lot of space. Egg cartons are too small for most transplants, and peat pots tend to dry out. In recent years, the soil block has made all these containers obsolete. It is a favorite of commercial growers, and it works just as well at home.

A seedling grown in a soil block can simply be planted in the ground. This avoids the shock to roots that occurs when seedlings are transplanted from flats into the garden.

A soil block is growing medium, such as soil, peat moss, compost, or any combination of these materials, that has been pressed into a compact 2-inch cube. The advantages are convenience and the elimination of transplant shock. Seedlings grown in soil blocks make the transition from "pot" to garden quite easily.

You can make your own soil blocks, or you can purchase commercial versions at a reasonable price. Commercial soil blocks are made of peat and may be wrapped in some kind of netting. They come as small flat pellets, and when you add water, each one expands into a block about 2 by 2 by 2 inches in size. You put the seed in the top of the block, and when the plant's first true leaves appear, it can be transplanted to another container or put out in the garden.

To make your own soil blocks, you will need a special press which can be found in many garden catalogs. The medium that you use can vary with what you have available and what you prefer. A common mix contains roughly equal amounts of peat moss, compost or soil, and sharp sand or perlite. Add water until the mix reaches the consistency of cooked oatmeal. Let it sit for an hour or so, and then compress this mixture with the soil block press. Pop out the little block of soil that holds its shape even when it is watered. Place the seed in the center of the top, and the roots will grow well even in that obviously compressed medium. When the seedling has its first set of true leaves, the soil block is ready to transplant to another container or to be placed out in the garden. Roots in this type of freestanding soil block avoid the sides of the block. They don't like to go past the surface of the soil in any direction, so they wind through the cube. With a good press you can make unlimited numbers of soil blocks at a very low cost. Whether you make or buy soil blocks, the technique is to start your seedlings under the lights in the block. When the seedling gets to be 2 or 3 inches tall, after it's gotten its first true leaves, you have several choices, depending on what season it is. In the early spring, you can put your seed-

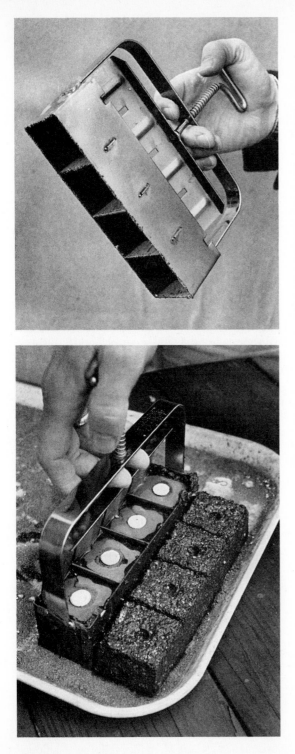

You can make soil blocks at home by using a commercial soil block press. A soil mixture is made and placed in the mold; then blocks are pressed out of the mold onto a tray, each one ready to receive a seed.

lings in Styrofoam coffee cups with holes punched in the bottoms. Add some potting soil so that you can keep the seedlings growing for another 3 or 4 weeks indoors. Later in the season, you can still put the soil block with each seedling in a coffee cup, but you can set them outside in a seedling box and let them grow another few weeks before placing them in the garden.

If you do not use blocks, you can start seedlings directly in containers. The key is to have a soil mix that drains well while simultaneously retaining moisture. You can buy ready-mixed seed starting material from any garden center. If you wish to make your own, a standard recipe is one part vermiculite, one part perlite, and two parts compost, potting soil, or garden soil. If you are a beginning gardener, you are wise not to use any soil from the outside garden in your seed-starting mixture. It may carry soil-borne fungal diseases, which will kill young seedlings before they even get a good start.

Water
Seedlings need to be watered when the medium is almost dry. Plants suffer as much from too much water as from not enough water. Generally, if the soil mix is appropriate, and humidity is adequate, you will need to water your seedlings every 3 to 5 days. They should not be allowed to look even slightly wilted for more than a day, or you will permanently retard their growth and ultimate productivity. Let the soil dry out sufficiently so the roots are forced to grow into the soil's air spaces as they search for water. Too much water, on the other hand, ruins the soil structure and fills up the critical air spaces. Soil that is continuously waterlogged has no air spaces to promote root growth, and root rot eventually sets in.

Water that has gone through a water softener should not be used since it contains potentially toxic amounts of sodium. To reduce the possibility of disease problems, always water the seedlings before noon so the leaves can dry before dark. Always use water that is at room temperature to avoid shocking the tender seedlings.

Temperature
Seedling root growth decreases when the temperature of the potting medium gets too cold or hot. If you are raising plants in a greenhouse or on a windowsill, soil temperature may occasionally get too high. Temperatures as high as 120°F are not uncommon in pots exposed to full sun in a sunny greenhouse or sun porch. Since root growth stops at 100°F, and slows at 85°F, such conditions are not tolerable. Use cheesecloth, agricultural fleece, or a fine netting to shade seedlings during the hottest part of the day. Another solution, if you don't have too many plants, is to move the seedlings into the shade in the afternoon. In any case, try to avoid having the growing medium's temperature exceed 85°F.

Fertilizing
Seedlings do not need any fertilizer until they get their first set of "true" leaves, actually the second set of leaves you'll see. Then you can begin giving them a very dilute solution of liquid fertilizer.

When fertilizing is overdone, salts accumulate in the soil mix to a toxic concentration. It is better to give frequent small feedings than occasional large feedings to very young seedlings. For example, if you normally mix 1 tablespoon of liquid fertilizer in a gallon of water, for the first month of a seedling's life, give it a solution with only 1 teaspoon of liquid fertilizer per gallon of water. A good general feeding program consists of this very dilute liquid fertilizer every week for the first month, and then the normal strength liquid fertilizer every 2 weeks until transplant time.

It is advisable to give your seedlings a dose of dilute liquid seaweed extract (1 teaspoon to a gallon of water) once before they are transplanted. The kelp solution reduces the problems caused by transplant shock.

Pest and Disease Control
Unhealthy seedlings may be victims of insects. Common insect problems include whiteflies, aphids, and mites. All of these insects can be easily controlled with a foliar spray of insecticidal soap, such as Safer's soap. Apply the spray to the undersides of leaves, and reapply it 3 to 5 days later to be sure of getting all the pests.

Few diseases bother seedlings unless you use soil from the outside garden. Damping-off, a fairly common fungal disease that leaves plants lying dead in their pots, occurs when the seedlings are allowed to stay in a damp condition. To avoid the disease, use a sterile soil mix and water only in the morning, before noon. To provide adequate ventilation for the plants, you may need to set up a small fan.

Brushing

If you've followed all the rules, and your seedlings still seem to be spindly and lack vigor, you should try the "brushing" technique. Research has shown that some form of mechanically induced stress caused by lightly brushing or rubbing the seedlings for a minute or so every day will produce stockier, stronger plants more resistant to transplant shock. Smaller seedlings can be brushed with a piece of paper folded over. Gently brush the plants so they bend over almost to horizontal, then let them spring back. As the plants get larger, simply brushing them lightly with your hand achieves the same result.

HARDENING OFF TRANSPLANTS

A plant is ready to transplant, either to the outside garden or to another larger container, when its roots have filled the container, but have not yet begun to grow around the outside of the soil ball. If the seedling is not transplanted at that time, it can be set back permanently. Most vegetables reach this stage between 4 and 6 weeks of growth. However, if a seedling's container is small, transplanting may be necessary in just 2 or 3 weeks.

As you move seedlings into progressively larger containers, use heavier textured mediums. The final transplanting medium should approximate the garden soil so the plant's roots will spread naturally into the garden soil.

Seedlings that have been raised indoors in generally constant conditions will suffer a major setback if placed directly outside into the garden. They need to undergo a gradual acclimation or "hardening off" process. This is true of purchased seedlings as well as homegrown ones. Such an acclimation should take place in the heat of summer as well as in the cool weather of early spring. Radical changes in air temperatures, whether cold or hot, can set trans-

plants back if they have not been given a chance to adjust beforehand.

In early spring, seedlings need to be acclimated to the harsh outdoors slowly, over a period of days or even a week. Set them outside during the day when the temperatures are above 40°F. Try not to set them in the direct sun, and shelter them from too much wind. Put them on a porch, under shrubs, or in a similarly protected place. Move them out a bit more each day for greater exposure to sun and breeze. Each night, bring the plants indoors. After 3 to 5 days of this acclimation or hardening off, they are ready to be transplanted outside. When nights below 40°F are predicted, cover the seedlings with cloches or agricultural fleece.

A cold frame is a good device for this hardening off process. Place the seedlings in the cold frame. On sunny days, open the cover an inch or so during the day and close it at night. As the days get warmer, open the sash wider, until, finally, you can remove the cold frame entirely when nighttime temperatures do not go below 35°F.

Many gardeners do not realize that the hardening off process is important for summer seedlings as well as spring ones. Plants raised indoors under lights, for example, are not going to react well to the heat of the summer sun. Before seedlings are moved into the garden where daytime air temperatures exceed 80°F, they should be hardened off. Place them outdoors overnight, and bring them in during the day. After a few nights, leave plants outside during the morning as well, bringing them in only during the heat of the afternoon. After another few days, they are ready to be transplanted outside. Even then, it is wise to shade new transplants during hot afternoons for at least a week to be sure they are not shocked and set back by the hot sun.

TRANSPLANTING SEEDLINGS

The best time to transplant seedlings into the garden is on a cloudy day, in the late afternoon or early evening. The transplanting process is hard enough on the plants without their having to cope with bright, hot sun on their first day in the ground. Do everything you can to minimize damage to the root system of each seedling, and to reduce any other unnecessary shock to the plants.

Dig a hole big enough to contain the root ball and deep enough so the plant is settled in at about the same level it rested in the container. Pour a little water into the hole before placing the seedling. After all the seedlings have been set, give them a thorough watering, without drowning them. A little seaweed extract in that water can help minimize transplant shock.

When the weather is stormy or too cold at setting out time, seedlings may be stored in a cool place such as the cellar, porch, or an outbuilding that maintains a steady temperature of 35°F to 40°F. If there is no natural light, position two 40-watt fluorescent tubes 12 inches above the plants, and keep them lit 14 hours a day. Most vegetable seedlings can be stored at optimum transplanting size for 2 weeks, and some can tolerate as much as 6 weeks in storage. Nevertheless, if they are ready, get them out into the soil as soon as you can.

One trick for protecting new transplants in danger of being hurt by frost is to give them a foliar spray of dilute seaweed extract just before a night of expected frost (1 tablespoon to the gallon of water). Seaweed applied just before frost helps stop cold damage by increasing the sugar content in plant cells, thereby lowering the freezing point of the sap.

SAVING SEEDS

Very few gardeners have such large gardens that they use up all the seeds from a single packet of a particular vegetable or herb. Consequently, it is tempting to save those extra seeds for next year. In most cases, seeds can be successfully stored for a year or more, but conditions must be correct to be sure the germination levels don't drop to 50 percent or below.

Seeds should be stored in a dark, cool, dry place. The best place is the freezer. Put seeds in a glass jar that also contains a dehumidifying packet of dried milk. The dried milk will absorb moisture. To make this dehumidifier, spread several layers of facial tissue and place 1 tablespoon of dried milk in the middle. Wrap up the milk and secure the packet with a rubber band. This is an effective dehumidifier for several months, but it should be replaced at least once during the winter. If the freezer is full, place the seeds in the refrigerator with the dried milk humidifier.

If you store your seeds anywhere else, such as a closet, cabinet, or basement, make sure they are kept as cool and as dry as possible. If you have any doubts about the viability of the seeds, it is best to purchase fresh seeds.

WATERING THE GARDEN

Watering the food garden is not all that complicated if you understand a few basic principles about how water penetrates the soil. Soil fills with water from the top down. The force of gravity causes the water to seep into the soil. Where it meets individual soil particles, water forms a thin layer around each particle. Under good drainage conditions, soil will hold back a definite amount of water against the force of gravity—this is called its *field capacity,* and it varies with differing soil texture and structure.

Plant roots use the power of suction to take water away from those soil particles until the water film is so thin that no more water can be sucked up by the plant. It is a regular war of the worlds down there, with soil and roots fighting for droplets of water. The gardener must make sure there is always enough water to satisfy the needs of the root systems, but not so much water that oxygen is denied to those same roots.

While the soil fills with water from the top down, it also loses water from the top down. Water is lost through transpiration by plant leaves and through evaporation from the soil surface. The rate of water loss depends on the temperature of the air and soil, the amount of humidity in the air, the amount of wind, and whether it is cloudy or sunny.

Deciding to Water

The plant has a very simple reaction to too little or too much water—it stops growing. When it stops growing, you are losing production both in size of fruit and in yield.

The problem is that when a plant starts to wilt from lack of water it has already stopped growing for a day or more. Don't get too excited about the temporary wilting that can occur on vegetables such as squash and cucumbers during the heat of the day in midsummer. This mid-afternoon wilting is not necessarily a sign of serious water trouble. When the sun is most powerful, photosynthesis is at its water-demanding peak. Temporary wilting shouldn't be ignored, but it is not automatically a cause for alarm. It is when the wilting extends beyond the heat of day, especially if it occurs in the morning, that you have a serious water shortage and must water immediately.

If possible, anticipate a plant's water needs *before* growth even slows down, much less stops. Try to keep the water supply as consistent as possible.

Keeping track of rainfall helps you avoid overwatering or underwatering your garden. It's a major source of information for deciding when to water the garden. Mount a rain gauge someplace in or around your garden, preferably in a place you can see from inside the house so you don't have to get wet to check it on a rainy day. A rain gauge is a plastic calibrated tube. Use it only when the temperature is well above freezing. In early spring and late fall, you must keep a watch out for possible overnight freezes, since this might crack the gauge.

If you don't want to purchase a commercial device, it is quite easy to use an old coffee can as a rain gauge. For quick and accurate measurements, mark a plastic straw in inches and fractions. After it rains, insert the straw to the bottom of the can, put your thumb over the top end of the straw, and withdraw it to read the depth of the rainfall. Remember to empty the can after each rainfall.

Keep track of the rainfall on a weekly basis. If, after a few days, you have not gotten ½ to 1 inch of

Using a gauge to keep track of rainfall helps you avoid overwatering or underwatering your garden.

rain, you should think about watering. You don't have to keep precise records on paper. Just keep rough track in your head.

There are two general approaches to watering the vegetable garden. You can use routine watering practices that are designed to give you good overall production, but won't win you any prizes at the county fair, or you can use plant-specific practices that give each plant the exact amount of water it needs when it needs it, with the express purpose of getting the absolute maximum production from each plant. For example, there are some vegetables for which watering at the right time is almost more important than watering all the time. Tomatoes, beans, and peas are crops that prefer additional water at flowering time to get the best production. The plant-specific watering technique obviously takes more knowledge and more time. It is more likely to be used by experienced gardeners. (See the discussions on the routine watering needs and the plant-specific watering needs in the individual entries for vegetables, fruit, and herbs in chapters 1 through 3 of this book.)

Deciding How Much to Water

Most gardeners tend to give vegetables too little water. This may be because gardens usually need the most watering during July and August, when gardeners find other demands on their time. Vegetables go through a dry/wet/dry cycle that stops and starts their growth over and over again. This stop/start routine seriously reduces the plants' productivity.

A general rule of thumb is to be sure your garden receives 1 inch of water a week from rain and watering systems. This may be too much water for some gardens, and too little for others. Soil with lots of compost, and mulched gardens that have a drip irrigation system, hold water longer and lose little or none from evaporation. The weekly need of these will be something less than an inch a week, probably between ½ inch and ¾ inch, depending on the season. Conversely, very sandy soils, containing little organic matter and unprotected by mulch, may need 2 inches of water a week.

An inch of water puts ½ gallon of water on each square foot of your garden. Likewise, ½ inch will then put ¼ gallon or 1 quart of water on each square foot of your garden. To get 1 inch a week on a 200-square-foot garden, you need about 100 gallons of water, less any rain that falls.

Now, watering the garden only once a week is not necessarily a good idea. Remember, consistency is more important than quantity in this case. You don't want the plants to go dry/wet/dry over and over again. If it does not rain, you may need to water your garden three times a week. That means putting about a quart of water on each square foot of garden space, resulting in about ½ gallon of water a week, less evaporation and runoff. If you are using a drip irrigation system, you can usually get what you need by running the system three times a week for about 20 to 30 minutes each time. If you get ½ inch of rain, wait 2 days and start your 20-minute watering cycle again.

Of course, you can overwater the garden, causing just as much harm as underwatering. If the soil gets saturated, it has less space for critical oxygen, and plant growth suffers. Overwatering is not a great problem if your soil drains very well. The excess water just passes on down past the roots of the plants. It is a problem in poorly drained soil. If puddles form on the surface of the bed and remain for more than a few minutes, you can suspect your plants have too much water. The best solution is to improve soil drainage using the techniques described in chapter 7. In the short term, you must stop all watering and let the soil dry before beginning your watering program again.

The objective of routine watering is to replace the moisture that is lost from transpiration so that moisture levels remain more or less constant. We know that water loss begins at the top of the soil and works its way down. We also know that a plant's root system is generally as deep in the soil as the plant is tall. Research on watering has indicated that 1 inch of water penetrates 24 inches in sandy soil, 16 inches in loamy soil, and 11 inches in clay soil. So when you water by drip irrigation for just 20 minutes, you still may be sending water down fairly deep, because the water will seep down toward that soil needing replenishment.

If you are not sure how much water your drip irrigation system releases in 20 minutes, simply place a coffee can under it and time how long it takes to fill it. You can then compute how much would have been released in 20 minutes. A 1-pound coffee can holds 1 quart of water.

The guideline of watering for about 20 minutes, two or three times a week, depending on rainfall, should not be followed blindly throughout the entire season. In the summer months, during very hot periods with little rain or breeze, you can increase watering to a half hour or more two or three times a week. August is the time for maximum production in the garden, so it is not the time to overlook the water needs of your plants. Feel the ground under the mulch to double check. It should always feel moist. It should never feel dry.

In the spring you may need to water new seedbeds by hand for a week or two until their root systems get down past the 2- or 3-inch depth where they can reach the water from the drip system.

In the fall, you can probably cut back watering to only 10 or 15 minutes twice a week, since plant transpiration slows down as the days get shorter and growth slows.

For master gardeners who know which plants need extra water at certain times in their life cycles, this routine approach to watering can serve as the base. Individual water supplements to certain crops can easily be done by hand in a relatively short period of time. For most of us, just holding to a basic watering program will make our gardens look better than they ever have in the past.

Using Drip Irrigation

Drip irrigation systems offer a number of important benefits to the backyard vegetable garden. Such a system uses much less water than the traditional sprinkler. You can assume that you will save at least 30 percent, and in some cases 50 percent, of your water over sprinklers or other methods of watering. Water in a drip system has no chance to evaporate or run off, because it is completely absorbed by the soil and never touches the leaves of the plants.

You can water your garden with a drip system in 10 seconds, the time it takes to simply turn it on. If your system has a timer, the watering is completely automated. You set the timer to a specified watering period and it automatically turns the water on and off.

A drip irrigation system provides a steady supply of moisture to the garden. Using drip irrigation also helps to prevent diseases, since water, which can carry diseases to plants, is not splashed around the garden.

Research has demonstrated that drip irrigation systems, especially those used in conjunction with mulch, increase the productivity of a garden. Plants have earlier blossoming, increased growth, and higher yields. Peppers grown with drip irrigation and black plastic mulch have produced more than twice the crop (120 percent) of peppers grown without drip irrigation and mulch. The same results have been shown in research with cantaloupes, eggplants, okra, summer squash, and tomatoes.

Because the water never touches plant leaves, many moisture-related diseases are avoided. Problems such as rust, mildew, and blossom damage are all reduced in gardens using a drip technique.

Another advantage is the cooling effect a drip system has on the soil. A properly managed drip irrigation system can be used to help keep down soil temperatures in the high heat of summer. This increases production, because plants grow more effectively in the cooler soil.

Finally, a drip irrigation system reduces the problem of soil compaction. When the soil is saturated with large amounts of water, its structure breaks down and compaction occurs. Drip irrigation reduces this problem because the water is applied to the soil so slowly that the structure of the soil is not affected.

A top-quality drip irrigation system will cost about 25¢ to 40¢ per square foot, or $50 to $80 for a 200-square-foot garden. These systems will last for decades with very little maintenance.

Types of Drip Irrigation Systems

There are at least three types of drip systems suitable for the backyard garden. They include drip soaker lines, porous soaker lines, and emitter systems.

Drip Soakers. The drip soaker system is simply a hose with lots of holes punched in it that allow the water to drip slowly out of the hose for its entire length. You lay the hose along the bed and turn on the water just a little bit so that the water seeps slowly into the ground. These hoses are found in most garden supply stores. They are used mostly for watering shrubs and flower gardens, but have a

number of disadvantages for vegetable gardens. Their most serious problem is that you can't control how much water is released into all parts of the garden uniformly. If you have more than one length of hose in a system, it is hard to regulate the pressure along the length of the hose. More water will come out close to the faucet, with much less water coming out at the far end of the system. Furthermore, these hoses are difficult to lay up and down a bed without having kinks develop at the bending points.

Porous Drip Soakers. Porous hoses are easier to handle and better suited to the vegetable garden. These are made from recycled automobile tires, with millions of little air spaces or holes in them. They sweat water along their entire length and are very durable. Such hoses last for 15 to 20 years. They can be placed on the surface of the soil or buried an inch or two below the surface. They won't be damaged by freezing, and can be left in the garden all through the winter.

Emitter Drip System. The emitter drip system is made up of a series of hoses laid throughout the garden. Each hose has nozzles imbedded in it. These nozzles are evenly spaced (15 to 20 inches is best), releasing drops of water along the length of the hose. These systems are also quite durable, but they take more maintenance than do the porous hoses. The emitters can clog up occasionally, but they are easy to replace. To reduce the chances of clogging or other damage, it is best to bring these hoses inside during the winter.

Installing a Drip System

Install drip lines in the spring on top of the growing beds and cover them with the black (or clear) plastic mulch that will stay in place for the duration of the season. You can lay the system long before the last frost, but don't use it until the danger of freezing water in the lines is past.

It is usually easiest to begin installing your drip system at the water source or "head end," and work out toward the garden. An ordinary lawn hose is used to carry the water from the head end to the system. Usually, you will have to cut and piece together various fittings to establish the whole system. The feeder lines in the beds are connected to the main supply line with various fittings to close off the end of a line or to take lines around corners. When working with PVC (polyvinyl chloride) tubing or porous hose, a hack saw and a measuring tape are about all you need to install the system.

Most drip lines irrigate a 2-foot-wide section, about 12 inches on either side of the drip line. That means you can lay the lines 24 inches apart to reach all the plants in the garden. Of course this estimate assumes you have normal, loamy soil. If your soil tends to be sandy and drains very quickly, you will want to place your lines just 18 to 20 inches apart to make sure all the plants are well irrigated.

You can set up a drip system for a 200-square-foot garden in an hour or two. Remember not to tighten plastic fittings with a wrench. Where you have plastic screw fittings, a piece of Teflon tape wrapped around the male end lets you control leaks with just hand tightening.

FERTILIZING THE GARDEN

The ideal approach to gardening is to first build the soil's fertility so that it can support healthy, productive plants. Once the soil is basically conditioned and well balanced, you need only to replenish those nutrients that are leached away or taken out by the plants each year. Follow the recommendations for creating good garden soil in chapter 7. In this chapter, you will find tips on replenishing lost nutrients, a process usually called fertilizing.

There are two approaches to fertilizing. You can fertilize your plants with a general, routine program that is designed to get acceptable or optimum production from your garden. With this optimum approach, you are just interested in normal, healthy crops, and not worried about growing the largest tomato in the neighborhood. Most gardeners will use the optimum approach to fertilizing.

If you are interested in getting that absolute maximum productivity from your food garden (the most fruit or the biggest fruit possible for that variety of plant), there are extra fertilizing steps you can take toward that goal. You can use a plant-specific approach to fertilizing the garden, giving each plant exactly the amount of fertilizer it needs, when it needs it. It is the plant-specific approach that can win you prizes at the local county fair. It is also the approach that takes more time and attention and more fertilizer. The plant entries in chapters 1 through 3 offer information on both types of fertilizing techniques, when appropriate to a particular plant.

Nutrient Amounts for Optimum Production

Nitrogen Requirements. Most vegetable crops require about ½ pound of actual nitrogen for every 100 square feet to produce well. If you grow two crops in 100 square feet, add 1 pound of nitrogen, using dried blood meal or cottonseed meal as the source. (See table 10, on page 500, for specific amounts of blood meal or cottonseed meal.)

Low. Less than 0.1 pound per 100 square feet
Medium. 0.1 to 0.3 pound per 100 square feet
High. 0.3 to 0.5 pound per 100 square feet

Phosphorus Requirements

Low. Less than 0.025 pound per 100 square feet
Medium. 0.025 to 0.075 pound per 100 square feet
High. 0.075 to 0.1 pound per 100 square feet

Potassium Requirements

Low. 0.1 pound per 100 square feet
Medium. 0.1 to 0.2 pound per 100 square feet
High. 0.2 to 0.3 pound per 100 square feet

If you desire maximum production, see the recommendations in the fertilizer segment of each plant entry in chapters 1 through 3.

Do not try to increase your garden's productivity by simply adding more and more fertilizer. Excessive fertilizing can cause as much harm to the food garden as adding no fertilizer. If you are seeking maximum productivity from your garden, you must address the individual needs of each vegetable, fruit, and herb in the garden. Some plants like lots of potassium and little nitrogen, and others prefer the reverse ratio. Therefore you must learn as much as you can about each plant before setting up your plant-specific fertilizing program. The box Nutrient Amounts for Optimum Production, on page 499, shows the relative amounts of each fertilizer that are required, depending on individual plant preferences.

Types of Fertilizer

There are a number of different types of fertilizer for the food garden. They all provide nutrients to varying degrees, but they differ in cost, availability, method of application, and duration of effectiveness.

Commercial Organic Fertilizers

Most commercial organic fertilizers come in a form that provides one of the three primary plant nutrients —nitrogen, phosphorus, or potassium. They usually come in a dry, granular form that can be applied directly to the garden. They act slowly to provide nutrients over a period of years. For some, an annual application is desirable; for others, biannual applications will do the job.

Nitrogen Fertilizers. There are a number of slow-release nitrogen fertilizers, such as blood meal or cottonseed meal. These dry nitrogen fertilizers tend to be expensive and are perhaps best for smaller gardens or for side-dressing plants that need lots of nitrogen. Manure and compost, discussed below, are also good sources of nitrogen.

TABLE 10.

Types of Fertilizers

Nutrient	Fertilizer	Amount for Optimum Production (lb./100 sq. ft.; coffee cans full)
Nitrogen	Blood meal, dried (12-3-0)	5; 3 every 2 years
	Cottonseed meal (7-2-2)	7–8; 4 every 2 years
Phosphorus	Rock phosphate (0-31-0)	15; 4 every 2 years
Potassium	Granite dust (0-0-5)	15; 4 every 2 years
	Greensand (0-1.5-5)	15; 4 every 2 years
	Wood ashes	8–10; 3 every year
	Fish emulsion	Apply a dilute solution biweekly or monthly as a snack rather than a main meal
All nutrients	Cow manure, dried (1.3-0.9-0.8)	10–15; 4–5 every year
	Manure, fresh (0.5-0.1-0.4)	40–50; 8 gal. every year in fall

Phosphorus Fertilizers. Commercial phosphorus fertilizers come in two forms, slow acting and quick acting. For the main meal of the garden, slow-acting fertilizers such as rock phosphate do the job. Rock phosphate can be added every 2 years to give you all the phosphorus you need. If you have an immediate deficiency, the quick solution is a foliar spray of diluted fish emulsion or some other liquid fertilizer. When they receive this fertilizer through their leaves, plants are able to absorb the needed phosphorus that may otherwise be bound up in the cool, wet soil.

Potassium Fertilizers. As with phosphorus, commercial potassium fertilizers come in two forms, slow acting and quick acting. The slow-acting potassium fertilizers come either in the form of granite dust or greensand. Both of these rock powders can be added every 2 years to give you all the potassium you need. If you have an immediate deficiency, the quick solution is a foliar spray of diluted fish emulsion or some other liquid fertilizer, or you can apply wood ashes, wetting them down thoroughly after the application.

Compost

Homemade compost is a perfectly good general-purpose fertilizer, containing some nitrogen, phosphorus, and potassium as well as almost the entire range of micronutrients.

Compost is relatively low in phosphorus, so you should apply rock phosphate directly to your garden, or add it to your compost pile. Compost acids aid in breaking down insoluble phosphate compounds.

Although the nitrogen content of compost will vary according to the materials used to make it and according to its age and how much it has weathered, compost made by the active method, in which the materials are chopped and turned, can provide most of the nitrogen your plants need all season. For highest nitrogen content, use compost made from hay, rather than from straw. About 75 pounds of leaves will produce compost with about as much nitrogen as a 5-pound bag of blood meal. In comparing the nitrogen content of manure and compost, aged cow manure is about 1.4 percent nitrogen and chicken manure is about 2.8 percent nitrogen. If your compost is made of leaves and grass, it will probably have about 0.8 to 1 percent nitrogen. That percentage is sufficient to give you the amount of nitrogen an average garden needs, about 0.6 pound for 100 square feet. This means you can supply your garden's need for nitrogen by adding a 1-inch layer of compost each spring.

Many gardeners use compost as a side-dressing or snack during the growing season. You will definitely improve individual plant performance with a few handfuls of compost spread around the base of each plant in the middle of the growing season.

Manure

Animal manure has been used as a general-purpose fertilizer by farmers and gardeners for centuries. Today it is not as readily available to gardeners as it was 50 years ago, but manure is still an excellent amendment to the food garden. You can buy dried manure in bags from the local garden center, or you can find a source of fresh manure.

Fresh manure can be harmful to plants in certain cases. Some fresh manures are "hotter," or higher in nitrogen, than others. Fresh chicken manure, for example, may burn plants. All manure will be safe if it is composted first. Otherwise, you need to be sure that it is 3 to 6 months old before you apply it to your garden.

Remember that fresh manure is somewhat perishable. Leaching from uncovered storage piles and loss of nitrogen through fermentation and drying can cut down its nutrient levels. Stored in the open, manure loses as much as 30 percent of its nitrogen in 1 week. Unless it is stored in a closed container of some kind, manure loses half its nitrogen in 6 months. However, the nitrogen that remains after this leaching becomes very stable, and still benefits the garden. Covering the manure pile will certainly reduce some of this leaching.

On a new garden, with questionable soil, you can add from 200 to 400 pounds of aged (3 to 6 months) undried cow or horse manure, or 4 to 8 bushel baskets (30 to 60 gallons) per 100 square feet. That is equivalent to an inch of manure over the whole surface of the garden. If you use commercial dried cow manure, use less, or about half as much as the fresh.

On an established garden with good soil, apply just 40 pounds of aged (3 to 6 months) undried cow manure, or a 1-bushel basket of horse manure (about 8 gallons) to each 100 square feet to supply nutrients for the entire season. That comes to about ⅛ inch over the surface of the garden. You can apply manure in the fall or in the early spring, about 3 weeks to a month before planting. If the manure is dried, use less. For example, 10 pounds of dried chicken manure or 10 to 15 pounds of dried cow manure is enough for 100 square feet.

Manure should be incorporated into the soil as soon as possible after spreading to retain its fertilizing value. Ideally, the manure should be mixed thoroughly with the top few inches of soil. Rotary-tilling is an excellent way to incorporate manure in small plots.

Manure or Compost Tea

Make a valuable liquid fertilizer by concocting a tea, "brown zinger." Suspend a cloth bag of manure or compost in a container of water, such as a 50-gallon drum or a rain barrel. Any manure is all right to use. You can even use dried manure. A good shovelful wrapped in a burlap sack is enough manure to make a nice tea after being soaked for a day.

Keep the container covered to slow the escape of nitrogen gas. The "tea" will be ready in a day. Dilute the finished product to a pale tea consistency. Pour it on the soil around the plants. If you use fresh manure to make your tea, keep the solution away from the stems or leaves of your plants, as they can be harmed by the high-nitrogen solution made from a manure that is not aged. The plants should be well watered before they are fertilized. The best time to apply liquid manure or compost is right after a rain.

When and How Much to Fertilize

If you add 1 inch of compost to your garden in the spring, use organic mulch during the growing season,

and grow cover crops during the winter, you won't need any other fertilizer for your food crops—ever. If you don't use compost, an application of a slow-acting fertilizer once a year will serve as a good substitute. (However, if you want maximum, rather than optimum, productivity from the food garden, you'll need to apply more fertilizer.) The following feeding program gives you plenty of produce with the least amount of time and effort. It gives you optimal productivity.

In somewhat oversimplified terms, you have three steps in a routine feeding program, assuming your soil is reasonably fertile to begin with:

1. Give plants their "main meal" for the entire season in fall or early spring.

2. During the growing season, give them some "snacks" to help them through the extra stress of summer sun and fruit production.

3. Finally, give them some "vitamins," in the form of a seaweed extract, once a month throughout the season to help the plants stay strong and healthy.

Main Meal

If you apply slow-acting fertilizer to the garden, you need only make one application each year to get average production from your crops. This is the so-called main meal. Supplemental feedings will make some improvement, but the single application of slow-acting fertilizer is really sufficient to keep the plants healthy and productive all season long.

You can choose from several types of fertilizers for this single application. Each will be discussed in detail later in this chapter; however, see table 10, on page 500, for the options and amounts of each needed for a one-time annual application.

Snacks

While the main meal is all plants need for average productivity, you can get a significant increase in the garden's overall productivity by supplementing that main meal with some periodic "snacks." This is not the intensive, high production, plant-specific approach mentioned earlier. Snacks are dilute applications of fertilizer that give plants a boost.

You can give your garden snacks as frequently as every month, or you can offer only one or two snacks during the growing season, preferably in midsummer: When plants are putting a great deal of energy into producing fruit, they can use the extra nourishment. Squash, corn, cabbage, pole beans, and nearly every other garden vegetable benefits from a summer booster feeding. Late-planted fall crops, usually set out where earlier crops have been harvested, need added fertilizer to replace nutrients already used. Berries and orchard fruit, which mature at the season's end, do well with more food.

You can apply dry, granulated fertilizer for snacks. Side-dress by working it lightly into the soil around the plant. Be careful not to use too much.

A more efficient means of supplying a snack is in liquid fertilizer form. Whether you apply the liquid fertilizer as a foliar spray, dampening the entire plant, or pour it into the soil, the plants will absorb the nutrients 20 to 30 times faster than from the dry fertilizer. Make the liquid very dilute so you are sure not to harm plants.

In most cases, a dilution of 1 tablespoon of any kind of liquid fertilizer to 1 gallon of water is sufficient. At that dilution you can give your plants snacks every month or as frequently as every 2 weeks without harming them. You may add a tablespoon of seaweed extract 2 or 3 times during the season to satisfy the vitamin requirement.

There are many fertilizers sold in garden centers that can be mixed with water and applied in liquid form. One favorite is fish emulsion, because

TABLE 11.

Main Meal

Make sure your garden receives the following amounts of nutrients for optimum production. These quantities are based on a 100-square-foot garden.

If you are using a complete commercial fertilizer that contains a slow-release form of nitrogen, you will need 1 pound, which is equivalent to 1 coffee can full or 4 cups. If you are combining various sources of nutrients to fertilize your garden, use one source of each nutrient in the amount given below.

Nutrient	Source	Application
Nitrogen	Compost (spring)	1 in.; 9 cu. ft.; 3 bushel baskets
	Dehydrated manure (spring)	20 lb.
	Dried chicken manure (spring)	10 lb.
	Aged cow or horse manure, undried (spring)	40 lb.
Phosphorus	Rock phosphate (fall)	2.5 lb.; about 1 coffee can full
Potassium	Granite dust (fall)	2.5 lb.; about 1 coffee can full
	Greensand (fall)	2.5 lb.; about 1 coffee can full

it has a much broader spectrum of micronutrients than many other liquid fertilizers commonly used. You can also use homemade manure or compost tea, which is a good source of nitrogen and costs little to make.

If you use any liquid fertilizer as a drench (pouring it directly into the soil), rather than as a foliar spray, it is best to apply it right after a rain or immediately after you have watered the garden. The fertilizer will spread more evenly in the moist soil and be more readily accessible to roots.

Although a liquid fertilizer is quickly absorbed by the roots of plants, there is still some loss, because some nutrients leach down past the roots. Applying liquid fertilizer as a foliar spray—spraying the leaves, stems, and fruit—has become an increasingly popular method of giving supplements to plants, because the plant gets 100 percent of the nutrient value of the fertilizer.

The best time for foliar fertilizing is in the early morning of a cloudy, humid day. Spraying in the evening leaves plants wet overnight, which could create disease problems. Set your sprayer to as fine a setting as possible for foliar feeding. A surfactant, that is, a product that helps the fertilizer stick to the leaves, will improve the absorption of the fertilizer.

Never use a sprayer that has been used to apply herbicides or insecticides. It is almost impossible to remove 100 percent of any residue from the tank, hose, and nozzle, and even a tiny bit can damage plants.

Vitamins

One of the most important steps in creating a healthy, productive food garden is to give your entire garden a dose of seaweed concentrate three or four times a year. Seaweed is sold as a liquid or powder concentrate of one or more varieties of kelp. It works much like a vitamin pill works for people. It is not a fertilizer as such, but it enhances the plant's general health and condition. It helps the plant absorb nutrients more effectively from the soil. It makes the fertilizer you use work better. Seaweed also

makes plants much more resistant to drought and diseases, and in some cases, increases a plant's insect resistance. It is a very valuable amendment.

Seaweed is totally safe, and provides some 60 trace elements that plants need in very small quantities. It contains growth-promoting hormones, doesn't leach, and has a slow release rate. It is a great source of vitamins and beneficial enzymes. Its carbohydrates help plants absorb otherwise unavailable trace elements. Spraying plants with seaweed extract stimulates leaf bacteria thought to increase the rate of photosynthesis.

If the seaweed is applied directly to the soil, rather than onto the plants, it stimulates soil bacteria. This in turn increases fertility through humus formation, aeration, and moisture retention. In this improved bacterial habitat, the nitrogen-fixing bacteria will fix more elements from plant residues and soil minerals.

A good general recipe for the powdered form, sold as kelp meal, is 1 pound of kelp meal per 100 square feet of garden applied each spring. You can divide this application into three or four portions of that pound and apply it once a month for the first 4 months of the growing season. If you use the liquid form, apply the spray once a month for the first 4 or 5 months of the growing season.

If you have fresh seaweed available, rinse it and apply it to your garden as a mulch, or you can compost it. Seaweed decays readily because it contains little cellulose. Furthermore, there's no need to worry about introducing weed seeds with seaweed mulch.

RECOGNIZING SIGNS OF NUTRIENT DEFICIENCIES

The best way to identify a possible soil deficiency is to look at the plants in your garden. Slightly nutrient-deficient plants are more susceptible to pests and diseases, and they have slower and smaller yields. As the deficiency worsens, these subtle signs are accompanied by more symptoms that are distinctive to each nutrient. However, the symptoms aren't always textbook-consistent, and they may be caused by more than one element shortage.

Nitrogen

Nitrogen is needed for all stages of plant growth. It is rapidly depleted from the soil, and so must be replaced almost continually, by adding manure, cover crops, blood meal, fish emulsion, or other fertilizers. The need for nitrogen ranges from low (less than 0.1 pound for every 100 square feet), to medium (0.1 to 0.3 pound for every 100 square feet), to high (0.3 pound or more for every 100 square feet) for different crops, but this nutrient should be readily available to all plants throughout the season.

Managing a Deficiency

Signs that nitrogen is lacking include very slow growth, stunting, and smaller than normal leaves. The leaves will begin to have a paler color, with the tips becoming yellow first. Eventually, the whole leaf will turn yellow. Lower leaves are affected first. In severe deficiencies, the undersides of the stems and leaves become bluish purple. The plants become spindly and drop older leaves. The fruit is small, pale green before ripening, and highly colored when ripe.

Because nitrogen is so soluble, a nitrogen deficiency occurs mostly on very light or sandy soils, where more leaching will occur. It can also occur in soils having a high organic content, when soil temperatures are around 40°F.

If you suspect a nitrogen deficiency, immediately give plants a foliar spray of diluted fish emulsion or some other liquid fertilizer. Apply it weekly until the symptoms disappear. Simultaneously, add some slow-release nitrogen-rich amendments to the soil to correct the deficiency. Add a 1-inch layer of compost or aged manure, or the appropriate amount of a commercial, slow-release nitrogen fertilizer. In the spring, you can plant legumes, such as peas, beans, and soybeans, to build up the nitrogen for crops that follow. In the fall, plant a legume cover crop, such as alfalfa or vetch, which can be plowed under in spring to provide a good supply of nitrogen for the next growing season.

Managing an Excess

Some gardeners, in their enthusiasm to feed their plants, apply too much quick-acting commercial fertilizer. This makes too much nitrogen immediately available to the plants. The result is a plant with far too much lush, green foliage and little or no fruit.

There is no short-term solution for excess nitrogen except to stop all fertilizing activity immediately. Rain and watering will carry away the excess over time. The long-term solution is to plant heavy feeders in that spot next year. This includes crops like corn and onions. (See the plant entries in chapters 1 through 3 for other heavy nitrogen users.)

Phosphorus

Phosphorus increases the rate of crop maturity, and it strengthens plant stems. It helps in building

TABLE 12.

Nitrogen Sources

The following are quick-acting nitrogen sources, which are either applied directly to the soil or applied to the leaves as a foliar spray.

Source	Application
Commercial liquid fertilizer	Apply weekly
Fish emulsion	Apply weekly
Manure tea	Apply weekly

The following are long-term slow-release nitrogen sources, which are sprinkled around each plant.

Source	Application
Blood meal, dried (12-3-0)	Once in spring
Compost	Once in spring
Cottonseed meal (7-2-2)	Once in spring
Manure, aged (0.5-0.1-0.4)	Once in spring
Manure, dried (1.3-0.9-0.8)	Once in spring
Soybean meal (6-0-0)	Once in spring

Key to Nutrient Deficiencies in Tomatoes

The following system helps you to identify that deficiency your vegetable plant may be suffering from. Although the example given is tomatoes, the effects of most deficiencies are similar for other vegetables. The exception is boron; it causes tip dieback and leaf distortion on most plants, but also causes specific problems such as browning heads in cauliflower, cracked stems in celery, and black heart in turnips.

To use the system below in identifying what deficiency your tomato or other vegetable plants may be suffering from, you must make a series of decisions. For example, starting with "A," pick the numbered statement that most closely matches the symptoms. The whole tomato plant—not just the leaves—has been affected, so you'd choose, "1," not "2." You are instructed to go to section "B." Are leaves small, or are they normal in size? You choose "1," and go to section "C." There you decide which of the three descriptions fits the symptoms, and you've identified the problem.

A 1. Effects general on whole plant . . . . B
   2. Effects principally on foliage . . . . D

B 1. Leaves small C
   2. Leaves normal in size. First indication, upper leaves turn dark green and may curl upward. Edges turn yellow, and leaves dry up and fall. Lower leaves normal. Stems fibrous and hard. Roots short and turn brown. Plant wilts, becoming weak and flabby. Fruit exhibits water-soaked lesions at blossom end. Common on acidic, highly leached soils . . . . . **Calcium**

C 1. The first symptom is very slow growth, followed by lighter green color and chlorosis (yellowing) in tips of leaves at top of plant. All leaves may be deficient in severe cases. Underside of stems and leaves becomes bluish purple. Plant becomes spindly and drops older leaves. Fruit small, pale green before ripening, highly colored when ripe. Most common on highly leached soils or on soils high in organic matter at low temperatures . . . . **Nitrogen**

C 2. Chlorosis is not a dominant symptom. Underside of leaf turns reddish purple. Color in web of leaf appears first in spots and then spreads to entire leaf. Stems slender, fibrous, and hard. Roots stunted. Fruit late to set and mature. Growth may be restricted. Availability reduced in acidic and alkaline soils and in cold, dry, or organic soils . . . . . . **Phosphorus**

C 3. Leaves turn dark purple to black while young. Terminal shoot curls inward, turns dark, and dies. Bushy appearance due to growth of new leaves below stem. Extreme brittleness of petioles and midribs. Fruit darkens and has dried areas. Symptoms vary widely from one vegetable to the next. Most likely on highly leached, acidic soils and on organic soils with free lime . . . . **Boron**

D 1. Leaves normal in size . . . . E
   2. Leaves small, yellow, or mottled, and may be necrotic (dead tissue cells). Internodes shortened. Some vegetables form "rosettes" of leaves. Reduced availability in acidic, highly leached, sandy soils and in alkaline and organic soils . . . . **Zinc**

E 1. First indication, ashen gray-green leaves at base of plant and working upward. Leaves develop a bronze or yellowish brown color. Leaf margins tanned, scorched, or have black necrotic spots, and specks develop along leaf veins. Margins become brown and cup downward. Young leaves become crinkled and curl. Tissue deteriorates and dies. Roots poorly developed and brown. Stems slender, become hard and woody. Fruit ripens unevenly. Symptoms may be more severe late in the growing season due to translocation of potassium to developing fruit. Most common on highly leached, acidic soils and on organic soils due to fixation . . . . **Potassium**

E 2. Lower leaves first affected. Veins of leaves remain dark green, area between veins becomes yellow and finally dark brown. Leaves brittle and curl upward. Tissue breaks down. Maturity of fruit delayed. Symptoms usually occur late in the growing season. Most common on acidic, highly leached, sandy soils or on soils with high potassium or calcium . . . . **Magnesium**

E 3. Terminal growth first affected. Leaves on upper section of plant become yellow. Young leaves chlorotic, but usually no necrosis. Symptoms rare on mature leaves. Distinct yellow or white areas appear between veins, and veins eventually become chlorotic. Most common on soils high in lime . . . . **Iron**

Reprinted from Foreman, Kim W. "Soil Deficiencies." *Organic Gardening* (July 1984): 36–41.

resistance to pests and diseases. It is necessary for proper fruiting, flowering, seed formation, and root branching.

Managing a Deficiency

A deficiency of phosphorus can show up as a reddish purple color on all the plant leaves, especially on the undersides, and in the veins and stems. The stems may appear purple, and the young leaves will be unusually small and darker colored than normal. As they mature, the leaves will become mottled and occasionally bronzed. Plants deficient in phosphorus suffer impaired metabolism, so the plant may develop very thin stems. Lush green foliage and every attribute of health except the appearance of fruit or flowers may also signify a phosphorus deficiency.

A phosphorus deficiency is more likely to occur on acid soils than on alkaline ones. It may also be a temporary condition in cold, wet soils. You are likely to notice a phosphorus deficiency in the early spring. Root systems are small at this stage, and cannot always get enough phosphorus to supply the plant's needs. Phosphorus is also less soluble in cold soil. The acids required to break it free of other elements need heat to function well. Phosphorus uptake can be enhanced by soil microbes. Unless the soil temperature and moisture content are hospitable, these microbes won't develop.

If you suspect a phosphorus deficiency, apply a foliar spray of liquid fertilizer. The plant can immediately absorb the phosphorus through the leaves. This is especially true if the soil is cold, making it difficult for roots to absorb it. Apply a dilute solution each week until the symptoms disappear. Fish emulsion or a commercial liquid fertilizer with a high phosphorus content will do the job. Wood ashes are very soluble and contain some phosphorus, so a light mulching of wood ashes around suffering plants can help eliminate the symptoms. Adding lots of compost helps increase the production of available phosphorus by microbial activity. Over the long term, build up the soil's phosphorus by adding rock phosphate powder to the garden in the fall.

TABLE 13.

Phosphorus Sources

The following are quick-acting phosphorus sources, which are either applied directly to the soil or applied to the leaves as a foliar spray.

Source	Application
Commercial liquid fertilizer	Apply weekly
Fish emulsion	Apply weekly

The following are long-term slow-release phosphorus sources, which are sprinkled around each plant.

Source	Application
Manure, dried (1.3-0.9-0.8)	Once in fall
Rock phosphate (0-31-0)	Once in fall

Managing an Excess

Too much phosphorus in the ground, often coming from excessive applications of super-phosphate fertilizers, can bind up trace elements such as iron, manganese, and zinc, and make those nutrients unavailable to your plants. Excessive phosphorus is a problem that occurs only very occasionally.

There is not much you can do to quickly reduce the phosphorus level in your soil. You should definitely not add any phosphorus-rich amendments to the soil for at least 2 or 3 years. Instead, add nitrogen and potassium amendments to bring them closer to balancing the excessive phosphorus, and then grow lots of plants to begin to extract that phosphorus from the soil.

Potassium

Potassium, or potash, is required for the formation of sugars, starches, and proteins in a plant. It is also needed for the action of certain enzymes. Potassium contributes to the cold-hardiness of many plants. It enhances the flavor and color of some crops, and is especially needed for development of root crops.

Managing a Deficiency

You can tell if your plants need potassium by looking at the leaves, starting at the bottom of the plant. As potassium moves through the plant, it travels from the lower, older leaves to the upper, younger ones. When there's a shortage of potassium in the soil, the lower leaves will be gray-green, and will begin to show a marginal yellowing or mottling. They turn brown later, and appear to be scorched. In some cases, different symptoms, such as bronze coloring with curling and drying of leaf margins, may show up. Symptoms may become more severe late in the growing season as the only available potassium moves to the developing fruit. A plant suffering from a potassium deficiency lacks vigor and has poor resistance to diseases, heat, and cold. Its fruit may be misshapen and small.

Potassium leaches from very light soils. It is most likely to be deficient in the upper layers of soil, since plants remove it from these levels. The quick solution to a potassium deficiency is a foliar spray of a liquid fertilizer, such as fish emulsion, applied weekly until the symptoms disappear. A side-dressing of wood ashes can also help the plant recover from the deficiency.

For a long-term solution to a potassium deficiency, add greensand, granite dust, seaweed, or animal manure to the soil. Hardwood ashes, a source of potash, can be applied at any time of the year. Since the nutrients in wood ashes leach quickly, you get the most value from them by storing them in a dry location, or by simply layering them in the compost pile as you would ground limestone.

Managing an Excess

There is not much you can do to quickly reduce the potassium level in your soil. You should definitely not add any wood ashes, manure, or other potassium-rich amendments to the soil for at least 2 or 3 years. Instead, add nitrogen and phosphorus amendments to bring them closer to balancing the excessive potassium, and then grow lots of plants to begin to extract that potassium from the soil.

Magnesium

Magnesium is needed in plants to support necessary enzyme activity.

Managing a Deficiency

Plants deficient in magnesium tend to be brittle. Lower leaves may turn yellow, but the veins remain green. Leaf edges show the changes first, turning yellow, then orange, and finally brown. Eventually, the whole leaf becomes brittle, curls upward, and may die. In a serious deficiency, many leaves die and fall prematurely. Deficiencies ordinarily show up late, near seeding time or fruit-set time, when the element is most needed.

Apple trees with a magnesium deficiency drop their fruit before it's ripe. One of the most popular varieties, McIntosh, is especially susceptible to this deficiency. The trees have particular trouble absorbing magnesium when in acid soils. Research has shown that all trees grown in soil with a pH below 5.5 showed signs of magnesium deficiency; half the orchards with a soil pH between 5.5 and 6.0 had deficiency symptoms; and trees grown in soils with a pH above 6.0 showed no sign of a problem. Since

TABLE 14.

Potassium Sources

The following are quick-acting potassium sources, which are either applied directly to the soil or applied to the leaves as a foliar spray.

Source	Application
Commercial liquid fertilizer	Apply weekly
Fish emulsion	Apply weekly

The following are long-term slow-release potassium sources, which are sprinkled around each plant.

Source	Application
Cow manure, dried (1.3-0.9-0.8)	Once in fall
Granite dust (0-0-5)	Once in fall
Greensand (0-1.5-5)	Once in fall
Wood ashes (varies)	Once in fall

6.0 seems to be the magic number, monitor your orchard soil so that the pH never drops below this level. Light soils leach magnesium easily, as do soils high in potassium or calcium.

The best quick solution to a magnesium deficiency is a foliar spray of liquid kelp or seaweed extract every 2 weeks until the symptoms disappear. For a long-term solution, apply dolomitic limestone to the soil. Dolomitic limestone is a slow-release source of magnesium. Well-mulched plants are not likely to show a magnesium deficiency because the organic material breaks down and adds magnesium, as well as other nutrients, to the soil.

Calcium

Plants need calcium for water uptake and cell development and division. Calcium also helps plants use nitrogen.

Managing a Deficiency

A plant with a calcium deficiency may develop weak stems and show poor growth. Its leaves will be normal in size, but young ones may be curled at the tips, and have wavy and irregular borders. Yellow spots can sometimes show up on the upper leaves.

TABLE 15.

Magnesium Sources

The following are quick-acting magnesium sources, which are either applied directly to the soil or applied to the leaves as a foliar spray.

Source	Application
Dissolved Epsom salts (1 cup/gal. water)	Apply weekly
Fish emulsion	Apply weekly

The following are long-term slow-release magnesium sources, which are sprinkled around each plant.

Source	Application
Compost	Once in fall
Dolomitic limestone	Once in fall

TABLE 16.

Calcium Sources

The following are long-term slow-release calcium sources, with the exception of wood ashes, which begin to break down immediately. In all cases, sprinkle material around the calcium-deficient plants.

Source	Application
Calcitic limestone	Once in fall
Clam or oyster shells	Once in fall
Dolomitic limestone	Once in fall
Manure, aged	Once in fall
Rock phosphate	Once in fall
Wood ashes	Once in spring

Fruit develops water-soaked lesions at the blossom end. Leaf borders of cabbage and other cole crops may appear burned.

Calcium deficiency is found mostly in acid soils, highly leached soils, and in soils with high potassium levels. Very dry soil may also be deficient in calcium.

Fruit growers should apply foliar calcium nitrate and calcium chloride to apples and pears to prevent fruit cracking, early drop, and other disorders associated with calcium deficiency. For a long-term solution, add dolomitic limestone to the soil.

Boron

Required by most plants in relatively small amounts, boron affects cell development, flowering, fruiting, and over a dozen other functions. It helps with the absorption of calcium, and when calcium is abundant, plants seem to need more boron.

Managing a Deficiency

A plant with a boron deficiency develops a strange bushy appearance. This is caused when the growing tips and new terminal buds die and the lower branches send out new shoots. Leaves turn dark purple to black while young. Leaf petioles and midribs are very brittle. Fruit darkens and has cracks or dried spots. Symptoms vary widely from one vegetable to the next. You will see browning of cauliflower, cracked stems of celery, and black heart in turnips.

A boron deficiency is most likely in highly leached, alkaline soils. It is a common problem in soils of the eastern United States.

The quick solution to a boron deficiency is a foliar spray of liquid kelp or seaweed extract every 2 weeks until the symptoms disappear. For a long-term solution, add granite dust, or plant cover crops of vetch or clover in the fall. Add rock phosphate to the compost pile, or add it to the garden in fall. Do not add lime to a boron-deficient soil, as the soil is likely to be close to alkaline already.

For fruit trees showing signs of boron deficiency, spray the newly opened blossoms with a boric acid solution, consisting of 0.02 pound of boric acid crystals in a gallon of water. (Handle boric acid carefully, as it is extremely toxic.)

Iron

Iron is involved in the control of certain metabolic reactions in food crops. It is also important in nitrogen fixation and in reducing nitrate in ammonia

TABLE 17.

Boron Sources

The following are quick-acting boron sources, which are either applied directly to the soil or applied to the leaves as a foliar spray.

Source	Application
Boric acid solution	Apply biweekly
Seaweed extract	Apply biweekly

The following are long-term slow-release boron sources, which are sprinkled around each plant.

Source	Application
Chicken manure, dried	Once in fall
Granite dust	Once in fall
Rock phosphate	Once in fall

TABLE 18.

Iron Sources

For a quick-acting source of iron, apply seaweed extract biweekly as a foliar spray.

The following are long-term slow-release iron sources, which are sprinkled around each plant.

Source	Application
Chicken manure, dried	Once in fall
Compost	Once in fall
Greensand	Once in fall
Wood ashes	Once in fall

for the synthesis of proteins. Finally, iron is necessary for the production of chlorophyll.

Managing a Deficiency

The symptoms of an iron deficiency are similar to those of a nitrogen deficiency. Through observation, however, you should be able to tell them apart. The leaves of iron-deficient plants often turn yellow, but retain green veins, whereas nitrogen-deficient leaves are uniformly yellow. Also, the leaves on the upper section of the plant become yellow from too little iron, but a nitrogen deficiency shows up first on lower leaves.

A high pH (above 6.8) and an iron deficiency often go hand in hand. Iron may be present in such a soil, but it is unavailable to plants. Often lowering the soil pH to 6.0 to 6.8 will eliminate the iron problem. Work peat moss manure, or other acid-building organic materials, into the soil. If the pH is normal, consider adding glauconite or greensand, two materials that supply iron.

CONTROLLING WEEDS

There are many reasons for having no weeds in the food garden. Weeds compete with plants for nutrients and water, especially if they're allowed to mature. Although weed competition early and late in the growing season has little effect on the yield of some vegetable crops, it is easier simply to eliminate all weeds from the garden, rather than worry about which plant can handle some weed competition and which can't.

Some weeds have what is called an allelopathic effect on your food crops. Allelopathy is any direct or indirect harm caused to a plant when another plant releases toxic chemicals. Such toxins may be secreted by living roots, leaves, or fruit, or leached from decaying plant residues.

Quack grass is one example. It is a stubborn, perennial nuisance throughout the northern United States and Canada. Also known as witchgrass or knotgrass, it has been known to chemically inhibit seed germination and growth of some food garden crops. In addition, investigators have discovered that the weed also inhibits the nitrogen fixation of legumes, such as soybeans, navybeans, and snapbeans. These effects are due to chemical interactions between the quack grass and neighboring plants. Potato yields were reduced by more than 20 percent when quack grass was allowed to grow for just 2 weeks after potato emergence. The longer quack grass was allowed to remain, the lower the tuber yields.

Therefore, there are certain weeds, like quack grass, that should not be allowed to reside close to certain vulnerable vegetables. Again, instead of worrying about which weed is a problem and which is not, it is best to learn how to eliminate all of them.

A more common way weeds harm the garden is by harboring pests. Weeds are even a problem in this respect after they die. Dead weeds with hollow stems left over winter in the garden can become rooming houses for harmful insect pests that return the next year to cause problems. Overwintering weeds can also host certain plant diseases, making your vegetables more vulnerable to infection from disease next year.

And last but not least, weeds spoil the appearance of the food garden. The more we can do to control weeds and even prevent them from emerging, the happier we will be.

Identifying Weeds

A good source for identifying weeds is your local County Extension Service, which is always concerned about reducing the population of noxious weeds in the area. You'll need to make a distinction between annual weeds and perennial weeds. Both types can

This weeding tool is handy not only for digging weeds out of the garden but also for any number of other gardening tasks, like making a row or transplanting young plants.

be pests in the food garden, but they present different kinds of problems, so you need to know which is which.

Annual Weeds

Most weeds that you see in a food garden are annuals. They seem to survive all abuse during the growing season, yet do eventually die at the end of the season. However, if you allow them to, they will spread thousands of seeds to guarantee their presence the next year. Annual weeds are highly prolific and produce enormous numbers of seeds per plant. For example, a single chickweed will produce 15,000 seeds, shepherd's purse will put out 40,000 seeds per plant, and good old lamb's-quarters is right up there with 70,000 seeds. These seeds lie in the soil, just waiting for the light and water they need to germinate. As you might guess, the key to controlling annual weeds is to control their seeding activity.

Perennial Weeds

It is the perennial weeds that can be the most serious problem in a food garden, and they need very direct attention. They are tough plants that often grow right through a heavy mulch. To control perennials, you must control their roots, but they tend to have amazing root systems, which make them extremely difficult to eliminate. Leafy spurge, for example, has roots that grow 4 to 8 feet deep, while Canada thistle's roots may penetrate to depths of 20 feet! It's no wonder that these root systems are very difficult to pull up completely. In most cases, if you leave just a little bit of the root in the ground, the weed will regenerate and appear again. If your rotary tiller happens to chop one of these roots into many small pieces, you will have propagated that villain and created a much more serious weed problem for yourself.

Some common annual weeds include (from left to right) lamb's-quarters, henbit, annual bluegrass, shepherd's purse, chickweed, and purslane.

Controlling Annual Weeds

There are a number of techniques for reducing garden weeds. These techniques either break the reproductive cycle of the weeds already in your food garden, or they keep new weeds from getting into the garden in the first place.

The best way to control annual weeds is to prevent them from emerging by cultivating the soil and then mulching the garden. Turn over the soil 10 to 14 days before planting your garden in the spring. This can be accomplished by plowing 6 to 8 inches deep, or by turning only the top 2 inches of soil. Most of the annual weed seeds that are on or near the surface will sprout within 2 weeks. At planting time, rake the soil lightly to destroy the tender young weeds. Rake or hoe to a very shallow depth, so that you wipe out the weed seedlings without bringing more weed seeds to the surface. Weed seeds require light to germinate. Those too deep in the soil to germinate may remain viable for many years. They are just waiting for you to bring them to the surface.

Now you can plant your vegetables, which will get a much better start with less competition from the annual weeds. Ten days after planting, cultivate the garden again around your new plants, still working at a very shallow level. Those three cultivations should keep the annual weeds from getting a foothold. They should remain under control throughout the season, so that occasional hand pulling is all that is

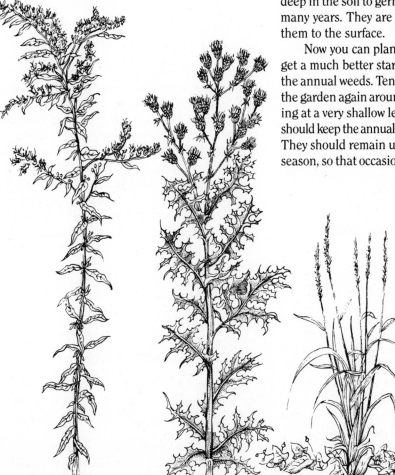

Some common perennial weeds include (from left to right) goldenrod, Canada thistle, quack grass, and bindweed.

necessary to keep them down. Mulching at this time will eliminate even this task.

If you don't use mulch in your garden or orchard, an effective way to break the reproductive cycle of annual weeds is to pull or cultivate those that do appear as soon as possible so that no seeds are produced and spread through the garden. Try to get rid of annual weeds within the first 3 weeks of their growth. If you pull a few weeds each time you are in the garden, the weed pulling never becomes an overwhelming task. Weeds are easiest to uproot right after a rain, when the soil is damp. Try very hard to pull up the roots, rather than just breaking off the stem.

In general, if you are able to pull up all the annual weeds that do appear, you will have only about half as many weeds the next year, and half again the third year. Eventually, you will reach the point where weeds are a very minor issue in your food garden. It typically takes gardeners 5 to 7 years of weeding to eliminate most of the annual weeds. If you mulch, annual weeds may be virtually gone in just 2 to 3 years. About half the weed seeds in the soil die each year without germinating.

Controlling Perennial Weeds

Perennial weeds, if they are a problem at all, require a different approach from that for annual weeds. Simply cultivating the soil and hand pulling these weeds only aggravates a perennial weed problem. A more systematic approach is needed.

To control perennial weeds by pulling them requires a very diligent effort. You need to catch every plant soon after it emerges from the soil. A weeding tool is handy for this task, because with it you can cut the roots down 4 to 5 inches. By doing this, you are able to completely cut off the weed's access to sunlight. After cutting the plant down a few times, it will eventually die. If you leave just a few portions of a perennial weed near the soil surface, you will continue to be plagued by the pest. Only if you are particularly persistent will you succeed in beating back perennial weeds by pulling.

Fortunately for those of us with less persistence, there is an herbicide on the market that is effective against virtually all perennial weeds. It is very specific, working only against those plants that it comes in contact with, and essentially harmless to other plants, the soil, people, and the environment in general.

The herbicide, called Superfast, is made of certain soap-based fatty acids, which act as a major desiccant to a plant that receives a single application. The plant loses its moisture in a matter of a few minutes and is dead within hours. The herbicide breaks down on the plant and harms nothing else in the garden.

Fall and Spring Cleanup to Control Weeds

In chapter 4, in the discussion on how to control insects, you are encouraged to do everything you can to attract birds to your garden, and you are strongly urged to follow a somewhat rigorous cleaning of the garden after the crops are harvested in the fall. These insect-control practices also reduce weed problems. You should do everything you can to prevent annual weeds from going to seed, but those few weeds that do go to seed attract seed-eating birds and may be somewhat controlled by the foraging of your feathered colleagues. When you cultivate a bed twice in the fall to expose the overwintering larvae of pest insects, you are also causing many of the hidden weed seeds to germinate. A light raking and subsequent winter chill will further reduce their numbers next spring.

Mulch to Control Weeds

Perhaps the best way to solve a weed problem is to use mulch during all or at least part of the growing season. Mulch does a number of good things for your garden, and weed control is one of them. A layer of mulch over the surface of the growing bed prevents annual weeds from getting a chance to even germinate. Those few weeds that pop up through the mulch where vegetable plants protrude are easily pulled by hand.

There are three kinds of mulch to consider for your garden. Plastic mulches are good in the early spring and late fall, since they warm the soil and help extend the growing season. Organic mulches, such as hay, straw, or chopped leaves, are good during the main part of the growing season because, among other things, they cool the soil. Finally, there are the new polypropylene fabric mulches, which tend to cool the soil, and which keep out the light needed for weed seeds to germinate.

One mulching technique is to use both plastic and organic types of mulch. Lay black plastic mulch in the early spring. In May or June, when the soil temperatures under the plastic reach intolerable levels, spread a 4- to 6-inch layer of organic mulch right on top of the black plastic mulch. This cools the soil during the hot summer months while continuing to prevent the growth of weeds. In the fall, when the soil temperatures drop, remove the organic mulch. A drip irrigation system laid under the black plastic mulch is a way to ensure that your plants get sufficient water.

Another mulching combination is layered newspapers covered with an organic mulch. Lay down five or six layers of newspapers, overlapped and anchored with dirt or stones. Cover these with 4 to 6 inches of straw, leaves, or other organic mulch. This heavy mulch will not overheat the soil and does not need to be moved for the entire season. It will do a good job of curtailing both annual and perennial weeds.

Black plastic, nonwoven mulching materials, or layered newspapers all control both annual and perennial weeds. If you prefer to use only organic mulch in your garden, then you will effectively control the annual weeds, although some of the more persistent perennial weeds may push their way through. A thin layer of finely shredded organic materials is more effective than unshredded loose material. Leaves and corn stalks should be shredded or mixed with a light material like straw to prevent packing into a soggy mass.

There is one caution here. Be careful not to reintroduce weed seeds into your garden with seed-filled compost or a weedy organic mulch, such as weed-filled hay or straw. Chopped leaves will have no weed seeds, and compost prepared by the active method (chopping and turning materials) should have only a few. To make old hay and manure almost weed-free, spread them on the garden soil in late winter. Water them well, and cover with black plastic. The weed seeds will sprout in a few days of warm weather, then will be killed by frost and lack of light. However, if you use a complete mulching system during the entire growing season every year, you don't care if you are bringing in more weed seeds, since they won't have a chance to germinate anyway.

Begin with a Weedless Food Garden

It makes little sense to create a food garden in the middle of a weedy site without first eliminating those troublesome pests. If you don't, you will be fighting an uphill weed-control battle for years. If you're building your food garden where there was formerly grass sod, it's unlikely that you'll face a serious perennial weed problem. If, on the other hand, your new garden is infested with a heavy growth of perennial weeds that may have been there for a few years, you're faced with a greater challenge.

There are three approaches to making a new garden site generally weed-free before you establish the garden. You can cover the site for a full year, you can solarize the site during a 6- to 10-week period in the summer, or you can use a safe herbicide.

Covering the Plot

An effective, but slow, way to deal with a serious perennial weed infestation is to heavily mulch the site and leave it fallow for a whole year. Blanket the area with a thick layer of overlapped newspapers and top that with several inches of bark or sawdust mulch. This will eliminate virtually all of your toughest perennial and annual weeds.

Solarizing the Soil

Solarizing your soil kills weed seeds as it destroys disease spores. It involves covering wet soil with clear plastic in the summer. After a few days of continuous summer sunlight, the soil temperature begins to soar, reaching 140°F at the surface and as high as 100°F 18 inches down.

This heat creates nearly 100 percent humidity in the water-soaked soil. The high heat and humidity over 4 to 6 weeks pasteurizes the soil, destroying many of the weed seeds near the surface. (See the discussion in chapter 5 for step-by-step instructions for solarizing a garden plot.)

The solarization process does not work uniformly for all weeds, but that is not a serious drawback. Research has shown that after 40 summer days under clear plastic, dayflower seeds, for example, were killed to a depth of a little over 4 inches, while sedges and barnyard grass seeds were killed to a depth of only 1½ inches; however, it took just 3 weeks to kill goosegrass seeds to a depth of 2 inches.

Using Herbicide

A safe, soap-based herbicide was described earlier. It can be used to clear a site of both perennial and annual weeds in about 2 to 3 weeks. Apply according to the directions on the package. This product is not harmful to the soil or the environment, and the site can be planted with vegetables 2 weeks after it has been sprayed.

New Developments in Weed Control

Researchers at Michigan State are developing a way to suppress weed growth in orchards and vegetable gardens using the naturally occurring toxins found in grain residues. This novel approach to weed management is based on allelopathy, the form of chemical warfare between plants described earlier. Chemicals leaching from a number of grain crops have been found to inhibit the germination of major weed species, or to severely stunt their growth. The selective nature of these allelopathic compounds led researchers to experiment with cover crops whose toxins might suppress weed species but not harm cash crops.

You can take advantage of a similar allelopathic effect in your garden by using a material called corn gluten meal to control weeds before they develop. Corn gluten meal is a by-product of the process that produces corn syrup, so it's safe to people and animals. But when it comes in contact with germinating seeds, it affects their fine "feeder" roots, killing off the seedlings within a few days. Corn gluten meal works against many common weeds, including dandelions, crabgrass, foxtail, lamb's quarters, and purslane. It is currently available commercially under the name A-maizing Lawn.

HARVESTING THE CROP

You've coddled and cared for the delicate seedlings, nourished and protected young plants, sprayed the fungi, brought out all arms against tarnished plant bugs, cucumber beetles, and all the other insect pests that tried to attack your plants. Finally, the time of harvest brings you just rewards. If you plan your harvest carefully, picking at the right times, your rewards will be the best that they can be.

Vegetables, Fruit, and Berries

As a rule, most food crops reach their peak flavor and nutritional value when they are still young and tender. As fruit and vegetables, and even berries, grow older and larger, their quality begins to deteriorate.

The best time to pick fruit and vegetables is in the early morning, just after the dew has dried. Harvesting in the morning catches them at their very freshest, with an extra crispness of texture imparted by cool night temperatures. Whether or not you harvest your food crops in the morning, the important thing to remember is to eat or store them right away. Allowing fresh fruit and vegetables to sit around neglected for more than a few minutes wreaks havoc with moisture and vitamin content. Greens start to wilt, beans go limp, carrots dry out, peppers lose their crunch, and fruit continues to ripen and get softer. More importantly, vitamin depletion begins with exposure to air. So, as soon as the vegetables are off the vine or the fruit is off the tree, you've got to decide what to do with them. If you must leave the produce outdoors for several hours, be sure to provide some shade. Shading, without fancy techniques like misting or packing in ice, works well to minimize the deterioration of all fruit, berries, and vegetables.

Herbs

The essential oil content of herbs typically reaches a maximum just before flowering, which is therefore the best time for harvest. For full aroma and flavor, cut the plants on a sunny morning after the dew has dried.

How to Harvest

The techniques for harvesting food crops will vary with the particular crop. Harvest tips are provided in each vegetable, fruit, and herb entry in chapters 1 through 3. As a general rule, remember to avoid picking any food crops when the plants are still wet from dew or rain. This helps to prevent unnecessary spread of diseases.

STORAGE

Vegetables and Fruits

Never wash fresh vegetables or fruits before storing them, since moisture encourages rot and tends to reduce the amount of water-soluble nutrients in the vegetables. The more cut surfaces there are, the greater is the chance for vitamin depletion, so cut only just before cooking. To maintain crispness, refrigerate most fresh produce, including beans, tomatoes, peppers, greens, broccoli, and cauliflower, in the crisper bin or in plastic bags. Store winter squash, sweet potatoes, white potatoes, and onions in a cool (45°F to 50°F), dry, dark area instead of in the refrigerator.

Herbs

If you plan to use the herbs fresh, place them immediately in a glass of water, cover them with some plastic wrap or a plastic bag, and keep them in the refrigerator until you are ready to use them.

If you are harvesting your herbs for drying, then you can prepare them for that process immediately. Herbs with small leaves are best dried by hanging bunches in a well-ventilated area (a paper bag with ventilation holes helps keep each bunch clean). Larger leaves can be spread on newspapers to dry, or gently heated in an oven with an open door. Leaves are sufficiently dry if they crackle when touched.

Store dried herbs in moisture-proof containers. Bottles allow easy checking of moisture levels, especially during the first few weeks after drying. Should any signs of moisture appear, redry the herbs. Storage life can be increased by avoiding direct sunlight and heat.

Sources for Equipment and Supplies

ANIMAL REPELLENTS AND TRAPS

Bonide Products, Inc.
2 Wurz Ave.
Yorkville, NY 13495

Bountiful Gardens
18001 Shafer Ranch Rd.
Willits, CA 95490-9626

W. Atlee Burpee & Co.
300 Park Ave.
Warminster, PA 18974

D. V. Burrell Seed Growers Co.
P.O. Box 150
Rocky Ford, CO 81067

Charley's Greenhouse Supply
1569 Memorial Hwy.
Mt. Vernon, WA 98273

Dalen Products
11110 Gilbert Dr.
Knoxville, TN 37932-3099

Dramm Corp.
P.O. Box 1960
Manitowoc, WI 54221-1960

Earlee, Inc.
2002 Hwy. 62
Jeffersonville, IN 47130

Gardener's Supply Co.
128 Intervale Rd.
Burlington, VT 05401

Gardens Alive!
5100 Schenley Place
Lawrenceburg, IN 47025

Great Lakes IPM
10220 Church Rd. N.E.
Vestaburg, MI 48891

Harmony Farm Supply
P.O. Box 460
Graton, CA 95444

Hartmann's Plantation, Inc.
P.O. Box E
310 60th St.
Grand Junction, MI 49056

Hydro-Gardens, Inc.
P.O. Box 25845
Colorado Springs, CO 80936

InterNet
2730 Nevada Ave. N.
Minneapolis, MN 55427

Kilgore Seed Co.
1400 W. First St.
Sanford, FL 32771

Orol Ledden & Sons
P.O. Box 7
Center & Atlantic Aves.
Sewell, NJ 08080

A. M. Leonard, Inc.
P.O. Box 816
Piqua, OH 45356

Liberty Seed Co.
P.O. Box 806
461 Robinson Rd.
New Philadelphia, OH 44663

Mellinger's, Inc.
2310 W. South Range Rd.
North Lima, OH 44452

Modern Farm
P.O. Box 1420
1825 Big Horn Ave.
Cody, WY 82414

The Natural Gardening Co.
217 San Anselmo Ave.
San Anselmo, CA 94960

Nature's Control
P.O. Box 35
Medford, OR 97501

Ohio Earth Food, Inc.
5488 Swamp St. N.E.
Hartville, OH 44632

Peaceful Valley Farm Supply Co.
P.O. Box 2209
Grass Valley, CA 95945

Plow and Hearth
P.O. Box 5000
Madison, VA 22727

Pony Creek Nursery
P.O. Box 16
Tilleda, WI 54978

Rodco Products Co.
2565 16th Ave.
Columbus, NE 68601

Stark Bro's Nurseries
   & Orchards Co.
P.O. Box 10
Louisiana, MO 63353

Tregunno Seeds
126 Catherine St. N.
Hamilton, Ontario L8R 1J4

The Waushara Gardens
N5491 5th Dr.
Plainfield, WI 54966-9239

BENEFICIAL INSECTS

A-1 Unique Insect Control
5504 Sperry Dr.
Citrus Heights, CA 95621

BioLogic
P.O. Box 177
Willow Hill, PA 17271
(Send a self-addressed stamped
envelope to receive information.)

Bountiful Gardens
18001 Shafer Ranch Rd.
Willits, CA 95490-9626

W. Atlee Burpee & Co.
300 Park Ave.
Warminster, PA 18974

Foothill Agricultural Research
510½ W. Chase Dr.
Corona, CA 91720

Gardens Alive!
5100 Schenley Place
Lawrenceburg, IN 47025

Harmony Farm Supply
P.O. Box 460
Graton, CA 95444

Hydro-Gardens, Inc.
P.O. Box 25845
Colorado Springs, CO 80936

Mellinger's, Inc.
2310 W. South Range Rd.
North Lima, OH 44452

The Natural Gardening Co.
217 San Anselmo Ave.
San Anselmo, CA 94960

Nature's Control
P.O. Box 35
Medford, OR 97501

Peaceful Valley Farm Supply Co.
P.O. Box 2209
Grass Valley, CA 95945

Plow and Hearth
P.O. Box 5000
Madison, VA 22727

Pony Creek Nursery
P.O. Box 16
Tilleda, WI 54978

Richters
P.O. Box 26
Hwy. 47
Goodwood, Ontario L0C 1A0

Smith & Hawken
P.O. Box 6900
2 Arbor Ln.
Florence, KY 41022

Spalding Laboratories
760 Printz Rd.
Arroyo Grande, CA 93420

COMPOSTING EQUIPMENT

Bonide Products, Inc.
2 Wurz Ave.
Yorkville, NY 13495

W. Atlee Burpee & Co.
300 Park Ave.
Warminster, PA 18974

Charley's Greenhouse Supply
1569 Memorial Hwy.
Mt. Vernon, WA 98273

Dalen Products
11110 Gilbert Dr.
Knoxville, TN 37932-3099

Earlee, Inc.
2002 Hwy. 62
Jeffersonville, IN 47130

Gardener's Supply Co.
128 Intervale Rd.
Burlington, VT 05401

Garden Way Mfg. Co.
102nd St. & Ninth Ave.
Troy, NY 12180

Harmony Farm Supply
P.O. Box 460
Graton, CA 95444

The Kinsman Co., Inc.
River Road
Point Pleasant, PA 18950

Orol Ledden & Sons
P.O. Box 7
Center & Atlantic Aves.
Sewell, NJ 08080

A. M. Leonard, Inc.
P.O. Box 816
Piqua, OH 45356

Liberty Seed Co.
P.O. Box 806
461 Robinson Rd.
New Philadelphia, OH 44663

MacKissic, Inc.
P.O. Box 111
1189 Old Schuylkill Rd.
Parker Ford, PA 19457

Mantis Mfg. Corp.
1028 Street Rd.
Southampton, PA 18966

Mellinger's, Inc.
2310 W. South Range Rd.
North Lima, OH 44452

Modern Farm
P.O. Box 1420
1825 Big Horn Ave.
Cody, WY 82414

The Natural Gardening Co.
217 San Anselmo Ave.
San Anselmo, CA 94960

Nitron Industries
P.O. Box 1447
Fayetteville, AR 72702

Peaceful Valley Farm Supply Co.
P.O. Box 2209
Grass Valley, CA 95945

Plow and Hearth
P.O. Box 5000
Madison, VA 22727

Richters
P.O. Box 26
Hwy. 47
Goodwood, Ontario L0C 1A0

Rodco Products Co.
2565 16th Ave.
Columbus, NE 68601

Smith & Hawken
P.O. Box 6900
2 Arbor Ln.
Florence, KY 41022

Stark Bro's Nurseries
& Orchards Co.
P.O. Box 10
Louisiana, MO 63353

Tregunno Seeds
126 Catherine St. N.
Hamilton, Ontario L8R 1J4

**DRIP IRRIGATION
SYSTEMS AND DEVICES**

W. Atlee Burpee & Co.
300 Park Ave.
Warminster, PA 18974

Charley's Greenhouse Supply
1569 Memorial Hwy.
Mt. Vernon, WA 98273

Dalen Products
11110 Gilbert Dr.
Knoxville, TN 37932-3099

Dramm Corp.
P.O. Box 1960
Manitowoc, WI 54221-1960

Gardener's Supply Co.
128 Intervale Rd.
Burlington, VT 05401

Harmony Farm Supply
P.O. Box 460
Graton, CA 95444

Hartmann's Plantation, Inc.
P.O. Box E
310 60th St.
Grand Junction, MI 49056

Hydro-Gardens, Inc.
P.O. Box 25845
Colorado Springs, CO 80936

International Irrigation
Systems
Box 360
1555 3rd Ave.
Niagara Falls, NY 14304

Orol Ledden & Sons
P.O. Box 7
Center & Atlantic Aves.
Sewell, NJ 08080

A. M. Leonard, Inc.
P.O. Box 816
Piqua, OH 45356

Liberty Seed Co.
P.O. Box 806
461 Robinson Rd.
New Philadelphia, OH 44663

Mantis Mfg. Corp.
1028 Street Rd.
Southampton, PA 18966

Mellinger's, Inc.
2310 W. South Range Rd.
North Lima, OH 44452

Misti-Maid
909 E. Glendale Ave.
Sparks, NV 89431

OFE International
P.O. Box 164402
Miami, FL 33116

Peaceful Valley Farm Supply Co.
P.O. Box 2209
Grass Valley, CA 95945

Raindrip
P.O. Box 5100
2250 Agate Ct.
Simi Valley, CA 93065

Rainmatic Corp.
828 Crown Point Ave.
Omaha, NE 68110

Rodco Products Co.
2565 16th Ave.
Columbus, NE 68601

Smith & Hawken
P.O. Box 6900
2 Arbor Ln.
Florence, KY 41022

Stark Bro's Nurseries
& Orchards Co.
P.O. Box 10
Louisiana, MO 63353

Submatic Irrigation Systems
P.O. Box 246
Lubbock, TX 79408

The Urban Farmer Store
2833 Vicente St.
San Francisco, CA 94116

Wade Mfg. Co.
1025 S.W. Allen Blvd.
Beaverton, OR 97005

EARTHWORMS

A-1 Unique Insect Control
5504 Sperry Dr.
Citrus Heights, CA 95621

Bountiful Gardens
18001 Shafer Ranch Rd.
Willits, CA 95490-9626

W. Atlee Burpee & Co.
300 Park Ave.
Warminster, PA 18974

Harmony Farm Supply
P.O. Box 460
Graton, CA 95444

Nature's Control
P.O. Box 35
Medford, OR 97501

Richters
P.O. Box 26
Hwy. 47
Goodwood, Ontario L0C 1A0

Rodco Products Co.
2565 16th Ave.
Columbus, NE 68601

FUNGICIDES

Bonide Products, Inc.
2 Wurz Ave.
Yorkville, NY 13495

W. Atlee Burpee & Co.
300 Park Ave.
Warminster, PA 18974

D. V. Burrell Seed Growers Co.
P.O. Box 150
Rocky Ford, CO 81067

Charley's Greenhouse Supply
1569 Memorial Hwy.
Mt. Vernon, WA 98273

Earlee, Inc.
2002 Hwy. 62
Jeffersonville, IN 47130

Gardener's Supply Co.
128 Intervale Rd.
Burlington, VT 05401

Gardens Alive!
5100 Schenley Place
Lawrenceburg, IN 47025

Harmony Farm Supply
P.O. Box 460
Graton, CA 95444

Hartmann's Plantation, Inc.
P.O. Box E
310 60th St.
Grand Junction, MI 49056

Kilgore Seed Co.
1400 W. First St.
Sanford, FL 32771

Orol Ledden & Sons
P.O. Box 7
Center & Atlantic Aves.
Sewell, NJ 08080

Liberty Seed Co.
P.O. Box 806
461 Robinson Rd.
New Philadelphia, OH 44663

Mellinger's, Inc.
2310 W. South Range Rd.
North Lima, OH 44452

The Natural Gardening Co.
217 San Anselmo Ave.
San Anselmo, CA 94960

OFE International
P.O. Box 164402
Miami, FL 33116

Ohio Earth Food, Inc.
5488 Swamp St. N.E.
Hartville, OH 44632

Pony Creek Nursery
P.O. Box 16
Tilleda, WI 54978

Richters
P.O. Box 26
Hwy. 47
Goodwood, Ontario L0C 1A0

Stark Bro's Nurseries
& Orchards Co.
P.O. Box 10
Louisiana, MO 63353

Tregunno Seeds
126 Catherine St. N.
Hamilton, Ontario L8R 1J4

The Urban Farmer Store
2833 Vicente St.
San Francisco, CA 94116

INSECT CONTROLS
AND TRAPS

AgriSystems International
125 W. 7th St.
Windgap, PA 18091

A-1 Unique Insect Control
5504 Sperry Dr.
Citrus Heights, CA 95621

BioLogic
P.O. Box 177
Willow Hill, PA 17271
(Send a self-addressed stamped
envelope to receive information.)

Bonide Products, Inc.
2 Wurz Ave.
Yorkville, NY 13495

Bountiful Gardens
18001 Shafer Ranch Rd.
Willits, CA 95490-9626

W. Atlee Burpee & Co.
300 Park Ave.
Warminster, PA 18974

D. V. Burrell Seed Growers Co.
P.O. Box 150
Rocky Ford, CO 81067

Charley's Greenhouse Supply
1569 Memorial Hwy.
Mt. Vernon, WA 98273

Concept, Inc.
213 S.W. Colombia
Bend, OR 97702

Dalen Products
11110 Gilbert Dr.
Knoxville, TN 37932-3099

Dramm Corp.
P.O. Box 1960
Manitowoc, WI 54221-1960

Earlee, Inc.
2002 Hwy. 62
Jeffersonville, IN 47130

Foothill Agricultural Research
510½ W. Chase Dr.
Corona, CA 91720

Gardener's Supply Co.
128 Intervale Rd.
Burlington, VT 05401

Gardens Alive!
5100 Schenley Place
Lawrenceburg, IN 47025

Garden Way Mfg. Co.
102nd St. & Ninth Ave.
Troy, NY 12180

Great Lakes IPM
10220 Church Rd. N.E.
Vestaburg, MI 48891

Harmony Farm Supply
P.O. Box 460
Graton, CA 95444

Hydro-Gardens, Inc.
P.O. Box 25845
Colorado Springs, CO 80936

Kilgore Seed Co.
1400 W. First St.
Sanford, FL 32771

Orol Ledden & Sons
P.O. Box 7
Center & Atlantic Aves.
Sewell, NJ 08080

A. M. Leonard, Inc.
P.O. Box 816
Piqua, OH 45356

Liberty Seed Co.
P.O. Box 806
461 Robinson Rd.
New Philadelphia, OH 44663

Mantis Mfg. Corp.
1028 Street Rd.
Southampton, PA 18966

Mellinger's, Inc.
2310 W. South Range Rd.
North Lima, OH 44452

Modern Farm
P.O. Box 1420
1825 Big Horn Ave.
Cody, WY 82414

The Natural Gardening Co.
217 San Anselmo Ave.
San Anselmo, CA 94960

Nature's Control
P.O. Box 35
Medford, OR 97501

OFE International
P.O. Box 164402
Miami, FL 33116

Ohio Earth Food, Inc.
5488 Swamp St. N.E.
Hartville, OH 44632

Peaceful Valley Farm Supply Co.
P.O. Box 2209
Grass Valley, CA 95945

Plow and Hearth
P.O. Box 5000
Madison, VA 22727

Raintree Nursery
391 Butts Rd.
Morton, WA 98356

Richters
P.O. Box 26
Hwy. 47
Goodwood, Ontario L0C 1A0

Spalding Laboratories
760 Printz Rd.
Arroyo Grande, CA 93420

Stark Bro's Nurseries
& Orchards Co.
P.O. Box 10
Louisiana, MO 63353

Tregunno Seeds
126 Catherine St. N.
Hamilton, Ontario L8R 1J4

The Urban Farmer Store
2833 Vicente St.
San Francisco, CA 94116

LIQUID ORGANIC FERTILIZERS

AgriSystems International
125 W. 7th St.
Windgap, PA 18091

Bonide Products, Inc.
2 Wurz Ave.
Yorkville, NY 13495

Bountiful Gardens
18001 Shafer Ranch Rd.
Willits, CA 95490-9626

W. Atlee Burpee & Co.
300 Park Ave.
Warminster, PA 18974

D. V. Burrell Seed Growers Co.
P.O. Box 150
Rocky Ford, CO 81067

Charley's Greenhouse Supply
1569 Memorial Hwy.
Mt. Vernon, WA 98273

Earlee, Inc.
2002 Hwy. 62
Jeffersonville, IN 47130

Gardener's Supply Co.
128 Intervale Rd.
Burlington, VT 05401

Gardens Alive!
5100 Schenley Place
Lawrenceburg, IN 47025

Harmony Farm Supply
P.O. Box 460
Graton, CA 95444

Hartmann's Plantation, Inc.
P.O. Box E
310 60th St.
Grand Junction, MI 49056

Kilgore Seed Co.
1400 W. First St.
Sanford, FL 32771

Liberty Seed Co.
P.O. Box 806
461 Robinson Rd.
New Philadelphia, OH 44663

Mantis Mfg. Corp.
1028 Street Rd.
Southampton, PA 18966

Mellinger's, Inc.
2310 W. South Range Rd.
North Lima, OH 44452

The Natural Gardening Co.
217 San Anselmo Ave.
San Anselmo, CA 94960

North American Kelp
41 Cross St.
Waldoboro, ME 04572

OFE International
P.O. Box 164402
Miami, FL 33116

Ohio Earth Food, Inc.
5488 Swamp St. N.E.
Hartville, OH 44632

Peaceful Valley Farm Supply Co.
P.O. Box 2209
Grass Valley, CA 95945

Pony Creek Nursery
P.O. Box 16
Tilleda, WI 54978

Richters
P.O. Box 26
Hwy. 47
Goodwood, Ontario L0C 1A0

Tregunno Seeds
126 Catherine St. N.
Hamilton, Ontario L8R 1J4

Otis S. Twilley Seed Co.
P.O. Box 65
Trevose, PA 19053

The Urban Farmer Store
2833 Vicente St.
San Francisco, CA 94116

ROW COVERS AND SHADING MATERIALS

Bountiful Gardens
18001 Shafer Ranch Rd.
Willits, CA 95490-9626

W. Atlee Burpee & Co.
300 Park Ave.
Warminster, PA 18974

Charley's Greenhouse Supply
1569 Memorial Hwy.
Mt. Vernon, WA 98273

Dalen Products
11110 Gilbert Dr.
Knoxville, TN 37932-3099

Earlee, Inc.
2002 Hwy. 62
Jeffersonville, IN 47130

Gardener's Supply Co.
128 Intervale Rd.
Burlington, VT 05401

Green Garden
R.D. #5, Box 275D
Somerset, PA 15501

Harmony Farm Supply
P.O. Box 460
Graton, CA 95444

Hydro-Gardens, Inc.
P.O. Box 25845
Colorado Springs, CO 80936

Orol Ledden & Sons
P.O. Box 7
Center & Atlantic Aves.
Sewell, NJ 08080

A.M. Leonard, Inc.
P.O. Box 816
Piqua, OH 45356

Liberty Seed Co.
P.O. Box 806
461 Robinson Rd.
New Philadelphia, OH 44663

Mantis Mfg. Corp.
1028 Street Rd.
Southampton, PA 18966

Mellinger's, Inc.
2310 W. South Range Rd.
North Lima, OH 44452

Modern Farm
P.O. Box 1420
1825 Big Horn Ave.
Cody, WY 82414

OFE International
P.O. Box 164402
Miami, FL 33116

Peaceful Valley Farm Supply Co.
P.O. Box 2209
Grass Valley, CA 95945

Smith & Hawken
P.O. Box 6900
2 Arbor Ln.
Florence, KY 41022

Otis S. Twilley Seed Co.
P.O. Box 65
Trevose, PA 19053

SPRAYERS

W. Atlee Burpee & Co.
300 Park Ave.
Warminster, PA 18974

D. V. Burrell Seed Growers Co.
P.O. Box 150
Rocky Ford, CO 81067

Charley's Greenhouse Supply
1569 Memorial Hwy.
Mt. Vernon, WA 98273

Dramm Corp.
P.O. Box 1960
Manitowoc, WI 54221-1960

Earlee, Inc.
2002 Hwy. 62
Jeffersonville, IN 47130

Gardener's Supply Co.
128 Intervale Rd.
Burlington, VT 05401

Garden Way Mfg. Co.
102nd St. & Ninth Ave.
Troy, NY 12180

Green Garden
R.D. #5, Box 275D
Somerset, PA 15501

Harmony Farm Supply
P.O. Box 460
Graton, CA 95444

H. D. Hudson Mfg. Co.
500 N. Michigan Ave.
Chicago, IL 60611

The Kinsman Co., Inc.
River Road
Point Pleasant, PA 18950

Orol Ledden & Sons
P.O. Box 7
Center & Atlantic Aves.
Sewell, NJ 08080

A.M. Leonard, Inc.
P.O. Box 816
Piqua, OH 45356

Liberty Seed Co.
P.O. Box 806
461 Robinson Rd.
New Philadelphia, OH 44663

MacKissic, Inc.
P.O. Box 111
1189 Old Schuylkill Rd.
Parker Ford, PA 19457

Mantis Mfg. Corp.
1028 Street Rd.
Southampton, PA 18966

Mellinger's, Inc.
2310 W. South Range Rd.
North Lima, OH 44452

The Natural Gardening Co.
217 San Anselmo Ave.
San Anselmo, CA 94960

OFE International
P.O. Box 164402
Miami, FL 33116

Ohio Earth Food, Inc.
5488 Swamp St. N.E.
Hartville, OH 44632

Peaceful Valley Farm Supply Co.
P.O. Box 2209
Grass Valley, CA 95945

PeCo Inc.
P.O. Box 1197
100 Airport Rd.
Arden, NC 28704

Plow and Hearth
P.O. Box 5000
Madison, VA 22727

Pony Creek Nursery
P.O. Box 16
Tilleda, WI 54978

Raindrip
P.O. Box 5100
2250 Agate Ct.
Simi Valley, CA 93065

Richters
P.O. Box 26
Hwy. 47
Goodwood, Ontario L0C 1A0

Smith & Hawken
P.O. Box 6900
2 Arbor Ln.
Florence, KY 41022

Stark Bro's Nurseries
   & Orchards Co.
P.O. Box 10
Louisiana, MO 63353

Recommended Reading

Books   Ball, Jeff. *The Self-Sufficient Suburban Garden.* Emmaus, Pa.: Rodale Press, 1983.

————. *Jeff Ball's 60-Minute Garden.* Emmaus, Pa.: Rodale Press, 1985.

Bilderback, Diane, and Dorothy Patent. *Backyard Fruits and Berries.* Emmaus, Pa.: Rodale Press, 1984.

Bubel, Nancy. *The New Seed-Starters Handbook.* Emmaus, Pa.: Rodale Press, 1988.

Carr, Anna. *Rodale's Color Handbook of Garden Insects.* Emmaus, Pa.: Rodale Press, 1979.

————. *Good Neighbors: Companion Planting for Gardeners.* Emmaus, Pa.: Rodale Press, 1985.

Cravens, Richard H. *Pests and Diseases.* Alexandria, Va.: Time-Life Books, 1977.

Creasy, Rosalind. *The Complete Book of Edible Landscaping.* San Francisco: Sierra Club Books, 1982.

Fryer, Lee. *The Bio-Gardener's Bible.* Radnor, Pa.: Chilton, 1982.

Hill, Lewis. *Pruning Simplified.* Emmaus, Pa.: Rodale Press, 1979.

Hirshberg, Gary, and Tracy Calvan, eds. The New Alchemy Institute Staff. *Gardening for All Seasons.* Andover, Mass.: Brick House Publishing, 1983.

Kourik, Robert. *Designing and Maintaining Your Edible Landscape Naturally.* Santa Rosa, Calif.: Metamorphic Press, 1986.

Logsdon, Gene. *Organic Orcharding.* Emmaus, Pa.: Rodale Press, 1981.

————. *Wildlife in Your Garden.* Emmaus, Pa.: Rodale Press, 1983.

MacNab, A. A. et al. *Identifying Diseases of Vegetables.* University Park, Pa.: Pennsylvania State University, 1983.

Minnich, Jerry. *The Earthworm Book.* Emmaus, Pa.: Rodale Press, 1977.

Minnich, Jerry, and Marjorie Hunt. *The Rodale Guide to Composting.* Emmaus, Pa.: Rodale Press, 1979.

The National Gardening Association. *Gardening.* Reading, Mass.: Addison-Wesley Co., 1986.

Yepsen, Roger B., Jr. *The Encyclopedia of Natural Insect and Disease Control.* Emmaus, Pa.: Rodale Press, 1984.

Magazines   *Avant Gardener,* P.O. Box 489, New York, NY 10028

The Green Scene, The Pennsylvania Horticultural Society, 325 Walnut Street, Philadelphia, PA 19106

Hort Ideas, Rte. 1, Gravel Switch, KY 40328

National Gardening, National Gardening Association, Depot Square, Peterborough, NH 03458

Rodale's Organic Gardening, Rodale Press, 33 East Minor Street, Emmaus, PA 18098

Hardiness Zone Map

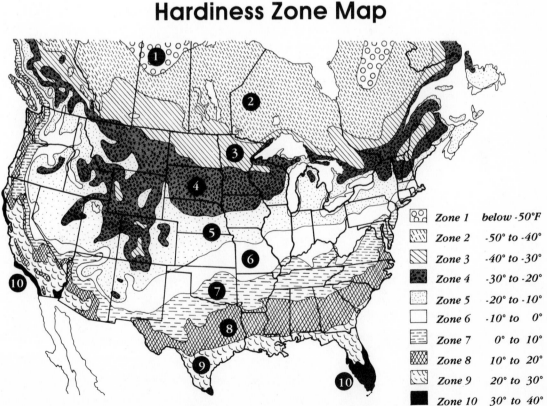

	Zone 1	*below -50°F*
	Zone 2	*-50° to -40°*
	Zone 3	*-40° to -30°*
	Zone 4	*-30° to -20°*
	Zone 5	*-20° to -10°*
	Zone 6	*-10° to 0°*
	Zone 7	*0° to 10°*
	Zone 8	*10° to 20°*
	Zone 9	*20° to 30°*
	Zone 10	*30° to 40°*

Average Minimum Temperatures for Each Zone

Index

Page references in *italics* indicate tables.